Trial *and* Triumph

ESSAYS IN TENNESSEE'S AFRICAN AMERICAN HISTORY

TRIAL
and
TRIUMPH

Edited by
Carroll Van West

THE UNIVERSITY OF TENNESSEE PRESS

Knoxville

𝖚𝖙𝖕

Copyright © 2002 by
The Tennessee Historical Society.

All Rights Reserved.

Manufactured in the United States of America.

First Edition.

All chapters previously published in
the *Tennessee Historical Quarterly*.

This book is printed on acid-free paper.

LIBRARY OF CONGRESS
CATALOGING-IN-PUBLICATION DATA

Trial and triumph: essays in Tennessee's
African American history/edited by
Carroll Van West.—1st ed.
p. cm.
Includes bibliographical references and index.
ISBN 1-57233-204-2 (pbk.: alk. paper)
1. African Americans—Tennessee—History.
2. Tennessee—History.
3.Tennessee—Race relations.
I. West, Carroll Van, 1955–
F445.N4 T75 2002
976.804'96073—dc21   2002004367

Contents

PART ONE

The Era of Slavery

Illustrations

Figures

Following Page 182

Map

African Americans and Tennessee History
Reclaiming Neglected Voices

Carroll Van West

It has been said that the colored people could not learn, but I say that that assertion is not true, for the scholars in our school are learning faster than those in the white schools.

—John J. Banks, Gallatin, 1869

Our duty is to show defense to the principles dear to the American people, and strive to elevate ourselves.

—Edward Shaw, Memphis, 4 July 1869

There is therefore only one thing left that we can do; save our money and leave a town which will neither protect our lives and property, nor give us a fair trial in the courts, but takes us out and murders us in cold blood when accused by white persons.

—Ida B. Wells, Memphis, 1892

If equality, political, economic, and social, is the boon of other men in this great country of ours, then equality, political, economic, and social, is what we demand. Why build a wall to keep me out? I am not a wild beast, nor am I an unclean thing.

—John Hope, Nashville, 1896

I am going to tell the truth. I am not guilty. I have
it said all the time that I did not do it and it is true.
I was not there. I know I am going to die and I have
no fear to die and I have no fear at all.

—Ed Johnson, before a Chattanooga
lynch mob, 1906

I wouldn't want none of my children, none of my
friends, to have to come through it, run, rocking and
rolling, over the hills and mountains that I come
over.

—Georgia Mae Turner, Fayette County, 1962

It's dehumanizing to be sent to the back door all the
time. So you have to square your shoulders . . . stand
a little taller if you can sit down at the table with
everybody else and not have to go to the kitchen.

—Robert Harvey, Knoxville, 1984

These are African American voices from Tennessee's past, words from a
sixteen-year-old boy in Gallatin to an accomplished university professor
from Nashville to a worker who was staring straight ahead at the hangman's
noose of a vicious lynch mob in Chattanooga. Historians say that their
lifeblood is finding, and understanding, the voices of the past, for through
them we gain insight to who we are—our accomplishments, our failures, and,
perhaps, our future. But for many years, historians routinely ignored these
voices—pretending either they could not hear those voices or that, when
heard, the voices had nothing important to say. The deafness of historians,
however, did not still these voices—they remained part of the historical
record—awaiting the eyes and hears of those who wanted to know the whole
story of Tennessee.

This collection of essays, published in the *Tennessee Historical Quarterly*
(*THQ*) between 1979 and 2000, demonstrate how historians have slowly
come to integrate African American voices into their interpretations of Tennessee's past, and how the people, places, and events of the state's African
American history point the way to new narratives of Tennessee history itself.

The scholars come from both within the state and from outside; they represent established historians, relative newcomers, and promising graduate students. While the majority of the published literature on Tennessee's African
American history has a tendency to look either at the 1850s and 1860s or the

1950s and 1960s, these articles cover two hundred years of history, from the frontier era of the 1790s to the statehood bicentennial of 1996. Scholars too have turned to the cities for most of their settings, but these chapters also present stories from Tennessee's rural counties and small towns, places such as Clinton, Cookeville, Fayette County, Franklin, and Haywood County.

This collection makes no claims to be the first to survey African American history in the Volunteer State. The essays instead follow a significant awakening in African American scholarship, best represented by historian Lester Lamon's admirable *Black Tennesseans, 1900–1930* (1977) and *Blacks in Tennessee, 1791–1970* (1981). In those same years, a host of scholars produced various articles, theses, and dissertations that explore various individuals and themes in the state's black history. Before those years, however, most of the early- to late-twentieth-century studies addressed African Americans in two very different ways: as incidental to history or as compensatory history.

Think, for a moment, of how many articles and books you have read that admitted the presence of African Americans in the past, but only as if they were background—present but largely voiceless, and certainly not actors who actually shaped the past. This is how historians, wittingly or not, portrayed Tennessee blacks in countless accounts; they were there, serving masters loyally, or being a pain in the neck, or living to their "true nature," or were a hindrance to southern progress and improvement as when the years of Reconstruction were invariably linked to befuddled, corruptible black legislators, Yankee carpetbaggers, and moral decline. The myths of the "lost cause" influenced many scholars to either ignore African American history or to engage it in the most derogatory stereotypes. To most white Tennesseans, the vivid images of *Gone with the Wind* may have had a Georgia setting, but they rang true, and embodied their understanding of past relations between blacks and whites in the Volunteer State.

With stereotypes defining mainstream perceptions, it is little wonder that authors by the late 1970s took pains to emphasize that African Americans were part of Tennessee history and that they contributed to that history in ways already recognized as historically significant, a type of scholarship that is called compensatory history. The early articles of this collection, such as Anita Goodstein's look at the Nashville frontier, Mechal Sobel's story of the creation of the black Baptist church in Nashville, and Bobby Lovett's study of black Civil War soldiers at Fort Negley, corrected three dominant false images of African Americans in nineteenth-century Tennessee history: that all blacks before emancipation were slaves and that slavery was a static institution (Goodstein and Sobel) and that blacks had no meaningful role in the military operations of the American Civil War (Lovett). Compensatory history is certainly preferable to stereotyped images of satisfied slaves, compliant workers, and deferential freemen. Indeed, as long as these false images persist, there is a need for counter examples of the reality of African American achievements and contributions. Several chapters in this collection present histories of black Tennesseans that challenge, and smash, the old stereotypes of shiftless workers and dedicated mammies. Marius Carriere points out both the contributions of, and the limits placed on, Memphis blacks in the ante-bellum era. Gary Edwards uses the Robert Cartmell diaries to expose the often hostile relations between slaves and masters in Madison County. Archaeologist Larry McKee turns to African American material culture as a way of reclaiming the everyday life of plantation slavery. Loren Schweninger relates the reliance of rural whites on the medical abilities of Doctor Jack, a self-trained African American doctor. Kenneth Moore recounts the bravery and military success of the United States Colored Troops in the aftermath of the battle at Fort Pillow. Paul Phillips discusses the relationship between the Freedmen's Bureau and educational institution building for African Americans. Elisabeth Perry's biography of the Girls Scouts activist Josephine Holloway points out how black professionals built meaningful institutions for nurturing young girls even in the face of direct, and indirect, race prejudice.

In the last decade, we have seen historical scholarship mature to a third phase: African American history is much more than a current academic fad, or a matter of political correctness. It is *integral* to an understanding of Tennessee history, and, in fact, represents a second creation narrative to the state's past. The bulk of Tennessee scholarship has focused on two heroic narratives, that of the early settlement era from 1770 to 1820 and that of the Civil War from 1861 to 1865. During these two periods, communities and traditions were established and basic principles defined and defended. African American scholarship also has two heroic narratives: that of the Reconstruction era, when communities and traditions were given institutional form, and that of the Civil Rights era, when basic rights were grasped and defended. The mainstream Tennessee history narratives and those of African American history have their differences: white settlers had numbers, technology, and laws in their favor while the black community builders of the late nineteenth century typically remained in the minority and faced legal hostility if not terrorist assaults. But African Americans emerged from the 1860s and 1870s with tight, cohesive communities, which nurtured them socially, culturally, and economically even as Jim Crow segregation stripped them of political power and encased them in a decidedly second-class citizenship by the time of the Tennessee Centennial Exposition in 1897. At that grand Nashville celebration, as Richard Couto's "Race Relations and Tennessee Centennials" documents, Booker T. Washington warned of a terrible future for the Jim Crow South—"no race can wrong another race simply because it has the power, without being narrowed and dragged down in its moral status"—but Michael Webb's account of the lynching of Ed Johnson in Chattanooga, one of too many other African Americans to suffer lynch-mob justice in the years to come, shows just how much white Tennesseans ignored black voices in the early twentieth century, debasing their own laws and constitution for the sanctity of "white man's law."

Scholars focusing on urban Tennessee, particularly Memphis, have done the most to help us understand the decades of institutional building that laid the foundation for black communities able to withstand the legal and economic onslaught of Jim Crow. Lisa Tolbert's study of the relationships between enslaved and freed blacks in antebellum Franklin points out the pre-emancipation roots of urban black neighborhoods. Dorothy Granberry uncovers the development of African American education in post–Civil War Brownsville. Underscoring the importance of class, Kenneth Goings and Gerald Smith interpret the transformation of Memphis's Civil War black community into three groups, with different goals and methods. Beverly Bond's overview of working class and professional African American women in Memphis raises the significance of gender to the state's history while Brian Page's analysis of how the Fourth of July in Memphis largely became an exclusively African American celebration is a reminder how Tennesseans embraced, or denied, the Union victory of 1865, and of how important fraternal lodges and sororities have been to African American identity. Turning to Nashville and its African American newspaper, the *Globe*, Christopher Scribner sheds light on how black pride and identity became commercial assets nurtured by turn-of-the-century businessmen, and how the black newspapers constantly provided counter images to the stereotypes distributed by mainstream media.

After decades of trials, African Americans stepped forward to claim their rights as full citizens during the 1950s and 1960s. Still viewed today as the great heroic era in Tennessee's African American history, the Civil Rights era was truly a time of war, and the stories of bravery, sacrifice, and triumph recounted by June Adamson in her article on the first school desegregation battlefield at Clinton, and Linda Wynn in her account of the Civil Rights movement in Fayette County, continue to inspire. But the articles by Cynthia Fleming on lunch counter desegregation in Knoxville and by Wali Kharif on school desegregation in Putnam County show that not all of Tennessee was a battlefield during those challenging years. White officials may have been supportive of peaceful desegregation and better race relations only out of fears of negative publicity, but compromise acceptable to both whites and blacks was possible. Since Adamson, Fleming, Kharif, and Wynn conducted extensive interviews with significant participants, strong, purposeful African American voices dominate these four interpretations of the Civil Rights era.

The articles found in *Trial and Triumph* reflect the growing maturity of Tennessee African American history scholarship. They remind us that traditional historical topics, such as religion, education, politics, law, war, and settlement are just as central to an understanding of black history as are the current topics of race, class, and gender. They further emphasize that the themes of religion, education, institution building, and civil rights have a key role in understanding black history. Most important, they emphasize that the voices of the African American past are not just for one part of Tennessee to listen to—they are for us all—because without them, Tennessee history is far from complete and can have only a limited meaning for the future.

Yet even this diverse array of topics and authors cannot do justice to the full breadth of the state's African American past; many other questions remain, and there are important issues still to be addressed. For example, comparable studies on the African American frontier experience in East and West Tennessee are needed to balance Goodstein's portrait of early Nashville. Since most of the published accounts have come from records of large plantations, the diversity of the slave experience across the state remains poorly understood. While it is now a given that black and white experiences were different during the Civil War, similar work is missing for the Spanish-American War, World War I, World War II, the Korean War, and the Vietnam War. Biographies of nineteenth-century black legislators, especially from rural counties, do not exist, except in brief sketches. We need more on the African American experience during the Great Depression and New Deal. Public housing and African American community building is another worthy twentieth-century topic. In its 2001 volume the *THQ* looked at the impact of Cumberland homesteads on plateau communities in the 1930s; we look forward to having an investigation of Haywood Farms, an African American project funded by the Farm Security Administration during those same years. Perhaps the most important topic awaiting scholarly scrutiny is the impact of urban renewal from the late 1950s to the 1970s on black institutions, neighborhoods, and even whole communities. What was lost, and what was gained, during those years is just as important to know as the legal and political fight for integration.

There are many other worthy questions, and much work to do in the coming years. It is our hope that this collection will encourage a greater appreciation of the symbiotic relationship between Tennessee history and African American history and will contribute to a fuller, more complete understanding of the people, places, and events that have shaped the Volunteer State.

THE ERA OF SLAVERY

Black History on the Nashville Frontier, 1780–1810

Anita S. Goodstein

FOR YEARS HISTORIANS DEPICTED TENNESSEE SLAV-
ERY AS LARGELY A STATIC INSTITUTION: WHAT WAS
TRUE IN 1861, AT THE BEGINNING OF THE CIVIL
War, also held for the frontier era of 1800. Anita
Goodstein's insightful research on roles played by African Americans in early Nashville history proves otherwise. Slavery on the frontier was different from what it
was like from the 1820s to 1860. She shows that not only
were the rules and laws regarding slaves and their relations with the larger white world less restrictive in the
early settlement period, she also found that free African
Americans gained a degree of autonomy, and their independent status later served as the basis for a sizable free
black community. She further developed a significant
theme in the history of slavery in Tennessee: a slave's
lot became increasingly circumscribed by both cultural
assumptions and legal realities as the nineteenth century
progressed. She introduces, as well, the theme that town
slavery was different from what was practiced on the
plantation—a theme further explored in the following
chapters by Carriere and Tolbert. Goodstein's varied
sources, including newspapers, wills, county court records,
deed books, and tax lists, remain potent evidence for
those interested in exploring other areas and themes of
frontier slavery.

For at least thirty years frontier factors affected the lives if not the status of black people in the Nashville area. The Indian fighting frontier was a long one in Davidson County's history, extending from the initial settlements in 1780 to roughly 1795; in the next fifteen years the total population grew from 3,613 to 15,608, and the slave population grew from 992 to 6,305. Even the tiny free black population climbed from the 6 people recorded in 1795 to 130 in 1810. From this time on, although population continued to grow, it did so by less dramatic increments; stockade and frontier stations had given way to village and settled hinterland.[1]

More than demography marked the period from 1780 to 1810 as frontier. Not until after the Creek Wars do the institutions of a settled community begin to characterize the Nashville area. Frontier society was almost by definition individualistic, lacking in community agencies: a fixed leadership, churches, schools, police. The very lack of institutional apparatus made for a paradox in the relationships of blacks and whites; slavery was at once more intimate and more commercial. This is not to say that Frederick Jackson Turner's stripping down process effectively altered the roles of either master or slave. Inherited status and traditional law remained operative.[2] The boundaries of black existence continued to be determined by the master. But the master's concern was, first, an almost frantic securing of land and more land, and, second, the making of a plantation, of a career or business, all of which left little energy for building community institutions.[3] The frontier did not as a result bring liberation to its black people. Indeed, black history stands as a major qualification of the frontier thesis whether that thesis is expressed in terms of political freedom or social mobility. But frontier history on the countryside and in the village did mark an episode of black history qualitatively different from settled plantation life and from the more complex patterns of urban life that would follow.[4]

The Indian fighting frontier meant immediately an increase in terror. Blacks were at least as vulnerable as whites; they were killed, scalped, kidnapped, and held for ransom.[5] In 1796 Governor John Sevier tried to teach The Little Turkey, a Cherokee chief, that "it is wrong to swap people for horses, for negroes is not horses tho they are black."[6] The irony rests in the schoolmaster.

The black pioneers of Nashville are, almost all of them, anonymous. Very rarely a given name appears in the record. Abraham, Anthony Bledsoe's servant and a fine marksman, shot and killed the Cherokee Mad Dog. Sam, James Bosley's "good waggoner and active plantation negro," was taken by the Creeks. Robert, James Robertson's servant, accompanied the first party of settlers in 1779, rode with his master through the Kentucky country in 1780, and lost his life in the Indian attack on Freeland's Station in 1781. More often reference is made only to the slave's owner. Witness the black woman who slept on the floor of Robertson's cabin and was ordered to throw the children under the bed when the Indians attacked. Witness the little black boy who fell from his perch on a horse behind Charlotte Robertson as the pioneers fled from Freeland's Station to the river bluff. The slave woman who desperately lightened a boat during an Indian raid on Donelson's flotilla is nameless. We are told that there were twenty-eight souls, both black and white, in one boat, which was left behind when smallpox broke out. That boat was later captured by the Indians. A rare note of humor in the dogged tale of the flotilla is supplied by the "African" asleep at the campfire when a Donelson party left hastily in fear of Indians. When they returned the next morning the African was still asleep, undisturbed.[7]

The legend of Jack Civil suggests another kind of black experience. Jack Civil was a free man of color, who probably accompanied the Donelson party and who was wounded and captured by Indians in the raid at Clover Bottom in 1780. Typically, one testimony to Jack Civil's existence is the attempt of the land speculator, Joseph Martin, to make good on Civil's preemption claim. Elijah Robertson gave his oath to seeing the transfer papers, which had been "lost by the badness of the weather." However, Jack Civil's name does not appear on James Robertson's list of preemptioners. Judge John Haywood's history, written in 1823 and the earliest account of the pioneers' story, reports only the wounding and capture by the Indians of Jack Civil and his son. W. A. Putnam's account, published thirty-five years later, reports that Jack Civil went over to the Indians and that after the Indian wars he "denied that he had ever killed or shot at a white person. It was generally believed he lied."[8] Evidently the legend grew over time; so also did white suspicion of a free black, who was perhaps more easily tolerated on the free-wheeling eighteenth-century frontier than by the southern historian writing two years before the Civil War. The sinister connotation, altogether absent from Haywood's work, is clear in Putnam's and tells us somewhat obliquely what would be the free black's experience as the frontier matured.

No white family except the Donelsons brought large numbers of slaves to the frontier initially. Extra mouths to feed were a liability and, perhaps more to the point, few pioneers had the wealth coffers of slaves represented.[9] Nevertheless, the number of slaves grew steadily. Most came with their masters from North Carolina or Virginia or Kentucky. Trading in slaves was limited in the 1780s, but sales began to mount in the next decade. Slaves were the property most sought after the land was secured. Indeed, one speculator sweetened his impressive land deals by binding himself to furnish Negroes to budding planters; another paid for land with slaves.[10] Recorded sales, gifts, and mortgages of slaves during the first twenty years (1784–1803) of the community's history involve approximately seven hundred black people, sufficient to tell us something of the frontier's impact on slaves.[11]

Above all there is the fact of sale itself. Although the number of sales in anyone year was not huge, each year the number of those who had experienced sale grew.[12] Sale meant at the least a new master, a new home, possibly a new work routine. It meant also an involuntary break with family and friends. The overwhelming number of sales were of a single slave, man or woman or child. Of the 452 transactions, only 116 involved transfers of more than one slave. Fifty-three of the 116 involved women and their children, the matriarchal families created by slavery. Only half a dozen of the 116 seem to have embraced what we might call a nuclear family: husband, wife, and children; 8 may have been transfers of couples, and perhaps 20 others may have included families. Significantly, not until 1802 does one find the term "family" used in a bill of sale to designate the slaves sold, and only once, in 1803, was a sale recorded in which the word "wife" was used.[13]

Sale into a frontier area would carry extra burdens of fear and distance from loved ones. Intensifying the trauma was the fact that these slaves were almost all young people. Of the ninety-eight men over sixteen for whom ages were reported, only nine were over thirty; of the eighty-three women, only eight were over thirty. Almost half of those for whom we have age data were under sixteen. It was not uncommon for children to be sold separately, away from parents or friends. Witness Aron, age six, sold to Andrew Jackson in 1791, and the fourteen year old, Sylvia, sold for two horse skins.[14] And even this terror could be aggravated. A fifteen-year-old girl was sold into the Chickasaw nation. A group of slaves was sold to a trader to the Illinois country. There was also the slave mother whose children had been sold before her master's family came out to the frontier; perhaps her pleas had prevailed, for later her master attempted to find the children his wife had sold.[15]

The unsettled environment of the frontier tended to underline the fact that slaves were property. A master's death, bankruptcy, or suit for debt in any slave area often meant the sale of blacks, and these situations recurred where physical danger was great and men were on the make. The mortgaging of blacks with or without land was a common practice, enabling the master to raise cash or, in one case, to guarantee delivery of a tobacco crop already paid for.[16] Sheriffs' sales of blacks for the unpaid debts of their masters were a source of bargain purchases.[17]

Even frontier conditions, however, did not overturn the fact that slaves were a peculiar property whose humanity made claims on their owners. When David Hay's "fellow" Blount was sold for debt on Hay's death, the buyer resold Blount to Hay's son, acknowledging the son's "greater right" and thereby, perhaps, a sense of "family." Elijah Robertson mortgaged thirteen of his slaves to Phillips and Campbell of Kentucky; after his death Robertson's children redeemed these slaves and divided them among themselves. In some cases blacks were sold with the provision that the seller could substitute others equally valuable within a given period. This is perhaps better evidence of a concern to maintain a given slave/white household. Some transfers were sales within a white family; others were gifts to daughters, sons, sons-in-law. When Anthony Foster, a Nashville merchant, sold a young woman to Bennett Searcy, he gave to Searcy's daughter a four-year-old girl, probably the child of the slave woman.[18] Despite such evidence of concern for individual slaves, the overwhelming testimony of the bills of sale points to the commercial interpretation of slave property. Impressive evidence of the ability of slaves to overcome sale and dispersion and to recreate the slave family does not minimize the impact of the trauma.[19] It does add to our understanding of the special circumstances of frontier blacks who had to and who did begin again the building of a family.

Frontier factors did not act all of a piece. The relatively small numbers of slaves on the frontier initially, the forced intimacy and shared dangers of the journey out, and the life of the stockades undoubtedly intensified the personal ties of blacks and whites in some cases. Some blacks certainly went armed. At the stations blacks helped build the cabins and the walls of the stockade, cooked, fetched water, and nursed. They hunted and dressed the pelts that were the community's first trade goods. Blacks moved with the white pioneers out to the countryside to tackle the job of breaking the land. Relative isolation there must have developed a special cohesiveness within the larger household particularly where the white family labored alongside the blacks. Most blacks and most whites were scattered across the countryside. Only a fraction remained in the village of Nashville, but here special conditions obtained.

In 1800, after twenty years as a frontier station and village, Nashville had a population of 345 people, of whom 154 were black.[20] Here all the factors that could affect black people on the frontier were in evidence and some, especially the commercial needs of a pioneering people, were exaggerated. Land speculators, merchants, self-made lawyers—all dealt in slaves. Indeed they used slaves almost as currency. One day in January 1789, speculator John Rice assigned a twelve-year-old girl, Jenny, to planter Robert Hays who the next day sold Jenny for 150 pounds to merchant William Taitt who immediately assigned the bill of sale to another merchant, Anthony Foster. A judgment against speculator Joel Rice was collected in part by the sale of Fran and her two children. One wonders about the fate of the child, Jemima, between ten and twelve years old, sold by John Marney to Thomas Blackamore, but redeemable by the merchant, Lardner Clarke. Then there is the case of a black woman belonging to banker George Deaderick; she was coming home from the spring with water one day in 1807 when she was stopped by a man and told "she was his property, and that she must go home with him." The lawsuit that ensued involved the property rights of Deaderick, not the abduction of a human being.[21] Business failures, debts, and shortage of capital all resulted in the sale of slaves. In addition, the hiring of slaves could mean a new master each week or month or year for the slave, and the hiring of slaves became a standard practice in town.[22]

Yet the other side of this insecurity has to be reckoned with, the wider and more diversified experience of slaves in town. Many life-styles were exhibited by Scottish merchants and Virginia squires, by pious Baptists, and free-thinking and drinking bachelors. The village was small enough so that black people could be aware of these different kinds of white people and the ways they interacted with black people. Which of the black community would not have known that Squire Thomas Molloy had fathered a slave daughter whom he cherished, that Senator Jenkin Whiteside kept a slave mistress, or, perhaps more to the point, that Robert Searcy was allowing Black Bobb to work his way out of slavery?

Wherever we have evidence of white men thinking about individual slaves they cared for, that evidence reveals complex and tortured responses to the traditional institutional restraints. Before his death in 1801 Thomas Molloy, Nashville's first lawyer, began the legal proceedings to emancipate and provide for Sophia, his slave and daughter. His will reveals his concern for her future, his evaluation of racial attitudes, and his conviction that Sophia could never make normal life choices. He urged that Sophia never marry; no black man would be worthy of her, and any white man who would marry her must be an "extravagant insensible person regardless of economy or honor, and the opinion of the world, and consequently would destroy the property and reduce the . . . girl to a wretched state of slavery and depression." Molloy's property was left to trustees who were to care for Sophia's "comfort and education" and, should she marry after all, determine how much she was to be allowed. Sophia did not marry but lived most of her adult life in Nashville with a brother who may also have been one of Molloy's children. Despite Molloy's concern for their emancipation, he and another brother had to earn their purchase money.[23]

Jenkin Whiteside's efforts to please and ultimately to emancipate and be free of his slave, the imperious Fanny, reveal another kind of situation. Because Whiteside was serving his term as U.S. senator in Washington, Fanny's care and emancipation were left to John Overton, the same lawyer who was left in charge of Sophia Molloy's estate. Overton had to deal this time with a woman who would not stay in the country where Whiteside had provided "she must have her cloathes washed and wood furnished and cut for her." Fanny insisted on coming to town and then complained bitterly about the dirt-floored cabin in which she was placed. Overton finally gave up a room in his office to Fanny. "It was my wish to do anything I could except raising the girl to equality with myself," he wrote in answer to Whiteside's frantic letters. Whiteside understood that his concern for Fanny, his attentions to her comfort and his anxiety that she trust his promise of emancipation—the most persistent of his concerns—did not follow accepted norms. "If I had reduced my Sentiments to the standard of public opinion I probably would not have taken any notice of her situation but . . . I must always act in such a manner as will satisfy my own conscience." This story has a pleasant resolution. Fanny was freed and reunited with her mother in Virginia.[24] And all of the town, black and white, must have been aware of her drama.

There was another kind of drama to observe as well. Gen. John Coffee was enraged and bewildered when his slave Ben turned on him "more personal abuse than I have ever received during my life." Ben had been an especially trusted slave, the man who carried messages from Coffee on the battlefield to Coffee's family during the War of 1812. Coffee's solution was to send Ben in irons to the Natchez country for sale. But first Ben was to be lodged in the Nashville jail for a few days as an example to other blacks.[25]

Neither Molloy nor Whiteside were native southerners brought up with the institutions of slavery. Molloy was an Englishman, Whiteside a Pennsylvanian. Indeed a surprising number of the merchants and lawyers of frontier Nashville were Europeans or Yankees. This did not prevent them from becoming slaveholders, but it may have left them more flexible in their responses to slaves and slavery. William Taitt, one of the principal merchants of the town from 1786 to 1816, was born in Scotland. It was he who first emancipated a slave in Davidson County and by the terms of his will emancipated four others and looked forward to the freeing of all his slaves on his wife's death.[26] Obviously emancipation was not confined to nonsouthern owners of slaves. What is suggested is that the frontier as a place of competing values where custom had not yet had time to gel must have played some part in these histories. In one rare case a slave owner freed an industrious slave because he wished her to "enjoy Liberty the birthright of all Mankind."[27]

Emancipation was and remained an unusual act in Davidson County; only eleven slaves, including Taitt's Nell, Sophia Molloy, and Fanny, were freed by the county court down to 1813.[28] Thus, the most important factor for black life in town was simply the substantial presence of black people, the opportunity for blacks to know other black people and to share friendship and experience with them, to build some life outside the purview of employer or master. In the 1780s, as the frontier station began to take physical shape, the lean-to kitchens were the living quarters of the slaves. But there were general meeting places very early, like the grounds around the tavern. Julius Sanders, Nashville's ordinary keeper, was indicted in 1785 for "allowing a number of Negroes to play at fives on the Sabbath at his battery."[29] One does not know which was the greatest offense: the assembling of the group of blacks, the gambling, or the gambling on Sunday. By 1800 there were perhaps one hundred houses in Nashville; the grand ones had many outhouses: kitchens, stables, smoke houses, slave cabins. The nine outhouses of tavern keeper and speculator William T. Lewis were assessed along with his one-and-a-half-story wooden mansion; William Betts, the carpenter, was taxed for only three outhouses. Merchant Taitt, who kept ten slaves, owned two houses and two outhouses. Slaves who lived with such rich men generally occupied one-room cabins, perhaps five or six to a cabin that ranged in size from twelve by twelve to thirty-one by eighteen feet.[30] Slaves who lived with less affluent masters or employers must have slept in lean-to sheds or kitchens not worth the tax assessor's trouble to enumerate. In these quarters the slaves ate and slept; they worked in the big house or in the master's store or at the wharf. They fetched water from the spring, shopped at the market house, heard a preacher on the public square, visited with each other in kitchens and "tippling" shops, and found, despite their own tight quarters, a place to dance and to talk.

Slaves knew that black people lived in and around Nashville under all the possible terms of freedom and servitude. The census of 1800 reported on three free persons of color living in Nashville. One must have been Nell, already an old woman of fifty-two when she was sold to Edgar and Taitt in 1789. In the next six years she managed to earn one hundred dollars to buy her freedom. Perhaps she earned her purchase money by washing clothes or cooking for some of Nashville's bachelors. Another free person must have been the tavern keeper Robert Rentfro. But most of the free black population of the frontier years must have acquired their freedom elsewhere. Of the seventy people whose free status was recorded in Davidson County between 1806 and 1818 less than a handful originated in the Nashville area. Most came from Virginia or North Carolina and a scattering came from other southern states, but one was a Pennsylvanian and one a sailor from Boston. The testimonials to free status give evidence of the variety of experiences of free black people. Anthony Gains was described as a Revolutionary War veteran "believed born in freedom." Eighteen people submitted manumission papers or records of their emancipations. Two could offer only evidence of false imprisonment; court acquittal evidently served as evidence of freedom here. Testimony to the free status of one's mother, or of one's parents, coupled often with evidence that one had been bound out as an indentured servant until twenty-one, sufficed in other cases. Two sailors offered certification of their status by a New York notary public. Nine people produced white witnesses, who testified that "he was always considered a free person from his birth," that "he was considered free in Baltimore and allowed to make contracts and receive wages," that the witness "knew him in Virginia," or that he knew "no one who claims her as property." Two men had "guardians" who testified that though they had worked out their purchase money, their masters, in New Orleans and in Natchez, could not legally emancipate them there. One young woman, Rachel Myers Norris, evidently wanted her freedom papers recorded since she was prepared to accompany her husband, a slave, "to the Western country." Her husband's master had promised "to respect her freedom."[31]

Not all free people sought or obtained registration of their free status. Undoubtedly it was the growth of the free black population after 1800 that provided the pressure to get these people identified and registered. Davidson County census returns reported 18 free persons of color in 1791, 6 in 1795, 14 in 1800, and, significantly, 130 in 1810. On the other hand judging by the skimpiness and sketchy quality of the evidence of free status that was accepted, there was no real effort to control or prevent free black immigration in these years.[32] The free black population was small, largely made up of transients and single men. Only 19 of the 70 people identified in the free passes were women; the data suggest only two nuclear families and only three families of mothers and children. A couple of the passes noted that the recipients were simply passing through Nashville. In perhaps half a dozen cases there is some evidence that the individual was to remain in Nashville or in Davidson County. The most notable was Sherwood Brian (or Sherrod Bryant), who located in the county in 1806, received his free pass in 1811, and by 1850 had become the richest free Negro in the state, owning twenty-two slaves and real estate, including a house and lot in Nashville worth fifteen thousand dollars. He had fathered eight sons and six daughters, a number of whom settled in Nashville.[33]

The transient nature of the free black population is of course not surprising in light of the research that has demonstrated that most poor people in nineteenth-century American cities tended to be temporary residents.[34] Steady work was hard to come by and harder for black people. As early as 1785 "a certain Mulatto fellow called Peter Barnett" had evidently been forced to indenture himself. In this case the county court freed Barnett from his indentures because there was no "valuable consideration given to the said fellow" to bind the contract. Again in 1798 another free black, Jeffrey Scott, felt compelled to indenture himself for six years to W. T. Lewis for forty-five pounds "and to be accommodated as Lewis does his own servants." Within six months Scott sued Lewis on grounds of assault and battery and false imprisonment. A long and involved court case led first to a mistrial and then to a finding for Lewis. Scott was desperately trying to hold on to his freedom despite the indenture agreement. In 1802 a free woman indentured herself and her children.[35] Undoubtedly there were opportunities for casual labor, but without special skills, tools or capital the free black could be reduced to a form of slavery or, more commonly, would be forced to move on. An 1804 advertisement for an apprentice and journeyman, which noted that "a black man would not be rejected," was a rare item.[36]

There were very few success stories like that of Robert Rentfro, a favored slave of Robert Searcy, who was given permission by the county court in 1794 "to sell Liquor and Victuals on his Good Behavior." Black Bob's enterprise earned his purchase money, and in 1801 many prominent residents of Nashville petitioned the state legislature for his emancipation. In 1803 the ex-slave bought lot 25 in Nashville from his former master, and for more than twenty years, as Robert Rentfro, he maintained a popular inn and livery stable at the sign of the Cross Keys on the north side of the public square.[37]

County records provide examples of many black lives that fit no rigid slave/free formula. There was Mary, whose mistress wanted to free her but whom the county court judged "too old to be hired out." The court was anxious to maintain legal responsibility for Mary with her mistress, but it provided that Mary could "pass and repass in the Town of Nashville." Presumably she had some way of earning her living in town. In another case a master simply recorded in the clerk's office his permission for his "slave Hannah to pass and repass during her good behavior." There were the four Ransom orphans, children of color, whom the court bound to Joel Lewis on the same terms, by and large, that it bound out white orphans. Each of the women was to be provided at age twenty-one with "a feather bed and furniture and a spinning wheel," each of the men with "two sets of clothes, and a horse, saddle, bridle worth $50."[38]

Some masters provided that slaves, though not emancipated, might live independently on their good behavior. Thomas Molloy allowed one slave "the priviledge [sic] of working and Doing for himself so long as he conducts himself as he Ought to do." John Blackamore allowed two men "the privilege of farming his plantation. They were to be permitted to keep all they could raise." Another master expected his slave to be able to support himself and provided that the slave be given access to the master's blacksmith tools.[39] Slaves who purchased their freedom had obviously been given time and often tools to accumulate the purchase price.

By the 1790s there were not only slaves and free people among the blacks in Nashville but also slaves who were rented from their masters by merchants and craftsmen seeking the labor of slaves without heavy capital investment.[40] These hired slaves were sent in from the countryside because of their special skills or just because greater profit could be made in town. Orphans were occasionally supported by the proceeds of their slaves' hire. Some masters who had not yet settled down to planting rented out their slaves. The hiring of slaves was a practice that flourished especially in urban areas where it was accompanied by inhibiting regulation. But the brass badges that hired slaves were required to wear in New Orleans, or the tickets they were required to carry in Charleston, were not adopted in the frontier village of Nashville.[41]

The practice of hiring blacks was sanctioned by custom and law, but the practice of allowing slaves to hire their own time, in effect to make their own labor contracts, to find their own food and shelter, and to live independently, also developed. The self-hire of slaves was technically illegal by the North Carolina statutes carried over to Tennessee and by Tennessee statutes, but these were obviously ignored in Nashville. In 1823 state law prohibited and ordered fines for self-hire, and yet four years later a municipal ordinance was providing expensive and complicated licensing procedures presumably to discourage and practice.[42] Only a few slaves could make these arrangements pay sufficiently to earn their freedom, but some did, witness Nell and Robert Rentfro. Some blacks were in effect set up in business as Rentfro was. For others it meant at least a freer existence if often a marginal one. Always self-hire must have provided an extra drive, a goal-oriented existence, and often a deeper despair. Hiring one's own time could be managed for any length of time only with an owner's permission. But the temptation to do it even without permission was a strong one. Andrew Jackson, for example, grew furious when his wife's maid washed clothes for people outside the family. He ordered that she be taken to the public whipping post and given fifty lashes should she try to do it again.[43]

Hiring one's own time could imply either long-term arrangements providing labor and skills or occasional labor provided with or without a master's permission. The town, of course, was the likeliest market for labor, services, and goods. A slave could raise vegetables or provide spring water or bake cakes for sale at revival meetings or in the market square. Slaves who "traded" were in effect hiring their own time. Some of Nashville's earliest ordinances were attempts to regulate this practice. In 1805 the town sergeant was ordered to inspect slaves who were trading. However, if the slaves had permission from their masters their goods could not be confiscated.[44] Slaves hiring their own time, and slaves trading goods and services became commonplace. Since the first practice was illegal and the second often illegal there exists no count of black people who lived on this basis. But especially in the years of rapid population growth after 1795 the demand for labor and the opportunities for profit encouraged the development of this different kind of slavery. England estimates that the number of virtually free blacks living in Nashville ultimately grew to be "perhaps as large as the number who were fully free." Certainly they fooled the census takers.[45]

Still, most blacks in Nashville remained slaves in the traditional sense. As the bachelor society of frontier Nashville gave way to families and more settled patterns of living for the white community, the slave quarters undoubtedly received more supervision. At the same time the growth of the village meant more black people, wider communication among them, and a life-style determined in part by contact with fellow slaves and the free men of color. Although slave quarters in town were physically closer to the white households than those in the country, the opportunity to lose oneself for shorter or longer periods in the busy streets along the river or off the square was also available. "Houses of entertainment," "Tipling shops erected on the highway, and in our Towns," run by and catering to blacks, were a source of complaint as early as 1799. Whites viewed them as corrupting agents, encouraging slaves to steal so that they might barter for liquor, and whites reacted with anxiety to the spectacle of a "numerous crowd of slaves" drinking whiskey. As the town grew, anonymity became one of its characteristics and any cluster of blacks became suspect.[46]

Nevertheless, the discipline of slaves was left almost entirely to masters and employers, despite the fact that municipal regulations governing the activities of black people were among the first to be spelled out by the corporation's government. In 1802 the Board of Commissioners tried to clarify the status of slaves in town but at the same time provided for the jurisdiction of masters. Slaves were not to trade nor to appear in the town on Sundays or after night-fall *without the permission of their masters*. No "riotous collection" of blacks, slave or free, were to be permitted and "no assemblies to dance after dark." [47] These regulations allowed considerable leeway for interpretation, and their enforcement was lax. Nashville, after all, had not even a night watch until 1810, and a Sunday patrol was not instituted until 1823. Significantly, the patrol was an answer to complaints that blacks were taking over the town and especially the market house and public square on Sundays.[48]

Certainly during Nashville's first two decades, the white community had little to fear from black people. Instances of criminal behavior by slaves were very rarely recorded. In 1791 Cato, Andrew Greer's slave, tried to steal a rifle from Charles Snyder's gun shop; in 1793, Dick, William Nash's slave, was accused of burning a barn; and in 1797 two slaves were accused of breaking into Abner Peak's meat house and stealing a "Quantity of Meat." These seem to be the only recorded instances of major crime. The special juries provided for trying slaves, composed of three justices of the peace and four freeholders and owners of slaves, were summoned and witnesses heard. Worth noting is that the punishment for the attempted theft of the rifle was the same as the punishment for the theft of the meat, thirty-nine lashes. However, we do not know what happened to Dick, who was reported to have told another slave that "he would put his knife" to any man who tried to whip him. Ominously, two pages of the court minutes are missing at this point.[49]

If the frontier community was too loosely organized to do much about its black population beyond using it, it is also true that opinion on the neces-sity and duration of slavery had not yet hardened. In 1803 the *Tennessee Gazette* published "by the request of a number of subscribers," *The African's Complaint*, a fierce denunciation of slavery which insisted upon seeing the slave as a son and lover torn from his home, "forced into a floating dungeon[,] . . . bartered as a slave, exposed to contempt and scorn, unjustly marked with the whip of tyranny—his labor unjustly extorted from him." Both republican and Christian principles were invoked to castigate slavery.[50]

Indeed the single strongest force battering away at frontier individualism was a religious revivalism that transcended racial distinctions. Early in Nashville's history Methodists and Baptists made a significant impact. Active concern for both black and white souls characterized these denominations. Through the mid-1820s many Methodists, especially in the ministry, insisted on a vigorous antislavery stance.[51] The Methodist circuit riders and Bishop Asbury himself preached to crowds of hundreds. In those crowds were black people drawn by the excitement, persuaded in some numbers by the message.

Lack of adequate church facilities in town meant that services were held in the open air, in camp meetings or on the public square, occasionally in the jail. Here there were no fixed galleries for blacks or designated black pews. The Methodists' suspicion of wealth and status, their identification with the poor and uneducated, and their insistence on feeling as opposed to ritual made them natural leaders in the effort to proselytize among blacks. In 1818 Nashville was made a separate charge of the Methodist Church and a year later the Nashville Station reported seventy-five white and twenty colored members. Within ten years black Methodists made up almost three-quarters of the membership of the Methodist churches of Nashville.[52]

In the countryside, Baptist churches welcomed blacks and whites who came to them "by experience." Baptists, like those organized in the Mill Creek Church, four miles from Nashville, disciplined their members, demanding of them chastity, sobriety, and church attendance. Very few of the prominent planters, speculators, and merchants were members of the Baptist Church. But some of their slaves were. Such masters must have welcomed church discipline for their servants. The Mill Creek Church insisted on a rigid Calvinism. On the other hand, the slaves, often freed, if only temporarily, from their masters' supervision, were admitted to new roles. In 1806 the Mill Creek Church "resolved that the Black Brethren at the time of the Church's Society Meeting have, and enjoy, the same liberty of exercising public gifts as white members do have or do enjoy." Black members were given the chance "to sing and pray with and exort [sic] . . . fellow servants," to exhort "within the Bounds of the Church," and to judge the worthiness of fellow blacks. If some of these statements indicate an attempt to restrict black enthusiasm to times and places where white supervision was available, they nevertheless do demonstrate that organized religion provided roles for black people to play that were outside the purview of institutional slavery. One cannot judge too precisely how much scope these new roles actually provided. Still, one is led to wonder by such cases as that of Becky, Anthony Foster's slave, who was tried by the Church for "living . . . in an improper way." Becky was "advised to change her Residence." Could she? Anthony Foster was not a member, but his brother, the pious Robert C. Foster, was a deacon and the church's clerk.[53]

Presbyterians were present as early as the 1780's but their proselytizing was restrained. A very few blacks were accepted into membership and the requirements for formal admission remained high. Occasionally an exceptionally talented black was encouraged. John Gloucester, who organized an African Presbyterian Church in Philadelphia in 1807, had been converted by Gideon Blackburn on the Tennessee frontier. Blackburn purchased and emancipated Gloucester and urged him to take up the ministry.[54]

The self-discipline internalized by black church members and the church discipline imposed in part by black brethren cannot be overlooked as significant factors in the development of black culture. Here lay some of the roots of the black churches that would continue to develop in the antebellum period. Although many more slaves experienced religion within the quarters than in formally organized white churches,[55] black participation in the frontier churches provided both a tradition and the stubborn reality of black members which white rejection of blacks in a later period could not erode.

The frontier decades, as compared with later years, marked a kind of ease in race relations. Jeffrey Scott did find two white lawyers to argue his case against W. T. Lewis, innkeeper, land speculator, and a powerful political figure. Though Anderson Lavender, schoolmaster, was fined only one cent for beating free Negro Bobb so that "his life was Greatly despaired of," this seemed to be the normal punishment for assault and battery cases where they involved only whites. What is to be remarked on is the finding of the white man guilty. Thirty-seven years later a Nashville jury would acquit a white man, who, before witnesses, murdered a newly freed black man.[56] Emancipation of slaves, though rare, met with no official obstacles in the frontier period. The petition for Robert Rentfro's emancipation was marked "reasonable and ought to be granted," but after 1831 Tennessee law provided that emancipation must be accompanied by departure from the state, and exceptions to that rule were hard to win.

Free blacks were technically able to vote until 1835 and at least four black citizens were enrolled in Davidson County's militia company in 1811: Caesar Prince, Robert Rentfro, Philip Thomas, and Christopher Christian. Prince had earned his freedom in much the same way as Robert Rentfro, by operating a tavern while still a slave. Christian bought a lot in Nashville in 1813 but disappears from the public record after the 1820 census. Thomas, who had acquired his first lot in Nashville in 1803, was described in 1820 when he secured the freedom of his second wife as "a free man of property [who] . . . has a family of children by a former wife who are free and on whose education much care and Expense have been bestowed." The court agreed that not only would it be a good thing to free Aggy Thomas, but also that any children she might have ought to be free. Of course, Thomas was to pay "a stipulated price" for his wife.[57]

Jeffrey Lockelier was born in 1788 to a free woman in North Carolina. At twenty-one, shortly after he had completed his indentures, he came to Nashville. He was caught up in the excitement of the Indian Wars, enlisted, and fought through the Creek campaigns, served at both Horseshoe Bend and New Orleans, and went on to fight in the Seminole Wars. The town gave him the complimentary title of Major Jeffrey and he got his living in Nashville as janitor of the court house. His was probably the only obituary of a black person published in the Nashville papers in the antebellum years. His war record and visits from President Jackson and General Coffee to his deathbed in the house of Col. Robert Armstrong were the distinguishing aspects of his life in the newspaper account—these and the fact that he died "a Christian." But by the time of Lockelier's death in 1830, the frontier phase of black history was over.[58]

How can we evaluate the first thirty years of black history on the Nashville frontier? Thousands of black people were brought or had come to the area. Their share of the violence and pain of frontier life was multiplied, for their coming was involuntary and often meant the trauma of separation from family and friends. While they helped to build farms and town they had also to recreate basic family structures, to rebuild shattered personal worlds. It was in this area by and large that what rewards and satisfactions they were to achieve had to come. For there were few places in town or on the countryside that were their own, no churches, no schools; a few parcels of town land, a farm or two, and a handful of "businesses," were owned by black people. On Sundays, despite protest, black people claimed the market square. Only fragments of the histories of the pitifully small numbers of "success" stories remain. Most black people remained slaves, legally a part of the households of masters or employers.

And yet the very absence of a fixed white establishment imposing coercive controls coupled with the reality of a growing and varied black presence, especially in town, marked a frontier phase of black history and made a difference in the quality of black life. Obviously such things as the relative ease of emancipation made a substantial difference to the few individuals who gained their freedom. But more important to most black people, slave and free, was the institutional atmosphere, the relative lack of agencies and energy directed toward the enforcement of racial codes. Allowing black people to hire their own time began in these early years and, although the practice did not always or often lead to legal emancipation, it did make for a different kind of slavery. The presence of practically free people became a constant, which all the agitation and legislation of the post frontier decades could not eliminate. In the same way, the presence of black members in the early churches laid the basis for black church leadership and black congregations. Free, practically free people, and slaves were together building something of a communal life. In the post frontier decades not only close family networks but also more formal institutions like schools and churches would be the impressive results.

Notes

1.

TABLE 1			
DAVIDSON COUNTY CENSUS RECORDS, 1790–1820			
Year	Total Population	Free Colored	Slaves
1790	3,459	18	659
1795	3,613	6	992
1800	9,620	14	2,936
1810	15,608	130	6,305
1820	20,154	189	7,899

SOURCE: Davidson County, Tennessee, 1790 to 1820 Censuses, United States Historical Census Data Web Page, fisher.lib.virginia.edu/census. Accessed 18 February 2002; for the 1795 census schedule, see Clarence E. Carter, ed., *The Territorial Papers of the United States* (Washington, D.C., 1936) 4:404.

2. Chase C. Mooney, *Slavery in Tennessee* (Bloomington, Ind., 1957). See chapter 1 for a discussion of the retention of North Carolina law. I should like to acknowledge a special debt to the pioneer studies of black history in Tennessee by Mooney and by James M. England. Mooney's work includes "Slavery in Davidson County, Tennessee" (Master's thesis, Vanderbilt Univ., 1936) and "Slavery in Tennessee" (Ph.D. diss., Vanderbilt Univ., 1939). England's work includes "The Free Negro in Davidson County, Tennessee, 1780–1860" (Master's thesis, Vanderbilt Univ., 1937) and "The Free Negro in Antebellum Tennessee" (Ph.D. diss., Vanderbilt Univ., 1941).
3. For further elaboration on the frontier characteristics of early Nashville, see Anita S. Goodstein, "Leadership on the Nashville Frontier, 1780–1800," *Tennessee Historical Quarterly* 35 (1976): 175–98.
4. The writing of black history in the last quarter-century has been remarkably productive. Historians have begun to address themselves to the complaint that studies of black culture in the slavery era have tended to be static. See especially Peter Wood, *Black Majority: Negroes in Colonial South Carolina* (New York, 1974); Ira Berlin, *Slaves without Masters: The Free Negro in the Antebellum South* (New York, 1974); Richard C. Wade, *Slavery in the Cities: The South, 1820–1860* (New York, 1964). Herbert G. Gutman in *The Black Family in Slavery and Freedom, 1790–1925* (New York, 1976) traces a "cycle of family destruction, construction, and dispersal" beginning in a newly opened plantation area. See also John W. Blassingame, *The Slave Community: Plantation Life in the Antebellum South* (New York, 1972); Robert W. Fogel and Stanley L. Engerman, *Time on the Cross* (Boston, 1974); Eugene D. Genovese, *Roll, Jordan, Roll: The World the Slaves Made* (New York, 1974). I hope by employing the term "frontier," covering the disruption of both white and black institutional patterns, to add to our understanding of the challenges faced by black people at a particular point in time.
5. See, for example, John Haywood, *The Civil and Political History of the State of Tennessee* (Knoxville, 1823), 128, 341, 379, 380; "Letters of Benjamin Hawkins, 1796–1806," in *Collections of the Georgia Historical Society* 9 (1916):174–75.
6. Sevier to The Little Turkey, 25 Aug. 1796, "The Executive Journal of Governor John Sevier," in East Tennessee Historical Society *Publications* 1 (1929): 119.

7. Jay G. Cisco, *Historic Sumner County, Tennessee* (Nashville, 1909), 219; "Letters of Benjamin Hawkins," 174; Haywood, *Civil and Political History*, 95, 130, 101–4; Thomas E. Matthews, *General James Robertson* (Nashville, 1934), 206–7, 210–12.

8. Davidson County Court Minute Book A, p. 49. All county records consulted are in the Tennessee State Library and Archives (hereafter cited as TSLA). A. W. Putnam, *History of Middle Tennessee* (Nashville, 1859), 119, 227; Haywood, *Civil and Political History*, 128, 218–20.

9. One reason given for the Donelsons' temporary retreat from Nashville in 1780 was the number of their slaves who would have to be fed out of the pioneers' meager store. Putnam, *History of Middle Tennessee*, 621. The inventory of John Donelson's personal estate in 1791 listed thirty Negroes "valued at $4,344 2/3 hard dollars." Davidson County Will Book 1, pp. 196–98.

10. Davidson County Deed Book B, pp. 111–13; Will Book 1, p. 164.

11. Davidson County Will Books, 1784–1803. Some of the slaves counted here were sold more than once in this period. On the other hand, records of slaves sold as part of the inventory of deceased masters have not been included.

12. Seventy-eight slaves were involved in the transactions recorded between 1784 and 1789. Between 1790 and 1803 the greatest number in any given year was eighty-four (1797), and the smallest number was twenty-five (1792).

13. Only in some cases were children clearly identified as those of the female slave sold with them, but where a woman was sold with young children, I have counted the group as a "matriarchal family." I have termed groups of slaves families or couples where the sexes and ages of the individuals make this possible. For the use of "family" and "wife" in bills of sale, see Davidson County Will Book 2, pp. 234, 378.

14. Will Book 1, pp. 240, 71

15. Will Book 2, p. 158; Will Book 1, pp. 179, 189, 220.

16. Will Book 1, p. 172.

17. See for example, Will Book 1, pp. 237, 248, 263, 270, 279, 280; Will Book 2, pp. 35, 98, 104, 118, 146; Will Book 3, p. 276.

18. Will Book 1, pp. 277–79; Will Book 2, pp. 94, 343–44; for provisos that a slave sold might be redeemed by substitution of another slave, see Will Book 1, pp. 96, 173, 244; Will Book 2, p. 9.

19. Gutman, *Black Family*, esp. chap. 4.

20. Davidson County, Tennessee, 1800 Census, United States Historical Census Data Web Page, fisher.lib.virginia.edu/census. Accessed 18 February 2002.

21. Will Book 1, pp. 86, 90, 97, 146; *State vs. Thompson*, in Helen T. Catterall, *Judicial Case, Concerning American Slavery and the Negro* (Washington, D.C., 1926–37), 2:483.

22. David B. Davis in a review of Gutman's *Black Family* argues that the hiring of slaves worked against the family stability Gutman is emphasizing. *American Historical Review* 82 (1977): 745.

23. Will Book 2, pp. 245–47; Estate Papers: Thomas Molloy, in Claybrooke Collection, TSLA; Davidson County Court Minute Book C, p. 390; Memorials and Petitions to the Legislature of Tennessee (1821), TSLA; England, "Free Negro in Davidson County," 6, 41.

24. Jenkin Whiteside to John Overton, 4, 10 Dec. 1809 and 4, 19 Jan. and 12 Mar. 1810, in Murdock Collection, Tennessee Historical Society, TSLA: Will Book 5, p. 88; Davidson County Court Minutes, January Sessions, 1810, p. 77.

25. John Coffee to John McLemore, 2 Jan. 1819, in Coffee Papers, TSLA.

26. Will Book 1–2, p. 32; Minute Book A, p. 299; Will Book 5, pp. 458–62; England, "Free Negro in Davidson County," 44–45.
27. Will Books 3–4, p. 239.
28. Mooney, "Slavery in Davidson County," 60, 62, 63. Mooney estimates that only fifty slaves were emancipated in the seventy-year period after 1790. England reports emancipations indicated in wills (although emancipation was not legal until the county court agreed to it) and, therefore, suggests a slightly higher figure.
29. Minute Book A, p. 91.
30. Mss. Tax List, 13th Assessment District, 1 Oct. 1798, TSLA.
31. England, "Free Negro in Davidson County," 10–19. Will Book 3, pp. 110, 184, 208, 233, 234, 236–42; Will Book 4, pp. 79, 112, 113, 121, 149, 167, 184, 186, 187, 195, 197, 201–3, 235, 236, 284, 346, 347, 375, 399.
32. England, "Free Negro in Davidson County," 22.
33. Ibid., 14, 15, 17, 18, 265, 266. Memorials and Petitions to the Legislature of Tennessee (1821), TSLA.
34. See, for example, Peter R. Knights, *The Plain People of Boston, 1830–1860* (New York, 1971), 121; Stephen Thernstrom, *Poverty and Progress* (Cambridge, Mass., 1964), 158–59.
35. Minute Book A, p. 78; Will Book 2, p. 134, Minute Book C, pp. 294ff. Scott's lawyers promised to appeal. England, "Free Negro in Davidson County," 131.
36. *Tennessee Gazette*, 26 Sept. 1804.
37. Minute Book B, p. 150; Memorials and Petitions to the Legislature of Tennessee 1801, TSLA; *Journal of the Senate at the First Session of the 4th General Assembly of the State of Tennessee, 1801* (Knoxville, 1801), 43, 48; *Tennessee Gazette*, 23 June 1802; *Clarion*, 18 Oct. 1808 and 11 Aug. 1812; *Nashville Whig*, 6 Jan. 1813; Reverse Index to Davidson County Deeds.
38. Will Book 4, p. 202; Will Book 3–4, p. 234; Minute Book C, p. 418.
39. England, "Free Negro in Davidson County," 41, 46, 83.
40. See, for example, Will Book 1, p. 276, Will Book 2, pp. 69, 167, 340.
41. Wade, *Slavery in the Cities*, 40. For the hiring and self-hire of urban slaves, see 38–54.
42. England, "Free Negro in Davidson County," 140; Mooney, "Slavery in Tennessee," 63; *The Laws of the Corporation of Nashville* (Nashville, 1828), 50.
43. John S. Bassett, ed., *The Correspondence of Andrew Jackson* (Washington, D.C., 1927) 3:87.
44. Caleb B. Patterson, *The Negro in Tennessee, 1790–1865* (Austin, Tex., 1922), 48.
45. England, "Free Negro in Davidson County," 154; see also 33–34, 139.
46. Davidson County Memorials and Petitions, 1799, 1813. At this point there was no evidence of the self-conscious planning to prevent alleys that Wade describes in a later period (in *Slavery in the Cities*, 61).
47. Minutes of the Board of Commissioners, Box N1, no. 11, TSLA; *Tennessee Gazette*, 22 Sept. 1802 and 3, 31 Aug. 1803.
48. *Nashville Whig*, 13 and 18 Oct. 1823.
49. Minute Book A, p. 411; B, pp. 119, 406.
50. *Tennessee Gazette*, 19 Oct. 1803.
51. Asa E. Martin, "Anti-Slavery Activities of the Methodist Episcopal Church in Tennessee," *Tennessee Historical Magazine* 2 (1916): 108; Patterson, *Negro in Tennessee*, 108–17.
52. John B. McFerrin, *History of Methodism in Tennessee* (Nashville, 1886), 3:64, 68, 81.

53. *The Conference Business of the Baptist Church under the Care of James Whitsitt, on Mill Creek, Davidson County,* Record Book, 1797–1814, TSLA.

54. Carter G. Woodson, *The History of the Negro Church* (Washington, D.C., 1921), 56–57.

55. Genovese, *Roll, Jordan, Roll,* esp. 232–54.

56. Minute Book C, 291–92 (1800); *Nashville Union,* 19, 22 Aug. 1837; *National Banner and Nashville Whig,* 21 Aug. 1837; Circuit Court Minutes, September Sessions, 1837, pp. 234, 265, 266, 268.

57. "Davidson County enumeration of militia companies," 1811, in TSLA: Putnam, *History of Middle Tennessee,* 303; Davidson County Court Minutes, 1817–1821, p. 436 (1820); Reverse Index to Davidson County Deeds.

58. Will Book 3–4, p. 237 (1809); Davidson County Court Minutes, pp. 435 (1820), 925 (1824), 420, 514, 556 (1826), 693 (1827); *National Banner and Nashville Whig,* 27 Sept. 1830.

Blacks in Pre–Civil War Memphis

Marius Carriere Jr.

MARIUS CARRIERE COMPARES THE EARLY HISTORY OF AFRICAN AMERICANS IN MEMPHIS TO OTHER ANTEBELLUM SOUTHERN CITIES AS documented in the earlier work of historians Richard Wade, Claudia Golden, and Kathleen Berkeley. He concludes that frontier Memphis residents held moderate attitudes about slavery and the presence of free blacks, as witnessed by the initial acceptance of Frances Wright's Nashoba community east of the town. In the early settlement years, enslaved and free African Americans enjoyed limited autonomy and a degree of freedom that disappeared due to more restrictive state laws and city ordinances in the 1840s and 1850s. Carriere's research is valuable for its analysis of slaves "hiring out," which allowed merchants, manufacturers, and professionals to employ slaves as hired help, with part of the fee going to the master and a small part being kept by the slaves, and of "living out," which meant slaves lived away from their masters. By the 1850s city officials attempted to control the popularity of "hiring out" and "living out," but their regulations met with little success. So, too, did the city try to circumscribe the numbers and opportunities of free blacks living in the Bluff City. But the size of the African American community continued to expand—and on the eve of the Civil War, this community "continued to be a vital and important part of Memphis."

The first blacks in Tennessee were slaves whom the fur traders of the late eighteenth century brought to carry the pelts back to the East. When the early settlers entered what would become Tennessee, they brought few slaves, but they brought enough in order to establish the institution of slavery. With the creation of the Washington District in 1776, these slaves, and blacks in general, were affected by the laws of North Carolina. While slaves were restricted in their travel, forbidden to bear arms, prohibited from owning property, and denied legally binding marriages, the North Carolina Constitution of 1776 permitted to all free adult males who paid taxes and who met the residency requirement the right to vote. The North Carolina manumission law, which had been rather liberal for the times, by July 1775 had been changed to permit emancipation only for "meritorious service." The first constitution of Tennessee recognized slavery, but it made no mention of free blacks being prohibited from voting, nor was there any prohibition on intermarriages. The status of emancipated blacks was not clear either.[1]

Not long after statehood, speculators and the United States government showed an interest in the area around the Fourth Bluff on the Mississippi River, land that would become Memphis. The government interest was military, but the speculators found land sales in the area disappointing. With a gradual increase in the population of the region, cotton became the dominant crop. However, it would not be until the late 1830s and the early 1840s that Memphis would be assured dominance in trade and commerce in the area, and not until then did the town appear to be headed toward becoming a major inland cotton center.[2]

With the increasing significance of cotton, Memphis grew. The 1840 population of Memphis was only eighteen hundred. Even with low cotton prices in the 1840s, however, the cultivation of that crop continued to increase, and as a result, the population of Memphis doubled between 1840 and 1845. It doubled again in the last five years of the decade. By the 1850s, "Memphis became the largest inland cotton market in the United States." The end of that decade witnessed Memphis having grown to the sixth largest city in the South.[3]

As it had in the eastern and middle parts of the state, slavery came to West Tennessee and Memphis. Yet the institution developed slowly. In fact, the total population of West Tennessee in 1820 was only about 2,500, while in Memphis the total residents numbered approximately 53. Ten years later the number of inhabitants of Memphis had increased to 663. Blacks (slave or free) were few in Memphis. By 1850 the black population of the city was 2,486, and in 1860, 3,882. Only 126 and 198 were free blacks in 1850 and

1860, respectively. The percentage of all blacks was 28 percent of the total population in 1850, and ten years later blacks constituted 17 percent of the total residents.[4]

In some ways attitudes toward slavery in Memphis could be described as moderate during the 1820s and early 1830s. It appears there were strong feelings for emancipation in the city at that time, and Memphians initially tolerated Frances Wright's Nashoba, the experimental community for the emancipation of slaves. Memphis even had a branch of the American Colonization Society. Tied to the sentiment for emancipation and to the philosophy of the American Colonization Society was the removal of the liberated blacks from the area. Additionally, even though three of the four local candidates for delegates to the 1834 constitutional convention favored emancipation, they were also in favor of deportation as part of the plan. Memphians also became less tolerant of Nashoba when Wright left and the community deteriorated into what some residents considered "an experiment in free love, racial equality, and amalgamation."[5]

Due to the small slave population during the 1830s and the early 1840s, the Memphis Board of Aldermen and the local newspapers were virtually silent on the general topic of blacks. But as population grew, so too did attention to the town's blacks. By the late 1840s, there is little difference in the kinds of ordinances passed by the aldermen and those of other southern cities. Reading these laws makes it clear that there was no question that the black population would be closely regulated during the pre–Civil War period. The state legislature had already approved restrictive laws. The usual legislation was all there. No one could trade with slaves unless the slave had a permit, no liquor could be sold to slaves, and towns had to provide for slave patrols. These were only a few of the restrictions and local communities, such as Memphis, were expected to pass ordinances that would apply to local circumstances.[6]

These city laws in Memphis, in addition to those of other southern cities, have led historians to speculate about the compatibility of slavery with urban life. In 1964 Richard Wade concluded that because urban areas gave blacks and slaves more freedom, this ultimately led to the decline of slavery in the 1850s. The realities of an urban existence, according to Wade, simply created a situation that eroded the distinctions between free men and slaves.[7] On the other hand, Claudia Goldin contends that slavery was not inimical to urban life. Why slavery declined in southern urban areas in the 1850s was more the result of what Goldin calls "elasticity values and the increase in the price of slave labor." What she is really saying is slave labor was too valuable to be used in cities at a time when cotton prices increased and a cheap, substitute labor force was available. This is what drew slaves out of the city. It did not mean an end to urban slavery; in fact, Goldin sees the probability that urban slavery, adaptable as it was, could have continued "in a more urban and industrial post-1865 South."[8]

One of the most useful examinations of slavery and blacks in Memphis before the Civil War is part of a 1980 unpublished dissertation by Kathleen C. Berkeley. In her first chapter she deals with the decade of the 1850s and, in particular, with immigrants and blacks. Berkeley, unlike Wade, does not believe urbanization is antithetical to the "southern way of life," and she specifically takes issue with Wade over the question of black residential patterns. Focusing on this residential issue, Berkeley concludes that in Memphis "slaves were living in close proximity to their masters." Therefore, there was no "breakdown in the master's authority" which Wade argues made slavery and urban life incompatible.[9]

There are many similarities between slavery in Memphis and slavery in other southern cities, and at times what Richard Wade, Claudia Goldin, Kathleen Berkeley, and other historians argue makes sense for Memphis. In other instances, Memphis is unique and does not easily fit their mold. However, slavery was important in Memphis right up to the Civil War, and owners did not regard slave labor as too costly for town use when cheaper immigrant labor would do. As far as Kathleen Berkeley's emphasis on the residential patterns, she makes too much over slaves living in close proximity to their masters. It is difficult to ascertain with much certainty if slaves were truly living in close proximity to their masters; judging from their worries about slaves who lived away from their owners, many masters believed that slaves "living out" were a real problem.

Indeed, the most common complaints about blacks in Memphis revolve around the freedom blacks enjoyed. The editor of one Memphis newspaper, the *Daily Eagle*, summarized the situation well when he attacked the practice of slaves hiring their own time, the practice of selling liquor and other goods to slaves, and the prevalence of numerous "negro resorts" throughout the city where slaves and free blacks congregated.[10] The editor warned Memphians that not only was the "traffic with slaves" against state laws, but the practice conflicted "with sound morality" and the controlling discipline of our slave population."[11] At the time this editorial appeared in the paper, the grand jury was in session and the writer urged Memphians to seek a legal remedy for these problems by complaining to that body. The grand jury would have to examine any violations of the laws.[12]

Of these different violations, the practice of slaves hiring themselves out bothered whites the most. This practice had begun during the early days of the city when slaves hired themselves to buy their freedom. Even before the slave population had grown very much, a few whites voiced opposition to "the liberal policies of the 1820s" which permitted slaves to earn their freedom in this manner.[13] Apparently, the rapid growth of the slave population had caught Memphians unprepared for the realities connected with urban slavery, particularly this problem of slaves hiring their own time. One resident complained about black drinking shops and the practice of slaves hiring themselves out. While he denounced the drinking shops as nuisances which demoralized the slaves, he reserved his harshest remarks for blacks hiring their own time. He wrote that "to permit a negro to hire his own time sends a slave to ruin as property, debauches a slave, and makes him a strolling agent of discontent, disorder, and immorality among our slave population."[14]

Even though Memphians were in violation of the law if they hired a slave without permission from the owner, the practice must have suited many whites, too. It is apparent that many masters were content to permit their slaves much latitude, and masters simply did not supervise their bondsmen well. A reporter in the *Memphis Daily Eagle and Enquirer* in February 1852 reminded everyone of the law requiring a written permit from the slave's master or his agent before hiring a slave. The writer warned that this practice was bad for both slaves and masters, and it weakened the institution. The author also wrote of another bad effect of hiring one's own time. Apparently what prompted this article more than anything else was the slave in question had been working for himself for almost a year and had paid his master nothing.[15]

Slaves continued to hire their own time throughout the 1850s. A writer in the *Memphis Daily Appeal* in the summer of 1853 reported how a female slave had been fined (her owner paid the fine) for hiring herself out without her mistress' permission. The editor of the same newspaper in 1855 wrote of the strengthening of the ordinance against slaves hiring themselves out without a permit, and in 1860 the *Daily Appeal* published the slave ordinances, reminding both black and white that no slave may hire his own time.[16]

An associated problem of hiring out was the practice of slaves living out—away from their masters or employers. The evidence for Memphis tends to refute Kathleen Berkeley's assessment that slaves living out was not a problem in Memphis, and free blacks and slaves were not living in close proximity to each other. She claims that Richard Wade is wrong in his conclusion that slaves living away weakened the authority of the master. In fact, she says slaves in Memphis lived in close proximity to their masters.[17] Berkeley also finds, again unlike Wade, that there was much evidence of residential segregation in Memphis before the war. Wade asserts that "few streets, much less than blocks were solidly black," but Berkeley argues that free blacks (along with the Irish) were "the most residentially segregated group from both the white community and the slave community."[18]

To be sure, many Memphians by the late 1850s were concerned about the growing sectional tension and the Free-Soil proclivities of the Republican Party, which Berkeley says accounts for the growing number and severity of the city regulations during that decade. However, the slave ordinances of the 1850s were the result of substantive problems, among which was the increasing practice of slaves living away from their masters.[19] Before the rise of the Republican Party and the more heightened sectional fears, the newspapers of Memphis were filled with comments about this arrangement. In 1849 a writer for the *Daily Eagle* deprecated the practice of slaves and free blacks living away from whites.[20] The next year, the Memphis Board of Aldermen responded with an ordinance prohibiting slaves from occupying, residing, or sleeping in any house "other than that of his owner or employer."[21] In 1853, a reporter for the *Daily Appeal* wrote about the arrest of a slave for living "away from the residence of her owner" and added that this offense has "become insufferable and must be suppressed."[22] Six years later, a petition to the board complained about a boardinghouse in which "blacks and low whites" resided and "whose customs were disgusting and immoral."[23] The city marshal, during the month of August 1858, arrested thirty-two blacks (slave and free) for "living in violation of the city ordinance," and in early 1861 the board investigated a number of blacks in the Fifth and Sixth Wards of the city living by themselves.[24] Memphis whites were very concerned about slaves living away from their masters.[25]

Just how much one should emphasize the fact that black residents had begun "to sort themselves out" by the late 1850s is debatable. For one thing, whites did not want blacks to sort themselves out. The city ordinances of that decade all worked to prevent that. As early as 1849 the complaint was heard in Memphis that "free Negroes cluster thickly around the borders and even around some central points in Memphis."[26] For another thing, in a city of less than three square miles, the point cannot be ignored that slaves and free blacks frequently associated with each other, too frequently for many white Memphians.[27]

While white Memphians struggled with the freedom they believed slaves gained by hiring out their own labor and by living away, apparently officials never came close to putting an end to the illegal trade with slaves. In particular, the selling of liquor to slaves continued unabated, and Memphians regarded it as one of the most disturbing problems in the city. A Tennessee law of 1813 provided for a fine of five to ten dollars for the unlawful trading with a slave, while another 1829 law allowed a fifty-dollar fine for selling liquor to slaves. By 1842 the Tennessee General Assembly approved more severe laws. By 1842, the penalty for selling liquor to slaves or permitting a free black to be drunk on one's premises was imprisonment for up to thirty days. The penalty for the same offence, by the late 1850s, had increased to a fifty-dollar fine and imprisonment.[28]

Throughout the 1840s and the 1850s, the Memphis Board of Aldermen attempted to enhance the state laws through its own ordinances that regulated the sale of liquor to slaves, in addition to any other illegal trade. The board levied fines, prohibited blacks from congregating in tippling houses, outlawed the selling of liquor to slaves on the Sabbath, and even banned the giving of spirits to a slave without the owner or employer's permission.[29] Despite such legislation, the city press reported that the practice was too common. One writer called for "more severe and more certain penalties" than presently in force. The problem had become an almost every day occurrence, and one resident predicted that if something was not done, he foresaw the "complete demoralization of the slave population."[30] A writer in the *Daily Appeal* reported in March 1855 that the grand jury believed the illegal trade in alcohol with slaves was a serious subject, which required the vigilance of both the police and the courts.[31]

From the police reports and the reports of the City Recorder's Court, it does appear that the police and the courts took seriously the admonition of the grand jury. A closer examination reveals that the fines levied against the guilty parties were not nearly as severe as the law allowed. For example, even though the recorder, in December 1853, pronounced the offense "too common an occurrence to pass over lightly," he fined one offender only ten dollars. The guilty party in this case was a repeat offender, and when she appeared before the same recorder, the fine remained ten dollars.[32]

Selling liquor to blacks, slaves in particular, remained a problem for the rest of the pre–Civil War period in Memphis. In the summer of 1856, the Memphis Board of Aldermen did attempt to strengthen the law prohibiting slaves from entering saloons without written permission of their owners. Convicted slaves would receive no less than twenty and no more than thirty-nine lashes on "the bare back," while the slave owner would be assessed costs of the punishment. The fine for the guilty saloon owner was twenty-five to fifty dollars for each offense.[33] Two years later, attempting to control the liquor sales in general, the board passed a 9:00 P.M. closing law for saloons. This would have primarily affected the white population, but slaves too would have found it more difficult to purchase alcohol. A Common Law Court judge ruled, however, that the board had no "power to limit the hours at which liquor should be sold."[34] To further frustrate city officers, the recorder continued to levy moderate fines against violators.[35]

Of all the realities associated with urban slavery that so concerned white residents of Memphis, probably none compared with the presence of free blacks. In most places in the South free blacks were few in number, indeed, and because the overwhelming majority of slaves resided in the rural areas of the South, free blacks and slaves had little if any contact. In an urban environment, however, slaves came into daily contact with men and women of the same color, some of whom were free—certainly not as free as whites, but free nonetheless. A few of the free blacks were not even from the South. In Memphis, an inland port city, there were times when free blacks from the North were in town. If liquor demoralized slaves and hiring their own time corrupted them, white Memphians were convinced that the presence of free blacks came close to snapping the bonds of slavery altogether.

Before the founding of Memphis, the Tennessee General Assembly had already provided that free blacks had to register in the county in which they resided. If they moved to another county, they had to register again, and free blacks from other states had to bring proof of their status and register. By 1842 free blacks had to renew their registration every three years. To prevent a large free black population from developing in the state, in 1831 the legislature required all manumitted slaves to be removed from the Tennessee. Ten years later the legislature reversed itself, but in 1849 Tennessee returned to the policy of removal. Despite the legislation, owners continued to emancipate their slaves without making any provision for their removal. Therefore, in 1852 legislators, fearing a growing indolent free black population, provided that these blacks could be hired out and their wages, if needed, be applied to their support. Then, in 1854, the law required that their wages be used to pay for their transportation to Africa. A bill that would have removed all free blacks failed in 1858, and in the session of 1859–60, the legislature failed to force free blacks into slavery.[36]

Even though the free black population of Memphis was negligible throughout the pre–Civil War period, the white citizens were no less alert than the legislature to what they considered a dangerous element. In the summer of 1848, when the number of free blacks was probably no more than one hundred (less than 2 percent of the total population),[37] the board passed an ordinance "to better regulate the conduct of free blacks within the city." This ordinance prohibited free blacks to be away from their homes after

10:00 P.M. without obtaining a pass from the alderman of their ward. The penalty for failure to comply was ten dollars and fifteen lashes.[38]

The presence of a small free black community, nevertheless, continued to threaten Memphis whites. One writer to the *Daily Eagle* in 1849 complained of the number of free blacks. He called them "a serious evil" in Memphis and believed it would be necessary to prohibit free blacks from living in the city and the state. This Memphian probably expressed the sentiments of many others in the city when he characterized free blacks as "immoral, unproductive, slothful and injurious to property—particularly slave property." He concluded that free blacks stood as the "unfailing cause of discontent, a dissatisfying contrast of the most utter indolence, before our slave population." He could not understand how a slave state permitted free blacks to live in the state, and he hoped the legislature would pass "stringent and salutary enactments."[39]

Other white Memphians agreed with this assessment. Most believed that free blacks presented too many problems for the South, particularly in towns and cities. Their litany of complaints is familiar: free blacks received stolen goods, they were thieves, and they were at best casual workers. But what concerned whites the most was the contrast free blacks offered to slavery. A free black, it was heard time and time again, was the "master of his own time . . . and the contrast is to breed discontent" among slaves.[40]

According to white Memphians, free blacks not only bred discontent, but they tried to lure slaves away to free states. One resident wrote the mayor in 1849 that the free black crew members of a packet steamer tried to entice slaves aboard to take them to a free state. Soon thereafter, the board of aldermen passed an ordinance that resembled those of other southern port cities. The ordinance prohibited steamboats arriving from the North to remain at the landing for more than three hours if it carried any "free black or mulatto." Violation of the ordinance carried a fifty-dollar fine for each free black or mulatto on board. Additionally, any free black so brought in on a boat who remained more than one hour after being informed by a city officer to leave would be arrested and jailed for thirty days. After being released, if the free black failed to leave Memphis within two hours, he or she would be imprisoned for another thirty days.[41]

By 1850 the number of free blacks living the city had reached 124, still a very small number but large enough to receive the close attention of city officials. The police kept a list of free blacks registered in the Recorder's Court and ascertained residence and employment. It treated those with no visible signs of support as vagrants. To encourage diligence, if not harassment, officers received two dollars for every arrest. Worse than any of these inconveniences was a potential loss of freedom. Any free black representing himself or herself as free but who had failed to register or who had no papers on their person while in public would be considered a slave and dealt with accordingly.[42]

While these measures satisfied some whites that the city's free black community was under proper control, a growing number of white Memphians decided that the laws did not go far enough; the best solution, in their mind, was for all free blacks to be removed from the state. Those who favored removal offered several justifications. Some whites, who admitted having friends among the free blacks, offered to end their relationship for the good of the community and proposed sending all free blacks north—at city expense.[43] One alderman proposed an ordinance that required the mayor to give free blacks sixty days' notice to leave the city. Another reminded the board that such an ordinance would conflict with state law and the proposal failed.[44] The board did resolve, however, to appoint a committee to study the problem, and arrests of free blacks appear to have increased at this time.[45] By the end of the 1850s, most whites concurred that removal was sound policy. One newspaper reported that in less than an hour, five hundred names had been signed to a petition calling for the expulsion of free blacks from Memphis.[46]

Unquestionably, whites found it difficult to control slaves and free blacks in Memphis before the Civil War. The contacts that blacks had with each other, free and slave, and with whites of all kinds, and the exposure of diverse situations was a far cry from what isolated rural blacks experienced in slavery. The constraints did break down. Masters in Memphis found it easier to send a slave on an errand without a written permit, and they gave their slaves other latitudes that would not have been possible on the plantation. Control of urban slaves was difficult, but that did not necessarily mean "slavery was in great disarray" and "was languishing," as Richard Wade argues was the case in other southern cities.[47] In this respect Memphis was different from the majority of southern cities. While Wade's research concluded that urban slavery was increasingly becoming incompatible with town life throughout the South, a similar pattern cannot be found in Memphis.[48] Wade certainly is correct to point out the significance of the difficulties of controlling slaves and free blacks. In Memphis, the restraints on blacks did receive constant attention and they do not appear to have been all that effective. Also, with so many people living in close proximity, it was next to impossible to keep slaves at a distance from whites and free blacks.

But in Memphis slavery and urban life were compatible; during the 1850s there was not a precipitous decline in the number of blacks, nor did

Memphis whites remove black males from the cities. In 1850 the black population of Memphis was 2,486.[49] The 1860 census shows that the black population had grown to 3,871, an increase of more than 56 percent. The increase for the slave population is about the same. This is far from a precipitous decline, and in spite of all the rhetoric and legislation during the decade, the number of free blacks in the city increased while the percentage of young males within the black community (19 percent in the 1850 census compared to 18 percent in the 1860 census) remained the same.[50]

One important pattern that Memphis shared with other southern cities was that there was a "persistent imbalance between the sexes" in southern towns.[51] In Memphis, 54 percent of the black population was female.[52] Throughout much of the urban South, however, the percentage difference was much higher. In 1850, according to a study of six southern cities by Leonard Curry, a typical city in the South had over one and a half females for every male; in Memphis the ratio was much lower at 1.1412:1, or about one and one-seventh females for every male. While that ratio increased in 1860, it only increased to 1.1666:1.[53]

These statistics indicate that, contrary to earlier conclusions by Claudia Goldin, strong agricultural demand in the Cotton South did not always lead to decreased slave population in southern cities.[54] As already mentioned, Memphians may have discussed and legislated the control of slaves, but the number of slaves increased by almost 60 percent between 1850 and 1860. Increased costs to masters do not appear to have been a problem, either. For example, during the 1850s, the city tax on slave property increased by only one-fourth of 1 percent while the fines imposed on masters as part of controlling slaves were minimal.[55] Nor did the availability of a substitute, low-cost immigrant labor lead to a decreasing urban black population. Even though the immigrant population dramatically increased during the 1850s in Memphis, for one reason or another Memphians continued to rely heavily on slave labor. A major factor for this reliance on slave labor would seem to be that Memphis, which experienced remarkable growth in the 1850s, needed as many workers as possible, including slaves, free blacks, and the newly arriving immigrants. In addition, being a slave owner carried with it important social distinctions. For the majority of white southerners, ownership of slaves was a status symbol. Just beginning to enjoy an accumulation of possessions and increasing prosperity, white Memphians defied the trend that was continuing in at least six of the older southern cities and heavily relied on the labor of slaves.

Demonstrating this commitment by white Memphis residents to slave labor is the 1858 debate over a tax on slaves for nonresidents of Memphis.

Apparently city officials wanted to secure additional revenue from masters who paid no taxes in Memphis but whose slaves worked in the city. This practice must have been widespread, for the board of aldermen to consider legislation to regulate it. Arguing against the ordinance, one alderman noted that the hotels of Memphis would be unable to acquire workers with such a regulation.[56] Further evidence of the demand for slave labor is the plan of the Memphis and Ohio Railroad to hire black workers and the willingness of the president of that railroad to pay thirty-one hundred dollars in 1860 for a house slave and his wife, the latter described as only a "good fair cook."[57] Then there was the use of a large number of slave laborers by a prominent Memphis construction firm until the proprietors of that firm retired in 1858.[58] There may have been an agricultural demand for more slaves, but the farmers and planters around Memphis must have acquired them from somewhere else.[59]

Memphians railed about controlling their slaves, about maintaining their authority over them, and they deprecated free blacks, liquor sales to slaves, and the practice of slaves hiring their own time and living out. City officials enacted and enforced numerous ordinances relating to blacks. Therefore, after examining the views of Memphis residents in the newspapers and reading the Minutes of the Board of Aldermen, it seems logical to assume that the 1860 census would reflect a decline in the slave population. Slaves, and blacks in general, simply were not tractable. Why would not Memphis follow her sister cities of the South in reducing what some perceived as a dangerous element? Instead, the black population (free and slave) increased by over 56 percent between 1850 and 1860. White Memphians continued to use slaves in various occupations despite the presence of large numbers of Irish and German immigrants.[60] There is no escaping the reality of how the black population, particularly the slave population, continued to be a vital and important part of Memphis as the antebellum period came to an end.

Notes

1. Edward Michael McCormack, *Slavery on the Tennessee Frontier: Tennessee in the Eighteenth Century*, ed. James C. Kelly and Dan E. Pomeroy (Nashville, 1976), 9–21.
2. Charles W. Crawford, *Yesterday's Memphis*, Seemann's Historic Cities Series No. 25 (Miami, 1976), 17; Gerald M. Capers Jr., *The Biography of a River Town, Memphis: Its Heroic Age* (Memphis, 1966), 57.
3. Crawford, *Yesterday's Memphis*, 18. The dramatic change in Memphis' fortunes is reflected in the shipment of cotton through the city. In 1840 only 35,000 bales worth $3 million went through, while in 1860 that had increased to 360,653 bales worth $18.5 million.
4. John E. Harkins, *Metropolis of the American Nile: Memphis and Shelby County* (Woodland Hills, Calif., 1982), 39; Capers, *Biography of a River Town*, 47, 110.

While there are those who would slight the importance of slaves in Memphis, vis-à-vis the new immigrants, it cannot be ignored that the slave population rose substantially in comparison to other southern cities in the 1850s.

5. Capers, *Biography of a River Town*, 68; Samuel Cole Williams, *Beginning of West Tennessee: In the Land of the Chickasaws, 1541–1841* (Johnson City, Tenn., 1930), 213. The constitutional convention not only ejected emancipation but also disfranchised blacks who had voted under the old constitution.

6. Caleb P. Patterson, *The Negro in Tennessee, 1790–1865* (Austin, Tex., 1922), 37–39, 46–47.

7. Richard Wade, *Slavery in the Cities: The South, 1820–1860* (New York, 1964), 243–48.

8. Claudia Goldin, *Urban Slavery in the American South, 1820–1860: A Quantitative History* (Chicago, 1976). The cheap, substitute labor force to which Goldin refers is the immigrant laborer.

9. Kathleen Berkeley, "'Like a Plague of Locust': Immigration and Social Change in Memphis, 1850–1880" (Ph.D. diss., UCLA, 1980), 11, 36, 48.

10. *Memphis Daily Eagle*, 8 Nov. 1849.

11. Ibid.

12. Ibid.

13. Bette B. Tilly, "The Spirit of Improvement: Reformism and Slavery in West Tennessee," West Tennessee Historical Society *Papers* 28 (1974): 30, 33, 35. By 1834 slaves could no longer buy their freedom.

14. *Memphis Daily Eagle*, 8 Nov. 1849.

15. *Memphis Daily Eagle and Enquirer*, 21 Feb. 1852.

16. *Memphis Daily Appeal*, 29 July 1853, 8 Aug. 1855, and 28 Dec. 1860.

17. Berkeley, "Like a Plague of Locust," 48.

18. Ibid., 48; Wade, *Slavery in the Cities*, 277.

19. Memphis did require slaves to carry a pass if they were away from their master's residence after curfew. Failure to have a pass could result in fines for the master. In 1839 curfew was 10:00 P.M. and the fine was two dollars. Memphis Board of Aldermen Minutes (hereafter cited as Minutes), 18 Mar. 1839, Shelby County Archives (hereafter cited as SCA). In 1851 slaves were given fifteen minutes to reach home after the curfew; by 1860 curfew was 9:00 P.M. Minutes, 1 Apr. 1851, SCA; *Memphis Daily Appeal*, 28 Dec. 1860. This does, in part, explain why many masters simply found it convenient to allow their urban slaves, who hired themselves out, to live close to their workplace.

20. *Memphis Daily Eagle*, 28 Dec. 1849.

21. Minutes, 27 Mar. 1850, VA-3, SCA.

22. *Memphis Daily Appeal*, 25 July 1853.

23. Ibid., 24 Aug. 1859.

24. Ibid., 4 Sept. 1858; Minutes, 2 Jan. 1861, VA-6, SCA.

25. The dissimilarity statistic, which Professor Berkeley utilizes, is a tool that has little relevance for the black population (slave or free) of Memphis. Additionally, as Leonard P. Curry in *The Free Black in Urban America, 1800–1850: The Shadow of the Dream* (Chicago, 1981) notes for free blacks, the index of dissimilarity has two major problems. One is the necessity of using ward boundaries which are too large to effect much accuracy and the other is how wards divide black residential areas thus distorting black residential patterns (55). Curry also demonstrates that in 1850, only two of six southern cities (Memphis is not included) had what he calls a "high level of racial residential concentrations." Four had residential concentrations

termed insignificant (56). This latter finding would seem to be consistent with what white Memphians were attempting to do at this time—to prevent free blacks from segregating themselves in neighborhoods where slaves frequently resided away from their masters. Then, too, Berkeley's slave figures come from the 1850 and 1860 census, figures reported to the census takers by masters who, I feel, would simply list those slaves that they owned or hired as living at the master's or owner's address. It is hardly likely that masters would have admitted to having knowledge that their slaves had broken the city ordinance prohibiting living away.

26. *Memphis Daily Eagle*, 8 Nov. 1849.

27. Berkeley, "Like a Plague of Locust," 35–36.

28. Patterson, *Negro in Tennessee*, 37–38, 46–48.

29. Minutes, 19 June 1841 and 27 Mar., 5 Nov., 17 Dec. 1850, VA-1 and VA-3, SCA.

30. *Memphis Daily Appeal*, 12 Apr. 1852 and 29 May 1855.

31. Ibid., 14 Mar. 1855.

32. Ibid., 8 Oct., 2 Dec. 1853 and 4 Jan., 27 Sept. 1854.

33. *Memphis Daily Whig*, 4 June 1856; *Memphis Daily Appeal*, 4 June 1856.

34. *Memphis Daily Appeal*, 28 Mar. 1858. Even though there was a 9:00 P.M. city curfew for slaves, there were numerous violations. As late as June 1860, the editor of the *Daily Appeal* admonished owners to keep their slaves home as required and reported that on one night three slaves had been taken into custody for violating the curfew. *Memphis Daily Appeal*, 7 June 1860. While the city attorney believed the city had the authority to close saloons at 9:00 P.M., the board did not appeal the decision and subsequently set the closing time at 11:00 P.M. *Memphis Daily Appeal*, 19, 22 Sept. 1858.

35. *Memphis Daily Appeal*, 11 Aug., 22 Sept. 1858 and 14 June, 20 Dec. 1860.

36. Patterson, *Negro in Tennessee*, 157–62. The state legislature expected that the local governments would see that no freed black would become a burden to the community and that local officials would carry out the will of the legislature in the matter of removal and garnishing of wages, but it appears that local officials hesitated to act. In part, the small number of free blacks across the state may account for the lethargy of local government.

37. The total population of Memphis was approximately eight thousand at this time; this number included about two thousand slaves.

38. Minutes, 20 May and 3 June 1848, VA-2, SCA.

39. *Memphis Daily Eagle*, 8 Nov. 1849.

40. *Memphis Daily Eagle*, 7 Dec. 1850; *Memphis Daily Appeal*, 25 July 1853 and 28 Dec. 1856.

41. Minutes, 10 Feb. 1849, VA-2, SCA.

42. Ibid., 27 Mar. 1850, VA-4, SCA.

43. *Memphis Daily Appeal*, 28, 30 Dec. 1856 and 7 Jan. 1857.

44. Ibid., 16 July 1856 and 7 Jan. 1857.

45. Ibid., 7 Jan. 1857, 30 Apr. 1859, 24 July 1859, 17 Aug. 1859, 2, 3, 19, June 1860, and 20 Dec. 1860.

46. Ibid., 18 Dec. 1860.

47. Wade, *Slavery in the Cities*, 243.

48. Ibid.

49. United States Seventh Census, 1850, Slave and Population Schedules, Shelby County, Tennessee.

50. United States Eighth Census, 1860, Slave and Population Schedules, Shelby County, Tennessee.
51. Wade, *Slavery in the Cities*, 263–64.
52. United States Seventh and Eighth Census, 1850 and 1860, Slave Schedules, Shelby County, Tennessee.
53. Curry, *Free Black in Urban America*, 8, 252, 254.
54. Goldin, *Urban Slavery*, 156.
55. *Memphis Daily Appeal*, 22 Sept. 1852; Minutes, 6 July 1859, VA-5, SCA.
56. *Memphis Daily Appeal*, 17 Nov. and 17 Dec. 1858. The ordinance passed, levying a tax of twenty dollars a year for each slave employed or hired in Memphis but owned by a nonresident.
57. J. P. Wood to Robertson Topp, 14 Dec. 1860; Robertson Topp Purchase Agreement (copy), 5 Jan. 1860; both in Robertson Topp Papers, Rhodes College, Memphis, Tenn.
58. *Memphis Daily Appeal*, 15 Oct. 1858.
59. Just how many urban slaves West Tennessee could have absorbed is questionable. Although the state was a net importer of slaves in the 1820s, by the 1850s it was a net exporter. Michael Tadman, "Slave Trading in the Ante Bellum South: An Estimate of the Extent of the Inter-Regional Slave-Trade," *Journal of American Studies* 13 (Aug. 1979): 215.
60. The occupations of slaves in Memphis would be too numerous to mention, but the most common job for female slaves was a domestic worker while male slaves commonly worked at construction, drayman, hotel, janitorial, and shipping related jobs.

Murder in Franklin
The Mysteries of Small-Town Slavery

Lisa C. Tolbert

*I*N TENNESSEE MOST ANTEBELLUM URBAN SLAVES LIVED IN SMALL TOWNS, NOT MEMPHIS, NASHVILLE, AND KNOXVILLE, THE STATE'S THREE LARGEST CITIES. Lisa Tolbert uses a forgotten murder case in Franklin, in which a slave was accused of murdering two white men in 1850, to shed light on the nature of small-town slavery. Of particular interest is how the testimony in the murder trial allows freed and enslaved blacks to speak directly from the past, giving their perspective on their routines and responsibilities. Since slaves had a "broad access to town space," Tolbert finds that slaves actively participated in a wide range of affairs, from prayer meetings, the routine of laundry and cooking, and endless daily chores to the numerous opportunities to visit with members of their own race. Yet town life had its drawbacks. Since comparatively few free blacks lived in small towns, there were no defined black neighborhoods where there could be some degree of separation from the white world. Nor did blacks answer to only one master; in a town setting, everyone knew each other, and white men had some police authority over town slaves, whether or not they were the owners. "The spatial and social proximity of mixed race households," argues Tolbert, "made small-town servitude distinctive."

The moon shone very bright on Main Street in Franklin Sunday night, 24 February 1850. Most of the town's fifteen hundred or so residents were at home asleep, but sometime between ten and eleven o'clock the quiet street filled with people. A prayer meeting had just ended at the home of Hannah Henderson, a free black woman who lived on Indigo Street. The slaves who had worshiped there walked leisurely toward their various places of residence, chatting in small groups spread out along Main Street. The tranquil scene changed abruptly when the moonlight revealed three men, two white and one black, wrestling in the street up ahead, near the Presbyterian Church corner. Someone cried, "Look there, they are about to take that negro." But the "scuffle" took a deadly turn. Before they could cry out for help, both white men lay dead in the street as the black man disappeared up the Columbia Turnpike, pursued only by the barking of dogs.[1]

The victims, William P. Barham and John G. Eelbeck, described as "respectable citizens" of Franklin, had both been stabbed in the heart.[2] Beside the bodies lay four slabs of bacon, which the murderer had dropped during the fight. It appeared that Barham and Eelbeck had attempted a citizen's arrest of a black man they accused of stealing the meat. Barham's heart had been "laid open, a piece cut off," along with one of his ribs. Doctors Ewing, Cliffe, and Morton all examined the bodies and determined that they must have been murdered by a powerful and skillful man, one who "had knowledge where the vital organs lay." Investigation of the crime scene and the search for the murderer continued through the night and into Monday morning. Sometime after breakfast on Monday, authorities arrested Henry, whose job at the local tannery made him skilled with the knife and thus a likely suspect.

The testimony at Henry's trial might be studied with interest as a dramatic murder mystery. But the trial transcript ultimately reveals a deeper mystery with broader historical implications than a simple whodunit tale. As the slave witnesses told what they had seen on that fateful Sunday night, they also exposed some of the mysteries of their own lives. Testimony at Henry's trial offers a rare glimpse of the everyday world of small-town slavery from the slave's perspective. The fact that the murders took place in a small town mattered.

Given their widespread distribution in the region, small towns remain surprisingly peripheral in the prevailing history of the antebellum South. Historians have learned much about the nature of rural and urban life in the antebellum South, but the regional landscape has been drawn largely as a map of contrasting extremes. Widely dispersed plantations and yeoman farmsteads composed the agrarian center,[3] while on the periphery, a few major

The Barham and Eelbeck murder scene in Franklin, drawn as an exhibit for Henry's 1850 murder trial and included in the court files of *Henry, a Slave v. State of Tennessee.* Tennessee State Library and Archives.

cities, largely riverine or coastal ports, emerged.[4] Elizabeth Fox-Genovese represents the prevailing consensus that even though small towns and villages were "ubiquitous" in the region, "southern towns primarily reflected the countryside."[5] The small-town South remains obscure, on one hand, subsumed by an undifferentiated rural countryside, and on the other assumed to be nothing more than an urban microcosm.

Small towns appear only incidentally in the landscape as a setting for social, political, and economic interactions among planters.[6] Yet slaves constituted nearly half of the population of Franklin in Williamson County in 1850.[7] The testimony at Henry's trial reveals the outlines of a system with own unique characteristics—a type of slavery that was qualitatively different compared to urban or rural forms of the institution. Furthermore, hearing this story from the perspective of slaves enables us to see more fully how slaves were active participants in town life.

Henry's routine on that fateful weekend in February reveals some of the patterns of work and leisure in a small town, where streets and shop floors rather than farm fields were the routine sites of action. Henry worked for

Samuel Tenneswood at the local tanyard on the Columbia Turnpike. Before sundown on Sunday evening, 24 February, Henry walked over as usual to Mrs. Doyle's house on the corner of Margin and Church Streets to get his employer's supper, which consisted of "a coffeepot and a plate of batter-cakes."[8] Catherine Doyle was the widow of a prosperous baker and business-man. Mourning, one of Doyle's four slaves, met Henry at the kitchen door. Henry always had to grab a piece of Doyle's stove wood to fend off the neigh-borhood dogs, and Mourning later remembered that she had accidentally kicked over the stick he had propped against the wall as she handed him the meal she had prepared. A similar stick would be found at the murder scene a few hours later. Henry balanced the components of Tenneswood's supper precariously, "coffee pot in one hand, and plate and stick in the other," as he set off to make his delivery.

Despite his evening errand for Tenneswood, Henry had had at least part of the day to himself. He spent some of his time off playing cards at Rags-dale's shop.[9] About one o'clock in the afternoon, Henry stopped at Ragsdale's gate to chat with Tom, slave of William P. Campbell, who was on his way to prepare the sacrament for the Sunday service at the Campbellite church.[10] Henry does not seem to have attended church or even the late-night prayer meeting at Hannah Henderson's house.

Henderson, a free black woman, lived on Indigo Street, a block up from Main, where a group of at least eleven or twelve slaves met for Sunday prayer, including Henry's neighbor, Isabella. Isabella worked for the Wells family who owned a carriage factory next door to Henry's current residence—the McConnell kitchen. Peter McConnell, a tobacconist from Pennsylvania, owned one slave, a forty-year-old woman named Susan. Henry "was in the habit of staying at night" with Susan in the kitchen, which stood at the back of a V-shaped lot where the Columbia Turnpike met Margin and Main Streets.[11] Susan and Isabella probably broke the monotony of cooking, laun-dry, and other housework by visiting across the unfenced property line between the McConnell and Wells households. When the prayer meeting at Hannah Henderson's ended around 10:30, Isabella took a roundabout route back to her employer's house, first visiting the household of her owner and then stopping by the McConnell kitchen to tell Susan the evening's news. Isabella noticed that Henry had returned to the kitchen to sleep.

Early Monday morning Henry rose before daylight and put on a clean white homespun shirt and his gray roundabout coat with its red flannel lin-ing. His first task was to cut the firewood Susan would need for cooking and laundry that day. He made the fire in the McConnell kitchen, slung the axe over his shoulder, and proceeded to his next job, sweeping the floor at King's grocery on the square. James King, who also lived in the store, had hired Jake Childress "to make fires for him." Jake had in turn employed Henry. For the past two or three weeks Henry had walked up Main Street early every morning to clean King's room, sweep out the store, and chop the firewood. Henry was used to seeing Jeff, slave of Hugh Duff, who started his work early at Short's stone yard near the grocery. Town slaves began their work day before sunrise, so Henry and Jeff were among the first town residents to appear on the public square Monday morning. Henry finished sweeping out the grocery just after daybreak, and once again slung the axe over his shoulder and walked back up Main Street to his job at the tanyard on Columbia Turnpike.

These circumstantial details of Henry's life are insignificant by themselves, but taken as a whole these ordinary activities and encounters begin to outline the contours of small-town slavery. From hard and bloody labor in the tanyard, to odd jobs and errands, to casual conversations and card games, Henry came into contact with other slaves more often than with white residents. Besides Susan, there was the neighbor Isabella; Jake, who exchanged chores with Henry; Jeff, who worked across the square from one of his early morning jobs; Mourning, who cooked supper for his employer; Tom, a church sexton; card players at Ragsdale's shop; and many others. Whether Henry took his walks in the pursuit of a particular work duty or as part of his own leisure time, town streets offered numerous opportunities for casual conversations with slaves and others he met along the way.

Through such interactions, Henry exerted a certain amount of flexibility and control over his work routine. Small-town streets were full of slaves running errands for their masters or employers, who took the same opportunities that Henry did to choose their own routes and stop to talk to friends and acquaintances along the way. Besides the flexibility of errand running, Henry was not under the close supervision of an overseer at the tanyard. His employer, Samuel Tenneswood, described Henry as "always attentive" and "perfectly honest." On occasion, Tenneswood left Henry to work alone because, as Tenneswood explained, "he knew what his work was." In addition to his full-time employment at the tanyard, Henry had also taken the initiative to arrange odd jobs to earn extra money. Small towns offered a variety of ways for slaves to earn some extra cash, and those opportunities were expanding in the prosperous 1850s.

Though most slaves were household servants like Susan and Isabella—cooks, washerwomen, stable hands, dining-room servants—Henry was one of the numerous slaves whose work took them beyond individual households.

His story suggests some of the ways that slaves used small-town hiring practices to shape their own lives. Samuel Tenneswood was Henry's employer, not his owner. A farmer named John Bennett, whose house stood on Main Street, actually owned Henry and eleven other slaves. But Henry's actions on that February weekend in 1850 show that he neither lived in the Bennett household nor worked as a field hand for Bennett. Before Tenneswood, George Neely had hired Henry for one year as a butcher. Indeed, in the last few years, Henry had performed a variety of jobs including butcher, wood hauler, and meat vendor, selling game he hunted in the vicinity of town. This pattern of localized hiring was more typical than the long-range hiring practices of some antebellum cities, where business was brisk enough to support hiring agents who connected slaves or their masters with potential employers. Hired slaves in the small town tended to have masters who lived in the town or county where they worked. Slaves themselves often took an active part in hiring negotiations in a small-town context.[12]

Henry's work and residential experience fits larger patterns of slave experience in Franklin. In 1850, 68 percent of households in town owned slaves.[13] Franklin's slaveholders certainly included the wealthiest town residents—merchants, physicians, lawyers—but slave owners occupied a broad range of social and economic positions in the small-town hierarchy. For example, there was John Burch, a shoemaker who owned a twelve-year-old boy; and John Short, a stone cutter who owned a twenty-year-old woman; and Elijah Porter, a mulatto laborer who owned a thirty-year-old woman, a four-year-old girl, and a two-year-old girl, probably his wife and daughters.[14] Peter McConnell was typical of most Franklin slaveholders who tended to own only one or two slaves.[15] But as Henry's story demonstrates, actual slave ownership was only part of the story of town slavery. Many householders not counted among slave owners nevertheless hired cooks, laundresses, and stable hands. Thus, widespread slave ownership and hiring practices distributed the slave population evenly across the townscape. African Americans lived and worked throughout the county seat, from the public square to the railroad depot, from Italianate townhouses to middle-class cottages and even a few laborers' cabins.

Deciphering the context of slave experience in Franklin suggests that small towns cannot be understood simply as urban microcosms. One of the most striking differences was the contrast between slaves and free black residents. The number of free black residents remained insignificant in county seats throughout the first half of the nineteenth century.

Only twenty-three free black men and women lived in Franklin in 1850, about 1 percent of the town's population.[16] Thus black residents were much more likely to be slaves than freemen. In contrast, on the eve of the Civil War, the largest population of free blacks in Tennessee resided in the city of Nashville and surrounding Davidson County.[17] Seventy-two percent of free blacks lived together near the waterfront and the public square, in the Second and Fourth Wards of the city.[18] There were no separate racial neighborhoods in the county seat to compare with the density of free black residents on the waterfront in Nashville. The defining characteristic of slave experience in the small town was living dispersed among white households.[19]

The spatial configuration of small-town slavery was also significantly different from rural patterns of the institution. Southern plantations were often described as townlike by observers searching for a metaphor to encompass the many buildings that composed the plantation landscape—from the master's dwelling to the barns and service buildings to the slave quarters.[20] Though the clustered buildings suggested a townlike appearance, the racial configuration of the plantation, where the dwelling of one white family was outnumbered by the dwellings of multiple slave families, was quite different from the racial integration of small-town Franklin. Likewise, small-town slavery was also distinct from rural neighborhoods where slaves lived widely scattered on smaller farms. Just as slave experience shows that small towns were more than urban microcosms, so it also demonstrates that the small town should not be subsumed seamlessly into the rural landscape.

One of the most striking aspects of town slavery was the apparent freedom of movement and broad access to town space that was an everyday part of the work slaves performed. Much to the slaveholders' dismay, however, slaves extended the broad access to town streets that was customary of their work routines into their leisure hours. Unlike rural farm labor, town business depended less on long agricultural cycles and more on a weekly routine that left many slaves with spare time, especially after business on Saturday night until work began again on Monday morning. One irate town dweller complained that "the most retired citizens were constantly subject to the most unpleasant arrogances from the disorder of which prevailed always on the Sabbath day among negroes and their more disreputable associates. The negroes . . . were in the habit of prowling about the streets, stealing everything they could lay their hands upon, from Saturday night till Monday morning."[21] In response, slave owners established a temporal boundary in the small town. The same streets that thronged with slave messengers and draymen during the day were forbidden territory after dark, when slaves presumably would be engaged in something other than their masters' business. The slave who murdered Barham and Eelbeck appeared to confirm the worst nightmares of white residents.

Franklin residents were predictably alarmed by the murders. "The deep-est solemnity of feeling as well as intense excitement, prevailed throughout our whole community," the local paper reported. The funeral was "attended by an unusually large and deeply affected gathering of friends and mourners," and stores closed to mark the solemn occasion. "A deep and settled gloom pervaded every heart and every home."[22] The news quickly spread beyond Franklin to Nashville and surrounding small towns.[23] But their "deep and set-tled gloom" did not lead to hysterical retaliation against the small-town slave community as a whole. Unlike the riotous aftermath of the Nat Turner rebel-lion in many southern communities, the murders of Barham and Eelbeck were not linked to an insurrection plot.[24] They were viewed, instead, as the act of a thief, working alone, caught while committing the crime. The fact that the crime was initially reported by slave witnesses probably averted any widespread suspicion of the slave community. Thus, when Henry was arrested, residents let the law take its course, confident of the outcome. Twenty years later, when the power of white residents was less assured, Henry might have been lynched. But in 1850, white residents emphasized the systematic delib-eration and ultimate justice of the process, and so, "after a patient hearing of all the evidence and the able argument of counsel, the jury . . . returned a verdict of guilty."[25]

Despite the local editor's supreme confidence that justice had prevailed, Henry was convicted primarily on circumstantial evidence. Only one eye-witness, a slave named Oney, identified him by name as the result of repeated questioning. The other eyewitnesses admitted only vaguely that one of the three men looked like a Negro. Jinney "could not say from his face whether he was white or black, only thought he was a negro because he had a load and had the dress and form of a negro." Similarly, Malinda believed that one of the men was a slave, not because she could distinguish the color of his skin, but "from his dress and walk and form—that he had on a sack coat and black cap. . . . She thought the other two men were white from their dress." Even Oney insisted that she "could not say positively" that Henry was the man she saw run up the Columbia Turnpike on the night of the murders. Henry, who did not testify during the trial, declared his innocence on the gallows to a crowd estimated at about four thousand spectators, "a great por-tion being negroes."[26]

Yet beyond the putative guilt of Henry, evidence presented at the murder trial raises important questions about law and order in a slave town. Testimony revealed that the accused murderer was not the only potential criminal in attendance. The slave witnesses themselves were guilty of breaking several laws of the town. For example, it was illegal for Hannah Henderson, a free black woman, to "entertain any slave in . . . her house or residence on Sunday, or between sunset and sunrise of any day."[27] Nevertheless, slaves testified that "there was a house full of negroes at prayer meeting that night."[28] Furthermore, it was illegal for these slaves to "be found from home after 10 o'clock at night" without written permission from an "owner or manager."[29] They risked arrest, not only by the watchmen but also by any "citizen" of the town. This explains the reaction of Oney, a slave who saw the "scuffle" between the three men on her way home from the prayer meeting. Believing that "white men were whipping [a] negro for being out so late . . . she pushed on home."[30] From the slaves' perspective, white residents could not be trusted to let them walk the streets in peace. Vulnerable to the arbitrary decisions of white residents, slaves might be punished for breaking curfew—or not.

In fact, despite these flagrant curfew violations, the trial testimony suggests an almost casual disregard on the part of Franklin slave owners for enforcing the letter of the law. They expressed no surprise or dismay about the prayer meeting at Hannah Henderson's, which seems to have been a routine gathering for the slaves in attendance. Dr. Ewing and Peter McConnell slept peacefully in their houses a few steps from the scene of the murders until their nervous slaves woke them to explain what had happened. Although laws regarding slaves convey an impression that social control in the county seat was rigid and absolute, town officials were never willing or able to enforce strict compliance from either white or black residents. Custom was frequently at odds with the law in the antebellum town, a situation which becomes more understandable when viewed in the larger context of small-town slavery.

The demographics of the antebellum county seat reassured white residents that any black person within town limits was almost certainly a slave. Widespread slave ownership and hiring practices among white residents fostered an enlarged sense of ownership that extended to African American town residents in general. Lax enforcement and casual disregard for the letter of the law demonstrate that white residents rarely felt any concerted threat from the slave community. Efforts to regulate time and space in the townscape of slavery were, ultimately, contradictory. On one hand, repressive legislation set clear racial boundaries that circumscribed the movements of slave residents. On the other hand, whites were confident that racial dominance was secured by more effective means than legislation and found it more convenient in practice to disregard the letter of the law.

Town slaves recognized the inconsistencies between law and custom and kept steady, though subtle, pressure on the system to enlarge their modicum of independence. They could exploit relationships with numerous whites to limit the authority of a single master. But control of this process was tenuous at best. Small-town whites compensated for the weakened authority of individual masters by giving white residents extensive powers over town slaves. For example, even though they were not officially deputized, Barham and Eelbeck had the authority to stop and take into custody the slave they had suspected of stealing hams. In effect, small-town slaves had multiple masters. Given the distinctiveness of small-town slavery, it is no coincidence then that the antebellum southerner who drew the clearest distinctions among urban, rural, and small-town life was a slave. We can only speculate about Henry's thoughts and attitudes, but the remarkable autobiography of one small-town slave opens a window onto the particular experience of slave residents in a small town. Harriet Jacobs, who grew up in Edenton, North Carolina, defined herself explicitly as a small-town slave. "How often did I rejoice that I lived in a town where all the inhabitants knew each other!" she declared. "If I had been on a remote plantation, or lost among the multitude of a crowded city, I should not be a living woman at this day."[31]

The essential distinction of town life, Jacobs felt, was intimacy, a strong contrast to isolation or anonymity. Jacobs exploited the social dynamic of the small town to her advantage when she rejected the unwanted advances of her master, Dr. James Norcum. She reasoned that she was protected by her abusive owner's concern for his own good name as a wealthy doctor and plantation owner in Edenton. "It was lucky for me that I did not live on a distant plantation," she carefully explained, "but in a town not so large that the inhabitants were ignorant of each other's affairs. Bad as are the laws and custom in a slaveholding community, the doctor, as a professional man, deemed it prudent to keep up some outward show of decency."[32]

But Norcum's public image was not the only reputation that mattered. Harriet's grandmother, Molly Horniblow, cultivated a powerful one of her own. Horniblow had secured personal freedom in 1828 and operated a bakery in the heart of town. "Her presence in the neighborhood was some protection to me," Harriet argued. The doctor "dreaded her scorching rebukes," but more important, "she was known and patronized by many people; and he did not wish to have his villainy made public."[33] The interactions of James Norcum, Molly Horniblow, and her influential white clientele illuminate the complex racial dynamic that distinguished southern towns.

Of course it was not the complexity of race relations that distinguished small towns from farms and cities. Interactions between white and black were rarely simple anywhere in the antebellum South. It was the spatial and social proximity of mixed race households that made small-town servitude distinctive.

Henry, who was ultimately executed for murder, might have come to a different conclusion about the protective possibilities of living in a small town where everybody knew each other. His daily movements were widely known. His occupation as a butcher and tanner of hides made him a handy murder suspect. (Doctors who examined the bodies of the murder victims agreed that they must have been inflicted by someone who "had knowledge where the vital organs lay" and "great skill with the use of the knife.") He lived with Susan in the McConnell kitchen along the murderer's getaway route.

Harriet Jacobs herself was victimized by small-town intimacy. When she became a fugitive, her escape was threatened by myriad possibilities of discovery. For a while, she was unable even to send her grandmother a message because "every one who went in or out of her house was closely watched."[34] For better or worse, lives of white and black were intimately intertwined in a small town where "all the inhabitants knew each other." Slaves managed to turn this situation to their own advantage whenever possible—negotiating employment and housing arrangements, for example—but communal intimacy brought its own dangers and limitations for small-town slaves.

Recent historians have emphasized the possibilities for community building on plantations where African American slaves were often the majority of residents.[35] Similarly, historians of urban slavery have found that free blacks and slaves who lived in antebellum cities were able to accumulate property, maintain separate households, form social organizations, build independent churches, in short, to create autonomous African American communities.[36] In small towns, by contrast, slaves did not have the opportunity to create physically segregated black communities. Nevertheless, antebellum town space was racially configured, its communities separated by powerful social customs. Yet Harriet Jacobs expressed her preference for town life as a slave, despite the seemingly limited opportunities for building communal autonomy in a place "where all the inhabitants knew each other."

The testimony presented at Henry's trial confirms Jacobs' assertion that the small-town South must be understood on its own terms. Above all, town slavery had the potential to produce extremely complex living and working arrangements which slaves themselves played an influential role in formulating. Compared to urban and rural population patterns, small towns composed a distinctive racial configuration of space. In the antebellum county seat, black and white residents lived closer together than they did in the countryside or in cities.

Scattered throughout town, slaves became architects of communal intimacy as they hauled water, delivered messages, and ran errands for white
employers. But forced dispersal constrained the slaves' ability to create their
own communal institutions. Still, in casual exchanges on the street, card
games in the back rooms of storehouses, the neighborly sharing of household
duties across unfenced back lots, slaves managed to create a kind of community. The story of Henry reveals the vital role slaves played in the construction of small-town society. Indeed, it is impossible to understand the
distinctive dynamic of small-town life in the antebellum South without taking into account the influence of slaves like Henry.

Notes

1. Material presented in this chapter appears in Lisa C. Tolbert, *Constructing
Townscapes: Space and Society in Antebellum Tennessee* (Chapel Hill, N.C., 1999).
I am grateful to my colleagues Bill Link and Bill Blair for their comments on an
earlier version of this essay, originally presented at the American Studies Association, Tennessee-Kentucky Chapter Regional Meeting in April 1996. Quotations
are from the trial transcript, *Henry, a Slave v. State of Tennessee*, Middle Tennessee
Supreme Court, Box 92A, Tennessee State Library and Archives.
2. Quotation is from trial transcript, *Henry, a Slave v. State of Tennessee*. A Nashville
newspaper described Barham as a member of the Oddfellows and Eelbeck as "a
Mason and a Son of Temperance." See *Nashville Daily Centre–State American*,
2 Mar. 1850. John Eelbeck was the son of a prosperous carriage maker in Franklin,
and William P. Barham's family owned a grocery store near the public square.
3. See, for example, Wilbur J. Cash, *The Mind of the South* (New York, 1941); William
R. Taylor, *Cavalier and Yankee: The Old South and American National Character*
(Cambridge, Mass., 1979); Eugene D. Genovese, *The World the Slaveholders Made*
(New York, 1969); James Oakes, *The Ruling Race: A History of American Slaveholders*
(New York, 1982); and Elizabeth Fox-Genovese, *Within the Plantation Household:
Black and White Women of the Old South* (Chapel Hill, N.C., 1988). While these
scholars construct very different arguments about the nature of southern society,
they all assume the centrality of the plantation. For two exceptions to this rule,
see Robert C. Kenzer, *Kinship and Neighborhood in a Southern Community*
(Knoxville, 1987), which develops the concept of distinctive plantation neighborhoods in Orange County, North Carolina, and Orville Vernon Burton, *In
My Father's House Are Many Mansions: Family and Community in Edgefield, South
Carolina* (Chapel Hill, N.C., 1985), which examines town and country in one
district of South Carolina.
4. See, for example, David R. Goldfield, *Cotton Fields and Skyscrapers: Southern City
and Region, 1607–1980* (Baton Rouge, La., 1982); Blaine A. Brownell and David
R. Goldfield, eds., *The City in Southern History: The Growth of Urban Civilization in
the South* (Port Washington, N.Y., 1977); and Claudia Dale Goldin, *Urban Slavery
in the American South, 1820–1860: A Quantitative History* (Chicago, 1976). Joseph
A. Ernst and J. Roy Merrens, "'Camden's Turrets Pierce the Skies!': The Urban
Process in the Southern Colonies During the Eighteenth Century," *William and*

Mary Quarterly 30 (Oct. 1973): 549–74; Leonard P. Curry, "Urbanization and Urbanism in the Old South: A Comparative View," *Journal of Southern History* 40 (Feb. 1974): 43–60; Lyle W. Dorsett and Arthur H. Shaffer, "Was the Antebellum South Antiurban? A Suggestion," *Journal of Southern History* 38 (Feb. 1972): 93–100; Blaine A. Brownell, "Urbanization in the South: A Unique Experience?" *Mississippi Quarterly* 26 (Spring 1973): 105–20.

5. Fox-Genovese, *Within the Plantation Household*, 5, 74.

6. For example, Elizabeth Fox-Genovese admits that small towns "constituted the focus of the lives of so many slaveholders, including planters." Ibid., 5–6. And James Oakes has acknowledged that small towns were the primary stage for slaveholders' social, legal, political, and religious activity. *Ruling Race*, 92.

7. Forty-two percent of Franklin residents were slaves (calculated from the 1850 manuscript census). The proportion of slave residents in antebellum Franklin was comparable to other Middle Tennessee county seats of the period.

8. For a history and provenance of the Doyle house, see Virginia McDaniel Bowman, *Historic Williamson County: Old Homes and Sites* (Franklin, Tenn., 1989), 140–41.

9. According to the 1850 census there were two Ragsdales in Franklin: Robert, a thirty-two-year-old shoemaker who owned nine slaves, and William, a twenty-one-year-old cabinetmaker who owned one slave. It is not clear which shop served as venue for the card game.

10. Middle Tennesseans often referred to members of the Church of Christ as Campbellites after the founder of the group, Alexander Campbell.

11. This was the testimony of I. L. Littleton at Henry's murder trial. See *Henry, a Slave v. State of Tennessee*.

12. Tolbert, *Constructing Townscapes*, esp. chap. 6, "Small-Town Slaves."

13. Franklin: 68 percent of households owned slaves (176 total households; 119 slaveholding households). Calculated from 1850 manuscript census. Franklin's slaveholding patterns were comparable to other Middle Tennessee county seats of the period. For example, Murfreesboro: 77 percent of households owned slaves (163 total households, 125 slaveholding households). Columbia: 52 percent of households owned slaves (297 total households, 155 slaveholding households). Shelbyville: 51 percent of households owned slaves (174 total households, 89 slaveholding households). In *Middle Tennessee Society Transformed, 1860–1870* (Baton Rouge, 1988), Stephen Ash estimated that 76 percent of "town families" in Middle Tennessee owned no slaves in 1860. During the 1850s, the slave population increased, although at a slower rate than the white population. In Murfreesboro, slaves had dropped to 41 percent of the population by 1860. Nevertheless, it seems unlikely that the proportion of slave owners should have declined as dramatically as Ash's figures suggest. Ash's calculations were based on a random sample that included residents of towns other than county seats. He used a quantitative definition of town population with no reference to the landscape or actual town boundaries. It is possible that slaveholding was more widespread in these four towns because the counties surrounding Nashville were the wealthiest in the region.

14. Under Tennessee law, freed slaves had to agree to leave the state for their new status to take effect. Families who did not wish to be split up often found it safer to hold members as slaves rather than to free them.

15. Franklin: 42 percent of slaveholders owned only one or two slaves. Calculated from the 1850 manuscript census. Compare this to other county seats in the region: Murfreesboro: 28 percent of slaveholders owned only one or two slaves. Columbia:

31 percent of slaveholders owned only one or two slaves. Shelbyville: 33 percent of slaveholders owned only one or two slaves.

16. Population statistics were calculated from the 1850 manuscript census returns. Free blacks in Franklin included twelve women and sixteen men. The same pattern holds true for other county seats in the region. Twenty free blacks lived in Murfreesboro, fourteen women and six men; twenty-two lived in Shelbyville, nine women and thirteen men; and twenty-six lived in Columbia, sixteen women and ten men. The small free black presence in Middle Tennessee county seats is consistent with population patterns described by Ira Berlin. He found that in the Lower South free blacks gravitated toward cities, while in the Upper South, free blacks remained primarily rural peasants. See *Slaves without Masters: The Free Negro in the Antebellum South* (New York, 1974), 181.

17. Nashville had 1,209 free black residents or 17 percent of free blacks in the state. As much as 18 percent of the total black population of Nashville was free in 1860. Anita Shafer Goodstein, *Nashville, 1780–1860: From Frontier to City* (Gainesville, Fla., 1989), 137. See Loren Schweninger, ed., *From Tennessee Slave to St. Louis Entrepreneur: The Autobiography of James Thomas* (Columbia, Mo., 1984), for a free black's perspective on antebellum Nashville.

18. Goodstein, *Nashville, 1780–1860*, 141. Ira Berlin notes that southern cities lagged far behind northern cities in the development of residential segregation. Although free blacks increasingly chose, or were compelled, to live in racially segregated districts within cities, there were few urban counterparts in the South to Boston's "Nigger Hill," Pittsburgh's "Hayti," and Cincinnati's "Little Africa." *Slaves without Masters*, 255.

19. "An Ordinance in Relation to Slaves" published in the Shelbyville newspaper, *Western Freeman*, on 17 December 1833, suggests that some slaves may have been living in separate households, unsupervised by whites. According to section 2 of the ordinance, "It shall not, hereafter, be lawful for any slave or slaves to occupy or reside in any house or houses within said corporation, unless he, she or they shall have been actually hired by and be then in the bonafide employ of some white person or persons within the corporation aforesaid."

20. John Michael Vlach, *Back of the Big House: The Architecture of Plantation Society* (Chapel Hill, N.C., 1993), 12.

21. *National Vidette*, 10 Jan. 1828.

22. News from the *Franklin Western Weekly Review* quoted in the *Nashville Daily Centre–State American*, 2 Mar. 1850; also *Daily Republican Banner and Nashville Whig*, 4 Mar. 1850.

23. The following list of newspapers contain articles about Henry's trial and execution: *Nashville Daily American*, 21, 22 Feb. 1851; *Nashville Daily True Whig*, 13 Jan. and 21, 22 Feb. 1851; *Daily Republican Banner and Nashville Whig*, 26 Feb. and 4 Mar. 1850, 22 Feb. 1851; *Nashville True Whig and Weekly Commercial Register*, 6 Dec. 1850 and 28 Feb. 1851; *Franklin Western Weekly Review*, 15, 29 Nov. 1850 and 10 Jan., 21, 28 Feb. 1851.

24. For example, Harriet Jacobs reports that in response to the Turner rebellion whites rioted in Edenton, North Carolina (hundreds of miles from Southampton, Virginia). Black residents were indiscriminately whipped and beaten, their property was destroyed, and a black church was demolished. Harriet Jacobs, *Incidents in the Life of a Slave Girl: Written by Herself*, ed. Jean Pagan Yellin (Cambridge, Mass., 1987), 63–68.

25. *Franklin Western Weekly Review*, 29 Nov. 1850.

26. Henry was executed in Nashville, along with another slave named Moses who had been convicted of murdering his master. The *Nashville Daily American*, 22 February 1851, reported that "the gallows [were] erected upon the Murfrees-boro turnpike, about two miles from the square. . . . An immense concourse had gathered to witness the execution." The two condemned men received last rites from a Catholic priest. "After the cords were adjusted, one of the negroes (we could not learn which) addressed the crowd as follows: 'Gentlemen, I am inno-cent. Gentlemen, you are hanging an innocent man. In all my life and fights dis hand never had any blood in it.' . . . The crowd present as spectators must have been about 4,000 a great portion being negroes." For descriptions of the execution and identification of Henry as the man who addressed the crowd, see also *Nashville Daily True Whig*, 22 Feb. 1851. At the gallows, "Henry spoke a few words to the crowd, declaring his innocence of the crime for which he had been convicted, and for which he had to suffer death. The clergyman of the Catholic denomination, who had attended the prisoners in their last days of earthly pro-bation, spoke in behalf of Moses, who also declared himself innocent. The boy Henry maintained a cheerful and indifferent appearance during the arrangement of the preliminaries, and mounted the scaffold with a smile upon his countenance. The countenance of Moses, however, indicated a state of mind more in unison with the circumstances that surrounded him, and seemed to indicate an apprecia-tion of the awful and sudden transition from lusty life to cold inanimate clay, and from time to eternity, which awaited him." See also *Nashville True Whig and Weekly Commercial Register*, 28 Feb. 1851, for similar description and assertion that Henry was the one who gave the speech at the gallows. There were many residents from Franklin among the crowd. The *Nashville Daily True Whig*, 21 Feb. 1851: "The city yesterday indicated the presence of an unusual number of strangers, notwithstanding the inclement weather, principally from the country. It was suggested to us that the execution today had drawn them in, but for the sake of humanity we hope this was not the case." Listed as "Arrivals at the Principal Hotels": E. M. Eelbeck of Franklin, registered at the City Hotel, and J. Bennett (Henry's owner) of Franklin at Union Hall.

27. *By-Laws of the Town of Franklin. Together with the Acts of Incorporation* (Franklin, Tenn., 1838).

28. *Henry, a Slave v. State of Tennessee.*

29. *By-Laws of the Town of Franklin.*

30. *Henry, a Slave v. State of Tennessee.*

31. Jacobs, *Incidents in the Life*, 35.

32. Ibid., 29.

33. Ibid.

34. Ibid., 97.

35. Vlach, *Back of the Big House*; Eugene D. Genovese, *Roll Jordan, Roll: The World the Slaves Made* (New York, 1972). Rhys Isaac argues that the communal ethos slave quarter presented a sharp contrast by the end of the eighteenth century to the increasingly privatized dwellings of slave owners, see *The Transformation of Virginia, 1740–1790* (Chapel Hill, N.C., 1982).

36. Elsa Barkley Brown and Gregg D. Kimball, "Mapping the Terrain of Black Rich-mond," *Journal of Urban History* 21 (Mar. 1995): 296–346; David R. Goldfield, "Black Life in Old South Cities," in *Before Freedom Came: African-American*

Life in the Antebellum South, ed. by Edward D. C. Campbell Jr. with Kym S. Rice (Richmond, Va., 1991), 123–53; Marie Tyler-McGraw and Gregg D. Kimball, *In Bondage and Freedom: Antebellum Black Life in Richmond, Virginia* (Richmond, 1988); Berlin, *Slaves without Masters;* Richard C. Wade, *Slavery in the Cities: The South, 1820–1860* (New York, 1964); Robert S. Starobin, *Industrial Slavery in the Old South* (New York, 1970).

They Can Never Both Prosper Together
Black and White Baptists in Antebellum Nashville

Mechal Sobel

*T*HE AFRICAN AMERICAN CHURCH WAS AN INSTITU-
TIONAL FOUNDATION FOR BLACK COMMUNITY AND
CULTURE IN THE NINETEENTH-CENTURY SOUTH.
This chapter highlights the significance of church building
in the African American history of Tennessee. Most older
black churches date to the Civil War/Reconstruction era,
yet a small number began earlier, as "mission" churches
in the era of slavery. Mission churches grew out of early
urban churches, which initially had mixed membership.
By the 1830s, however, most white congregations chose
to segregate blacks—while retaining control over their
religious practices—by creating separate missions.
Mechal Sobel tells the story of one successful mission,
that of the First Baptist Church in Nashville. Sobel
found that its numerous black members were determined
to achieve as much independence as possible in the mission's operation. In 1853 Nelson Merry, the mission's first
ordained African American minister, expanded its membership and increased its visibility and significance in the
black community. Merry and his congregation worked
hard to maintain its own quasi-independence into the
Civil War. Finally, in 1865, Merry's mission was granted

independence and became the First Colored Baptist
Church (today the Spruce Street Baptist Church). Out
of slavery, Sobel reminds us, grew an institution that
remains of vital importance to Nashvillians today.

While over 170 independent and fully recognized black Baptist
churches were constituted prior to 1864, many southern black Baptists, particularly in the last two decades before the war, accepted and even welcomed a quasi-independent mission or branch status as their best option, in part because they believed it might lead to total independence.[1] Their overt subservience allowed them room for significant separate development, which they did not have as members of mixed congregations.

The black mission of the First Baptist Church in Nashville achieved such near-independence. This black congregation eventually had an ordained black pastor who celebrated the ordinances, a separate meetinghouse and baptistery, a separate Sunday school, and an all-black business meeting. Notwithstanding all these privileges, full equality was not granted to this particular congregation in the slave period. Nashville's black Baptist mission fell just short of independence by the crucial distinction that it remained a mission and could at any time be legally closed by the white church.

Nashville's almost independent black Baptist mission was countenanced and even supported by white, slave-owning Baptists. It was not seen as a threat to white supremacy. Rather than altering the subservience of blacks it freed the whites to have a separate religious life while it demarcated black inferiority and was a means of building a black infrastructure to support the social system.

Black Baptist experiences in Nashville began with the city's first Baptist congregation, which, when constituted in 1820, welcomed blacks.[2] Nearly closed by defections to the newly formed Church of Christ, it was not until 1831 when the Rev. Peter S. Gayle was called to serve that the congregation began to expand. By that time most Baptist churches were already moving away from the fully shared biracial church life that had characterized much of their earliest history in America. Nevertheless, as continued to happen all over the South, blacks, primarily slaves, joined or rejoined Nashville's mixed church. Included among the new black members was Reverend Gayle's slave Lewis, who had accompanied the pastor to Nashville and applied for admission together with his owner.[3] Lewis's case, similar to many others, suggests the peculiar *relative equality of treatment* accorded these black members, who were not full participants. Blacks and whites were admitted together, gave oral evidence of their conversions together, and were baptized together, dismissed together, and criticized for similar reasons (except for the occasional black runaway who was immediately excluded).[4] Blacks and whites were called "sister" and "brother," although black status was always noted as "servant of," "belonging to," or "free man (or woman) of color." The term "slave" was never used. It is a sign of white concern that much trouble was taken to check out the church backgrounds of slaves. Their old churches, often in other states, were written to if the applicant had no formal church letter of dismission in hand, and letters were sent out to slaves' new churches. When an occasional member again defected to the Church of Christ, the formal reaction was much the same regardless of race. A committee was sent to talk with the defector, white or black, and only if this effort failed was the individual excluded.[5]

The issue that most significantly distinguished black discipline from that of whites was that of slave marriage and remarriage, a particular problem for both slaves and white Christians. Many churches agonized over the issue of slaves' marriage vows. How were they to be regarded when slaves were sold away from their spouses? Some churches formally resolved the problem, deciding that inability to live near or with a spouse would be regarded much as a separation due to death. Both individuals could then remarry. Most churches could not bring themselves to make such a formal pronouncement, although in practice they often concurred. The Nashville church, without recording any debate or soul searching on this issue, came to regard the city limits as the blacks' universe. If an "ex" spouse was within the city limits, the slave could not remarry. Thus on 20 April 1831, "Brother Frederick, (belong[ing] to Judge Campbell) was excluded for having two wives living in Nashville at the same time."[6]

At the constitution of the church its members had covenanted to "give ourselves to each other, in the Lord, to watch over, and perform each relative duty." The institution of slavery was not mentioned. As seen, blacks and whites were accepted together and dismissed together, but blacks in this church did not vote, nor did they "choose" to criticize whites. Duties and privileges were "relative" to status.

Sixteen years later, 8 July 1836, on the occasion of their moving into their own church building (which had a balcony for blacks), the members of the Nashville church wrote a new covenant. This actually repeated the avowal of absolute Christian equality earlier voiced, but now it was made explicit that Christian equality and perpetual slavery were not enemies,

[handwritten margin note:] Know your place

although the word "slavery" never appears: "Every member of this Church shall be subject alike to her jurisdiction; but no member shall, in consequence of connection with her, be deprived of any right, of any kind, social, domestic, political, &c. which as a man and a citizen he may lawfully and innocently exercise."[8] The new minister, Rev. R. B. C. Howell, who had replaced Gayle in August 1834, undertook a special outreach to the blacks, based on what were mixed emotions and biased reasoning. As he was later to explain,

> It is very well known by all who are familiar with the subject, that colored people require special teaching. [Their minds are of a peculiar caste; their temptations, and trials, are unlike those of others; they are generally dull of apprehension;] they are for the most part, strongly inclined to fanaticism; and as church members they are litigious, and difficult to govern. A sermon which to a cultivated white congregation, would be highly instructive and useful, is of very little worth to the colored people present, not that the language, and style, are not perfectly simple, and well understood by them, but especially because the amount of thought is more than they can grasp, and the train of ideas not in a familiar direction.[9]

Howell had come to Nashville from Norfolk, Virginia, where there was an unusual black church that had begun as a mixed church. In 1816 all twenty-five white members, with the exception of the pastor, an Englishman, the Rev. James Mitchell, disaffected both by Mitchell's pro-black attitudes and the numerous blacks, left the First Baptist Church, Norfolk, to found a separate church.

Howell took this history to heart and would not risk its recurrence: "No instance, in any city or village, can now be recollected, in which the colored part of the church, when taught exclusively in the same assembly with the white, was prosperous, or if they were, in which the white part of the church did not dwindle and come to nothing. The two classes require different forms of instruction. They can never prosper together." Howell was later to claim that, basing his actions on this reasoning, he himself was responsible for separatist black developments. He claimed that from the time of his arrival in 1834 he invited blacks to meet separately with him, both on Sunday evenings and on one weekday night. He remembered lecturing and questioning the black congregation in a manner very different from his white-oriented behavior. He compared the didactic black sessions to an "ordinary High School

examination." Howell did note, however, that in his absence from black meetings two blacks, licensed by the congregation, preached.[10]

The church minutes record a somewhat different origin of black meetings. On 8 November 1834, the church "agreed that the coloured members
might hold prayer meetings once a month (on Friday evenings)." However,
after only two months, the church "rescinded the order permitting the coloured
brethren to hold prayer meetings."[11] The church was clearly ambivalent, and
there was no record of Howell's involvement.

From the beginning of January 1837 the phrase "the colored members"
began to be used consistently in church affairs. The "colored members"
reacted as a group to new black admissions, and they had disputes among
"themselves." White committees were appointed to look into these various
issues as well as the specific question of blacks meeting separately.[12]

By January 1841 a special separate black meeting was legitimized by the
presence of the pastor, deacons, and clerk. This became an annual tradition, a
time of taking stock, when the black roll book would be reviewed and black dis-
ciplinary cases discussed.[13] As a result of this practice we know that as of January 1841 there were 99 black members as compared to 255 white members in
Nashville's Baptist church.[14] The church then took the decision to constitute a
standing committee of whites to consider black problems. Clearly by 1849
black church life was less integrated with white church life than before.

Other changes in black status were concurrently taking place as symbolized by the dropping of the honorifics "brother" and "sister." From 1839
on these terms were rarely used for blacks.[15] It is true that within a few years
the terms were in most cases dropped for whites as well, but in their stead
whites were called Mr., Miss, or Mrs., while blacks were called by name alone
and most often just by their first name.

It was at this juncture that the "colored members" again asked for the
private use of the church, and that a black preacher, George Brents, joined
the congregation.[16] Brents, or Brentz, was a free man who came to Nashville
in November 1841 from Greensboro, Kentucky. There "he had been in the
habit of addressing his Brethren of colour in public," and he continued doing
so at Nashville's mixed church until about 1847. (By 1848 he had left
Nashville to become the pastor of an independent black church, the Second
African, in Lexington, Kentucky.)[17]

Either with the white Reverend Howell or with Brents or another black
preacher, Anderson,[18] as seems more likely given the later events, the blacks
continued to develop autonomous traditions, reporting to the yearly meeting

on the state of their congregants. The recounting of religious conversions, and the ordinances of baptism and the Lord's Supper were administered in the white or mixed church, but blacks clearly continued to meet separately as well.

In January 1846 the colored members officially broached the issue of building a separate black church. Although some whites had strong reservations or "prejudices" against such a separate black institution, no public debate was held. It was here perhaps that Reverend Howell's approval was of most import, as the whites immediately acted to implement the black request albeit under white control. A committee of seven whites was appointed to "contract for and hold in trust" a building which would be either "a branch of this church or . . . an independent church."[19] No public complaints were made by either side, and apparently most whites and blacks welcomed the move. It would give both blacks and whites more "privacy" and more clearly separate their experiences, without threatening the whites in any way. It was a privilege given by the whites, but with the understanding that it could be withdrawn at any time.

The extent of self-determination given was such that in principle, the whites were not loath to consider a black preacher for such an independent black church, but the black reality, as they found it, did not meet their needs. By July 1847 the white leaders of the church were investigating the abilities of black preachers, charged specifically to judge "whether the coloured ministers were capable of imparting that sound Doctrinal instruction so essential in this case."[20]

It is likely that Anderson and Brents were gone by this point, because the only black interviewee was "coloured preacher" Brother John Dodds. When first tested, Dodds proved too embarrassed to perform well, and when finally ready to be retested, proved not "sufficiently well informed to take charge of a church," although his interrogators did think he "possessed some talent and correct views of many of the leading points of Scripture."[21]

Not having found a black preacher of proper stature, the white committee did not simply choose a white preacher but sat down to confer with Brother Davidson and the colored members respecting the best course to pursue.[22] Brother Samuel Davidson was a white licentiate who had been taking an active interest in black affairs since the beginning of 1847. At this conference of blacks and whites it was agreed that, given the "insufficiency" of black leadership, a separate black church would be sanctioned under the spiritual direction of an "efficient" white brother, who would consult with the white pastor, but be paid by the black members.[23] It was clear that Davidson was the "efficient" white that everyone had in mind. By November 1847 he had arranged for black use of the City School House, once used by the mixed church.[24] With Davidson as minister, the blacks immediately began to hold regular separate Sunday evening worship services and Sunday afternoon school sessions while once every three months the Lord's Supper was brought to their black church by the white minister and deacons. This black "mission" was allowed to act on all cases of discipline, although the decisions were to be submitted to the white church for "sanction." Approval was generally given pro forma.[25] Clearly, formulated hopes were held out for the future of the black congregation legitimating the white efforts on a high moral plane involving the conversion of the African heathen. "The belief is confidently entertained that with the proper attention and fostering care, the Mission is destined to develope [sic] itself into a well organized Church and take a high stand among sister Churches, and likewise become a powerful auxiliary in sending the light of truth and salvation to the benighted land of their forefathers."[26]

By the end of 1849 some 250 blacks were attending the mission, although only 102 were members. Services were held both Sunday morning and afternoon, about 50 students attended Sunday school, and many blacks attended the monthly black business meetings and irregular extra prayer meetings as well.[27] All black church life was in this mission-church. It was varied, rich, and well organized. There was no occasion on which blacks needed to participate in the white activities.

Now, however, some whites worked in and with the black church. In addition to the white preacher, a white Sunday school superintendent was appointed, and over the years several whites helped with the teaching. Blacks, however, *were taught to read!* By December 1849 it was proudly recorded, "Several of our old members have learned to read and are greatly delighted with the privilege of reading the Bible."[28] Whites also contributed to Reverend Davidson's salary and to the black church fund.[29]

Although whites originally filled the major status positions, the activities at the black church definitely stimulated black leadership. In June 1849 Henry Howard, a black member, requested a license to preach, and a three-man white committee, including the pastor, granted him a one-year (renewable) license.[30] Howard, however, apparently was not the leader that the church was looking for, and the search for a black pastor continued, especially in the face of Davidson's growing disaffection from the time-consuming job and white congregant Thomas B. Ripley's temporary substitution.[31]

After some five and a half years of entirely separate existence, the right man was found. On 9 March 1853, Brother Nelson Merry "was by a unanimous vote of the [white] church licensed to preach the Gospel."[32] Merry was not new to the church, and perhaps it had been difficult for both blacks and whites to recognize the leadership qualities of one who had long been a "boy" among them and had served in the menial task of sexton. Born a slave, Merry had been freed by his owner's will at about the time of his baptism in November 1845.[33] He was then twenty-one and apparently supported himself by working for the church. Black tradition has it that Reverend Howell tutored Merry and prepared him for the ministry, but Howell's detailed memoirs strangely make no reference to this.[34] Whatever the preparation, eight years later Merry was recognized as having a call to preach and the stature for the pastorate.

Reverend Howell, for all his ambivalence about blacks, later acknowledged that Merry was far superior to the whites who had served the mission. Comparing him with the white Reverend Davidson and his successor Ripley, Howell concluded that "Nelson G. Merry . . . is perhaps the ablest, the most judicious, and certainly the most successful of the three."[35]

After Merry's licensing in March 1853, the white church and the black mission moved rapidly toward almost separating the black church. In November the blacks, for the first time, selected their own deacons, although they still submitted their names to the white church for "sanction," and "Nelson Merry was at the same time chosen by them as their Pastor."[36]

The status of the black mission was not debated. Formally it was to remain a mission of the white church until the end of the Civil War, but as of 29 November 1853 it would have an ordained black preacher, who could and would administer the ordinances, and black deacons, self-chosen. It would continue to hold its own business meetings and conduct all the business of a regular Baptist church. Nevertheless, until 1863 a white committee would still be charged with reporting back to the white church on the blacks' spiritual condition, and real veto power, apparently never used, would still be vested in the white church's hands. The whites of Nashville's First Baptist Church gave the blacks functional autonomy but retained legal superiority.

Merry's ordination was a serious and formal affair. An ecclesiastical council was convened at white Reverend Baker's Nashville home, composed of three ordained white Baptist preachers, S. Baker, J. R. Martin, and J. R. Graves. It heard Merry narrate at length "his religious experiences, the evidences of his call to the ministry and [his] views of doctrines." Satisfied, the council voted to ordain him that very evening, an event which had no doubt been planned prior to his examination.[37]

The ordination service was held in the First Baptist Church (white). It was a special Wednesday evening service devoted solely to this task, including special prayers for the blacks, a special "charge" to Merry as a black Baptist preacher, and the presentation of a Bible and the formal right hand of fellowship. When Merry then left the First Baptist Church he was a fully ordained Baptist minister, but uniquely his call had not come from a full or complete Baptist church but from what remained technically a mission.[38]

Merry was twenty-nine when he took over the pastorate. He served the black mission-church from 1853 until his death in 1884, a period of thirty-one years. For the first ten of these years Merry had to consider white reactions particularly closely inasmuch as his church was not fully independent and his congregants were largely slaves. Merry succeeded in both keeping white intervention at a minimum and creating a thriving black church even in a period when the mother (white) church was having membership difficulties.[39] A lot was purchased, a house of worship was raised and soon "greatly enlarged" due to the growing need, and a separate baptistery was built.[40] Between 1853 and 1863 the only formal relationship with the white church continued to be its legal right to supervision. The ordinances and the disciplining of its members were consistently taken care of within the black "mission" by blacks. Merry's prewar success became known in wider Baptist circles, and he himself became involved in the broader black community. In fact, he traveled to the North, and by 1859 was a member of the interstate black missionary group, the American Baptist Missionary Association, working together with black ministers from Massachusetts to Missouri.[41]

The internal dynamics of the black church's life are more difficult to detail in this last period of quasi-independence. Reports to the white church were pro forma, and white church interference apparently negligible, although no doubt whites "spoke to" Pastor Merry, Deacon Walker, and others when they wanted some particular action taken. As a result, few records of this period were preserved.

This black-white relationship lasted until 1863, when "owing to the disturbed condition of the country" the white church rarely had possession of its own building (which was appropriated by the Union Army), the white minister Howell was temporarily jailed, and the mission committee could not "discharge its duties." In contrast, the black church met continuously and, notwithstanding some forced removals of blacks, grew enormously during the war period. Nashville became a center for emancipated slaves, and between 1863 and 1865 the black church more than doubled its membership.

It was not until March 1865 that the blacks, writing as members of the First Baptist Church and not as a "mission," politely asked for permission to be independent:

> We, the colored members of the First Baptist Church of Nashville Tennessee
>
> Do hereby Petition to your honor for a separate [*sic*] and Independent church to be known by the name of the First Colored Baptist Church, Nashville, Tennessee.
>
> We most cordially thank you for the kindness done us in times past we also wish you would grant us a clear deed to the lot on which our house now stands. Our membership is now about 500. We your Brethren in love and respect.[42]

"Done by order of the church." As at the black mission's origin, but this time in a period of traumatic dislocation, the white church recorded no debate nor opposition. Under hostile military occupation, with the "enemy" supporting black independence, there was little to debate. In September 1865 the deed was transferred and the First Colored Baptist Church was independent.[43]

There had never been a period of open conflict between white and black Baptists in Nashville. [Most whites had welcomed the growing separation between white and black church lives, but as long as whites were masters they retained the right to oversee the black "mission."] It was only when blacks had been emancipated and whites reduced in status that they "granted" blacks full independence. In fact, the white Baptists of Nashville granted full rights to the blacks only at the point at which the whites themselves felt they had "no rights." Only then, when they themselves were ironically crying that "we [white people] are a herd of abject slaves,"[44] were they willing to regard the black church as equal.

Notes

1. Of the 116 known black Baptist churches in the slave South, at least 75 were formally constituted and technically independent while 31 were branches or missions. There were no doubt many more branches, unrecorded in the official records. These churches are analyzed in Mechal Sobel, *Trabelin' On: The Slave Journey to an Afro-Baptist Faith* (Westport, Conn., 1978).

2. This church was known as Nashville Baptist Church until 1859, when it became the First Baptist Church. It was also sometimes known by its location, as Spruce Street Baptist Church, but as this was the building later given to the blacks, the black church was later known as Spruce Street Church.

3. Nashville Baptist Church was reduced to five members in 1825. See Lynn E. May Jr., *The First Baptist Church of Nashville Tennessee, 1820–1970* (Nashville, 1970), 1–41; and Ambrose Bennett, *108th Anniversary, Spruce Street Baptist Church* (Nashville, 1956), 9. The records of the church can be found in the manuscript minutes of the Southern Baptist Historical Commission, Nashville (hereafter cited as FBC Minutes). On blacks joining, see, for example, entry for 4 May 1831, when Brother Reuben Butcher, free man of color, and Brother Pompey, servant, "having withdrawn from the Campbellites," were admitted. See also entry for 7 May 1831. As of August 1836, seventy-one blacks had been admitted, seven of them free. One of these free blacks was a slave owner. On 20 March 1833 is this entry: "Brother Isham McLundy property of James (a free man of color) received by letter." It is interesting that the slave had a surname, no doubt his previous owner's, while the free black did not.

4. The FBC Minutes for 18 September 1833 notes a runaway's exclusion. See entries for 17 Oct. 1832 for interracial admissions to church, 9 June 1932 and Dec. 1833 for interracial dismissions, and 14 June 1834 for a report of "Sister Mary, Servant of Col. Wilson's" death.

5. See, for example, entry in FBC Minutes, 27 Jan. 1833: "The clerk appointed to write to the church on Mills Swamp, Isle of Wight County, Virginia, concerning Anthony, a servant, formerly a member of said church." See also entries for 20 Mar. 1833 and 7 Dec. 1833.

6. FBC Minutes, entry for 20 Apr. 1831. There is extensive comparative material on other churches handling of the issues of slave "rights." See, for example, Harrison W. Daniel, "Virginia Baptists and the Negro in the Antebellum Era," *Journal of Negro History* (Jan. 1971): 1–16.

7. FBC Minutes, entry for 22 July 1820. While the policy on black voting was not explicitly stated, the minutes are very detailed and make no reference to blacks participating in either the voting or the criticisms of whites. Nor is disenfranchisement mentioned, suggesting that the policy of extending the franchise to free white males (legalized in a state charter in 1858) was the original policy in this church. There is evidence that black and even slave congregants in other congregations criticized whites, and that in some cases free blacks voted.

8. Article 7 of "Covenant," FBC Minutes, 8 July 1836. May, *First Baptist Church*, 71.

9. Bennett, *Spruce Street Baptist Church;* FBC Minutes, May and 11 July 1831; R. B. C. Howell, "A Memorial of the First Baptist Church, Nashville, Tennessee, 1820–1863," manuscript in Southern Baptist Historical Commission, Nashville, vol. 2, 215–16.

10. See Reuben Jones, *A History of the Virginia Portsmouth Baptist Church Association* (Norfolk, Va., 1950); Howell, "Memorial," vol. 1, 216 (emphasis added by Sobel).

11. FBC Minutes, 8 Nov. 1834 and 10 Jan. 1835.

12. Ibid., 8 June, 15 July, 11 Apr., and 1, 12, 19 May 1837.

13. Ibid., Jan. 1841, Dec. 1842, Jan. 1844, Jan. 1845, and Jan. 1846.

14. Ibid., 27 Dec. 1840; 7 Jan. 1841.

15. After that time, "brother" was used with reference to a black preacher but not to a lay member.

16. FBC Minutes, 10 July 1841. That year was also the time of a massive revival at the church. In 1841 alone, 140 members were added, including many blacks. Between 1820 and 1842, 143 blacks had joined the church, including slaves and freedmen. According to May, *First Baptist Church*, 54, there were 337 church members, but less than 80 were black.

17. FBC Minutes, 13 Nov. 1841; Minutes of the Elkhorn Association, Kentucky, 1848, p. 1.

18. Brents and Anderson were the two black preachers mentioned by Howell in the reference cited above. Anderson may have been (1) Cufee Anderson, a pastor at Oakland African, Georgia, (2) Thomas Anderson, pastor of 3rd African, Savannah, Georgia, or (3) John R. Anderson, pastor of St. Louis Second Colored.

19. FBC Minutes, 10 Jan. 1846.

20. Ibid., 7 July 1847.

21. Ibid., 4 Aug. and 8 Sept. 1847.

22. FBC Minutes, 8 Sept. 1847. James Dickinson, slave of a Mrs. McKay, was another black preacher, licensed in 1843. According to Lynn May's *First Baptist Church,* 72 and 130, his ownership was given to the deacons in 1846, so that he might serve the black mission, but he apparently was not considered adequate for the role of minister

23. FBC Minutes, 17 Feb., 7 July, 8 Sept., and 6 Oct. 1847.

24. Ibid., 10 Nov. 1847; May, *First Baptist Church,* 71–72.

25. FBC Minutes, 5 Jan., 8 May, and 11 July 1848.

26. Ibid., 17 Jan. 1849.

27. Ibid., 23 Dec. 1849.

28. Ibid., 7 Feb. and 23 Dec. 1849; M. B. Pilcher and T. W. Haley were whites teaching blacks. May, *First Baptist Church,* 110.

29. In 1849 Nashville blacks, mostly slaves, contributed $28.00 to charity, $33.00 to the building fund, and paid Pastor Davidson $42.40. When Davidson's salary was found insufficient, the white church agreed to supplement it. In 1850 they were to pay $125, the blacks $100, and Davidson would "would deduce his usual $75 dues or donation to the church so that in total his salary was $300. FBC Minutes, 17 Jan. and 23 Dec. 1849.

30. FBC Minutes, 6 June 1849; May states that Howard was ordained, but this is not confirmed in the minutes. *First Baptist Church,* 130.

31. See FBC Minutes, 4 July 1849, when Davidson temporarily left and was replaced by Ripley. Later it was reported that Davidson could not give the blacks "enough time." FBC Minutes, 23 Dec. 1849. When Davidson left for California, Ripley again took over for some time, but he then returned to his old home, Portland, Maine (he had originally come from Lynchburg, Virginia). Howell, "Memorial," vol. 1, 217.

32. FBC Minutes, 9 Mar. 1853.

33. FBC Minutes, 9 Nov. 1845: Nelson. (A Coldman is suing for his freedom in Lemmon [Lincoln?] County . . . will of Betsy Merry recd. for Baptism."

34. Bennett, *Spruce Street Baptist Church*, 9.

35. Howell, "Memorial," vol. 1, 217.

36. FBC Minutes, Oct. and 20 Nov. 1853. Louis Butler, Daniel Walker, Aaron Jennings, Joseph Morsell, and Anderson Pritchett were selected as deacons.

37. Ibid., 29 Nov. 1853.

38. Normally, ordination in the Baptist Church is given to those called by a church to serve as pastor. A church can, however, license many to preach even for areas outside of the church so licensing.
39. In 1854 the Baptist church had 407 members (206 blacks, 201 whites); in 1863, 520 members (243 blacks, 277 whites); in 1865, 735 members (500 blacks, 235 whites). May, *First Baptist Church*, 70, 206; N. H. Pius, *An Outline of Baptist History* (Nashville, 1911).
40. Howell, "Memorial," vol. 1, 218.
41. American Baptist Missionary Association, Minutes, 1859, 1860; Lewis C. Jordan, *Negro Baptist History* (Nashville, 1930).
42. FBC Minutes, 16 Apr. 1865.
43. Ibid.
44. Howell, "Memorial," vol. 1, 419.

Doctor Jack
A Slave Physician on the
Tennessee Frontier

Loren Schweninger

COMMON MISCONCEPTION IS THAT SLAVES WERE FIELD HANDS, DOMESTIC SERVANTS, OR MANUAL LABORERS. A REALITY NOT SO OFTEN acknowledged is that some slaves possessed talents and abilities that [whites highly prized, and because of those talents, these same slaves sometimes were able to carve out new lives as freedmen.] Through a careful reading of legislative petitions and period newspapers, Loren Schweninger has found the story of one such individual, Doctor Jack, a slave doctor who worked in several Middle and West Tennessee communities before gaining his freedom and moving to Nashville in the 1850s. Once again, a historian had turned to an unexpected source—petitions to the Tennessee General Assembly—to uncover the story of a remarkable individual. This brief chapter presents the critical primary documents from which the contributions of Doctor Jack to nineteenth-century life may be partially decoded.

During the decades before the Civil War, few slaves in Middle Tennessee achieved a reputation as enviable as that of Doctor Jack, a healer of remarkable talents who—if we are to believe the testimony of numerous whites—surpassed the abilities of the best white physicians. Like most slaves, much of Jack's life is shrouded in mystery, but glimpses of his career can be gleaned from several unique petitions to the Tennessee General Assembly and a number of "Certificates," or testimonials about his accomplishments.

Born about 1783, "Doctor Jack," as he came to be known, first appears in the written record when he was about forty-nine years old and had worked as a healer for many years. By then, he was owned by William H. Macon of Maury County, who permitted him to move about the countryside through six counties, including Maury, Bedford, Giles, Hickman, Williamson, and Lincoln, practicing medicine. So enthusiastic were his patients about his cures that when a law was passed in 1831, shortly after the Nat Turner revolt, to halt slaves practicing medicine, a group of patients sent a petition to the legislature seeking a special exemption. They knew "this boy" well, they said, and although he was a slave, they knew about his "character for honesty and fair correct deportment." Moreover, he was unequaled as a physician. Although no exemption was granted, Doctor Jack continued his "practice" in succeeding years. As he moved about from farmhouse to farmhouse and plantation to plantation he not only relied on his reputation but also carried with him testimonials from his various patients explaining how he had, in a matter of days or weeks, cured them of longstanding ailments. Some of these testimonials were sent along with the petition seeking an exemption from the law. Also in the packet of materials was a statement on using natural remedies to combat disease. While its authorship is unknown—it was signed "An old observer"—the ideas it contained certainly reflected Doctor Jack's philosophy: "I believe that nature has wisely (& graciously) formed roots, & herbs, to meet every complaint incident to the human species, & that [if] men would study to grow acquainted with them & their uses, & would drench less with drugs, the world would be people'd a great deal sooner, & mankind would enjoy a great deal more health & strength."

Most of the profits from Jack's practice went to his owner, who sent along instructions that those who wished to engage Doctor Jack should send their notes to Macon payable by Christmas Day of that year. But when the master moved to Fayette County some residents became concerned about a slave being allowed such freedom of movement. Moreover, there was always the fear among whites that rather than healing, black physicians might take retribution on their masters or other whites. There were cases where instead of administering cures slaves poisoned slave owners or members of their families. In 1843, some residents of Fayette County protested against Jack's practicing medicine. But again, other whites came to his defense. A group of more than one hundred farmers and planters, some of whom had known Doctor Jack for twenty years, said he was <u>humble and unassuming, peaceable and quiet</u>, and possessed "great medical skill, particularly in obstinate disease of long standing." Although he was now about sixty years old, they said, he remained an extraordinary physician. They asked that any fine that might be imposed on his master by the Fayette County Circuit Court be remitted to the owner.

Perhaps the most remarkable defense came in the same year not from the male recipients of Jack's expertise but from <u>a group of women</u> who knew what he had done for their families and the families of their friends and neighbors. In the entire South, there are only a handful of extant petitions to state legislatures by groups of women seeking redress of grievances. Among them is one from "Ladies residing in Tennessee" in behalf of Doctor Jack. He was honest, honorable, and skillful, and he was especially adept in handling "obstinate cases of long standing." The women "ought not to be denied the privilege of commanding his services." Unfortunately, only glimpses of Jack's exceptional accomplishments are to be found, but there is little doubt that those who spoke on his behalf were accurately describing his talents. Most who wrote on his behalf agreed with the general proposition that slaves should not be permitted to move about without supervision. And most were firmly wedded to the South's "peculiar institution." Nor would they have anything to gain by praising a black man who did not deserve their praise or who had not, in fact, brought people back from the brink of death.

The final written record concerning Doctor Jack came neither in the form of testimonials nor petitions, however, but from an unexpected source. In 1853 in Nashville's first business directory, an eight-word advertisement, appeared: "Jack, Root Doctor. Office 20 N Front St."[1] The same announcement appeared in 1859.[2] How he had done it is not known, but this information shows that Doctor Jack had gained the status of a free man. The next year, on the eve of the Civil War, the records of the Nashville City Cemetery told of the final chapter in his extraordinary career: interred in plot number 168 in the Negro section was Jack Macon, free man of color age eighty, color black, died of "old age." He was "know [sic] as Dr. Jack."[3]

The Documentary Sources about Doctor Jack

1. The Middle Tennessee Petition Concerning Doctor Jack

To the Honl. The Legislature of the state of Tennessee—
The subscribers having understood and learnt that an
act was passed at the last Session of your Honl. body,

Entitled "An act to amend the Laws of this State in relation to the government of slaves and for the persons of color," one Section of which makes it an indictable offense for "any owner or other person having charge of any slave or slaves, to permit him or them to go about the Country under pretext of practicing medicine or healing the Sick." Without pretending to question the [wisdom] of this law, as one [of a] general character that [sic] or denying that in its general operation it may not be productive of much good, yet we would most respectfully ask of your Honl. body to [modify] its general operation so far as to permit, a negro man, named Jack, the property of Mr. William H. Macon of Maury County, t[o] practice as he has been heretofore doing. We ask this from a full Knowledge of the Character, of this boy though he may be a *slave*, yet in the opinion of the undersigned, his character for honesty and correct deportment, is fair [an]d not often excelled by many who profess to possess more than he does—In his profession, we speak from our knowledge of his practice we are free & happy to say that he has practised with great & unparalled success, for many years, none having any cause to complain of either a want of fidelity or success among his patients. We are residents the Several Counties of Maury, Bedford, Giles, Hickman, & Williamson, and Lincoln, and ask the passage of this Law, granting permission to this [man] to practice, with firm belief that the public good will be advanced by its pas[sage] from our Knowledge of the character of this boy, and his practice for Several years—

Subscribers from the County of Maury
[signed]

A. L. Pickard
Johnston Craig
Reuben Reynolds
Milledge S Durham Dr
Ezekiel Hogg
Jos B. Wallace
Stephen Smith
Jos A Estes

John F Carr
Wm B Brown
Jansen Colkeil [?]
Edward Grimes
James Grimes
henry Grimes

[Doctor Jack has] bin healing diseases more or less for the last Six or Seven years and has done much good and not any harm [to anyone] that ever has bin laid to his charge
[signed]
John Boon

Subscribers from Bedford County
James Y. Green
Hugh McClelan
James McClelan
C. C. Cathey Dr
J N Rainey Jr
Edward Walker
Wm J Sanders
[torn page]
John M Dawson
Thomas Atkerson
Milton Powell

I do Certify that I have bin acquainted with the general character of Dr Jack for the past Three years and know him to be an honest faithfull slave, I am also acquainted with his skill in the art of healing disease and know it to be very good and not easy to be exceed he has [torn page]
This is to certify that I had a case of sickness in my family caled by the phisitions the D[ropsy?] & baffled the[ir] skill which I do believe Dr Jack has made a firm cure wheather or not his medicine cured or no I cant tell but this I do c[e]rtify that sencible releaf was felt on taking the first dose & continued to mend & is at this time in good health—
[signed]
[illegible] . . .[4]

2. Terms for engaging with Doctor Jack

Those who wish to Imploy Jack, must send me their notes, payable on the 25th of decr- next

William H. Macon

(Certificate)

3. Testimonials for Doctor Jack

State of Tennessee }

Giles county }

I do (hereby) certify that my wife (Amelia) was taken unwell about the first of Augst 1829—she complain'd of great misery in the back & loins, together with a numbedness in her thighs, which threw her to bed about the 19th of the same month.

I immediately applied to a physician, who (formerly) waited on my family—from whom she took medicine for about six weeks without receiving any benefit—I then applied to another, who (I thought) to be the best physician in the county, who attended on her about one month without the least (apparent) benefit, but she still grew worse & it was the opinion of the most of my neighbors that she must sink under her complaint (if not speedily remov'd)

In this case she was when about the first of decr following I imploy'd Doctor Jack (a colored man) belonging to William Macon of Maury County, Tenn—ten miles west of Columbia, who undertook her, he commenced with roots, & (to my great astonishment) in a few days she began to amend, & in a few weeks was up & attending to her ordinary business of life—& I believe she is as well (at this time) & enjoys as good health as she has done for several years—

Given under my hand, July 6th *1830*

[signed]

Wade Barret

Certificate 2nd

I do (hereby) certify, that a colour'd woman, belonging to me was taken unwell about the 25th of last augst &

appear'd to be labouring under the same complaints of my
wife, in the (above case) or nearly so, she also took medicine from the same physicians, & about the same length of
time, but to no profit, she continued to grow worse until I
imlpoy'd Doctor Jack (named in the above certificate) he
commenced giving her medicine, & in a few weeks, restored
her to good health— & she continues to enjoy it— Given
under my hand.

    July 6th *1830*
    [signed]
    Wade Barrett

Certificate 3rd

    I do (also) certify that I had a colour'd boy about nine
years of age—who was taken about the first of last March,
with pains in his limbs, which (finally) settled in one of
his thighs a little above the Joint of his knee which pain'd
him exceedingly, & put on every appearance of a white-
swelling, after he was confined to bed for about two weeks,
I applied to Doctor Jack, & in a few days he began to
amend, & appears (at this time) to be well Given under
my hand

    July 6th *1830*
    [signed]
    Wade Barrett

    I do certify that the persons spoken of (in the above
certificates) are all enjoying good health, at this time—
Given under my hand—Jany, 1st, 1831

    [signed]
    Wade Barrett

Certificate 4th

State of Tenn. Maury co. Jany, 5th 1831 I do hereby certify,
that I myself was labouring under the complaint call'd the
dispepsia, or indigestion for about 4 years, in which time I
imploy'd a physician but receiv'd no benefit— about the
first of last m[a]rch I imploy'd Doctor Jack, & from that
time I began to amend, & continued to amend, & I think I
am (now) as well as I ever was— & having an acquaintance

with Doctor Jack, & his success, I believe him to be a very
honest man a useful Doctor, & can do a great deal in that
complaint

Given under my hand the day & above date
[signed]
Larkin Dearen . . .

State of Tennessee }
Hickman County }

I do Certify that my wife was taken unwell about the
20th of March 1830 She had bin afflicted for ten years with
a tremendous bad cough and I applied to three different
physicians but they could not help her I then imployed
Doctor Jack a negro belonging to William H. Macon of
Murry County and he Commenced Doctoring her with
roots and she was relieved of her Affliction in a short time,
I believe she injoys good health at this time given under my
hand May the 8th day 1831

I believe that Doctor Jack is a good and faithfull Doctor to what he undertakes
[signed]
Alston Jones

D[ecember] 15th 1831
State of Tennessee }
Bedford County }

I do Certify that my Wife has bin Dise[as]d with the
Tetter in the Bowels for Ten years or more and never has
been intirly well We have appeal to as Good Doctors as any
in the Cuntry and som of them Stated She never Could be
cured and Docter Jack was pasing through the neighborhood and wife insisted that I should Send for him and I did
so and from the time he commced Giving her medicine she
m[e]nded and she has become int[i]rly well in a very short
[time] —and therefore we are bound to Give him the praze
of any other Docter
[signed]
Isaac Rainey [?]

This is to certify that some time in the summer of 1829 that I had a negro man in a low lingering way & sunk under his complaint so rapidly that soon became entirely unfit for service, his disease seemed to threaten an imediate disolution when I Employd A negro man call'd Doctor Jack belonging to Wm Macon of Maury county, Ten. who commencd to do[c]tor him with indigenous roots & to my Surprize in a few weeks reli[e]ved him of all his complairits & in a few months I belive made a perfect cure the negro is now well & fit for the hardest service given under my hand this 2nd day Dec. 1829

[signed]

L [?] Harwell

State of Tennessee Maury County September 29, 1831

I Do certify that I had the Bowell complaint for two years and ten months a great [part] of the time verry sever, often Reduced very Low, and could find no relief from any medicine I could get in that time. I applied to Doctor Jack, by taking his medicine and following his directions, I got relief immediately In one Two or three Months I became a Sound Man of said complaint, and therefore I have Reason to give Doctor Jack the Reference and honor as a physician

[signed]

Joseph Linn

Maury County Tennessee

This is to certify that I had a negro man afflicted with a pain in his side for two months, I employed the best physicians of Columbia to attend him, but he received no benefit from their attentions, I then called upon Doctor Jack and he produced a cure in two weeks.

[signed]

Thomas Stone

March the 20 1829

Hickman County Tennessee

I do certify that Doctor Jack has attended on my negro woman in the year 1828 and cured her of the bloody flux that is as far as I ever tryed him— I believe he is an excellent Doctor for that complaint

[signed]

Gilbert Nichols[5]

4. Fayette County Petition on Doctor Jack

To the Legislature of the State of Tennessee—

The undersigned, citizens of Tennessee, respectfully petition the Honorable Legislature of the State, to repeal, amend or so modify the Act of 1831, chap. 103, S 3 which prohibits Slaves from practicing medicine, as to exempt from its operation a Slave named Jack, the property of William H. Macon, Esq. of Fayette County.

The undersigned are acquainted with the Slave Jack and his medical attainments, (some of us have Known him for 20 years & some for a shorter period) and state, that in his disposition he is humble unobtrusive, peaceable and quiet; and in his morals altogether irreproachable, possessing great medical skill, particularly in obstinate diseases of long standing, and capable of great usefulness to the community in which he may reside. Doctor Jack is about 60 years of age, and has been a public practitioner of medicine 16 years, giving offence to no one, creating no disturbance, and until recently, meeting no disturbance in the quiet pursuit of his business.

For these reasons the undersigned request that the Laws of the State may be so changed as to permit "Doctor Jack" to continue the practice of the healing art.

The undersigned would further petition the Hon. Legislature to remit any fine or penalty that may be imposed by the Circuit Court of Fayette County upon the master of said slave for permitting sd slave to practice medicine contrary to Law, for the people are as much in fault as the master—August 1843.

[signed]

Duke Williams

Whitfield Boyd

B H Henderson

D I Henderson
Wm. L. Lacy
Benj Watkins
B. W. Williamson
W. G Cole
Henry W Sale
Nicholas Long
John A. Winfrey
L C Moore
Alex Boyd
T G Boyd
W E Hall
James E Mason Senr
[ninety-nine additional signatures][6]

5. The Ladies' Petition Concerning Doctor Jack

To the Legislature of Tennessee

The undersigned, Ladies residing in Tennessee, respectfully petition the, Honourable Legislature of the State to repeal, amend, or so modify the Act of 1831 c. 103, S. 3 which prohibits slaves from practicing medicine as to exempt from its operation a slave named Jack the property of William H. Macon, Esq. of Fayette County.

We believe "Doctor Jack" to be honest, honourable & skilful, especially in obstinate cases of long standing; and that the [people ought not to be denied the privilege of commanding his services]—August 1843 *his services > his freedom*

[signed]

Mary M. Williams
Mary F Ballard
Lucinda Henderson
Lockey M Boyd
Mary J Henderson
Julia A. Lacy
Frances A Watkins
Eliza J Williamson
Phe Behall
Frances C Mason

Nancy Sale
Mary B Macon
Charlotte C Winfrey
Julia A Boyd
Ann Taylor
Susan Booth
Ann M Kirkland
Casandra Wilson
Eliza P Alston
[forty-eight additional signatures][7]

Notes

1. *The Nashville General Commercial Directory* (Nashville, 1853), 36.
2. *Nashville City and Business Directory, for the City of Nashville* (Nashville: E. G. Eastman & Co. [1859], p. 87.
3. Records of the Nashville City Cemetery, 1846–1860, 16 May 1860, Nashville Room, Public Library of Nashville and Davidson County, Nashville. The editor wishes to thank Carol Kaplan of the Nashville Room for providing him with this information as well as the 1859 *Business Directors* citation.
4. Legislative Petitions, Petition of Residents of Maury, Bedford, Giles, Hickman, Williamson, and Lincoln Counties to the General Assembly, ca. 1832, no. 11-1832-la-4, reel 12, Tennessee State Library and Archives, Nashville (hereafter cited as TSLA). Some of the petition's pages are torn, and some of the signatures are illegible or too faint to decipher. The extant signature pages reveal that 121 residents signed the remonstrance.
5. Legislative Petitions, Testimonials Concerning Doctor Jack, 1829–31, no. 294-1831-1-7, reel 12, TSLA.
6. Legislative Petitions, Petition of Citizens of Tennessee to the Legislature, Aug. 1843, no. 189-1843-1-2, reel 17, TSLA. Petition presented in the house by Representative Fisher on 1 November 1843 and transmitted to the senate the next day. *Journal of the House of Representatives of the State of Tennessee at the Twenty-fifth General Assembly, Held at Nashville, on Monday the 25 Day of October; 1843* (Knoxville, 1844), 180; *Journal of the Senate of Tennessee at the Twenty-fifth General Assembly, Held at Nashville* (Knoxville, 1844), 190.
7. Legislative Petitions, Petition of the Ladies of Tennessee to the Legislature, Aug. 1843, no. 189-1843-3-4, reel 17, TSLA. This petition was transmitted to the senate by the clerk of the house, 2 Nov. 1843. *Journal of the Senate of Tennessee at the Twenty-fifth General Assembly, Held at Nashville* (Knoxville, 1844), 190.

Slaves and Masters in Antebellum Madison County
Slave Life in Rural West Tennessee

Gary Edwards

ONE OF THE MOST DIFFICULT CHALLENGES FACING HISTORIANS OF SLAVERY IS TO DETERMINE THE SLAVE'S PERSPECTIVE ON ANTEBELLUM LIFE. SLAVES left little direct evidence in the form of diaries, letters, and documents, but previous chapters have shown that unexpected sources—court cases, legislative petitions, local government records—can give insight on how African Americans coped with slavery. In this chapter, Gary Edwards takes a traditional source, a diary by a prominent Madison County planter, but reads it for the information that the planter indirectly or directly divulges about his slaves and their everyday routines. By reading between the lines, Edwards paints a vivid picture of an owner's attitude to his slaves, as well as the different, often subtle, ways that African Americans rebelled against their condition or adapted the owner's demands to their own perceived needs and wants. Their resistance met with floggings, vicious beatings, and sales outside of the plantation, breaking bonds with family and home. "Antagonism between master and slave," Edwards asserts, "was a natural component of a society based upon racial inequality." A few slaves escaped by running away—but slave patrols caught and returned most, back to their lives of toil and violence. The Cartmell diary, if one needs reminding, is a stark, grim document of the hardships of slavery on Tennessee's plantations.

Reminiscing about his privileged boyhood in antebellum Madison County, Tennessee, planter's son John Johnston savored memories of the halcyon days of the Old South. He happily recalled the perceived racial harmony of his region, noting that the local plantations "were cultivated with well-trained and docile slaves who in the main were well cared for and were happy and contented." E. F. Alexander, the son of a Jackson carpenter agreed, adding that "there was by fare a better feeling then between the colared [sic] race and the white race than there is today."[2] Yet the diarist and young planter Robert Cartmell presented a less felicitous image of the peculiar institution. "I am obliged to keep a good watch dog," he wrote in 1854, "or have everything stolen by negroes." Constantly irritated by his slaves' petty theft, Cartmell asked his wealthy brother-in-law John Bond to purchase for him some Osage orange seeds. At maturity, they produced a thorny tree with excretions which caused severe skin inflammation. "I want to try to make a hedge around [the] garden and small orchard," proclaimed the exasperated planter, "and bid defiance to negroes . . . and all other animals."[3]

Twentieth-century scholarship has produced different interpretations about the essence of slavery in the Old South. Some studies have substantiated Robert Cartmell's consistent frustration with his human property. Kenneth Stampp's *Peculiar Institution* (1956) represented a significant effort to combat the previous notion, commonly shared up to that time, that slavery represented a suitable arrangement for a racially inferior people. Utilizing psychological analogies drawn from Nazi concentration camp prisoners, Stanley Elkins's *Slavery* (1959) illustrated the provocative "Sambo" thesis in reference to the antebellum caricature of the obedient servant. This interpretation viewed the plantation system itself as producing generations of docile adult-children incapable of breaking free from this personality type. Elkins's thesis received a potent rebuttal in John Blassingame's *Slave Community* (1972). Blassingame argued that slaves, when able, acted as individuals instead of surrendering to the mass conformity of the loyal Sambo stereotype. Two years later, Eugene Genovese's *Roll, Jordan, Roll* (1974) pointed toward slaves' acceptance of Christianity and its message of individual worth, which enabled them to combat the Sambo image. Genovese also explored the concept of paternalism, which, he asserted, had to do with responsibilities and rights based on the vantage point of masters and slaves, respectively. That same year, Robert William Fogel and Stanley Engerman's *Time on the Cross* also appeared. With a strong emphasis on quantitative evidence, this work examined daily aspects of slave existence and produced, in general, a more favorable assessment of slavery. However, Fogel and Engerman's favorable picture of the peculiar institution was highly criticized. Historical scholarship in the past generation has continued this debate over the general nature of slavery. The bondsmen and bondswomen of Madison County, Tennessee, demonstrate that antagonism between master and slave was a natural component of a society based upon racial inequality.[4]

Antebellum Madison County is representative of Tennessee's southwestern sector, which proved to be a large slave owning and cotton growing region. However, it is quite divergent from the remainder of West Tennessee, which existed as an area dominated by small farmers and generally fewer slaves. In general, Madison County provides an excellent example of a significant plantation region on the eve of the Civil War.[5]

Only scattered bits of surviving evidence illuminate the complex nature of the master and slave relationship in Madison County. Virtually all of this information is biased toward the vantage point of the master, but the views of slaves can still be discerned despite the prejudicial tone of the evidence. The best known source about white-black relationships in antebellum Madison County are the daily entries Robert Cartmell made in his diary during the 1850s. Cartmell's detailed diary provides excellent insight into the inherent conflict between slave and master in Madison County. It was a struggle which remained largely unknown or ignored by young men like Johnston and Alexander, who in their adolescence rarely served as taskmasters. By contrast, Cartmell's daily contact with his slaves often led to confrontation. In Madison County slaves were far from contented, and many resisted in both active and passive ways.

Born and raised in Jackson, the seat of Madison County, Robert Cartmell possessed strong religious convictions, a college education and the economic advantages of a wealthy father. The elder Cartmell set his oldest son on the road to prosperity when he purchased a new plantation and gave Robert his old one. Beginning in 1850, the twenty-two year old recorded the events that occurred on his 755-acre estate on the outskirts of town. Utilizing some of his father's slaves, as well as all of his own, he had anywhere from fifteen to twenty-eight bondsmen during this period. Because of the paucity of sources from this era, any examination of slave life in Madison County becomes, by default, a profile of Robert Cartmell and his view of slave society.[6]

In Madison County slaves fulfilled a critical economic role. For those whites who could afford sufficient numbers of them, their labor created profits sufficient to provide their masters considerable comfort. For those who owned only a few, their toil added to a master's material well-being without elevating him to the stature of a planter. However, for all whites slavery established an economic boundary between those who owned human property and those who did not. In 1860, two out of five white families in Madison County owned at least one slave. Six percent of white families possessed twenty or more, and thus comprised the class of affluent planters. Another 35 percent had less than twenty slaves. Of these, one-tenth were professional men—attorneys, doctors, merchants, clergymen—whose social status equaled that of the planter class. The remaining owners were small farmers, who more often than not worked in the fields alongside their human property. The remaining 59 percent of Madison County's white families owned no slaves and received little direct benefit from the institution.[7]

In common with white yeomen and tenant farmers, slaves structured their lives by an agricultural calendar. Plowing, planting, hoeing, and harvesting marked each season's cadence. In contrast to the yeomen and the tenant, however, slaves were not the master of their destiny; they always toiled for the benefit of others. Madison County bondsmen labored at a wide variety of tasks; cultivating cotton emerged as their most important chore. Planters deemed the harvesting, ginning, and baling of cotton vital to their quest for profit, and they assembled every available hand at the onset of these tasks. Robert Cartmell recorded in September 1853, "I commenced with the trash gang picking cotton on the 12th." His meticulous records reflected the importance that all planters attributed to this effort. Each fall he kept an elaborate chart that tracked the harvest's progress. Listing the slaves' names and the days of the month they picked, he carefully chronicled each day's yield. Dick, one of his favorite workers, gathered more cotton than anyone else through the harvest of 1853. On one memorable day, he picked an impressive 180 pounds of the precious fiber. Children worked as well, "to carry dinner, go after water, etc." If Cartmell could be considered typical, Madison County planters gleaned their fields of the last strand of the crop. His record of the 1853 harvest indicated that he had at least a few slaves picking deep into winter, a task finally concluded on 9 February 1854.[8]

In addition to the work dictated by the agricultural cycle, such as preparing fields, planting, and harvesting, Cartmell's slaves toiled in numerous other ways. They engaged in winter chores such as cutting wood, fixing ploughs, knocking down cotton and corn stalks, and gathering manure. They also dug livestock ponds, fenced in orchards, and built a cistern and a gin house.[9] Slaves skilled as craftsmen proved exceptionally useful to their masters. Cartmell's bondsman Dave acquired a reputation for his various abilities, particularly his talent for carpentry. When not working alone in the plantation's shop, Dave received assistance from the slave Dick in "making a wagon body." Dave also wove baskets and proved so popular that Cartmell's mother once requested to borrow him for "2 or 3 days after he is done ginning."[10]

Slaves who were too old to work in the fields still performed useful tasks. Looking back on life in the Madison County town of Denmark, Thomas Reid recalled that on his family's plantation, "the older negros" worked at spinning and weaving. Aunt Candice, an elderly slave belonging to the family of Cartmell's mother, had rheumatism to the degree that she did little work. Cooking "a little for negroes, was all she did," Cartmell explained.[11]

Ordinary farm work occasionally provided physical dangers. One of Cartmell's slaves was run over by a wagon and "very badly bruised" he recorded. "If the wagon had been heavily loaded," thought Cartmell, "the probability is that it would have killed him." However dangerous the work place, slaves had more reason to fear the well-laid lash than any accident.[12]

Violence remained a constant but unpredictable variable in their lives. Masters and overseers expected bondsmen not only to provide labor but also to offer proper deference to their master's race. When they did not receive both in anticipated proportions, the consequences could be savage. Cartmell's slave Dave received a whipping because of his lethargic cotton picking. "I gave him a good one," his owner recorded. The effects of these encounters did not always have the desired effect. On one Saturday, Cartmell whipped his slave "Big Mary" only to discover on Monday that "Mary [was still] complaining."[13]

Floggings often became a part of a slave's life, even before adulthood. When trying to repair his cellar, Cartmell recorded, "Had to chastise 3 of my boys pretty severely this evening[.] John, Ned and Dave, all three under 15 years of age. . . . I struck John 10 or 15 licks for triffling." Cartmell then ordered his young slaves to the cotton patch, but they ran away instead. Apparently the trio wandered several miles down the road before they became scared and returned late in the evening. "I whipped them," wrote Cartmell, "thinking it might prevent something of the kind when they become older."[14] Eight years later, however, Cartmell continued to have trouble with John. One day as the slaves commenced spring plowing, Cartmell believed he had caught John in a lie. "I took him to some peach trees," Cartmell recorded, "and while I was cutting some switches and telling him to take his coat off, he broke and run." As John raced across a clover field, Cartmell charged his horse in pursuit. At that moment, a man Cartmell did not know appeared to assist in the developing chase. "I got him to go one way and I another," wrote Cartmell. With the outcome never in doubt, the two men rapidly overtook the slave. An agitated Cartmell recalled that he gave the stranger the horse to hold "and ———— John plenty of peachtree."[15]

Occasionally slaves received exceptionally vicious beatings. Cartmell's younger brother Martin served as his overseer when he left on a two-week trip. Upon his return the two had a heated discussion over Martin's severe disciplining of one slave. "I thought it wrong to beat a negro with a big hickory stick," Cartmell explained. Martin "has laid Josh up so as to be unable to plow, arms bruised and swollen. He said I could go to hell [if] I did not like it."[16]

Although working for their masters consumed the greater portion of slaves' lives, it did not consume all of their time. Slaves sometimes employed their free time in tending their own gardens. This labor gave them time away from their masters as well as providing an important supplement to their meager diet. In the spring Cartmell occasionally allowed his slaves time for this task, giving "the negroes balance of day from about 10 A.M. to break them up some patches." Another day he allowed his slaves to have "part of the evening to plant some watermelons." However, weeks often went by before slaves received more time for this project or others. "Gave the negroes the day," Cartmell recorded. "I had given them no time for the past four weeks."[17]

Slaves did, however, receive some regularly scheduled breaks. Masters and bondsmen alike deemed Sunday as a day of rest, and many slaves attended church services with whites. The records of St. Luke's Episcopal Church in Jackson documented several slave burials in the 1850s. In the Methodist church, A. B. Jones remembered that "after the Holy Communion was administered to the whites, the negroes were served." However, certain limitations came with this liberty. Referring to this aspect of slave life, E. F. Alexander recalled, "we had white Preachers to Preach the gospel to them."[18]

Alexander's recollection reflected a primary white fear endemic in the Old South. Slaves could not be allowed to congregate unsupervised and were discouraged from preaching to one another for fear that black ministers might espouse explosive ideas of freedom. White evangelists, on the other hand, propounded the all-important biblical edict "Slaves obey your masters." Nevertheless, such moments offered ephemeral glimpses of freedom as masters might allow slaves the opportunity to walk to and from church unmonitored.[19]

Christmas gave slaves their best opportunity for leisure during the entire year. Each December most owners allowed their slaves a large measure of liberty, and many took this opportunity to congregate in Jackson. By 1859, however, Cartmell believed this practice had gotten out of hand. Returning from a holiday visit into town, he noted that the "negroes [were] monopolizing things in general." The next Christmas proved more ominous as Lincoln's election and the looming war cast a shadow over many masters' generosity. "Rather a quiet Christmas," Cartmell noted. "Fewer negroes about town than usual, their masters keeping them at home."[20]

Sometimes slaves received an unexpected respite from their labors. One winter Cartmell's slaves had the unusual pleasure of a ten-day period of minimal supervision while their master attended jury duty. Two days before finishing his responsibility, Cartmell wrote irritably that "negroes [were] doing little or nothing and will not until I get off the jury." Such prolonged breaks from daily toil were exceedingly rare.[21]

A few particularly fortunate slaves had a certain economic latitude in that they were allowed the privilege of charging items at the local country store under their masters' names. These slaves' accounts show a wide array of purchases. Tobacco, ribbon, cologne, ear drops, blankets, boots, and hats were common acquisitions. The store's proprietor listed the slave's name under that of his master, who usually settled the account at the end of the year. Such indulgences went, no doubt, only to the most trusted servants. The mere chance to step inside any store and experience the wonderful sights and fragrances within gave the slaves an abbreviated splash of color in their normally drab routine.[22]

Not all diversions received the master's blessing. After sundown slaves might venture away. Under cover of darkness, they traveled to other plantations or to one of the few free black households in the county. Once there they enjoyed simple amusements or conducted religious services unencumbered by white intervention. This covert communication served to bind the extended black community. Masters knew that this type of activity could not be completely squelched. When one of Cartmell's slaves could not be found early one morning, he suspected the bondsman still might be out "on some of his sly missions." Such risks, however, posed very real dangers for slaves caught off their plantations after dark.[23]

The normal cycles of birth, sickness, and death among the slaves called for special attention. Masters anticipated births among their slaves as they watched their labor force grow. Cartmell succinctly recorded one such event on his plantation: "Easter had a boy child this evening." All births were not necessarily welcomed. Cartmell also owned a teenage mulatto he referred to as Yellow Mary. The coming of this young woman's first child brought an unpleasant surprise. Cartmell recorded with consternation that "Mary, Yellow, was delivered of a boy—white at that." With indignation he continued, "I had rather have no negroes than white ones." The advent of a pale complexioned slave child caused severe confusion in a culture premised on racial distinctions.[24]

When slaves became seriously ill their masters sent for medical aid. While Cartmell often requested Dr. Snider for his servants, he favored the more skilled Dr. Fenner for his family. When the slave Easter became sick, Snider made the initial visit. However, he soon became concerned over her condition. Cartmell noted, "[Snider] felt somewhat uneasy and advised me to go in for Fenner." In accordance with the medical technology of the day, Snider's cures could often be worse than the disease. For high fever, quick respirations, and rapid pulse, Snider prescribed an expectorant and then bled the patient. Despite such tactics, slaves, like their white contemporaries, generally recovered provided they were not already too ill.[25]

In addition to physical ailments, mental illness occasionally intruded upon the slave quarters. Cartmell's slave Big Mary appeared acutely afflicted with some type of catatonic disorder. "She moves like a snail," Cartmell observed, "stands in one place for hours, chews her food and spits it out. The negroes say she eats dirt . . . [and] has not sense enough to keep out of the fire." The care of such persons created an impediment for both master and bondsman.[26]

Death, of course, deprived the master of his slave's services. Dick, one of Cartmell's favorites, became ill in the winter of 1857 and succumbed within four days. His passing marked the first such occurrence on Cartmell's relatively new plantation. While hoping that Dick might yet live, Cartmell summarized the slave's role: "Dick is certainly the main stake here among the negroes—old and settled—trusty . . . a great help to me." Later that spring Dick's namesake and eleven-year-old son also died unexpectedly. The burial must have been a melancholy occasion for Cartmell's slaves, as he recorded, "Buried Dick by the side of his Daddy." Death from contagious diseases could exact a high toll on slave children. Cartmell's neighbor "Pic" Jones lost three children to whooping cough within a few days.[27]

For the slave, being sold might be as unsettling as the death of a loved one. More than anything else, it reminded them that they could never truly control their own destiny. The motives behind this act took many forms. Abner Taylor, one of the county's more affluent planters, had to sell one of his slaves to pay his railroad tax. The county revenue collector apparently gave Taylor no other option. Cartmell witnessed the sale in town, observing that the elderly Taylor "was bitterly opposed to the tax, in fact he spoke against it as well as he could." The unfortunate slave, a mere boy of ten, had no voice in the unfolding drama. He played the pawn's role while others bickered over the justice of taxation.[28]

Occasionally slaves were sold to avoid personal problems on the plantation. Cartmell purchased Yellow Mary as a sixteen-year-old house girl for his wife Mary Jane, but soon found the two incompatible. Describing Yellow Mary as "very smart and rather headstrong," Cartmell had little desire to sell the girl but did so because "Mary Jane did not like her." The young, light-skinned woman's fondness "for white men" proved a further embarrassment for Cartmell and his wife, who had no wish "to raise a gang of white children [who were] negroes too." He lamented, "I felt sorry to see the negro and her child go . . . [and] would not have sold her if she had suited." Thus the lives of Mary and her infant were reduced to a business transaction when Cartmell deeded her to the slave merchant William Witherspoon.[29]

While the slaves of Madison County lived in the shackles of bondage, they found ways to tug at those chains and occasionally to break free from them altogether. One of the slaves' most frequently employed means of resistance consisted of compromising the amount of work their masters required of them. Toil constituted the primary component of their life, but they would not satisfy their owners' quota if at all possible. Cartmell at first believed that his slaves would shell corn at night simply because he wished it. But he soon discovered that without direct supervision his slaves, who had already spent a long day in the field, had little heart for the task. Cartmell finally faced reality and purchased a corn sheller. "The negroes waste a good deal shelling by hand," he wrote in exasperation, "and are not very nice about it and sometimes neglect it."[30]

Unsupervised work always provided ample opportunity for slaves to engage in passive resistance. When Cartmell sent his hands to hoe his fruit trees, he noted with irritation that they "did not finish orchard but ought to have done so." His bondsmen took this opportunity not only to relax but also to air some personal grievances. Later that evening Cartmell checked their progress only to discover that "John and Mary had had a fight and a general napping." A similar problem developed when Cartmell set his slaves to baling cotton on an especially cold January day. "They made 5 bales which is about all they had done and took them almost all day to do that." He speculated, "I guess they were hovering over a fire."[31]

Other resistance entailed more risks and potential punishment if caught. Hunger produced strong motivation for slaves to help themselves to the bounty of their master's table. "Noticed today where one of my hogs had been killed in the field and cleaned in a deep gully," observed Cartmell, who then speculated the culprits to be "some of my own negroes." Deception of this magnitude required careful planning and cooperation on the part of several slaves.[32]

Distrust of his slaves plagued Cartmell. More than once he believed that slaves had attempted to enter his home to rob him. "A negro attempted to get in the house last night before the doors were closed," he surmised, and "was discovered by [slave] girl, Mary, when she went to lock the door." He specified the consequences in no uncertain terms: "If I see any person moping about my house or trying to get in I will certainly shoot them." He further snapped, "This negro or some other has been here several times but was prevented from getting in or was scared off by my dog."[33]

Running away was a major form of resistance. In one stroke slaves could deprive their masters of property and labor as well as attain freedom for themselves. In 1849, Madison County attorney Frank Gamewell discovered that his slave Peter absconded under the guise of attending a meeting at the Cane Creek Church. Gamewell speculated that he "may attempt to pass himself as a free man (as he reads and writes pretty well)." Having come from South Carolina only a year earlier, Peter may have intended to return perhaps in an effort to rejoin family members.[34]

Peter most likely planned his escape ahead of time, calculating the most opportune moment, but for others, running away was a spur-of-the-moment decision. Cartmell's valuable bondsmen Dave gave his master abundant frustration as a result of one such impulse. A fellow planter, Mr. Deberry, happened by and took it upon himself to supervise Dave in his work. The slave's response to his behest was not the submissive reply that the patrician expected. Deberry then "collared him" and "a scuffle ensued," wrote Cartmell. The "scuffle" likely became a swirl of flailing fists and ripped clothing as "Dave got away after tearing all his [own] clothes off." This absence of clothing proved to be a minor inconvenience for the recalcitrant slave, who eluded detection for four days. Captured several miles away near the large plantation of William Hunt, Dave returned home. Lamenting the trouble with this individual and others, Cartmell postulated that slaves never became "too old to *whip* if not too old to run away."[35]

Several months later, Dave attempted a more carefully planned escape. He contacted a slave blacksmith, who had been hired out in Jackson and the two headed north together. Cartmell called upon fellow planters John Bond and Mr. Deberry to assist in their retrieval. When this proved fruitless, Cartmell thought back to other problems: "I have not the least doubt that [Dave] has been at the head of the men trying to get in this house on several occasions." The next day Cartmell's anger grew as he contemplated how Dave, "a rascal," had delayed the completion of his cotton ginning. "He had not the least provocation or cause for running away," wrote a bitter Cartmell. "Nothing but a settled and determined determination to go to a free state and enjoy the sweets of free negro liberty." Within two days Dave and his companion attempted to cross the Obion River in Weakley County, where the blacksmith was apprehended, but Dave managed to slip through. Cartmell became more hopeful that Dave would be caught now that he no longer had assistance. He waited several days before he heard from a jailer in Kentucky. There Dave's saga ground to a halt less than thirty miles from the Ohio River and freedom. Cartmell and his father made the journey north, where, he wrote, "I found the identical Dave there lodged in jail." He summarized the total cost of the slave's exploits: "Including expenses traveling, his board, blankets, and shirt, he cost between $90 and $100 to get him out of jail, beside trouble of going after him, [and] riding through cold."[36]

Several years later another of Cartmell's slaves tried to escape. Ironically, this bondsmen had the name Little Dave to distinguish him from the older malcontent. When Little Dave could not be found near the plantation one morning, Cartmell quickly went into town. There he received assistance from a man named Butler who owned several blood hounds. A search of four hours produced no sign of the missing slave. Meanwhile, Little Dave made his way to the plantation of Cartmell's father, where he spent the night. He continued north, and his master had no news concerning him for nearly a month. On a hunch Cartmell responded to an advertisement in the Trenton, Tennessee, newspaper where an eighteen-year-old slave had been put in jail. Little Dave told the jailer he came from Arkansas and belonged to a man named James Whittlington. Cartmell made the trip to Trenton, where he "found Dave calling himself John . . . $27.65 expenses . . . getting Dave out of jail."[37]

For slaves who attempted escape or simply to slip out for the evening, the slave patrol represented the greatest threat to their success. The patrol symbolized white society's constant fear: slave rebellion. Its primary function served as a safeguard against any activities of insubordination. A slave belonging to the planter William Darnall had an encounter with the patrol in Madison County. Found away from the plantation and without a pass, the slave attempted to get away when he was injured by members of the patrol. Darnall sued patrol leader James Tomlinson for his slave's fifteen-dollar medical bill, but the attempt proved unsuccessful. Justice Caruthers delivered the court's opinion, which reflected the community's concern, when he stipulated that "the institution and support of the night-watch and patrol . . . are indispensable to good order, and the subordination of the slaves, and the best interest of their owners."[38]

While the slaves of Madison County never engaged in organized rebellion, the dread that they might do so remained with their masters. The fear reached such proportions in 1856 that the county's slaves went without their regular Christmas holiday. "There is some apprehensions of a general rising of negroes" wrote Cartmell. "North of this in several places a scheme has been detected and a good many negroes have been hung." He continued, "The negroes are to a great extent cut off from their usual enjoyment. At any event they are closely watched."[39]

The early stages of the Civil War served to heighten white anxiety about their slaves. Even as the first Confederate volunteers headed north in the spring of 1861, Madison Countians believed they had uncovered a full-scale insurrection near Pinson Mound. A full company of soldiers came by rail from Memphis and numerous shotgun-carrying locals met them. The truth turned out to be so distorted as to be embarrassing. "Proved to be a false report," Cartmell wrote, "started by some fellow shooting off a repeater 4 or 5 times in front of a house where some women were."[40]

The advent of the Civil War also provided some slaves with an opportunity to settle old grievances. Late in the war, John Johnston and Hewett Witherspoon attempted to return to duty in the Confederate cavalry. To elude detection from Union patrols, Hewett spent the night at the home of a Mr. Dickerson. Johnston recalled that one of Dickerson's slaves informed nearby soldiers of young Hewett's hiding place. "There was a negro who had some sort of grudge against Witherspoon," Johnston remembered, "and he went down to their camp and informed them that a rebel soldier was spending the night at Dickerson's." The slave's grievance could have very well been against the entire Witherspoon clan, one of Madison's largest slave-owning families.[41]

Evidence of a broader slave community, reaching beyond the individual plantation, is manifested by planters who shared and swapped slaves with their friends and relatives. Cartmell had access to extra labor from his father's many bondsmen. On one occasion his father loaned him "two men [for the] balance of week." When his brother-in-law needed construction laborers, Cartmell "sent 3 hands to help Mr. Bond raise his gin house." He also sent "5 hands . . . to help Pic Jones," one of his closest friends. When repairing a bridge abutment near his home, Cartmell counted that he had "3 of Pic Jones hands 4 of Hurts 3 of Bonds and 4 of mine." This interaction between slaves from various areas quite likely served to keep many of them informed of the news and events of their extended community.[42]

If Robert Cartmell and his bondsmen provide any clue, in antebellum Madison County the relationship between master and slave bears little resemblance to the subservient Sambo. The planter's unyielding frustration and the slaves' consistent recalcitrance can be summarized by returning once again to Cartmell's own words. "Negroes are an unpleasant animal to have anything to do with," he surmised, "requiring constant watching, they feel an interesting in nothing, *only punctual* in coming *regularly* when their meat [supply] gives out." Cartmell punctuates the tumultuous nature of their coexistence by offering this final observation: "Negroes . . . are a mean, unprincipled, rogish, lazy set only fit to fret a man's life out of him." Clearly, Madison County slaves attempted to assert themselves on an individual level while providing their masters with both economic security as well as mental anguish.[43]

Notes

1. Robert H. Cartmell diary, 24 Mar. 1855, Robert H. Cartmell Papers, Tennessee State Library and Archives, Nashville (hereafter cited as Cartmell diary).
2. John Johnston, "Memoirs," Confederate Collection, Tennessee State Library and Archives, Nashville (hereafter cited as TSLA), 4; E. F. Alexander, Tennessee Civil War Veterans Questionnaires, TSLA (hereafter cited as TCWVQ).
3. Cartmell diary, 22 Aug. 1854 and 24 Mar. 1855.
4. Kenneth Stampp, *The Peculiar Institution: Slavery in the Antebellum South* (New York, 1956); Stanley M. Elkins, *Slavery: A Problem in American Institutional and Intellectual Life* (Chicago, 1959); John W. Blassingame, *The Slave Community: Plantation Life in the Antebellum South* (New York, 1972); Eugene D. Genovese, *Roll, Jordan, Roll: The World the Slaves Made* (New York, 1974); Robert W. Fogel and Stanley L. Engerman, *Time on the Cross* (Boston, 1974).
5. Lewis C. Gray, *History of Agriculture in the Southern United States to 1860*, 2 vols. (1933; reprint, New York, 1949), 2:873.
6. Cartmell diary, 27 July and 3 Aug. 1853; Eighth U.S. Census, Agricultural Schedule, 1860: Madison County, Tennessee, 7.
7. Eighth U.S. Census, Slave Schedule, 1860: Madison County, Tennessee. All statistics in this chapter were generated by using Statistical Package for the Social Sciences (SPSS).

8. Cartmell diary, 30 Sept. 1853, "Cotton Picking Chart," 1853–54.
9. Ibid., 28 Feb., 1 Oct., 2 Dec. 1853 and 23 May, 27 Sept. 1860.
10. Ibid., 1 Oct. and 6 Dec. 1853.
11. Ibid., 24 Jan. 1856, Thomas Reid, TCWVQ.
12. Ibid., 2 Aug. 1853.
13. Ibid., 23 Apr. 1855 and 8 Mar. 1856.
14. Ibid., 13 Aug. 1853.
15. Ibid., 20 Mar. 1861.
16. Ibid., 26 May 1858.
17. Ibid., 17, 22 May and 8 July 1854.
18. St. Luke's Episcopal Church Records, Burials, 1855–62, Tennessee Room, Jackson–Madison County Library; A. B. Jones and E. F. Alexander, TCWVQ.
19. *West Tennessee Whig,* 31 Aug. 1849.
20. Cartmell Diary, 27 Dec. 1859 and 25 Dec. 1860.
21. Ibid., 22 Jan. 1855.
22. Rogers and Hearn Store Ledger, 1858–59, TSLA; in Emma Williams, *Historic Madison: the Story of Jackson and Madison County, Tennessee* (Jackson, Tenn.: Madison County Historical Society, 1946), 207.
23. Cartmell diary, 30 Oct. 1854. A detailed look at the lives of free blacks during this period can be found in Steve Baker, "Free Blacks in Antebellum Madison County," *Tennessee Historical Quarterly* 52 (Spring 1993): 56–63.
24. Cartmell diary, 1 Oct. 1857 and 18 Mar. 1859.
25. Ibid., 1 Dec. 1855 and 12, 16 May 1857.
26. Ibid., 27 Sept. and 19 Dec. 1859.
27. Ibid., 27, 31 Jan., 13 May, and 6 Nov. 1857. For an examination of how slaves coped with death, see David R. Roediger, "And Die in Dixie: Funerals, Death, and Heaven in the Slave Community, 1700–1865," *Massachusetts Review* 22 (Spring 1981): 163–83.
28. Cartmell diary, 22 Apr. 1854.
29. Ibid., 25 Sept. 1857 and 15–16 Dec. 1859.
30. Ibid., 2 Mar. 1855.
31. Ibid., 17 June 1859 and 7 Jan. 1854.
32. Ibid., 25 Nov. 1859.
33. Ibid., 12 Sept. 1854.
34. *West Tennessee Whig,* 31 Aug. 1849.
35. Cartmell diary, 24, 28 June 1854.
36. Ibid., 30–31 Oct. and 2, 15 Nov. 1854.
37. Ibid., 28 May and 3, 27 June 1861.
38. Harvey Gresham Hudspeth, "Forgotten Whig: The Life and Times of Howell Edmunds Jackson, 1832–1895" (Ph.D. diss., Univ. of Mississippi, 1994), 72–73.
39. Cartmell diary, 23 and 25 Dec. 1856.
40. Ibid., 27 May 1861.
41. Johnston, "Memoirs," 38–39.
42. Cartmell diary, 6 Dec. 1853, 23 July 1857, 7 Apr. 1858, and 18 Aug. 1859.
43. Ibid., 7 Jan. 1854 and 13 Mar. 1860.

Archaeological Study of Slavery and Plantation Life in Tennessee

Larry McKee

RCHAEOLOGY IS AN EFFECTIVE WAY OF GAINING INFORMATION ABOUT THOSE TENNESSEANS WHO LEFT LITTLE TO NO WRITTEN RECORDS but did leave valuable information in the archaeological remains of their dwellings and places of work. In his study of plantation slavery, Larry McKee summarizes years of excavations at the slave quarters of the Hermitage, the Nashville home of President Andrew Jackson, along with other properties across the state. He finds that the material culture of slavery suggests that planters structured the physical environment so to keep slaves in, and remind slaves of, "their place." Also, the evidence indicates that there was no hierarchy between house servants and field hands at the Hermitage; rather, there was a black community structure "based on cooperation, valued talents, and personal qualities." Slaves broke the monotony of a pork-dominated diet from their owners by catching raccoons, squirrels, rabbits, fowl, and fish. They also took discarded items, from marbles to ceramics, and reused them to advantage. They had weapons, judging from the firearm artifacts gathered by the archaeologists, and they carried over African religious practices.

Over the last three decades archaeological research has emerged as an exciting way to study the lives of enslaved African Americans in Tennessee and the rest of the Americas. The power of this research comes from its ability to circumvent documentary silences and ambiguities on slavery, revealing, through sometimes unexpected and surprising discoveries from the ground, what has been lost and hidden about the past.

Archaeological research on slavery is also about spreading the word on new information and new perspectives on the topic. Excavation results have proven to be a powerful way of getting people to look beyond their usual minimized understanding of the past based on dates and names absorbed from grade school history textbooks. Archaeology's emotional appeal, linked to popular notions about treasure and mysterious discoveries, also plays an important role in engaging the public's attention. Excavations at slave dwelling sites often turn up eye-catching evidence, which challenges and even contradicts common perceptions about plantation life. In taking the research toward deeper questions about the interaction between race, economics, politics, and culture in American history, archaeology also can encourage the public to see the steady flow from the past to the present. This is, of course, the point of studying history.

The central focus of archaeological research is on material culture—the tangible items which come from excavation sites. These sources inform us about slave life in two ways. The first is as the residue of everyday life, with bones telling about diet and standing structures and architectural remains telling about shelter and levels of crowding and discomfort while other items—about everything from clothing to children's activities—give insight to spirituality. But excavated evidence goes beyond serving as just a passive record of human activity in the past. Things left in the ground can provide a view of how artifacts and the built environment surrounding enslaved African Americans actively structured life and became tools and weapons in the tense struggle between master and slave.[1]

The structures and details of the layout of a farm or plantation are perhaps the strongest evidence of the influence of inanimate objects on the structure of social life. Plantation housing for both blacks and whites was always more than just shelter from the weather. The opulence of plantation "big houses" certainly provided owners and their families with luxurious comfort, but these buildings also signaled to all who was in charge. The owners' personal residences also served as effective markers within the landscape, defining and supporting what passed as the "natural order" of the social hierarchy. In the same way, dwellings provided for slaves, usually small in size and minimal in amenities, were the product of forces other than just the desire to keep costs down. Standing in sharp contrast to the highly visible big house, and usually situated and arranged in precise order, plantation community housing was intended by planters to keep slaves, literally and figuratively, in their place.[2] Almost every category of the physical world of plantation life, from fences to food to diet, can be read in a similar way. The challenge is to use the evidence not only to see the master's intentions, but to see the slave's responses as well. How did the occupants of the slave quarter alter their homes, add to their rations and meager clothing allotments, and find ways to buy and barter for possessions? To what degree did these actions help to subvert the planters' plans for complete domination of their chattel? What comes out of the ground at sites associated with slave life can reveal not only what went on but also how it went on.

The archaeological study of slave life in the United States had its beginnings in the 1970s, and Tennessee played a prominent role in the development of this research from the start. During the 1970s, Richard Polhemus, working at the Tellico Blockhouse site in East Tennessee, and Sam Smith, working at the Hermitage, each uncovered and analyzed somewhat unexpected evidence about enslaved residents. Their findings have remained central to some of the most important and intriguing questions within the archaeological study of slave life.

Polhemus's contribution to the field came from his 1977 analysis of ceramic fragments excavated at the Tellico Blockhouse site, a late-eighteenth-century trade and military installation near Knoxville.[3] The artifact collection included a type of pottery known in the archaeological literature of the time as colono-Indian ware. During the previous three decades, archaeologists had been finding pieces of such handmade, low-fired, unglazed vessels on seventeenth- and eighteenth-century sites up and down the eastern seaboard. The widely accepted interpretation of this material was that it had been made by surviving Indian groups as items to be traded with white colonists.

Polhemus called attention to the obvious differences between the so-called colono-Indian ware shards and the locally produced Cherokee pottery unearthed at the Tellico site. He linked this difference to the known presence of African American slaves in residence at the blockhouse, concluding that the distinctive ceramics "are not likely to have been made by Indians at all." He went on to make another important observation: "The uniform presence of blacks on all sites producing "colono-Indian" ceramics and the consistency in forms represented throughout its area of occurrence strongly indicate that such ceramics should more properly be called "colono-black" rather than "colono-Indian." (His recommended name change never took root, and these days this ceramic is referred to as colono ware.) Polhemus's breakthrough insight was fueled by years of research on colonial sites in South Carolina and, serendipitously, a visit he made during the same period to the West African nation of Ghana. He reported that traditional potters still at work there made vessels that looked identical to the American colono Indian ware, and the two could only be distinguished "through a detailed analysis of the composition of the paste and temper."[4]

The long ignorance, in both senses of the word, of the probable role of African American slaves in the production of colono ware is a good example of the common discounting of the ability of slaves to take action or to have any significant input in determining the conditions of their enslavement. Ironically, production and use of colono ware comes to an end practically everywhere around 1800, largely due to the widened availability at the time of cheap mass produced vessels from newly industrialized English potteries. Few if any colono ware fragments have been recovered at Tennessee sites other than the Tellico Blockhouse.[5]

Sam Smith, on the staff of the Tennessee State Division of Archaeology for most of the last three decades, became involved with the archaeological study of slave life as a graduate student at the University of Florida. There his advisor was the late Charles Fairbanks, one of the acknowledged founders of archaeological research on plantation sites. Smith's work at the Hermitage during the 1970s was largely intended to recover evidence of Andrew Jackson's early years at the site, specifically in terms of what was left in the ground around the two standing log cabins known as the First Hermitage. Due to the nature of the site and the background he brought to the research, Smith turned up at least as much evidence of the site's later use as a slave quarter as he did about its original use as the Jackson family residence. Smith's research has served as a rock-solid foundation for more recent work at the Hermitage and at many other Tennessee sites associated with slavery.

Smith was successful not only in confirming the archaeological visibility of the Hermitage slave community, but also in establishing the best routes for future research to follow in making use of this visibility. His 1976 site report and his 1977 article "Plantation Archaeology at the Hermitage: Some Suggested Patterns"[6] highlight the project's discoveries, with special attention given to recovered evidence on architecture, diet, the plantation's layout, and the rich array of recovered furnishings and personal items. Smith was perhaps the first to note the consistent presence of blue glass beads on slave dwelling sites, an association that has since blossomed to the point that anyone work-ing on such sites anywhere in the Americas now expects to find such beads. Published studies exploring the meaning of blue beads have men-tioned a variety of explanations, from clothing and body adornment to use as identifying markers on sewing equipment to being an expression of African religious tradition.[7] Like much else that comes out of the ground at these sites, a single ironclad explanation will no doubt always remain elusive.

In 1988 the Ladies' Hermitage Association instituted an in-house archae-ological research program, in part to ensure proper care of the site's significant archaeological resources and in part to conduct research on what this resource could reveal about the plantation's history. Although the slave com-munity was not the program's original intended focus, it soon came to be because of staff and public interest and the extraordinarily rich remains asso-ciated with slave dwelling sites on the property. The program's centerpiece is an annual large-scale summer excavation crewed by Hermitage staff, student interns, and volunteers. The summer dig has focused on slave dwelling exca-vation in eight of the eleven years since the program's inception.

Probably the single most important accomplishment of recent archaeo-logical research at the Hermitage has been to relocate the extensive presence of the slave community on the property. Surprisingly, not a single map of the Hermitage dating to the antebellum period has yet come to light, and men-tions of the layout and array of plantation buildings and facilities in primary documents about the site are rare and ambivalent at best. Over the past twenty-five years of excavation twenty separate slave dwelling units have come to light. This is enough to account for the housing of Jackson's entire number of slaves, made up of over 140 individuals at its high point in the 1840s. Only three slave dwellings remain standing on the property (two duplexes and one single-family dwelling), underlining the importance of the discovery in presenting a more complete picture of the plantation to visitors.[8]

The Hermitage slave dwellings are clustered in three areas: near the Jackson family mansion, at the First Hermitage (which became a quartering area after the Jacksons left it to move into the first version of the current brick mansion in 1821), and at the field quarter, located a third of a mile north of the big house. These separate dwelling areas seem in keeping with prevailing notions about the division of plantation slave communities into "classes" linked to work duties, with the cook and other house servants living near the mansion and the field hands housed in close proximity to the crops that they tended. The fact that the Hermitage's current property includes the location of all three of these clusters of slave housing provides enormous research opportunities for the archaeological study of all segments of the plantation community.

So far the most surprising element of this plantation-wide research has been the lack of many differences in the archaeological remains associated with the three housing clusters. Housing in all three areas was of a standard size, based on twenty-square-foot single rooms assigned to individual families. The artifact collections (or assemblages) associated with each slave house lot at various locations on the property are also surprisingly similar in terms of the quantity, quality, and diversity of items.

It would appear that the scholarly and popular perception of a community hierarchy with the house servants on top and the field hands at the bottom did not apply at the Hermitage. A 1995 dissertation by Brian Thomas explored this topic at length. Thomas concluded that such an "antagonistic" model of slave community structure was imposed and manipulated by planters as a method to divide and conquer their chattel. He also concludes that the archaeological record at the Hermitage reveals a different model of community structure, defined by the community members themselves, and based on cooperation, valued talents, and personal qualities rather than on task assignments. His use of documentary sources revealing many cases of Hermitage slave marriages between house servants and field hands adds compelling support to his argument.[9]

Questions about the quality and quantity of the slaves' food supplies are always central to the issue of how slaves were treated by their owners, and archaeological research on dietary remains has added a great deal of evidence unavailable from any other source. Emanuel Breitburg of the state of Tennessee's Division of Archaeology has carried out studies of the animal bones recovered from Hermitage excavations since the 1970s.[10] One very strong pattern jumps out from his research: the prevalence of pig bones found in association with all Hermitage households, from the mansion on back to the field quarter. Translating the bone evidence into dietary terms suggests that pork made up between 70 and 90 percent of the meat portion of the diet for all Hermitage residents, with beef and mutton only consumed about 10 or 20 percent of the time. This is not too surprising, given southern dietary preferences and the fact that approximately two hundred hogs, representing about *nine tons* of useable meat, were slaughtered every year at the Hermitage.

The monotony of the core diet at the Hermitage was apparently lessened through the varied efforts of slave households to supplement their rations from other sources. Small mammals (opossum, raccoon, squirrel, and rabbit), fowl (chicken, turkeys, ducks, and geese) and aquatic resources (turtles, fish, and mollusks) are all represented in the collections of animal bones from Hermitage households. One unexpected and important element of the collections is that the percentages for these different animal bones vary wildly from dwelling to dwelling, suggesting that each family pursued different strategies in trying to put an adequate amount of food on their tables.

Other kinds of artifacts consistently found around Hermitage slave dwellings include ceramics, bottle glass, nails and other architectural debris, buttons and sewing equipment, and children's toys such as marbles and small china dolls. The richness and variety of the collections are somewhat of a surprise in terms of the common perceptions of slave life. It remains open to interpretation whether the quantity and quality of the artifacts left by the Hermitage slave community is a "trickle-down" effect related to Andrew Jackson's wealth and high social standing or whether this is a reflection of the abilities of the Hermitage slave community to obtain and accumulate these goods on their own.

Some artifacts recovered from Hermitage slave dwellings provide more direct challenges to specific contemporary assumptions about slave life. Items related to firearms—lead shot, gun flints, percussion caps, and even broken firing mechanisms found at almost all the excavated slave households—point to some consistent access to weaponry within the Hermitage slave community. Such discoveries have been made at other slave dwelling sites, and are actually in keeping with documentary sources referring to the use of slaves as wild game hunters on some plantations. What immediately strikes our own sensibilities about this is the contradictory images of armed, unsupervised slaves wandering around the countryside. On deeper consideration, the combination of firearms and slaves provides telling insights about the level of trust and acceptance of the status quo between master and slave. It also points out that violence and armed insurrection was not necessarily an immediate acceptable option for those held in bond. The discovery of evidence of literacy (albeit indirect) in the form of eyeglasses, writing slates, slate pencils, and initials carved in bone artifacts, and the consistent presence of coins at Hermitage slave household sites allows for similar recognitions about how the specific dictates of plantation life were often open to negotiation and accommodation.

Another strong pattern seen in the archaeological record of slave life at the Hermitage is the presence of small storage pits or root cellars beneath slave dwelling floors. So far such pits have been found in association with every slave dwelling explored through excavation at the Hermitage, with the exception of the standing log structure known as Alfred's Cabin. All are rectangular in shape, ranging in size from just over two feet on a side up to one measuring 6.5 by 7.5 feet. These features have also been regularly encountered on slave dwelling excavations in Virginia, North Carolina, and Kentucky, but are not found on Low Country plantations along the Georgia–South Carolina coast. This regional difference is probably linked to climate, since the pits primarily functioned to hold potatoes, apples, and other storable vegetables and fruits at stable temperatures during the winter months. The strong correlation between these cellars and slave dwellings has encouraged speculation that the features represent a continuity with African architectural forms, but little in the way of corroborating ethnographic evidence from Africa has been found. My interpretation is that these features are of European origin, soon adopted by enslaved Africans in North America as a very practical way to add secure storage space to dwellings which otherwise had little or nothing available in the way of cupboards or chests.[11]

Perhaps the most intriguing and telling thing about the Hermitage root cellars is the wide variation seen from dwelling to dwelling in terms of position in the building, size, and wall construction details. Most are found in close proximity to the hearth area, but some are much farther away. In about half the examples there is only one cellar, while in the other half there are multiple chambers, sometimes connected, sometimes not. The most common size is about 4 feet long by 2.5 feet wide, but others are only half that long. One example, within the brick dwelling known as the triplex near the Jackson family mansion, measures 6.5 feet by 7.5 feet. In most cases the walls and the floors of the cellars are lined with brick, but some were just left as squared-off holes dug down into the site's stiff clay subsoil. The root cellar tradition spans the two distinct phases of slave dwelling construction at the site, which roughly coincides with the Jackson family's move from a log dwelling to a newly constructed brick mansion in 1821. (The final version of the mansion kitchen, constructed after the structure's 1834 fire, also includes a substantial root cellar accessible through a trap door in its plank floor.) There is also clear evidence of frequent remodeling and reconfiguration of the cellars by the dwelling occupants, perhaps as a result of partial collapses, perhaps due to changes in the household or changes in the intended uses of the storage space.

The wide variation in the size and placement of the root cellars in the Hermitage's slave dwelling can be interpreted as material evidence of some limited autonomy of individual enslaved families within the otherwise stifling system of plantation discipline. Although the dwellings provided for the slave community are numbingly standardized in terms of size and configuration, these cellars were obviously added later, with little or nothing in the way of a specified plan. This would seem to be a telling bit of evidence about how each family had a certain amount of independent control over how they used and transformed their own dwellings.

Another surprisingly consistent find at the Hermitage has been of artifacts related to African American spirituality and folk beliefs. Although conjure work and "root doctoring" have long been recognized as an essential element of African American culture under both slavery and freedom, at the Hermitage the number of recovered items indirectly and directly associated with these activities has been an overwhelming surprise.[12] Every household so far investigated at the Hermitage has produced several items such as smoothed stones, glass beads, concentrations of prehistoric stone tools, pierced coins, small brass charms in the shape of a human fist (Fig. 24), quartz crystals, and deliberately reshaped ceramic fragments and animal bones, all which can be lumped within the loosely defined category of spiritual artifacts. It is admittedly hard to pin down the specific meanings or uses of these things, but there are some obvious links to documented African American folklore and to finds of identical items at slave dwelling excavations throughout the eastern United States and in the Caribbean.[13] The wide array of such recovered artifacts points to some very active belief systems making use of and transforming what were mostly mundane items into culturally charged forms. These retain enough "flash" to still catch the eye of the late-twentieth-century observer. Finding, writing about, and displaying these artifacts to the interested public is probably the most exciting element of the archaeological study of the African American past.

The personality and public life of Andrew Jackson, the owner of the Hermitage and its slave community, obviously had a significant but mostly indirect impact on the site's archaeological record. Jackson was no Jefferson, in the sense that he left behind little in the way of writings on his personal philosophy of plantation and slave management and no expressions of moral anxiety over slave ownership. His overall pragmatic approach to the world certainly guided his experiences as a planter and his view of slavery as an accepted part of economic and social life.[14] Those enslaved at the Hermitage benefited in some ways from being his property, especially in terms of the stable family life within the community enabled and encouraged by his long-term ownership of the Hermitage. Jackson was obviously well aware of public scrutiny of his personal life as he advanced on the national stage, and the standing buildings and archaeological remains at the Hermitage are clear evidence of his attempt to showcase his plantation as an example of the southern ideal of slave ownership guided by benign paternalism. The huge size of his slaveholding, which at its peak of over 140 individuals was about four times the size needed to conduct efficient farming, was in part due to his reluctance to sell individuals and open himself to the charge of profiteering through slave trading and "breeding." The twenty-square-foot size used for nearly all the Hermitage slave dwellings was fully 25 percent larger than the usual "mean" dimensions of sixteen-square-foot houses cited in surveys of slave accommodations.[15] This supposedly ample size, along with the common use of brick for these dwellings after 1820, was no doubt recognized as "enlightened" by the many curious visitors who came to meet and personally assess Jackson at his plantation home. One challenge in presenting the Hermitage to modern visitors is to avoid continuing this showcasing in terms of the constant need to provide a context for the notion that Jackson was a "good" slave owner. This is made easier by allowing people to walk around and even enter the extant slave dwellings at the site, and to consider for themselves what it was like to raise a family in such minimally "ample" spaces.

This study only reviews the highlights of archaeological research at the Hermitage. The evidence collected so far, along with the continuing investigations at the site, will support decades of further analysis into the nuances of slave life at the Hermitage. Topics ripe for deeper study include everything from clothing production and seamstress activities to the material culture of childhood to the particulars of house yard use and layout. The Hermitage provides a rich context for studying slave and plantation life, in terms of the large land base, the extensive (albeit patchy) documentary sources on the site, the supportive staff and governing board, and the ready-made national interest and audience for the resulting interpretations.

One challenge within what is otherwise an ideal setting for research is in comparing and fitting Hermitage finds and interpretations with work done at sites associated with the African American past elsewhere in Tennessee and the rest of the nation. The Hermitage was unusual in many ways during its antebellum heyday, and the question of whether or not discoveries at the site will be useful in addressing slave life in general remains to be answered. One solution to this dilemma is to consider the site not on a completely separate plane from other research settings, but at the far edge of the continuum in terms of size, the social stature of its principal owner, and the level of research attention it has received. The challenge then becomes to use other sites and other project results to view other selected spots along this continuum.

A site known as the Gowen farmstead provides some strong evidence of a place closer to the middle of the continuum of the African American experience in antebellum Tennessee. Its value as a comparison to the Hermitage is enhanced by the fact it was occupied during the same time period, and it was located about ten miles from Andrew Jackson's home, on property now under one of the runways at the Nashville International Airport.[16] The site was originally the residence of William Gowen (1720–1790), an immigrant from South Carolina who moved to the Nashville area from South Carolina in 1779. The following year Gowen became one of the signers of the Cumberland Compact. By the 1820s a third generation of Gowens was living on and working the property, which had evolved into a prosperous farming operation producing cotton, tobacco, corn, and livestock. With four hundred acres and fifteen enslaved African Americans in 1820, the Gowen operation could be counted as either a large farm or a small plantation, depending on the particulars of the definition being applied. The numbers clearly put the Gowens at the higher end of the economic spectrum in Middle Tennessee, but still below the uppermost status of Jackson's holdings at the Hermitage.

Archaeological research on the site took place in 1991 and 1992, prior to the construction of a new airport runway across the area. The work revealed subterranean evidence of a number of long-gone buildings clustered together in a way that allows some clear insights into the farm's organization. A stone foundation, measuring about forty-one feet by thirty feet, with two fireplace bases and the remnant of a possible portico entrance, sits at the center of the cluster and probably served as the Gowen residence. Two nearby foundations, much smaller in size and in line to the rear of the main house, represent some kind of food storage facilities, one possibly an icehouse.

Two other buildings, each off to one side of the main house, probably served as slave residences. One of these, measuring approximately twenty-two feet by eighteen feet, left only ephemeral traces of its outline, suggesting it was a log building propped up on limestone piers. Associated pit features and ash deposits are very reminiscent of what was found beneath the surface adjacent to Hermitage slave dwellings.

The second Gowen farmstead structure identified as a slave residence was much more substantial and probably also served as the site's kitchen and food production center. It measured forty-five feet by twenty feet, with a central fireplace serving its two rooms. Excavation uncovered an unusually large root cellar measuring nine feet by nine feet within one of the two rooms.

Artifacts recovered from the root cellar and general deposits associated with the kitchen/residence signal its occupancy by enslaved African Americans.

Along with the usual array of ceramic fragments, bottle glass, and animal bones commonly found around nineteenth-century dwelling sites, digging here produced some unusual items which have also been recovered at a number of other known slave dwelling sites throughout the southeastern United States, including the Hermitage. These include a pierced Spanish coin, four glass beads, a complete conch shell, and another marine shell with a hole drilled through it. Although these are just a few of the hundreds of thousands of artifacts from the site, taken together, in association with one another, with the architectural setting, and in the context of discoveries made at other slave-associated sites, encourages the interpretation that these are clear markers of the presence of a slave family in residence in this building.

Using this artifact cluster to identify, at least hypothetically, the cultural affiliation of the building's residents is just a first step. The pieces also suggest some deep connections between those enslaved at the Gowen farmstead and slaves at operations spread across the entire South, connections which marked a separate cultural identity defined and maintained by the slaves themselves rather than one imposed by those who claimed ownership. Although these odd trinkets may seem too trivial to be used in positing such a grander scheme, these are best read as representing only the visible, enduring, and material evidence of broader customs and traits which left little or no trace: language, body presentation and posture, foodways, folk beliefs, and the general shared perceptions of self, family, community, and the rest of the world.

This intriguing set of kitchen/slave residence artifacts is given an additional charge of meaning from the fact that the property's original owner, William Gowen, was of mixed race. An affidavit dating to 1792 refers to him as a free mulatto, and his son, James H. Gowen, was falsely arrested as a possible runaway slave in Sumner County in 1804, "suggesting the physical characteristics of William and his children were recognizably African."[17] The Gowen family's racial identity certainly adds complexity to the analysis of the archaeological research. The family's history before coming to Tennessee is a little unclear, especially in terms of William Gowen's forebearer's apparent prosperity and his various previous residences in Virginia, North Carolina, and South Carolina. This suggests he might have been the offspring of a liaison between a white planter and a black woman, possibly one of his slaves. The transitional nature of the family's racial identity is underlined by the fact that one of William Gowen's daughters, Christiana, married an important Nashville founding resident, Capt. John Rains. "The fact that William Gowen and his descendants were able to establish themselves as successful planters highlights conditions prevalent during a brief period of Tennessee's history when established social relations of race and caste were eased by a frontier situation. . . . No doubt these conditions changed as the frontier settlement matured."[18] The Gowen family apparently "passed" from its mixed race status to full uncontested identity as white sometime during the antebellum period. Certainly many other Americans did this throughout the nineteenth century and well into the twentieth. What is surprising from our perspective is that the Gowens made the switch while maintaining membership within a community that was fully aware of their mixed status.

Archaeologically, the Gowens present themselves as white. Excavation of the main house at the Gowen farmstead turned up no cluster or even single example of the "obvious" slave-related artifacts found in the kitchen/residence. The family apparently rejected any items which would identify them as being anything other than white, probably in part because it would send the wrong message and in part because such items would be meaningless and useless, from a cultural perspective, to them. This is the easiest way to read the evidence, conveniently ignoring the many layers of social ambiguities involving the Gowens, their slaves, and the rest of the inhabitants of Middle Tennessee at this time. Historical archaeology has yet to define study methods and procedures to deal with the social and racial complexities offered by such situations as the Gowen farmstead. Of course the same can be said about other disciplines studying the past. What archaeology does do in an effective way is bring to light physical evidence, otherwise largely unavailable from the more traditional sources on history, which allows the researcher at least some insights into some unusual, but intriguing, situations like the Gowen farmstead.

A common pitfall in conducting archaeological research on the African American past is an overly tight, compartmentalized focus blocking out recognition of the broader social world surrounding the sites under study. In the eighteenth and nineteenth centuries most of Tennessee was a place where the free and the enslaved were in close physical and cultural proximity, making it both difficult and unwise to segment the past into separate spheres of black and white.

An important painting showing a prominent antebellum Nashville family provides an example of this interaction, with intriguing links to the archaeological study of slave life in Tennessee. Painted in about 1825, and now a part of the collection at the Cheekwood Museum of Art in Nashville, the large portrait shows the Ephraim Hubbard Foster family. One member of the family, a young girl, stands on a windowsill with an odd feathered hat on her head and a large coin or medallion, decorated with an eagle, strung around her neck. Like most of Nashville's elite during the first third of the nineteenth century, Ephraim Foster had close dealings with Andrew Jackson. This connection carried over to the family's choice of portraitist, Ralph E. W. Earl, best remembered for his many dramatic portraits of Andrew Jackson. The medallion around the young Foster child's neck provides another link to the Hermitage, since a visually identical piece, also pierced, was recovered during the excavation of one of the slave dwellings near the Jackson family mansion. Six other pierced coins have been found from three other slave dwelling sites on the property, and such finds are common at other sites and are usually understood to be related to folk beliefs about bringing luck and warding off evil.[19]

One reading of the connection between coins from slave dwellings and the medallion shown in the Foster family portrait is that it represents the presence, and at some level the acceptance, of an alternate meaning and use for coins, one derived from an African American tradition. The Fosters would have of course made use of a slave as a nanny for their children, and it may be the coin was present around the child's neck as the result of the influence of such an individual. What each participant in this exchange—parent, child, and slave (and of course Earl the painter, a longtime resident at the Hermitage)—believed about the meaning and function of the talisman/medallion is unrecoverable from our vantage point. This should not discourage conjecture that the portrait and the related documentary and archaeological sources that provide it context signal some strong but usually silenced connections between black and white antebellum Tennesseans. An engaging image of a smiling little girl with an unusual taste in accessories is admittedly a long way from the dirt and sweat of an archaeological site, but it is this kind of give and take between different lines of evidence that provide value and strength to the interpretations of what we dig up.

The African American past in Tennessee should continue to be a topic of archaeological interest for a long time to come. The state has a wide array of sites throughout its various regions ready to sustain extended study, and many questions remain to be explored. Time and place strongly influenced slavery in Tennessee, and archaeology should continue to make some major contributions to understanding the distinctions and continuities between the lives of slaves on small slaveholdings in East Tennessee, on middling operations in the Central Basin, and on the large cotton plantations in the area around Memphis. Although plantation life has been the major focus of the work so far, the ground should also yield some exciting information on the ways newly freed African Americans dealt with the harsh social and economic realities of the decades after emancipation in both rural and urban settings. One continuing challenge in doing the work will be to bridge the gaps between "pure" academic studies, "public" research (in museum and cultural resource management contexts), and the average citizens who are the ultimate consumers, in one form or another, of the work. Success in making these linkages will come through a focus on the idea that Tennesseans of all racial and ethnic backgrounds are eager to learn more about the state's heritage, and that a broadened knowledge and understanding of the past can make a crucial contribution in dealing with our present and our future.

Notes

I would like to thank my former employer, the Ladies' Hermitage Association, and James Vaughan, the former executive director of the Hermitage during my years there, for their boundless support and enthusiasm for archaeology's value and potential in studying the recent path. Over the last decade, additional financial support for archaeological research at the Hermitage has come from Earthwatch, the Martin Foundation, the Massey Foundation, and the National Endowment for the Humanities.

1. Mary C. Beaudry, Lauren J. Cook, and Stephen A. Mrozowski, "Artifacts and Active Voices: Material Culture as Social Discourse," in *The Archaeology of Inequality*, ed. Robert Paynter and Randall H. McGuire (Oxford, 1991); Paul Shackel and Barbara Little, "Post-Processual Approaches to Meanings and Uses of Material Culture in Historical Archaeology," *Historical Archaeology* 26, no. 3 (1992): 5–11.

2. See Larry McKee, "The Ideals and Realities Behind the Design and Use of Nineteenth-Century Virginia Slave Cabins," in *The Art and Mystery of Historical Archaeology: Essays in Honor of James Deetz*, ed. Anne E. Yentsch and Marcy C. Beaudry (Boca Raton, Fla., 1992); Dell Upton, "White and Black Landscapes in Eighteenth-Century Virginia," in *Material Life in America, 1660–1860*, ed. Robert Blair St. George (Boston, 1988); and John Michael Vlach, *Back of the Big House: The Architecture of Plantation Slavery* (Chapel Hill, N.C., 1993).

3. Richard R. Polhemus, *Archaeological Investigation of the Tellico Blockhouse Site* (University of Tennessee Report of Investigations No. 26 and Tennessee Valley Authority Publications in Anthropology No. 16, Norris, 1979).

4. Ibid., 258–59, 282–83.

5. For a more detailed discussion of colono ware, see Leland G. Ferguson, *Uncommon Ground: Archaeology and Early African America, 1650–1800* (Washington, D.C., 1992).

6. Samuel D. Smith, ed., *An Archaeological and Historical Assessment of the First Hermitage*, Tennessee Division of Archaeology, Research Series No. 2 (Nashville, 1976); Samuel D. Smith, "Plantation Archaeology at the Hermitage: Some Suggested Patterns," *Tennessee Anthropologist* 2, no. 1 (1977): 152–63.

7. Linda France Stine, Melanie A. Cabak, and Mark D. Groover, "Blue Beads as African-American Cultural Symbols," *Historical Archaeology* 30, no. 3 (1996): 49–75.

8. See Larry McKee, "Summary Report of the 1990 Hermitage Field Quarter Excavation," *Tennessee Anthropological Association Newsletter* 16, no. 1 (1991):

1–17; Larry McKee, "Summary Report on the 1991 Hermitage Field Quarter Excavation," *Tennessee Anthropological Association Newsletter* 18, no. 1 (1993): 1–17. A variety of other manuscript reports are on file and available through the archaeology office at the Hermitage.

9. Brian W. Thomas, "Community Among Enslaved African Americans on the Hermitage Plantation, 1820s–1850s" (Ph.D. diss., State Univ. of New York at Binghamton, 1995).

10. Emanuel Breitburg, "Faunal Remains from the First Hermitage," in Smith, *Archaeological and Historical Assessment*; Emanuel Breitburg and Larry McKee, "Exploring Dietary Diversity within Archaeological Communities: Some Tennessee Examples" (presented as part of the symposium "Zoological Contributions to Historical Archaeology" at the annual meeting of the Society for Historical Archaeology, Kingston, Jamaica, Jan. 1992).

11. McKee, "Ideals and Realities," 204–6; Larry McKee, "The Earth Is Their Witness," *Sciences* 35, no. 2 (1995): 36–41.

12. For an extended discussion of the topic, see Aaron E. Russell, "Material Culture and African-American Spirituality at the Hermitage," *Historical Archaeology* 31, no. 2 (1997): 63–80.

13. Theresa A. Singleton, "The Archaeology of Slave Life," in *Before Freedom Came: African-American Life in the Antebellum South*, ed. Edward D. C. Campbell Jr. (Charlottesville, Va., 1991); Laurie A. Wilkie, "Secret and Sacred: Contextualizing the Artifacts of African-American Magic and Religion," *Historical Archaeology* 31, no. 4 (1997): 81–106.

14. Robert V. Remini, *The Legacy of Andrew Jackson: Essays on Democracy, Indian Removal, and Slavery* (Baton Rouge, La., 1988).

15. Eugene Genovese, *Roll, Jordan, Roll: The World the Slaves Made* (New York, 1974), 524; James O. Breeden, ed., *Advice Among Masters: The Ideal in Slave Management in the Old South* (Westport, Conn., 1980), 114–39; Bernard L. Herman, "Slave Quarters in Virginia: The Persona Behind Historic Artifacts," in *The Scope of Historical Archaeology: Essays in Honor of John L. Cotter*, ed. David G. Orr and Daniel G. Crozier (Philadelphia, 1984), 262.

16. Kevin E. Smith, "The Airport Runway Expansion Project: Archaeological Survey and Testing of the Gowen Tract, Davidson County, Tennessee," manuscript on file, Tennessee Division of Archaeology, Nashville, 1991; Guy G. Weaver, Jeffrey L. Holland, Patrick H. Garrow, and Martin B. Reinbold, "The Gowen Farmstead: Archaeological Data Recovery at Site 40Dv401 (Area D), Davidson County, Tennessee," manuscript report produced by Garrow and Associates, Memphis, Tennessee, for the Metropolitan Nashville Airport Authority and Tennessee Division of Archaeology, 1993.

17. Weaver et al., "Gowen Farmstead," 326.

18. Ibid., 327.

19. Newbell Niles Puckett, *Folk Beliefs of the Southern Negro* (Montclair, N.J.: 1968 [1926]), 314–15, 391; Russell, "Material Culture," 68; Theresa A. Singleton, "The Archaeology of Slavery in North America," *Annual Review of Anthropology* 24 (1995): 131.

PART TWO

EMANCIPATION, RECONSTRUCTION, AND JIM CROW TENNESSEE

Nashville's Fort Negley
A Symbol of Blacks' Involvement
with the Union Army

Bobby L. Lovett

UCH OF TENNESSEE'S CIVIL WAR HISTORY HAS IGNORED THE CONTRIBUTIONS MADE BY AFRICAN AMERICANS, BOTH AS CONTRABAND laborers for the Union army and as soldiers in the United States Colored Troops (USCT). Bobby Lovett's work, from his 1976 study in *Civil War History* to his recent book about African Americans in Nashville, has done much to dispel the myth that blacks were nothing more than interested bystanders during the war years. His study of Fort Negley emphasizes the strategic value of contraband labor to the Union occupation. It also demonstrates that inexperienced black soldiers could fight, and fight well, in defending Fort Negley and other fortifications during the Battle of Nashville in late 1864. Finally, Lovett relates the fort's rather strange history after the Civil War, from being an occupation post to a forgotten pile of dirt, lumber, and stone, and then, its twentieth-century history as a restored historic site in the New Deal to once again being a forgotten pile of stones. When Lovett published this study in the *Tennessee Historical Quarterly* twenty years ago, he ended on an optimistic note that the fort would soon be reopened to the public. In 2001 Tennesseans still await the restoration and reopening of this "symbol of blacks' involvement" in the Civil War.

To tell the history of Fort Negley, the historian must relate the story of the Union army's occupation of Nashville, the building of numerous fortifications, and the involvement of local blacks in the building of the forts and filling of vital positions in the Union army. Soon after the fall of Forts Donelson and Henry, the Confederate Army of Tennessee retreated to Nashville. Upon the advice of engineers, however, the Confederate army command and Governor Isham G. Harris gave orders to abandon Nashville. On 22 February 1862, the Army of Tennessee retreated southeastward to Murfrees-boro. Confusion set in as citizens rushed to evacuate their belongings before the Yankees arrived in Nashville. The town's Negroes hid in order to avoid being forced to load and drive supply wagons; however, a few unlucky black residents were discovered in their hiding places and taken to Murfreesboro.[1]

During the earlier stages of the Civil War, the Confederate Army of Tennessee had attempted to use Negro labor from Kentucky and Middle Tennessee. But slave masters generally resisted the efforts to impress their expensive slaves for dangerous military duty. In June 1862, the Tennessee General Assembly tried to obtain military laborers by passing the Act to Draft Free Negroes, but Tennessee only had seventy-three hundred free blacks, most of whom were too old, crippled, too young, or too unwilling to serve the Confederate military. Chief engineer for the Army of Tennessee, J. F. Gilmer, attempted to "procure Negroes from their [Kentucky] masters to work on the entrenchments for defending the city of Nashville against land approach" but failed.[2]

At last, Gen. Ulysses S. Grant's Union Army of the Ohio began to occupy Nashville on 23 February 1862, when the gunboat *Diana* docked at the foot of Broad Street. On 25 February, the Sixth Ohio Volunteers' regimental band paraded down Broad playing "Hail Columbia" as slaves and Unionist residents danced in the street. In March 1862, President Abraham Lincoln appointed Senator Andrew Johnson of Tennessee as the military governor of occupied Tennessee. Johnson, a former tailor and East Tennessee slave master, assumed the rank of brigadier general for the Tennessee Volunteer Forces. Elias Polk, a free Negro, went with a delegation of pro-Union citizens to Murfreesboro in order to accompany Johnson on the train to Nashville. Upon the military governor's arrival, crowds of Negroes, Unionists, and Federal soldiers cheered and lined the streets as Johnson led a parade in his honor. Those pro-Confederate citizens who had not fled the city watched in utter disgust as Yankees and runaway slaves took over their town.[3]

Governor Johnson was nervous and apprehensive about being kidnapped and hanged as a southern traitor. He began to pressure the Union army and secretary of war, Edwin Stanton, to fortify the town heavily with an enclosure of forts. Unlike their enemy predecessors, the Union army engineers believed that Nashville could be defended against great odds with a ring of forts and a garrison of at least six thousand men. The city was undulating and rocky, with beautiful, picturesque scenery, and it was surrounded, lying like a vast amphitheater, by a range of hills. It occupied six square miles, three miles long by two miles wide.[4]

During the late summer of 1862, Gen. Don Carlos Buell took his army out of Nashville in pursuit of the Confederate army into Kentucky, leaving six thousand troops under Gen. James S. Negley to hold Nashville.[5] Johnson now began to demand immediate erection of fortifications for the city. He tried to convince Lincoln and Stanton that he was better able to command and position Nashville's troops than was General Negley. However, neither Buell nor any other Federal official was about to risk the charge of a Union army garrison in Johnson's hands. Yet General Buell did respond to the governor's sense of urgency and also realized that the Confederate army could double back and take the city. To make matters worse, indeed, it was rumored that Confederate cavalry units under Nathan Bedford Forrest might attack the city during the late summer of 1862. Buell ordered Capt. James Sinclair Morton, a West Point graduate of 1851, from Philadelphia, to take a detachment of men and go to Nashville to help Negley fortify the city. Buell told Morton, "We should be in the edge of the city to command the principal thoroughfares and other prominent points"; Buell also sought to quiet Johnson's fears by ordering Morton, to "devise some defenses also around the capitol building."[6]

Captain Morton was born in 1829, the son of Dr. Samuel G. Morton of Philadelphia. He was among the best of Civil War military engineers and was later promoted to brigadier general. His command was called the Pioneer Brigade, which was equipped with its own arms, ammunition, clothing, axes, hatchets, saws, files, spades, shovels, picks, hammers, augers, nails, spikes, rope, wagons, mules, and whatever was needed to go in advance of the army in order to prepare or repair bridges, fortifications, railroads, and roads.[7]

After forcing the Confederate army to retreat from Kentucky toward Murfreesboro, Buell wired the Nashville command on 6 August 1862 and ordered them to call upon local slave masters for hands to be employed in Morton's Fort Negley project. With the Confederate army less than one hundred miles to the east, Morton assured Buell that the planned fort would be secure "against any attack except regular approaches and investments."[8] Of course, the Union army under General Buell was supposed to catch the

Confederate army before it could attack Nashville. But the Confederate army commanders were masters of deception and well schooled in the tactics of evading the clutches of the numerically superior Union army.[9]

For this reason, among others, the completion of Nashville's military fortifications was rushed ahead with all deliberate speed. Morton wired Buell: "I lost 48 hours trying to get Negroes, teams, tools, cooking utensils, and provisions. Only 150 Negroes so far, no tools, teams, etc. I wanted to employ 825 Negroes by the 11th." But Morton found that he needed about two thousand blacks, including local free Negroes, to complete Fort Negley. On 12 August Col. John F. Miller, post commander, ordered the *Nashville Daily Union* and the *Nashville Dispatch* newspapers to print notices that Rebel slaveholders of Davidson County were to supply one thousand slaves with "daily subsistence and axes, spades or picks with terms of payment to be made known by Certificates of Labor, which will be furnished after the service shall have been performed."[10] Part of Morton's problem was that he had no money to pay the local blacks who wanted to be paid by the day, whereas, ironically, they had worked for nothing as slaves. In order to pay the laborers and keep them on the project, General Negley issued Special Orders No. 17 (17 October 1862), which ordered "a known contributor to the rebel cause to be required to advance the money to Captain Morton."[11] Unionist citizens, a minority in Nashville, cheered the Negley decision and hoped that all Rebel sympathizers would be similarly punished.

It was known, indeed, that local slave masters tried every trick in the book to keep slaves from coming into contact with the Union army. The slaves were told that the Yankees were cannibals who would eat them alive. Until blacks learned better, Yankee cavalry often had to run some rural slaves down and force them to walk to the Nashville labor camps.[12]

Notwithstanding, Nashville was an ideal place to find skilled blacksmiths, carpenters, coopers, shoemakers, stone masons, and wagon makers. In spite of slavery, local blacks resided in the center of town, mostly integrated among their masters and patrons. A small concentration of prosperous free blacks resided east of Spruce Street (Eighth Avenue) between Crawford and Cedar (Charlotte) Streets. Nashville had the largest free black population of any Tennessee town and three semi-independent black church congregations, including the First Colored Baptist Church, which was pastored by a free black named Nelson Merry.

Meanwhile, Morton designed some temporary defenses for the city. General Negley positioned some regiments of cavalry, which were sent to the city for that purpose, around the town along with several batteries of artillery.

Siege guns and rifle pits occupied South Nashville, and the fires of Federal camps lit up the night sky in every direction. To feed the growing number of Negro laborers and soldiers, Negley took his army south to Franklin and foraged eighteen thousand bushes of corn as well as bacon, cattle, flour, hams, and horses. It took twenty railroad cars to transport the loot.[13]

Morton forged ahead with the construction of Fort Negley, designed to be the pivot point of Nashville's defenses. On 7 November 1862, the First Michigan Engineer Corps made their way into the city to build three bridges over Mill Creek in order to reopen the Nashville-Chattanooga Railroad, allowing additional supplies to flow into the city. Nashville now had eleven thousand troops in town, enough to provide detachments of cavalry to round up more black laborers and to guard them against Confederate raiders. The Union cavalry surrounded the Colored Baptist Church during its services and marched the able-bodied members of the congregation off to the Fort Negley construction site on St. Cloud Hill.[14] Julius Casey, a former slave, recalled that the Federals took two of his older brothers and one sister. Another former slave, Francis Batson, remembered that [the Union army's constant raiding and labor impressment caused the young black children to become frightened and to run when they saw the "blue mans" (Union soldiers) coming.][15]

During the course of construction, long, impressive lines of wagons went back and forth carrying away felled trees and blasted rock. The blacks chopped St. Cloud Hill completely bare of trees in order to give the fort's guns an unimpaired view of the surrounding terrain and to provide no places for the enemy to hide. Children fourteen to fifteen years old, women, and men were camped on the St. Cloud Hill, some living in tents and others sleeping out in the open. Women and young adults pushed wheelbarrows, cooked the food for the laborers, washed clothes, and frequently served as teamsters for wagons. Black stone masons blasted the rock, fashioned the stone, laid the walls, and dug the underground magazines.[16] Curious citizens could clearly see the construction site from a point near the Murfreesboro Pike.

Although the blacks were often forced to labor without adequate food, warm clothing, shelter, or pay, they were willing to defend their creation with their lives. On 5 November 1862, before the fort was completed, Gen. Nathan Bedford Forrest ordered the city to surrender. With approximately three thousand men, he attacked the city near the Lebanon and Murfreesboro Pikes, east of Fort Negley. The Negro laborers sent a delegation to the officer of the day and asked to be armed for the protection of themselves and the fort. Their request for guns was denied, but the army allowed them to make a symbolic stand armed with axes, shovels, and spades.[17]

The Federals, nevertheless, had sufficient forces to defeat the Confederates. Rachel Carter, a pro-Confederate resident, wrote in her diary on 5 November 1862 that one of the artillery shells from the fight "struck Mrs. Trimble's smokehouse."[18] In fact, Mrs. Trimble's smokehouse was east of the guns of Fort Negley and in the general vicinity of today's Cameron–Trimble Bottom, Nashville's oldest black neighborhood. As night came and a drizzling rain fell, Forrest's cavalry fled to the east, leaving the city in the hands of the Union army and its black allies. Some twenty-three Confederate soldiers were captured, and the Union army suffered twenty-six men wounded and nineteen men missing.[19]

At the least, this demonstration convinced the Union army's Nashville command that black labor was vital for the release of white soldiers from time-consuming labor chores. By using Negro laborers, the army could put more white soldiers *au fort du combat.* Before, the army allowed slave masters to search the camps and reclaim their runaway slaves. As late as 7 August 1862, for example, the *Nashville Daily Union*, a pro-Union newspaper, published a notice for two twenty-three-year-old runaways named Foster and Edmund who belonged to Dr. John L. Cheatham and his brother, William S. Cheatham. Slaves were yet worth three hundred to thirteen hundred dollars apiece. A short time earlier, Davidson County Sheriff Jim Hinton ran an advertisement in the local papers: "July 18, 1862. A Negro man, who says his name is Henry and belongs to Matt Scruggs, Bedford County, Tennessee, age about 28, 5 feet 7 inches high, weighs 155 pounds, color black. The owner is requested to come forward, prove property and pay charges as the law requires."[20] On 27 February 1863, the Nashville Union army command issued an order prohibiting the return of fugitive slaves to their masters. Further, the Nashville provost marshal threatened to arrest any law officer caught arresting Negroes to be sold or transported to masters.[21]

Nearly a year later, on 4 February 1864, the Union army ordered Capt. Ralph Hunt of the First Kentucky Volunteers to establish a contraband camp in the area of the Chattanooga-Nashville Railroad Depot.[22] A larger contraband camp was built on the east side of the Cumberland River, north of Edgefield and near the Louisville-Nashville Railroad tracks; it initially held over two thousand Negroes. A third contraband camp was located south of Broad Street between Front and Cherry Streets; it was called "Black Bottom." A former slave, Joseph Fowley, recalled that "they had contraband camps, and men, women and children had to be guarded to keep the rebels from carrying them back to the white folks."[23]

After a short time, the Federal government investigated the notoriously inhuman conditions of Nashville's contraband camps. Although camp superintendent Ralph Hunt was accused of stealing supplies meant for the blacks and selling them in his downtown store, nothing ever came of the charges. Attempts were made to "colonize surplus Negroes" on locally abandoned farms. This colonization effort was similar to the later Freedmen's Bureau's 1865 relocation program in Memphis, which was designed to force thousands of unemployed blacks to leave the urban camps and relocate in the countryside where the cotton crop was suffering from lack of pickers. Undoubtedly, such a relocation effort accounted, in part, for Nashville's Negro population not rising above ten thousand during the war years.

At any rate, the contraband camps and the influx of black laborers into town served the Union army's purposes by 1865 and at little cost to the government. Between August 1862 and April 1863, for example, the army paid black workers only $13,648.00 of the $85,858.50 that was owed them. One author, Peter Maslowski, who has studied Union military occupation of Nashville, estimates that between six hundred and eight hundred blacks died working on fortifications in the Nashville area during the whole occupation period.[24]

By 7 December 1862 Fort Negley was completed.[25] Captain Morton's report included praise for the blacks: "To the credit of the colored population be it said, they worked manfully and cheerfully, with hardly an exception, and yet layout upon the works at night under armed guard, without blankets and eating only army rations. They worked in squads, each gang choosing their own officers; one was often amused to hear the Negro captains call out: 'You boys over there, let them picks fall easy, or they might hurt somebody.'"[26]

The creation of the Negro laborers and the Union army engineers was impressive. The topmost structure was constructed of twelve-foot erect timbers. On the parapet surrounding the outside of the stockade, the artillery rested on carriages which rolled about on smooth planked flooring. This flat area for the artillery operations was protected by three-foot-high ramparts, nine-foot-thick embankments of earth walled with stone. The ramparts on the east and west side of the stockade had projected redans. Below the east and west ramparts and parapets were scarps, steep slopes, which were in turn protected by a glacis, a smooth, gentle slope. At the bottom of these hills on the left and right side of the south section of the fort were two groups of four blockhouses, which were really bombproofs topped with railroad iron, timbers, and dirt. Each blockhouse had embrasures or openings for riflemen's guns.

The bastioned blockhouses were protected by a salient system that projected out from the fortification. Above the bastion was a stoned scarp, protecting the first two blockhouses, an entrenchment connecting the two parallel blockhouses, another stoned scarp rising above the entrenchment, and the other two blockhouses rising above the scarp, with a passage way between the blockhouses. The fort's entrance was on the north side with a gentle slope; visitors passed a sharp salient, a gateway, a timber-structured guardhouse, and a loop-holed bombproof flanking the gate. And on top of each corner of the wooden stockade were rounded gun turrets.

Adapted to the local situation, Fort Negley was a copy of an old European architectural system, a repeat of the Castillo de San Marcos, built by the Spaniards of St. Augustine, Florida. San Marcos used a bastion system which was developed by sixteenth-century European military engineers. The fort was polygonal. Eight lower salients, four on the east and west sides, projected from the fort; each of these salients had broad parapets (apparently for infantrymen), stone scarps, and glacis. Again, each set of four blockhouses had a salient; thus the fort resembled a many-sided star. There was no "dead" space in the design, and every inch of ground could be covered by defenders. The enemy had to climb the bastions, scale the glacis, jump over the ramparts, cross the parapets, climb another glacis, scale a scarp, jump over another rampart, and fight the defenders behind the main parapets and ramparts, before setting siege to the troops and horses behind the stockade. But if the enemy chose to come in from the south side, he had to face the murderous rifle fire from the blockhouses as well.

The entire fort consumed a staggering 62,500 cubic feet of stone and 18,000 cubic yards of dirt. It occupied a space of 600 by 300 feet and claimed fifty-one acres of St. Cloud Hill. It was 620 feet above sea level, some 150 feet above the surrounding terrain, and two miles south of the city limits.[27] A typical garrison for Fort Negley was described in 1864 as the "12th Indiana Battery and Battery C of the 1st Tennessee Light Artillery Volunteers." Occasionally, various infantry regiments camped on the lower part of the hill, including the 105th Illinois Volunteers and the Thirty-third Indiana Volunteers.[28]

Fort Negley's first major military role was in the Battle of Nashville on 15–17 December 1864. After taking Atlanta, Gen. William T. Sherman sent Gen. George H. Thomas and twenty thousand troops hurrying back to Tennessee to set up a defense against the Confederate Army of Tennessee, which was moving across northern Georgia and northern Alabama. Inevitably it was headed for Nashville, in hopes of drawing Sherman back from his intended march through Georgia. Fort Negley became the pivot point of Thomas's defense at Nashville. Thousands of soldiers from Wisconsin, Illinois, Indiana, Ohio, and other northern states camped near St. Cloud Hill while dining on boiled beef, beans, baker's bread, coffee, and occasionally some rabbits, squirrels, turkeys, and other wild game. Some of the soldiers thought that Nashville was "quite a nice place for the South."[29] Thomas collected nearly fifty thousand troops by obtaining reinforcements from Chattanooga and Missouri and some thirteen thousand black troops.

Thomas made heavy use of local blacks as forced laborers. He used the labor organization techniques that had been perfected by the building of Fort Negley and the building of the Northwestern Military Railroad. Between August 1863 and March 1864, Governor Johnson and the Union army impressed thousands of blacks into labor battalions of ninety-eight persons each—with white officers, a cavalry escort, and Negro labor captains—to build a railroad from Nashville seventy-five miles to Johnsonville on the east bank of the Tennessee River. Fully 20 percent of the black laborers were women, and the ages of the black laborers ranged from fourteen to fifty-five. The completion of the Northwestern Railroad made it logistically possible for Sherman to launch his famous march through Georgia. Union steamers brought supplies to Johnsonville, where they were shipped on cars to Nashville warehouses, and on to Sherman's staging area at Chattanooga. Thomas sought to resurrect this system in order to expand Nashville's fortifications. One former slave remembered being captured by the Federals as he made his escape from a Murfreesboro plantation. He recalled that General Thomas seldom was able to provide the black laborers with sufficient rations, and he added, "We would kill a beef, cut off the head, take out the insides, skin it, and cut the meat into big chunks. Then we would put our meat on a long-forked pole, one end buried in the ground and the other slanting up and pointing toward the fire. It would make me awful sick at times, and I would throw up a lot."[30]

General Thomas's engineers had a problem in recruiting an adequate supply of black labor. For instance, many of Middle Tennessee's black males between the ages of eighteen and forty-five were mustered into the military, leaving few able-bodied Negroes for labor duties. On 10 September 1863, the Bureau for the Recruitment of United States Colored Troops was established at 38 Cedar Street (Charlotte Street). Similarly, recruitment stations were established at Clarksville, Columbia, Lynnville, Murfreesboro, Pulaski, Shelbyville, Tullahoma, and Wartrace. Even the black laborers who had completed the Northwestern Railroad project were marched to their camps, sworn into Federal service, armed, and trained as soldiers. Consequently, the Davidson County area contributed to the filling of five infantry and two artillery units, including the Second U.S. Colored Light Artillery Battery A and the Ninth U.S. Colored Heavy Artillery Battalion, which used 380 free black Ohioans to complete the organization. Additionally, two infantry regiments were organized at the Clarksville contraband camps; the units relied heavily on recruiting runaway slaves from Kentucky. The Fourteenth U.S. Colored Infantry Regiment was organized at the Gallatin contraband camp and recruited slaves from Robertson, Sumner, and Wilson Counties. Four infantry regiments were organized at Pulaski's contraband camps and consisted of so many runaways from northern Alabama that the regiments were at first named the First, Second, Third, and Fourth Alabama Infantry Regiments of African Descent; but they were later renamed the 101st, 106th, 110th, and 111th Regiments of the United States Colored Troops.[31]

Equally important, after finding the local agricultural economy to be devastated because of the scarcity of black labor and pro-Union citizens lustily protesting their financial ruin, on 10 November 1863 the army command at Nashville issued orders to prevent this growing economic-political disaster by directing Union officers to take no more than "one-half of any loyal master's slaves."[32] For even Sherman took two Middle Tennessee black regiments and black laborers to be used as supply troops and teamsters during his long march through Georgia. Therefore, Thomas's engineers found few black laborers for impressment. As a result, on 1 November 1864 General Thomas issued orders to recall black soldiers and white garrisons from their Middle Tennessee posts. These troops, along with available black laborers, worked on the fortifications.[33]

Thomas's job was made easier because of the existing fortifications that had been built by Captain Morton in 1862. These fortifications included the capitol building, which had been fortified and named Fort Johnson; Fort Casino, which overlooked Fort Negley; and Fort Morton, which in turn protected Fort Casino. In contrast to Fort Negley, these forts were smaller and consisted of earth parapets, timber-reinforced blockhouses, crushed-stone glacis, and dozens of light artillery pieces. Nevertheless, the area these forts would help to defend was very important to the Union. The District of Nashville included the defense of the Nashville-Chattanooga Railroad as far as the Duck River, the Nashville-Decatur Railroad as far south as Columbia, the Northwestern Railroad southwest to the Tennessee River, the Louisville-Nashville Railroad to the Kentucky state line, and the posts of McMinnville, Clarksville, Fort Donelson, and Nashville—the apex of the iron quadrangle.

From 1 November to 1 December 1864, the black workers and the Union army soldiers struggled through heavy rains to complete the ring of forts. Fort Morton, situated on Curry's Hill near Granny White Pike and Jackson Street, was reinforced. Next in line to the north, Fort Houston was built near Belmont and Broad Streets and named after Russell Houston, a strong Union supporter, who allowed his home to be blown up to make way for the fort. Fort Houston was designed to hold over thirty-five guns and to protect the Charlotte Pike. A small fort was built on Hill 210 by the 182d Ohio Volunteers in the shape of an octagon, with blockhouses and underground magazines to protect the Northwestern Railroad and warehouses in West Nashville. Fort Dan McCook was built just east of Fort Negley; it held twenty-six guns for the cover of the main fort and the Nashville-Decatur Railroad.

On the present site of Fisk University's Jubilee Hall, Fort Gillem (later named Fort Sill) was constructed. Fort Gillem was built by a native of Jackson County, Tennessee, Gen. Alvin Gillem, and the Tenth Tennessee Volunteer Regiment. Fort Gillem was about 120 feet square with narrow ditches, walled with stone, 6 feet high, with emplacements for eight artillery pieces. North of Fort Gillem was Fort W. D. Whipple (Redoubt Donaldson); between Forts Gillem and Whipple was Hyde's Ferry Fort (Fort Garesche) on the south bank of the Cumberland River, built by the Eighty-second Ohio Volunteers in November 1864. The Fifteenth Illinois Volunteer Regiment built a small redoubt on the north side of the Cumberland River in order to cover the Louisville-Nashville Railroad. Fort Negley was expanded at a cost of twenty thousand dollars by adding the interior double-cased blockhouses and entrenchments. The inspector of fortifications, Gen. Z. B. Tower, wrote to Thomas with this request: "If I can secure a black regiment, some 200 men, which have been promised, it will be a great gain."[34] By 30 November over ten thousand black troops were working on the fortifications and carrying out reconnaissance patrols on alternate days beginning 1 December and ending 13 December. The entire fortifications project cost an estimated $300,000 plus $130,000 for Fort Negley. The city of Nashville was enclosed within a ring of twenty-three forts, redoubts, and fortified bridges.[35]

From September to October 1864, Hood's army encountered much resistance from the black and white Union garrisons at Decatur and Sulphur Trestle, Alabama, and Pulaski and Johnsonville, Tennessee. Many black soldiers lost their lives and hundreds more were shipped as prisoners to Mobile, Alabama. Further, Hood's army of thirty-six thousand caught Gen. John Schofield's Union army of twenty-three thousand at Franklin and forced it to fight. Although the federals lost two thousand men, the Confederates lost six thousand men and six of their best generals; moreover, while the enemy slept on that night of 30 November 1864, Schofield abandoned his dead and wounded and sneaked across the Harpeth River and arrived safely in Nashville, thirty miles away, on 1 December. After receiving Schofield's reinforcements, General Thomas had nearly twice Hood's troop strength.

And yet, General Hood unwisely turned his battered army toward Nashville instead of retreating into the deep South. Hood could not turn back because he had slept on too many dreams and had made a personal pledge to President Jefferson Davis to carry out a successful campaign. As the Army of Tennessee approached Nashville on 2 December, they saw a formidable fortress gleaming with new forts, behind which more than fifty thousand Union troops waited. The gods cursed the Confederates by blasting the Nashville area with a winter storm that left glistening ice. A Maury County Confederate soldier said, "Being in range of the guns of Fort Negley, we were not allowed to have fires at night." During the day, however, an unspoken truce allowed both sides to gather firewood.[36]

On the cold, foggy morning of 15 December 1864, the ice melted and the guns of Fort Negley came alive to signal the start of the Battle of Nashville. Out of a mist came the dark, shining faces of seven regiments of U.S. Colored Troops, who advanced on the enemy's right flank near Brown's Creek—east of the guns of Fort Negley. Patsy Hyde, a former slave, recalled the moment: "When dey wuz fighting at Fort Negley, de cannons would jar our house. The soldiers' band played on Capitol Hill: 'Rally round the flag boys, rally round the flag.'" Another slave remembered that "when the Yankees on Capitol Hill gave the signal—God bless your soul—it sounded like the cannons would tear the world to pieces. I could hear the big shells humming as they came; they cut off trees like a man cutting weeds with a scythe."[37]

Two days later, the Confederate army was in mass retreat. They left behind ten thousand prisoners and sixty-eight pieces of artillery. One Negro soldier, Joseph Fowley [Farley], who joined the Union army along with his father at the Clarksville contraband camp, recalled the Confederate soldiers were captured just as bare-footed "as they could be." He said, "I brought my gun from Nashville right here to Clarksville and kept it for 25 years."[38] The Negro troops took part in the pursuit of Hood's army as far south as central Alabama. Nashville's Seventeenth Colored Troops Regiment won personal recognition for bravery from General Thomas and the *New York Times* (19

Dec. 1864). The Battle of Nashville was one of the last major military actions of a dying Confederacy that surrendered in April 1865.

What some men create, other men let wither and die. In short, Fort Negley and its sister forts were not monuments that a defeated South wanted to preserve. The forts were gradually forgotten and allowed to go into ruins. In 1865, Fort Negley was renamed Fort Harker; and in 1867, the Union army abandoned the fort. Fort Harker became the secret meeting place for the Nashville Den of the Ku Klux Klan, which was active until 1869. In that year the Nashville Klan defied a government ban against public demonstrations and marched through the streets to Fort Negley, where they burned their robes and officially disbanded.[39] Until the late 1890s, citizens took wagons and streetcars out to the fort at Chestnut and Ridley Streets and held Sunday picnics, just as in prewar days.

Years later, during the Great Depression, Fort Negley was restored and opened to the public. The Works Progress Administration (WPA) provided funds to put Davidson County's unemployed to work in a restoration project. According to the *Nashville Tennessean* (31 Jan. 1936), the Fort Negley restoration project became one of the top WPA programs in the state. When the WPA workers finished the project in 1937, they left a crudely chiseled stone at the entrance, which read, "Fort Negley, Restored by the WPA, 1936." The Tennessee WPA Federal Writers' Project, which was designed to put unemployed writers to work, compiled histories of the state's forts, including a two-page overview of the history of Fort Negley.[40] The restored fort was a city park until 1941, with a "museum." The WPA workers attempted also to restore the subterranean magazines; they built some stone walkways to make the fort and the "museum" more accessible to visitors. A drainage ditch, covered with natural stone, encircled the bottom of the hill. Aerial photographs that were taken in 1941 and preserved by the Tennessee Department of Conservation revealed a road of rough gravel and a parking lot on the north side near the entrance of the fort.[41]

With the coming of World War II the fort was forgotten and allowed to be overgrown by weeds and other vegetation. Not until the Civil War Centennial celebration of 1964 did the Nashville Committee for the Civil War Centennial include a tour of the old fort, and local college professors came out to speak on the history of the fort. In 1975, the Metro Historical Commission made application to have the fort placed on the National Register of Historic Places.[42] On 14 May 1979, according to the *Nashville Tennessean*, the Metro Historical Commission and the Council on Abandoned Military Posts jointly suggested that the city restore the fort. In August 1980, a feasibility study was completed for the Metro Historical Commission with the recommendation that the fort be made into a recreational historic park at a projected cost of $145,521.38.[43]

Though covered with vines and trees, and hidden from easy view, Fort Negley continued to serve as a monument to local African American and Civil War history. The fortress and its sister forts served as symbols of the uneasy alliance between the Union army and local blacks in their successful campaign to preserve the Union and destroy slavery. Consequently, much history was hidden beneath Fort Negley and its sister fortifications, including the lost histories of thousands of black laborers, the contributions of thirteen thousand black Union soldiers, and the blood and tears of thousands of black women.

The Fort Negley project was the Union army's first heavy use of local black labor. It set the precedent for using black laborers on all large Middle Tennessee Union military projects. Such use, one might reflect, made the [Union officers realize the utility value of maintaining contraband camps— ready sources of black laborers and Negro soldiers.] Indeed, the Union army fully utilized both in winning the war. Hence, the influx of Negroes into Nashville doubled the black population between 1862 and 1865.

Finally, one might argue that the Union army's labor system, which was first induced by the need to build Fort Negley, the Northwestern Railroad, and other military projects, acted as a catalyst for the development of black Nashville communities. Ironically, the Union army's efforts to control the local Negro population for military purposes caused a disintegration of antebellum controls over slaves and free blacks. Freed at last from the legal restraints of black codes and slave codes, the free blacks and the former slaves built communities in Nashville and Edgefield that were complete with economic, political, and social institutions, including a black-owned drugstore, a black-edited newspaper (the *Colored Tennessean*, 1865–66), and a branch of the Freedmen's Savings and Trust Company bank. In 1865 the Union army and the Freedmen's Bureau attempted to force thousands of Negroes to relocate on rural farms; however, the black migration into Nashville continued into the twentieth century. On the whole, although the Union army occupied Nashville in 1862 without any intention of becoming involved in the social and political questions of slavery and Negro affairs, the army and its agencies served as grudging agents for social change in Nashville and paradoxically were responsible for the genesis of ghettoizing blacks due to segregating and concentrating them into local contraband camps.

Notes

1. Stanley F. Horn, "Nashville During the Civil War," *Tennessee Historical Quarterly* 4 (1945): 3–22.

2. J. F. Gilmer to Lt. Col. W. W. Mackall, Bowling Green, Kentucky, 7 Dec. 1861, *The War of the Rebellion: A Compilation of the Official Records of the Union and Confederate Armies* (Washington, D.C., 1898) (hereafter cited as OR), ser. 1, vol. 52, pt. 2, 233.

3. H. W. Crew, ed., *History of Nashville* (Nashville, 1890), 101–2.

4. Doug King, ed., *Nashville City Directory, 1865* (Nashville, 1865), 1–10.

5. Stanley F. Horn, *The Army of Tennessee: A Military History* (1941; reprint, Indianapolis, 1952), 394–411.

6. OR, ser. 1, vol. 26, pt. 11, 268; Mark M. Boatner, *The Civil War Dictionary* (New York, 1959), 571; Morton authored several books on fortifications; Paul M. Angle, ed., *Three Years in the Army of the Cumberland: The Letters and Diary of Major James A. Connolly* (Bloomington, Ind., 1959), 37–39; Thomas Jordan and J. P. Pryor, *The Campaigns of Lieut.-Gen. N. B. Forrest* (Dayton, Ohio, 1973), 179.

7. *Annals of the Army of the Cumberland* (Philadelphia, 1864), 181–91; Mead Holmes, *Soldier of the Cumberland: Memoirs of Mead Holmes, Jr., Sergeant for Company K, 21st Regiment, Wisconsin Volunteers* (Boston, 1952); Fred A. Shannon, *The Organization and Administration of the Union Army, 1861–1865*, 2 vols. (Cleveland, 1928); Thomas Van Home, *History of the Army of the Cumberland: Its Organization, Campaigns, and Battles* (Cincinnati, 1875). Note: the Corps of Engineers and the Corps of Topographical Engineers merged as the Corps of Engineers. The Engineering Department and the Pioneer Corps made heavy use of hired and impressed black labor.

8. Buell to Morton, Kentucky, 6 Aug. 1862, and Morton to Col. J. B. Fry, Nashville, 13 Aug. 1862, OR, ser. 1, vol. 26, pt. 2, 326–27.

9. Jordan, *Campaigns of Lieut.-Gen. N. B. Forrest*; Frederick A. Dyer, ed., *A Compendium of the War of the Rebellion: Numbers and Organization of the Armies of the United States*, 3 vols. (New York, 1959).

10. *Nashville Dispatch* and *Nashville Daily Union*, 13 Aug. 1862.

11. *Nashville Daily Union*, 18 Oct. 1862.

12. Buell to Morton, Kentucky, 20, 29 Aug. 1862, OR, ser. 1, vol. 26, pt. 11, 408.

13. "Yanks in Nashville," in the *Chattanooga Rebel*, 12 Oct. 1862, quoted by the *Nashville Daily Union*, 18 Oct. 1862. The Union army recognized the claims of area citizens for properties destroyed by the Federal army; see Report on Nashville Defenses, OR, ser. 1, vol. 49, pt. 3, 197.

14. *Annals of the Army of the Cumberland*, 194, includes a sketch of the Negroes leaping from the church windows; *The Official Atlas of the Civil War* (New York, 1958), plate 134, contains an illustration of blacks working on Fort Negley, as reported in OR, ser. 1, vol. 49, pt. 3, 15 Oct. 1862.

15. Slave testimony found in George P. Radwick, ed., *The American Slave: A Composite Autobiography, God Struck Me Dead: Religious Conversion Experiences of Ex-Slaves*, vol. 18 (1941; reprint, Westport, Conn., 1975), 121–25; Mechal Sobel, "'They Can Never Both Prosper Together': Black and White Baptists in Antebellum Nashville, Tennessee," *Tennessee Historical Quarterly* 38 (1979): 296–307; Works Progress Administration, Federal Writers' Project, Tennessee slave narratives, in Radwick, *American Slave* 16: 3, 68.

16. OR, ser. 1, vol. 49, pt. 3, 196–98. The 15 October 1862 report by the chief inspector of fortifications, Gen. Z. B. Tower, does not mention a secret tunnel; however, local rumor has it that Fort Negley had a secret tunnel that permitted Union soldiers to emerge from the Old City Cemetery just east of the fort. A recent (1980) engineering report did not confirm the existence of a tunnel but did not rule it out; archaeologists will have to have the final word.

17. The Photographic History of the Civil War, 10 vols. (New York, 1957), 3:266–70 and 248–58 contain illustrations and actual photos of Fort Negley in 1864 and just prior to the Battle of Nashville.

18. Louise Davis, "Box Seat on the Civil War: Rachel Carter's Diary," Nashville Tennessean Magazine, Apr. 1979, 6–11.

19. Davis, "Box Seat on the Civil War," 6–11; Nashville Banner, 16 Dec. 1961; Juanita Gaston and Samuel Shannon, Cameron-Trimble Neighborhood Project: A Pictorial Guide (Nashville, 1979), 1–10.

20. Nashville Daily Union, 10 Aug. 1862.

21. Nashville Dispatch, 27 Feb. 1863.

22. This camp was between Church and Demonbreum Streets. Benjamin "Pap" Singleton held his organizational meetings for the Black Exodus to Kansas in the former Edgefield contraband camp between 1877 and 1879. A housing project and interstate highways occupy the Edgefield site. Urban renewal also cleaned the blacks out of "Black Bottom," the Crawford Street area, and the Church/Demonbreum area. Some moved into the Napier and Taylor housing projects.

23. "Unwritten History of Slavery," in Radwick, American Slave 19:128–29.

24. Peter Maslowski, Treason Made Odious: Military Occupation and Wartime Reconstruction in Nashville, 1861–1865 (Milwood, Ill., 1978), 100–112; Porter Nimrod Diary and Notebook, 1861–1898, Manuscripts Division, Tennessee State Library and Archives, Nashville (hereafter cited as TSLA).

25. Nashville Banner, 16 Dec. 1862.

26. Annals of the Army of the Cumberland, 620–33.

27. Metro Historical Commission, "Fort Negley, Davidson County, Tennessee," National Register of Historic Places Nomination Application, 21 Feb. 1975; Fort Negley: A Study for the Metropolitan Historical Commission (Nashville, 1980), A-1.

28. Angle, Three Years, 37–39; Frank L. Byrne, ed., The View from Headquarters: Civil War Letters of Harvey Reid (Madison, Wis., 1965), 121–26; Photographic History of the Civil War, 248, has a photo of a battery manning the fort; Southern Battlefields: On and Near the Lines of the Nashville, Chattanooga and St. Louis Railroad (Nashville, 1956); Della Yoe, "Fort Negley," in Federal Writers' Project, Tennessee Forts and Fortresses (Nashville, 1940), TSLA; Bruce Grant, American Forts Yesterday and Today (New York, 1965), 58; Federal Writers' Project, Tennessee: A Guide to the State (New York, 1939); Harold L. Peterson, Forts in America (New York, 1964), 1–25.

29. Byrne, View from Headquarters, 121–26; Susan K. Parman, "The Battle of Nashville" (Master's thesis, George Peabody College for Teachers, 1932).

30. Radwick, American Slave, 116. It is likely that nearly two thousand blacks served in the Confederate Army of Tennessee as laborers and personal servants to officers. Some of the black Confederates received state pensions as a result of the 1906 Confederate Pension Act being amended in 1921 to include former black servants. Nearly three hundred Colored Men's Pension Applications are filed at the TSLA, Nashville. However, Thomas's Union Army of the Cumberland used thousands of black laborers as part of his Quartermaster Corps, Engineering Corps, Pioneer

Corps, Medical Department, and Subsistence Department. For this reason, Thomas was able to place a huge number of soldiers in the battle itself. It is likely that Union blacks and Confederate blacks made some abrasive contact during the Battle of Nashville.

31. The Negro in the Military Service of the U.S., 1630–1866, National Archives and Record Service, Washington, D.C.; Compiled Service Records of Military Units in Union Organizations: U.S. Colored Troops, Tennessee, part of RG 94, NARS; Bobby L. Lovett, "The Negro's Civil War in Tennessee, 1861–1865," *Journal of Negro History* 59 (1976): 31–50; Dudley T. Cornish, *The Sable Arm: The Negro in the Union Army, 1861–1865* (New York, 1956), 248–49; George Washington Williams, *A History of the Negro Troops in the War of the Rebellion, 1861–65* (1888; reprint, New York, 1968), 273–90.

32. Special Orders No. 301, Department of the Cumberland, Nashville, 10 Nov. 1863, Adjutant General's Office, RG 21, TSLA; *OR*, ser. 1, vol. 31, pt. 3.

33. General Orders No. 43, Department of the Cumberland, Nashville, 1 Nov. 1864, Adjutant General's Office, RG 21; Lovett, "Negro's Civil War in Tennessee," 31–50.

34. Tower to Thomas, Nashville, 1 Nov. 1864, *OR*, ser. 1, vol. 49, pt. 3, 755–81; William Waller, *Nashville in the 1890s* (Nashville, 1970) contains a map showing the approximate positions of the old forts; Thomas to Gen. Rousseau, Chattanooga, 31 Jan. 1864, *OR*, ser. 1, vol. 33, pt. 3, 203.

35. Tower's 1865 Report, *OR*, vol. 49.

36. Samuel R. Watkins, *Maury County Grays: First Tennessee Regiment, C.S.A.* (Nashville, 1882), 225; J. F. C. Fuller, *Decisive Battles of the U.S.A.* (New York, 1942), 292–323; Horn, *Army of Tennessee*, 394–411; Stanley F. Horn, *The Decisive Battle of Nashville* (Baton Rouge, La., 19.56); William J. McMurray, *History of the Twentieth Tennessee Regiment Volunteer Infantry, C.S.A.* (Nashville, 1904), 329; Crew, *History of Nashville*, 198–201.

37. Radwick, *American Slave*, 116.

38. "Unwritten History of Slavery," 121; *Battles of the Civil War: A Pictorial Presentation, 1861–1865* (New York, 1960), includes a color illustration of Thomas's black troops attacking the Confederate positions on Overton Hill (Peach Orchard Hill) on 16 December 1864, where the blacks suffered greatly; however, the Negro troops took the hill. A Metro Historical Commission marker designates the site near the corner of Harding Place and Franklin Road.

39. Yoe, "Fort Negley," 1–2, is brief but informative.

40. Ibid.; see also Directory of WPA Manuscripts, TSLA.

41. Photos of Fort Negley Restoration, Department of Conservation Photographs, TSLA.

42. Metro Historical Commission, Fort Negley National Register Application.

43. *Fort Negley.*

Fort Pillow, Forrest, and the United States Colored Troops in 1864

Kenneth B. Moore

S SOON AS THE GUNS WERE QUIET, AND THE CONFLICTING REPORTS WERE FILED, THE BATTLE OF FORT PILLOW BECAME ONE OF THE most controversial of the Civil War. The controversy continues: Were African American troops massacred as they surrendered, or was the battle just another terrible bloodbath in which most of the casualties were African American soldiers? Kenneth Moore follows recent scholarship in labeling the battle as a massacre, but his focus is not on the controversy; rather, he analyzes the battle's impact on USCT soldiers across the state. Moore finds that Fort Pillow, whether heroic victory or deliberate massacre, became an albatross around the neck of Confederate general Nathan B. Forrest. USCT soldiers who faced Forrest in the months after the battle fought with great determination and vowed to offer no quarter in their desire for revenge, and to show that black troops would fight bravely, to the last man if necessary, to stop Forrest's raids. The result, Moore emphasizes, was that the Confederates suffered losses they could ill afford in 1864, and Forrest himself received increased attention from Union commanders, thus lessening his overall effectiveness in the Western theater. At the same time, the USCT gained experience and a reputation as brave soldiers; by the end of 1864, they were "professional, seasoned fighters."

On 12 April 1864, Gen. Nathan Bedford Forrest's force of about fifteen hundred Confederates attacked and surrounded Fort Pillow, Tennessee, a stronghold on the Mississippi River fifty miles above Memphis.[1] By 3:00 P.M. the Confederates had gained advantageous positions outside the fort. Forrest asked for a surrender, but Maj. William F. Bradford, commander of the 557 black and white Union troops, refused in spite of the Southerners' overwhelming numbers and strong positions.[2] After unsuccessful negotiations with Bradford, Forrest did not hesitate to attack.

The bugler sounded the charge, and with a yell the Confederates vaulted in unison over the eight-foot parapets and fired into the Union ranks from an sides. Outnumbered almost three to one, the blue line wavered and broke under the tremendous weight of the volley. A wave of Confederates charged into the fort as the Union men retreated toward the river in confusion, some firing back, others only running. Rebel sharpshooters on surrounding hills opened fire on the white and black troops as they neared the banks of the Mississippi River, thus adding to the turmoil and carnage. As their sharpshooters continued a withering fire, the charging gray invaders closed in from three sides while the river prevented escape. Many Union soldiers tried to swim for freedom but were shot in the water or drowned. According to several reports, Union troops threw down their arms in surrender but were shot nonetheless. The battle was over within twenty minutes. The black regiments suffered over 60 percent casualties, and the Northern press and politicians labeled it the "Fort Pillow Massacre."[3]

The Northern press and government popularized this event and stigmatized Forrest by labeling him a butcher—a reputation that quickly spread through the Union army, especially to the regiments of the United States Colored Troops (USCT) stationed at Memphis, Tennessee. If captured in battle, black troops already knew they would be returned to slavery or sentenced to manual labor. They were also aware that in every theater of the war Confederates sometimes shot down black troops instead of taking them prisoner. The soldiers of the USCT had good reason to fear the next encounter with Forrest.

The USCT's feelings of apprehension and anger were first apparent at the Battle of Brice's Crossroads in northern Mississippi on 10 June 1864. They sought to avenge the Fort Pillow massacre but soon found themselves in the midst of a chaotic Union disaster. However, from the Battle of Tupelo in July to the Battle of Nashville in December 1864, the USCT improved as professional soldiers. As they gained experience, they performed coolly under fire despite the menial status accorded them by their adversary. Nevertheless, Forrest's brutal reputation prompted black troops to realize they may meet a more horrible fate. Rumors, the press's focus on Fort Pillow, and indeed the caution exhibited by Union commanders at Memphis, all seemed to intensify the fear that Forrest would repeat the butchery committed on 12 April 1864.

This notoriety also adversely affected Forrest's command in direct and indirect ways. Perhaps the most direct impact is that the controversy brought Forrest into the limelight. The Union command intensified its focus on the Confederate raider just when he needed to be invisible—as Gen. William T. Sherman split the Deep South. Indirectly, Forrest's various battles in Mississippi gave valuable experience to the previously untested black troops. Perhaps most important, the fighting of the spring and summer of 1864 in northern Mississippi, northern Alabama, and West Tennessee proved to Union commanders that black troops would indeed fight, and fight hard, prompting their increased use in the Union army. Ultimately, the "success" of Fort Pillow became a weight on Forrest's back that contributed to his army's eventual demise in the war and, furthermore, its notoriety created a stigma that dogged Forrest until his death.

Maximum publicity was given to Fort Pillow and Forrest throughout the North in the spring of 1864. On 16 April, the *New York Times* headlined the battle with a detailed description of the atrocities. The story described the Rebels as "devils incarnate" and "fiends." Men were said to be buried alive but were dug up before they suffocated. Descriptions informed Northerners that men were shot, bayoneted, and burned after an attempted surrender. The *Times* headlined the event for three days and reported further details through 20 April.[4]

Other newspapers also devoted great attention to the battle in Tennessee. It remained a front-page story for four days in the *New York Herald* and the *New York Tribune*.[5] The *Herald* reported that President Abraham Lincoln, while speaking in Maryland, promised quick and decisive retribution if the accounts proved to be true. The president, unlike many, questioned the validity of the reports.[6] Horace Greeley's *Tribune* certainly did not doubt the story's validity. Its entire front page on 23 April was devoted to Fort Pillow.[7]

In Memphis, headquarters of the black troops in the Western theater, the *Bulletin* of 23 April described the battle as "barbarous, savage, and unworthy of savages." The *Chicago Tribune* recounted Forrest's past as a slave trader and said, "Let no quarter be shown to these dastardly butchers of Forrest's command while the war lasts." The *Daily National Intelligencer* of Washington also covered the story extensively.[8] By the end of April, the name of Nathan Bedford Forrest in the North was synonymous with the murder of black troops.

The Fort Pillow massacre also gained the attention of the United States Congress. The Joint Committee on the Conduct of the War quickly dispatched Senator Benjamin F. Wade and Representative Daniel W. Gooch to Cairo, Illinois, to question survivors of the battle. Gooch, an Ivy League graduate from Massachusetts, was a noted Republican congressman who had studied law and had been a member of the Massachusetts bar since 1846.[9] Benjamin F. Wade, also an accomplished lawyer, was a senator from Ohio who studied medicine at one time and was judge of the Third Judicial Court of Ohio from 1847 to 1851.[10] Significantly, Wade was a Radical Republican and abolitionist, and his son, Henry, was a commander of black troops.[11]

Gooch and Wade reported that Forrest, indeed, had committed atrocities. They wrote that the garrison was "indiscriminately slaughtered" and the Rebels murdered, "sparing neither age nor sex, white or black, soldier or civilian." Men were reportedly shot down in lines execution-style, and civilians and soldiers alike were hacked with sabers amid cries of "no quarter, no quarter, kill the dammed niggers; shoot them down!" The congressmen elaborated that Forrest ordered the carnage to continue into the night and the following day. Men were shot, burned, and buried alive. Union survivors testified that their dead were nailed to doors of the dwellings in the fort and were left as horrible effigies to the plight of the black troops.[12]

Wade and Gooch exaggerated the fight and its aftermath. The interviews were not conducted objectively. Unsubstantiated stories were accepted if they served the Republicans' purposes. One black survivor, for example, claimed he witnessed Forrest directing the massacre. He described the Confederate general as "a little bit of a man."[13] Forrest, in fact, was six feet tall, not small for those times.

The congressmen framed their questions to elicit certain responses. W. P. Walker, a sergeant in the Thirteenth Tennessee Cavalry, USA, reported that during the battle he was shot in the arm, shoulder, neck, and eye. Gooch asked Walker who shot him and why. Walker stated that a Rebel private not only wounded him with a pistol but also told the bloodied Yankee that a Confederate general had ordered him to do so.[14] Such a conversation in the midst of battles seems unlikely, but Gooch's line of questioning masterfully extracted the anticipated answer: a Confederate general was responsible for the massacre.

The report had other shortcomings as well. It neglected to include relevant evidence that cast a dim light on the congressmen's interpretation of the battle. Washington's *Daily National Intelligencer* printed a revealing account which posited that Fort Pillow was as much the fault of the garrison as it was that of the Southerners. The *Intelligencer's* correspondent reported that an "intelligent Irishman" witnessed the event. Blacks, the Irishman reported, "immediately ran away," in contrast to their white comrades, who "surrendered as soon as the rebels entered the fort." The black soldiers, "not understanding matters" due to their inexperience and "being afraid of falling into the hands of the rebels," hurriedly "ran away with their arms and occasionally fired on their pursuers."[15] Thus, surrendering Union men were killed because a number of their comrades continued to fight with guns in hand. Whether or not the views of this source are to be lent much credence is certainly questionable. But this contemporary account shows another perspective that the joint committee clearly ignored. Their report was, at least partly, a manifestation of the investigators' own bias. They wrote down what they expected and, indeed, wanted to hear. Referring to this report, Secretary of the Navy Gideon Welles succinctly stated, "I distrust Congressional committees. They exaggerate."[16] Nonetheless, the exaggerated report on Fort Pillow convinced many and was a useful propaganda tool for the North.

While Gooch and Wade investigated the battle, the Union army quickly retaliated. On 17 April 1864, five days after the battle, Gen. Ulysses S. Grant announced he would no longer exchange prisoners as a result of Fort Pillow.[17] In Washington, meanwhile, U.S. government officials debated several avenues of action. Secretary of War Edwin M. Stanton not only endeavored to disallow prisoner exchanges but also wanted to indict Forrest and Gen. James R. Chalmers, Forrest's subordinate who led the initial attack at Fort Pillow, for war crimes.[18] Stanton also urged holding Confederate prisoners hostage for insurance in case any more atrocities were committed against Union soldiers. Secretary of State William H. Seward also advocated holding Confederates until their government guaranteed no more hostilities toward black troops.[19]

Gideon Welles recorded in his diary that Lincoln's cabinet discussed wholesale retaliation—"killing man-for-man."[20] Welles, Secretary of the Interior John Palmer Usher, and Attorney General Edward Bates opposed such a policy.[21] Welles justifiably questioned how the Rebel commanders could be punished if they could not be captured. Would the United States government consult Gen. Robert E. Lee or the Confederate government? He admitted that the entire affair was "beset with difficulties." The cabinet concluded that President Lincoln should declare the responsible Confederates "massacre outlaws" and further stipulated that any federal officers who captured the accused should detain them for a trial. This was the most they could do, for their options were extremely limited within the confines of the continuing war.[22]

Following the battle, Forrest retired into Mississippi and soon issued statements defending his actions at Fort Pillow. He denied any massacre took place, but his sentiments were clear in his report of the battle. He admitted that the Union loss was heavy, "upward of 500 were killed," and that "the river was dyed with the blood of the slaughtered for 200 yards." He boldly asserted, "It is hoped that these facts will demonstrate to the Northern people that negro soldiers cannot cope with Southerners."[23] General Chalmers also displayed a harsh prejudicial attitude in his report of 20 April. He claimed that his brigades "taught the mongrel garrison of blacks and renegades a lesson long to be remembered."[24] These statements exhibit the very prejudices that angered black Union troops and worried Union commanders. By summer 1864, they would get an opportunity to vent their frustration.

In early June, Union general Samuel D. Sturgis was preparing his new army in Memphis for an invasion of Mississippi and intended to destroy Forrest and to prevent him from hindering Sherman's invasion of Georgia. The Fifty-fifth and Fifty-ninth U.S. Colored Infantries and Company F of the U.S. Colored Artillery were ready for a fight. They took an oath on their knees to show the Confederates no mercy, or "no quarter," as they termed it, and wore black badges that read "Remember Fort Pillow."[25]

The black brigade, commanded by Col. Edward Bouton, marched with vengeful determination through Mississippi. The Reverend Samuel A. Agnew, a white resident of the area, found the soldiers "especially insolent" in their attitude. They endeavored to "show Forrest they were his rulers." Agnew confirmed that the black troops wore badges reading "Remember Fort Pillow" and that they carried a black flag which signified their unwillingness to take prisoners. William Witherspoon, a Confederate private, recalled that the black soldiers boasted they were going to whip Forrest and bring him to justice.[26]

Their opportunity arrived on 10 June 1864, when Forrest attacked Sturgis's army on the Ripley Guntown Road, near an intersection called Brice's Crossroads. The battle raged through most of the hot, humid day and soon turned into a Union disaster. After a spirited fight, Sturgis's heat-exhausted troopers could no longer bear the weight of Forrest's attacks and began to retreat. The black brigade, which initially guarded the wagon train in the rear, covered the retreat that soon became a panic-stricken melee of Union soldiers running back to Memphis. The Fifty-fifth and Fifty-ninth Regiments were hastily thrown into the chaotic battle as the rest of the army was breaking up. They fought stubbornly despite constant flanking movements by Forrest's men. Bouton's brigade suffered heavy losses: 800 casualties out of 1,350 men, although many of these were listed as missing and 312 were characterized as "slightly wounded."[27]

Colonel Bouton reported on 17 June that during the battle he "was left entirely cut off" and was "surrounded by several hundred" of the flanking Confederates. The black troops massed around their colonel and "fought with terrible desperation." Some, Bouton reported, "having broken up their guns in hand-to-hand conflict, unyielding, died at my feet, without a thing in their hands for defense." The black brigade managed to break out and started a splintered retreat. As ammunition ran low, they gathered caps and balls thrown away earlier by the retreating white regiments ahead of them. They fought their way back to Memphis over the next two days.[28]

Brice's Crossroads was a victory in the field for Forrest and a humiliation for Sturgis, but it demonstrated the potential of the black troops. Their stubbornness in the fight helped prevent the destruction of the entire force. On the morning of 11 June, for example, the Confederates attacked at Ripley, Mississippi, to cut off the Union retreat to Memphis. Formed up and fighting with no more than ten rounds of ammunition per man, troopers from the Fifty-fifth and Fifty-ninth Regiments led two spirited charges that drove the Rebels back two hundred yards and allowed the rest of the Union army to continue up the road. In fact, the black soldiers held off Forrest's cavalry for sixty miles before reaching Collierville, Tennessee, where the command was reformed to protect the rear as the army moved into Memphis.[29]

Union commanders had nothing but praise for the performance of the black brigade. Colonel Bouton reported that his men were "deserving of great credit for the bravery with which they fought in the main engagement."

General Sturgis praised them when he wrote, "The colored troops deserve great credit for the manner in which they stood to their work."[30]

From the Confederate perspective, however, the black brigade did not deserve such praise. Henry Ewell Hord, a private in Forrest's command, recalled that the blacks had "sworn before they left Memphis never to take any of Forrest's men prisoners," but conversely, he wrote, "they did not put up much of a fight—seemed more intent on getting rid of their equipment and plunder." Another Rebel veteran recalled that the blacks threw down their guns without firing a shot and "bounded off with the fleetness of a deer."[31]

The black troops were inexperienced in contrast to their adversaries who were seasoned veterans. The Fifty-ninth Regiment, for example, had been training for a year and was considered disciplined and certainly ready for a fight. But they had not yet seen a large-scale engagement, and certainly not one with Forrest.[32] The Battle of Brice's Crossroads, significantly, was lost by the time the black brigade was put into action. The Union army was, in fact, running away, like a panicked mob. Witherspoon and Hord certainly witnessed black troops running, as was the entire Union army. In comparison, the black brigade regained some semblance of order, which was evident at the skirmish at Ripley.

Brice's Crossroads also demonstrated that fears were rampant within the black soldiers' ranks and among their white commanders. Agnew recalled that many blacks were frantic after the battle. They reportedly asked, "Would Mr. Forrest kill them?"[33] William Witherspoon wrote that his unit encountered surrendered federal soldiers, black and white, who were fighting among themselves. The whites were "endeavoring to force the negroes away and the negroes equally determined on staying with the [white] Yanks. The Yank afraid to be caught with the negro and the negro afraid to be caught without the Yank."[34] Union colonel Arthur T. Reeve, commander of the Fifty-fifth Colored Infantry, recalled that his troops did not intend to take prisoners. And he himself "fully expected to be killed if captured." Forrest's reputation "made the Federals afraid to surrender," and, in turn, this "greatly exasperated" the Confederates. A Southern artilleryman recalled Brice's Crossroads to have been "more like a hunt for wild game than a battle between civilized men."[35]

The desperation displayed by the black troops incited the Rebels to a fever-pitch, causing more chaos. Private Witherspoon related that when he and his comrades were exhausted from the heat and from the chase of the Union army someone cried out, "Here are the d[amne]d negroes!" Black

Union troops were forming a line of battle in the Rebels' front when immediately "new life, energy and action coursed through our bodies." The Southerners charged in a "maddening rush" and drove the Federal troops back, with the spirited fighting costing heavy black casualties.[36]

The intensity of the battle and the black troops' state of mind drew an adamant protest from General Forrest. After the battle, he wrote to Union General Cadwallader C. Washburn, commander of the troops in Memphis. Northern commanders in Memphis, Forrest argued, were aware of the vengeful oath taken but ignored it, thereby putting Forrest's soldiers in jeopardy, as well as the black troops. Forrest confessed to Washburn that Brice's Crossroads "was far more bloody than it would otherwise have been but for the fact that your men evidently expected to be slaughtered when captured" and related that neither side "felt safe in surrendering, even when further resistance was useless." Union prisoners captured by the Confederates admitted that they "expected no quarter." Forrest inquired as to how Washburn was going to treat Confederate prisoners taken at Brice's Crossroads and admitted that he wished to continue the prisoner exchange as before.[37]

Washburn replied to Gen. Stephen D. Lee, Forrest's superior and claimed that, despite the absence of evidence, another massacre of black troops occurred at Brice's Crossroads, much like the one at Fort Pillow. He warned Lee that such actions would "lead to consequences hereafter fearful to contemplate." The Union general also wrote, "If it is intended to raise the black flag against that unfortunate race, they will cheerfully accept the issue."[38]

The Union army was extremely suspicious of Forrest's methods. In Washburn's letter to Lee, he admitted that he worried about the fate of the black regiments in Sturgis's command until he learned that Lee, not Forrest, was in command of the Confederate forces. Then he was satisfied that atrocities would not occur.[39]

General Washburn demanded that Forrest and Lee unequivocally state their policy in regard to captured black soldiers. If they were to be treated as prisoners, Washburn was satisfied. On the other hand, if they were to be returned to slavery or slaughtered, he had no choice but to let their oath of no quarter stand. He further cautioned that if Confederate policy was not specifically outlined, he would leave the black troops in his command to their own devices. In other words, he would overlook any atrocities they might commit in the future.[40]

General Forrest responded, citing the generic Confederate policy: "I regard captured negroes as captured property and not as captured soldiers." He went on to say that it was not his place to decide Confederate policy; that responsibility belonged to the Confederate government. He would whole-heartedly obey any directive it issued. He elaborated, noting that "it is not the policy nor the interest of the South to destroy the negro—on the contrary, to preserve and protect him."[41] In conclusion, Forrest delivered his own warning to Washburn of dire consequences if the Union army continued to leave the treatment of Confederate prisoners to the discretion of vengeful black troops.

The Confederates were concerned not only about the treatment of their soldiers, but also about the desperate fighting that had been occurring. Refer-ring to the oath taken by black troops before Brice's Crossroads, Forrest stated, "Had I and my men known it . . . the Battle of Tishomingo Creek would have been noted as the bloodiest battle of the war." Forrest even threatened to hold Union prisoners hostage to insure the fair treatment of Confederate prisoners and demanded that Washburn forbid the black flag to prevent his troops from taking more oaths of "no quarter."[42]

The Confederate government reaffirmed Forrest's policy toward black prisoners, although it had been relaxed over the previous year. When news reached Richmond in 1863 that black troops were being raised in the North, the Confederate Congress proclaimed that white officers in command of black troops could be put to death and that the black rank and file would be dealt with according to the laws of the state in which they were captured.[43] This policy was later rescinded, however, when President Lincoln retaliated by promising the same treatment for Confederate prisoners.[44]

Black prisoners were typically used for manual labor if not returned to slavery. In a letter dated 22 April 1864, CSA president Jefferson Davis ordered Lt. Gen. Leonidas Polk, who was in Alabama, to hold black prison-ers who were escaped slaves until they could be recovered by their owners. Black prisoners from Fort Pillow were shipped to Mobile to work on fortifi-cations. And black troops captured in Alabama in September 1864 were forced to work on railroads.[45] This was not the Union's idea of how prison-ers of war should be treated. To compound the problem, the prisoner exchange was discontinued. This alienated the black troops and heightened tensions between the Northern and Southern armies because without the exchange, prisoners, in effect, were abandoned. This increased the likeli-hood of mistreatment, especially for blacks. Forrest's admissions, the rumors of his barbarity, and Grant's policy gave black troops few options.

The war of words soon ended in July, nearly one month after Brice's Crossroads, when the USCT encountered the Confederate raider on a hot and dusty day near Tupelo, Mississippi. Union general Andrew Jackson Smith was ordered to dispose of the relentless Forrest with another foray into

Mississippi, and Colonel Bouton's black brigade was again called on to fight. It consisted of the Fifty-ninth, Sixty-first, and Sixty-eighth U.S. Colored Infantries and Battery I of the Second U.S. Colored Light Artillery—a "total aggregate exclusive of brigade staff" of 1,899 men.[46]

The Union troops initially guarded the wagon trains in the rear of the column, but when Smith ordered a forced march to Tupelo, this inactive role changed. Forrest attacked the rear of the moving column, hoping to cause confusion within the Union ranks. Despite constant harassment from Forrest's troops, the black soldiers maintained their order as General Smith moved his fourteen-thousand-man army east toward Tupelo. For the first time, a Union army did not disintegrate as a result of Forrest's move-and-hit tactics. Forrest defeated three armies under Samuel D. Sturgis, William Sooy Smith, and Abel D. Streight by using the same style of warfare. The black troops, however, did not panic and protected Smith's rear "by moving in close order."[47] Edwin C. Bearss, a historian of the Brice's Crossroads and Tupelo campaign, concluded that the black brigade "acquitted itself with honor" by holding Forrest's men in check.[48]

Bouton reported on 25 July that his men "opposed [the Confederates] with a will and determination highly commendable." He further conveyed that the battle "was a severe test of the soldierly qualities and power of endurance of my men." He elaborated that his command "was under fire over half the time and was in line of battle an average of over ten times." They withstood an artillery barrage from their rear and flanks for a "full three hours." But the black brigade managed to remain calm and marched in column "with men closed in ranks without wavering."

Bouton's troops proved a point. They fought Forrest's troopers in heated engagements, including hand-to-hand combat a number of times.[49] General Smith reported on 25 July that the black brigade "fought excellently well" and wrote that their effectiveness eliminated his "prejudice of twenty years standing."[50] The USCT certainly had improved on its performance at Brice's Crossroads. More important, Smith's army once more had pinned Forrest in Mississippi.

Forrest would again encounter the USCT. In September 1864 he attacked a well-defended fort in Athens, Alabama, which was garrisoned by the 106th, 110th, and 111th Colored Infantries, as well as the white Third Tennessee Cavalry and Ninth Indiana Cavalry.[51] Col. Wallace Campbell commanded the garrison of 571 Union soldiers, close to the size of the command at Fort Pillow months before. After a two-hour artillery barrage, Forrest sent a message to Campbell demanding "an immediate and unconditional surrender." He warned that he had a "sufficient force" to take the fort and informed Campbell of the consequences, relating that "white soldiers shall be treated as prisoners of war and the negroes returned to their masters." This was the standard manner in which Forrest asked for surrender, and Campbell was clearly intimidated by it. He believed that the Confederate force contained upward of ten thousand men because of its deceptive movements. Campbell was convinced that his garrison would be massacred if he did not accept Forrest's terms.[52]

The black troops and several of the officers did not want to surrender, especially to Forrest. But Campbell lost his nerve and surrendered the fort. A Union officer recalled that the men nearly revolted and were only brought into line by gunpoint. The black troops "would prefer to die than to be transferred to the tender mercies of General Forrest and his men," the officer asserted.[53]

Later controversy surrounded the affair at Athens. While in captivity in Mississippi, the surrendered officers wrote a report critical of Campbell's decision. They pointed out that Campbell did not fully consult his officers before he capitulated. They maintained that the fort was well defended and the soldiers were in good spirits and thus could have fought on. Each officer who surrendered against his will signed the report to clear his name.[54] This report was important to the blacks who were trying to gain respect as soldiers in what had been a white man's war.

Three days after Athens, Forrest attacked the Fourteenth U.S. Colored Infantry, which defended a ridge near Pulaski, Tennessee. Commander of the Fourteenth, Col. Thomas I. Morgan, reported that "the massacre of colored troops at Fort Pillow was well known to us, and had been fully discussed by our men. . . . He and his troops heard rumors that General Forrest "had offered a thousand dollars for the head of any commander of a 'nigger regiment.'" Despite this, the black troops exclaimed, "Colonel, dey can't whip us, dey nebber get de ole 14th out of heah, nebber. Nebber drives us away widout a mighty lot of dead men."[55] The 14th repulsed Forrest, and he retreated east to Murfreesboro. The USCT had finally defeated the man they considered responsible for Fort Pillow.

The Fort Pillow massacre was a motivating factor for the USCT. They fought with spirit, and high casualties were apparent due to each side's reluctance to surrender. Historian Bobby Lee Lovett estimates that the black troops were partly responsible for 2,234 casualties inflicted on Forrest's command from February to December 1864. These were men the South could not replace, whereas the 2,242 lost from the black brigades were replaced by the Union without much difficulty. In fact, the casualties in the string of battles from April to December 1864 prevented Forrest from engaging in offensive operations.[56] These battles, moreover, achieved no strategic victory for the South. They only served to waste men who could have been better used elsewhere.

The black troops also played an important role in keeping Forrest away from Sherman's invasion of Georgia. Sherman was well aware of Forrest's ability and kept track of him at all times. He mentioned Forrest in almost every dispatch during the Atlanta campaign and called him "the very devil." Not long after the Battle of Brice's Crossroads, Sherman exclaimed that Forrest must be stopped: "If it costs 10,000 lives and breaks the Treasury. Tennessee will never have peace until Forrest is dead."[57] Sherman, as it turned out, was overly cautious of Forrest because the invasions from Memphis served their purpose. Whether or not the Confederate cavalry commander could have actually affected Sherman's invasion can only be left to speculation. The fact remains that the invasions into Mississippi prevented Forrest's active role in Georgia or East Tennessee.

Nathan Bedford Forrest was himself deeply affected by the Fort Pillow massacre. It stigmatized him until his death. His obituary in the *New York Times* read, "Forrest would be remembered only as a daring and successful guerilla cavalry leader were it not for the one great and indellible [sic] stain upon his name." It further pointed out that he spent the rest of his life defending his war record. He reportedly almost fought a duel with U.S. cavalry general Judson Kilpatrick because he apparently called Forrest a murderer.[58]

The effects of the Fort Pillow massacre can easily be exaggerated. Although capturing the interest of the nation, how much influence did it actually have? Mistreatment of black soldiers was certainly not limited to this theater of the war or to Nathan Bedford Forrest. It was pervasive from Virginia to Arkansas. Moreover, even though the Northern newspapers extensively reported the event, what did Northerners really think about the massacre? After all, they were not without their share of racism and prejudice. We have to ask if the war in this theater would have turned out differently if there had not been a Fort Pillow. Of course, speculation is a dangerous endeavor, but this question shows that Fort Pillow's full and exact impact is immeasurable.

It did make its mark, however. The attention Forrest received was detrimental because stealth was his livelihood. It created a focus on him that could not have been comfortable. It further incited and motivated the black troops, which, in turn, increasingly angered the Confederates. Casualties were heavy as a result. Indeed, John Hubbard, who was in Forrest's cavalry, admitted after the Memphis raid in August that their lines were "becoming shorter."[59] It also slowed the recruitment of black troops. In Missouri, for instance, Gen. William A. Pile reported on 21 May 1864 that enlistment of blacks had "nearly ceased" with only two hundred men reporting in the previous month. He explained that potential black soldiers were looking forward to the farming season and were deterred by the affair at Fort Pillow in April.[60]

The USCT emerged from the spring and summer of 1864 as professional, seasoned fighters. They gained fighting experience at Brice's Crossroads and Tupelo and, as at Fort Wagner, South Carolina, these battles proved that black men were indeed able combatants. Soldiers of the USCT further confirmed this at the Battle of Nashville where they helped drive John Bell Hood's army from the capital city on 16 December 1864. They comprised 15.9 percent of the front-line attackers at Nashville and played a vital role in the victory.[61] Indicative of the Union's increasing confidence in black soldiers, the USCT regiments fought on the front lines with their white comrades at the Battle of Nashville; whereas months earlier, at Brice's Crossroads and Tupelo, they had guarded supply trains. Recognizing the USCT's resolve, Union general George H. Thomas, the Rock of Chickamauga, confidently declared, "Gentlemen, negroes will fight."[62] And from the summer of 1864 to the end of the war, the United States Colored Troops not only fought but also compiled a courageous and distinguished record of combat in their battles in Mississippi, Alabama, and Tennessee.

Notes

1. This summary of the battle follows those presented in several different accounts. See Charles W. Anderson, "The True Story of Fort Pillow," *Confederate Veteran* 3 (Jan. 1895): 322–26; Robert Selph Henry, *First with the Most: Forrest* (New York, 1991), 248–62; Albert Castel, "Fort Pillow: A Fresh Examination of the Evidence," *Civil War History* 4 (1958): 37–50; John Allan Wyeth, *That Devil Forrest: The Life of General Nathan Bedford Forrest* (New York, 1959), 299–341. For further information on Fort Pillow, consult Lonnie E. Maness, "The Fort Pillow Massacre: Fact or Fiction?" *Tennessee Historical Quarterly* 45 (Spring 1986): 287–315; Charles Robinson, "The Fort Pillow 'Massacre': Observations of a Minnesotan," *Minnesota History* 43 (Spring 1973): 186–90; John Cimprich and Robert C. Mainfort, "The Fort Pillow Massacre: A Statistical Note," *Journal of American History* 76 (Dec. 1989): 830–37; Ibid., "Fort Pillow Revisited: New Evidence about an Old Controversy," *Civil War History* 28 (Dec. 1982): 293–306; John L. Jordan, "Was There a Massacre at Fort Pillow?" *Tennessee Historical Quarterly* 6 (1947): 99–133.

2. Bradford assumed command after the original commander, Maj. L. F. Booth, was killed in the initial attack. It should be noted that this was not the Confederates' first encounter with black troops. In the Battle of Moscow, Tennessee, on 3–4 December 1863, Confederate cavalry had a sharp skirmish with the Sixty-First

Colored Regiment and the Second West Tennessee Memphis Light Artillery of African Descent. The black troops fought well despite their inexperience. See Bobby Lee Lovett, "West Tennessee Colored Troops in Civil War Combat," *West Tennessee Historical Society Papers* 34 (Oct. 1980): 53–70; L. D. Bejach, "Documents and Brief Notes: The Battle of Moscow, Tennessee," *West Tennessee Historical Society Papers* 27 (1973): 108–12.

3. Joseph T. Glatthaar, *Forged in Battle: The Civil War Alliance of Black Soldiers and White Officers* (New York, 1990), 156.

4. *New York Times*, 17–20 Apr. 1864.

5. They printed the same descriptions given in the *Times; New York Herald*, 16–23 Apr. 1864; *New York Tribune*, 16–20 Apr. 1864.

6. *New York Herald*, 17 Apr. 1864.

7. *New York Tribune*, 23 Apr. 1864.

8. Bobby Lee Lovett, "The Negro in Tennessee, 1861–1866: A Socio-Military History of the Civil War Era" (Ph.D. diss., Univ. of Arkansas, 1978), 64; Jack Hurst, *Nathan Bedford Forrest: A Biography* (New York, 1993), 178–79; *Washington Daily National Intelligencer*, 18–23 Apr. 1864.

9. U.S. Congress, *Biographical Directory of the United States Congress: 1774–1989* (Washington, D.C., 1989), 1071.

10. Ibid., 1989.

11. Hans L. Trefousse, *Benjamin Franklin Wade: Radical Republican from Ohio* (New York, 1963), 214–17, 316.

12. U.S. Congress, Joint Committee on the Conduct of the War, *Fort Pillow Massacre* (Washington, D.C., 1864), 1–27.

13. Ibid., testimony of Jacob Thompson, 10. For a more extensive critique of the Joint Committee's report, consult Henry, *First with the Most*, 259–68.

14. Congress, Joint Committee, *Fort Pillow Massacre*, 32.

15. *Washington Daily National Intelligencer*, 23 Apr. 1864. This account was given by the *Intelligencer* after it had already printed descriptions of the battle that laid the blame with Forrest.

16. Gideon Welles, *The Diary of Gideon Welles: Secretary of the Navy under Lincoln and Johnson*, with an introduction by John T. Morse Jr. (New York, 1911), 2:23.

17. Hudson Strode, *Jefferson Davis: Tragic Hero: The Last Twenty-Five Years, 1864–1889* (New York, 1964), 29.

18. Edwin M. Stanton to President Lincoln, 5 May 1864, in War Department, *War of the Rebellion: A Compilation of the Official Records of the Union and Confederate Armies* (Washington, D.C., 1890–1901) (hereafter cited as OR), vol. 7, ser. 2, 113.

19. Joe H. Mays, *Black Americans and Their Contributions Toward Union Victory in the American Civil War, 1861–1865* (Lanham, Md., 1984), 34.

20. Welles, *Diary*, 24.

21. Dudley Taylor Cornish, *The Sable Arm: Negro Troops in the Union Army, 1861–1865* (New York, 1956), 176.

22. Welles, *Diary*, 24–25.

23. Report of Nathan Bedford Forrest on Fort Pillow, 15 Apr. 1864, OR, vol. 32, ser. 1, pt. 1, 609–11.

24. Report of Gen. James R. Chalmers on Fort Pillow, 20 Apr. 1864, OR, vol. 32, ser. 1, pt. 1, 623.

25. In correspondence after the Battle of Brice's Crossroads, Gen. Cadwallader C. Washburn, the commander of the Union forces in Memphis, admitted that such an oath was taken, although not in the presence of the Union commander. See

Washburn to Forrest, 19 June 1864, OR, vol. 32, ser. 1, pt. 1, 588–89 and Forrest to Washburn, 14 June 1864, ibid., 586.

26. Reverend Samuel A. Agnew, "Battle of Tishomingo Creek," Confederate Veteran 8 (1900): 402; Robert Selph Henry, ed., As They Saw Forrest: Some Recollections and Comments of Contemporaries (Jackson, Tenn., 1956), 134.

27. Edwin C. Bearss, Forrest at Brice's Crossroads and in Northern Mississippi in 1864 (Dayton, Ohio, 1979), 143; Glatthaar, Forged in Battle, 165; Report of Colonel Edward Bouton, 17 June 1864, OR, vol. 39, ser. 1, pt. 1, 127.

28. Report of Colonel Edward Bouton, 17 June 1864, OR, vol. 39, ser. 1, pt. 1, 127.

29. Joseph T. Wilson, The Black Phalanx (New York, 1968), 362–64.

30. Report of Colonel Edward Bouton, 17 June 1864, OR, vol. 39, ser.1, pt. 1, 127; Wilson, Black Phalanx, 365.

31. Henry Ewell Hord, "Brice's Crossroads from a Private's View," Confederate Veteran 12 (1904): 529; Henry, As They Saw Forrest, 124.

32. Robert Cowden, A Brief Sketch of the Organization and Services of the Fifty-Ninth Regiment of the United States Colored Infantry, and Biographical Sketches (Dayton, Ohio, 1883; reprint, Freeport, N.Y., 1971), 47; The Fifty-fifth and Fifty-ninth Regiments had seen some action at the Wolf River and on Big Hill, Tennessee. See Lovett, "West Tennessee Colored Troops," 61–62.

33. Agnew, "Battle of Tishomingo Creek," 402.

34. Henry, As They Saw Forrest, 134.

35. Wilson, Black Phalanx, 348–49.

36. Henry, As They Saw Forrest, 124.

37. Forrest to Washburn, 14 June 1864, OR, vol. 32, ser.1, pt.1, 586–87.

38. Washburn to Gen. Stephen D. Lee, 17 June 1864, OR, vol. 32, ser. 1, pt. 1, 587–88.

39. Ibid., 587.

40. Ibid., 586–89.

41. Forrest to Washburn, 25 June 1864, OR, vol. 32, ser. 1, pt. 1, 590.

42. Forrest to Washburn, 23 June 1864, OR, vol. 32, ser. 1, pt. 1, 591–93.

43. Morris J. Macgregor and Bernard C. Nalty, eds., Blacks in the United States Armed Forces: Basic Documents, vol. 2, In Civil War and Emancipation (Wilmington, Del., 1977), 196–97.

44. Mays, Black Americans, 32.

45. Jefferson Davis to Gen. Leonidas Polk, 22 Apr. 1864, in Dunbar Rowland, ed., Jefferson Davis: Constitutionalist: His Letters, Papers, and Speeches (Jackson, Miss., 1923), vol. 6, 233; Gen. Dabney H. Maury to General Cooper [regarding Fort Pillow prisoners], 20 May 1864, OR, vol. 7, ser. 3, 155; Lovett, "Negro in Tennessee," 89.

46. Report of Colonel Edward Bouton, 25 July 1864, OR, vol. 39, ser. 1, pt. 1, 300.

47. Recollection of John Milton Hubbard in Henry, As They Saw Forrest, 175.

48. Bearss, Forrest at Brice's Crossroads, 185–89.

49. Report of Colonel Edward Bouton, 25 July 1864, OR, vol. 39, ser. 1, pt. 1, 301–3.

50. Report of Andrew J. Smith, 5 Aug. 1864, ibid., 253.

51. The USCT also saw some action on 21 August 1864, when Forrest raided Memphis. After the initial shock of the dawn attack wore off, the black soldiers, like those in the Sixty-first USCT, aided their white comrades in driving the Confederates from the city. This attack forced Gen. A. J. Smith to return from his foray into northern Mississippi, but ended as another example of Forrest's audacity. See reports in OR, Aug. 1864, vol. 39, ser. 1, pt. 1, 468–84; Juan Rayner, "An Eyewitness Account of Forrest's Raid on Memphis," West Tennessee Historical

Society *Papers* 12 (1958): 134–37; Jack D. L. Holmes, "Forrest's 1864 Raid on Memphis," *Tennessee Historical Quarterly* 18 (1959): 295–321.

52. Report of Colonel Wallace Campbell, 24 Nov. 1864, OR, vol. 39, ser. 1, pt. 1, 520–23.
53. Hondon B. Hargrove, *Black Union Soldiers in the Civil War* (London, 1988), 191.
54. Report of Lt. J. D. Hazard, 17 Oct. 1864, OR, vol. 39, ser. 1, pt. 1, 525.
55. James M. McPherson, *The Negro's Civil War: How American Negroes Felt and Acted During the War for the Union* (New York, 1965), 231.
56. Lovett, "Negro in Tennessee," 83–84; Lovett, "West Tennessee Colored Troops," 53, 70.
57. Hurst, *Nathan Bedford Forrest*, 198; William T. Sherman to Edwin M. Stanton, 15 June 1864, OR, vol. 39, ser. 1, pt. 2, 121.
58. *New York Times*, 30 Oct. 1877.
59. Henry, *As They Saw Forrest*, 189.
60. Report from Gen. William A. Pile to Adj. Gen. Lorenzo Thomas, 21 May 1864, in Ira Berlin, Joseph P. Reidy, and Leslie S. Rowland, eds., *Freedom: A Documentary History of Emancipation: 1861–1867*, ser. 2, *The Black Military Experience* (Cambridge, England, 1982), 251.
61. Lovett, "Negro in Tennessee," 95–109.
62. Hargrove, *Black Union Soldiers*, 193.

Education of Blacks in Tennessee during Reconstruction, 1865–1870

Paul David Phillips

PAUL PHILLIPS'S SOLID DISSERTATION ON THE FREEDMEN'S BUREAU IN TENNESSEE HAS NEVER BEEN PUBLISHED IN FULL, BUT KEY PARTS OF HIS research have appeared in various articles, including this one from the *Tennessee Historical Quarterly* in 1987. Phillips asserts that the building of schools was a crucial institutional development in the creation of black communities after the Civil War. In his review of the Freedmen Bureau's program across the state, and through his use of the agency's records and contemporary newspaper accounts, Phillips found dedicated teachers and a more than willing African American audience. He also found a debilitating paternalism among federal officials, woefully inadequate funding and institutional support, and an alarming level of violence directed at closing black schools. Most whites considered the idea of educational advancement for African Americans repugnant. By 1869–70, the level of violence and antagonism became such that it was apparent to Tennessee blacks that if they were to have schools, they would have to find the resources and commitment to make them possible. Despite the obstacles, Phillips concludes, the Reconstruction years witnessed "a significant beginning" for primary and higher education for Tennessee's African Americans.

Shackled in ignorance for nearly two and a half centuries of slavery and barred by law from receiving even the least rudimentary education, blacks emerging from bondage placed their faith in education as the essential key to freedom. Early during the Civil War, abolitionist-inspired Yankee teachers, dedicated to the social and moral regeneration of blacks by way of the classroom, began flocking to the South. So great became the faith of the teeming throngs of former slaves in the magic of education that they placed an almost overwhelming demand on their mentor-benefactors for book learning, which, they believed, would unlock doors of opportunity in freedom. Many accepted the simple notion that "anyone devoted to his books was on the road to freedom; anyone ignorant of books was on his way back to slavery."[1]

As the Union armies fought their way into the South, thousands of slaves, fleeing from their masters, sought refuge within the Federal camps. The presence of these contrabands of war (the label attached to slave refugees before the Emancipation Proclamation) provided the American Missionary Association, a rising plethora of other northern benevolent societies, and the teachers whom they enlisted, a longed-for educational opportunity among blacks. The schools at Fortress Monroe, Virginia, and the Sea Islands of South Carolina, established in 1861 and 1862, respectively, led the way in a movement, which would soon spread to sixteen states and the District of Columbia.[2] In late 1862, John Eaton Jr., army chaplain in Gen. Ulysses S. Grant's command, set in motion a massive program of contraband education in the Mississippi Valley.

When General Grant's Army of the Tennessee swept southward through the Tennessee and Mississippi Valleys in 1862, it was met by an army of escaping slaves from West Tennessee and North Mississippi plantations and farms. His army threatened by refugee inundation, Grant ordered Eaton to establish a contraband camp for black refugees at Grand Junction in Hardeman County, Tennessee. According to Grant's order, they were to be organized into "suitable companies for working . . . picking, ginning, bailing all cotton now cut and ungathered." And Eaton was charged with the responsibility of providing for all of their needs.[3] When Grant moved his army to Memphis in December 1862, Eaton moved his contraband camp to President's Island, a point just below the city, where it remained until the end of the war. Meanwhile, Grant enlarged Eaton's jurisdiction by appointing him general superintendent of contrabands for the department. From the end of 1862 to March 1865, Eaton had charge of a constantly expanding contraband camp system.[4]

Although Eaton's initial charge was aimed at organizing work details to harvest crops for both government and private employers, to build roads, bridges, earthworks, and to cut wood for the military, he said, "Employment and protection were necessities preceding instruction in order only,—not in importance."[5] He organized grammar and industrial schools and staffed them with army chaplains, northern teachers sent by benevolent societies, and "such other men as were likely to feel the importance of this matter."[6] Writing many years later about his educational work in the Mississippi Valley, Eaton expressed his frustrations caused by his informal relations with the teacher sending societies, which left him in a strictly advisory role without authority to superintend the schools. He also found his work hampered by a lack of funds to build schoolhouses and provide desks and uniform books for his students.[7] It was not until late September 1864 that Eaton received authorization from Adj. Gen. Lorenzo Thomas enabling him to establish effective control over the schools.[8]

Nevertheless, in his report for the schools under his jurisdiction for the quarter ending 31 March 1865 he could boast that thousands had learned to read. His report showed that 7,360 pupils with an average attendance of 4,667 were enrolled in fifty-one schools, taught by 105 teachers.[9] So much progress had been made in such a short time, said Eaton, that the freedmen were "unfitted . . . for being chattels. They were no longer creatures whom it would be safe to re-enslave."[10] Eaton's schools met in abandoned or confiscated buildings, in barns and stables or under the shade of a tree. Davis Tillson, the Freedmen's Bureau official who inspected the camp at President's Island, gave the schools a good report but was critical of the overall camp management, which he said was so poorly arranged that "it will be found impossible to educate the race to habits of neatness, thrift and industry amid such surroundings."[11]

Among the books used in Eaton's schools to teach reading was the *Freedmen's Primer or First Reader*, published by the American Tract Society. The statement of purpose in the preface of the book corresponded directly with basic aims of the northern benevolent societies: "To teach freedmen to read and write and to instruct them in religious truth, in various domestic, social and civil duties to which freedom has introduced them."[12] Like other readers widely used, the *Primer* was designed not only to teach reading but also to teach Christian morality. One lesson answered the question, What is it to be free?

> We are free! we are free! cry the boys. What do they
> mean? What is it to be free?

"We may work for whom we will, and have our pay for
it," says Luke. True. But when you get your pay, what will
you do then? "We will save up all we can, and buy a farm."
Good. Mind that you do it. Look out that you do not lose
all you earn in some bad way. Do not buy rum with it, nor
vile weed that some men chew.[13]

The inclusion of the Ten Commandments and the Lord's Prayer gave the
Primer a distinct Christian content.

In addition to the book learning schools, which taught reading, writing,
arithmetic, and geography, Eaton's camps established industrial schools to
teach sewing. Freedwomen were taught the skill of making new clothing and
also the art of alteration from the clothes sent south by the benevolent societies and from the throwaway soldiers' uniforms furnished by the army quartermaster. For those who could not attend during the day, night schools were
provided.[14]

Following the Union victory at Chattanooga in late 1863, additional
contraband camps, including those at Nashville, Gallatin, Clarksville, Hen-
dersonville, and Murfreesboro, spread the work of education across Middle
Tennessee. The lack of adequate facilities to house the schools, the lack of
equipment, including desks or seats, and the short supply of textbooks were
constant obstacles to the educational process. But the stories of heroic
teachers and students who overcame these physical barriers were many. The
school at Gallatin, which had six hundred pupils and only nine teachers,
often met in the open air. Later it met in a dirt floor stable for which officials
paid a high rental.[15] Lelitia Faurat, teacher at Murfreesboro, described her
first day at school on a cold January morning as follows: "The house was very
open, there being many places where the hand could be thrust through the
shackling boards which were nailed up in place of broken windows and
doors." Her first impulse was to leave, but "two much-interested colored men
were engaged trying to nail some coffee-sacks over open spaces which there
were no boards to cover, and their cheerful earnestness in telling me how
much labor they . . . had spent on the house . . . gave me courage to take
hold of the work uncomplainingly."[16] On the first day sixteen scholars hud-
dled around two broken stoves.

In spite of the difficulties, freedmen demonstrated an earnest desire to
learn. Annie Casper, teacher at Murfreesboro, reported that a freedman of
eighty-five learned the alphabet in two days. He said, "I only want to get so
I can read a chapter in the Bible." Within five weeks, according to Miss

Casper, he had accomplished that feat.[17] Teachers at the contraband camps contended that Negro children learned as rapidly as whites and that blacks had a greater desire to learn.[18]

At the end of the war, Gen. Oliver Otis Howard, commissioner of the newly established Freedmen's Bureau, undertook the Herculean task of educating the multitudes of freedmen who crowded into the existing schools and into the additional facilities established under bureau and society auspices. These makeshift, poorly equipped schools, which housed large, ungraded classes, understaffed by teachers whose competencies were sometimes questionable, could hardly have been less inviting and less promising. The myriad severe shortcomings notwithstanding, Gen. Clinton B. Fisk, assistant commissioner of the bureau in Tennessee and Kentucky, reported that freedmen were "hungering and thirsting" for knowledge and "the cry from plantation, town and city" was "come over and help us."[19] In a letter to the secretary of a benevolent society, Fisk wrote, "The colored people will be educated—they imperatively demand it."[20]

In his *Plain Counsels for Freedmen: In Sixteen Lectures*, Fisk drove home the importance of education to freedmen: "You must learn to read, write, and cipher, in order to make you able to get on well in the world as a free man, and you will need all your leisure evenings to do this." He further counseled that it might be "dull, hard work" for a time to "sit down and study your book," while "Peter Puff is hopping around the ballroom like a monkey with Betty Simple," but after a time it would not be so hard, and "it will pay richly in the end."[21] In his lecture "The Little Folks," Fisk said, "You cannot well overestimate the value of education. It is worth more to your child than money. Education makes the mind stronger, gives greater vigor and endurance to the body, and adds to the years of a man's life." He followed this extravagant claim to the physical and mental virtues of education with a more rational economic assertion that education "opens numerous roads to competence and wealth. An educated man gets higher wages than an uneducated man and he may do many more things." Therefore, he urged parents, "send your children to school while they are small, and keep them there as long as you are able. Do not fallout with their teachers when they are chastized."[22]

Fisk directed his county superintendents to encourage the establishment of plantation schools, but they apparently never were widespread. In the spring of 1866, Benjamin P. Runkle, subassistant commissioner of the Memphis district, reported to Fisk that many freedmen in West Tennessee had left the plantations and had gone into the city. Runkle felt that some of them would become vagrants and paupers, but most of them, he said, had come for the express purpose of getting an education both "for themselves and for their children" in the bureau schools. And he believed that this movement of freedmen from the rural areas to the city would continue as long as planters failed to provide schools for them.[23]

The *Memphis Bulletin* contended that planters did not provide schools because they were themselves in poverty caused by "stealing and peculation," and that it was "simply absurd" to talk about their establishing freedmen's schools. It was not prejudice, the *Bulletin* maintained, but the devastation of the war and the confiscation program of the government which left farmers in straitened circumstances causing them to drag their feet in establishing schools for children of the freedmen.[24] Earlier in a letter to his superior in Washington, Fisk optimistically forecast that prejudice against "nigger schools" was disappearing and that planters were recognizing the fact that the education of freedmen's children was a "just demand, which would produce a harvest of contented and profitable labor."[25] There is evidence that Fisk had some small success in persuading planters to provide educational opportunities to children of freedmen.[26]

The Freedmen's Bureau provided a much-needed centralized organizational structure for the total program of freedmen's education. Among the officers on Howard's staff at Washington was John W. Alvord, superintendent of education, who had the general oversight of schools in the bureau districts. Teachers sent out by the benevolent societies were responsible both to their sponsoring societies and to the district superintendent on the assistant commissioner's staff.[27] Responsibility for the day-to-day operation of the schools was shared by the Freedmen's Bureau, benevolent societies, and, to an increasing degree, the freedmen themselves.[28]

The academic day schools, which ran on a schedule of six to sometimes eight hours a day, were designed for children, but all ages actually attended, while the night schools, which met for two or three hours each evening, were for parents and working adults. In addition to the academic schools, the societies operated Sabbath schools, which were designed to accomplish the moral and spiritual regeneration of their charges. These schools received the strong encouragement of Fisk but were dealt considerable criticism by his successors in the assistant commissioner's office. William P. Carlin charged that the Methodists were making "the extension of their church the primary object in Tennessee and education only an incident of their work." He did admit that he was "somewhat inclined" to the Episcopal Church but quickly added, "I have never had, and could not possibly have any sectarian feeling against any denomination."[29] John R. Lewis charged that the societies put the expansion of their denomination first and the education of freedmen second.[30] Some of the teachers seemed to believe that education should follow conversion. Mary Leewood, teacher at Johnsonville, took special pride in her Sabbath school, which, she said, was sorely needed because Johnsonville was "the wickedest place I ever was at." She added, "I intend to do all I can to get the people together on Lords day and teach them that they Must Keep the Sabbath Holy" because the people showed little respect for the Sabbath. She continued, "I trust that the wickedness of the wicked may soon come to an end and Christ Kingdom may be built up hear at Johnsonville by God's help. I will do all I can to bring it about."[31]

Scarcity of funds plagued the freedmen's schools throughout their brief tenure. With no appropriation in the first year of bureau operations, the schools were dependent on the War Department for transportation for teachers, for rations for teachers at commissionary rates, and for government and confiscated buildings adapted for school use.[32] Beginning in 1866, small annual appropriations of a niggardly-minded Congress provided some support for the schools. This money (twenty-five thousand dollars in 1866) was available for building, rental, and repair of school buildings and asylums (for the care of orphans).[33] By 1867, when society funds began to dwindle, bureau officials began to interpret appropriations bills very loosely so that they could pay a part of the teachers' salaries from money designated for school building rental and repair. Such a use of the funds was critical to keeping teachers in the field.[34] Commissioner Howard approved the plan, which provided for the transfer of titles to many bureau schoolhouses to benevolent societies and to freedmen. The bureau would then pay a monthly rental fee (Howard set the amount at ten dollars) to supplement the teachers' salaries. David Burt, Tennessee superintendent of education in 1867, warned, "We must keep the plan a little private" because the benevolent societies might discontinue all support.[35]

In the summer of 1867, Burt made a speaking tour of northern cities in an effort to gain renewed support for freedmen's schools. He reminded his audiences that the surest way of "redeeming the South" was through the education of freedmen. The greatest need, he said, was for voluntary contributions to pay teachers' salaries.[36] Bureau officials at the national level also campaigned for continued benevolent support of the schools. Just six months before the bureau closed its work, John W. Alvord asked his subordinate in Tennessee to forward "any interesting incidents, striking facts, or pleasant anecdotes" which were "illustrative of any point in our work, or trait in the character of the freedmen and their children" which he might use to encourage private benevolent support for the schools.[37] Maintaining a continuous effort on the part of the benevolent societies proved difficult, but society support did outlast that of the bureau.

On their part freedmen, despite their grinding poverty, provided increasing support for the schools through purchasing lots and raising money by subscription to erect buildings. In the summer of 1870, when the bureau closed its educational work, blacks owned 55 buildings and grounds of the 106 freedmen's schools in the state.[38] They paid salaries of teachers, raised money for the white teachers' board, boarded black teachers in their own homes, raised up teachers in their own communities, and paid tuition fees for their children to attend the schools. Their support of the schools varied directly with the fortune of their crops. For example, the poor harvest of 1867 left many freedmen so destitute that they could not support the schools, and some closed in the winter of 1867–68 because of lack of funds to pay the teachers. In Smyrna, an impoverished black offered to share his corn and bacon with a struggling teacher and his wife.[39]

The lack of adequate physical facilities came under sharp attack from bureau officials and teachers. "The policy of huddling a few hundred children and adults together in some old shed or barn, or worn-out Government building, and calling it a school," said John Ogden, bureau superintendent of education, "is a ruinous one," because "when their schools are of such a ridiculous character, nothing inspiring to manhood or womanhood can be taught in them."[40] He urged that land in small lots be purchased or leased and buildings bought or erected as soon as possible at all important places. These schools might then become the "exponents of a higher civilization, the stepping stone of *right thinking and right living*."[41] To meet the statewide need for new buildings, the appropriations bills were construed loosely again so that freedmen might begin construction on a lot to which they had a clear title, and when they had exhausted their resources, the bureau would supply funds (from fifty to five hundred dollars) to complete the building.[42] Commissioner Howard expressed his enthusiasm for the program when he said that the erection and repair of school buildings and the employment of teachers was the most important educational work of the Freedmen's Bureau in Tennessee in 1868.[43] In fact, the school building and repair program outreached the ability of the societies to commission teachers and pay their salaries, and the bureau had more buildings than teachers to "keep school" in them.[44]

A knotty problem, which the bureau found hard to resolve, was that of securing and retaining competent teachers. At the very outset of bureau operations, Ogden expressed the fear that the bottom of the barrel would be scraped, that those teachers who could not find employment in northern schools because of their incompetence would drift to the South. In a circular designed to head off such migration, he stated, "If there are any poor broken down teachers in the north, let them stay there, but let the good ones be sent here, where they are needed."[45] Evidence that some of those "poor broken down teachers" sifted through the societies' screening net is amply documented in the bureau records.[46] These records contain both letters and monthly school reports illustrating some teachers' incompetence.

An example of such letters is one written by Leander Grant, teacher at Cleveland:

> Cleveland, Tenn., May 21, 1867
>
> Mr. Bert General Superintendent of education for the State of Tenn.
>
> Dear Sir
>
> I take pleasure in informunning yoo that we are goin on pretty well with our Sunday School I resevd those Sunday School Books on the 9th for which we all send our sinser thanks and to you littl Son of hoom you Spoke and all the soopeople we have as our Hous will accomidat We ecspect to have our School hous up soon and then we will still have an in crsec in nomer we ar endevering to mov forward withoor School Hous and hoop to hav it completted soon for we are much in ned of it.
>
> Yours most respectfuley
>
> Leander Grant

Six months later Grant attached a short letter to a blank school report. In the note he explains why he has not yet "taken up School": "The reson is we are destitut of a floor in our Hous . . . the pupils have a ling way to come to School and the weather is very bad and for this resons I shal return this report blanke."[47]

A Mrs. Brasher, "conservative" teacher at Brownsville, was not qualified, said Burt, because she "insists on occasion that the Milky Way is the equator."[48] Sometimes the zeal of the teacher might compensate for lack of teaching ability, as in the case of Mrs. Mary Truesdell, who taught the first freedmen's school in Athens. Burt confessed that she was not a first-rate teacher, "yet her zeal for the work and her acts of kindness to the colored people are such that she may be doing them as much good as could some other teacher with more literary ability but less heart and perseverance."[49] The opinion of many southerners, said Burt, was that anyone could teach "niggers." One man recently from "Kentuck" who had been unable to find a job applied to the Freedmen's Bureau for a teaching position. He said that he had never "teached," but "reconed he could lam niggers to read right smart."[50] George L. White, acting superintendent of education, personally examined a Mr. Carr from Springfield in reading, writing, and spelling and concluded that he was a fair reader, a poor speller, and a poor writer. "I cannot say that I think him qualified to teach a school properly," White noted, "but he seems to be in a state of progress and has some good ideas of teaching. He would evidently be useful if employed." White concluded his report of this rather bizarre episode by saying that Carr came to the examination late and had to leave early to return to Springfield and White was unable to make a thorough examination.[51]

Rebecca Winchester, teacher of the West Union School at Charlotte, demonstrated much confused ignorance in filing her June 1869 Monthly School Report. A few of the questions on the form and her answers follow:

> Question: Of what grade?
> Answer: the lowest I think
> Question: Is rent paid by freedmen?
> Answer: No sir
> Question: How much per month? (related to the
>   previous question)
> Answer: $80
> Question: Is your school supported by an educational
>   society?
> Answer: No Sir
> Question: What society?
> Answer: Homes Mission

Fortunately, none of her thirty-seven students were studying in the "higher branches" (at least she did not report any), but twenty were reported in "advanced reading." Attached to W. B. Hankal's teacher's report, November 1869, was a note with the request "Send me a Report Mad out in stile then I will Know how to fill Beter." His report showed a need for a model to follow.[52] At Shelbyville, John Dunlap reported that one of his teachers "positively declined keeping her register."[53]

Assistant Commissioner Carlin refused to pay the salaries of incompetents and in response to a request for Freedmen's Bureau assistance at Cumberland, he refused to pay a teacher on the grounds that he was not qualified.[54] L. T. Drake, public school superintendent at Jonesboro, lamented the scarcity of good teachers, which he said was the greatest hindrance to the education of blacks. He charged that there was not a black teacher properly qualified, and that most local white teachers were afraid to teach blacks because they would be ostracized by their neighbors.[55] Reverend W. B. Williams, agent of the American Missionary Association, said that his trip to Memphis had "banished from my mind that almost anyone will do to teach at colored schools. The very best teachers are demanded here, so that their work will command the respect of all the intelligent people of the South." They are required "in order to demonstrate to all men the capacity of the blacks to acquire knowledge. Only the most skillful workmen can show fairly the quality of material in which they work." And it is important that blacks who should become "teachers of their own race should never become acquainted with any save first class schools."[56] Bureau officials did praise those teachers and schools, which they believed were doing a good job. Based on his continuous evaluation of the schools in Nashville, Carlin stated categorically that the schools were "flourishing" under "well-qualified and zealous" teachers.[57]

To meet the chronic teacher shortage crisis, normal schools were established first in Nashville. In the fall of 1865, John Ogden pointed up the impracticality of employing northern teachers. He contended that $100,000 spent in training one hundred teachers "would do much more towards educating freedmen of the South than three times that sum spent in supporting Northern teachers."[58] In the absence of normal schools, he instructed teachers to set aside classes in their academic schools to train prospective teachers.[59] Fisk University became the first normal or teacher training school for freedmen in Tennessee.

Fisk School, named in honor of Clinton B. Fisk, bureau chief in Tennessee and Kentucky, was established on 9 January 1866 under the auspices of the American Missionary Association and the Western Freedmen's Aid Commission. By 1867 the school was incorporated as Fisk University and organized into three departments: the Academic, which included grammar and high school; the Normal, which admitted pupils over fifteen who could demonstrate their ability to teach; and Collegiate, which offered ancient and modern languages and higher mathematics. The most distinctive characteristic of the incorporation, said John Ogden, who had left his bureau post to become Fisk principal, "has been, from the beginning, a Normal, or training school for colored teachers."[60] The first Normal School class of twelve began in November 1867, and a second class of ten began in January 1868. Each student in the Normal School practiced teaching in the Model School, which had about sixty primary pupils ranging in age from four to fourteen years old. Ogden alternated meeting the teachers' classes on a daily basis in his recitation room, "where I give them a sound drill, both in theory and practice, together with a review of their course of studies from day to day."[61]

The early years at Fisk were especially difficult for both faculty and students. The faculty was overworked, underpaid (when paid at all), and poorly fed. Students suffered even greater deprivation from want of funds to pay tuition and from lack of clothes to protect them from the winter cold. Upon exhausting their meager resources, many students would spend from five to six months each year teaching in freedmen's schools in surrounding counties. And there was no certainty that they would be paid for their efforts. Barefoot students would be compelled to stay at home and miss school in the most severe weather. While white faculty might be socially ostracized by the local white community, their black students were harassed, intimidated, and physically abused. Nevertheless, dedicated faculty and determined students persevered.[62]

Following the establishment of Fisk, normal schools began to multiply across the state, including Central Tennessee College and the Normal and Theological Institute (later Roger Williams University) both at Nashville, and at Columbia, Murfreesboro, Chattanooga, Knoxville, and Clarksville.[63]

State provision for common schools for both blacks and whites, to be supported by a state property tax through the Public School Law of March 1867, evoked an enthusiastic response from Freedmen's Bureau officials. In an open letter to the black population, published by the *Nashville Daily Press and Times* under the caption "What do you think of the colored schools opened by the city? Shall we attend them?" Burt advised, "By all means patronize the schools." The "charity schools," he said, were "an abnormal method of education," schools which were never intended to be permanent but were designed to "meet your wants until schools could be established for you by the State and city laws." Primary education, he said, should be supported by local taxation and the charity schools could become academic, normal, and/or collegiate institutions.[64]

Before the law went into effect, both Nashville and Memphis began to establish public schools on their own authority. In January 1868 the school of Memphis authorized John H. Barnum, agent of the American Missionary Association and the Western Freedmen's Aid Commission, to open schools for freedmen as he deemed necessary. He was authorized to employ teachers at a salary of seventy-five dollars per month and expend half of the Memphis school fund.[65]

But before any state school funds could be made available for public schools, a school population census had to be taken. Because of several obstacles causing delays in taking the census, including threats on the lives of the census takers if they counted the black population, it was not taken for more than a year after the law was enacted. With the exception of Memphis and Nashville, the public school system existed only on paper. According to a Nashville newspaper by October 1868, only eleven schools had been organized under the common-school law.[66] Burt then made an appeal to the northern benevolent societies to continue their support of the freedmen's schools, and cautioned his teachers against their taking precipitate action in closing bureau and society-sponsored schools.[67] To a teacher in West Tennessee, Burt advised, "It will be time to close your work . . . after you see an effort made there under the new law and not before."[68]

In 1869, when the public school system was finally established (in some rural areas, especially in West Tennessee, no common schools existed), bureau officials began to relinquish control of the freedmen's schools to the public system. However, because public school funds were scarce to non-existent, county superintendents of public instruction often appealed to the bureau and to the societies for funds to build schoolhouses. And the bureau gave schoolhouses and money to the civil authorities to assist in erecting other schools.[69] Teachers of black schools often complained that they received no salary from the public school system and appealed to the bureau for pay.[70]

In December 1869 the legislature repealed the common-school law and placed responsibility for public education on the counties. County courts were empowered to levy property taxes for school support and were directed to provide for separate schools for whites and blacks.[71] This act temporarily ended the brief experiment of state-supported public schools.

Throughout the short tenure of the bureau schools, the freedmen's burning desire for learning remained constant. From across the state from bureau agents, teachers, and the press came glowing reports of the achievements of freedmen in the classroom. A Nashville newspaper reported that a fifty-six-year-old woman walked more than a mile each day to sit in a primary class. "Oh, what a spectacle it is to see," reported the paper, "this old lady wending her way through the streets with her school books in one hand and a cane in the other, while she looks out through glasses upon a world in which fifty years of her life were spent as a slave."[72] From Pulaski, a letter published in the *Nashville Daily Press and Times* signed "colored friends" expressed appreciation and praise for the freedmen's schools and teachers and high expectations of the schools: "Abraham Lincoln made our bodies free, and we hope that good schools will make our minds free and enlightened."[73]

Freedmen's Bureau teachers congratulated their students on their ability to master "easy lessons" and reported that the alphabet spread through a school "like a contagious epidemic." The children, they said, "take it from each other as they would the measles or whooping cough."[74] S. H. Melcher, bureau agent of Fayette County, said that once blacks gain confidence in their ability to learn, their desire for knowledge increases and "should it go on for a generation there must be some bright minds among this once despised and persecuted people."[75] In reporting on a school in Columbia, Samuel Potter, bureau agent, said, "The school is going along finely, and the children are learning just like a streak."[76]

That blacks learned as rapidly as whites and showed a much greater desire to learn was a major assessment made by bureau agents and teachers. William Stanton, teacher at Gallatin, expressed what appeared to be the consensus view: "The members of our school, taken altogether, are making as rapid progress as any class of white children that I ever saw." He added, "The Negroes seem to feel more interest in learning than white children usually do."[77] George Judd, bureau agent at Pulaski, went a step further in his evaluation as he told how children took their learning home to teach their parents. Given the combined efforts of parents and children, "there are many whites who will have to look sharp or they will have hard work to keep equal with the Negro, much less their Superior," he predicted.[78] Benjamin Runkle, bureau agent at Memphis, marveled at the interest which freedmen manifested in education: "That a race kept in total ignorance for more than a century should conduct themselves as well as they do, should be so earnest in their desires, and so eager and persevering in their efforts to acquire an education is a matter of astonishment."[79] But David Burt put the issue of black versus white ability and quickness to learn in balance when he said, "The Negroes as a class display very much the same important elements of character that the white race might be justly disposed to do under the same circumstances. Their minds [are] just as susceptible of improvement, expansion and culture as those of whites—neither greatly more nor greatly less."[80]

Not every teacher shared the enthusiasm expressed by many about the progress of freedmen in the schools. Ella Gray, teacher at Charlotte, reported that most of her twenty-six students were "very hard to manage," and only two or three could be called industrious.[81] Harriet Hall, teacher at Kingston, reported at the end of her school session in June 1868 that she did not plan to return because "six months teaching among the colored people seems quite sufficient," but she did recommend her cousin and implied that she would be willing to return as an assistant.[82]

In 1869, the *American Missionary* published letters from students in Gallatin who responded to their teacher's request to thank their northern friends for their support given to the school. The following letters were published in the September 1869 issue:

> Gallatin Tenn June 7th 1869
> Kind Friend
>
> The majority of colored people of our town are gaining steadfast footing year after year and we feel thankful toward the Northern people for their assistance. Before the rebellion we were not allowed the privilege of attending school but now we have a flourishing school and competent teachers for which we are grateful. It has been said that the colored people could not learn, but I say that that assertion is not true, for the scholars in our school are learning faster than those in the white schools.
>
> John J. Banks, Age 16

> Gallatin Tenn June 1st 1869
> Kind Friend
>
> This is the first time I have ever tried to write to any of our northern friends. We have a pleasant school and good kind teachers and school mates. I feel very much interested in our school. It is true I am very small but the small can do something, I want to be useful while I am young, and when I grow up I hope to make a useful woman. l am trying to serve the Lord who is so good and kind to all. I want to see the day when our race will be educated. We are learning very fast and if we keep on will be able to teach others.
>
> Alice Tompkins, Age 11

These letters reflect the influence of the teacher in instilling a strong sense of pride in the personal achievements of the students and in the promised uplift of all blacks through the classroom.

Slave Narratives, prepared by the Federal Writers' Project between 1936 and 1938, contain recollections of a few former Tennessee slaves concerning their schooling or lack of it following emancipation. Emma Grisham of Nashville said of her brief schooling, "I went ter schul at Fisk a short time, w'en hit wuz neah 12th 'en Cedar, en a w'ile down on Church St. Mah teacher allus bragged on me fer bein' clean en neat. I dint git much schuling, mah daddy wuz lak mos' ole folks, he though ern you knowd yo a, b, c, s en could read a line, dat wuz 'nuff. En he hired me out. Dunno w'at dey paid me, fer hit wuz paid ter mah daddy."[83] Another Nashvillian, Moesy Hudson, who attended Fisk for a short time, said, "But i diden git ter go long 'nuff ter git en edj'cation."[84] Ann Matthews, also of Nashville, said, "I didnt go ter schul, mah daddy wouldin let me—Said he needed me in de fiel wors den I needed schul."[85] Joseph Leonidas Star of Knoxville said that he "had considerable schoolin, went to my first school in the old First Presbyterian church. My teachers was white folks from the North. They give us our education and give us clothes and things sent down here from the north. That was just after the surrender."[86]

According to bureau records, enrollment in freedmen's schools in Tennessee reached a peak in March 1868 of 10,077, with an average daily attendance of 7,213. The nearly 70 percent average daily attendance is impressive when one considers all the obstacles of distance to the schools (some walked six miles), foul weather, cold schoolhouses, sickness, and farm demands. Statistical records belie, indeed, any charge of education being a mere novelty to freedmen. It is true that this enrollment represented no more than 10 to 12 percent of the black school-age population in the state.[87] The report showed that there were 128 schools (Burt estimated that as many as 20 schools with an estimated 600 pupils were not reported), 175 teachers (126 white and 49 black), 2,098 paying tuition totaling $1,262.15 (about 60 cents per pupil), 48 schools graded with two to five grades, and 1,600 pupils over sixteen years of age. The number of students engaged in different levels and courses of study included: 1,103 in alphabet, 3,548 able to spell and read easy lessons, 4,390 advanced readers, 2,475 in geography, 4,041 in arithmetic, 554 in higher branches (including grammar and physiology), 3,654 in writing, and 151 doing needlework. There were 8 industrial schools with 200 studying sewing and knitting. Six normal schools were functioning with 130 pupils.[88]

The closing of school sessions was often used as an occasion for a public exhibition demonstrating the work of the students. Such an exhibition was held in Memphis on 4 May 1868 under the direction of J. H. Barnum, superintendent of the free colored schools. The students demonstrated their academic skills through declamations, reading, dialogues, recitations "interspersed with favorite National songs and excellent tableaux, representing a variety of scenes, with closing gymnastic exercises." An appreciative audience tossed bouquets of flowers on the stage at the end of each performance.[89] Park Brewster, teacher at Elizabethton, had closing exercises at his school both in the spring and summer sessions in 1868. Parents and friends who came heard exercises in reading, spelling, writing, singing, declamation, and arithmetic, and Brewster said, "They think the children have learned wonderfully."[90] At his school closing exhibition in May 1867, Henry C. Eddy, teacher at Springfield, said that everyone was pleased and "white people [were] astonished."[91]

White hostility proved to be the most ominous threat to the bureau schools. Teachers were threatened, intimidated, beaten, driven away and their schoolhouses destroyed. In the Memphis riots of May 1866, twelve schoolhouses were destroyed and twenty-five teachers were thrown out of work and driven out of town. The teachers received a terse anonymous note whose message was clear: "You will take notice that we have determined to rid our community of Negro-loving fanatics and philanthropic teachers of our former slaves. You are one of the number, and it will be well for you if you are absent from the city by the 1st of June. Consult your safety."[92] When the federal commander of the garrison at Memphis told the teachers that he could not protect them but would give them transportation out of the city, most of them accepted his offer and fled.[93] The teaching of freedmen was indeed a hazardous occupation.

K. J. Sample, bureau agent at Lebanon, charged that prejudice was so great there against northern teachers that "many . . . would starve a Yankee teacher if they could thereby prevent the freedmen from being educated."[94] A teacher in Hardeman County was attacked at his boardinghouse and dragged some distance to an old field, where he was choked, beaten, turpentined, tarred and painted in the face, and forced to promise to leave town the next morning.[95] Isaac Newton, teacher at Somerville, was assaulted and forced to leave town, and a troop of twenty-five soldiers was required to escort him back and protect him in reopening his school.[96] Thomas Wells and Israel Aiken, two young black students from Fisk, opened a school at Dresden where, on the night of 2 September 1869, they were dragged from their beds to the woods. There most of their clothes were torn off, their backs were lacerated with whips, and they were warned to stop teaching "niggers" and sent running for their lives to a "hail of bullets."[97] At Clarksville, the white owner of a building, which freedmen wanted to rent for a school, said that he would rather "burn it to the ground than rent it for a 'nigger school.'"[98] Arson was indeed a popular weapon used by the opponents of freedmen's schools.[99] Violent white opposition to freedmen's schools occurred all across the South, but there was a lack of universal agreement about its cause. In his pioneering study of black education in the Reconstruction era, Henry Lee Swint said that white reaction to the freedmen's schools was "definite, decided, and violent." White opposition, said Swint, did not stem from Negro education per se but from the presence of the Yankee schoolmarm, who did not confine her instruction to the three Rs nor even to the higher branches, but who instructed her charges in the volatile field of partisan politics.[100] Martin Abbott's study of the Freedmen's Bureau in South Carolina echoed Swint's thesis that white opposition to Negro education centered around the northern teachers and their alleged political indoctrination of blacks following the 1867 installation of Radical Reconstruction.[101] In his trenchant study of the bureau, George R. Bentley contended that by 1867, when Radical government was forced on the southern states, black education was already firmly established. And the bitter, violent opposition to the northern teachers engaged in political propagandizing was ineffective in curbing the growth of the freedmen's schools.[102] In another study of freedmen's education, Ronald E. Butchart charged that southern white opposition was aimed against any kind of black education and not simply against "Yankee cultural imperialism."[103] Butchart has brought the historiography on white reaction to the freedmen's schools back to the view of many contemporary observers of the bureau, including the viewpoints of bureau officers.

David Burt, who held the office of bureau superintendent of education longer than any other, bluntly stated that opposition to the freedmen's schools on the grounds of the presence of the Yankee teacher was no more than a subterfuge: "It is really the purpose to help the ex-slaves to knowledge and man-hood that is odious, whether a Northerner or a Southerner attempts its execution."[104] Criticizing those who said "If the negroes are to be educated, let the Southern people do it as it ought to be done," Burt countered, "[Those] who say we understand the negro best, may know him as he was some years ago, but the negro of today is the very thing they do not understand. They are ignorant of his progress, and of his aspirations."[105] Evidence from bureau records seems to uphold Burt's charges. Local white teachers, who were sympathetic to teaching freedmen, did not because they feared social ostracism or worse. And those who dared breach local social convention sometimes suffered abuse.[106] White reaction was mixed on the issue of whether education would make blacks better or poorer workers. W. E. B. Du Bois charged that whites opposed the education of blacks because whites feared educated blacks.[107] Perhaps Du Bois was right, but the bottom rail stayed on the bottom.

In his study of O. O. Howard and the Freedmen's Bureau, William McFeely contended that much of the work of Commissioner Howard and the bureau served to preclude rather than promote the advancement of freedmen. Howard failed to make sympathy for the plight of freedmen a qualification for service in the bureau, said McFeely, and, consequently, instead of working for the interests of blacks, many officers of the bureau worked for former masters' interests. Not only did Howard's bureau deny freedmen the promised "forty acres and a mule," he said, but the bureau schools did not prepare them for meaningful freedom but kept them on hold.[108] It is true that Fisk and his subordinates actively encouraged education for freedmen, but Fisk also advised blacks to return to work for their old masters. Romanticizing the relationship between ex-master and ex-slave in a manner reminiscent of slavery apologists, Fisk admonished blacks to "think kindly of your old master." Why? Because "you will, in most cases, find him as kind, honest, and liberal as other men. Indeed he has for you a kind of family affection, and . . . he desires to see you do well in life."[109] Undoubtedly, most bureau officials from the top down could parrot similar paternalistic attitudes.

The quality of freedmen's schools, with their secondhand cast-off books and equipment, second-rate teachers, and dilapidated buildings, reflected an overarching paternalism. The manifestation of the highest idealism on the part of abolitionist-inspired teachers was not sufficient to accomplish the transformation of former slaves into educated, self-reliant citizens in the brief tenure of the bureau schools. And when free common schools were established, relatively few whites voiced opposition to segregated schools for freedmen.

Nevertheless, a significant beginning was made both in primary and in higher education for blacks. Du Bois credited the bureau with the establishment of the free school system among blacks and the spread of the idea of common schools among all people in the South.[110] Granted that only a small minority of the black school-age population was brought into the schools, and most of those gained only rudimentary knowledge of reading and writing, their mentors soon learned that they had both "the capacity and the perseverance necessary to permanent intellectual progress."[111] Fisk University, among other institutions of higher learning for blacks, stands as a living testimony to the educational efforts of the Freedmen's Bureau and contributory agencies in the Reconstruction era.

Notes

1. John Eaton, *Grant, Lincoln and the Freedmen* (New York, 1907, Reprint, 1969), 208. The basic source materials used in this study include the official records of the Freedmen's Bureau and local newspapers of the era; studies of the bureau used here include George R. Bentley, *A History of the Freedmen's Bureau* (Philadelphia, 1955); William S. McFeely, *Yankee Stepfather: General O. O. Howard and the Freedmen* (New Haven, Conn., 1968); Martin Abbott, *The Freedmen's Bureau in South Carolina, 1865–1872* (Chapel Hill, N.C., 1967); Paul D. Phillips, "A History of the Freedmen's Bureau in Tennessee" (Ph.D. diss., Vanderbilt Univ., 1964); studies used on education of blacks include Joe M. Richardson, *A History of Fisk University, 1865–1946* (University, Ala., 1980); Oliver O. Howard, *Autobiography of Oliver Otis Howard* (New York, 1907); Robert C. Morris, *Reading, 'Riting, and Reconstruction: The Education of Freedmen in the South* (Chicago, 1981); Ronald E. Butchart, *Northern Schools, Southern Blacks, and Reconstruction: Freedmen's Education, 1862–1875* (Westport, Conn., 1980); Henry L. Swint, *The Northern Teacher in the South, 1862–1870* (Nashville, 1941).
2. Morris, *Reading, 'Riting, and Reconstruction*, 1 and 7.
3. Eaton, *Grant, Lincoln and the Freedmen*, 5 and 20.
4. Ibid., 26.
5. Ibid., 193.
6. Ibid.
7. Ibid., 194–95.
8. Ibid., 196.
9. Ibid., 204; Schools included in his report were located at Memphis, Vicksburg, Natchez, Helena, Vidalia, Little Rock, Pine Bluff, President's Island, Davis Bend, and camps around Vicksburg.
10. Eaton, *Grant, Lincoln and the Freedmen*, 204–5.
11. Davis Tillson to William T. Clarke, 10 July 1865, in Selected Records of the Tennessee Field Office Bureau of Refugees, Freedmen, and Abandoned Lands, 1865–1872, National Archives, Washington, D.C. Microfilm copies of these records are on file in the Tennessee State Library and Archives (hereafter cited as TSLA). (All subsequent unidentified letters and circulars are in this collection and are hereafter cited as BRFAL.)
12. *Freedmen's Primer or First Reader* (Boston, 1864).
13. Ibid., 40.
14. Eaton, *Grant, Lincoln and the Freedmen*, 200–201.
15. Alexander York to Clinton B. Fisk, 5 Aug. 1865, BRFAL.
16. *Second Annual Report of the Western Freedmen's Aid Commission* (Cincinnati, 1865), 38.

17. Ibid., 40.
18. York to Fisk, 5 Aug. 1865, BRFAL.
19. Fisk to Howard, 13 July 1866, BRFAL.
20. Fisk to Jacob S. Willetts, 23 Apr. 1866, BRFAL.
21. Clinton B. Fisk, *Plain Counsels for Freedmen: In Sixteen Lectures* (Boston, 1866), 23.
22. Ibid., 38–39.
23. Runkle to Fisk, 4 Apr. 1866, BRFAL.
24. *Memphis Bulletin,* 26 Dec. 1865.
25. Fisk to Howard, 9 Dec. 1865, BRFAL.
26. *American Missionary,* Jan. 1866, 19.
27. From 1865 to 1870, the following men served as superintendent of schools in Tennessee: Alexander M. York, 28 July–18 Aug. 1865; John Ogden, 18 Aug. 1865–23 Aug. 1866; David Burt, 30 Aug. 1866–22 Apr. 1868; James Thompson, 13 May 1868–17 May 1869; and C. E. Compton, 17 May 1869–15 July 1870.
28. Burt to Carlin, 4 June 1867 and 9 Mar. 1868, BRFAL.
29. Carlin to Howard, 10 Mar. 1868, BRFAL.
30. 39 Cong. 2 Sess., Senate Exec. Docs., No. 6 (1276), 132.
31. Mary Leewood to R. S. Rust, 15 Feb. 1870, BRFAL.
32. Bentley, *Freedmen's Bureau,* 171.
33. Howard to Lewis, 26 Nov. 1866, BRFAL.
34. Burt to A. P. Nicks, 23 May 1867; Alvord to Howard, 26 Sept. 1867, BRFAL.
35. Burt to Erastus M. Cravath, 14 Sept. 1867, BRFAL.
36. Burt to Carlin, 12 Aug. 1867, BRFAL.
37. Alvord to Compton, 3 June 1869, BRFAL.
38. Compton's Report, 1 June 1870, BRFAL.
39. A. B. Clinton Douglas to Burt, 19 Feb. 1868; W. L. McEwen to Burt, 22 Nov. 1867, BRFAL.
40. John Ogden, Circular Letter, 31 Dec. 1865, BRFAL.
41. Ibid.
42. Compton to Howard, 24 Dec. 1869; Burt to Carlin, 1, 4, 14 May, 4 June 1867, and 18 Apr. 1868, BRFAL.
43. 40th Cong., 3d sess., House Exec. Docs., No. 1 (1367), 1058.
44. Bentley, *Freedmen's Bureau,* 173.
45. Ogden, Circular Letter, 3 Oct. 1865, BRFAL.
46. The American Missionary Association supported some 2,638 teachers in the South between 1866 and 1869; candidates for teaching positions were required to have good standing in an evangelical church, full academic training, and teaching experience.
47. Leander Grant to Burt, Dec. 1867, BRFAL.
48. Burt to Carlin, 27 Dec. 1867, BRFAL.
49. Ibid., 14 May 1867, BRFAL.
50. Report of the Freedmen's Schools for Feb. 1868, in *Nashville Daily Press and Times,* 10 Mar. 1868.
51. White to W. P. Carlin, 9 May 1868, BRFAL.
52. Monthly School Report, Nov. 1869, BRFAL.
53. Monthly School Report, Jan. 1867, BRFAL.
54. Carlin to J. C. McMullin, 4 Dec. 1867, BRFAL.
55. Drake to Compton, 4 Aug. 1869, BRFAL.
56. *American Missionary,* Mar. 1867, 61.

57. Carlin to A. P. Ketchum, 5 Feb. 1867, BRFAL.
58. Ogden, Circular Letter, 3 Oct. 1865, BRFAL.
59. Ibid.
60. *American Missionary,* May 1868, quoting a letter from Ogden, 29 Feb. 1868, 192.
61. Ibid.
62. Richardson, *History of Fisk University,* 9–12 and 16–19.
63. *Nashville Union and Dispatch,* 11 Feb. 1868.
64. *Nashville Daily Press and Times,* 13 Sept. 1867.
65. Fred S. Palmer to S. W. Groesbeck, 9 Dec. 1867, BRFAL.
66. *Nashville Daily Press and Times,* Oct. 1868.
67. Burt to J. Miller McKim, 18 Oct. 1867, BRFAL.
68. Burt to Isaac M. Newton, 18 Sept. 1867, BRFAL.
69. Palmer to James G. Leash, 15 June 1869, BRFAL.
70. Samuel Walker to Compton, 8 Feb. 1870; W. L. Copeland, Monthly School Report, Feb. 1870; David Bronson, Monthly School Report, Dec. 1869, BRFAL; sixty-five schools closed in 1870 for lack of funds.
71. Acts of Tennessee, 1869-70, chap. 33, pp. 41-42.
72. *Nashville Daily Press and Times,* 8 May 1867.
73. Ibid., 10 June 1868.
74. American Freedmen's and Union Commission Circular, 5 Feb. 1866, BRFAL.
75. Melcher to Fisk, 1 Mar. 1866, BRFAL.
76. Potter to Fisk, 23 Sept. 1865, BRFAL.
77. York to Fisk, 5 Aug. 1865; *Second Annual Report of the Western Freedmen's Aid Commission,* 33-34.
78. Michael Walsh to Carlin, 7 Dec. 1867, BRFAL.
79. Runkle to Fisk, 4 Apr. 1866, BRFAL.
80. Burt to Carlin, 20 July 1867, BRFAL.
81. Ella Gray to Burt, 26 Feb. 1868, BRFAL.
82. Harriet Hall to James Thompson, 13 June 1868, BRFAL.
83. Federal Writers' Project, *Slave Narratives: A Folk History of Slavery in the United States* (Washington, D.C., 1936–38), interviews with former slaves, TSLA.
84. Ibid.
85. Ibid.
86. Ibid.
87. Burt to J. Miller McKim, 18 Oct. 1867, BRFAL.
88. State Superintendent's Monthly School Report, Mar. 1868; the report showed schools classified according to how they were financed, and of the 128 schools, 58 were society schools, 34 bureau schools, and 36 private schools, BRFAL.
89. *American Missionary,* July 1868, 51-52.
90. Park Brewster to Burt, 2 Apr. 1868, BRFAL.
91. Teachers' Monthly School Report, May 1867, BRFAL.
92. 39th Cong., 1st sess., House Report No. 1 (1274), 261.
93. Ibid.
94. Walsh to Carlin, 7 Dec. 1867, BRFAL.
95. Palmer, Monthly Report, 10 June 1868, BRFAL.
96. Palmer to W. H. Bower, 12 July 1868, BRFAL.
97. H. S. Bennett to Reverend M. E. Strieby, 4 Sept. 1869, BRFAL.
98. Maggie Horton to Burt, 21 April 1868, BRFAL.
99. Ogden to Fisk, 31 Dec. 1865; Potter to Fisk, 23 Sept. 1865, BRFAL.

100. Swint, *Northern Teacher in the South*, 92-94 and 133-36.
101. Abbott, *Freedmen's Bureau*, 95.
102. Bentley, *Freedmen's Bureau*, 179-83.
103. Butchart, *Northern Schools*, 181-83.
104. Burt, Report of Freedmen's Schools, Feb. 1868, quoted in *Nashville Daily Press and Times*, 10 Mar. 1868.
105. *Nashville Daily Press and Times*, 15 June 1867.
106. William Green to Burt, 5 Dec. 1867, BRFAL.
107. W. E. B. Du Bois, *Souls of Black Folk in Three Negro Classics* (New York, 1965), 234.
108. McFeely, *Yankee Stepfather*; 3, 7, 73, 105-6, and 322.
109. Fisk, *Plain Counsels for Freedmen*, 11-12.
110. W. E. B. Du Bois, "The Freedmen's Bureau," *Atlantic Monthly* 87 (Mar. 1901): 361.
111. Alvord, *Report on Schools and Finances of Freedmen*, July 1866; Phillips, "History of the Freedmen's Bureau," 181, 199, and 228.

Origins of an African American School in Haywood County

Dorothy Granberry

HE PREVIOUS CHAPTER EXPLORED THE INSTITU-
TIONAL BUILDING OF AFRICAN AMERICAN SCHOOLS
STATEWIDE. DOROTHY GRANBERRY'S ORIGINAL
research concentrates on Haywood County, which has
one of the highest percentages of black population in
Tennessee, and the role that African Americans played
in establishing their schools. Granberry found that local
African American ministers were crucial actors, linking
the schools to newly established black churches and
other existing community networks. While the Freedmen's Bureau provided some assistance and know-how,
"these former slaves established countless numbers of
early schools, many beyond the reach of the Freedmen's
Bureau, and, whenever feasible, they exercised their
preference for black controlled schools." In fact, when
public support for schools was not forthcoming, local
blacks funded and built schools of their own. The
Brownsville School, established by 1868, was the most
important. Later known as Dunbar School, it remained
in use into the early twentieth century, nurturing a
sense of community and black pride that served local
African Americans well during the trials of Jim Crow
segregation.

Schools for African Americans sprang up all across the South following emancipation. They were set up in the dust of marching armies, in the tents of contraband camps, in cabins and bush arbors of plantations, in rustic hamlets and in sophisticated towns and cities. While much has been written about the contributions of the Freedmen's Bureau and northern missionary societies to this enterprise, comparatively fewer accounts exist that chronicle the actions of the formerly enslaved African American community in establishing these schools and the extent to which these actions were declarations of this community's freedom and independence. The following account of the origins of a school for African Americans in Haywood County will examine this issue through an exploration of the sociopolitical context in which the school emerged, the involvement of African American community leaders, and the evolution of the school into a community enterprise with linkages to a network of African American institutions.

Haywood County is located in West Tennessee and is one of two counties in the state with a historically black majority. Large numbers of persons of African descent came into the county as slaves in the 1830s and 1840s, mainly from southern Virginia and contiguous parts of North Carolina, resulting in the population becoming majority black by 1850. Blacks continued to move into this fertile agricultural region through the mid-1870s. Some county districts were as much as 75 percent black five years after the end of the Civil War. Consequently, the population was substantially African American until the Great Migration of the twentieth century reduced the overall population and the proportion of blacks to little more than half.[1]

In 1866, an estimated 41 percent of all persons living in Brownsville, the county seat, were black. Most were former slaves, although less than 1 percent had been free prior to the war. Economically, the town was comparatively well off. Although large planters in the area had suffered sizable losses as a result of emancipation, the war had brought little actual physical damage and the local economy had rebounded and was robust. Business was booming as a result of the high price of cotton. Immigrant merchants and other newcomers were establishing retail businesses around the court square. Signs of prosperity were everywhere, speculation was rampant, and storage space for bales of cotton commanded exorbitant rents.[2]

A subdistrict office of the Freedmen's Bureau was operating in the town. It had been established in the fall of the previous year under the direction of R. C. Scott. Most social, religious, and educational institutions, such as churches and private white academies, were functioning, including those that had suspended operations during the war. There was still social upheaval in the vicinity in the form of vigilante attacks in outlying areas, but blacks were beginning to solidify their steady expansion of freedom's boundaries. African American churches and other benevolent associations were slowly being weaved from the threads of former clandestine networks. Blacks were acquiring lots and houses, as well as tools and equipment necessary for independent living. Crops, mainly cotton and corn, were planted and harvested just as before and during the war. A difference, however, was that freedmen now farmed independently or made contracts with landlords for cash payments or crop shares in exchange for their labor.[3]

The Emergence of a School

It is within this context that Brownsville's first documented school for African Americans appeared about a year after Lee's surrender at Appomattox. This private day school was run from the home of its female teacher. The first three-month session extended from mid-April to the end of June 1866. The school closed in July due to excessive heat and reopened the next month. When it resumed in August, the student body consisted of twenty male and twenty-seven female African Americans younger than sixteen years of age. To sustain the school, each of the forty-seven students paid tuition of one dollar per month plus a twenty-five-cent wood tax in the winter. The teacher thought her students were improving rapidly since most had come with no prior literacy skills. Few of them could distinguish one letter of the alphabet from another when they began school. As a result of their diligence and effort, she expected all would be reading well by Christmas.[4]

This early school appears to have been overcrowded from its inception. Instruction had begun in April 1866, and by October the teacher was reporting that she had experienced a continuing lack of success in locating a larger space. Two months later she recessed school indefinitely and despaired of ever finding suitable accommodations.[5] By February 1867, she had reopened the school and had devised a plan to address the space problem. She proposed to build a new house for her family and to use the house she was occupying as a school building which she would rent for five dollars a month, presumably to the Freedmen's Bureau. Her plan rested on a request that the bureau make her a loan of fifty dollars to help with the construction of her family's house. She expected to be able to repay the loan during the year, possibly within three months. The Superintendent of Education for Tennessee, the Reverend David Burt, reviewed her proposal and sent word he would visit Brownsville on

21 February 1867 to investigate her case. Apparently, the outcome of the visit was at least partially favorable, for in May 1867, the school was still in operation with an enrollment of sixty-eight students, an increase of twenty-one over that of the year before. The school also appears to have broadened its curriculum. Of the sixty-eight students, twenty were older than sixteen and only nine were persons just beginning to learn the rudiments of literacy.[6]

The teacher of this first school was Harriet A. Turner, a white woman who was assisted by her mother. Little is known about the personal identity of Turner or the circumstances by which she came to teach at the freedmen's school. She was most likely a local woman. In 1870, a Harriet Turner was living in Brownsville, and a Turner family is known to have been members of the white Baptist church during this period. This church had also been the church of at least two leaders in the local black community. The fact that Turner's mother lived in Brownsville and that Turner gave David Nunn, Mr. Syms, and Dr. Whitelaw, local whites, as references to the Freedmen's Bureau to vouch for her school support this conclusion. Furthermore, there is no known evidence to indicate Turner was a teacher sent by a benevolent association. In fact, Freedmen's Bureau letters and reports indicate her school was independent of that agency and other external organizations.[7]

Turner's school had ceased to exist by 1868, or at least she was no longer the active teacher. There are a number of reasons this school may have closed. Primary among these is that some aspect of social relationships between blacks and whites had changed in such a way that a school for blacks operated by a white woman was no longer tenable. Although no known terrorist raids were made on the school for blacks in Brownsville, there was pronounced white opposition in rural county districts as indicated by attacks in the form of schoolhouse burnings and beating of teachers.[8] White antagonism was particularly virulent against white teachers. While this certainly is a compelling explanation for the end of Turner's teaching in the school for blacks, it does not eliminate other possible interpretations. For example, it is possible that the termination of Turner's teaching may only reflect the demands of her responsibilities as a female and mother. In 1870, she had two dependent children, a seven-year-old son and a two-year-old daughter.[9] Thus, she may have left teaching because of pregnancy or other child-care duties. Yet another credible explanation is that the black community preferred to have its school taught by an African American. Therefore, when such a person became available, the community terminated Turner's services. Reports to the Freedmen's Bureau of blacks preferring black teachers to white teachers, coupled with the fact that by October 1868 the school in Brownsville had "two colored teachers," add weight to the plausibility of this set of circum-stances accounting for Turner's exit.[10]

Whatever Turner's reason for leaving teaching, a likely contributing fac-tor was the establishment of a second tuition school for African Americans in Brownsville. Apparently, there were community forces who desired a more permanent school than one operating from a private dwelling. At the end of March 1867, nearly two months after Turner's proposal to the Freed-men's Bureau, local agent R. C. Scott wrote David Burt that he had "post-poned writing . . . until our Colored friends had accomplished something permanent toward establishing a fine school in our (T)own." He reported that blacks had secured six hundred dollars in contributions to be used toward the purchase of a lot costing fourteen hundred dollars. The lot con-tained a good house and was well situated. Scott indicated he considered the price to be fair and that the community had made a good deal. The bureau was asked to make a one-time contribution of five hundred dollars or what-ever amount possible if it could not provide the amount requested.[11]

Two weeks later, it appears circumstances arose that led to the deal's can-cellation. In a letter dated 12 April 1867, Scott informed Burt that the deal was called off because the lot was too close to the public square and some prop-erty owners in the area had objected. However, another lot had been located and purchased which, although unimproved, was located near Scott's dwelling. Scott felt the proximity to his residence was an asset as it would afford him the opportunity to give the school his protection should the need arise. His letter also indicates that the deed for the school lot had been assigned to a group of trustees selected by the African American community.[12]

Although the Freedmen's Bureau provided assistance in the establish-ment of this second school, the efforts of the local African American com-munity formed its foundation. The bureau's representative in May 1867, J. L. Poston, noted this in a report to the state superintendent of education in Nashville:

> The freed people of this town have purchased their lot, paid
> for it and have a good title, have raised by subscriptions
> about ($900.00) nine hundred dollars ($500.00) five hun-
> dred of which is collected & now in the Treasurer's hands.
> ($300.00) Three hundred of the remainder on subscription
> can be relied on as good. They have contracted for the build-
> ing of this House at ($1175.00) eleven hundred & seventy-
> five dollars, leaving a balance to be received by subscriptions

or otherwise of ($375.00) three hundred seventy-five dollars.
If the Bureau can consistently aid them it will be thankfully
received, if not they intend to complete the building, try to
raise the balance next fall. They have not yet decided as to
teacher, will want your opinion on the subject.[13]

The trustees for the school were Mortimore Bond, Charles Somerville,
Thomas Claiborne, Frank Peebles, Samuel Williams, Martin Winfield, and
Hardin Smith.[14] For the school site, they purchased nearly one acre of land
on the Estanaula Road in April 1867 at a cost of $146.29 from S. B.
Hotchkiss, a local white merchant. Mortimore Bond was evidently the leader
of the trustees, the school deed being indexed by his name.

The individuals in this group, like countless other postbellum African
Americans across the South, clearly viewed themselves as responsible for
and capable of making provisions for their community's educational needs.
Their confidence in this regard is evident in their stated intention to proceed if the Freedmen's Bureau was unable to provide aid. Undoubtedly, a factor contributing to this certitude was the trustees' justified faith in their
contingency plan. They planned to raise the remaining funds during the fall
of 1867 from persons, most likely local blacks, who would then have money
from the harvested cotton crop. This intracommunal solicitation of funds
was a widely used fund-raising mechanism in southern black communities.
Therefore, these leaders knew the technique was workable since it had been
repeatedly used in soliciting the community's support for benevolent causes
such as church buildings, burials, and care for the sick and homeless. One of
the school trustees, the Reverend Martin Winfield, had recently raised a sizable amount for the building of the black Baptist Church by asking atten-
dees at a revival service to each donate one dollar.[16]

The newly built school was a two-story frame structure that cost $1,175
to construct. Freedmen's Bureau agent Scott took an active part in planning
its design, which incorporated features that would allow the building to
accommodate growth in both enrollment and curriculum. When construction was completed, the school contained four well-proportioned rooms with
wide hallways on both floors. Large glass windows on all sides admitted light
and fresh air. The structure's clapboard siding was painted white, and a
cupola sat atop the roof.

In 1868, the Brownsville African American community owned this
school building free of any debt. There were 2 black teachers instructing 109
students. One of the teachers was E. H. Freeman. The identity of the other

is unknown. Average daily attendance was 75, and a broadened curriculum was in place. Fifty students were spelling and reading easy lessons, 55 were advanced readers, 35 were studying geography, 40 were studying arithmetic, and 35 were learning to write. Only 5 of the students were older than sixteen. The school was still without acknowledged support from any educational society or the Freedmen's Bureau but did receive some support in 1868 from the Tennessee General Assembly through the Common Schools Act of 1867.[17]

The school building was in use from the late 1860s to the 1910s, when it was destroyed by fire. Photographs made at the turn of the century indicate the building was not new at that time and could easily have been thirty or thirty-five years old. Furthermore, the site corresponds to the locality described in the 1867 deed, and no evidence of the construction of a second building on this site has been found. The first name of the school was the Freedmen's School at Brownsville. During the 1880s it was called the Brownsville City School for Coloreds. Sometime during the 1890s, its name was changed to Dunbar,[18] most likely in honor of the Reverend Marion Dunbar, a leader of the black Baptist church and an associate of John Gloster, the principal at that time.[19]

The Community Leaders

The men selected by the Brownsville African American community were chosen because of their standing in the community. They were ministers or craftsmen skilled in the mechanical arts. Most were relatively well off, mature family men, able to read and sometimes write. Their children and family members were for the most part literate or in the process of becoming literate. These seven men were members of either the Baptist or Methodist Church, the two predominant religious groups among both black and white Brownsvillians during this period. At least four of the seven trustees were members of the Baptist Church: Mortimore Bond, Frank Peebles, Martin Winfield, and Hardin Smith. Both Martin Winfield and Hardin Smith were ordained Baptist ministers and were performing marriage ceremonies by 1865. Frank Peebles was one of the original seven deacons ordained in the black Baptist church by Martin Winfield. Sam Williams and Thomas Claiborne were Methodists.[20]

Mortimore Bond was a brick mason who had gained his freedom prior to the Civil War and had assisted in the building of the county courthouse in the 1840s. By 1870, forty-seven-year-old Bond had real estate worth one thousand dollars and a personal estate worth seven hundred dollars. He was married and the father of five children. Both he and his fourteen-year-old son Andrew, who would serve as a Haywood County constable in the 1880s, could read, but neither could write. A twelve-year-old daughter, Ellen, could write as well as read. This discrepancy between the literacy skills of two children relatively close in age is possibly due to family circumstances. The Bond family lived outside the Brownsville city limits, so it is possible that Ellen was allowed to board in town and attend school while Andrew could not be spared for so long a period of time and was therefore taught to read by his father or some other person. Two household farmhands in their early twenties, Sandy Tucker and G. Grant, could read but not write. Neither Bond's wife, Maryetta, nor his three younger children, ages eight to three, could read or write.[21]

Charles Somerville, age forty in 1870, was a shoemaker with real estate valued at five hundred dollars and a personal estate of two hundred dollars. Neither he nor his wife was literate, though their eleven-year-old son James, who had presumably attended school at some time, could read and write.[22] Little else is known about Somerville and his family.

Thomas Claiborne apparently died before mid-1870 since he does not appear in the federal census that year, and his wife is listed as a widow in the 1872 Brownsville City Directory. In 1867, Claiborne had purchased a town lot and house from David A. Nunn for fifteen hundred dollars. Later court records show David A. Nunn attesting to the lot being the property of Harriet Claiborne. In 1870, Harriet Claiborne had real estate valued at fifteen hundred dollars and a personal estate of five hundred dollars. She and her twenty-seven-year-old son Robert, who was a blacksmith, were illiterate. However, her younger son, eighteen-year-old Thomas, a porter, could read and write.[23]

Martin Winfield, a former slave, was forty in 1870 and had been a Baptist minister for twelve or more years. He reportedly had $250 worth of real estate and a $200 personal estate. He could read and write, having been taught these skills by his former owner, James Winfield. Martin's two oldest children, William and Joseph, ten and eight years old, had attended school during 1869 and were also literate. Winfield was the organizer and first pastor of the black First Baptist Church in Brownsville, a position he held until his death in 1883.[24] His early training in the ministry was under the tutelage of the Reverend Thomas Owen of the white Brownsville Baptist Church.[25] By the 1880s, the Winfields were active in local politics and their oldest son, William, served as registrar for Haywood County during this period.[26] Prior to his election as registrar, William Winfield was a teacher in the Brownsville school, and by the turn of the century he had become a well known and respected minister in the black Baptist church.[27]

Hardin Smith, born in 1829, was a Baptist minister, the organizer of the Woodlawn Baptist Church seven miles outside Brownsville and its minister from the church's founding in 1866 through 1922, when he retired.[28] Smith assisted in the founding of several other Baptist churches in the county, notably Freedonia (now spelled Fredonia), Good Hope, and Mount Zion, all located in Stanton.[29] He, too, had been trained in the ministry by Thomas Owen and the Baptist Home Mission Society.[30] In 1870, his real and personal estates were valued at five hundred dollars and two hundred dollars, respectively. Smith could both read and write. His son, Edward Smith, says that his father learned to read from his experiences with the children of his owner, William H. Loving. However, the Reverend T. O. Fuller in his book *The History of Black Baptists in West Tennessee*[31] reports that Smith's second daughter, Sarah Smith Beard, claimed she taught her father to write. Hardin Smith's three oldest children, Mariah (age twelve), Sarah, (age nine), and George (age seven), along with a relative or charge, Mat Jones (age eleven), had all attended school during 1869 and could read and write. Sarah became one of the early teachers in the Brownsville school. Five more of Smith's twenty-two children became teachers and taught in Haywood County. Smith's wife, Jane Rucker Smith, unlike the wives of the other trustees, could read. In 1870, the Smith household also contained a thirty-five-year-old teacher, James Scott, born in Ohio, Harry Bennett, a tailor, and Smith's sister, Elizabeth. Neither Bennett nor Elizabeth could write.[32]

The last two trustees, Samuel Williams and Frank Peebles, apparently did not own real estate in 1870.[33] Williams was a forty-three-year-old minister with a personal estate valued at three hundred dollars. He could read and write. His twenty-four-year-old wife or daughter, Patsy, could also read. Frank Peebles was a fifty-five-year-old farm hand living in a household with a fifty-four-year-old wife, a twenty-five-year-old daughter, and a five-year-old grandson. He and Charles Somerville were the only trustees who were illiterate.

The Evolving School

To understand fully the character of the school at Brownsville, three points must be considered: the form the developing school took, the bases on which this black community made its choices for school trustees, and the community's goals for the school. John Blassingame has observed that the understanding of the psychosocial world of slavery resides in illumination of the role of religion and the church in southern life during this period. Cornelius's work on black literacy during enslavement strongly corroborates this observation.[34] The emergence of African American community leadership in Brownsville had its roots in this matrix. The school leaders were the products of a convergence of remnants of African culture and its emphasis on community, the group's hopes for a better world that initially took substantive form in their religious organizations during enslavement, and their individual experiences and initiatives.

At the time of the establishment of the Freedmen's School, African American communities, like the one in Brownsville, were repeatedly making choices that would result in their exercising maximum control over their schools. These former slaves established countless numbers of early schools, many beyond the reach of the Freedmen's Bureau, and, whenever feasible, they exercised their preference for black-controlled private schools. Furthermore, these communities had definite ideas as to the type and quality of education they desired. A letter to the Freedmen's Bureau from neighboring Fayette County notes blacks in that area preferred female teachers because of parental concerns that their daughters learn the intricacies of appropriate feminine behavior.[35] These preferences and patterns reflect the conscious adaptation of existing models to meet the needs of a people struggling for a place in the sun in a still hostile environment.

Many black community leaders of this era had some familiarity with the tuition model, a common form of education in the South until the establishment of public schools during the last quarter of the nineteenth century. The Brownsville white community had a long record of providing schools and education for its children. From the inception of the county in the 1820s, many whites with means hired tutors for their children and established tuition schools on their properties. The two dominant local religious groups, the Baptists and Methodists, had histories of active involvement in the establishment of educational institutions. Consequently, by the time of the Civil War, there were several tuition schools in the town and surrounding area. Most were affiliated with religious denominations and many continued to operate during the military conflict. The Baptists had established the first female college in the area, and the Methodists had established the first school in the county.[36]

The identified black community leaders were associates of these churches and their white leadership. This relationship had begun prior to emancipation when both blacks and whites were members of the same churches. For example, both Martin Winfield and Hardin Smith had personal relationships with the religious, educational, and business leadership of the white community. They were initially trained in the ministry by the pastor of the local white Baptist church and received training from the American Baptist Home Mission Society. Winfield and Smith brought to their leadership posts experiences with formal educational models as well as sustained interactions with persons instrumental in the development and implementation of schools.

The ability to read undoubtedly contributed to possessors of this skill coming to occupy community leadership roles such as minister, mediator, and so on. Although illiterate blacks were licensed as preachers and exhorters during the antebellum period, for those like Winfield and Smith who had become literate, this skill was a key ingredient in the services they provided their community. Literacy was a means of gaining and protecting freedom and rights. For this reason, Smith was an ardent supporter of education. During the early years of his ministry, he began traveling about the county with newspapers and books reading to those unable to read. He continued this practice throughout his long life.[37]

The pre-emancipation experiences of Winfield and Smith which resulted in their becoming literate were not atypical. Charles Roberts, writing in the 1870s, noted that it was not unusual for slave owners, many of whom were active in religious affairs, to have house servants instructed in reading and writing, although no such training was provided for the masses of slaves who worked the plantation fields.[38] While we do not know the extent to which Roberts's assertion held true for Haywood County, evidence indicates that by 1870, blacks twenty-five years and older who could read were as apt to be field hands as skilled mechanics and less likely to be purveyors of personal services. Of course, these data may be comments on the economic reality of freedom more so than on practices during enslavement. During the seven years following emancipation, cotton prices were exceptionally high, creating greater economic opportunities in farming than in service. Consequently, former house servants sought to make a free living in the more economically productive area of farming.

Just as economic realities determined occupation, gender influenced which blacks brought literate skills to freedom. In 1870, black males residing in Brownsville, who were twenty-five or older, had a higher literacy rate than comparable females. Approximately one-quarter of this male cohort was able to read compared to about 4 percent of the female cohort. This means that the literacy of the men at the forefront of the movement to create a school for blacks was not an aberration in their community. They were part of a core of literate males in Brownsville. Additional educational information must be examined to determine whether the pattern of male dominance in literacy is found for community members younger than twenty-five, the first group to benefit from the initial schools.[39]

Class rosters for the early years of the black school at Brownsville do not exist. However, it is known that among the early students were H. C. Owen, Alex Moody, and Primus Lane.[40] The 1870 census reveals that a number of black Brownsville children attended school in 1869. A major goal of the school at Brownsville, in addition to making basic literacy available, was to use education as an avenue for prepared participation in social and political life. When students had mastered all areas offered through the local school, an impressive number of them were sent beyond Brownsville to places like Roger Williams University in Nashville for additional schooling. Some of these students were Sarah Smith, Matthew Jones, Albert Austin Lott, and William Winfield, who pursued additional studies at Roger Williams during the late 1870s and early 1880s.[41]

Although the school in Brownsville appears to have been founded as a joint effort by both Baptists and Methodists, it was the black Baptists of Brownsville through their association with Roger Williams University who appear to have emerged as the principal community leaders behind the school. By the late 1880s the school in Brownsville was the leading school for blacks in the county. John R. Gloster, a graduate of Lemoyne and Roger Williams, headed the school from 1887 until 1915, when he and his family moved to Memphis and Howe Institute.

Gloster and his wife, Dora Morris Gloster, also a teacher, came to Brownsville in 1887 from Roger Williams University. Their arrival was a result of the recruitment efforts of the Reverend T. R. Searcy, an associate of Hardin Smith, and the minister who replaced Martin Winfield at the black First Baptist Church.[42]

Although the Glosters had religious, social, and possibly ideological ties to the Brownsville community, neither appears to have had family connections to Haywood County. John Gloster was a native of Memphis with family ties in Mississippi, and his wife, Dora, was from Hopkinsville, Kentucky.[43] As head of Dunbar School, Gloster continued the tradition of black community leadership built on a linkage of church and school. In addition to being an educator, Gloster was an associate minister of the Brownsville black First Baptist Church. He wrote a newspaper column, "In Colored Circles," for the white-owned local newspaper, the *Brownsville States Graphic*. The column reported school events, teacher training, and news from the surrounding black community such as deaths and fires. John Gloster was also a founder and active member of the West Tennessee Education Association.

The Glosters were parents of four children, all of whom were born in Brownsville. One of their children, Dr. Hugh M. Gloster, became a noted educator, serving as a faculty member at Hampton University in Hampton, Virginia, and president of Morehouse College in Atlanta, Georgia.

Clearly, the early leaders of the movement to create a school for the education of African Americans in Brownsville saw their community as an entity capable of meeting the challenge of education for a newly freed people. They, like J. Willis Menard of the Louisiana Educational Relief Association, felt it was their responsibility "to mark out on the map of life with their own hands their future course or locality in the great national body politic."[44] The community's willingness to accept outside assistance if available—but determination to make their school a reality if aid was not forthcoming—is compelling evidence of this perspective. The raising of the initial funds for the school site and structure, plus paying tuition for their children's education, resoundingly underscores the initiative and willingness of the African American community and its leadership to participate fully in the preparation of its people, especially its children, for economic and political viability. Undoubtedly the church, the Baptists first and later the Methodists, played a significant role in the school coming to fruition and being able to survive.

These churches, through their teacher training colleges—Roger Williams in Nashville and LeMoyne in Memphis among the Baptists, and Lane College in Jackson among the Methodists—provided training sites for the graduates of the Brownsville school, as well as recruitment sites for early teachers who were not native to the county. The outlook exemplified by the actions of these early community leaders survived despite the setbacks caused by Jim Crow. As in many places across the South, it was this viewpoint which was the smoldering ember that sparked the fire of the movement to tear down the walls of racial segregation.

Notes

1. See Seventh (1850), Ninth (1870), Twelfth (1900), Thirteenth (1910) and Fourteenth (1920) Censuses of the United States, Population Schedules, Haywood County, Tennessee; Chase C. Mooney, "Some Institutional and Statistical Aspects of Slavery in Tennessee," *Tennessee Historical Quarterly* 1 (Sept. 1942): 209; Haywood County Chancery Court Records 1867–1870; Statistical Information brochure, Brownsville, Tennessee, Chamber of Commerce.
2. Estimate is based on population listed in Ninth (1870) Census; *The Goodspeed History of Tennessee: Lauderdale, Tipton, Haywood and Crockett Counties* (1887; reprint, Easley, S.C., 1978).

3. Richard A. Couto, *Lifting the Veil: A Political History of Struggles for Emancipation* (Knoxville, 1993); excerpt from John A. Taylor's diary in *Taylors of Tabernacle* (Brownsville, Tenn., 1957).

4. Freedmen's Bureau, Teacher Monthly School Report, 1866–1868, Microfilm Roll 52, Tennessee State Library and Archives, Nashville (hereafter cited as TSLA); Harriet A. Turner to Mr. Burt, 27 Oct. 1866, Freedmen's Bureau Records, Microfilm Roll 47, Tennessee State Univ. Library, Nashville (hereafter cited as TSUL).

5. H. A. Turner to Mr. Burt, 23 Dec. 1866, Freedmen's Bureau Records, Microfilm Roll 47, TSUL.

6. H. A. Turner to Rev. D. Burt, 6 Feb. 1867, and Endorsement by D. Burt, Freedmen's Bureau Records, Microfilm Roll 47, TSUL.

7. See Ninth (1870) Census for Brownsville, Tenn.; "Brownsville Baptist Church," in *History of Haywood County Tennessee, 1989* (Marceline, Mo., 1989), 264; Harriet A. Turner to Mr. Burt; Teacher Monthly School Report, 1866–1868.

8. Freedmen's Bureau agent reports to the State Office of Education indicate that in rural districts of Haywood County there was often marked opposition to schools for blacks and that whites burned a number of schools. Selected Records of Freedmen's Bureau, Letters Sent by Districts of Brownsville-Cleveland, 7 Mar. 1866–25 Mar. 1871, Microfilm Roll 15, TSLA.

9. See Ninth (1870) Census.

10. Ronald E. Butchart, *Northern Schools, Southern Blacks, and Reconstruction: Freedmen's Education, 1862–1875* (Westport, Conn., 1980), 173; Teacher Monthly School Report, 1866–1868.

11. Butchart, *Northern Schools*, 173; R. C. Scott to D. Burt, 30 Mar. 1867, Selected Records of Freedmen's Bureau, Microfilm Roll 47, TSUL.

12. R. C. Scott to Colonel Burt, 12 Apr. 1867, Selected Records of Freedmen's Bureau, Microfilm Roll 47, TSUL.

13. Butchart, *Northern Schools*, 111–12; Letters Sent by Districts of Brownsville-Cleveland, 7 Mar.; 1866–25 Mar. 1871.

14. Haywood County Deed Books, vol. Z, Jan. 1867 to June 1868, 96.

15. Vincent P. Franklin, *Black Self-Determination: A Cultural History of African American Resistance* (Brooklyn, N.Y., 1992); Janet Duitsman Cornelius, *When I Can Read My Title Clear: Literacy, Slavery and Religion in the Antebellum South* (Columbia, S.C., 1991); and Butchart, *Northern Schools*, 111–12, 126.

16. "History of the First Baptist Church, 311 E. Jefferson Street," in *History of Haywood County Tennessee, 1989*, 254–56.

17. Teacher Monthly School Report, 1866–1868; Couto, *Lifting the Veil*, 36.

18. Teacher Monthly School Report, 1866–1868; *Roger Williams University Catalog*, 1888, 1889, 1900, Southern Baptist Historical Library and Archives, Nashville; Ms. Willie Bell Leigh Rawls, interview with author, Detroit, Mich., Dec. 1990. Rawls relates that her mother, Nannie Bell Whitelaw Leigh, who was born in 1889 and began school at Dunbar in 1895, said the school was known as Dunbar when she first enrolled.

19. John Gloster, who came to Brownsville in 1887 to teach at the school for blacks, was a Baptist with roots in Mississippi and a member of the black Baptists' North Mississippi, East Arkansas, West Tennessee and General Association. In 1890, the Reverend Marion Dunbar, a leading black Baptist in Mississippi and the pastor of Mount Helm Baptist Church in Jackson, Mississippi, from 1867 to 1890, died. It is

believed that Gloster and other Baptists in Brownsville named the school Dunbar in memory of Marion Dunbar. See Patrick Thompson, *History of the Negro Baptists of Mississippi* (Jackson, Miss., 1898), 32.

20. "History of the First Baptist Church, 311 E. Jefferson"; *Woodlawn Baptist Church Centennial Booklet* (Brownsville, 1966); Haywood County, Tennessee, Marriage Docket: 1859–1866, TSLA. Thomas Claiborne's surviving family were members of a Methodist church, which possibly suggests Claiborne's religious affiliation. Although Mortimore Bond's descendants have been associated with the Church of Christ since its inception in the 1880s, it is possible that Mortimore was a Baptist prior to the 1880s. A large number of Bonds, both black and white, were Baptists.

21. See "Mortimore 'Malt' Bond Family" in *History of Haywood County, 1989*, 11. According to Bond family lore, Andrew was a constable during the 1880s, however, no corroborating documentation has been discovered. Political letters to the Brownsville newspaper in September 1905 verify that there were local black constables, though no names of individuals are mentioned. See Ninth (1870) U.S. Census.

22. Based on information in the Ninth (1870) U.S. Census.

23. *1872 Brownsville City Directory*, typescript, TSLA; Haywood County Deed Books, vol. Z; Ninth (1870) United States Census.

24. "History of the First Baptist Church, 311 E. Jefferson Street"; T. O. Fuller, *History of the Negro Baptists of Tennessee* (Memphis, 1936), 83–85.

25. "History of the First Baptist Church"; Edward Smith, son of Reverend Hardin Smith, to Ms. Willie Bell Leigh Rawls, 1967, copy in author's possession; *Woodlawn Baptist Church Centennial Booklet*; "Thomas Owen," in *History of Haywood County, 1989*, 156.

26. *Goodspeed History.*

27. O. P. Hamilton, *The Bright Side of Memphis* (Memphis, 1908), 146–47; Fuller, *Negro Baptists of Tennessee*, 33.

28. Smith to Rawls; Fuller, *Negro Baptists of Tennessee*; *Woodlawn Baptist Church Centennial Booklet.*

29. *Fredonia M. B. Church Commemorative Booklet* (Privately published, 1958); Fuller, *Negro Baptists of Tennessee*, 32.

30. Smith to Rawls; Fuller, *Negro Baptists of Tennessee*, 83–85; *Woodlawn Baptist Church Centennial Booklet.*

31. Fuller, *Negro Baptists of Tennessee*, 83–85.

32. Based on information in the Ninth (1870) United States Census.

33. Ibid.

34. John Blassingame, *The Slave Community* (New York, 1972); Cornelius, *When I Can Read My Title Clear*, passim.

35. Butchart, *Northern Schools*; Henry Lee Swint, "Reports from Educational Agents of the Freedmen's Bureau in Tennessee," *Tennessee Historical Quarterly* 1 (1942): 51–80 and 152–70; N. Shublinger to Rev. Mr. Burt, 14 Nov. 1866, Letters Sent by Districts of Brownsville-Cleveland, Freedmen's Bureau Records, TSUL.

36. Brief accounts of early schools are found in *History of Haywood County, 1989* and the earlier nineteenth-century source of *Goodspeed History.*

37. Fuller, *Negro Baptists of Tennessee*, 83–85; Smith to Rawls.

38. Charles E. Roberts, *Negro Civilization in the South* (Nashville, 1880).

39. An analysis of the relationship between occupation listed in the 1870 United States Census and literacy was made using a Chi-square. Males may have outnumbered

Students and their teacher pose in front of the combination school and Methodist church in Alexandria, DeKalb County, c. 1910. W. E. B. Du Bois attended services here as a young man and later wrote about them in his classic work, *The Souls of Black Folk*. Photograph courtesy of Carroll Van West.

Slave quarters, Fairvue Plantation, Sumner County. Photograph by Carroll Van West.

Slave cabins at Wessyngton, Robertson County. Washington Family Papers, Tennessee State Library and Archives.

Lower Redoubt, Fort Johnson, Johnsonville State Historic Area, Humphreys County. United States Colored Troops manned this Tennessee River fort until the end of the Civil War. Photograph by Carroll Van West.

Morristown College,
Hamblen County, and
Jubilee Hall, Fisk University,
Nashville. In the Recon-
struction era, urban African
Americans established private
colleges and universities.
Photographs by Carroll
Van West.

Fraternal lodge gathers on grounds of Craigs Chapel AME Zion Church, Loudon County, c. 1900. Photograph courtesy of Carroll Van West.

Children pose in
a settlement near the
Mississippi River in
West Tennessee, c. 1900.
Manuscripts Photograph
Collection, TSLA.

Two powerful Memphis families pose for a late-nineteenth-century portrait.
Left to right: Josiah Settles, Fannie McCullough Settles, Mary Church Terrell,
Robert R. Church, and Anna Church. Photograph courtesy of Memphis/Shelby
County Public Library and Information Center, Memphis and Shelby County Room.

Noah W. Parden and Styles L. Hutchins ably defended accused murderer Ed Johnson before a Chattanooga mob viciously lynched him in 1906. Threatened with violence, both attorneys moved to Oklahoma. Photographs courtesy of the Chattanooga–Hamilton County Bicentennial Library.

Cotton pickers near Memphis, c. 1920. Photograph courtesy of Memphis/Shelby County Public Library and Information Center.

(Above) Interior, St. Paul AME Zion Church, Johnson City, Washington County, and (below) Woodlawn Baptist Church, Nutbush, Haywood County. These two National Register–listed churches, built at opposite ends of the state in the 1920s, speak to the cultural and religious significance of the church to African American life in the Jim Crow era. Photographs by Carroll Van West.

Dickey Barber Shop, Rives, Obion County. This National Register–listed octagonal frame building represents the types of African American trades that whites deemed acceptable in the Jim Crow era. Photograph by Carroll Van West.

"Typical Negro Cabin and Some of the Children" is what public health expert Dr. Harry Mustard titled this photograph, taken during his survey of rural living conditions in Rutherford County during the mid-1920s. Harry Mustard Collection, Tennessee Historical Society Collection, TSLA.

Administration Building, Tennessee State University, Nashville. This classical revival landmark centers the TSU historic district. Photograph by Carroll Van West.

Lincoln School, 1930, and Lincoln School, 2000, Pikeville, Bledsoe County. Built with support from the Julius Rosenwald Fund, Lincoln School was a community center for African Americans in the Sequatchie Valley. Photographs courtesy of the author.

Cemeteries, such as Mount Olivet Cemetery in Jackson, are significant cultural landmarks in African American neighborhoods across the state. Photograph by Carroll Van West.

The bedroom where the Rev. Martin Luther King Jr. rested before his assassination in 1968 is preserved in the National Civil Rights Museum in Memphis. Photograph by Carroll Van West.

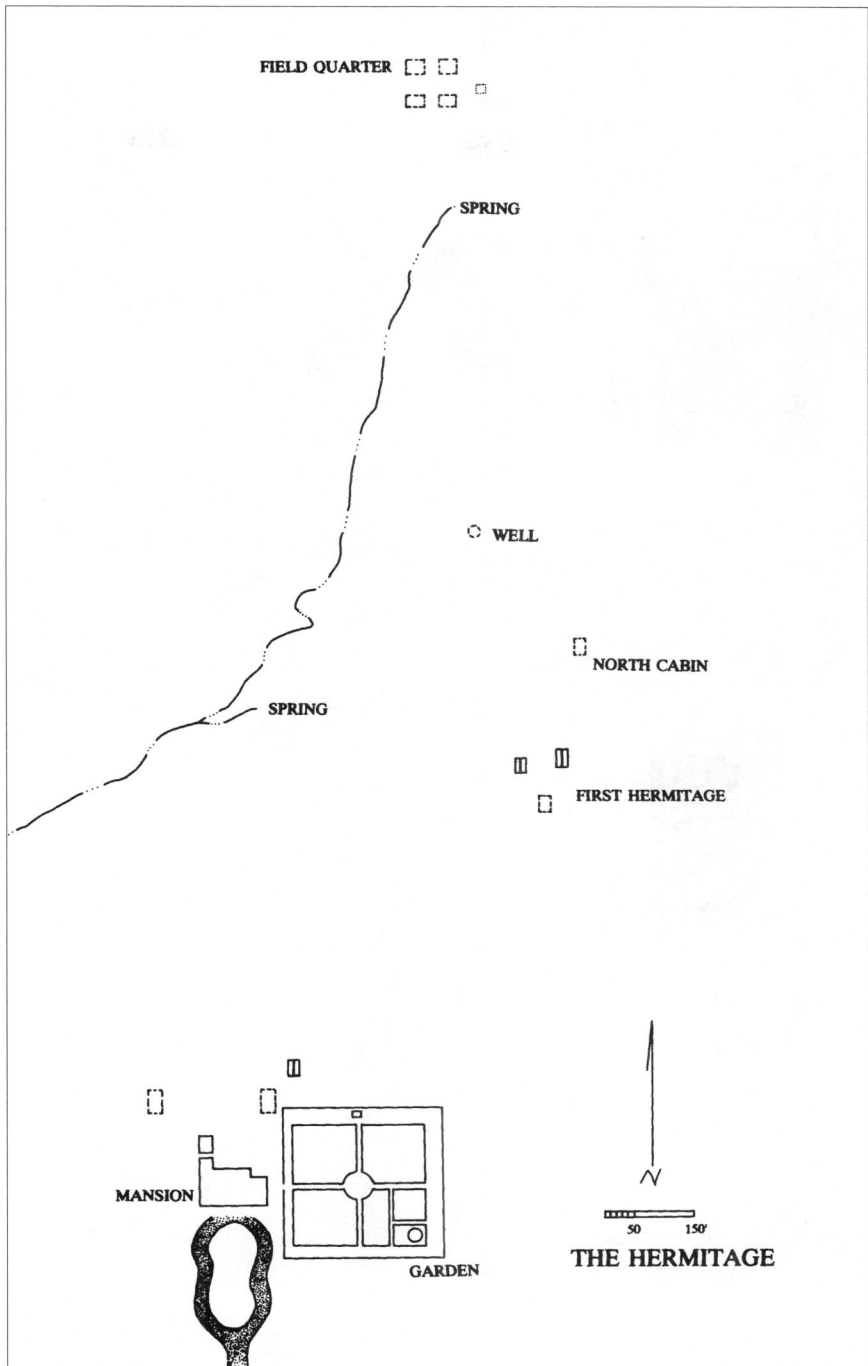

Location of Slave Quarters at the Hermitage. Illustration courtesy of Larry McKee.

Overview of the excavation of cabin 3 in the field quarter. Photograph courtesy of Larry McKee.

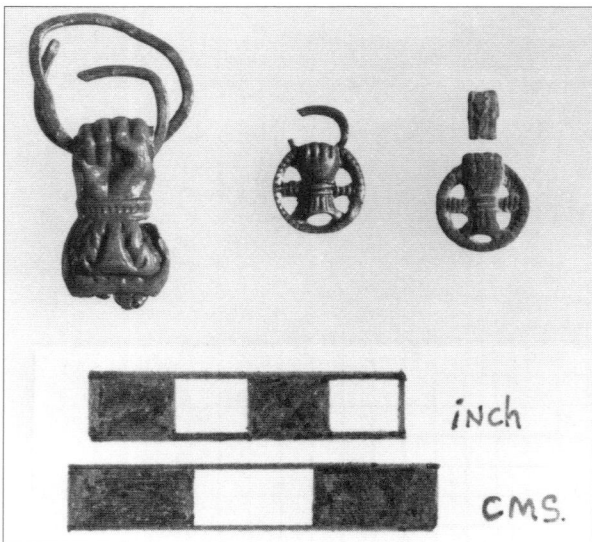

Copper charms excavated at the Hermitage. Photograph courtesy of Larry McKee.

females because of the dangers associated with knowing how to read during slavery or because males had greater opportunities to learn to read. Existing evidence suggests that when educational training became available after emancipation, females were as likely as males to be educated. Future analysis are planned to look at the relationship between gender and education for younger cohorts through 1900.

40. Fuller, *Negro Baptists of Tennessee*, 83–85.

41. *Roger Williams University Catalog*, 1879, 1880, 1881, 1882, Microfilm copies, Southern Baptist Historical Library and Archives, Nashville.

42. Dr. Hugh Gloster, interview with author, Atlanta, Ga., 1990; Fuller, *Negro Baptists of Tennessee*, 83–85. Hugh Gloster is the only surviving child of John and Dora Gloster.

43. Gloster, interview.

44. James D. Anderson, *The Education of Blacks in the South, 1860–1935* (Chapel Hill, N.C., 1988), 10.

Stand by the Flag
Nationalism and African American Celebrations of the Fourth of July in Memphis, 1866–1887

Brian D. Page

THE FOURTH OF JULY IS THE MOST CELEBRATED OF AMERICA'S CIVIC HOLIDAYS, BUT FOR THREE DECADES—A GENERATION—AFTER THE CIVIL WAR, many white Tennesseans ignored the Fourth as a holiday. Brian Page explores this phenomenon in Memphis, where until the 1890s only the African American community, and white Unionist supporters, honored the meaning and symbolism of the Fourth of July through parades, gatherings, and patriotic speeches. His research extends beyond the mere dichotomy of white-black reactions to explore the significance of the African American organizations that participated in the annual Fourth of July parades. The power of public parades and rituals can be as powerful as the spoken word, and Page analyzes the Fourth celebrations as true community expressions of black pride and aspirations. This chapter also is the first of three that address the development of freed African American communities and institutions in post–Civil War Memphis. The Bluff City became the largest urban center in the state, and home of the state's largest African American population, in the late nineteenth century. Page, Bond, and Goings and Smith

provide invaluable insight to the individuals and institutions that turned Memphis into a cultural hearth for
black identity and achievement.

On 4 July 1866, African Americans in Memphis, led by the Sons of
Ham, a recently established mutual-aid association, organized a parade
and picnic to celebrate the birth of American independence, thus beginning
a long and important cultural tradition within the African American community.[1] They celebrated this national holiday in the shadows of the hor-
rendous Memphis massacre of 1 May 1866, which had resulted in the death
of forty-six African Americans.[2] This atrocity did not curb African Americans' assertions of freedom, or their affirmation of their rights within the
social and political landscape of this southern city.[3] For the first generation
after emancipation, celebrating the Fourth of July became a rite of identity,
history, and memory for African Americans, who made the day their own
unique event in contrast to the general indifference shown by local whites
to the holiday. A careful examination of these holiday celebrations, in fact,
uncovers important truths about the construction of nationalism and racial
identity in the urban South after the Civil War.

For most white residents of Memphis, the traditional holiday of the
Fourth of July lost much of its meaning during the war years. It seemed some-
how inappropriate to celebrate nationalism in the midst of a war to destroy
that nation. It especially seemed inappropriate to whites concerned about the
reversal of race relations that accompanied the Federal occupation of the city.
In June 1862, Memphis fell to Federal forces, and the city soon became the
destination for a large number of African Americans. After the war, the *Memphis Daily Avalanche* commented that "the city is literally swarming with these
ragged and dirty vagabonds, who are seriously looking for the sweets of freedom."[4] The number of African Americans in Memphis indeed rose from
3,882 in 1860 to 15,525 in 1870.[5]

The mere numbers of African Americans unnerved some whites. Elizabeth
Meriwether, a member of an affluent family in Memphis, noted the change
in notions of power and equality among African American citizens after her
return to the city following the war: "Men but lately released from slavery, men
but a degree removed from savagery sometimes do terrible things when suddenly entrusted with power. . . . Any stranger, seeing those negroes would have
supposed the Blacks, not the Whites, were masters in the South. . . . As I saw

those things that first morning in Memphis, and as I myself experienced them the thought came to me that, if negroes were to dominate life in the South, it would be better for us to emigrate."[6]

To whites such as Meriwether, African American occupation soldiers were especially a problem; they were an explicit reminder of the war and implied notions of equality. On January 23, 1866, the *Memphis Daily Avalanche* commented, "The system of Negro garrisons in the South carries with it its own commentary of uselessness and wantonness. . . . It disturbs all the natural feelings of the white man; it corrupts the whole Negro population of the South; it puts before their eyes a picture of their race, which raises their expectations above all reason and discontents them with the plain tasks of labor."[7] In March 1866, the *Memphis Daily Avalanche* even claimed that "riots and mobs were unknown among us until the Negro troops were quartered here."[8]

For many whites, the nation equated with black soldiers which, in turn, meant social anarchy. These Memphis residents thus had little regard for either the Union or for any holidays celebrating the nation. At a congressional hearing following the May massacre, a Union general reported on a lack of patriotism. He commented that "if a love of the Union and the flag was considered loyal he would look upon a large majority of the people of Memphis as not being loyal." The general observed that the United States flag was only displayed at three locations in Memphis: Army headquarters, the Freedman's Bureau, and the office of the *Memphis Post*. This lack of patriotism was found throughout the region. Retired major general Carl Schurz commented after touring the South that there was "no national feeling" in the region.[9]

White rejection of the Fourth of July's celebration of the words of the Declaration of Independence did not soon disappear. In 1867, the *Memphis Daily Appeal* reported that "the Fourth can at present be appropriately celebrated by only one class in the South—the radicals, and as a partisan holiday."[10] The *Memphis Daily Post* reported in 1869 that the Fourth was "celebrated . . . only by our Germans and our colored citizens." Furthermore, the newspaper commented that "the rebel press groans about oppression and tyranny" and white southerners "do not have it in their hearts to celebrate as in the glory years of the past."[11] As late as 1888, it was noted that "since the late war between the States, the Fourth of July has become, in the South, a day of minor importance."[12]

It might have been a day of minor importance to whites, but to African Americans in Memphis, the Fourth of July was one of the major public holidays; the words of the Declaration of Independence finally seemed to be more than mere promises. There is a long history of African American celebrations that have their roots in slavery. In antebellum slave communities, for example, African Americans gathered to celebrate Pinkster Day and Election Day in the rural countryside and on the outskirts of cities. Urban African Americans celebrated West Indies Day or designated their own emancipation as a holiday.[13] Antebellum recognition of Independence Day had often been a method of protest. Frederick Douglass, in his famous speech in Rochester, New York, on the character of this national holiday, stated, "Your high independence only reveals the immeasurable distance between us. The blessings in which you, this day, rejoice are not in common." Furthermore, Douglass lashed out, "this Fourth of July is yours, not mine."[14] Prior to emancipation, the words of the Declaration proclaiming equality and freedom from tyranny rang hollow for most African Americans.

Then during the Civil War came the celebration of Emancipation. On 1 January 1867, for example, the Sons of Ham and other social and benevolent associations organized an emancipation celebration and led a parade through the city streets. Undoubtedly these individuals were energized by the promise of freedom. Many of the same organizations that participated in this event contributed to Independence Day celebrations in Memphis.[15]

The Fourth of July celebrations shared common characteristics with these earlier public demonstrations. African Americans celebrated with dancing and singing until the late hours of the evening, a common characteristic of slave festivals.[16] Historians have noted further a strong cultural connection between the traditional holiday barbecue and slave festivals.[17] Barbecues were used to celebrate the Fourth in Bartlett, a neighboring town in Shelby County, in 1882 and in Memphis in 1884.[18] In addition, the Independence Day events had direct precedents in other Reconstruction era demonstrations. In Memphis on 1 August 1866, in recognition of West Indian emancipation, African Americans called for the right to vote, to serve on juries, and to hold office.[19] On 27 February 1867, Horatio Rankin, a local African American politician, urged African American citizens to "stand by the flag" in order to demonstrate that "they were worthy of complete equality."[20]

The Independence Day commemorations were more than patriotic expressions. They could be used to build a memory for the future as a promise of better days to come and a medium for encouraging moral improvement and preparing African Americans for citizenship. Free, but confronted with slavery and discrimination, African Americans struggled to define what it meant to be black and American.[21]

In Memphis, from 1866 to 1887, there were nineteen accounts of Fourth of July celebrations in local newspapers. Reference was made to these public events in every year except 1871 and 1886. Sixteen of the accounts made specific reference to the organizations that participated. Leading the way were the newly established mutual-aid and benevolent organizations that had emerged from black churches throughout Memphis. These organizations pooled together their resources in order to help African American neighborhoods,[22] creating a vital community framework. In Memphis it is possible to construct a more complete picture of this institutional infrastructure from the limited amount of records left behind. From 1866 to 1874, over two hundred various organizations deposited money in the Freedmen's Savings and Trust Company. These deposit ledgers include the names of members who served as officers and some contain biographical information about the participants. Furthermore, names can be cross-referenced with Memphis city directories and relevant newspaper articles, presenting a more visible description about the nature of these organizations.[23]

The level of mutual-aid society involvement in the Independence Day celebrations provides insight to the range of people, and the range of motives, involved in these public commemorations. In general Fourth of July celebrations emerged within the context of a large, poor, and unskilled African American population.[24] Armstead Robinson, in his study on African American organizations in Memphis, has previously identified a split between religious and benevolent groups and those engaged in political activity. While political leadership lay within the more skilled middle class, the community's institutional infrastructure was dominated by those organizations with a religious and benevolent purpose.[25] In addition, unskilled women led the majority of these associations.[26] In other words, not only was the black community able to organize for the benefit of others, but it was also largely the result of leadership and involvement from unskilled African Americans, especially women.[27]

Two benevolent groups in particular dominated Independence Day ceremonies. The Sons of Ham and the Independent Pole-Bearers, in thirteen of these celebrations, materialized as the leaders and organizers of these public ceremonies. These two associations planned parades leading the participants down the streets of Memphis and organized picnics in various parks in the city. Other African American societies including both sexes in Memphis participated in these celebrations. Some groups that were particularly visible included the Daughters of Ham, the Daughters of Zion, the Sisters of Zion, the Sons of Zion, the Mechanics Benevolent Association, and St. John's Relief Society.[28]

The Sons of Ham was formed prior to the Civil War and had a good deal of influence in Memphis during Reconstruction. In the early 1870s, its members were able to carve out an influential space for themselves in local politics.[29] They were also one of the first to plan and lead a Fourth of July celebration in 1866, when they organized a picnic and parade.[30] The leaders of this association consisted of carpenters, drivers, porters and upholsters. However, officers were not solely limited to the skilled and economically stable. There were two accounts of an unskilled working-class African Americans attaining an established position within the Sons of Ham. As a result, some general laborers, although it was rare, were elected as officers. In addition, many of the leaders could not be located in various city directories suggesting that they may have been new to the area, most likely lacking a sufficient job, or that they did not hold a stable residence or job in Memphis. The leadership framework within the Sons of Ham, however, leaned toward the economically established.[31]

The Independent Pole-Bearers was another association that would contest for a leadership role in African American celebratory events. Reference to the society first appears in 1868, when they participated in a parade organized by the Sons of Ham. Gradually, the Independent Pole-Bearers would eclipse the Sons of Ham politically and socially in Memphis.[32] By 1874, the Independent Pole-Bearers were leading the parades;[33] they continued to dominate the Fourth of July celebrations into the 1880s. The leadership structure of the Independent Pole-Bearers resembled the Sons of Ham in that it leaned heavily toward the skilled and middle-class members of African American communities. However, here again, this did not rule out the possibility of a general laborer gaining an official office within this association. Of eight known members of the Independent Pole-Bearers three represented the unskilled working class.[34] As a result, characteristics of these two groups suggest that the organization of Fourth of July celebrations was initiated by the more skilled and prosperous within the African American communities but did not exclude members of the working class.

Other organizations participating in the parades, picnics, and sociopolitical gatherings underscore the inclusive character of these public celebrations. The Daughters of Zion was a very influential benevolent organization in Memphis during the Reconstruction era.[35] First mentioned in the 1867 parade organized by the Sons of Ham, its members participated in many of these ritual events and even created their own celebrations. In 1875 and 1877, the Daughters of Zion organized a social gathering at the Exposition building in Memphis.[36] The Daughters of Zion included many members of the African American working class. Many of the officers were unskilled daily laborers who washed and ironed clothes for money. Martha Ware, a washerwoman and a victim in the Memphis Massacre, was a prominent member. Some of the women also listed as their husbands unskilled men who cut wood or worked on farms to make a living.[37]

The Sisters of Zion and the Sons of Zion also participated in the celebrations. The Sisters of Zion consisted of washerwomen, housekeepers, and cooks, whereas the Sons of Zion included farmers, daily laborers, draymen, bricklayers, barbers, and clerks.[38] A pattern that emerges in these associations reflects a trend toward the participating male organizations being led by members of the African American skilled and middle class, while female organizations tended to be under the leadership of the unskilled working class.

Group affiliation provides some characteristics of the participants in these celebrations, but it is impossible to gauge how many people were in each of these organizations. The *Memphis Daily Post* suggested that the United Daughters of Ham consisted of over one hundred members in the 1868 celebration.[39] In 1868, the Daughters of Zion listed over three hundred members in their organization.[40] While exact numbers are lacking, it is possible to get a feel of these celebrations to determine just how large these public events were in Memphis. The information revealed suggests that these celebrations consisted of a rather large portion of the African Americans in the Memphis area, with thousands participating. The Memphis newspapers, for instance, frequently remarked on the size of the crowds that joined together on this national holiday. On 4 July 1866, the *Memphis Daily Post* reported that "the colored people turned out in mass to see them [the parade], and crowds accompanied them to the grove." In 1867, the paper estimated that two thousand were in attendance and in 1869, 1875, and 1877, the papers suggested that five thousand African Americans joined together to celebrate.[41] The accuracy of these numbers is unknown, but the numbers indicate a consistently large display of celebratory fervor. In fact, there is some evidence to suggest that these Fourth of July celebrations helped construct a community from a dispersed population.[42] In 1872, the *Memphis Daily Appeal* reported that "several car loads with them [African Americans] arrived from Brownsville. Several other car loads with them [African Americans] arrived by the Charleston road." The paper also commented that they arrived by "foot, on horseback, by river, by wagon, . . . and made an immense army."[43] At the very least, the Fourth of July in

Memphis established bonds of fellowship and severed the distance between African Americans in the area.

The celebrations served other functions as well. They were fund raising events for the various mutual-aid and benevolent organizations. In 1866, the Sons of Ham "organized for benevolent purposes," with the money raised used "to increase the benevolent fund." The Sons of Ham, in 1879, planned a picnic "for the purpose of raising funds to replenish their treasury, the amount so received to be dispersed among the sick and . . . burial for destitute members."[44] By joining together and projecting an image of solidarity, African Americans could instill a sense of belonging and, in the process, build a community.

The different celebrations between 1866 and 1867 shared certain components. One of the most revealing was the parade, which usually was the first event of the day followed by a public gathering at a park, picnic grove, or building.[45] A typical African American parade at this time followed a prescribed order. The 1869 celebration, which was organized by the Sons of Ham, proceeded in this order: the chief marshal of the Day, the grand marshal of the different societies mounted on horseback, a musical band, the United Sons of Ham, the Benevolent Society No. 1, the Union Forever Society, and the Independent-Pole Bearers. From that point, the list of parade order continued, ending with the Gymnastic Society.[46] On other occasions various military organizations such as the M'Clellan guards led the parades. Parades are hierarchical by nature and undoubtedly reinforced the ranked order of the different societies. The working class or the socially marginalized would often use parades to secure respectability for their individual and collective identity. The standard norms of neatness, order, and patriotism served to mold other public ceremonies.[47] In Memphis the order and appearance of the participants were consistently noted. In 1866, the *Memphis Daily Post* commented that "all were neatly dressed in holiday attire."[48] The *Memphis Daily Appeal*, in 1879, reported the participants in the parade gave a "fine soldiery appearance," and in 1872 they noted that there was "not a single disturbance." The attention to order and appearance in these celebrations was as much a self-conscious attempt to gain respect in society as it was a reflection of the standards of contemporary celebrations.[49]

A popular way to distinguish between groups, and classes, was the use of flags and banners. Each group designated itself with flags and banners. In 1867, the African American participants were "drawn up in line and decorated with regalia of their several orders." The various associations, in 1869, marched in procession, with "each society bearing a banner, with the name of the society and the date of organization . . . wearing the regalia of his order." Again in 1879, the various societies carried "flags and banners" as they marched through the streets of Memphis. Also, certain individuals were often selected to lead their organization. In some cases, one member of an African American society would be elected to head the whole parade, elevating him to a heightened level of pride and self-respect.[50]

Dress was also a distinction among the parade participants.[51] Frequently it would be mentioned that the participants were "neatly dressed in holiday attire" or dressed in an "endless variety of costumes." On the Fourth, various military organizations would parade "in their handsome uniforms." Other times the appearance and dress of the participants would simply be noted as being in "full regalia."[52] Regardless of the phrase used to depict the appearance of the African Americans who participated, clothing played a vital role in the picture they presented. Clothing could undoubtedly depict class and affluence, but also could be used to transcend a working-class experience. For the independent barber or blacksmith it could designate his position in the community. Likewise, for the washerwoman or laborer who paraded through the streets, dress could claim a position of respectability in their own community, and the larger society.

Another obvious distinction in the parades was between men and women. While both male and female organizations participated, the manner in which they paraded sometimes differed. In the 1875 procession, male and female societies paraded together but with a "carriage containing the queen of the day and maids of honor." In addition there were "twelve carriages containing female members of the societies."[53] This may have been a reflection of Victorian sensibilities designating the street as a male terrain. In most of the processions reference was not made to different modes of transportation, however, this did not mean that men and women paraded equally. Another gender distinction in the African Americans parades was the time of the parade. On 4 July 1868, the female organizations paraded separately from the men. The *Memphis Daily Post* reported that the male societies gathered at a "later hour" than the female organizations. In 1869, the women assembled to parade at nine in the morning, while the men gathered together at eleven in the morning.[54] A final difference was the length of the parade. In 1868, the female societies not only gathered at an earlier hour, but also traveled a shorter parade route. The route for women was considerably shorter in the celebration of 1869. The male organizations proceeded down a total of eight streets, compared to three for the female societies.[55]

No matter the differences in length, time, and transportation, African American women were included in these public occasions but given a less visible public role. One can only speculate on the role these women played behind the scenes.[56]

The parades were not radical demonstrations, but they sometimes reminded whites that local African Americans had power, and that they were willing to go beyond their traditional neighborhood boundaries. African American military companies, such as the McClellan guards and the Zouave cadets, with both names representing direct reference to the Union army during the Civil War, participated in these Independence Day celebrations, leading parades and congregating at the designated place for social gathering. On 4 July 1878, according to the *Memphis Daily Appeal*, the McClellan guards "engaged in a competitive drill" and determined a winner at the end of the evening. The drill reflected traditional military standards of the day and the goal of precision and order, as they revealed "careful and good timing."[57]

The majority of the parades occurred in the northern part of the city beyond the traditional area for African Americans. The parade routes expanded on the emancipation celebration of 1867 enlarging their scope of the city. Of the sixteen parades mentioned during this period, the information revealed suggests that most of them followed the same pattern. These parades generally proceeded along streets north of Vance Street up to Poplar. This physical area can be understood as the core of Memphis during Reconstruction. The region south of this area contained the majority of the African American population. The southern part of these parade routes would usually be the point of origin, and, depending on the destination, the various African American societies would either proceed north or march north and return south at the end. The reports on these parades usually noted that the participants marched through the "principle streets" in Memphis. Some make reference to the actual streets in these processions. Their primary destinations reflect the character of these parades.[58]

The parade sometimes began at the hall of one of the African American organizations. In 1868, the participants gathered at the hall of the Sons of Ham on Gayoso Street and proceeded to march through the city. The parade often ended at another destination, Court Square. In 1875, the *Memphis Daily Appeal* noted that "in and around Court Square the Negroes congregated in great numbers." Again in 1887, it was reported that "the city was crowded with colored people yesterday [4 July] and Court Square seemed to possess a special charm for them."[59] The question to be raised is what exactly was this "special charm"? Court Square undoubtedly contained a number of conscious and subconscious meanings for the African Americans who occupied this space. Court Square was a seemingly established public place for the citizens of Memphis. It was not only public but also extremely visible to both black and white residents. Public spaces represented a common ground for African Americans to reinforce their rights as American citizens in the larger white communities. The Fourth of July not only provided an opportunity to celebrate freedom, but, more important, to affirm equal rights.

Another destination was the Exposition Building, a few blocks behind Court Square, where in 1875 and 1877 the Daughters of Zion led a Fourth of July celebration. These social gatherings differ from the others in that they occurred in an enclosed space. However, the building existed as a public accommodation for the citizens of Memphis. Therefore, African Americans were still able to celebrate in the public sphere and assert their rights.[60]

Other times the parade would come to an end at the Memphis and Charleston Depot where the participants would take railroad cars to the Fair Grounds on the outskirts of the city. In 1867, the *Memphis Daily Post* reported that "a train of cars ran from the city to the picnic grounds at short intervals throughout the day, carrying immense crowds." The *Memphis Daily Appeal* noted in 1874 that the various African American societies "paraded the streets, finally hitting at the Charleston Depot, whence they were conveyed to the Fair Grounds."[61]

African Americans paraded down Main, Poplar, Second, Adams, Madison, and Union. The marches also paraded down Gayso, DeSoto, Beale, and Vance.[62] Not only would the parades march past the Beale Street Church, a large African American church constructed shortly after the Civil War, but they would also continue though established white sections of town.[63] The marchers proceeded in full public view, thus expanding the boundaries of their urban environment.

Additional celebratory events took place at parks and picnic groves in the city. The various African American societies congregated at Alexander Park, James Park, Estival Park, and Humboldt Park. Two parks, Alexander and James, were located on Vance Street in the southern part of the city, which seems to validate the conclusion that African Americans tended to congregate in socially prescribed areas. In 1869, however, the participants paraded to Mrs. Preston's grove located at the head of Court Street. While this was most likely a private area, the location of the picnic grove suggests it would have placed African Americans within reasonable visibility for the white residents of Memphis.[64]

What happened at the celebrations? Almost always the organizers would read a copy of the Declaration of Independence. Then leading citizens addressed the crowd. A particularly useful year to study is 1867, in the midst of the political battle over African American voting rights in Tennessee, when celebrations took place at two different locations in Memphis. President's Island, the location of one of the largest contraband camps in the South during the Civil War, was the site of one gathering. Edward Shaw, a leading African American politician, addressed the crowd there, claiming that the holiday was a "celebration of the freedom of America." Furthermore, African Americans "could now join in with this celebration, and would show that they were worthy of their freedom." Gen. W. J. Smith, a white Memphian and federal officer, declared that he "was glad to see them [African Americans] out to celebrate the national day of American Independence." General Smith went on to comment that "all patriotic citizens, white and black, could meet on common ground and in a common cause."[65] White newspaper reporters gave a slanted view of the day's speeches; the Memphis Daily Appeal reported that the participants were led by "radical white politicians . . . designed for grinding the political axes."[66]

Another celebration, led by the Sons of Ham and other organizations, took place at the Memphis Fair Grounds.[67] This event drew a larger crowd than the one at President's Island, probably due to the nature of the participants. President's Island's organizers were much more affluent than the majority of the African American population in Memphis. Edward Shaw, a future county commissioner; A. T. Shaw, a white law clerk; and John Harris, a black lawyer, led this gathering.[68] At the fair grounds, leadership came from the benevolent organizations.

At the 1869 event, approximately five thousand citizens attended the celebration. After the parade, leading citizens of Memphis addressed the crowd. Reverend William Murphy urged his fellow African Americans to "stand up and be worthy of our freedom." Furthermore, Reverend Murphy suggested that instead of money for lawyers and doctors they should contribute to "building churches, schoolhouse, and dwellings for themselves."[69] Edward Shaw then delivered one of the most poignant interpretations of the meaning of the Fourth of July for African Americans. Shaw suggested that the Fourth of July was an African American holiday, stating, "I claim the privileges we now enjoy came through the Declaration of 1776." Reaffirming his place within American history, Shaw related, "I believe that I am as much included in that declaration as was General Washington." Furthermore, Shaw asserted that "our duty is to show defense to the principles dear to the American people, and strive to elevate ourselves."[70]

What happened at Independence Day celebrations began to change by the mid-1870s. Affluent white residents of Memphis had been leading a charge to wrestle control away from the current city government and thus to gain control of the African American voting class. In January 1874, an Irish and African American coalition had been able to make substantial gains in the election of city officials, sparking a political movement led by Memphis' leading citizens in order to gain command of local events. The People's Protective Union, led by members of the elite, urged for the repeal of Memphis' city charter on financial terms. One aspect of this elite movement was aimed at gaining the support of African Americans through political reconciliation. In December 1874 various African American leaders designated their support for the Democratic Party, marking a further political reconciliation.[71]

The nature of this new alliance became apparent in the 1875 Independence Day celebration. In some ways, that year's celebration was business as usual. The Independent Pole-Bearers and Hezekiah Henley, an African American blacksmith, led the Fourth of July celebration. It began with a parade, including a variety of African American associations from the Sons of Ham to the Daughters of Zion. The event climaxed with a visible political gathering at the Memphis Fair Grounds with an estimated crowd of five thousand participants.[72] But at the fair grounds, the new political reality became apparent through the variety of African Americans and white Americans, including Gen. Nathan Bedford Forrest, who gave speeches. The *Memphis Daily Appeal* reported that "the Independent Pole-Bearers had invited a number of prominent Southern gentlemen," and that "there was no little anxiety as to the probable result of this meeting." Furthermore, "from the number of societies and the display made by them, it was evident that the Negroes intended making at least jollity yesterday."[73]

By 1887, African Americans had celebrated the Fourth of July in Memphis for twenty-one years. On 4 July 1887, the Independent Pole-Bearers "marched along the principle streets," but judging from newspapers, they also quietly marched out of the history of Fourth of July celebrations.[74] African Americans in Memphis did not stop celebrating Fourth of July altogether, but the nature of these celebrations changed. The long parades and large crowds disappeared, replaced by simple and small social gatherings of various members of the African American communities.[75] Two years later, in 1889, the *Memphis Daily Appeal* suddenly claimed that "patriotism among the colored citizens was no less extant than with his Caucasian brother." There was a social gathering at the African American Carfield Orphan Asylum, where "most of the colored divinities and celebrities attended and good feeling prevailed." By five more years, on 4 July 1894, the Memphis African

American recognized the national holiday by "going way off by himself" to celebrate.[76] The evidence suggests that the Fourth of July seemed to have lost that "special charm," which made prior celebrations so unique, to the social and legal dictates of Jim Crow and second-class public citizenship.

Social and political landscapes in Memphis changed markedly in the 1880s. In 1879, when Memphis lost its city charter, the political power of African Americans was diminished when the city became a taxing district of Shelby County under the auspices of the Tennessee legislature. The state government appointed various city officials and citywide elections replaced ward representation, hindering the impact of the African American vote. In 1883, the Civil Rights Act was overturned in the Supreme Court, paving the way for segregation. Finally in 1889, the state of Tennessee successfully established Jim Crow, limiting the political and social rights of African Americans. In the 1880s, there emerged in the South what has been traditionally called the "nadir" period for African Americans. In Memphis, this sense of increased hostility in the South altered the nature of these Fourth of July celebrations.[77]

Disfranchisement and Jim Crow segregation helped to pave the way for a rapid embrace of Independence Day by Memphis whites. In 1891, it was noted that "for many years after the war this legal holiday was not observed in the South, but as social bitterness engendered by that fratricidal struggle fades into forgetfulness, the observance grows more universal—and in a few years the day will be celebrated throughout the Southern land just as much as in the North."[78] Again in 1894, it was stated that the Fourth of July "seems to mean more to the South as time rolls on than it did."[79]

But for Memphis African Americans, the Fourth of July once again became a far-off promise of equality as the words of the Declaration of Independence were voiced, but proved to have little meaning, in the Jim Crow South.

We study these events in an attempt to relate meanings of patriotism and citizenship within African American communities. After the Civil War, the Fourth of July emerged as an African American holiday, demonstrating the nationalistic spirit of African Americans. Furthermore, on this national holiday African Americans revealed their American characteristics by incorporating their history into the nation's identity. African American politicians and individuals of Memphis encouraged members of their communities to demonstrate race progress by standing by the flag. Perhaps as a testament to their nationalistic spirit, the *Memphis Daily Appeal* commented that independence "has a peculiar charm, now that they are released from servile bondage, and stand free as American citizens."[80]

On the Fourth of July, African Americans were able to carve out a space for their past in American history and a place for their experience in America's destiny. That they were unsuccessful is a testament to the powers of change. However, it does not mean that African Americans ceased to reveal their American identity, only that it materialized in different forms. African Americans continued to live in search of dignity and self-respect regardless of the historical situation. The very fact that we examine African American Fourth of July celebrations separately from the larger society is a reflection of the differences imposed on them from the dominant majority. As a generation of white southerners turned away from the Fourth of July, African Americans celebrated it fervently, reinforcing their perspective of freedom, but more important, they commemorated this national holiday as Americans.

Notes

1. *Memphis Daily Appeal,* 5 July 1866, p. 5.
2. There has been a wide variety of historical literature written on the Memphis Massacre. For a sampling, see the following: Eric Foner, *Reconstruction: America's Unfinished Revolution, 1863–1877* (New York, 1988), 261–62; Walker Barrington, "'This is the White Man's Day': The Irish, White, Racial Identity, and the Memphis Riots," *Left History* 5 (Fall 1997): 31–55; Kevin R. Hardwick, "Your Old Father Abe Lincoln Is Dead and Damned: Black Soldiers and the Memphis Race Riot of 1866," *Journal of Social History* 27 (Fall 1993): 109–28; Bobby L. Lovett, "Memphis Riots: White Reaction to Blacks in Memphis, May 1865–June 1866," *Tennessee Historical Quarterly* 38 (Spring 1979): 9–33; George C. Rable, *But There Was No Peace: The Role of Violence in the Politics of Reconstruction* (Athens, Ga., 1984), 33–45; Altina L. Waller, "Community, Class and Race in Memphis Riot of 1866," in *Journal of Social History* 18 (Winter 1984): 233–46. The massacre resulted in a Joint Congressional Committee Investigation, providing the most detailed information in the record of the Thirty-ninth Congress. See 39th Cong., 1st sess., HR 101, in E. B. Washborne, chairman, *Memphis Riots and Massacres,* in the series *Mass Violence in America* (New York, 1969).
3. I approach this subject in agreement with the fact that various public rituals contain implicit and explicit meanings that broaden our understanding of the history of a particular group of people or period of time. They not only help translate the social and political landscape for historical purposes but also serve as a viable method for constructing a collective memory. Parades and public celebrations are viable tools for uncovering history. Two studies influenced my understanding of public rituals as historical evidence: Susan G. Davis, *Parades and Power: Street Theater in Nineteenth-Century Philadelphia* (Philadelphia, 1986) and Mary Ryan, "The American Parade: Representations of the Nineteenth-Century Social Order," in *The New Culture History,* ed. Lynn Hunt (Berkeley, 1989), 138, 139. Parades can be used to define the urban landscape uncovering social and political realities. See Peter Gould and Rodney White, *Mental Maps* (Middlesex, England, 1974), 34; D. W. Meinig, ed., *The Interpretation of Ordinary Landscapes: Geographical Essays* (New York, 1979), 2–6. Also, two studies in particular that discuss the use of African

American public rituals used for claiming their right to civic space. See Elsa Barkley Brown and Gregg D. Kimball, "Mapping the Terrain of Black Richmond," and Shane White, "It Was a Proud Day," in *The New African American Urban History*, ed. Kenneth W. Goings and Raymond Mohl (Thousand Oaks, Calif., 1996), 73–76, 41–42. In addition, public celebrations are useful methods for constructing the collective memory of a particular group of people. See Genevieve Fabre, "African American Commemorative Celebrations," in *History and Memory in African American Culture*, ed. Genevieve Fabre and Robert O'Meally (New York, 1994), 72–91.

4. *Memphis Daily Avalanche*, 3 Mar. 1866, p. 2.

5. Population Schedules of the 9th Census, 1870, City of Memphis, Wards 1–10. Several Sources were used to develop a historical and demographic perspective of the city of Memphis. See Kathleen C. Berkeley, "'Like a Plague of Locust': Immigration and Social Change in Memphis, Tennessee, 1850–1880" (Ph.D. diss., Univ. of California at Los Angeles, 1980), 111, 125; Gerald Capers, *The Biography of a River Tow: Its Heroic Age* (New Orleans, 1966), 107, 108, 163; William D. Miller, *Memphis During the Progressive Era, 1900–1917* (Memphis, 1957), 5–7; Armstead L. Robinson, "Plans Dat Comed from God: Institution Building and the Emergence of Black Leadership in Reconstruction Memphis," in *Toward a New South? Studies in Post–Civil War Southern Communities*, ed. Orville Vernon Burton and Robert C. McMath Jr. (Westport, Conn., 1982), 187; David M. Tucker, *Black Pastors and Leaders: Memphis, 1819–1972* (Memphis, 1975), 5–7; Howard Rabinowitz, *Race Relations in the Urban South, 1865–1900* (New York, 1978), 61.

6. Elizabeth Avery Meriwether, *Recollections of 92 Years, 1824–1916* (Nashville, 1958), 164, 167.

7. *Memphis Daily Avalanche*, 23 Jan. 1866, p. 2.

8. Ibid., 20 Mar. 1866, p. 2.

9. *Memphis Riots and Massacres*, 32; *Memphis Daily Avalanche*, 3 Jan. 1866, p. 1; 4 Jan. 1866, p. 2.

10. *Memphis Daily Appeal*, 6 July 1867, p. 3.

11. *Memphis Daily Post*, 6 July 1869, p. 1.

12. *Memphis Daily Appeal*, 5 July 1866, p. 5.

13. William B. Gravely, "The Dialectic Double Consciousness in Black American Freedom Celebrations, 1808–1863," *Journal of Negro History* 67 (Winter 1982): 303, 304; White, "It Was a Proud Day," 20–23; William Wiggins, *O Freedom: Afro-American Emancipation Celebrations* (Knoxville, 1987), xx, 26–32.

14. Frederick Douglass, *The Life and Writings of Frederick Douglass*, vol. 2, *Pre–Civil War Decade, 1850–1860* (New York, 1950), 189, 190.

15. *Memphis Daily Post*, 2 Aug. 1866; 2 Jan. 1867, p. 4.

16. In these Fourth of July celebrations dancing and singing was consistently reported. See *Memphis Daily Post*, July 1866–69; *Memphis Daily Appeal*, July 1867–87.

17. See note 28.

18. *Memphis Daily Appeal*, 6 July 1884, p. 4; *Memphis Daily Appeal*, 6 July 1882, p. 4.

19. John Cimprich, *Slavery's End in Tennessee, 1861–1865* (Tuscaloosa, Ala., 1985), 104; William G. McBride, "Blacks and the Race Issue in Tennessee Politics, 1865–1876" (Ph.D. diss., Vanderbilt Univ., 1989), 17, 118, 133; *Memphis Daily Post*, 2 Aug. 1866, p. 8.

20. *Memphis Daily Post*, 27 Feb. 1867, p. 8.

21. Fabre, "African American Commemorative Celebrations," 72–91; Gravely, "Dialectic Double Consciousness," 302–12; Benjamin Quarles, "Antebellum Free Blacks and the 'Spirit of 76,'" *Journal of Negro History* 41 (Jan. 1976): 229–42.

22. Foner, *Reconstruction*, 90, 95; Lawrence Levine, *Black Culture and Black Consciousness: Afro-American Folk Thought from Slavery to Freedom* (New York, 1977), 268 and 269; Rabinowitz, *Race Relations in the Urban South*, 140–43, 198, 199, 210. This pattern also resembled that of free black communities in the North prior to the Civil War. See Gary B. Nash, *Forging Freedom: The Formation of Philadelphia's Black Community, 1720–1840* (Cambridge, Mass., 1988), 5, 210, 259, 272, 273.

23. The Freedman's Bank was established in 1865 in Memphis but went bankrupt in 1874. Many African Americans in the community lost all of their savings, including the various mutual-aid and benevolent societies. See the Registers of Signatures of Depositions in Branches of the Freedman's Saving and Trust Company, 1865–1874, Memphis, Tennessee, National Archives, RG 101, Microfilm copies, Memphis Public Library. Some of the biographical material, relating to the members of these societies, was obtained from the deposits slips of the Freedman's Saving and Trust Company. However, in most cases the deposit slips provided the names and the various city directories supplied their occupation. *Boyle and Chapman's Memphis Directory, 1876*, Memphis Public Library; *Edwards Annual Directory to the City of Memphis* 1869, 1870, 1874, Memphis Public Library.

24. Robinson, "Plans Dat Comed from God," 47.

25. Ibid., 73, 91.

26. Kathleen Berkeley, "Colored Ladies Also Contributed," in *The Web of Southern Social Relations: Women, Family, and Education*, ed. Walter J. Fraser Jr., R. Frank Saunders Jr., and Jon L. Wakelyn (Athens, Ga., 1985), 181–203. African American women were both African Americans and women, not one or another. See Berkeley, "Colored Ladies Also Contributed," 184; Elsa Barkley Brown, "Negotiating and Transforming the Public Sphere: African American Political Life in the Transition from Slavery to Freedom," *Public Culture* 7 (Fall 1994): 107.

27. African American women were both African Americans and women, not one or another. See Berkeley, "Colored Ladies Also contributed," 184; Elsa Barkley Brown, "Negotiating and transforming the Public sphere: African American Political Life in the Transition from Slavery to Freedom," *Public Culture* 7 (Fall 1994): 107.

28. *Memphis Daily Post*, July 1866–1869; *Memphis Daily Appeal*, July 1867–1887.

29. In 1869, it was reported that the Sons of Ham would be celebrating their eleventh anniversary. See *Memphis Daily Post*, 2 July 1869, p. 4. The Sons of Ham were also influential in local politics during the early 1870s. See Tucker, *Black Pastors and Leaders*, 27.

30. *Memphis Daily Post*, 3, 5, 6 July 1866, p. 8.

31. The names and occupations of members of the Sons of Ham were obtained by cross-referencing deposit slips of the Freedman's Savings and Trust Company with city directories. See note 44. Also, the Sons of Ham and their officers were listed in the 1874 and 1876 city directories. See *Boyle and Chapman's Memphis City Directory, 1876*; *Edwards Annual Directory to the City of Memphis, 1874*.

32. *Memphis Daily Post*, 7 July 1868, p. 4. In these celebrations the Independent Pole-Bearers gradually replaced the Sons of Ham as the leaders and organizers of these events. The Sons of Ham continued to have various picnics in the city throughout the 1870s. However, no mention is made to the Sons of Ham in the 1880s.

33. *Memphis Daily Appeal*, 5 July 1874, p. 4.

34. Unlike the other African American societies, information for the Independent Pole-Bearers came solely from the Memphis city directories. See *Boyle and Chapman's Memphis Directory, 1876*; *Edwards Annual Directory to the City of Memphis, 1874*.

35. Berkeley, "Colored Ladies Also Contributed," 181, 193, 182.

36. *Memphis Daily Appeal,* 6 July 1867, p. 3; 6 July 1875, p. 1; 6 July 1875, p. 1.
37. Information on the Daughters of Zion was compiled from the Freedman's Saving and Trust Company. See the Registers of Signatures of Depositions in Branches of the Freedman's Saving and Trust Company.
38. Information on the Sisters of Zion came from the deposits slips of the Freedman's Saving and Trust Company. See note 51. However, information of the Sons of Zion came from both the Freedman's Saving and Trust Company and Memphis city directories. See note 44.
39. *Memphis Daily Post,* 7 July 1868, p. 4.
40. Ibid., 9 July 1868, p. 4.
41. *Memphis Daily Post,* 6 July 1866, p. 8; 5 July 1867, p. 8; 6 July 1869, p. 4; *Memphis Daily Appeal,* 6 July 1875, 6 July 1877, p. 1.
42. African American mutual-aid and benevolent organizations not only provided support but also were used to build a community. See Nash, *Forging Freedom,* 210.
43. *Memphis Daily Appeal,* 5 July 1872, p. 4.
44. *Memphis Daily Post,* 3 July 1866, p. 8; 6 July 1866, p. 8; *Memphis Daily Appeal,* 5 July 1879, p. 4.
45. *Memphis Daily Post,* July 1866–1869; *Memphis Daily Appeal,* July 1867–1887.
46. *Memphis Daily Post,* 2 July 1869, p. 4.
47. Davis, *Parades and Power,* 21.
48. *Memphis Daily Post,* 6 July 1866, p. 8.
49. *Memphis Daily Appeal,* 5 July 1879, p. 4; *Memphis Daily Appeal,* 5 July 1872, p. 8. These celebrations were not radically different from other nineteenth-century commemorations. Genevieve Fabre suggests that Independence Day celebrations could be used to offset white culture by creating a separate public ritual. In Memphis, African Americans also reflected contemporary festivities of the dominant society. See Fabre, "African American Commemorative Celebrations, 76, and Davis, *Parades and Power.* As African Americans embraced freedom, they did so in their own image. Joel Williamson asserts that African Americans were the "most American of Americans." Joel Williamson, *The Crucible of Race: Black-White Relations in the American South Since Emancipation* (New York, 1984), 49.
50. *Memphis Daily Post,* 5 July 1867, p. 8; 7 July 1868, p. 4; 2 July 1869, p. 4; 6 July 1869, p. 1; *Memphis Daily Appeal,* 5 July 1872; 5 July 1879, p. 4. William Wiggins notes that the American flag was a popular symbol in Emancipation Day celebrations. See Wiggins, *O Freedom,* 95.
51. In antebellum slave festivals dress was one way in which African Americans could transcend their marginal situation. In post-emancipation parades clothes became a way to designate class and status. See White, "It Was a Proud Day," 28; Brown and Kimball, "Mapping the Terrain of Black Richmond," 76; Robin D. G. Kelly, *Race Rebels: Culture, Politics, and the Black Working Class* (New York, 1994), 50.
52. *Memphis Daily Post,* 6 July 1866, p. 8; *Memphis Daily Appeal,* 5 July 1872, p. 4; 5 July 1882. The "regalia" of the participants was often mentioned is some form or fashion. See *Memphis Daily Post,* 5 July 1867, p. 8; 7 July 1868, p. 8; *Memphis Daily Appeal,* 6 July 1867, p. 3.
53. *Memphis Daily Appeal,* 6 July 1875, p. 1.
54. *Memphis Daily Post,* 7 July 1868, p. 4; 2 July 1869, p. 4.
55. Ibid.
56. Historians have noted the communal aspect of voting that included female participation. See Darlene Clark Hine and Kathleen Thompson, *A Shining Thread of Hope: The History of Black Women in America* (New York, 1998), 158–60.

57. *Memphis Daily Appeal*, 6 July 1878, p. 4.
58. Reference was made to a parade in every year except 1870, 1871, 1878, 1884, 1885, and 1886. In 1868 and 1869, the specific parade route was listed. See *Memphis Daily Post*, 3 July 1868, p. 4; 2 July 1869, p. 4.
59. *Memphis Daily Appeal*, 6 July 1875, p. 1; 5 July 1887, p. 8.
60. Ibid., 6 July 1875, p. 1; 6 July 1877, p. 1.
61. *Memphis Daily Post*, 5 July 1867, p. 8; *Memphis Daily Appeal*, 5 July 1874, p. 4.
62. Ibid.
63. Elsa Brown and Gregg Kimball have suggested African American parades proceeded past various establishments that designated Race Progress. See Brown and Kimball, "Mapping the Terrain of Black Richmond," 83.
64. *Memphis Daily Post*, 2 July 1869, p. 4.
65. Ibid., 5 July 1867, p. 8.
66. *Memphis Daily Appeal*, 6 July 1867, p. 3.
67. Ibid., 6 July 1867, p. 3; *Memphis Daily Post*, 5 July 1866, p. 8.
68. *Edwards Annual Directory to the City of Memphis*, 1870.
69. *Memphis Daily Appeal*, 6 July 1869, p. 4.
70. Ibid.
71. The Fourth of July celebration in 1875 represented a break in African American support for the Republican Party. See Berkeley, "Like a Plague of Locust," 298–355. Joseph Cartwright concludes that the reform movement initiated by the Memphis elite was, in fact, directed at limiting black political power. See Cartwright, *The Triumph of Jim Crow: Tennessee Race Relations in The 1880s* (Knoxville, 1976), 120. For a discussion on African American societies and reconciliation, see Tucker, *Black Pastors and Leaders*, 31–34. For the most in-depth analysis of this reform movement, see Lynette Boney Wrenn, *Crises and Commission Government* in *Memphis: Elite Rule in a Gilded Age City* (Knoxville, 1998).
72. *Memphis Daily Appeal*, 6 July 1874, p. 1. For information on Hezkiah Henley, see *Edwards Annual Directory to the City of Memphis*, 1874. Also, for a discussion on the celebration of 1875 in the context of politics, see Tucker, *Black Pastors and Leaders*, 32–34.
73. *Memphis Daily Appeal*, 6 July 1874, p. 1.
74. Ibid., 5 July 1887, p. 8.
75. It must be remembered that just because there was no mention of an African American Fourth of July celebration does not necessarily mean that one did not occur.
76. *Memphis Daily Appeal*, 5 July 1889, p. 4; *Memphis Commercial Appeal*, 5 July 1894, p. 5.
77. Cartwright, *Triumph of Jim Crow*, 76, 119, 120, 138, 139, 145; Foner, *Reconstruction*; Evelyn Brooks Higginbotham, *Righteous Discontent: The Woman's Movement in the Black Baptist Church* (Cambridge, Mass., 1993), 4, 5; Valeria W. Weaver, "The Failure of Civil Rights 1875–1883 and Its Repercussions," *Journal of Negro History* 54 (Oct. 1969): 368–82.
78. *Memphis Appeal Avalanche*, 4 July 1891, p. 4.
79. *Memphis Commercial Appeal*, 4 July 1894, p. 5.
80. *Memphis Daily Appeal*, 5 July 1876, p. 4.

Every Duty Incumbent upon Them

African American Women in Nineteenth-Century Memphis

Beverly G. Bond

EVERLY BOND'S INTENSIVE RESEARCH INTO THE ROLE OF GENDER IN SOUTHERN HISTORY HAS CONCENTRATED ON AFRICAN AMERICAN WOMEN in Memphis. This chapter emphasizes the central role that women played in a wide range of events and institutions, from the stability and feasibility of the free black community in the era of slavery to the creation of black churches and schools in the post–Civil War years to the fight against Jim Crow in the late nineteenth century. As her ample evidence demonstrates, "gender matters as much as race and ethnicity in social, political, and economic relationships." Bond especially sheds light on the importance of women's clubs and organizations in late-nineteenth-century Memphis. Moreover, her stories of such determined women as Ruthie Anna Maria Boyd, Ida B. Wells, Virginia Broughton, and Julia Britton Hooks show how individual women made a difference, whether the battle was to purchase freedom for a family member or demanding a stop to the senseless lynching of innocent black men. Bond documents how "African-American women created identities as freed people that challenged assumptions of their innate immorality and

degradation, emphasized protection of family and community, and stressed economic agency and assertion of
their personal and property rights."

Scholars and lay observers of nineteenth-century Memphis generally
frame their stories from an elite white male perspective.[1] African American men are cast as laborers (dock workers, draymen, or field hands), politicians (Edward Shaw), or businessmen (the Robert Churches, Sr. and Jr.).
African American women are virtually ignored. The scarcity of specific evidence on the private lives of African American women and the tendency to
generalize the African American experience may, in part, account for this
silence. However, ignoring the black female experience suggests to readers
that gender was and is insignificant to the experiences of African Americans.[2] Historians of women's history have demonstrated that this is not the
case; gender matters as much as race and ethnicity in social, political, and
economic relationships.[3]

African American women's voices enrich our understanding of life in
the rural and urban South. A closer reading of local newspapers, court proceedings, and other public records coupled with this recent scholarship
reveals that African American women played significant but unexamined
roles in nineteenth-century Memphis.

African Americans composed 17 percent of the Memphis population in
1860. Nearly 4,000 slaves and 176 free blacks lived and labored in the city
and more than half were women. Slave women were publicly and privately
bartered and bequeathed from the earliest days of Memphis settlement. They
were sold in Memphis slave markets where prices for young girls twelve to
eighteen years old ranged from six hundred to eight hundred dollars in the
1850s. Women with skills—cooks, seamstresses or nurses, for example—
commanded even higher prices.[4]

The purchase or gift of a female slave was often viewed as an investment.
Ownership of a slave woman entailed the right to control and profit from her
sexuality as well as her labor since the status of African American children
depended on the status of their mothers. Their "reproductive" labor was as
much a part of an enslaved woman's contribution to her owner's household as
her "productive" labor. Thomas Jefferson once noted, "A woman who brings
a child every two years is more profitable than the best man on the farm [for]
what she produces is an addition to capital, while his labor disappears in mere
consumption." Shelby County slaveholder Joseph Smith left his pregnant

wife and "heirs in prospect . . . [money] to be put on interest until it becomes sufficient to purchase a negro girl for the benefit of the young child in prospect." David Dunn bequeathed two four-year-old slave girls (Phillis and Fanny) to his granddaughter Mary. The enslaved children would be taken from their mothers and raised as servants to their young mistress, but Dunn's bequest also secured Phillis and Fanny's future services as producers of human resources for Mary's economic well-being.[5]

Slave families were broken up to settle estates or relieve the owner's widow or orphaned heirs of the burdens of management, to raise revenue for land purchases or other investments, to resolve personal crises in a household, or to compensate for declining agricultural production. Some investors also speculated in the market for slaves just as they did in land, cotton, or tobacco. A Memphis slave named Emily, for example, was traded three times within one year, first for seven hundred dollars' worth of land in Arkansas, then for real estate in Memphis, and finally for cash. Although her value declined slightly in the course of these transactions, her owners were assured of recovering their loss whenever she produced a child.[6]

In West Tennessee, as in other parts of the South, interracial liaisons between slave women and their white owners were not uncommon. Slave women might refuse or resist the sexual overtures of their owners, but they had no legal recourse since the rape of a slave woman was not considered a crime. Nor could African American women count on other whites, including white women, for support and protection. Nineteenth-century America was a patriarchal society in which women—black or white, slave or free— were the "property" of their fathers, husbands, or masters. It is impossible to estimate the frequency or character of interracial sexual relationships, however, historian Joshua Rothman suggests, in a recent essay on Virginia slave owners, that these relationships were "rarely secret": "Most people in the small communities that composed much of Virginia's landscape knew precisely who was engaged in such illicit sexual conduct, and they gossiped among themselves accordingly. Despite legal and cultural sanctions against such connections, however, whites almost never exposed them to open public or legal discussion, except when useful as a means of gaining personal advantage."[7]

Public discussion or recognition of interracial sexual relationships involving white men and slave or free black women appears in three different ways in Memphis. First, in contemporary or historical accounts of long-term romantic and companionate relationships between prominent white men and free black women. The wife of Memphis' first mayor, Marcus

Winchester, is alleged to have been a free woman of color (Mary Winchester); the couple had eight children before her death about 1840. The Winchesters probably married in Mary's home state of Louisiana since Tennessee state statutes prohibited such unions. Memphians were aware of the relationship, and early historians commented on Mary Winchester's "good works" and the couple's friendship with reformer Frances Wright, who lived in Shelby County off and on between 1825 and 1829, keeping her Nashoba plantation until her death in 1852. However, an 1837 city ordinance, probably directed at the Winchesters' interracial union, forced the family to move out of the city to property in the county.[8] In another instance, free woman of color Maria Mercer lived with Isaac Mercer for many years. When Mercer died in 1851, he left his property to Maria and her (or their) eight children noting that "the woman or girl Maria may select any prudent person she may think *proper* to *assist* her in the management of her property given to her and the children."[9]

A second way to publicly acknowledge an interracial sexual relationship was when white male slaveholders freed and provided financial support for particular African American women and their children. Long-term sexual liaisons between slave women and their owners may or may not have been romantic and companionate, but inequities in power and elements of force in these relationships cannot be ignored.[10] While the wills of several men do not specify the nature of their relationships with slave women, the documents suggest that more productive labor was at stake. The women and their children were freed and bequeathed money or property for support in Tennessee or to pay for migration to free states or territories. In most of these cases, there were no white wives or children involved. In his 1850 will Caesar Jones freed eighteen of his slaves and left one female slave, Matilda Mead, and her five children two thousand dollars in state stock bearing 6 percent interest. Jones's brother was to oversee this investment and provide Mead with income from the interest that accrued from the stock. When there was a white family involved, their well-being had to be considered to limit contestation of the will or community censure. For example, Zenas Mellon left sixty acres of land to his slave Frances "to live on should it be her choice or to be sold for the purpose of sending her to some free state or island." But Frances was to receive the land only after Mellon's wife Marinda died, unless Marinda decided to free the slave woman (and honor the bequest) earlier.[11]

Another way for interracial relationships to be acknowledged involved white men who were arrested for fraternizing with African American women. The men in these cases were poor or working class, outsiders or immigrants whose standing in the community placed them outside the margins of "respectability." James Richardson drew community criticism to Frances Wright's utopian community of Nashoba in rural Shelby County when he publicly announced in June 1827 that he was living with the "nearly white" Josephine Lalotte. The Nashoba community was subsequently attacked as a "brothel" where miscegenation and free love were openly practiced. This, combined with economic difficulties, led Wright to take the slaves she intended to free to Haiti and abandon the project. In another instance, John Rocco, identified as "an Italian gentleman," was fined five dollars for "promenading the streets with a colored woman . . . the same being contrary to the city ordinance."[12] While interracial sexual relationships that involved influential or powerful men could skirt state and local miscegenation laws, powerless men or outsiders with little social, political, or economic standing could expect to receive public censure for their illicit (and illegal) affairs.

In antebellum Memphis enslaved women had few legal safeguards to protect their persons, their property, their families, or their communities but through various means, they resisted reasonable demands on their labor, abuse of their children, separation from family and friends, and physical and sexual abuse. Slave women malingered at assigned tasks, sabotaged equipment or labor projects, or fought abusive owners or overseers. Cooks stole food from the kitchen to take to their own children, or, in extreme cases, poisoned their owners. Women working in the fields physically attacked overseers who tried to whip the women or their children. Women acted alone in these attacks or had the overt or covert support of other women. When the riding boss on a Somerville farm in Fayette County tried to whip one woman for working too slowly, she "tore every rag clothes he had on offen him." And when an overseer had workers dig a hole in the ground so that an overseer could whip a pregnant woman, the woman's mother told him that "if he put her daughter there in that hole she'd chop him in pieces wid her hoe. He found he had two to conquer and he let her be." Fannie Alexander, who was interviewed in the 1930s, remembered an occasion when the women working in a field attacked the overseer with their hoes and would have killed him if he had not run away. House servants also developed strategies for protecting themselves and their families. Cooks, seamstresses, weavers, or other domestic workers took their daughters with them when they worked in the owner's household either to train the girls in specialized tasks or to shield them from harder work in the fields or from sexual or physical abuse. Women also escaped or hid friends and relatives who were escaping. When eighteen-

year-old Hannah, a hired slave, ran away from her Memphis employer, her
owners expected that she was "lurking in the neighborhood of Germantown
or Holly Springs," where she probably had friends or relatives who would
help her.[13] Enslaved women perceived themselves as more than bound laborers. They were wives, mothers and daughters, and members of communities
that extended beyond the limits of their owner's households. Some also saw
the possibilities of life as free women modeled in the behavior of free women
of color.

State laws, local ordinances, fear of arrest, and exile from the state limited the social and economic activities of and interaction between slaves and
free people of color in antebellum Memphis. The small free African American population in Memphis included the freeborn sons and daughters of free
black women. Others were freed in their owner's will, purchased their own
freedom, or had their freedom purchased by family members. Free African
American women diligently pursued autonomy despite their marginality.
Most were poor, working women who lived under the constant shadow of
poverty that might force them to indenture their children or possibly drive
them back into slavery. Other more prosperous women owned property and
rented rooms to other free blacks, hired slaves, or white immigrants. Free
black women existed on the margins of the city's economy and competed
with hired slave women and working-class white women for jobs as domestic
workers, washerwomen, cooks, and nurses.

In the 1860 census, thirty-two of the forty-six free black women for whom
an occupation was given were listed as washer women or washer/ironers. Two
women combined washing with gardening or ironing, three were seamstresses, and five were servants in "bagnio" houses or brothels. Thirty-one of
the seventy-four free black households in Memphis and Shelby County in
1850 were headed by women; ten years later the number had risen to forty-
three of ninety-four households. The women in these households, as *femme
soles*, controlled their own property but lived in a social and economic environment that encouraged two-person, male-headed households. Female-
headed households had less income than those headed by free black men or
where both men and women worked; female-headed households were more
vulnerable to hard times and poverty. Free black men and women were limited to service jobs but the services men performed generally garnered higher
wages than those done by women. By 1860 the total value of the real estate
of female-headed African American households in the city was only half
that of husband-wife households. The most prosperous free black men were
skilled barbers and blacksmiths, but the most profitable women's jobs were

in the lower paying area of domestic work: cooking, washing, sewing, and nursing.[14]

The households headed by the four wealthiest free black women claimed real estate valued from $4,000 to $6,000 and personal property valued from $750 to $6,000. Only 15 percent of free black women in the entire South owned $2,000 or more in property, but four Memphis women (Martha Preston, Milly Swan, her sister Charity Swan, and Agnes Alexander) were in this income category. All four women earned some portion of their income as washerwomen. Milly Swan was a freeborn woman who worked as a farmer and washerwoman. She bought land and slaves in her own name in the 1840s and 1850s, purchased Bob Price and his daughter Harriet and several other slaves, freed and eventually married Bob, then helped him acquire land and slaves. The Prices purchased and operated a farm in rural Shelby County. The 1860 census placed the value of her personal property and real estate [after Price's death] at $12,000.[15] Ruthie Anna Maria Boyd, a hired slave who worked as a washerwoman, eventually amassed enough money to buy her freedom as well as several lots in South Memphis. When she died in 1852 she left her property to her white lawyer so that he could sell it, then purchase and free her husband and son.[16] Other free African American women operated laundries, purchased dray wagons which they either leased to other free blacks or to hired slaves, bought land and slaves (most often other family members), and participated in the African American religious congregations, Sabbath schools, and secular organizations in the city. The free black community in Memphis was small, but it was a stable community that became the basis for more extensive community building during and after the Civil War.

The African American population in Memphis rose from nearly four thousand in 1860 to over sixteen thousand by 1865. During the Civil War, thousands of slaves migrated to the city from plantations in the Mississippi Delta and found shelter in three contraband camps—Fiske, Shiloh, and President's Island—and in shantytowns in South Memphis. Union military officials who recruited soldiers from the African American men in the camps had little use for the large numbers of women who accompanied their husbands, sons, and fathers to the city. A few women found work in the army and contraband camps or in the city as cooks and domestic laborers. Many more unemployed women, however, were put to work harvesting crops on abandoned plantations on President's Island or were encouraged to return to Mississippi Delta farms. White missionary associations and church groups conducted relief work and established schools in the camps and at the Canfield Orphan's Asylum (for African American children).

Missionaries also encouraged African Americans to formalize their marriages and sometimes performed mass weddings in the contraband camps. One white missionary teacher, Lucinda Humphrey, described a "Thanksgiving Day" wedding of twenty-seven couples conducted at Camp Fiske on 20 August 1863. Men and women promised to "love and cherish" their spouses, to support them with "honorable . . . industry and energy," and "to be true to the thought of her [or him] . . . carefully avoiding improper intimacy with any other." Humphrey also noted that "many of the women were adorned with bits of ribbons in various colors. As I said before, many of these had been living together, but it is a law of the camp that all such shall be legally married. The were furnished with marriage certificates, neatly printed bearing a picture of the 'old flag.'" Military officials restricted claims for support and access to enlisted men to women who were legally married to their husbands.[17]

The dramatic population increase in Memphis encouraged entrepreneurship, community building, and freer expression of dissent among African Americans.[18] Black women became more independent, autonomous women by legitimizing their marriages, searching for and reclaiming families, abandoning dress styles and behaviors associated with slavery, and challenging whites on the streets and in the courts. White southerners, however, saw these changes as signs of African American retrogression into savagery. One newspaper noted: "Congo black, brass kettle tint and whiter hues mingle like the waters, and rush down the hill of life with more impetuosity . . . bandanas have gone into the rag-bag and are seldom seen. Fashionable Dinah's perspiring brow is no longer mapped with the 'domestic' of many hues. The finest of fabrics, fringed with the most delicate lace, and redolent of sweetest perfumes, shade her languishing eyes, and confine her corkscrew tresses. The world moves and Africa jogs apace."[19] Elizabeth Avery Meriwether, a white Memphian who returned to the city after several years behind Confederate lines, considered the "ugly, gaudily dressed negro women" and the arrogant black soldiers who refused to step off the sidewalk for white "ladies" an indication of the depths to which the city had sunk as a result of emancipation.[20]

How African American women responded to the infamous Memphis racial massacre of May 1866 also provides insight to how women were shaping their new public identities. Many of the women who testified before the commissions created to investigate the riot hoped to receive restitution for personal suffering and property losses. Their actions also indicated a refusal to accept white privilege over their bodies or their property. African American women who were robbed and/or sexually assaulted in the racial massacre refused to quietly accept the role of victim. While attacks on some women were clearly opportunistic, other women linked assaults and robberies to previous confrontations with white neighbors or the local police or to their personal and economic connections to military personnel quartered at Fort Pickering. Harriet Armour, whose husband was stationed in the fort, was alone in her small shanty when five white men broke in, robbed her, and raped her. She told military and civilian fact-finding commissions that she felt powerless to fight back and did not resist her attackers. Her husband, like other black soldiers in the fort, and her neighbors were also unable to come to her assistance. Other women were brutalized after rioters found pictures of Lincoln on their walls, blue uniforms in their closets or trunks, money they had earned from working at the fort, or possessions they were holding for men in the fort.[21] The responses of these "new women" in speaking out about their assaults probably sounded the proverbial "fire bell in the night" for white Memphians because, as historian Catherine Clinton noted, "it is difficult to fathom the fear created by a black woman fighting back. . . . Such vocal, direct black female resistance combined with the fear of male retaliation, fueled white hysteria during the post war era."[22]

African Americans assumed more responsibility for the care of the poor, sick, and elderly in their communities as the War Department and the Freedman's Bureau discontinued services in the late 1860s. Women sometimes shared housing and advised each other on saving money, opening bank accounts, starting businesses and educating children. They organized mutual-aid and self-help associations that promoted community social welfare projects and provided sick and death benefits.[23]

Women were leaders in about one-third of the black associations that were active in the city between 1866 and 1899 and churches were the "organizational base" for many of their social welfare activities.[24] Clubs like the Daughters of Zion, the Baptist Sewing Circle, the Advent Benevolent Society, and the Sons and Daughters of Canaan raised funds for religious, educational, benevolent, and social welfare work, to provide direct aid to the poor, and to support a freedman's hospital.[25]

Professional and elite women shared leadership responsibilities with unskilled working-class women, but the latter were, according to historian Kathleen Berkeley, the core of the black female community leadership and played key roles in institutional development until the late nineteenth century. Working-class seamstresses, laundresses, or domestics consistently led women's clubs during this period. Charlotte Armor, a housekeeper and Jennie Bickford whose husband was one of hundreds of African American dray men, served as president and treasures of the Daughters of Zion. Seamstress Martha Ann Ware was a member of Queen Esther's Court #8 and treasurer of a Masonic Society.[26]

These early associations were replaced by the 1890s by church missionary societies or clubs like Busy Bee or Ruth Circle in which working-class women still played important leadership roles. Professional and elite women (schoolteachers or the wives of business and professional men) were active in literary and cultural societies like the Lyceum or the Liszt-Mullard Music Club or secular and social welfare organizations like Coterie Migratory Association, the Phillis Wheatley Union, or the Orphans and Old Folks Home Club. This split in women's groups reflected the growing impact of socioeconomic class in late-nineteenth-century Memphis.

The migrations of rural blacks, devastating yellow fever epidemics, expanding business and professional opportunities for African Americans and racial segregation changed the character of the city. African Americans constituted about 30 percent of the South's urban population during this era, however, by the end of the nineteenth century African Americans were 55 percent of the population in Memphis. Black and white migrants brought rural values and life-styles, but many had little education and few skills. Their experiences with city life did not always live up to their expectations; wages were better than in the rural countryside, but the expenses of city life swallowed up the extra income. Poverty and behavior separated the rural migrants from better educated and affluent professionals and elites and, although united by race, Memphis' black communities were increasingly divided by class.

All African Americans, however, faced increasing racial segregation in the last quarter of the century. From the 1870s through the 1890s, the Tennessee legislature initiated some of the South's first Jim Crow laws with restrictions on intermarriage and provisions for segregated schools, public accommodations, and transportation.[27] African Americans responded to segregation by challenging laws or customs which seemed to take back privileges they had enjoyed since the end of slavery or by accommodating and strengthening African American institutions. By the turn of the century black churches, black-owned groceries and other businesses, schools staffed by all-black teachers and administrators, and hospitals run by black physicians suggested the presence of a substantial professional and elite class. But poor farmhands, stevedores, draymen, and domestics still made up the bulk of the city's black population.

Historians Kenneth Goings and Gerald Smith have suggested that there were three black "communities" in late-nineteenth-century Memphis: the "talented tenth" of educated, economically secure elite blacks who struggled for recognition of their social and political rights; an "accommodationist" sector of professionals who favored racial "harmony" rather than demands for inclusion or entitlement; and a migrant community who refused to accept the "place" allotted to them by white Memphians. The late-nineteenth-century migrant community was more likely than the talented tenth or the accommodationist to take personal action against racism. In many ways, migrants "planted the seeds of protest against racial injustice in the city."[28]

African American women fit well into these three categories.[29] But women also shifted their responses from resistance to deferential defiance (submissiveness masking resistance) to accommodation based on particular situations and life experiences. In the 1880s, Memphis teachers Ida B. Wells and Julia Britton Hooks provided examples of defiant resistance similar to that of some post–Civil War freedwomen. Hooks and Wells were migrants to the city—Hooks from Kentucky and Mississippi, Wells from Mississippi—but they were not part of the city's population of illiterate rural blacks.

Julia Hooks was born in Kentucky in 1852 and educated in an interracial program at Berea College. She worked as a teacher at Berea and later in Mississippi before coming to Memphis and accepting a teaching position in the public schools in 1876. During the 1870s, theaters in Memphis accommodated integrated audiences, and Hooks, like other middle-class and professional elites, attended performances in these facilities. However, Julia Hooks was arrested in 1881, charged with disorderly conduct and fined five dollars for creating "a little civil rights commotion" at a local theater. Hooks dressed in what one newspaper called her "best store clothes" and she stood patiently in line with other theatergoers waiting to buy her ticket.[30] But she "abused the ticket-seller roundly" when the he passed over her to sell tickets to white women and children, "shook her fist" at the policeman who tried to remove her and "dared him to touch her," and tried to take a seat in the section reserved for white patrons.[31] Although local newspapers described Hooks's behavior as "obstreperous, insulting and disorderly," one African American observer challenged these accounts and noted that the evidence presented in the case actually demonstrated that the policemen had assaulted Hooks.[32]

Three years later Ida B. Wells was forcibly removed from a first-class car on the Chesapeake, Ohio & Southwestern Railroad while she was traveling between her school assignment at Woodstock in rural Shelby County and her home in Memphis. Wells won her subsequent court case against the railroad company but the company appealed and the Tennessee Supreme Court

overturned the lower court's ruling.[33] Ida B. Wells began her career as a jour-
nalist as editor of a newsletter published by the Lyceum, a culture club of
local black teachers. By the end of the 1880s Wells owned and edited her
own newspaper, the *Memphis Free Speech*. In 1892, she launched an anti-
lynching campaign in her newspaper after a local lynch mob murdered three
black businessmen. The killings underlined the weakness of the idea that
proper African American "character building" would convince whites to be
more tolerant. Advocates of this strategy held that hard work, church attendance, education, temperance, and sexual abstinence before marriage—in
other words, a middle-class life-style—would improve race relations in the
city. However, as Wells noted after the 1892 lynchings, "The city of Memphis had demonstrated that neither character nor standing avails the Negro
if he dares to protect himself against the white man or become his rival. . . .
There is therefore only one thing left that we can do; save our money and
leave a town which will neither protect our lives and property, nor give us a
fair trial in the courts, but takes us out and murders us in cold blood when
accused by white persons."[34]

Wells's study of past lynching incidents concluded that few occurred
because African American men assaulted white women. Rather they were
responses to social, political, and economic challenges by African Americans. Her friends were not murdered because they attacked a white woman
but because one had opened a grocery store that competed with a neighboring white business. "Nobody in this section of the country believes the old
thread bare lie that Negro men rape white women." Wells went on to say
that "if Southern white men are not careful, they will over-reach themselves
and public sentiment will have a reaction; a conclusion will then be reached
which will be very damaging to the moral reputation of their women."[35]

Wells's critique inflamed whites, who attacked her newspaper office and
threatened her life. She decided to leave Memphis permanently. She later
noted that her newspaper, *Free Speech*, was run out of town "so that the colored people might be more easily controlled."[36] While her voice was stilled
in Memphis, Wells took her attack on lynching to national and international audiences with the publication of pamphlets on racial violence and
support of black and white women's groups. She even suggested that the
"Winchester rifle should have a place of honor in every black home and it
should be used for that protection which the law refuses to give."[37]

While Wells fled the Bluff City, other African American women stayed to
demand that laws and courts apply to whites and blacks equally. In 1894, Julia
Hooks wrote a strong but measured response to the shooting of six black men

at Kerrville in northern Shelby County. The men were arrested on charges of barn burning, waylaid by a group of white men on the way to the Memphis jail, and shot to death. In a letter published in the *Memphis Commercial Appeal* of 5 September 1894, as "An Appeal For Mercy," Hooks thanked local leaders for their antilynching responses to the Kerrville incident and noted that African Americans "wanted to remain peaceful, law-abiding, patient people here, and though we are not without our faults as human creatures we beg that protection in life, liberty and the pursuit of happiness which is guaranteed by out State's constitution, and we in our humbleness lean upon you to assist in all that will make us a good, happy and contented people. Without protection we are helpless in our land and country."

Hooks's demands for racial justice were cloaked in the rhetoric of deference to white authority. She spoke in a nonthreatening, conciliatory voice at a time when the governor and many of the "better class" of Memphis whites also criticized the murders. The newspaper editors assumed that the author of the letter was a man (Hooks signed her comments "J. A. H.") and noted that the writer's "wail from the heart" acknowledged white superiority and only asked for basic rights which "Southern white men will see to it that he has," since, in the spirit of southern chivalry, "the shield of the strong . . . [must be] thrown about the weak."[38] As with her foremothers in generations past, Hooks looked to this "better class" of white Memphians for support and protection from the lawless white working classes. The acceptability of this feminine voice suggested that only African Americans who used this tone would be admitted to interracial dialogues. African American men in Kerrville marched defiantly behind the wagons that brought the victims' bodies back to their homes. Black men also attended public meetings in Memphis on the Kerrville murders and contributed to a widows and orphans fund, but black men's voices were muted in this discourse on race. But two weeks after the publication of "An Appeal for Mercy," Julia Hooks advised Memphis black men to pay their poll taxes and vote for higher educational funding. Her deference was a vehicle for demanding African American citizenship rights.[39]

In the 1880s and 1890s African American social and cultural organizations, led by teachers and the wives of middle-class business and professional men (the social and economic "elite"), assumed more prominent positions in the community.[40] Working-class women were still active in religious clubs and benevolent societies, but their activities received less publicity in local media than those of the elite.

Virginia Broughton, the first African American woman in the South to receive a college degree from Fisk University in 1875, was a teacher and administrator in the Memphis schools for 12 years before leaving for a career as a religious activist. Broughton supported demands for stronger roles for women in Baptist congregations. She opposed interpretations of the Bible that limited the active involvement of women in churches and rejected the idea of female subservience to male authority. "Woman's ultimate allegiance" according to Virginia Broughton, was "to God, not to man."[41] Broughton has been described as "the forerunner for womanist biblical interpretation" and one of the "intellectual leaders of the cause of Black Baptist womanhood between 1880 and 1900."[42] She traveled as a Baptist missionary throughout the Mississippi Delta and organized women in Bible study groups or "Bible Bands." Bible Bands encouraged women to push for "the Bible plan of church government in the discipline of members, in supporting churches, and in preaching and teaching the gospel." They condemned intemperance, tobacco use, excessive eating and dressing, church fairs and festivals, and other "worldly amusements." This woman-centered "feminist theology" also supported black women's philanthropic and charitable work, encouraged them to become self supporting and to "value the dignity of labor," and idealized home, family, and motherhood.

Broughton further advocated the use of local newspapers to promote women's causes by bringing their ideas to a wider audience and championed cooperation between black and white women on local and national social issues.[43] Broughton supported the establishment of a women's convention within the National Baptist Convention, worked with national Baptist women's groups to establish the Training School for Girls in Washington, D.C., wrote numerous religious tracts and pamphlets, edited the Woman's Messenger, and published two books, *Women's Work, as Gleaned from the Women of the Bible* (1904), and *Twenty Year's [sic] Experience of a Missionary* (1907).[44] In the 1890s, she was active in several local women's organizations and chaired the Education Committee Negro Department of the Tennessee Centennial in 1897.

Influential women like Virginia Broughton and Julia Hooks led reform and social welfare activities in their communities. They blended a sense of shared oppression with a desire to use the moral authority of womanhood to improve conditions for African Americans. Their actions coupled an elitist critique of the values and behavior of others in their communities with the realization that neither their social and economic status nor the fact that they were women guaranteed immunity to the humiliations of Jim Crow segregation. Women were the moral centers of their households, their communities, and the race as a whole. They were the guardians of home and hearth who provided a comfortable, tension-free environment for men to return to from activities in the competitive workplace. As the primary caregivers, women nurtured, educated, and provided spiritual direction for children. Writer Lillie E. Lovinggood noted in the *Afro American Encyclopedia* (1896), "If the hand that rocks the cradle rules the world, the home is a great field for woman. The Negro race needs homes, not hovels and pens. Christian character is built most largely there . . . [and a woman's sphere is] anywhere that she can do good.[45] Virginia Broughton admonished black parents to "do their whole duty in bringing up their children, for upon this depends the future welfare of our race."[46]

Washington, D.C., educator Anna Julia Cooper described African American women as the "fundamental agency under God in the regeneration, the retraining of the race, as well as the ground work and starting point of its progress upward."[47] This vision of womanhood drew upon post–Revolutionary War ideals of "Republican motherhood" and what historian Barbara Welter identified as nineteenth-century ideals of "true womanhood." Woman's political roles in the new nation were not those of voter or officeholder. Instead, their primary responsibilities as "Republican mothers" were to train their sons for citizenship in a democracy and their daughters as future "Republican mothers." "True women" created households that were private domestic sanctuaries for men from the public world of paid labor and politics. In addition to their household and child-rearing responsibilities, "true women" were submissive to the authority of their fathers and husbands, sexually pure and circumspect in their behavior toward men, and religiously pious.[48]

In classrooms, religious congregations, and community organizations middle-class and elite black women expanded these prescribed roles to include their own racialized ideals of womanhood.[49] African American women's success or failure as "true women" reflected not just on their individual household obligations but on their roles as race women.[50] One writer noted, "No race can rise above the morals of its women, and for that reason the women of our race should be careful, and strive to do nothing that will retard our progress," and another cautioned that if African Americans were to be a "great race in this great nation of races, our women must be largely instrumental in making it so."[51]

Although Ida B. Wells questioned the reliance on "character building" in improving race relations, Julia Hooks considered "character building" the solution to racial problems. In "Duty of the Hour," an essay published in *The Afro-American Encyclopedia*, Hooks encouraged African Americans to "seek faithfully to bring to the front true womanhood that will not make any nation ashamed; honest, reliable, and industrious manhood that will not disgrace civilization. . . . Let us make it the duty of the hour to garnish with art, strengthen with acquirement, and elevate with eloquence and good character, the great and transcendent theme which commands so many true and willing votaries throughout the whole dominion of the civilized world."[52]

Hooks noted that character building prepared children for their eventual roles as voters and leaders of the "State." As such, it was too important to leave to mothers, whether they were "mothers of wealth, or the mothers of the poorer classes of children." Hooks felt that "home work" had to be supplemented in tax-supported compulsory public schools.[53] Hooks also favored the private educational and social welfare work black women took on in their churches and community organizations. While many black women continued to work in traditional women's organizations (sewing circles, church clubs, fraternal orders, and cultural and literary clubs), new associations with clearly reformist objectives—often tied to national agendas—developed in the late nineteenth century. Temperance, suffrage, maternal and child welfare, and the employment of a police matron were prominent issues tackled by African American women's clubs.

For example, Julia Hooks, Daisy Harvey, and several other women organized the Orphans and Old Folks Home Club in 1891. They held concerts and other activities to raise funds, which they used to purchase about twenty-five acres of land on Hernando Road where they built a home for orphans and elderly women.[54] The Ruth Circle, Busy Bee, and other women's groups within African American churches made similar efforts to care for destitute blacks. In 1894 Julia Hooks also established the Phillis Wheatley Union, a branch of the Woman's Loyal Union of New York. Both the national and the local unions directed their efforts at "uplifting . . . fallen humanity, regardless of race, color, or nationality, the improvement of the condition of women morally, intellectually, financially and civilly, and to assist in the elevation of the youths of the land."[55] In 1910 African American clubwomen established a branch of the National League for the Protection of Colored Women to address the needs of young female migrants. The group hired a matron to meet trains and assist women who came for short visits, to offer protection from unscrupulous employment agents and boarding house operators, and to help those seeking permanent or temporary employment. The League eventually opened a women's shelter in the city.[56]

In 1905 several African American women's organizations in the city united to form the City Federation of Colored Women's Clubs, which later affiliated with the National Association of Colored Women's Clubs. Mary

Church Terrell, daughter of Memphis businessman Robert R. Church, was NACW'S first president. Representatives of two Memphis women's organizations, Coterie Migratory Assembly and the Hooks School Association, attended the first NACW national meeting in Washington, D.C. Social service, the betterment of black women, and racial uplift—the primary goals of the NACW and its affiliated clubs—mirrored the work Memphis women had been involved in for several decades.[57]

Although women's clubs and reform activities in the city, as in the nation, remained segregated, instances existed in which individual black women interacted with white women for common goals or in which white organizations sought the support of black women in mutually beneficial programs. But historian Rosalyn Terborg-Penn suggests that segregation in women's organizations not only mirrored race relations in American society but also was a function of prevailing stereotypes of black women—the assumption of their innate immorality.[58] And writer Phyllis Marynick Palmer noted that the image of African American women as "bad" women juxtaposed with that of white women as "good" women made cooperation difficult since "white women could not free themselves from the feeling that they were better than black women; nor could they work with black women to overcome the stigma black women experienced."[59]

Local newspapers continued to portray African American women as inherently immoral and criminal. G. P. M. Turner, editor of the *Memphis Daily Scimitar,* declared in 1886 that "it is not *now* as it has been that colored women were harlots" (emphasis added). Fifteen years later a *Memphis Commercial Appeal* writer commented that "the truth of the matter is . . . the negro is corrupted at the source. When immorality is almost universal among the women of a race; its doom is sealed."[60] For white women there were few advantages to be gained by gender solidarity given these widely publicized viewpoints.

When black and white women worked together it was in separate organizations and often with very different motivations behind their seemingly common goals. Black and white women worked for women's suffrage, temperance, and local reforms like the employment of a police matron. A report presented at the suffrage meeting in Washington, D.C., in 1880 included a letter from Elizabeth Avery Meriwether concerning suffrage petition work in Memphis. She described two petitions she had prepared: one containing 130 white women's signatures and the other—solicited by a black woman identified only as Meriwether's maid—containing 110 black women's signatures. Although Grace Prescott's study of Memphis suffrage suggested that the belief black women were "more slaves of their husbands than they had ever been of white masters" motivated their petition, black women also saw political involvement as a tool for improving racial as well as gender conditions. African Americans considered male suffrage not as the opportunity for men to express their individual citizenship rights but as the communal property of black families.[61] The disfranchisement of black men was, in effect, the disfranchisement of all African Americans. In the same way, the enfranchisement of women held the potential of bringing thousands of black families back into the electorate.

National suffrage leaders who campaigned in the city in the 1890s spoke to black and white audiences, but at segregated meetings. When Susan B. Anthony and Carrie Chapman Catt visited Memphis in January 1895, they addressed white women at the Nineteenth Century Club, the Woman's Club, and the Woman's Council. They spoke to black women at a meeting of the Coterie Migratory, a women's literary and social club, and at Tabernacle Baptist church. Both meetings were open to the public, but more elite and middle-class African American women probably attended the Coterie Migratory meeting than the church gathering. Although there is no report of what Anthony and Catt said to black women at either of these meetings, it was probably not the same message they delivered to white women's groups. Newspapers reported that Anthony and Catt told white audiences that Anglo-Saxon supremacy could be achieved in the South by coupling woman suffrage with an educational requirement.[62] But four months earlier, Julia Hooks had encouraged African American women to see to it that "colored citizens of Memphis and Shelby County do their whole duty in promptly complying with the law in regard to the payment of their poll tax." Payment of the poll tax was a prerequisite for voting, which Hooks assumed black men would continue to do. She coupled this admonition with requests for a petition to the state legislature for enactment of legislation for compulsory education and larger school appropriations. Women like Julia Hooks would have seen woman suffrage as a way of advancing their own racial agenda, not guaranteeing Anglo-Saxon supremacy.[63]

African American women were also active in the temperance movement. Mrs. C. H. Phillips, wife of the pastor of Collins Chapel CME Church, was president of a local chapter of the Women's Christian Temperance Union in 1886. The following year two Memphis women represented fourteen African American temperance unions in Tennessee at the state conference of the WCTU.[64] For African American women, temperance was also linked to racial uplift, character building and the feminist theology of black Baptist women.[65] Historian Marsha Wedell's finding that "black women were organized into [temperance] unions, with the impetus coming from white women," does not take into account the strong support for temperance in the black community. In 1860 African Americans organized a "society for the benefit of destitute colored people," which fined its members for chewing tobacco and public intoxication and the Colored Temperance Organization in Memphis was established by 1866. African American women's groups also incorporated calls for temperance into their church-based clubs and mutual-aid societies.[66]

The police matron issue, like temperance, reflected race, class, and gender in the city. The most visible advocates for the appointment of a police matron were teachers or the wives of the business and professional elite, who saw the matron as a missionary to city's "unfortunate" women. As one white woman writer noted, "The hope of the world is in its women—women who live on a high plane in the clear atmosphere, possessing unselfishness, thoughtfulness, broadmindness [sic]. . . . The more depraved the woman the greater the need for her being put under the care of a pure, good woman."[67] But city administrators resisted the appointment of the matron on the grounds that most of the female prisoners in the South were African American women who would not benefit from a matron's presence and no "self-respecting" white woman would take on such a job. African American women who worked with white women on this issue were teachers and the wives of black businessmen and professionals. Julia Hooks was well received when she spoke to a meeting of the Nineteenth Century Club on the importance of this issue for all Memphis women.[68]

In the aftermath of the Civil War, African American women created identities as freed people that challenged assumptions of their innate immorality and degradation, emphasized protection of family and community, and stressed economic agency and assertion of their personal and property rights. Some women responded to racism and discrimination with individual protests and demands that society recognize basic human and civil rights. Other women built on traditions of female networking and community organization and formed mutual-aid associations and religious societies. Still others supported a feminist theology, which advocated stronger roles for women in churches. The interracial cooperation of Memphis women on issues like temperance, suffrage, and the appointment of a police matron, however, did not reflect a sisterhood that superseded race. Women's actions mirrored the racial and gender roles and relationships of nineteenth-century society. The issues that black and white women collaborated on were concerns shared by women as social housekeepers and moral guardians of their communities. The issues that divided them reflected their racial identities.

By the end of the nineteenth century, African American women in Memphis had constructed ideas of womanhood that emphasized their roles as workers, wives, mothers, and race women. Virginia Broughton captured the essence of this ideal of African American "true womanhood" in an 1895 article for the special "Woman's Edition" of the *Memphis Commercial Appeal*. Broughton declared that African American women "now realize their responsibilities as never before, and from the weight of this realization they are organizing their forces to better prepare themselves to perform, in the best manner, *every duty incumbent upon them*, from the cellar to the garret; in the home; or their lot in the church and other religious organization, and in the world" (emphasis added).[69]

Notes

1. Gerald M. Capers, *The Biography of a River Town, Memphis: Its Heroic Age* (New Orleans, 1966); James D. Davis, *The History of the City of Memphis* (Memphis, 1873); J. M. Keating, *History of the City of Memphis and Shelby County, Tennessee* (Syracuse, N.Y., 1888); William Miller, *Memphis During the Progressive Era, 1900–1917* (Memphis, 1957); J. P. Young, *Standard History of Memphis, Tennessee: From Study of the Original Sources* (Knoxville, 1912).
2. More recent works that have included analysis of African American women's roles in the city's history include Kathleen Berkeley, "'Like a Plague of Locust': Immigration and Social Change in Memphis, Tennessee 1850–1880" (Ph.D. diss., Univ. of California, Los Angeles, 1980) and "'Colored Ladies Also Contributed': Black Women's Activities from Benevolence to Social Welfare, 1866–1896," in *The Web of Southern Social Relations: Women, Family and Education*, ed. Walter Fraser Jr., R. Frank Saunders Jr., and Jon L. Wakelyn (Athens, Ga., 1985), 181–203; Miriam DeCosta-Willis, ed. *The Memphis Diary of Ida B. Wells* (Boston, 1995); Linda O. McMurry, *To Keep the Waters Troubled: The Life of Ida B. Wells* (New York, 1998).
3. Margaret Ripley Wolfe, "The Feminine Dimension in the Volunteer State," *Tennessee Historical Quarterly* 55 (Summer 1996): 112–29; Darla Brock, "'Our Hands Are at Your Service': The Story of Confederate Women in Memphis," West Tennessee Historical Society *Papers* 45 (1991): 19–34; Connie L. Lester, "'Let Us Be Up and Doing': Women in the Tennessee Movements for Agrarian Reform, 1870–1892," *Tennessee Historical Quarterly* 54 (Summer 1995): 80–97; Jane Crumpler DeFiore, "'Come and Bring the Ladies': Tennessee Women and the Politics of Opportunity During the Presidential Campaigns of 1840 and 1844," *Tennessee Historical Quarterly* 51 (Winter 1992): 197–212.
4. Robert A. Sigafoos, *Cotton Row to Beale Street: A Business History of Memphis* (Memphis, 1979), 32–33.
5. Shelby County Wills Book, vol. 1, wills of Joseph Smith (1834) and David Dunn (p. 91); Jefferson quoted in Colin A. Palmer, *Passageways: An Interpretative History of Black America*, vol. 1, *1619–1863* (Fort Worth, Tex., 1998), 102.
6. *William Brown v. William Neely*, 1867, Shelby County Quarterly Court.

7. Joshua D. Rothman, "James Callender and Social Knowledge of Interracial Sex in Antebellum Virginia," in *Sally Hemmings & Thomas Jefferson: History, Memory, and Civic Culture*, ed. by Jan Ellen Lewis and Peter S. Onuf (Charlottesville, Va., 1999), 88.

8. Davis, *History of the City of Memphis*, 31 and 73; James E. Roper, "Marcus B. Winchester, First Mayor of Memphis, His Later Years," West Tennessee Historical Society *Papers* 13 (1959): 18; James E. Roper, "Marcus Winchester and the Earliest Years of Memphis," West Tennessee Historical Society *Papers* 21 (1962): 342–50; Betty Tilly, "The Spirit of Improvement: Reformism and Slavery in West Tennessee," West Tennessee Historical Society *Papers* 28 (1974): 29.

9. Shelby County Wills, vol. 2, Isaac Mercer (1851), no. 1015; Memphis Tax Assessment Book, 1852, p. 45, Memphis and Shelby County Archives (hereafter cited as MSCA). Isaac Mercer obviously trusted Maria Mercer's judgment, however, growing animosity toward free blacks may have prompted her to sell the property and leave the city the following year. She transferred ownership of her land to Joseph Clouston, a free black man, and is not listed in any subsequent public records.

10. See Adele Logan Alexander, *Ambiguous Lives: Free Women of Color in Rural Georgia, 1789–1879* (Fayetteville, Ark., 1991); Kent Anderson Leslie, *Woman of Color, Daughter of Privilege: Amanda America Dickson, 1849–1893* (Athens, Ga., 1995).

11. See the wills of Caesar Jones, 1850 (no. 890), Thomas Lea Smith, 1851 (no. 1038), O. G. Kennedy, 1854 (no. 1380), Andrew Rembert, 1845 (Will Book 1, pp. 318–22), Shelby County Probate Court, MSCA.

12. "Nashoba," James Roper Collection, no. 156, Mississippi Valley Collection, Ned McWherter Library, Univ. of Memphis, Memphis, Tennessee; *Memphis Daily Bulletin*, 10 July 1862.

13. George P. Rawick, ed., *The American Slave: A Composite Autobiography* (Westport, Conn., 1972), 11:193 (Anna Williamson); vol. 8, pt. 1, p. 41–43 (Lucindy Allison), 30–31 (Fannie Alexander); *Memphis Weekly Eagle*, 24 Apr. 1846. See also Mary Ellen Obitko, "'Custodians of a House of Resistance': Black Women Respond to Slavery," in *Black Women in United States History*, ed. Darlene Clark Hine et al. (New York, 1990), 3:1–14, and Debra Gray White, *Ar'n't I a Woman: Female Slaves in the Plantation South* (New York, 1985), 76–83.

14. Some free black female-headed households actually included husbands who were slaves in the city or the county. In a few instances, enslaved husbands were allowed by their owners to hire their time to city residents.

15. David Tucker, *Black Pastors and Leaders: Memphis, 1819–1972* (Memphis, 1975), does not describe any specific role for women within the early black congregations until after the Civil War and even then it is primarily one of organizing groups to do fund raising or to provide social welfare services.

16. A picture of Milly Swan Price's activities can be drawn from records in the Memphis and Shelby County Archives (MSCA). See Shelby County Quarterly Court, Bob Price pay receipts , MSCA; Shelby County Probate Court, Bob Price will (no. 2081); Bob Price deed, Shelby County Deed Book 11, p. 87; Milly Swan deed, Shelby County Deed Book 23, p. 141; Tax assessments for Milly Swan, South Memphis Property Tax Assessment Book, 1847–49, and Memphis Property Tax Assessment Books, 1851–58, MSCA; Bob Price and Milly Swan, Shelby County Marriage Records, Book 1, MSCA. For information on Ruthie Anna Maria Boyd (Bayliss), see petition for emancipation (Ruthie Anna Maria Boyd), Shelby County Quarterly Court, MSCA; Ruthie Anna Maria Boyd, Will no. 1210, Shelby

County Probate Court; R. Bayliss or Rutha Bayliss estate, Memphis Property Tax Assessment Books, 1851 and 1852, MSCA.

17. Berkeley, "Like a Plague of Locust," 149–54; Lucinda Humphrey, 20 Aug. 1863, American Missionary Papers, National Archives and Records Administration, Washington, D.C.

18. Freedmen's Bureau, Subdistrict of Memphis, Rental Agent's report, 18 Aug. 1865. In July 1865, a Freedman's Bureau census of the African American population in Memphis and on nearby President's Island, where contraband camps had been established revealed that there were 16,509 blacks in those areas alone—9,735 of whom were women.

19. *Memphis Public Ledger,* 7 Sept. 1867.

20. Elizabeth Avery Meriwether, *Recollections of 92 Years, 1824–1916* (McLean, Va., 1958), 154.

21. Beverly G. Bond, "Till Fair Aurora Rise: African American Women in Memphis Tennessee, 1840–1915" (Ph.D. diss., Univ. of Memphis, 1996), 69–70, 90, 97–98.

22. Catherine Clinton, "Bloody Terrain: Freedwomen, Sexuality, and Violence During Reconstruction," in *Half Sisters of History: Southern Women and the American Past,* ed. Catherine Clinton (Durham, N.C., 1994), 144.

23. Berkeley, "Colored Ladies Also Contributed," 181–82.

24. Freedmen's Bureau, Subdistrict of Memphis, Chief Surgeon's Correspondence, J. M. Grove, 28 Aug. 1865, and A. C. Swartzwelder, 21 Nov. 1865; Berkeley, "Colored Ladies Also Contributed," 193.

25. Berkeley, "Colored Ladies Also Contributed," 181–82.

26. Ibid., 194.

27. John Hope Franklin, *From Slavery to Freedom,* 7th ed., (New York, 1994), 263; Robert E. Corlew, *Tennessee: A Short History,* 2d ed., (Knoxville, 1981), 361.

28. Ibid., 133–40.

29. Kenneth Goings and Gerald L. Smith, "'Duty of the Hour': African-American Communities in Memphis, Tennessee, 1862–1923," *Tennessee Historical Quarterly* 55 (Summer 1996): 136.

30. DeCosta-Willis, *Memphis Diary,* 40; Earnestine Jenkins, "Julia Britton Hooks," in *Black Women in America: An Historical Encyclopedia,* ed. Darlene Clark Hine, Elsa Barkley Brown, and Rosalyn Terborg-Penn (Bloomington, Ind., 1993), 572–73. Hooks became increasingly dissatisfied with the education provided for black students in the city's schools and eventually resigned her position. She opened a private kindergarten and elementary school, the Hooks Cottage School, as well as the Hooks School of Music.

31. *Memphis Commercial Appeal,* 13 Mar. 1881.

32. Ibid., 15 Mar. 1881.

33. Alfreda M. Duster, ed., *Crusader for Justice: The Autobiography of Ida B. Wells* (Chicago, 1970), 18–20.

34. Ibid., 52.

35. Jacqueline Jones Royster, ed., *Southern Horrors and Other Writings: The Anti-Lynching Campaign of Ida B. Wells, 1892–1900* (Boston, 1997), 52.

36. Ibid., 68.

37. Ibid., 70.

38. *Memphis Commercial Appeal,* 5 Sept. 1894.

39. Ibid., 22 Sept. 1894.

40. Many were recent migrants who represented what some white Memphians derisively referred to as the "imported" element in the black community. They were more likely to have been influenced by "missionary" teachers from the North or to have attended northern schools and their life-styles and values initially seemed at odds with what southern whites considered appropriate behavior for blacks. Julia Hooks, Ida B. Wells and Virginia Broughton were among the most prominent and active of these women.

41. Evelyn Brooks, "The Feminist Theology of the Black Baptist Church, 1880–1900," in *Black Women in United States History*, ed. Darlene Clark Hine et al. (Brooklyn, N.Y., 1990), 1:37.

42. Marcia Y. Riggs, *Can I Get a Witness? Prophetic Religious Voices of African American Women: An Anthology* (Maryknoll, N.Y., 1997), 31; Brooks, "Feminist Theology," 32–33.

43. Brooks, "Feminist Theology," 37–46.

44. Virginia W. Broughton, "Twenty Year's Experience of a Missionary" (1907) in *Spiritual Narratives*, ed. Sue Houchins (New York, 1988), 7–8; Brooks, "Feminist Theology," 33; Thomas O. Fuller, *History of the Negro Baptists of Tennessee* (Memphis, 1936), 81. Broughton also served on the Women's Committee for the Negro Building and exhibitions at the Tennessee Centennial of 1897.

45. James T. Haley, *Sparkling Gems of Race Knowledge Worth Knowing* (Nashville, 1897), 109.

46. Ibid., 98.

47. Anna Julia Cooper, *A Voice from the South* (New York, 1888), 28.

48. Barbara Welter, "The Cult of True Womanhood: 1820–1860," *American Quarterly* 18 (Summer 1966): 151–74.

49. Brooks, "Feminist Theology," 42.

50. Haley, *Sparkling Gems*, 181.

51. Ibid., 79 and 81.

52. Selma S. Lewis and Marjean G. Kremer, *The Angel of Beale Street: A Biography of Julia Ann Hooks* (Memphis, 1986).

53. *Memphis Commercial Appeal*, 22 Sept. 1894.

54. Jenkins, "Julia Britton Hooks," 573.

55. *Memphis Commercial Appeal*, 14 Feb. 1895; Goings and Smith, "Duty of the Hour."

56. George W. Lee, *Beale Street: Where the Blues Was Born* (New York, 1934), 62.

57. Mary Church Terrell's parents, Robert R. Church Sr. and Louisa Ayers Church, divorced when she was six years old and Mary ("Mollie") moved to New York City with her mother. She attended an integrated school connected with Antioch College in Ohio and Oberlin College Academy. After graduating from Oberlin College in 1884, Mary Church lived with her father in Memphis for a year before beginning her teaching career at Wilberforce University and later in Washington, D.C., at M Street Colored School. She married Robert H. Terrell in 1891. Although she maintained ties with her Memphis family, Mary Church Terrell lived most of her life outside the city and her activities in the African American women's club movement reflect national trends rather than specific events in Memphis. See Beverly Washington Jones, *Quest for Equality: The Life and Writings of Mary Eliza Church Terrell, 1863–1954* (Brooklyn, N.Y., 1990), 3–16, 24, and Mary Church Terrell, *A Colored Woman in a White World* (New York, 1940).

58. Rosalyn Terborg-Penn, "African-American Women and the Woman Suffrage Movement," in *One Woman, One Vote: Rediscovering the Woman Suffrage Movement*, ed. Majorie Spruill Wheeler (Troutdale, Oreg., 1995), 146.

59. Phyllis Marynick Palmer, "White Women/Black Women: The Dualism of Female Identity and Experience in the United States," *Feminist Studies* 9 (Spring 1983): 157–58.

60. *Memphis Scimitar*, 3 Dec. 1886; *Memphis Commercial Appeal*, 2 Aug. 1901; DeCosta-Willis, *Memphis Diary*, 185–86; Cynthia Neverdon-Morton, *Afro-American Women of the South and the Advancement of the Race* (Knoxville, 1989), 223.

61. Grace Elizabeth Prescott, "The Woman Suffrage Movement in Memphis: Its Place in the State, Sectional, and National Movements" (Master's thesis, Memphis State Univ., 1963), 21; Darlene Clark Hine and Kathleen Thompson, *A Shining Thread of Hope: The History of Black Women in America* (New York, 1998), 158.

62. *Memphis Commercial Appeal*, 18 Jan. 1895.

63. Terborg-Penn, "African-American Women," 138; Dorothy Salem, *To Better Our World: Black Women in Organized Reform, 1890–1920* (New York, 1990), 37–40; *Memphis Commercial Appeal*, 22 Sept. 1894. The Memphis suffrage movement declined between 1900 and 1906, and when it was revived it was dominated by women who held even more firmly to the belief that "enfranchisement of females would ensure the rule of whites."

64. Marsha Wedell, *Elite Women and the Reform Impulse in Memphis, 1875–1915* (Knoxville, 1991), 92–93.

65. Broughton, "Twenty Year's Experience," 22. Broughton included the "temperate use of all good things and total abstinence from poisons, tobacco and liquors" among the fundamental principles to "Christian development as women."

66. Wedell, *Elite Women*, 67–68; *Memphis Daily Argus*, 19 Oct. 1860.

67. *Memphis Commercial Appeal*, 14 Feb. 1895.

68. Wedell, *Elite Women*, 91–92.

69. *Memphis Commercial Appeal*, 14 Feb. 1895.

Duty of the Hour
African American Communities in Memphis, 1862–1923

Kenneth W. Goings and Gerald L. Smith

KENNETH GOINGS AND GERALD SMITH BELIEVE THAT THE NARROW FOCUS OF MANY STUDIES OF AFRICAN AMERICANS IN THE URBAN SOUTH have distorted the true nature of the black urban experience by focusing too much on the visible and vocal black middle- and upper-middle-class of professionals and merchants, the group often identified as the "talented tenth." By the beginning of the Jim Crow era in Memphis history, they found three distinct African American communities: (1) the talented tenth, who urged "racial uplift and to seek racial redress through legal channels"; (2) the accommodationists, who accepted second-class citizenship as a way of ensuring harmony between the races; and (3) the much larger migrant community, who often individually resisted attempts to keep African Americans in "their place" and provided a foundation for the development of insular black institutions and neighborhoods—crucial havens of support and safety in the Jim Crow era. The concept of three different African American approaches to white domination can carry over to other Tennessee cities and towns, meaning that the patterns found in Memphis between emancipation and the mid-1920s were present throughout the state.

Out of the three strategies, especially the willingness to resist shown by the migrant group, would emerge the Civil Rights movement of the mid-twentieth century.

On Friday evening, 21 September 1894, African American women of Memphis held a mass meeting at the Beale Street Baptist Church, the oldest African American church in the city. The purpose of this gathering was to organize a local Phyllis Wheatley Union and seek improvements in the conditions of African American women. Among those attending were six widows whose husbands had been recently lynched less than twenty miles from Memphis in what was one of the worst mass killings in the history of Tennessee. The lynchings had shaken the entire Memphis African American community; mass meetings were held in several churches for the victims' families in order to raise money on their behalf. The gathering of African American women at the Beale Street Baptist Church served as another occasion in which funds were collected for the widows of the lynchings.[1]

Julia A. Hooks, a prominent African American schoolteacher in Memphis, delivered the meeting's main address, titled "Duty of the Hour." In her presentation to the audience, Hooks solicited support for the public education of African American school children: "We women must unite on plans and means by which we may be able to deal directly with wickedness and crime rather than their causes. We must show to the tax payers this necessity, and they will agree with us. Strength and nobility of character can be secured by well-directed efforts in the schoolrooms."[2]

Hooks was praised by the *Memphis Commercial Appeal*. "She is a thoroughly educated woman," it observed, "and has done much for the uplifting of the colored race." In 1896 Hooks's essay, "Duty of the Hour," was published in the *Afro-American Encyclopedia*, where she emphasized more clearly her argument. According to Hooks, "Character building is to be considered the 'Duty of the Hour.' Some people argue that this belongs to the home, but in how many homes do we find it neglected on account of ignorance[?] Every child," continued Hooks, "has the possibilities of becoming a blessing or a curse to the State. . . . It is the duty of the State to see that her subjects grow up with noble characters. It is her fault, and she alone must bear the blame for every vicious act, for every diabolical crime done and perpetrated within her borders if she [neglects] this duty."[3]

Apparently Hooks believed, as did other African American elites, that "character building" and moral teachings would socially and economically uplift African Americans and prevent them from becoming the victims of violent crimes committed by whites. To be sure, this was a warped interpretation of the status of African Americans and the conditions they faced during the late nineteenth and early twentieth centuries. Although Hooks's suggestions received wide attention from local and national publications, they did not reflect the concerns and solutions of Memphis' entire African American population.

Hooks represented the ideals of the "talented tenth," and her beliefs were centered on assimilation as a means of gaining the equality and respect of white Memphians. But Memphis' African American population was diverse. African American leaders and their foot soldiers were not always in unison with one another on matters involving racial progress and race relations. This division was, in part, a consequence of the city's ever increasing black population. That different African Americans from different places were migrating to Memphis at different times created a complex and diverse black community. While the African American community became more diversified in its class, education, and residential tenor, black survival skills used to challenge racial violence and discrimination in Memphis became more elastic.

Due to the economic and political influence of the talented tenth on the development of African American communities in the North and South, scholars have overly concentrated on the role they played in community development. Writing in 1944, Gunnar Myrdal argued that "though the upper class is relatively small in numbers, it provides the standards and values, and symbolizes the aspirations of the Negro community; being the most articulate element in the community, its outlook and interests are often regarded as those of the community at large."[4] Basing his conclusions about African Americans in Memphis on the activities of the city's talented tenth, Lester Lamon in *Black Tennesseans, 1900–1930* claims "fear and a dulling environment held resistance in check in West Tennessee." Although Lamon acknowledges that "the firm dedication to accommodation that had characterized Tennessee's various black communities in 1900 deteriorated noticeably during the next fifteen years," his study neglects to identify the black communities on a statewide or local basis.[5] Had Lamon completely pulled back the veil to examine black Memphis, he would have found at least three communities bound by racial discrimination but differing in ideologies. The accommodationist position he writes about was simply a stand taken by one segment of the African American community.

At least three African American communities existed in Memphis between 1890 and 1920. Each represented the activities and ideologies of a particular African American group. First, there were those who composed the talented tenth. Most had secured an education, made economic investments in the city, and achieved an elite status in the community. They utilized the political and judicial systems whenever they could, but believed their duty of the hour was "character building" so that whites would have a more positive perception of all African Americans. Second, there were the accommoda-tionists, including black professionals who refused to challenge segregation and racial discrimination in the city. For them, the duty of the hour was to promote "harmony" between the races by accepting second-class citizenship for African Americans. The third community consisted of migrants who ignored attempts by the Memphis white community to keep blacks in their "place." Many of the migrants participated in individual acts of resistance to racial indignities. As their numbers increased, they established an insulated African American community surrounded by schools, churches, business neighborhoods, and social organizations that met the needs of all black Mem-phians. This was important considering the city's racial climate.[6]

Similar to other southern communities, Memphis restricted the social and political rights of African Americans after the Civil War. Whereas in 1867 the Tennessee General Assembly extended to African Americans the right to vote, it subsequently enacted legislation that systematically weak-ened the citizenship rights of African Americans. In 1870 the state's consti-tution mandated segregated public schools and outlawed interracial marriages. In 1881 the general assembly required separate railroad coaches for black and white passengers. Eight years later lawmakers passed several bills ostensibly for the purpose of electoral reform yet also designed to mini-mize the influence of the black vote in the state.[7] Still, Memphis had a thriv-ing African American population long before its northern counterparts—Chicago, New York, and Detroit. After the federal occupation of Memphis in 1862, African Americans began working assiduously to advance the condi-tion and status of their communities. Following the race riot of 1866, black Baptists and Methodists formed societies such as the Avery Chapel Building Fund and the Daughters of Zion No. 1 Building Fund to rebuild their churches. Black fraternal orders of Masons and Odd Fellows had established chapters in Memphis by the end of the 1860s. There were also several black schools, churches, and mutual-aid societies in the city by the end of Recon-struction. Additionally, in 1870, the American Missionary Association established Lemoyne Normal Institute. Within three years, 280 students were receiving instruction from the school's black and white faculty mem-bers. According to Armistead L. Robinson, in his study of black leadership in Memphis, the "evidence suggests that in Memphis the recently freed managed to survive the emancipation experience without relying either upon crime or upon agencies of public welfare."[8]

While each black fraternal organization had its own handshakes, secret passwords, and rituals, all of them assured their members that they would receive financial assistance in paying medical expenses. Yet following the race riot of 1866, divisions in the African American community became more apparent in Memphis. Elite African Americans petitioned the Freedmen's Bureau with a solution to resolve the problems that led to the riot. In their view, the newly arrived black migrants should be sent back to the countryside. According to Armistead Robinson, "The interest in reducing racial tensions within Memphis loomed larger in the calculations of these prosperous blacks than the safety and well-being of their poorer fellow blacks. Clearly, social class conflicts existed within the black community of Reconstruction Memphis."[9]

Meanwhile, elite African Americans, whose groups comprised both the talented tenth and accommodationist communities, appeared to be making significant racial progress. Between 1865 and 1890, black fraternal orders even played an important role in local politics. More than ten blacks served on the city council while several others were appointed assistant attorneys general, wharfmasters, and coal inspectors during the 1870s. Thomas Cassells and Isaac F. Norris were elected to the state legislature in 1881. Yet the influence of black fraternal orders declined as black confidence in the Republican Party withered and as whites adopted the black clergy to represent the black community.[10]

During the 1880s, the Reverend R. N. Countee, pastor of Tabernacle Missionary Baptist Church, the Reverend B. A. Imes from Second Congregational Church, and the Reverend W. A. Brinkley from the Washington Street Baptist Church led the criticism of black secret societies. Countee believed members of his congregation affiliated with these organizations should contribute to the church's treasury instead of their fraternities. Brinkley decided to oust the members of his church who refused to renounce their membership in these kinds of organizations.[11]

In 1880 Countee and Brinkley founded the Memphis Baptist and Normal Institute for West Tennessee Baptists. Members of black fraternal orders were not allowed to teach at the school, thus exacerbating the conflict that already existed between the two groups. Meanwhile, the school won considerable approval from the white community. According to historian David Tucker, "The Institute founders had shrewdly designed a curriculum which combined academic, religious, and industrial training, and therefore had a wide appeal. . . . Cooperation between the local white power elite and black ministers, for the support of Howe, as the Institute came to be called after its largest donor, would continue over the years accruing to the ministers important white contacts and greater prestige in the community."[12]

Black Memphians were divided over choosing their leaders and determining their relationship with whites. The evidence suggests they were not monolithic in their behavior and attitude toward the white community. Because it was centrally located in the mid-South, Memphis had an ever-changing black population. Consequently, most newcomers to the city were rural migrants who believed that Memphis offered an abundance of employment, educational, and housing opportunities. More than half of the persons migrating to the city were born in Mississippi, while at least one-fourth came from Arkansas, Alabama, and Louisiana.[13]

Memphis was attractive to African Americans because it offered an urban community with strong ties to a rural economy. In 1873 the Cotton Exchange was founded in the city. Factors loaned money to nearby planters and purchased their crop on the spot. The factors, in turn, sold the crop and received a commission and payment for whatever supplies or loan they had originally given to the planter. Because the Cotton Exchange was also engaged in the wholesale and retail grocery business it became the "center of trade in the Mid-South."[14]

Besides witnessing an increasing number of black migrants, Memphis experienced the arrival of white farmers from Mississippi and Tennessee who moved to the city during the 1880s and 1890s. They were, according to Gerald Capers, "a simple and virtuous country folk, but stubborn and often unlettered." In 1900, writes Capers, "Memphis presented a strange paradox— a city modern in physical aspect but rural in background, rural in prejudice, and rural in habit." Actually, noted one local historian, "Memphis was a small town with a lot of people in it."[15]

The presence of rural white migrants in Memphis created significant differences in the white community just as the presence of black migrants led to greater stratifications in the African American community. Elite whites who could utilize cheap black labor and who sought the political support of African Americans made friendly overtures to the black community while working-class whites were threatened by their presence. Yet black migrants were inspired by the opportunities urban life offered. Three black newspapers were being published in the city by the end of the 1880s: the *Memphis*

Watchman, the *Living Way*, and the *Free Speech and Headlight*. Socially, Memphis remained an exciting place for African Americans. Beale Street, in particular, was described as the "Main Street of Negro America." Both whites and blacks owned businesses on Beale Street; however, except for the Pee Wee Saloon, blacks owned enterprises from Hernando to Fourth Street. They included Charlie Carner's Movie House, Jackson's Drug Store, Smith's Café, and Gillis Brothers Hotel among others. Beale Street was where W. C. Handy popularized the blues. It was where African Americans met on the weekends to mix socially in the restaurants, saloons, and gambling dens. Because the atmosphere was clouded with crime and vice, one minister observed, "It seems that the devil left hell on a vacation, stopped over at Memphis, sat down on Beale Street and rewrote the Ten Commandments leaving the NOT out of each Commandment."[16]

Black migrants to Memphis took advantage of various employment opportunities not related to plantation labor. They worked on the levee, the steamship lines, and in the lumber industry.[17] Denied opportunities in skilled labor, some African American migrants were hired as cooks and maids and in other service occupations reserved specifically for them. By 1920, however, African Americans comprised only 39 percent of the Memphis work force. This figure was a reflection of the continued migration into the city not only of African Americans but also of whites from the fields and small towns of the region. These white migrants were moving into traditional "Negro" jobs and displacing African American workers.[18]

But the economic situation was not all bleak. African American migrants continued to provide a clientele for African American professionals and business people. Besides the growth of African American businesses, there were increases in the number of doctors, lawyers, and teachers. African Americans also owned and operated grocery stores, barber and beauty shops, saloons, funeral homes, and other businesses that served the African American community.[19]

Although there were enough economic opportunities in Memphis to continue to attract African American migrants, the problem of the color line remained an important issue during the years immediately following emancipation. For instance, Robert Church Sr. and Samuel J. Ireland, two African Americans, boarded a streetcar on Poplar Street on 16 December 1867. The conductor ordered them to stand on the platform, but they refused since a recent state law did not require separate seating for the races. After being ejected from the car by the conductor, Church and Ireland filed a complaint against him, claiming he had violated the "Common Carriers Law." It is not known how this case was resolved, but apparently Church and Ireland naïvely expected their newfound rights would be protected.[20]

As the late nineteenth and early twentieth centuries progressed, the reality of racial discrimination and racial violence created serious problems facing all segments of the African American community. Class, education, and generational differences influenced the shaping of Memphis' three African American communities. But the real passion and protest for justice was more clearly defined by the attitudes and actions of Africans Americans as they were subjected to racial inequality. The responses of the talented tenth were much different from the accommodationists and migrants.

In 1881 Julia Hooks was charged with disorderly conduct in a Memphis court when she complained about the segregation of theater seats. She was fined five dollars for the incident. Yet, in spite of this incident, Hooks maintained her philosophy devoted to "character building," which assumed that if all African Americans adopted a better character, the racial discrimination she faced would dissipate. Hooks's act of protest was not uncommon. According to historian Dorthy Sterling, "Black women with education and social standing rankled at the discriminate, legally enforced system of segregation in transportation." They believed they deserved first-class treatment when they paid first-class prices.[21]

Another incident, which received more publicity than the Hooks case, involved Ida B. Wells, a migrant to the city of Memphis who managed to achieve a notable standing in the African American community. In 1884 Wells, a young schoolteacher, challenged customary segregation on railroad cars in Tennessee. Wells had purchased a first-class train ticket in Memphis to ride to the school (at Woodstock, Shelby County) where she taught. The conductor refused to take Wells's ticket as she sat in the ladies' car, which was reserved for whites. He insisted that she sit in the smoking car (front car) and even tried to wrestle her out of her seat. But Wells fought for the seat and "fastened her teeth in the back of his hand." Determined to get Wells off the car, the conductor solicited assistance from a baggage man and finally removed her from the train.

Wells filed a lawsuit against the Chesapeake & Ohio & Southwestern Railroad Company. Her first attorney, T. F. Cassells, was black but he was bought off by the railroad company. A white attorney, Judge Greer, took over the case and won it in circuit court. According to presiding Judge J. O. Pierce, the railroad company had violated Tennessee's 1881 statute that prohibited railroads from seating blacks in second-class cars while charging first-class fare. An 1882 statute mandating equal first-class accommodations for the races had also been violated. Therefore, the court awarded Wells five hundred dollars in damages.[22]

Three years later, the Supreme Court of Tennessee reached a different conclusion. After listening to the testimony of a witness, the court was convinced there was no one smoking on the front car as Wells had claimed and that the conductor had stopped her before she entered the rear. Consequently, the lower court's decision was reversed.[23]

Although Wells lost her case, her reputation as a race leader and anti-lynching crusader was enhanced following the mob execution of three African American males in Memphis in 1892. As the coeditor of *Free Speech and Headlight,* Wells used her position to convey to the public her anger over the lynching of black men. Not only did she write about lynchings, she spoke throughout the Northeast and even traveled to England to speak out against the brutal crime.[24]

Wells's articles stirred up the black and white communities of Memphis. On 7 June 1892, the city's black and white leaders met at the Cotton Exchange Building to discuss the apparent differences in the community. The meeting had been requested by black leaders who included several attorneys, ministers, and politicians. According to the *Memphis Appeal-Avalanche,* the highlight of the evening was a paper read by the Reverend B. A. Imes, who had served as pastor of the Second Congregational Church for more than a decade. In his message before the interracial meeting, Imes wanted whites to differentiate between "law-abiding" African Americans and the "individual negro criminal" in order that the rights of the former would be protected. He did not question the dubious reasons whites chose to lynch blacks. A few weeks after the interracial meeting, Imes and about a dozen of the "most prominent & respected" African Americans in Memphis prepared a statement for the press further distancing themselves from the writings of Ida Wells: "We desire to put on record a most positive disapproval of the course pursued by Miss Ida Wells through the medium of the *New York Age,* in stirring up, from week to week, this community and wherever that paper goes, the spirit of strife over the unhappy question at issue. We see no good to come from this method of journalism on either side."[25]

Clearly, African Americans differed on issues involving race. Julia Hooks, Ida B. Wells, and B. A. Imes represented the behavior of merely one community in Memphis—the "talented tenth." They wanted blacks to have equal rights but within the constraints and approval of the white community. Hooks, Wells, and Imes were not the only members of the talented tenth community in Memphis. Josiah Settles and Benjamin F. Booth were noted attorneys in Memphis during the same period. In 1905 Settles and Booth argued the case of Mary Morrison, who refused to accept a seat on the newly established Jim Crow streetcars of Memphis. Although they lost the case in the state supreme court, their participation in the trial indicated, once again, that the talented tenth community was not rigid in its response to racial discrimination. Some were simply more outspoken than others on the race issue.[26]

One of the most successful members of the talented tenth community was Robert R. Church Jr. In 1912, at the age of twenty-six, he returned to Memphis upon the death of his wealthy father, Robert R. Church Sr. The younger Church became an active businessman and politician in the community. In 1916 he was the logical choice to replace the late Josiah T. Settles on the Republican State Executive Committee but was passed over. Working from within the party had not brought due recognition and power. Church needed an organization base; thus, in 1916 he founded the Lincoln Republican League. Challenging the party's lily-white policy, the Lincoln League ran its own slate of candidates in the 1916 local elections. Although Democrats won every office, Lincoln League candidates out-polled lily-white Republicans four to one. Church proclaimed that after the elections the league had become the "regular Republican Party."[27]

Throughout his political life in Memphis, Robert Church Jr. would have to contend with Edward Hull Crump, a southern business "progressive" origin-ally from Mississippi. Crump was elected mayor of Memphis in 1909. He quickly pushed to change the city council–mayor system of government to a commission system in which each commissioner would be elected at large. This ensured an all-white commission. One commissioner would be mayor and have veto power over any commission action. Serving as mayor from 1910 to 1916, Crump developed a political machine that would ensure his statewide political influence until the mid-1950s.[28]

The relation between Robert Church Jr. and "Boss" Crump, at least until 1932, was a symbiotic one. In 1911 Church, along with two other local African American business leaders, Bert Roddy and Harry Pace, cashiers at the Solvent Savings Bank, formed the Colored Citizens Association of Memphis. It is through this organization that they endorsed Crump and his candidates for political office. As long as African Americans voted for him and his Democratic machine locally, Crump had no objection to Church urging his supporters to vote Republican on the state and national levels. In exchange for these votes, Crump dispensed limited patronage to the African

American community. He supported the request for a black park, paved some neighborhood streets, and did not attempt to disfranchise African American voters.[29]

The African American community, through some of its leaders, remained very active in politics even under the adverse conditions of the first two decades of the twentieth century. But racial violence was a constant problem in Memphis, and the white press tended to portray African Americans in a negative light. African Americans most often appeared in the white Memphis press when they were charged with some criminal offense. The *Commercial Appeal* claimed that racial integration was a "gross absurdity" and that the United States retained black troops in order to punish white students from West Point who established a poor record.[30]

Concerned about the increased racial violence, Bert Roddy tried unsuccessfully to create a local chapter of the National Association for the Advancement of Colored People (NAACP) in 1914. It was not until three years later, following the lynching of an African American male named Ell Persons, that Memphis finally established a chapter. But not all African Americans in Memphis were pleased by the political and civil rights measures pushed by the talented tenth. Some chose to promote racial harmony in spite of resistance. As Willard Gatewood has noted in his book, *Aristocrats of Color*, "At one extreme, were those who shunned involvement in racial affairs altogether and withdrew into the safe oasis of their own making in an effort to isolate themselves from the conflict and tensions of race."[31] These persons were accommodationists who had adopted the public philosophy of Booker T. Washington.

Four very important and prominent individuals who represented the accommodationist position were Robert Church Sr., G. P. Hamilton, principal of Kortrecht High School, the Reverend Sutton E. Griggs, and the Reverend Thomas O. Fuller. Born in Holly Springs, Mississippi, in 1839, Church was the mulatto son of Capt. Charles B. Church, owner of several steamboats that traveled the Mississippi River from New Orleans to Memphis. As a young man, Robert Church worked as a steward on steamboats. After the Civil War, he invested in real estate, saloons, and hotel businesses. When Memphis was in debt and lost its charter following the yellow fever epidemics of 1878 and 1879, Church purchased the first taxing district bond. In 1890 the *Indianapolis Freeman* reported Church's wealth to be a quarter of a million dollars.[32]

The greatest manifestation of Church's wealth was the park and auditorium he built in Memphis in 1900. Located on Beale Street near Fourth and

Turley, the site offered blacks a place to hold carnivals, graduations, and conventions. The *Planters Journal* described the facilities as "one of the largest
and most profitable investments in the city. . . . It is beautifully landscaped
with walks and handsomely kept grounds with flowers which show unusual
taste in their arrangements."[33] Church was quite influential in developing
the prestigious image of the black community. In 1906 he founded the Solvent Savings Bank and Trust Company, the city's first black bank since
Reconstruction. Within four years, it was the most successful black bank in
Tennessee with $86,568 in deposits. In 1910 two black funeral home direc-
tors, H. Wayman and J. Jay Scott, opened the Fraternal Savings Bank, giving the African American community at large another symbol of growth and
development.[34]

In spite of church's wealth, the *Memphis Commercial Appeal* observed
that he had "not obtruded his affairs or his personality upon others. He has
been unostentatious and unpretending. . . . He has minded his own business."[35] The elder Church had endeared himself to the white community in
1901, when he contributed one thousand dollars toward a fund established
to defray the entertainment expenses for a reunion of the United Confederate Veterans. In making his contribution to the event, Church stated, "I
have tried to be liberal at all times and to help along this city whenever I
could but I can say that I never gave a cent in my life so cheerfully or gladly
as I gave that check to the veterans' entertainment fund." Unlike his son,
the older Church was more accommodating of the racial climate. He had
obviously put the 1867 streetcar incident behind him, ultimately capitulat-
ing to the racial etiquette of the era.

G. P. Hamilton was another accommodationist. In 1908 Hamilton published *The Bright Side of Memphis*, highlighting the various African American institutions, professionals, and business leaders in the city. Hamilton
made a point of noting in the book, "The relationship between the two races
in Memphis is as friendly and cordial as can be reasonably expected. Occasionally there may be rash and intemperate men of both races who, if not
restrained by the conservative element, would possibly try to jeopardize this
friendly relationship and cause unnecessary friction and strife; but the great
majority of both races are sincerely desirous of peace."[36]

Similar to Church and Hamilton, Sutton Griggs, pastor of the Tabernacle Baptist Church, saw positive race relations in Memphis. Griggs
worked to create an "institutional church" that would effectively work as a
social welfare agency within the African American community. The church
provided recreational activities, moral training, and employment services.

The latter two activities brought Griggs to the attention of the Memphis Chamber of Commerce, which, through its Industrial Welfare Committee, funded a large part of his activities. All were concerned about labor leaving the mid-South area. A tireless worker who preached accommodation, Griggs urged African Americans to stay in the South with their "true" friends during the great migration.[37]

The Reverend Thomas Oscar Fuller was pastor of the First Baptist Church and became principal of Howe Institute in 1902. Three years later, Fuller opposed staging a boycott of Memphis streetcars in response to the legal establishment of segregation on this form of transportation. In a letter to the *Commercial Appeal,* Fuller stressed the need for "perfect harmony and cooperation between the races."[38] It was a message assured to receive white support as well as wide publicity throughout the city. Yet despite this kind of rhetoric, it was the third and largest African American community, comprised of migrants, which would actually have the most significant influence on building black Memphis.

African American migrants came to Memphis in search of economic opportunities that would allow them to escape the rigid racial structures of the agricultural South. And, upon arriving in the city, many refused to follow the racial etiquette accepted by older African Americans and others who had become acculturated to urban life. The migrants planted the seeds of protest against racial injustice in the city. Yet, unlike the talented tenth and accommodationists, the migrants held the least prestige in Memphis. They were the least educated and had little contact with the white community. They worked in low-paying unskilled jobs, lived in shotgun-style houses, and were despised by the talented tenth and accommodationists for their uninhibited behavior. Additionally, being migrants, they experienced daily harassment from the local police, who were concerned with maintaining control over the growing African American population.

By 1900, Memphis had become the third largest city in the South. African Americans comprised 49 percent of the more than 102,000 residents living in the city and 55 percent of the 153,000 total population for Shelby County. For the next twenty years, the African American population did not drop below 37 percent in either Memphis or Shelby County.[39]

African American migration provided a constant boost to black institutional growth in Memphis. Whites complained, however, of farm or labor shortages and streetcar congestion. Because of the large number of rural migrants coming into Memphis, police officers had "orders to stop all suspicious-looking negroes and search them." The police department even hired "Negro spotters," local African Americans who could identify the city's new black residents and point them out to officers.[40]

But the extent of how far race relations had really deteriorated was evident in the newspapers. There were numerous examples of police attacks against African Americans during the second decade of the twentieth century. It was, in part, an effort to harass migrants into leaving the city. Yet the African American migrant community did not passively accept these attacks. Instead, they engaged in an interracial struggle with white Memphians. When they were insulted or physically attacked by whites, black migrants often responded with an aggression uncharacteristic of the talented tenth and the accommodationists. On a number of occasions, migrants even resorted to physical force to defend themselves.[41]

Racial contestation in Memphis was most apparent on the city's streetcars. Even though "officially" segregated, they were one of the few places where African Americans and whites came into direct and regular contact with each other. Several newspaper accounts reveal African Americans arguing with streetcar conductors and refusing to surrender their seats to whites.[42] Clearly, these people were not accommodationists or members of the talented tenth. They were part of a community whose members often engaged in individualized acts of resistance. For them, the duty of the hour was confrontation.

However, "fighting back" did not stop the attacks. On 22 May 1917, Ell Persons, a woodcutter, was lynched just outside the city limits for allegedly raping and murdering a young white girl.[43] Neither the talented tenth, nor the accommodationists, nor the migrants armed themselves to defend him. Perhaps the "communities" felt overwhelmed by the number of armed whites descending on Memphis, or perhaps they felt Persons was guilty and deserved what he got. While it is not possible to definitely know why no "community" came to his defense it is entirely possible that the explanation lies in the fact that Persons had no clear ties to any "community." Ell Persons was not a member of the talented tenth. He was an itinerant woodchopper, a migrant to the area who lived a relatively isolated existence in a woods outside of Memphis. While assertive in defending themselves and members of "their" group, the talented tenth had not shown any inclination to make a strong defense of the migrants or the poor during the late nineteenth and early twentieth centuries. Their duty of the hour was still to work for racial uplift and to seek racial redress through legal channels. The accommodationists could not, in keeping with their duty of the hour, come to his defense. To interfere with the mob would only put their lives in jeopardy and would do nothing to "foster harmonious race relations." For those migrating to Memphis, one would have thought, their duty of the hour would have included the defense of another migrant. But one must remember that in pursuing racial justice migrants had often sought individualized strategies that were not necessarily inclusive of other African Americans. Although Ell Persons was a migrant, he was clearly not one of them. And so, tragically, he was left alone as each group continued to pursue its own duty of the hour, even though no strategy was inclusive enough to guarantee racial justice in Memphis.

Notes

1. *Memphis Commercial Appeal*, 2, 6, and 22 Sept. 1894.
2. Ibid., 22 Sept. 1894.
3. Ibid., Julia A. Hooks, "Duty of the Hour," *Afro-American Encyclopedia* (Nashville, 1896), 333, 335.
4. Gunnar Myrdal, *An American Dilemma: The Negro Problem and American Democracy* (New York, 1944), 2:689–708.
5. Lester Lamon, *Black Tennesseans, 1900–1930* (Knoxville, 1977), 3, 19.
6. As of 1920, thirty-five thousand of the city's sixty-one thousand African American population lived in the southeastern section of the city, according to T. J. Woofter: "All kinds of homes from cottages to shacks were mixed together." See T. J. Woofter, *Negro Problems in Cities* (New York, 1928), 104; Charles Williams Jr., "Two Black Communities in Memphis, Tennessee: A Study in Urban Socio-Political Structure" (Ph.D. diss., Univ. of Illinois at Urbana-Champaign, 1982), 109, 114, 139–40.
7. Joseph H. Cartwright, *The Triumph of Jim Crow: Tennessee Race Relations in the 1880s* (Knoxville, 1976), 18, 104.
8. David M. Tucker, *Black Pastors and Leaders: Memphis, 1819–1972* (Memphis, 1975), passim. Three very important studies of Memphis' African American community include Kathleen Christine Berkeley, "'Like a Plague of Locust': Immigration and Social Change in Memphis, Tennessee, 1850–1880" (Ph.D. diss., Univ. of California at Los Angeles, 1980), passim; Armistead L. Robinson, "Plans Dat Comed from God: Institution Building and the Emergence of Black Leadership in Reconstruction Memphis, 1865–1880," in *Toward a New South? Studies in Post–Civil War Southern Communities*, ed. Orvil Vernon Burton and Robert C. McMath Jr. (Westport, Conn., 1982), 82; Gloria Brown Melton, "Blacks in Memphis, Tennessee, 1920–1955: A Historical Study" (Ph.D. diss., Washington State Univ., 1982), 18.
9. See Robinson, "Plans Dat Comed from God," 95. Robinson writes, "This group of entrepreneurs and artisans insisted that it was 'for the welfare of a large portion of the present colored population of this city that they should be made to go into the country where their labor is needed by the farming community.'"
10. Melton, "Blacks in Memphis," 6–7, 14–15.
11. Tucker, *Black Pastors and Leaders*, 35–37.
12. Ibid., 39.
13. David M. Tucker, *Memphis Since Crump: Bossism, Blacks and Civic Reformers, 1948–1968* (Knoxville, 1980), 14.

14. Robert A. Sigafoos, *Cotton Row to Beale Street: A Business History of Memphis* (Memphis, 1979), 67.

15. Gerald M. Capers, *The Biography of a Rivertown: Memphis, Its Heroic Age,* 2d ed. (Privately published, 1966), 207; Historian Charles Crawford as quoted in Ann Trotter, "The Memphis Business Community and Integration," in *Southern Businessmen and Desegregation,* ed. Elizabeth Jacoway and David Colburn (Baton Rouge, La., 1982), 285.

16. Fred L. Hutchins, *What Happened in Memphis* (Memphis, 1965), 44.

17. See Melton, "Blacks in Memphis"; Berkeley, "Like a Plague of Locust"; Joel Roitman, "Race Relations in Memphis, Tennessee, 1880–1905" (Master's thesis, Memphis State Univ., 1964), 71, 74, 75; David M. Tucker, "Miss Ida B. Wells and Memphis Lynching," *Phylon* 32 (Summer 1971): 113, 116.

18. Denoral Davis, "Against the Odds: Postbellum Growth and Development in a Southern Urban Black Community, 1865–1900" (Ph.D. diss., State Univ. of New York at Binghamton, 1987), 50–55.

19. Melton, "Blacks in Memphis," passim.

20. *Memphis Daily Post,* 17 Dec. 1867.

21. Hooks, "Duty of the Hour," 332–39; *Memphis Commercial Appeal,* 13 Mar. 1881.

22. Alfreda M. Duster, ed., *Crusader for Justice: The Autobiography of Ida B. Wells* (Chicago, 1970), 18–19; Mildred Thompson, "Ida B. Wells-Barnett: An Exploratory Study of An American Black Woman, 1893–1930" (Ph.D. diss., George Washington Univ., 1979), 24–26.

23. *Chesapeake, O & S.R. Company v. Wells,* Tenn. 4 SW, 85 Tenn 613, 627; Thompson, "Ida B. Wells-Barnett," 24–26.

24. Duster, *Crusader for Justice,* 58, 61–63, 66–67; Thomas C. Holt, "The Lonely Warrior: Ida B. Wells-Barnett and the Struggle for Black Leadership," in *Black Leaders of the Twentieth Century,* ed. John Hope Franklin and August Meier (Urbana, Ill., 1982), 43; Tucker, "Miss Ida B. Wells," 118–22.

25. For biographical information on Imes and his work in Memphis, see Tucker, *Black Pastors and Leaders,* 41–54, and *Memphis Appeal-Avalanche,* 8, 30 June 1892.

26. Lamon, *Black Tennesseans,* 32.

27. Ibid., 56–58.

28. Ibid., 45–46.

29. William D. Miller, *Mr. Crump of Memphis* (Baton Rouge, 1964), 103; Lamon, *Black Tennesseans,* 56–58.

30. Thomas Harrison Baker, *The Memphis Commercial Appeal* (Baton Rouge, La., 1971), 206.

31. Willard B. Gatewood, *Aristocrats of Color: The Black Elite, 1880–1920* (Bloomington, Ind., 1990), 300.

32. Annette E. Church and Roberta Church, *The Robert R. Churches of Memphis: A Father and Son Who Achieved in Spite of Race* (Ann Arbor, Mich., 1974), 5–13; Hutchins, *What Happened in Memphis,* 101.

33. Church and Church, *Robert R. Churches,* 13–15; Hutchins, *What Happened in Memphis,* 101.

34. Lamon, *Black Tennesseans,* 188–90; David M. Tucker, *Lieutenant Lee of Beale Street* (Nashville, 1971), 17.

35. *Memphis Commercial Appeal,* 30 Jan. 1901, 1.

36. G. P. Hamilton, *The Bright Side of Memphis* (Memphis, 1908), 9.

37. Randolph M. Walker, *The Metamorphosis of Sutton E. Griggs: The Transition from Black Radical to Conservative, 1913–1933* (Memphis, 1991), 26–28, 46.
38. Lamon, *Black Tennesseans*, 32.
39. Melton, "Blacks in Memphis," 21; Capers, *Biography of a Rivertown*, 207.
40. *Memphis Commercial Appeal*, 10 Aug. and 11 Nov. 1916.
41. Ibid., 6, 14 Aug., 29 Oct., 11 Nov., and 4 Dec. 1916; *Chicago Defender*, 24 Apr. 1915; Melton, "Blacks in Memphis," 21; U.S. Department of Interior, Bureau of Education, *The Public School System of Memphis, Tennessee*, Bulletin 50, 1919 (Washington, D.C., 1920), 13; U.S. Department of Commerce, Bureau of the Census, *Negroes in the United States, 1920–1932* (Washington, D.C., 1935), 3. We believe that migrants were well represented in the incidents cited above. In 1918, for example, the National Bureau of Education surveyed the parents of white and African American students in the public school system. They found that less than 2 percent of the 11,871 white parents and less than 5 percent of the 3,801 African American parents had been born in Memphis. In addition, the census shows that 53.6 percent of the African American population in Memphis was born outside Tennessee. In the state's next largest city, Nashville, only 8.4 percent were born outside Tennessee. It is very likely that migrants were heavily involved in these incidents. We have been unable up this point to trace many of the individuals involved in these altercations through the census and or police records for several reasons. The great mobility of the population during the years of this study and the rapid development of neighborhoods on the fringe of the city where migrants, at least initially, lived were not as closely tallied by census takers as the more established neighborhoods. We also have not been able to identify their birthplaces from police records because, for this time period, most have been destroyed, lost, or "misplaced." We are still searching through city and county records. Our evidence about the identity of these individuals, migrant/working class, is thus circumstantial. However, we base our assessment on several factors. Perhaps the most important factor is the description of the individuals dress and language in the newspapers. Even given the racist news reporting of the white press in Memphis, this coverage does give some indication of class background. It should be noted that during the time of this study when African American elites went out into the public they were almost universally dressed extremely well because they wanted to make sure that they would not be mistaken for "ordinary" African Americans. Also, the location of these incidents gives some indication of who was involved. While police harassment could and did affect African Americans all over the city, most of the incidents took place in the southern and southeastern parts of the city. These neighborhoods were the reception areas for the migrants. Also, increasingly over the time period of this study, the talented tenth and accommodationists were coming to an "understanding" with "Boss" Crump, while poorer African Americans were still clearly targets for police harassment and attacks. Increasingly, they were spared these assaults.
42. As for the incidents on the streetcars, we have additional but still circumstantial evidence that the individuals involved were migrants or working-class African Americans. Throughout this period, the talented tenth were removing themselves from streetcars to avoid the kinds of behavior we have described. In addition, the incidents on the streetcars generally took place on lines that ran to or through migrant and working-class neighborhoods. *Memphis Commercial Appeal*, 14 Aug., 22 Oct., and 10 Nov. 1916.
43. *Memphis Commercial Appeal*, 22 May 1917.

Race Relations and
Tennessee Centennials

Richard A. Couto

IGID SEGREGATION CODES WERE IN PLACE
THROUGHOUT THE STATE BY THE TIME OF THE
TENNESSEE CENTENNIAL EXPOSITION IN 1897.
Richard Couto, a political scientist, takes that event to
look at race relations in turn-of-the-century Tennessee.
He reviews the disfranchisement laws that ended most
African American participation in the state's politics by
such capable leaders as James Napier and Samuel McElwee
and evaluates the response to that diminished citizenship
voiced by different individuals in the black community.
Of special interest is his comparison of the centennial
period speeches of the Alabama educator W. H. Councill,
nationally prominent leader Booker T. Washington, and
John Hope, then a professor at Roger Williams College in
Nashville. Hope's impassioned question—"Why build a
wall to keep me out?"—met with no answer then, and for
decades to come. Couto ends with a provocative conclusion, frankly asking, Were the 1990s—a decade of church
burnings and judicial reverses—so different from the
1890s? "Looking at the past," Couto gently reminds us,
"may provide a better view of our present that affects the
actions we take to shape our future."

I began to wonder how one recognizes history and one's role in making it
when I was completing a previous book. My research required that I study

in considerable detail race-related events in the 1890s, including Tennessee's first centennial celebration. I acquainted myself with the people of that decade and realized that they pursued, protested, or propitiated the erosion of the democratic rights and constitutional guarantees of African Americans established in the 1860s and 1870s. I wondered if they knew the significance of what they were doing and the profound impact their actions would have for most of the next century. I wondered if I would have had any sense of the importance of the events of that decade and if I understood the importance of the 1990s, my own decade.

Centennials prompt such questions and ruminations. We look back to see how we got here. We look at the lives of others to understand how people like us handled situations similar to ours. The latter view provides us a glimpse into human beings as history makers, people with choices that influence the history that follows. The second centennial of Tennessee offers a chance to look back at the events, ideas, and choices of the past. It also offers us the chance to look at modern events and ideas and the choices that they present to us for the history that we will make. The 1990s was a dramatic decade of decision making about race relations in Tennessee and America, no less than the 1890s decade was. As students of history, we can recognize the significance of the 1890s. As makers of history, we establish the future significance of our own time, in part by what we make of the present as well as the past.

Getting Along Pleasantly and Peaceably: White and Black People of the South

At the time of its first centennial, Tennessee, like the rest of America, was revising laws and policies regarding race relations. The legal forms of segregation, quasi-legal forms of restrictions on civil rights, and extralegal forms of subordination and violence replaced radical democratic reforms of the 1860s that enfranchised freedmen, established free public education for all children and established the civil rights of African Americans. Nationally, lynching reached record highs in the 1890s. In Tennessee about ten African American men were lynched annually during that decade. Additional laws permitted separate but equal facilities but ignored the gross disparities between the facilities for one race and the other. Throughout the South, new laws restricted the access of African American men to the ballot and then to the registration rolls.

Tennesseans participated in this disfranchisement. Registration laws and a poll tax got most African American voters off the rolls and saw to it that they could not get back on. Other laws invalidated the ballots of most of the remaining African American voters. Over the course of a decade, African American influence at the polls disappeared, the total number of voters dwindled, and the all-white Democratic Party dominated Tennessee politics.[1] These Tennessee efforts on racial restrictions got a boost at the national level. In 1896 the U.S. Supreme Court decided that "separate but equal" provisions for racially segregated facilities did not violate the federal constitution and extended this doctrine to public schools. Its decision in *Plessy v. Ferguson* formally inaugurated the Jim Crow era.

As the U.S. Supreme Court deliberated on that case, the Negro Department of the Tennessee Centennial Exposition dealt with racial policy restrictions and a low tide of African American expectations. Its work expressed eloquently the new spirit of race relations of the times. The Spanish Renaissance architecture of the Negro Building exhibited the contemporary absorption with Spain and its empire. Within a year of the exposition's start, America would be at war with Spain and, in six months, it would put on Spain's faded mantle of empire. In doing so, the country also accepted southern views on the necessity and appropriateness of recognizing differences among races. This meant the superiority of the white race and the requirement that white people accept the subordination of people of other races and wait with patience as these people acquired the education and prosperity to govern themselves. The colonial experience of the United States exported the justification of racial repression, prevalent in the South in the 1890s, across the oceans to Cuba, the Philippine Islands, and Puerto Rico.[2]

The Negro Building of the Tennessee Centennial Exposition offered white southerners an opportunity to explain the racial repression of African Americans in the South to white northerners. According to the official history of the exposition, "The South has been misunderstood and grossly misrepresented, and it therefore hoped that investigation will do what argument has failed to accomplish." The Negro Building offered whites from the North the opportunity to investigate how "the white race in the South has shown its friendliness by affording the negro race a splendid opportunity to show what they can do, and they will rejoice to find that the opportunity has been wisely and magnificently improved." The accomplishments of African Americans, displayed in the three hundred exhibits in the Negro Building, rebutted northerners who "so often accused Southerners of a lack of consideration for the negro." On a more positive note, the exhibit, according to the official history of the centennial, demonstrated that "the white and black people of the South understand each other perfectly and do, if left to themselves, get along as pleasantly and peaceably as any two races that ever dwelt together in any other country or in any other age."[3]

Determined Reaction and Defeated Republicans

The planning of the Negro Department's exhibit involved prominent African American men, whose sinking political fortunes exemplified changes in American and Tennessee race relations that belied the official historical account. James C. Napier, among the most prominent African American Republicans in Nashville during his lifetime, initially chaired the executive committee of the Negro Department of the centennial management. He had been an agent for the Freedmen's Bureau and a regular participant of the Conventions of Colored Men in the 1860s and 1870s. He testified before Congress in 1870 on the atrocities of the Ku Klux Klan. He held federal appointments from Reconstruction to 1884. In 1896 he bucked the white tide in the Republican Party; he ran for Congress and lost. At the end of the century, he became closely associated with Booker T. Washington and headed Washington's National Business League.[4]

This league provided Washington's answer to other efforts to organize the African American middle and professional classes that eventually resulted in the formation of the National Association for the Advancement of Colored People (NAACP). Napier's marriage tied him to the family of James M. Langston, and Napier's political fortunes reflected those of his father-in-law. Langston had a brilliant career. He was born to a slave mother and her white master. In his will, Langston's father freed all his slaves and provided for their move from Virginia to Ohio. Educated at Oberlin College, which produced several abolitionist leaders, Langston served as the general inspector of education for the Freedmen's Bureau from 1867 to 1870. In October 1868 Langston assumed responsibilities as dean of the newly formed law department of Howard University in Washington, D.C. He left that position when President Benjamin Harrison appointed him minister to Haiti, a foreign service position reserved for African Americans. Next, Langston assumed the presidency of Virginia Normal and Collegiate Institute, now Virginia State University, in Petersburg, Virginia.

In 1888, amid very turbulent times, Langston entered politics. The Democratic Party of Virginia gained ascendancy over the Republicans in the mid-1880s. Race was key to their triumph. African American men had provided the Republican Party its strength since the 1860s, but by the mid-1880s, election changes, which lowered the number of African American registrants, meant that Republicans could muster majorities only in places with solid majorities of African American residents. Petersburg, in Virginia's Fourth Congressional District, was one of them. In 1888 Langston ran for the seat of this district. He faced a Democratic opponent, naturally, but he also faced efforts in the Republican Party to push prominent African American leaders, such as he was, into less visible roles. The lily-white Republican movement of Virginia and elsewhere attempted to win over Democrats and hold on to the diminishing number of African American voters who had little reason to support the Democratic Party in the South. The election outcome was disputed. State officials of the all-white Democratic Party certified the Democratic candidate as the victor. Congressional committees, with Republican majorities, certified Langston the winner, and he eventually took the seat late in the first session of the Fifty-first Congress. Every Democratic member in the House of Representatives left the chamber as he was sworn in. Langston's 1890 reelection was contested as well, but this time he did not fight for his seat. Democrats controlled the House after the 1890 election, and Langston had no chance of prevailing in a Democratic-controlled House on an appeal of the certification of a Democrat's victory by the state Democratic administration. In 1892, Langston refused the Republican nomination for the Fourth Congressional seat and bowed to the changed circumstances that made it impossible for an African American to win in the face of inter- and intraparty opposition.[5]

James Napier's unsuccessful bid for Congress in 1896 simply indicated that the changes Langston faced in Virginia prevailed in Tennessee by that time. Napier's reputation in Tennessee grew enormously because of his relation to Langston. However, as African Americans, both men faced dwindling political opportunities. White political leaders had found ways to stymie the election of black candidates even in districts with a majority of black residents.

Samuel McElwee, more than Napier, indicated the change in political climate as Tennessee approached the centennial anniversary of its statehood. Much younger than either Langston or Napier, McElwee was educated in the schools of the Freedmen's Bureau that Langston and Napier administered. McElwee attended Oberlin briefly and then Fisk University in Nashville. He earned his degree at Fisk while serving in the Tennessee General Assembly, having been elected in 1882 at the age of twenty-two to represent Haywood County. In 1888 violence and fraud interrupted his electoral bid for a fourth term. Shortly after returning to Haywood County from the August National Republican Convention, McElwee faced armed groups of white men who saw to it that candidates of the all-white "citizens ticket" won the primary elections. These armed bands roved Haywood County intimidating African American voters, just as the Ku Klux Klan had done twenty years before. On election day in November, men with rifles again roamed through the county. They stood by ballot boxes and places where ballots were counted "to squelch any inclinations among the defeated Republicans [such as McElwee] to rise."[6]

After 1888, the Democratic Party consolidated its grip on state government and Republicans in Tennessee began a lily-white movement giving McElwee few political opportunities. The general assembly that met in 1889 began the systematic disfranchisement of African American voters in the state. Haywood County soon felt little influence from its African American residents at the polls. The duly elected officials at the state and local level had instituted laws and practices that legalized the restrictions on African American voting that terror and fraud had achieved. The latter would no longer mar the electoral process, but no African American would go to the Tennessee General Assembly until the 1960s. No African American would succeed McElwee from rural West Tennessee. With his political base in Tennessee eroded, McElwee turned to Washington and sought the Haitian diplomatic appointment from the Harrison administration. That post, however, went to Frederick Douglass. Left with few political options, McElwee turned to law practice in Nashville and joined with prominent local African Americans of his time, such as James Napier.

We Are Now on Trial: The First Centennial

McElwee served with Napier on the original committee of the Negro Department of the Centennial Exposition. McElwee had considerable experience with such exhibitions. He had served on a committee for the New Orleans Exposition in 1885 and had been active in promoting fairs for African Americans during his time in the general assembly. McElwee served on the executive committee of the Negro Department for a while but apparently dropped his participation before the Negro Building at the exposition opened. There is no mention of him among the committee members at any of the major events at the building. He withdrew several months after Napier resigned as chairman of the executive committee.

The reasons for the McElwee and Napier withdrawals are lost in unrecorded history—as is much of the history of race relations.[7] Undoubtedly, they had to deal with the ambiguity of cooperating in a display of African American pride arranged by white officials in separate events and buildings for African Americans. Some prominent African American leaders totally discouraged participation in expositions of this type anywhere. For example, Ida B. Wells, a one-time Memphis newspaperwoman and now a national columnist and antilynching advocate, had opposed African American participation at the Columbian Exposition (also known as the World's Fair) in Chicago in 1893. She contrasted the funds needed to stop lynchings with the funds requested to defray the expense of a most comfortable day of praise at the Chicago World's Fair, 17 August, to be known as "Afro American Jubilee Day." She added, "Even if the condition of our race was not so serious in this country, the whole thing is lacking in dignity, self-respect and judgment to say nothing of good taste." She found the idea especially appalling at a time which coincided with the first anniversary of a Memphis riot in which three African American male—her friends—were killed in "one of the most diabolical lynchings in the country. . . . The idea of a separate day at the fair in which the race is to pace before the world in an attitude of worship and supplication, is a mockery on its face."[8]

In her opposition to Negro Day in Chicago, she differed with Frederick Douglass, who showed her how to use such a token event as a platform. He gave a speech that day that articulated the alienation of the African American. It protested the reconciliation of northern and southern whites that came at the expense of excluding African Americans from American life in general and the Columbian Fair in particular.[9]

Unlike Douglass, some Tennessee African Americans interpreted their overall inequality as a challenge to themselves rather than the nation. Unlike Wells, these same African Americans took pride in the quality of arrangements for the centennial. In Nashville the Negro Bureau leaders stressed the symbolic significance of the Negro Building that was much more than a day "to pace before the world." Richard Hill, chairman of the executive committee of the Negro Department of the Centennial Exposition, explained at the cornerstone ceremony:

> We are now on trial—the most severe test as to what we have done, and are now doing, since our emancipation. The American people have spent no small amount of money and energy for our intellectual and moral training. Many are now asking, "What has it all amounted to?" . . . Now is the time to prove all this. The managers of the Tennessee Centennial have given us, at a cost of nearly $13,000, the most beautiful building on the grounds (250' x 100', three stories), and have placed it on the prettiest site. The Southern railroads have generously offered to bring our exhibits and return them free of charge. *They have also granted us equal railroad accommodations.* In fact, everything that could

be done for us has been done, except to make the exhibits. Our duty, then, is plain. If we fail to do it, it will be to our everlasting shame.[10]

By all accounts, the organizers of the Negro Building and exhibit passed their trial by gratitude. June 5, 1897, was Negro Day at the Tennessee Centennial. It prompted close inspection of the exhibits, which won approval from the press and other visitors. The *Nashville American,* in the strange style of speaking of African Americans as if they were not privy to newspaper coverage, reported that the opening parade "was not only the longest and the most imposing colored parade ever seen in Nashville, but it was unquestionably composed of the best elements of the Negro race that Tennessee could produce."[11] The parade had its curious and ironic elements. African American workers from the Nashville, Chattanooga, and St. Louis Railroad carried a banner "thoughtful and courteous" toward their employer: "We are never refused a reasonable request."[12] When 100 African American veterans of the Grand Army of the Republic reached the Negro Building, they were greeted with the strains of "Dixie." A delegation from New York reported that "this Negro building stood out prominently as a tangible evidence of the possibilities of freedom and opportunity and of the inherent ability of the Negro to rise to the importance and dignity of American citizenship."[13] The white organizers of the centennial displayed their beneficence by reducing admission prices on Negro Day to twenty-five cents for adults and ten cents for children. This permitted record crowds of African Americans to attend.

Follow the Advice These Orators Have Given You

The ceremonies at the Negro Building rewrote the common history of white and black Tennesseans into a history of "us" and "you." Speaker after speaker at programs in the Negro Building portrayed the efforts of the past to provide for the political participation of African Americans as mistakes. In place of politics, African Americans had the opportunity to prove themselves worthy of the esteem of Anglo-Saxons and the benefits of that esteem. The official history of the exposition explained the disfranchisement of African Americans as a positive step toward reducing the confusion of the black race. Without the vote, the average African American could concentrate on hard work at low wages, rather than politics, as the surest means of improvement.[14] Several African American speakers who appeared at the Negro Building during the exposition underscored this message of white southerners to white northerners and of Tennessee whites to Tennessee blacks. Professor W. H.

Councill, principal of the Agricultural and Mechanical College for Negroes in Normal, Alabama, spoke at the opening ceremony on 5 June 1897. His school was one of the seventeen land grant colleges established for African Americans. Councill spoke of an educational system that taught obedience and dignity even in the face of oppression:

> This kind of higher industrial education is the only kind he [the Negro] needs now and is essential to his salvation. . . . Teach obedience to law, obedience to legally constituted authority, which alone can give protection to life and property and security to society. Teach him that the human mind can form no loftier ideal than that of triumph of right through the supremacy of the law; that no one who violates the humblest law of the land can be an ideal man. . . . Teach him that men and races grow from within; *that congressional enactments can not make us a race. The race must make itself.* Teach him that he belongs to a glorious race, which stands before its God with its hands unstained by human blood. . . . Teach him that it is better to be persecuted than to persecute. . . . Teach him that man, that race, is superior which does superior things to lift mankind to superior conditions. Teach him that it is the superior man, the superior race, which does the most for its country, fights most nobly for man, and lives closest to God."[15]

Councill's new creed of self-improvement before political improvement had wide acceptance among former white political allies and even some African Americans. George F. Hoar, U.S. senator from Massachusetts, helped establish the Free-Soil Party and represented the abolitionist tradition in the Republican Party. As a remnant of that tradition, he also eschewed politics. Speaking to the law class of Howard University in 1894 on "The Opportunity of the Colored Leader," Hoar spoke as an elder statesman on race relations. He told the new attorneys that "the solution of what is called the negro question in this country is to be found in the strength, purity, courage, and loftiness of the individual soul."[16] He was not disappointed in the reversal of policies and law because improvement for African Americans "must come, not by virtue of any laws, but by their own virtue."[17] Paradoxically, Hoar, a political leader, deflated the importance of politics. "The political conduct of the colored man," he noted, "is of far less importance at the present time than that personal conduct by which he is to manifest his personal worth among his neighbors and associates."[18] Hoar recounted that some Republicans had challenged him on this position. One Republican from Massachusetts, Hoar recalled, pointed out the problems of African Americans to gain admission to training and employment in the higher professions, such as the law, and their inability to get a fair reward for their efforts in politics or in employment. Hoar rejoined his critic with "the first great lesson of American life. . . . The words 'obstacle' and 'opportunity' mean exactly the same thing."[19]

Councill pushed Hoar's views further in his remarks on Negro Day at the Tennessee Centennial. He found opportunity even in the obstacles of slavery. Councill pointed to slavery as a time of oppression by Caucasians but gains for African Americans. "We received much more from slavery than did the slave-holder."[20] Councill did allow there was a Caucasian problem, however: "In view of what the negro has done for this country, in view of what the white man has done for the negro, will the white man continue and enlarge the work of encouragement to the struggling race; or will he use the shotgun instead of the Holy Bible; the bloody knife instead of the spelling-book? These are problems for Caucasian brains."[21]

Swept up by the emotions of the dedication of the Negro Building and the opportunities within restrictions that Councill and others had described, J. W. Thomas, president of the exposition management, passed up his opportunity to add to the oratory of the day. He simply underscored the wisdom of setting aside politics for individual efforts for improvement: "If you will follow the advice which these orators have given you, you will make more material progress in the next five years than you have made in the last thirty. I address you as fellow citizens for though the colored race may have a different complexion and differ in intellectual attainments from the white race, we are still fellow-citizens of one great nation under one great flag. As President of the Centennial Company I welcome you to these grounds and to the Exposition. It is as much yours as ours."[22]

Prologue and Protest of the New Freedom of Jim Crow

Councill was only a precursor to the major proponent of industrial education for African Americans, Booker T. Washington. Washington came to Nashville and the Negro Building in August 1897 to commemorate Emancipation Day. He repeated the themes of a famous speech he gave two years earlier at the Cotton Exposition in Atlanta. At that exposition, he urged African Americans to accept their situation and to "cast down your bucket where you are."[23] Washington's prominence came in large measure from the popularity of his views among white people, who listened to him selectively. They heard that political efforts of the past were mistaken, so their past repression and present restrictions were perhaps justified. They heard that slavery had positive features that could contribute to solving problems of the day. Finally, Washington's white audiences could hear that the economic progress of African Americans awaited their own effort and their civil rights awaited their economic progress. There remained nothing for white people to do but to be kind to African Americans as the latter made efforts to reduce racial inequality on their own. Washington found immense financial reward for his views from white philanthropists, who supported his educational efforts at Tuskegee Institute and related programs.

Washington, without doubt, voiced the predominant views on race for his times, but not everyone, white or black, agreed with him. One African American who criticized Washington was John Hope, a faculty member at Roger Williams College in Nashville. Later, Hope would become president of Morehouse College in Atlanta, a school that went far beyond industrial education for African Americans. On Washington's birthday in 1896, at a time midway between the Atlanta and Tennessee expositions, Hope addressed the Negro Debating Society of Nashville with a rebuttal of Washington's position of racial equality:

> If we are not striving for equality, in heaven's name for what are we living? I regard it cowardly and dishonest for any of our colored men to tell white people or colored people that we are not struggling for equality. If money, education, and honesty will not bring to me as much privilege, as much equality as they bring to any American citizen, then they are to me a curse, and not a blessing. God forbid that we should get the implements with which to fashion our freedom, and then be too lazy or pusillanimous to fashion it. Let us not fool ourselves nor be fooled by others. If we cannot do what other free men do, then we are not free. Yes, my friends, I want equality. Nothing less. I want all that my God-given powers will enable me to get, then why not equality? Now, catch your breath, for I am going to use an adjective: I am going to say we demand social equality. In this republic we shall be less than freemen, if we have a whit less than that which thrift, education, and honor afford other freemen. If equality, political, economic, and social, is the boon of other men in this great country of ours, of *ours*,

then equality, political, economic, and social, is what we demand. Why build a wall to keep me out? I am no wild beast, nor am I an unclean thing.[24]

Hope implied a political role for white people in addition to personal kindness. They could help African Americans take down walls that impeded racial equality or at least not impede the work of African Americans to take the walls down alone. While Washington did not go as far as Hope did on racial equality, he did have other more controversial tenets of his belief. He shared some of them with his Nashville audience. Washington's major appeal, especially to African Americans, was to turn the deprivation and past repression of African Americans, which he acknowledged, into a moral advantage. Pride and dignity were within the reach of African Americans, if they looked inward for their capacity to suffer the wrongdoing of others toward them:

> I propose that the negro take his place upon the high ground of usefulness, forgiveness, and generosity, and that he invite the white man everywhere to step up and occupy this position with him, and if the white man can not accept the invitation we will then prove that this is a white man's problem rather than a negro problem. No race can wrong another race simply because it has the power, without being narrowed and dragged down in its moral status. We are a patient, humble race. There is plenty in this country for us to do. Away up in the atmosphere of goodness, forbearance, patience, and forgiveness, the workers are not many or overcrowded. If others would be little, we can be great; if others would be mean, we can be good; if others would push us down, we can push them. Character, not circumstances, makes the man.[25]

As a small voice in the desert, Washington, in Nashville in 1897, also heralded the mutual interests of whites and blacks that whites ignored at their own great risk:

> My white friends, we are bound together by a tie which we can not tear asunder if we would. There is no escape; you must help us raise the character of our civilization or yours will be lowered.
>
> My friends of the white race, we are one in this country. The question of the highest citizenship and the complete education of all concerns eight million of my people and

sixty million of yours. We rise as you rise; when we fall you fall; when we are strong you are strong; when we are weak you are weak; there is no power that can separate our destiny. No member of your race can harm the weakest or meanest of my race without the proudest and bluest blood in your civilization being degraded. The negro can afford to be wronged; the white man cannot afford to wrong him. Unjust laws or customs injure the white man and inconvenience the negro.[26]

This modest message of mutuality largely escaped the ears and understanding of most white Tennesseans in the 1890s. As the nineteenth century closed, the condition of African Americans had not changed much since the beginning of Reconstruction. What change had occurred was revoked and reinterpreted. The most notable changes of the 1890s were the recision of hope for civil rights, the muffling of protest about the economic conditions of African Americans, and the abandonment of politics as a means to address and redress race relations. The clearest message of the age—Washington's— spoke of loyalty to the political and economic system of the time and to the people who conducted it. In less than half a century, the country had moved from radical steps toward equality for African Americans during Reconstruction to their systematic exclusion from political, educational, and social institutions. As the twentieth century began, the fight for equality of African Americans was a rear guard action against measures to exclude them further from white-controlled institutions. The Negro Building of the Tennessee Centennial Exposition indicated the triumph of Washington's Tuskegee Creed. Less heeded were Hope's rebuttal and even Washington's views on mutuality. The splendid separation of the Negro Building inspired speaker after speaker to extol the building as an example of what white and black southerners could do together and separately despite the political oppression of the time.

A New Centennial, Another Decade of Reaction

Ironically, as Tennessee celebrated its second centennial, the 1990s stood in a similar relationship to another, better-known decade, the 1960s. Tennessee, like the rest of the nation, revised laws and policies regarding race relations. Radical democratic reforms of the 1960s removed barriers to voting registration and the election of minorities, enforced constitutional provisions for integrated schools, and reestablished the civil rights of African Americans and other Americans who faced discrimination. The 1990s brought a reaction to these reforms. U.S. Supreme Court decisions limited affirmative action and the provisions of the 1965 Voting Rights Act. Republican majorities in both houses of Congress limited or eliminated social programs of the 1960s intended to benefit Americans with low incomes, including a disproportionately high number of African Americans. Violence lurked just below the surface of a growing white male backlash against the federal government.[27]

Some parallels of the race relations, a century apart, were eerie. Educational reforms of the 1860s had strong opposition. Schools for the freed children were often burned and their teachers harassed and impeded. By the 1890s, reactions created separate schools for white and black children with grossly unequal funding bases. The 1960s desegregation of Tennessee's public schools spawned new forms of segregation and inequality. New racial residential patterns segregated some schools anew in the 1990s and created funding disparities among school districts that guaranteed new forms of inequality. Instead of extolling industrial arts education for African Americans, however, the 1990s offered family values as the building blocks for racial equality. The sad state of public education prompted reinterpretation, among members of both races, liberals and conservatives, about some of the positive aspects of school desegregation that were missing.[28]

Similarly, political changes provided parallels for the second and first centennials. The ascendant national political parties of the reforms of the 1960s and the 1860s reached the nadir of their political influence in the 1990s. The labels of Democrats and Republicans were reversed, of course, but the issues of the nineties decades, a century apart, bore a striking resemblance. In particular, the efficacy and primacy of politics, including the role of the federal government in race relations and other matters, stood out, with the 1890s providing a silhouette to the 1990s.

Without a doubt, the Civil Rights Act of 1964 and the Voting Rights Act of 1965 provided the most gains for African Americans since the Civil Rights Acts of the 1860s and 1870s and the Thirteenth, Fourteenth, and Fifteenth Amendments to the Constitution. In the mid-1990s nearly five thousand African Americans held elective office across the South. These numbers reflected the gains that women and other ethnic groups made in winning elected offices. In the face of resistance to these democratic reforms, the U.S. Supreme Court and Congress, until recently, upheld and extended them. When the Court faltered, Congress continued with reforms. It amended the Voting Rights Act in 1982 and made illegal any arrangement that had the consequences of vote dilution, whether intentional or not. The results were extraordinary. Hundreds of cities, towns, and counties switched from at-large systems to district voting. Districts with predominantly racial or ethnic minorities elected members of their own groups in record numbers. The changes affected Congress as well. Congressional redistricting after the 1990 census increased the number of majority black and Latino districts from twenty-nine to fifty-two. Twelve new predominantly black districts sent twelve new black representatives to Congress. In 1992 the Congressional Black Caucus grew to forty members.[29]

Reaction became as pronounced as reform. The Reagan administration and a minority in Congress opposed the 1982 changes. They charged that minority-controlled districts would polarize the races and invite a quota system into political representation. It took several Reagan and Bush appointees but eventually the U.S. Supreme Court joined the reaction. In the case of *Shaw v. Reno* (1993), the high court called into question the constitutionality of redistricting to remedy racial discrimination. Associate Justice Sandra Day O'Connor wrote that the redistricting plan of North Carolina "bears an uncomfortable resemblance to political apartheid." The phrase stood history on its head. It implied that race-based remedies should be precluded as primary solutions to race-based problems. The court raised grounds to reverse the gains of affirmative action in political representation just as they questioned the recent history of affirmative action in social and economic contexts of American life.[30]

This decision touched the lives of Tennesseans. It provided the grounds to overturn a decision of the federal district court for West Tennessee that the 1992 legislative redistricting in Tennessee violated the U.S. Constitution. In 1993 the district court found that voting discrimination had occurred since the 1960s "and that official discrimination in voting is not entirely in the past." The court found that the 1992 senate reapportionment plan of the general assembly violated the Voting Rights Act "by affording black voters in [W]est Tennessee less opportunity than other members of the electorate to participate in the political process and to elect representatives of their choice."[31] The state appealed this court's decision to the U.S. Supreme Court, contending that remedial plans would violate *Shaw*, which was decided shortly after the district court's finding. The decision to use a race-based solution to a problem of racial discrimination ran counter to the new direction of the U.S. Supreme Court. As the Supreme Court opened the 1995–96 session, its first order of business included vacating the remedy of constructing one or two more Senate districts with a majority of voting-age African Americans that would provide African American candidates more opportunity to be elected, as they had when Samuel McElwee represented Haywood County.[32]

No less than before, the 1990s also had voices, many of them African American, that assured the white majority that social and economic inequality between races was irremediable, perhaps justified, and almost certainly beyond politics. U.S. Supreme Court Justice Clarence Thomas is one contemporary spokesman of this conservative credo. Shelby Steele is another.[33] The credo of contemporary conservative African Americans embodies a retreat from racial integration and justifies a decline in public resources and programs to reduce racial and other forms of inequality. Thomas Sowell explains that inequality follows from differences of race and culture among people.[34] Richard Hermstein and Charles Murray similarly argue that intelligence has a genetic foundation.[35] Both works, like many others, disavow any policy provisions or political agenda. However, both provide ample reason to avoid political solutions to race relations and racial inequality. If African Americans have less intelligence, on average, and if their culture, on average, hinders their work ethic, then politics is powerless to remedy inequality. Cultural change is best done from within. Affirmative action and even minimum-wage laws, at least for Sowell, do more harm than good.

We know these discussions well. What we do not realize is how they echo the discussions of the nineteenth century that obstacles are opportunity, that work at wages inadequate for a livelihood builds character, and that personal character and minding one's business are the best and surest avenue to political change. Then, as now, we have advocates of inequality who found good in slavery as we can find good in the era of segregation, who lampooned the democratic reforms of two decades ago as misguided if not perverse, and who urged departure from the political arena and entrance to the arena of individual effort and hard work in humble circumstances. Then as now, there is considerable political realignment and reaction to disparage and dissipate reforms to redress racial inequality.

Students and Agents of History

We celebrated the second centennial of Tennessee's statehood as students and agents of history. Looking at the past may provide us a better view of our present and may affect the actions we take to shape our future. Of course, how we view the present influences our interpretation of the past. For example, my class of college students watched a segment of the television series *Eyes on the Prize* that covered the Nashville sit-ins. Those events of 1960 provided a training ground for important leaders of the Civil Rights movement: James

Lawson, John Lewis, Dianne Nash, and the Reverend C. T. Vivian, to name only a few. Mayor Ben West gave his personal assessment that the segregation of lunch counters was wrong, a major, if not unprecedented, admission of a white elected official in the South. The campaign demonstrated the power of nonviolence and provided the grounds for other groups and leaders, such as the Southern Christian Leadership Conference (SCLC) and Martin Luther King Jr. to adopt nonviolence as a primary tactic. The nonviolent campaign elicited violent reactions, including beatings and dynamite blasts. Police intervention was heavy handed and one sided. The courts weighed in against the demonstrators as disturbers of the peace. One judge literally turned his back to the arguments of the demonstrators' attorney. The segment never fails to provoke strong feelings of outrage and to stimulate class discussion among students separated by four decades and, seemingly, a world apart from these events. It did on this particular day as well. After class, I went over to the one student from Nashville and asked her about her thoughts and feelings. She said, "I did not feel very proud of my hometown."

I thought about her comment a lot. She obviously identified with the white people in the video depicted as thugs beating the demonstrators or as officials enforcing "peaceful" racial subordination. Perhaps that identification is important and appropriate, but I wondered, what will it take, for her, for me, for all of us to understand the mutuality of that event and every event like it? What will it take for black and white people to talk about our centennial or our Civil Rights movement rather than ours and yours or, even worse, ours and theirs? What will enable white people to take pride in the efforts of African Americans, and some few white allies, to move this nation closer to the social and democratic equality that all Americans espouse?

These changed perceptions undoubtedly require that we recognize our bonds to those who went before us. We understand clearly now, as students of history, the choices made by the celebrants of the first Tennessee centennial to promote, protest, or propitiate the demands of Jim Crow. Less clear to us, but no less certain, is that we were making history as we celebrated the second centennial of Tennessee statehood. Our choices, no less than those people like us a century ago, will shape the century of our children, their children and their children, no less than the choices made a century ago shaped our century and its history of reform and reaction. Perhaps we will understand the words of Martin Luther King Jr. on mutuality better than the last centennial's celebrants understood Booker T. Washington, that whites and blacks are in "an inescapable network of mutuality . . . a single . . . garment of destiny." Perhaps the knowledge of the first centennial in some small way can assist us in maintaining some hope in the efficacy, if not the primacy, of politics for race relations. Perhaps that knowledge can inspire us to forge a new century of mutuality that transcends being together, separate and unequal.

Notes

1. Joseph H. Cartwright, *The Triumph of Jim Crow* (Knoxville, 1976), 116; J. Morgan Kousser, *The Shaping of Southern Politics: Suffrage Restriction and the Establishment of the One-Party South, 1880–1910* (New Haven, Conn., 1974); Richard A. Couto, *Ain't Gonna Let Nobody Turn Me Round: The Pursuit of Racial Justice in the Rural South* (Philadelphia, 1991), 228–33.
2. C. Vann Woodward, *The Strange Career of Jim Crow*, 2d rev. ed. (New York, 1966), 69–74.
3. Herman Justi, ed., *Official History of the Tennessee Centennial Exposition* (Nashville, 1898), 193. For a general study of race relations in Tennessee, see Lester C. Lamon, *Blacks in Tennessee, 1791–1970* (Knoxville, 1981).
4. Cordell Hull Williams, "The Life of James Carroll Napier from 1845 to 1940" (Master's thesis, Tennessee State Univ., 1955). In 1911 Napier received another federal appointment and served as registrar of the United States Treasury under President William Howard Taft. He resigned that position rather than establish separate-but-equal facilities for African Americans within the office. President Woodrow Wilson instituted Jim Crow facilities throughout the federal government. Nancy J. Weiss, "The Negro and the New Freedom," in *The Segregation Era: 1863–1954*, ed. Allen Weinstein and F. O. Gatell (New York, 1970), 129–42.
5. John Mercer Langston, *From the Virginia Plantation to the National Capital: An Autobiography* (reprint, New York, 1969), 438–520; George Freeman Bragg, "John Mercer Langston," manuscript, Schomburg Center for Research in Black Culture, New York Public Library (hereafter cited as Schomburg Center).
6. Richard A. Couto, *Lifting the Veil: A Political History of Struggles for Emancipation* (Knoxville, 1993), 49–79.
7. Gloria McKissack suggests that the extensive change of membership of the executive committee came with Napier's departure. The change meant men of less status and prestige replaced the most prominent elite of the African American community. "Late Summer: AfroAmerican Nashville, 1890–1899," in *From Winter to Winter: The Afro-American History of Nashville, Tennessee, 1870–1930*, ed. Bobby L. Lovett (Nashville, 1981), 103–34. The written record of these events is simply too inadequate to discern the reasons of McElwee and the others for their departure.
8. Wells wrote this in a column, "The Reign of Mob Law: Iola's Opinion of Doings in the Southern Field," *New York Age*, 18 Feb. 1893, Ida B. Wells Collection, Box 5, Folder 1, Department of Special Collections, Joseph Regenstein Library, Univ. of Chicago.
9. Alfreda M. Duster, ed., *Crusader for Justice: The Autobiography of Ida B. Wells* (Chicago, 1970), 115–19; see also Frederick Douglass, et al., *The Reason Why the Colored American Is Not in the World's Columbian Exposition* (n.p, 1893), and Elliott M. Rudwick and August Meier, "Black Man in the 'White City': Negroes and the Columbian Exposition, 1893," *Phylon* 26 (Winter 1965): 354–61.
10. Justi, *Official History*, 196.

11. New York Commission, Report of the New York Commission of the Tennessee Centennial Exposition, 1897, 22, Schomburg Center.
12. Ibid., 26.
13. Ibid., 40.
14. Justi, Official History, 193.
15. Councill's speech as quoted in ibid., 198.
16. George F, Hoar, The Opportunity of the Colored Leader: An Address to the Law Class of Howard University (Washington, D.C., 1894), 117, Schomburg Center.
17. Ibid., 15.
18. Ibid.
19. Ibid., 5.
20. Justi, Official History, 197.
21. Ibid.
22. New York Commission, Report of the New York Commission, 39.
23. Justi, Official History, 202–3.
24. Ridgely Torrence, The Story of John Hope (New York, 1948), 114–15.
25. Justi, Official History, 202–3.
26. Ibid.
27. Sheila Wissner, "Fear, Suspicion of Government Cause Surge in Tennessee Militias," Nashville Tennessean, 3–6 Sept. 1995.
28. Couto, Ain't Gonna Let Nobody, 190–213.
29. American Civil Liberties Union (ACLU), Reaffirmation or Requiem for the Voting Rights Act? The Court Will Decide (New York, 1995). See also Chandler Davidson and Benard Grofman, eds., Quiet Revolution in the South: The Impact of the Voting Rights Act, 1965–1990 (Princeton, N.J., 1994).
30. ACLU, Reaffirmation or Requiem; Ellen Spears, "Recent Decisions Troubling, but Limited," Voting Rights Review (Summer 1994): 1ff. Several other articles deal with the aftermath of the Shaw decision. Linda Greenhouse, "By 5–4, Justices Cast Doubts on U.S. Programs that Give Preferences Based On Race," New York Times, 13 June 1995.
31. Rural West Tennessee African-American Affairs Council v. Ned McWherter. et al., 836 F. Supp. 453 (W.D. Tenn., 1993).
32. Ibid. The court explained a violation occurs if "a voting procedure . . . has the "result" under the "totality of the circumstances" of affording black voters less opportunity than white voters "to elect representatives of their choice." The "totality of the circumstance" includes seven specific factors including racially polarized voting and the effects of past discrimination. An analysis of West Tennessee election results from 1983 to 1992 suggests that African American candidates have little chance of winning an election in a majority white district, including an at-large election. The cohesion of white voters for white candidates is extremely high. Consequently, it takes an unusual set of circumstances for an African American candidate to win. Evidence in the trial showed a pattern of extreme racial polarization in elections from 1983 to 1992. In fifty-eight elections with white and black candidates, thirty-two of them resulted with extreme polarization of 160 percent or more. That is, the percentages of blacks voting for a black candidate and of whites voting for a white candidate equaled 160 or more. Twelve of them resulted in substantial polarization, more than 140 but less than 160. The presidential primary races of 1984 and 1988, with Jesse Jackson as a candidate, were the most polarized races in the six-county region. These election

results confirm the findings of Earl Black and Merle Black reported in *Politics and Society in the South* (Cambridge, Mass., 1987). In places where African Americans make up 25 to 50 percent of the voting-age population, an African American candidate needs to have 90 to 95 percent of the African American vote and 35 to 40 percent of the white vote. In general, given the degree of racial polarization in voting, an African American candidate needs to have close to 40 percent of the white vote. Other evidence in the trial showed clearly that different degrees of poverty impacted past forms of racial discrimination, for example, education and employment, which, in turn, hindered the political participation of African Americans. The measures of socioeconomic status from the 1990 census indicate a wide disparity between African Americans and whites in each of the six counties in rural southwest Tennessee, which continues the historic inequality between members of each race. The area provides a bench mark of need for the state. In each of the other counties, black per capita figures are less than 50 percent of the white per capita income: Fayette (41.9 percent); Haywood (49.6 percent); Madison (43.8); and Tipton (48.7). In addition to African Americans lagging within their counties, their counties fall far behind the per capita income of the state, which was $12,255 in 1990. These income differences translate into vastly different rates of poverty between African Americans and whites. In the six-county area, 38.1 percent of African Americans are reported below poverty level incomes compared with 11.9 percent of whites. The rate of poverty among African Americans ranged from a high of 45.3 percent in Tipton County to a low of 36.4 percent in Hardeman County.

33. Shelby Steele, *The Content of Our Character: A New Vision of Race in America* (New York, 1990). See also George M. Frederickson, *The Arrogance of Race: Historical Perspectives on Slavery, Racism. and Social Inequality* (Middletown, Conn., 1988), 80–88.
34. Thomas Sowell, *Race and Culture: A World View* (New York, 1994).
35. Richard J. Hermstein and Charles Murray, *The Bell Curve: Intelligence and Class Structure in American Life* (New York, 1994).

Nashville Offers Opportunity
The *Nashville Globe* and Business as a Means of Uplift, 1907–1913

Christopher M. Scribner

FRICAN AMERICAN BUSINESSES PROVIDED NEEDED SERVICES AND PRODUCTS TO THE BLACK COMMUNITY DURING THE JIM CROW era. Christopher Scribner uses the early history and development of the *Nashville Globe* to review the impact that the black press had on African American business development. Scribner is also interested in how the black press in Nashville reflected the influence of the ideas of self-help and self-improvement identified with the philosophy of Booker T. Washington as well as the praise for a communitarian philosophy most closely associated with W. E. B. Du Bois. The editorial philosophy of this Nashville newspaper, in general, embodied the concept of "accommodative resistance" to Jim Crow Tennessee, meaning that the newspaper protested racial injustices but also accepted the idea that African Americans must pull themselves up to respectability and success and not expect much help from white society. Scribner emphasizes the importance of R. H. and Henry Boyd to both the newspaper and other black commercial enterprises. The themes of racial solidarity, race pride, and self-improvement met with a popular reception in the black community, allowing the *Globe* to establish itself as a black Nashville institution by the time of World War I.

During the latter part of the nineteenth century and early twentieth century, conservative black leadership, self-reliance, and a separate economy characterized life in the black urban South. African Americans, however, faced increasing challenges to their economic and business efforts, and they confronted restrictive racial customs and institutionalized Jim Crow. Although African Americans did not retreat altogether from the racially inclusive ideas of the black leader Frederick Douglass, after 1895 the power and influence of Booker T. Washington pointed blacks toward a new strategy in the achievement of full citizenship that had much to do with accommodationism and business enterprise.[1] Within Tennessee, the Washingtonian philosophy had its detractors, but it also found strong adherents, especially in Nashville among the city's black middle class.[2]

In 1906 four African American businessmen founded the *Nashville Globe*. They wanted to provide information to the city's blacks during a streetcar boycott, the result of a new Jim Crow ordinance. According to an article celebrating the newspaper's first anniversary, the *Globe*'s founders expected it to act as a "much-needed weapon of defense, a champion of its people who are unjustly villifed [*sic*] in every section of this now great country."[3] "The object of the *Globe*," the editors wrote, "is to interest Negroes in business,"[4] which they considered the most effective means of racial uplift. The four original officers—Henry A. Boyd, Dock A. Hart, J. O. Battle, and Charles Burrill—all worked for the National Baptist Publishing Board (a prosperous black-owned religious press) and had extensive contacts in the city's black middle class.[5]

In advocating a strong role for business achievement and by linking segregation to economic opportunity, the *Globe*'s editors generally accepted the pillars of "conservatism, patience and material progress"[6] that supported Booker T. Washington's program. Washington appealed to the black urban middle class through organizations like the National Negro Business League, which he formed in 1900. Thus, the *Globe* provides a window to study black activity following the era historian Rayford Logan termed the nadir of black life in America.[7] The editors, however, refashioned Washington's gospel to fit local conditions during the newspaper's first decade in print. They borrowed as well from the ideas of W. E. B. Du Bois, who after 1903 increasingly publicly opposed Washington and his policies. While better known for his demands for political and civil equality and liberal arts education, Du Bois also believed that business offered opportunity for black advancement.[8] Du Bois, however, contended that economic pursuits benefited the race only if businessmen acted as community philanthropists, not as individuals seeking to maximize profits.[9]

The *Globe* editors' attempts to define areas of autonomy for African Americans in Nashville contained internal tensions. These tensions expose the limitations of the black middle class' self-help message in the age of segregation. The curious mixture of optimism and pessimism embedded in the newspaper's doctrine marked a fundamental dissonance. The editors had an elemental faith in blacks' meritorious achievement, yet they also acknowledged the barriers obstructing black progress. Part of this inconsistency resulted from the dual nature of the black newspaper as both a business enterprise and an organ of protest. Business concerns made the editors keenly aware of the difficulty of black economic independence. In response, the *Globe* adapted the idea of community responsibility to its business philosophy, modifying its message of individualism and boot-strap capitalism.

In his study of Mississippi during the Jim Crow era, historian Neil McMillen argues that African Americans adopted a strategy of "accommodative resistance" to meet white oppression.[10] Nashville's black middle class espoused a similar tactic of limited protest.[11] The newspaper's bullish commercial attitudes undergirded its acceptance of accommodation. Accommodation should be understood as a "double-edged" adjustment[12] to the political and social reality that confronted African Americans in the early-twentieth-century South. It was a tactical retreat, one that did not threaten the established order and enhanced elements of black life.[13] The newspaper sought to promote progress, but the editors were careful not to create unreasonable expectations. The elevation of the businessman as race leader, and the doctrine of self-help mixed with community involvement, defined the *Globe*'s accommodationist stance because it restricted advancement to delineated areas.

A product of the 1905 streetcar boycott, the newspaper's business philosophy resembled that of the protest's leaders. Indeed, boycott organizer R. H. Boyd, Henry Boyd's father and secretary of the National Baptist Publishing Board (NBPB), was the chief financial backer of the weekly. In reaction to a new segregation ordinance, R. H. Boyd and a several of Nashville's leading black businessmen formed the Union Transportation Company. They bought several steam cars to provide black-operated transportation.[14] In a letter he wrote to the *Nashville Banner* during the boycott, R. H. Boyd contended that a separate black streetcar line would end the current problems as well as the need for Jim Crow.[15] Boyd believed that racial separation, a product of white prejudice, must be manipulated for racial advancement. African Americans thus should work within the enforced system of separation to achieve equality by self-reliance and business acumen. Segregation, to extend his argument, was unfair not because it separated the races but because it led to inequality and inferior treatment.

Although the bus boycott and the Union Transportation Company ultimately failed, the *Globe*'s editors sought to publish news of business achievement. They searched for stories that "would tend to uplift rather than to degrade . . . members of our race."[16] Like his father, Henry Boyd perceived business advantages in the restrictions of the racial caste. The denial of civil equality and meaningful political opportunity forced blacks to seek fulfillment through business and to experience a world of their own. The *Globe*'s editors saw no contradiction in their assertion that whites would accept black business and evidence that whites would deny black equality. An editorial agreed with black real estate entrepreneur T. Clay Moore's claim that the "white man knows no prejudice when it comes to dollars and cents."[17] Reports that challenged the idea of color-blind commerce, like the unwillingness of a New York–based insurance agency to handle African American customers, provoked a sanguine response. The refusal, the *Globe* noted, provided an opening for a shrewd businessman.[18]

The most notable aspect of the *Globe*'s economic philosophy was the idea that business must be based on competitive principles. Businesses should seek profits, not dispense charity, an assumption directly at odds with Du Bois's notion of business philanthropy. It followed that a "painstaking and energetic" businessman would succeed. Failure, on the other hand, resulted from poor moral character, laziness, or "slothfulness," not the restrictions of the racial caste.[19] Still, the *Globe* modified Washington's individualistic ethic. The editors, for example, could not suggest that the Union Transportation Company had failed because of poor character or insufficient effort. Businessmen, therefore, were role models and the foundation for community development. Businessmen had a responsibility to the community, and the community, in turn, owed loyalty to black businesses. As black businesses increasingly catered to a black clientele in the twentieth century. race pride along with racial solidarity emerged as a fundamental tenet of the economic creed.[20]

As a first step in this communitarian philosophy, businessmen must hire black workers to insure a separate, self-sufficient economy. The *Globe*, seeking to teach by example, gloated, "The news matter of this great edition was written by Negroes, the type matter set by Negroes . . . the presswork by Negro pressmen on presses owned, controlled, and operated by a Negro institution. . . . In fact, it is a Negro production from beginning to end."[21] The newspaper kept a vigilant watch for businesses that broke this rule. It criticized a graduating class at Meharry Medical College for having its graduation announcements printed at a white-owned shop in Philadelphia instead of keeping the business within the race in Nashville.

Nothing revealed the newspaper's attitudes about community obligation quite like its articles about black-owned financial institutions. Banks were both symbols of success as well as essential community establishments. Banks and bankers personified the importance of the commercial spirit and the need for racial solidarity. At the same time, financial pragmatism had to accompany racial unity. A banker could not rely on moral support or sympathy to support his bank. "It takes money, and nothing else," an editorial commented, "to make a bank go."[22] Banks also evidenced the frustrations of black businesses. The newspaper often implored its readers to save in the race institutions so the institutions could realize their full potential.

Features about banks were the most regular business stories in the newspaper. Reports of the annual meetings of Nashville's black-owned banks dominated the newspaper each January. The articles documented the financial health (total assets, monthly transactions, and dividends for the stockholders) of each bank and devoted space to the speeches of the bank presidents. Nashville had two: the One-Cent Savings Bank, started by R. H. Boyd and James C. Napier in 1904, and the People's Savings Bank, begun by Robert Fulton Boyd, a local physician not related to Henry Boyd, in 1909. The newspaper welcomed the city's second bank as a sign of Nashville's prosperity, and wrote that it was glad to see "younger Negroes" involved in banking. "The growth of banking institutions among our people," an editorial commented, "is the natural sequence of their material progress—their accumulation of wealth, their intellectual acquirements and their participation in business affairs."[23] To show that this financial energy existed beyond Nashville, the *Globe* featured banks throughout the state and the South. Banks from Birmingham, Alabama, and Muskogee, Oklahoma, occasionally advertised in the newspaper.[24]

The editors believed banks could stimulate the race's latent business activity while simultaneously restoring its pride and confidence. The newspaper quoted R. H. Boyd in his annual address to the One-Cent stockholders: "[The bank] came upon the scene not for the purpose of investing and accumulating money for the stockholders, neither for the purpose of paying salaries to the

officers, but for the purpose, first, of restoring confidence in the already industrious colored citizens and training young men in financial dealings."[25]

Banks had a more pragmatic purpose, too; white banks often spurned
blacks who sought credit. "Negroes have found out that the only way to get a
financial standing and rating in the commercial world," another editorial read,
"will be to open their own financial concerns."[26] Community obligations cut
both ways. Local blacks had to support the businessmen and keep commerce
within the race; businesses could not prosper without black patronage.

The *Globe* labored to overcome the reservations of elements of the black
community about saving in the black-owned banks. Comments from the
presidents of the two banks indicated that a fraction of Nashville's African
American community (and middle class) saved at the race institutions. R. H.
Boyd noted in 1907 that if all Nashville's blacks saved at the One-Cent, the
total transactions would more than quadruple the $500,000 it averaged its
first three years.[27] The *Globe* chastised those who did not, and offered no
sympathy for blacks who lost money when a local white bank failed in 1909.
In the same edition, it praised the black banks for avoiding trouble during
the panic of that year. An editorial further claimed that the city's "rank-and-
file" were more loyal than the "scores of men of means . . . who absolutely
refuse to have anything to do with these banks."[28] R. F. Boyd implored his
bank's stockholders to elect to the board of directors "only those who have
enough confidence in this bank at least to deposit here."[29]

Such examples led an editorial to lament that in business matters blacks
brought "his brother down to this cold, double proposition: 'Can you give me
better service than the white man and can you make a me a cheaper price?'"[30]
The editors believed educated African Americans judged their "fellowmen"
more harshly. This was a serious charge because business aspirations depended
on racial solidarity. Instead, the newspaper urged "brotherly cooperation."
Thus, the *Globe* often ignored these examples as it attempted to encourage
local support for black banks and business in general. At times, the newspaper commented that blacks would rather frequent a black-owned shop,
even if they must pay dearer prices.[31]

Another essential element of the newspaper's commercial philosophy
was the belief that[black business could develop and sustain race pride.]The
National Negro Doll Company, founded by Henry Boyd in 1908, exemplified the newspaper's message of race pride.[32] The doll venture combined
uplift and good economic sense. Boyd started the company along with his
father because white companies sold African American dolls so distasteful as
not to be "acceptable to a gorilla, a chimpanzee, or even a baboon."[33] The

Boyds hoped that black dolls would instill pride and confidence in girls and teach them of the "beauty and graces . . . of the well-developed and refined American Negro woman."[34] This appeal to African American women was typical of the *Globe*. Its editors usually portrayed women as consumers and rarely portrayed them as owners and investors in local businesses. The doll venture also highlights the small size and interdependence of Nashville's black middle class, of which the Boyds represented a significant element. The doll company frequently advertised in the newspaper, and as reciprocal support the newspaper ran occasional articles and editorials praising the business.[35] It also displayed the dolls in its offices.

The newspaper commended both the dolls' social benefits and the loyalty of black consumers. Henry Boyd claimed sales had been made in every state and that the African American dolls were sold at church fairs in such diverse states as New Jersey, Kansas, and California.[36] Success, however, led to an article in the local white press about the imminent financial collapse of the doll company. The *Globe* considered the attack unfounded and irresponsible; an article speculated that white merchants, upset about their own declining doll sales during the Christmas season, had spread the allegations.[37] This incident, the editors believed, proved the African American market offered opportunities for advancement and new challenges. To meet growing demand, the business proposed to build a factory in Nashville, which would mean, the *Globe* imagined, "the employment of hundreds of Negroes and the advancement of Nashville in many lands."[38] To further its efforts to instill race pride and improve the treatment of blacks in Nashville, the newspaper advised its readers to stay away from a grocery store in which the proprietor beat up a black customer who challenged the owner's attempt to overcharge him. If one could not shop in black stores, the newspaper counseled its readers to shop where they received acceptable treatment.

Despite its communitarian strain, the *Globe*'s business ethic remained rooted in individualism. In its essence the business message also was anti-elitist: anyone could succeed without special privileges, education, or rank. Advancement required prudence and thrift. As such, the *Globe* in an April 1909 editorial lauded a local businessman who had remarked that an absence of debt caused his high spirits. The editorial noted that he could take pride because "building up is hard and tedious" while failure is easy. The newspaper rejoiced when the largest black business escaped the city's financial panic of early 1908 because of careful planning during good times. A black business could succeed if it operated "not by accumulating a large bank account, as some would suppose, but by the economical and wise management during prosperous and undisturbed seasons."[39] Businessmen had to remember they served as a model for the community and the foundation for its development. Repeated coverage of A. N. Johnson's successful funeral business showed the newspaper valued hustle and innovation as well.

In 1907 the *Globe* announced Johnson's arrival in Nashville from Montgomery, Alabama, to open "the finest undertaking establishment in the South."[40] The laudatory full-page article was accompanied by another page and a half of congratulatory letters, from Booker T. Washington and R. H. Boyd, among others. Johnson, like the *Globe*'s editors, believed that "business draws no color line and that business development will wipe out racial differences to a large extent."[41] The undertaking establishment was a point of civic pride and the *Globe* kept a watchful eye on it. Two years later an article, under the headline "The Wonderful Growth of A. N. Johnson's Undertaking Business,"[42] claimed that Johnson's innovations, like the ladies' room and the baby hearse, had spurred his business. The next year it noted that Johnson had performed 375 funerals even though he had known few people when he arrived. Johnson knew how to succeed because of proper business principles, not a reliance on sentiment, the editors maintained. The newspaper reported that "this is a new era. The people want their money's worth . . . and the competent man knows it."[43] The message: skill guarantees achievement. Of course, the *Globe* neglected to mention that undertakers were often the most prosperous businessman because they did not have to compete with whites. Johnson, moreover, had obviously not started from scratch; letters from Boyd and Washington show his reputation preceded him.

A portion of the newspaper's business message, with its confidence in bootstrap capitalism and the openness of economic opportunity, represented an unabashed strain of early-twentieth-century urban boosterism. In this way, the *Globe* mirrored white urban dailies in the Progressive era. Boosterism reflected the editors' desire to present "the bright side of the race question in our home city to the whole world."[44] The weekly lauded Nashville as the nation's best city for black business. A January 1913 edition of the *Crisis*, the organ of the NAACP, extolled Nashville's economic vigor.[45] Nashville's African American business district, centered on Cedar Street (now Charlotte Avenue) between Fourth and Fifth Avenues North, had a reputation as one of the most thriving in the nation in the early twentieth century. The north side of Cedar Street in 1912 (moving east to west) included the Brown (professional) Building, the People's Savings Bank Building (which included the bank, a real estate company, and the offices of a local business organization), a tonsorial parlor, a laundry, a barber shop, a printer, Johnson's undertaking establishment, a men's clothing store, a dry cleaners, the Majestic Theater, a café, a second professional building, a soda shop, and a tailor's shop.[46] The *Globe* implored entrepreneurs to take advantage of the possibilities, great and small. Its editors predicted that blacks "can have as great success with a peanut stand as he can with a bank, and will be looked upon in the commercial world with the same respect and confidence."[47] The men of the *Globe* pointed out that the absence of black-owned shoe, hat, clothing, and bookstores represented opportunities for black entrepreneurs. The *Globe* championed business leagues as both a form of local boosterism and as a community organization that could protect and further black commercial activity.

Nashville had a local chapter of the National Negro Business League, an organization formed by Booker T. Washington in 1900.[48] The *Globe*, however, criticized the local chapter's somnolence. It only sent delegates to the national convention, the newspaper noted. An association should provide more than inspirational speeches, the *Globe* contended; it should disseminate useful information, teach practical business skills, and create jobs. Henry Boyd acted on his newspaper's message. In November 1907 he and several younger local businessmen, including Johnson and Moore, formed the Nashville Business and Professional League to "stimulate" new businesses and share information.[49] In February 1909 the *Globe* scolded both local black business groups for taking a "snooze," but the next month it said both were showing signs of a general revival. Editorials in the newspaper, which kept a close eye on the leagues, persistently repeated the need for effective organization. One editorial intoned, "We believe that a well organized association, on the order of a board of trade or a merchants association, where the men could come together once a month, would be of great benefit. The members could help each other in the way of suggestion, and by frankly pointing out to each other their defects, but always in the spirit of mutual interest."[50] African American businessmen also could learn from the organization and united efforts of Nashville's white business community. The *Globe* placed the slogan of the local white board of trade, "Nashville Offers Opportunity," on its masthead in 1911. An editorial claimed that improved relations with the white business organization could lead to jobs for black contractors.[51]

The newspaper's optimism at times waned and pessimism flared. An April 1910 editorial spoke of a dangerous time for black commerce: "If the enterprises now conducted by the Negro should receive reverses the whole race would be in danger of being reduced to serfdom for all time to come."[52]

Such pessimistic attitudes, however, appeared infrequently in the *Globe*. More typical was a February 1909 editorial which boasted, "So seldom does a Negro concern fail that the whole city is stirred when it happens."[53] The newspaper rarely reported failure outright; one had to read between the lines. A celebratory article about a new business often masked a flop—as did a series of articles between 1907 and 1913 noting the nearly annual opening of the Economical Steam Laundry Company—under different management and different names.[54] The problems of changing ownership did not concern the editors; rather, they offered endless stories about the laundry's bright future.

The usual message of optimism and achievement could not compensate for real limits of black businesses in an age of Jim Crow segregation. Rather than provide ammunition for whites who asserted that blacks were incapable of running their own business, the *Globe* focused on African American success—large or small. In an October 1907 issue, a picture accompanied the story of an electrician who left a white employer to begin his own business. "Step by step the Negroes are pressing out into all lines of business, and are putting their enterprises on firm bases," the *Globe* reported.[55] This type of story was an occasional feature for several years. The opening of Gray's Grand Grocery earned nearly equal coverage as bank news. But barriers could not be ignored. Even Johnson's attempts to reach beyond a traditional black business proved elusive. In February 1912 he opened the Majestic Theater in the heart of the African American business district on Cedar Street. The *Globe* enthusiastically observed the construction, which it reported was more than "child's play." The newspaper then bemoaned the sparse crowds that followed the opening. Should not blacks be willing to pay more to patronize a theater where they did not have to enter through a muddy alley and could sit anywhere once inside, an editorial asked. The *Globe*'s editors remained cognizant of the barriers facing black entrepreneurs because they were businessmen themselves. In seeking advertisements, for example, the *Globe* learned it could not rely on African American business support alone. A significant percentage of the *Globe*'s advertisements came from white-owned businesses. During the first ten years of the newspaper's existence, moreover, the percentage and quantity of white advertisements increased while the number of black advertisements dropped slightly. For instance, a 1907 issue ran forty-five advertisements from black-owned establishments and twenty-three from white-owned enterprises. Five years later, an issue contained more advertisements from whites than blacks (twenty-nine to twenty-eight).[56] White advertising remained a consistent and important source of the newspaper's income. The *Globe* also accepted advertisements from white-owned businesses that competed with black-owned enterprises, like tailors and dry-goods stores. The editors did not directly confront this contradiction.

The newspaper urged racial solidarity and also entreated readers to shop at stores that advertised on its pages. The editors' position indirectly addressed the tensions of their reliance on white advertising and their philosophy of racial pride. For one, the *Globe* demanded equal treatment in white-owned stores, and it claimed that the stores that advertised in the newspaper treated blacks fairly. Thus, an element of the newspaper's race pride philosophy called for African Americans to receive (or fight for) equal treatment in white-owned stores. The *Globe* believed the white stores that advertised with it provided that respect. Several issues in 1909 included "the *Globe* Coupon," which guaranteed its readers good service and a "square deal" in the shops that advertised. Also, the *Globe's* editors reacted caustically when white businesses slighted their advertising agent. "We gather from the refusal of white stores to deal with our agent," the newspaper remarked, "that they have all the business they want and do not need black patronage."[57] As another way to promote race pride, the *Globe* refused to accept advertisements for "beauty" products like hair straighteners and skin bleaches. One editorial contended that "a man as black as pitch is just as comely as the fairest man if he has the same self-pride."[58]

The newspaper modified Booker T. Washington's intense individualism because it knew firsthand the limits of business opportunity. The newspaper itself was not an independent venture. The Boyd family subsidized the newspaper in its early years, primarily through National Baptist Publishing Board (NBPB) advertisements. Moreover, at a dinner celebrating its first anniversary, the editors praised R. H. Boyd as one who had helped the paper in its first year. In a 1907 issue of the newspaper (its second year), the NBPB's advertisements represented about 40 percent of the total advertising space and 20 percent of the total space in the newspaper. But a year and a half later, Boyd's business had reduced its advertising even though the total advertising space of the newspaper increased. The Board's advertisements represented about 16 percent of the total advertising space and less than 10 percent of the total space in the newspaper.[59] These percentages decreased slightly over the next several years. Still, the 1913 edition of the *City Directory* listed R. H. Boyd as president of the Globe Publishing Company (it was the first year it named company officers) though the newspaper's masthead never included his name.

The *Globe* survived its early years (and lasted until 1960) because of special circumstances: the Boyd family's wealth. Most African American businesses were not so fortunate. Despite the newspaper's claims to the contrary, the early twentieth century was a difficult economic era. The percentage of black males in unskilled and service occupations rose between 1890 and 1910, from 70 to 80 percent of the work force, which meant a concomitant drop of the percentage of black men who held skilled positions or were professionals. Also, black laborers received lower wages than their white counterparts due to their inability to join local unions.[60] Most African American businesses were risky, short-term ventures. A sampling of the *Nashville City Directory* between 1907 and 1917 highlights this economic insecurity. Even though they comprised one-third of the city's population,[61] blacks accounted for less than 5 percent of the city's contractors and operated less than 10 percent of neighborhood businesses such as grocery and dry-goods stores. Businesses in which blacks were disproportionately active, like barber shops and restaurants, were usually short-lived. Tracking of individual shops reveals that few of these enterprises stayed in business over a period of several years.[62] Black business opportunity declined as social and economic circumstances changed in the new century, too. For example, in 1907, 24 of 43 expressmen and 46 of approximately 120 fuel dealers in Nashville were black; however, by 1917, African Americans comprised just 14 of the 42 expressmen and 11 of the 57 fuel dealers.

In spite of these limitations (of which the *Globe*'s editors doubtlessly were aware), the newspaper continued to champion business and economic pursuits as the surest path of racial and personal advancement. "In the meantime, while the Negro is complaining," an editorial stated, "he is going forward buying homes, opening new business enterprises, decreasing his illiteracy and advancing in most every way of life at a rate that will compare favorably with that of any other race in America."[63] Blacks bought homes in the same areas in northwest Nashville, the *Globe* contended, not because of legal barriers but because they wanted friendly neighbors. A 1912 editorial, which announced that "the day will never come when there will be a black Nashville and a white Nashville," echoed that idea.[64] Separation was not segregation; a black world need not be inferior to a white world. While divided, the *Globe*'s editors believed both black and white Nashville pursued similar opportunities and aspirations.

Furthermore, social separation offered opportunities for businesses and fostered racial solidarity. African American neighborhoods "afford a splendid opportunity for Negroes to do business along various lines," an editorial avowed, while avoiding the slights of white merchants who profited from black trade.[65] The newspaper reported that M. V. Battle moved his drug store from South Nashville to North Nashville near Fisk University because physicians in his former neighborhood had not cooperated with him. He had, the newspaper reported, received the pledges of doctors in North Nashville to support his new pharmacy, the only one in the neighborhood.[66] The newspaper also promoted home ownership, which would benefit both the individual and black real estate ventures.[67]

The newspaper promoted its ideas of individualism, communitarianism, and race pride in other avenues as well. The *Globe* took a strong stand on several social issues. In 1909 a series of editorials criticized the white administration of Fisk University for firing several black teachers and replacing them with whites. The newspaper wondered if the time had come for a black university president. Education was a key issue because it provided opportunity. Both Henry Boyd and Dock Hart served on a citywide committee that helped bring the new state-funded black industrial training school, Tennessee Agricultural and Industrial (now Tennessee State University), to Nashville in 1909. The newspaper also urged political participation. It called voting a "high privilege" and chastened blacks who did not pay their poll tax. Expressing its typical independence, the *Globe* also argued that blacks should split their votes between the major parties, depending on which would offer greater concessions.[68] Still, much of this message was conservative; it placed a burden on African Americans to prove worthy of change. One 1911 editorial called for blacks to display their best behavior on streetcars to ensure continuance of their limited Jim Crow rights.

The editors promoted business because they believed an economic foundation best supported advancement within a restrictive racial system. Moreover, it matched their middle-class beliefs in thrift, industriousness, and property ownership because "character, wealth and intelligence is the bedrock upon which you must rest your fight for your manhood rights."[69] This strategy of accommodative resistance, or protest within well-defined limits, spoke to and for the city's black middle class, those who occupied the relatively few positions of privilege in the city. It justified their leadership but offered little to the African American majority. For the black middle class, somewhat immune to the daily debasement of segregation, separate was not necessarily subordinate. But the message changed when circumstances affected their semiprotected status. When the state legislature altered Nashville's voting from ward to at-large elections in 1913, diluting the black middle class' voting strength, they again (as with the 1906 Jim Crow streetcar ordinance) felt the encroachment of segregation.[70] In a rare moment of vehemence, a *Globe* editorial recognized the stifling effects of legalized segregation, screaming, "But as yet no one has been able to advance a single argument that the scheme can do other than harm the Negro. The more the matter is discussed the plainer it is that the perpetuators of this diabolical plot are endeavoring to crush the life out of the Negro; to chill his ambition; to check his progress."[71]

The optimistic rhetoric and the more militant message above were not easily squared. The dissonance revealed the limitations of the former message. The heightened tensions during World War I, the start of the black migration to cities and northward, and a new generation of African Americans who began to demand greater equality in the 1920s weakened the business message (and the Washingtonian dogma). In coming decades, African Americans, as well as the editors of the *Globe*, would seek new ways to carve out racial autonomy and a racial identity in Nashville and elsewhere.[72] The *Globe*'s business philosophy had helped to invigorate Nashville's black middle class, but African Americans would in time seek new ways to remedy unfair racial conditions. Ironically, not until the 1960s—after the demise of the black weekly—would Nashville's blacks take lasting steps toward racial equality.

Notes

1. For a discussion of Washington's influence and his ideas, see August Meier, *Negro Thought in America, 1880–1915: Racial Ideologies in the Age of Booker T. Washington* (Ann Arbor, Mich., 1966); Louis R. Harlan, *Booker T. Washington: The Making of a Black Leader, 1856–1901* (New York, 1972); and *Booker T. Washington: The Wizard of Tuskegee, 1901–1915* (New York, 1983). For a perceptive study of southern urban blacks in the late nineteenth century, see Howard Rabinowitz, *Race Relations in the Urban South, 1865–1900* (Urbana, Ill., 1980).

2. For general studies of Nashville's black community in this period, see Faye Robbins, "A World-Within-a-World: Black Nashville, 1880–1915" (Ph.D. diss., Univ. of Arkansas, 1980); Lester Lamon, *Black Tennesseans, 1900–1930* (Knoxville, 1977); Don H. Doyle, *Nashville in the New South* (Knoxville, 1985). There is also a section on Tennessee in Henry L. Suggs, ed., *The Black Press in the South, 1865–1979* (Westport, Conn., 1983).

3. *Nashville Globe*, 18 Jan. 1907, 1.

4. Ibid., 6 Sept. 1912, 2.

5. Hart, *Globe* president, was general foreman of the National Baptist Publishing Board until he resigned in 1913, manager of Work Brothers and Hart Music Publishing Company, and vice president of the People's Savings Bank; Boyd, the manager of the newspaper, was assistant secretary of the NBPB, manager of the Negro Doll Company, and a board member of the One-Cent Savings Bank and an Atlanta insurance company; Battle, the editor, was in charge of the bookbinding department at the NBPB. He died on 3 March 1909. Burrill, the treasurer, left the newspaper in 1911 due to poor health. The newspaper replaced neither Battle nor Burrill. Boyd and Hart appeared to have editorial control from the start.

6. C. Vann Woodward, *Origins of the New South, 1877–1913* (Baton Rouge, La., 1951), 359.

7. Rayford Logan, *The Negro in American Life and Thought: The Nadir, 1877–1901* (New York, 1954). There were source limits that defined the period of my study. There are no extant *Globe* copies for its first year. Copies exist for the periods 1907–13, 1917, 1918, and 1930–60. Copies are on microfilm at the Tennessee State Library and Archives, Nashville.

8. One Washington scholar noted that business was one area where Washington and Du Bois were in general agreement. Louis Harlan, "Booker T. Washington and the National Negro Business League," in *Seven on Black: Reflections on the Negro Experience*, ed. William Shade (New York, 1969), 76.

9. In an editorial in the *Crisis*, Du Bois wrote that black businessmen must view their work "as a philanthropy, as a means of group employment and group gain, not for making millionaires, but for making a large class of well-to-do citizens." *Crisis*, Oct. 1913, 290.

10. Neil R. McMillen, *Dark Journey: Black Mississippians in the Age of Jim Crow* (Urbana, Ill., 1989).

11. Lamon contends the city's influential educated and professional elite followed the teachings of Washington (*Black Tennesseans*, 176, 187). None of the general histories of Nashville provides a precise estimate of the size of the city's black middle class, although Lamon calls it "sizable" (*Black Tennesseans*, 219). If one defines the city's middle class as those working in the professions or in business pursuits, a study of the city's occupational patterns in 1910 would place between 10 and 20 percent of the city's blacks in that class. See Robbins, "World-Within-a-World," 319, 321.

12. The ideas in this argument are derivative of Eugene Genovese's arguments regarding slavery and the role of the slave preacher in *Roll, Jordan, Roll: The World the Slaves Made* (New York, 1974), 222, passim.

13. Rabinowitz claims that in the 1890s, Nashville's African Americans turned away from politics toward economic activism (*Race Relations*, 238). Beginning in the late 1880s, a series of acts in the Tennessee legislature diluted black political power. For a fuller story, see Doyle, *Nashville in the New South*, 140–74.

14. For a complete story of the streetcar boycott, see August Meier and Elliot Rudwick, *Along the Color Line: Explorations in the Black Experience* (Chicago, 1976). They note that the Union Transportation Company failed because insufficient capital meant the businessmen could not buy enough cars to provide regular and reliable service, and that some of the steam cars could not traverse Nashville's steep hills.

15. *Nashville Banner*, 27 Sept. 1905, p. 6.

16. *Nashville Globe*, 4 Sept. 1909, p. 5.

17. Ibid., 20 Aug. 1909, p. 2.

18. Ibid., 11 Jan. 1907, p. 4.

19. Ibid., 2 Dec. 1910, p. 4.

20. Meier, *Negro Thought*, 140.

21. *Nashville Globe*, 4 Sept. 1909, p. 4.

22. Ibid., 13 Feb. 1911, p. 4.

23. Ibid., 9 Jan. 1909, p. 4.

24. As an example, see ibid., 6 Jan. 1911 edition.

25. Ibid., 12 Jan, 1912, p. 8.

26. Ibid., 16 Aug. 1907, p. 4.

27. Ibid., 8 Jan. 1908, p. 1.
28. Ibid., 13 Feb. 1911, p. 4.
29. Ibid., 12 Jan. 1912, p. 1. Apparently, previous board members had not deposited with the bank.
30. Ibid., 12 Jan. 1910, p. 4.
31. Ibid., 4 Aug. 1911, p. 4.
32. Henry was the manager and his father was listed as the company's owner (and later as its president).
33. *Nashville Globe*, 18 Dec. 1908, p. 1.
34. Ibid., 21 Dec. 1909. The newspaper compartmentalized its coverage of the city's women. Women rarely received coverage in news stories, but a section of the newspaper ("Miladi's Notebook," originally "City Items") contained social news such as marriages, receptions, women's club meetings, and the like.
35. The newspaper promoted other black businesses in this manner, although not with the same vigor as it did the doll company. Editorials praising the industriousness and talents of the new proprietor often appeared in the same issue as the article announcing the opening.
36. *Nashville Globe*, 3 Dec. 1909, p. 3.
37. Ibid., 3 Dec. 1909, p. 3. The *Globe*'s story noted that the local article (it did not mention the newspaper or the date of the article) had been picked up by newspapers throughout the country. The newspaper quoted from the article by the "local correspondent," who claimed that black's responded to the doll sales-men's pitch by saying of their offspring, "Dey's jist as good as anybody's chilluns, and is gwine to have pretty white folks dolls to play wid."
38. Ibid., 13 Dec. 1908, p. 3.
39. Ibid., 5 Jan. 1908, p. 1.
40. Ibid., 13 Sept. 1907, p. 2.
41. *Report of the Eleventh Annual Convention of the National Negro Business League* (Nashville, 1911), 30.
42. *Nashville Globe*, 17 Sept. 1909, p. 3.
43. Ibid., 11 Feb. 1910, p. 2.
44. Ibid., 7 Aug. 1908, p. 5. See Blaine Brownell, *The Urban Ethos in the South* (Baton Rouge, La., 1975) for general argument about similarity of black and white boosterism.
45. *Crisis*, January 1913, 112.
46. *Nashville Globe*, 1 Nov. 1912, p. 1.
47. Ibid., 15 Sept. 1911, p. 4.
48. Links between elements of Nashville's black elite and the National Negro Business League emphasize the strong relationship between Washington and the city's middle class. Nashville formed its NNBL chapter in 1902. Both R. H. Boyd and James C. Napier, a black attorney and politician, served on the NNBL's executive committee; Napier as its chairman. Furthermore, Nashville's participants in the NNBL's annual meeting in 1911 needed to register at the *Globe*'s offices. Napier succeeded Washington as president of the NNBL in 1915 and served until 1917.
49. *Nashville Globe*, 22 Nov. 1907, p. 6.
50. Ibid., 2 Dec. 1910, p. 4.
51. Ibid., 29 Mar. 1912, p. 4.
52. Ibid., 22 Apr. 1910, p. 4.
53. Ibid., 26 Feb. 1909, p. 1.

54. Ibid., 22 Mar. 1907, 27 May 1910, 17 Feb. 1911.
55. Ibid., 4 Oct. 1907, p. 3.
56. Ibid., 5 July 1907 and 5 July 1912. While just one example, the study of the newspaper during this period makes it appear to be a legitimate generalization.
57. Ibid., 1 Feb. 1907, p. 4.
58. Ibid., 3 Sept. 1909, p. 4.
59. Ibid., 18 Jan. 1907, 1; for comparison of the NBPB advertisements see ibid., 2 Feb. 1907 and 3 July 1908.
60. Robbins, "World-Within-a-World," 138–40.
61. According to the 1910 United States Census, 36,523 out of a total population of 110,523.
62. This information comes from a study of the *Nashville City Directory* for the years 1907, 1912, 1914, and 1917.
63. *Nashville Globe,* 7 June 1912, p. 4.
64. Ibid.
65. Ibid., 6 Aug. 1912, p. 4.
66. Ibid., 1 Aug. 1913, p. 1.
67. A front-page story noted the growth of the Star Realty Company from six thousand dollars to twenty-five thousand dollars as it developed lots near Fisk University. Ibid., 21 Feb. 1913.
68. See the 27 Aug. 1909 and 29 July 1910 issues for political arguments.
69. *Nashville Globe,* 13 Jan. 1991, p. 2.
70. For a full story of this change, see Doyle, *Nashville in the New South,* 171–77.
71. *Nashville Globe,* 21 Nov. 1913, 4.
72. Lamon, *Black Tennesseans,* 230–300.

God Bless You All—I Am Innocent
Sheriff Joseph F. Shipp, Chattanooga, and the Lynching of Ed Johnson

Michael Webb

UNDREDS OF PEOPLE, RESIDENTS AND VISITORS
ALIKE, STROLL DAILY ACROSS THE WALNUT
STREET BRIDGE, ENJOYING ITS VIEWS OF THE
Tennessee River and downtown Chattanooga. On the
night of 19 March 1906, a far different group marched
along the bridge—it was a brutal lynch mob, ready to
hang and then shoot an innocent black man, Ed Johnson,
in the name of racial vengeance. Lynching was the most
violent way that whites kept African Americans "in their
place" during the Jim Crow era. According to one count,
lynch mobs murdered approximately two hundred blacks
in Tennessee between 1882 and 1930. Michael Webb
details one grisly murder, that of Ed Johnson of Chattanooga, and the important legal and political ramifi-
cations of this failure to uphold the rule of law and
protect the rights of the defendant. Whereas other chapters in this section emphasize more positive themes—
especially how African Americans made the most out of
limited opportunities—Webb's sad tale is a powerful
reminder that, in the end, whites rarely felt compelled to
respect the rights of any African American in the Jim
Crow era. Beneath the veneer of racial calm in early-
twentieth-century Tennessee lay a far different reality:
that of the noose and mob demands for justice.

Ed Johnson's final words were "God bless you all—I am innocent."[1] Moments later he lay dead at the feet of his executioners. Lynched from the County Bridge (later renamed the Walnut Street Bridge) in Chattanooga, his body riddled with more than fifty gunshot wounds, Johnson fell victim to a fate all too common to southern blacks in the early twentieth century. He was twenty-four years old. His death, during the evening of 19 March 1906, came within hours of the U.S. Supreme Court's decision to stay his execution. Completely indifferent to the high court's ruling, a small band of vigilantes assumed the role of judge, jury, and executioner.

Two months earlier, Nevada Taylor, a nineteen-year-old white woman, notified police that she had been robbed and sexually assaulted in a cemetery near her home during the early evening of 23 January 1906. The crime, vilified in a local newspaper as one "which heat[s] Southern blood to the boiling point and prompt[s] law-abiding men to take the law into their hands," was allegedly perpetrated by a young black man.[2] It was for this crime that Johnson had been accused, convicted, and sentenced to death in a Chattanooga court. The Supreme Court's last-minute intervention had seemingly spared him the hangman's noose. But the locals, demanding swift and deadly retribution, had taken it upon themselves to carry out his execution. Such groups were rarely punished during this time. Indeed, between 1900 and 1929 various local and state courts presided over eight cases that involved fifty-four accused lynchers. The legal system's unwillingness to punish those who were convicted is evident by the outcomes of these cases. While only a small number of those accused were actually convicted of participating in lynch mobs, their punishments ranged from meager fines to short jail terms.[3]

Those who participated in Ed Johnson's murder must have been confident that they also would avoid punishment for their actions. If the circumstances of this lynching had been similar to the hundreds that preceded it, they would have been correct. Ed Johnson's name would have become just another entry into the numerous lists of faceless lynching victims. But Johnson's death became significant because it marked the first time in American history that the United States Supreme Court would involve itself in a lynching case. U.S. Attorney General William H. Moody declared that "for the first time we now have a national lynching, one which the federal government must and will punish."[4] When Hamilton County sheriff Joseph F. Shipp was notified by the Court of its decision to hear Johnson's case and stay the death sentence, responsibility for the incarceration and safety of his prisoner assumed a different dimension. Ed Johnson was now a federal prisoner and his death, in the face of blatant disregard for the Supreme Court, would not quietly fade away. The circumstances surrounding Johnson's murder presented the federal government with its first opportunity to prosecute a lynch mob. It set in motion a chain of events that kept Chattanooga in the national headlines for the next three years.

When Trinity University president John C. Kilgo commented on the 1906 Atlanta race riots, he remarked that the pervasiveness of lynching was traceable to the race demagoguery practiced by southern newspaper editors.[5] During the investigation, incarceration, trial, and subsequent lynching of Ed Johnson, various articles published in Chattanooga newspapers supported Kilgo's blanket indictment of southern editors. The *Chattanooga News* called the assault of which Johnson was accused "a crime without parallel in [the] criminal annals of Hamilton County." The article brazenly predicted that "had the brute who committed the crime been caught or if he is yet caught his life would hardly be his for more than a minute in the hands of these men."[6] The men to which the article referred were those private citizens who had organized themselves into search parties within hours of learning of the assault. Known for their reputations as mobs that "hang first and inquire afterward," these search parties, or posses, often formed the first link in a chain of events that resulted in most lynchings.[7] Still another article had threatened that when the "brute" was brought to justice, "he shall suffer death in the most frightful form the human mind can conceive. This seems to be the sentiment, which has impregnated St. Elmo, and not that suburb alone, but the entire city and vicinity."[8]

These responses were typical of southern newspapers when reporting the rape of a white woman, especially if the alleged perpetrator was a black man. At this early juncture, even before a suspect was arrested, the inflammatory rhetoric expressed in these articles effectively sanctioned violent retribution. These newspaper accounts provided a clear validation of Arthur Raper's conclusion that lynching "is but a product of community standards, and consequently will not be condemned by that community."[9]

Nevada Taylor was assaulted in the Forest Hills Cemetery at about 6:30 P.M. on 23 January 1906. Her father, William Taylor, a popular and respected member of the St. Elmo community, was the caretaker of the cemetery. It was widely known that Taylor walked the same route through the cemetery upon her return home from work each evening. She told police officers that upon approaching the cemetery gate, she "heard footsteps behind her and turned only to be caught in the powerful arms of a negro man, whom she cannot identify." She was choked into unconsciousness with a leather strap as the rapist "accomplished his terrible purpose." Because it was dark when the assault occurred, Taylor could only provide officers with a vague description of the assailant: a black man, five feet eight or slightly taller (about her height), wearing dark clothing and a black hat. In fact, Taylor would never positively identify her attacker. The leather strap, two feet in length with a slit in one end, was left at the scene by the assailant. Aside from the minor injuries to Taylor's neck, this strap was the only physical evidence of the assault.[10]

On 24 January, James Broaden was arrested as a suspect or as someone who knew "something of the perpetrator of the St. Elmo crime." Answering the victim's sketchy description, Broaden's criminal reputation was known to the local police. Through his former employment with R. F. Fowler Grocery, a business located near the crime scene, police surmised that "his knowledge of the 'lay of the land' about the spot where the crime was committed . . . might easily have [allowed him to] become possessed of the knowledge that his intended victim reached her home at a certain hour each evening." But the search did not end with the arrest of Broaden, for information had been received by the sheriff's department that led to the investigation of another suspect. Ed Johnson, an illiterate, twenty-four-year-old manual laborer and "well known as a hanger on at various saloons in South Chattanooga," was arrested the following morning.[11]

Because police records are no longer available, an interview granted to the *Chattanooga Daily Times* by Sheriff Shipp provides the most reliable record of events leading to Johnson's arrest. Shipp stated that shortly before Taylor's train arrived at the St. Elmo station, a witness, Will Hixson, had observed a black man answering Johnson's description loitering in the vicinity. Hixson claimed to have recognized the suspect because he remembered asking him for a match on the previous day. He also told police that the suspect was nervously twirling a leather strap. Accompanied by Hixson, the police searched the downtown "red row" district before locating Johnson on Whiteside Street, near a pool room he was known to frequent. Citing the need "to protect him from a mob that was forming [more] than on account of belief in his guilt," Shipp immediately took Johnson into custody.[12]

The most challenging task confronting Shipp and his department was protecting the two prisoners from an enraged community. In the aftermath of the arrests, rumors circulating throughout Chattanooga convinced Shipp that a lynch mob was planning to kill Johnson and Broaden. In fact, he was warned by several citizens that plans were underway for an assault upon the jail that very evening. After consulting with Judge Samuel D. McReynolds of the criminal court, Shipp ordered Johnson and Broaden transported to

Nashville for safekeeping. Unaware that Johnson and Broaden had been taken from the city, a mob of three thousand men descended upon the jail at nightfall. They not only demanded the suspects in the Taylor assault, but two other black prisoners—Floyd Westfield, accused of murdering police officer Lon Rains, and Ed Smith, accused of assaulting a white girl at the Vine Street Orphanage—were objects of the mob's rage. Over the course of four hours the jail was barraged with gunfire, rocks, and sledgehammers while the bloodthirsty mob screamed "bring them out" and "kill the niggers." A metal battering ram was used to break down the jail's front door, while random gunshots injured three spectators and destroyed every window in the building. The intensity of the attack prompted Governor John I. Cox to order the local militia into service to protect the jail and the officers inside. Although the presence of five hundred armed troops quickly brought the disturbance under control, the somewhat calmer mob remained unconvinced by Judge McReynolds's assurances that Johnson and Broaden were not in the jail. They continued threatening police officers and engaging in sporadic violence until McReynolds found a way to placate them.[13]

Upon hearing the commotion at the jail, members of the chamber of commerce adjourned their meeting and hurried to McReynolds's aid. Several notable civic leaders from Chattanooga's past were counted among the chamber members. John A. Patten, president of the Chattanooga Medicine Company; Demitrious M. Steward, noted manufacturer and entrepreneur; T. C. Thompson, Chattanooga's first mayor following the enactment of commission government in 1911; and Milton B. Ochs, managing editor of the *Chattanooga Daily Times*, were among those who assisted McReynolds in negotiating with the mob. The mob leaders and chamber members successfully forged an agreement that allowed a small group of mob members access to the jail so they could ascertain for themselves that the prisoners were absent. After a tour of the jail satisfied them that Johnson and Broaden were not there, the frustrated mob, amid further threats to have their way with the prisoners, began disbanding by 11:30 P.M.[14] If Johnson and Broaden had been in the jail during the attack, it is doubtful the mob have abandoned their intentions to kill them. Shipp's decision to remove them from Chattanooga not only saved their lives, but probably the lives of Westfield and Smith as well.

Immediately following the attack, the *Chattanooga Daily Times* used a scathing editorial to denounce the mob. Claiming that Chattanooga had been "shamed by the riotous demonstrations of the ugly mob," the editorial demanded the arrest of those who had engaged in the attempt to lynch the prisoners and in the wanton destruction of property.[15] Judge McReynolds

responded to the riot by charging the grand jury with the responsibility to
investigate the mob and to summon before the court those who could be
identified as participants. It was this same grand jury that in only a few days
would hand down a criminal assault indictment against Ed Johnson. But the
Daily Times' condemnation and McReynolds's grand jury charge eventually
proved to be nothing more than empty rhetoric. No charges were ever filed
against any of the participants. Not only did private citizens refuse to identify
members of the mob, both local newspapers, despite having eyewitnesses on
the scene, refused to come forward with information. Community silence,
typical in the aftermath of mob violence, had already taken root in Chattanooga. Which of the two suspects would be indicted for the assault? This
dilemma was resolved when at the request of Sheriff Shipp, Nevada Taylor
traveled to Nashville for the purpose of identifying her attacker. Upon arriving, Taylor was ushered into a darkened interrogation room thought to
resemble the conditions she had experienced on the night of the assault. It
was here that she confronted Johnson and Broaden for the first time. Shipp
ordered both men to speak alternately, first using their normal voices, then
lower, menacing voices. They were also ordered to move about the room so
that Taylor might observe their silhouettes in the darkness. Despite earlier
statements that she was unable to identify her attacker, Taylor showed little
difficulty in accusing Johnson. She told Shipp that "from that negro's general
figure, height and size; from his voice, as I can distinctly remember it; from
his manner of movement and action, and from the clothing he wears, it is to
my best knowledge and belief that the man who stood on your left [Johnson]
was the one who assaulted me." She added that she believed in Johnson's
guilt because he deliberately tried to disguise his voice—just as Shipp had
requested! This "almost positive identification" of Ed Johnson, coupled with
testimony from a "well known white man [Will Hixson], whose word is
regarded as the very image of truth by his friends," proved sufficient for the
grand jury to indict Johnson. Following the indictment, Judge McReynolds
appointed local attorney Robert T. Cameron to the unpopular task of representing Johnson. Attorneys W. G. M. Thomas and Lewis Shepherd were also
appointed to assist with Johnson's defense.[16]

Still concerned for his safety, the sheriff's department implemented a
series of measures to protect Johnson during what was sure to be a trial
charged with emotion. Judge McReynolds also ordered that the general public be excluded from viewing the trial. With the exception of those directly
involved in the proceedings, only the local press were to be permitted access
to the courtroom. Furthermore, asserting an interest in preventing any further

mob violence, McReynolds determined that Johnson's trial would proceed expeditiously. Anticipating a defense motion for a change of venue, a move viewed by McReynolds as a way to delay the trial, the judge stated publicly that such a motion would be denied.[17] As a result, Johnson's attorneys would never broach the issue in open court. On 6 February 1906, within hours of his secret return to Chattanooga, the highly publicized trial of Ed Johnson was underway.

Led by Tennessee Sixth District attorney general Matt Whitaker, the prosecution opened the trial by calling Nevada Taylor as its first witness. Taylor's testimony contained significant contradictions with regard to her ability to identify the assailant. When asked specifically if Johnson was the assailant, she merely replied, "I believe he is the man." Frustrated with Taylor's inability to offer a positive identification of Johnson as her assailant, the jury itself recalled her to the stand during the third day of the trial. During a period of direct questioning by the jury foreman, Johnson, wearing dark clothing and a black hat, was ordered to stand directly in front of Taylor. Neither Johnson's attorneys nor Judge McReynolds objected to this unusual request. With the defendant standing less than three feet from her, Taylor once again stated that she "believed" him to be the assailant. C. E. Bearden, one of the jurors, became so frustrated with Taylor's response that he "became more and more nervous and began to weep, and almost rising to his feet, cried, 'Miss Taylor, as God sees you, can you say that is the negro, the right negro?'" Taylor calmly responded, "I would not take the life of an innocent man, but I believe that is the man."[18] Despite the prodding, she never offered positive identification.

Will Hixson, the only witness placing Johnson near the crime scene prior to the attack, provided the most damaging testimony to Johnson's case. He testified to not only seeing Johnson near the crime scene, but to observing him twirling the leather strap presumably used in the assault. When asked if he might be mistaken about the defendant's identity, Hixson claimed that he was certain because not only did he know Johnson worked at the St. Elmo Rock Church, he had observed him there on several occasions. But when he allegedly began searching for Johnson on the day following the assault, Hixson testified, "I hunted over Mountain Junction, Alton Park, St. Elmo, Whiteside street, East and West Ninth streets and I finally saw him at the rock church talking to a negro."[19] Why did Hixson not begin his search at the St. Elmo Rock Church if he knew that Johnson worked there? In fact, St. Elmo was located closer to his own place of employment, the Chattanooga Medicine Company, than the first areas he searched.

Successfully defending Johnson necessitated a dual strategy. The defense needed to mitigate the damage done by Hixson's testimony, and they needed corroborating witnesses to support Johnson's claim that he was at the Last Chance Saloon on Whiteside Street when Taylor was attacked. When they began presenting their case on the afternoon of the second day, the defense immediately attacked Hixson's credibility. They asserted that Hixson's testimony was fabricated and motivated by greed. He had in fact resigned from the Chattanooga Medicine Company on the day prior to notifying Sheriff Shipp that he had knowledge of the assailant's identity. Hixson, they argued, was sufficiently motivated to accuse Johnson, or in fact any black suspect, because it would entitle him to claim the $500 reward that had been offered for the assailant's capture. Harvey McConnell, a black laborer, was called as the first defense witness. McConnell, it was hoped, would undermine the veracity of Hixson's statement that he previously knew the defendant and his place of employment. McConnell testified that he had, in fact, spoken with Hixson concerning various black laborers employed at the church. When Hixson asked for their names, he replied that the only one familiar to him was Ed Johnson. Upon receiving this information, Hixson told McConnell that it was Johnson who was suspected of assaulting Taylor. What he failed to mention, however, was that at this particular time it was only he who suspected Johnson. In further testimony, McConnell stated that as he spoke to Hixson he noticed Ed Johnson standing directly across the street. When he summoned Johnson to join them, Hixson promptly left the scene. Upon being recalled to respond to McConnell's testimony, Hixson simply denied having spoken with him concerning either Ed Johnson or the Taylor assault.[20]

Johnson's alibi rested upon his claim that he was in South Chattanooga at the Last Chance Saloon between 4:30 and 10:00 P.M. William Hunnicut, an employee of the Chattanooga Packing Company, was among several witnesses called to corroborate his claim. Hunnicut testified that at approximately 6:00 P.M., he saw Johnson "sitting by the stove in the pool room, which is under the saloon proper." Two other witnesses, J. G. Groves and John Jackson, both "frequenter[s] of the Last Chance Saloon," also testified to having seen Johnson at the tavern during the time the assault occurred.[21] The prosecution attempted to undermine Johnson's alibi by raising a question concerning the exact time that he was supposedly at the saloon. The prosecution's strategy centered upon the question of whether the clocks in the tavern were reliable. According to witnesses, two clocks were in the saloon, each hanging on opposing walls of the establishment. The clock located on the south wall "was a small 'crazy' one, which when wound up usually ran less than an hour before becoming tired and stopping."[22] The clock that hung on the north wall was thought to be more reliable. Which of the two clocks did defense witnesses use to establish the time they saw Johnson? The prosecution's argument could only be valid if all of the defense witnesses had used the same slow clock. But would all of them have used the same clock to support Johnson's alibi, on the same evening, and at about the same time? The answers to these questions never surfaced during Johnson's trial. Eight witnesses, five black and three white, testified under oath that Johnson was at the saloon when the crime occurred.

The replacement of the clock, shortly after Johnson was taken into custody, broaches another questionable aspect of the case. J. G. Brooks, the "mysterious clock man," testified that he when replaced the clock in the saloon, he also destroyed both the old clock and the "memorandum in regard to the clock" because he "had no further use for it."[23] During the time he replaced the clock. Brooks was in the company of three deputies of the Hamilton County Sheriff's Department. This action becomes significant by virtue of when the clock replacement supposedly occurred. Apparently, the clock was replaced following Johnson's arrest and subsequent statements that he made regarding his alibi. Did a faulty clock really exist? If not, testimony from defense witnesses would have been more difficult to undermine and Johnson's alibi would have been more compelling. If the clock did exist, why did the police department allow the destruction of a piece of evidence that could have essentially made the prosecution's case? In the end, despite their being unable to either confirm or deny the existence of a faulty clock, the jury sided with the prosecution's version of events. Unfortunately for Johnson, the jury was more willing to accept the faulty clock theory than the testimony of eight eyewitnesses. On Friday morning, 10 February 1906, the jury returned a guilty verdict against Ed Johnson.

Accompanying the verdict was their recommendation that he be sentenced to death by hanging. Upon hearing the verdict, Johnson exhibited the same stoic persona that had become his trademark throughout his highly publicized incarceration and trial. When he was permitted to address the court, Johnson once again proclaimed his innocence. And perhaps because he did not know what else to say, the convicted man closed with a muffled "thank you."[24]

In the hours prior to Johnson's official sentencing a committee of six Chattanooga lawyers took under advisement the question of whether the jury's verdict would withstand the scrutiny of appellate review. Robert

Pritchard, Foster V. Brown, and J. H. Cantrell joined Cameron, Thomas, and Shepherd in comprising the committee. In fact, Thomas, an inexperienced criminal lawyer, had previously voiced misgivings about the trial and hoped that the committee would in some way enable them to share in the burden of deciding Johnson's fate. But in the end it was Foster Brown, not Thomas, who displayed the most concern, for Johnson's right to appeal the verdict. Brown was unable to persuade the other members that the only way to guarantee fairness for Johnson was through the appeals process. But when his argument fell on deaf ears, he acceded to the majority opinion. The committee unanimously concluded that Johnson had received a fair and speedy trial, was convicted by a jury of his peers, and was represented by competent legal counsel. Furthermore, they believed that the verdict would withstand appeal. They also agreed that nothing more should be done in defense of Johnson because they feared that an appeal would lead to further mob violence. Later that afternoon, Thomas and Cameron laid aside their sworn obligation to defend their client when they addressed Judge McReynolds prior to his passing sentence and announced their acceptance of the verdict.[25]

Only minutes before, Thomas and Cameron had convinced Johnson that he should acquiesce to the committee's findings, that pursuing further legal recourse would serve neither his nor the community's best interest. Indeed, they painted a bleak picture of his situation: "If you are an innocent man, you . . . were found in bad company. . . . And it looks like you must lose your life on [that] account. The jury would not believe your bad company. If you die, Ed, and you are innocent, your bad company will be the thing that kills you, because the jury refused to believe anything they said." Fearing death at the hands of a lynch mob if the verdict was appealed, Johnson took the advice of his attorneys and resolved to accept punishment for a crime that he still denied committing. Johnson's attorneys, under the absurd pretense of protecting him from a mob during his final days, had effectively persuaded him to die legally. When Judge McReynolds set Johnson's execution date to occur within thirty days, the condemned man once again accepted the news without emotion. Asked if he wished to make a final statement to the court, Johnson, in a solemn and almost inaudible voice, muttered, "I haven't got much to say, only I am an innocent man. I reckon I'll have to suffer, and it's all right."[26] He was immediately remanded to the Knox County Jail to await his execution date.

Noah W. Parden and Styles L. Hutchins, two highly regarded black attorneys, immediately took up Johnson's case. Their intervention, at the behest of Johnson's father, was met with mixed sentiments among Chattanoogans. Although Parden and Hutchins claimed to have heard from several whites who supported their effort to win a new trial for Johnson, the *News* reported that such efforts were "deplored by the better element of the race." One editorial noted that "Johnson is a convicted man and resort to the Federal arm in the hope of saving his neck, or prolonging his life is ill advised and calculated to bring about more trouble than his miserable neck is worth." On 13 February, Parden notified Judge McReynolds that he intended to file a motion seeking a new trial and stay of execution. Included among the several points contained in the motion was their assertion that Johnson was convicted solely upon circumstantial evidence that failed to warrant a guilty verdict, that the jury overstepped its authority when the foreman compelled the defendant to provide self-incriminating evidence, and that both Johnson and his attorneys had been subjected to a systematic pattern of intimidation. These trial errors, they asserted, provided sufficient proof that Ed Johnson had been deprived of a fair trial.[27]

The new defense team faced a major legal obstacle: too much time had passed before their appeal was filed. Since Johnson's father retained them after the verdict, they were unable to file an official new trial motion within the legally allotted three-day period. With Johnson officially sentenced on Friday and the motion not being heard until Tuesday, the inclusion of Sunday meant that four days would elapse. Owing to this special circumstance, only Judge McReynolds could grant the necessary waivers to clear the path for a new trial. But the judge quickly proved unsympathetic to their plight, noting in a Monday that in his opinion the trial errors that the defense intended to use as the basis of their motion failed to establish sufficient grounds for granting a new trial. Undeterred by McReynolds's open opposition, Parden pressed his request for special consideration. Were not Sundays, he inquired of McReynolds, usually excluded when fixing the time allowed for filing appeals? McReynolds was unmoved. Soon after disposing of the remaining docket, McReynolds dismissed his court and departed Chattanooga for an extended Florida vacation.[28]

Parden and Styles next filed a writ of error with the Tennessee Supreme Court. The merits of Johnson's appeal prompted the court to review the case even though its next term would not convene until September. On 4 March the state supreme court dealt a serious blow to the defense. Yet another legal technicality, the absence of Judge McReynolds's signature on the bill of exceptions contained in the writ, compelled the court to vote for its dismissal.

Despite Parden's argument that he had been unable to obtain McReynolds's signature because he had left the city, the court would not be swayed from its decision.[29]

With Johnson's time quickly ticking away, the defense filed a writ of habeas corpus in federal court that enumerated six violations of his constitutional rights. They maintained that Johnson had been compelled to provide self-incriminating evidence, was soon to be deprived of his life without due process, had been denied a public trial by a jury of his peers, and had been deprived of adequate counsel in the final stages of his trial, equal protection under the law, and the right of appeal pursuant to the Tennessee criminal code. It was, declared Parden, "the most remarkable trial ever witnessed in a court of justice." The charges set forth in the writ proved so compelling that federal Circuit Judge C. D. Clark decided to hear the supporting evidence. On 7 March, upon his arrival in Knoxville to take custody of Johnson, Sheriff Shipp received notification of Judge Clark's decision. He was ordered to have Johnson in Clark's courtroom on the following Saturday, during which time evidence pertaining to the writ would be heard.[30]

Before the federal court, Parden argued that his client's right to avoid self-incrimination under the Fifth Amendment was violated at the moment the jury required him to stand before Taylor in open court while wearing a hat and dark clothing. And, during the questioning, when one of the jurors shouted, "If I could just get at him, I would tear his heart out," Parden told Judge Clark that McReynolds "did not rebuke him by word or jesture [sic] or disapproving look." This intimidation, he noted, exemplified what Johnson and his attorneys were forced to endure throughout the trial proceedings and clearly undermined his ability to receive a fair trial.[31] Parden complained of Johnson's supposed surrender of his right to appeal and the court's refusal to grant a change of venue for the highly publicized trial. Parden noted that Johnson's lawyers had intimidated him so effectively that he felt compelled to accept a death sentence. The outbreak of mob violence following Johnson's arrest sent a clear signal that his trial necessitated removal to another city. Parden admonished Johnson's attorneys for failing to file the motion simply because public statements by Judge McReynolds indicated that he would refuse to hear it. In fact, Parden continued, McReynolds's decision was not likely arrived at by thoughtful deliberation but was the product of an intimidating *Chattanooga Daily Times* editorial that predicted more mob violence if a change of venue were to be granted.[32] Parden also pointed that Johnson had been deprived of a public trial by a jury of his peers since no blacks were included on the jury. Deputy Court Clerk J. P. Pemberton denied Parden's allegation. He testified that at the time of Johnson's trial, the names of between two hundred and five hundred blacks were among the four thousand contained in the jury pool. He insisted that at no time were the names of potential black jurors removed from the selection box. In denying earlier defense motions for a reconstituted jury, McReynolds claimed that reconstituting the jury would lead to Johnson's murder at the hands of a mob. This ruling clearly demonstrated, Parden contended, that intimidation played a controlling role in the trial. Furthermore, Johnson's right to a public trial had been violated when the courthouse and the courtroom designated for the trial had been cordoned off by police officers. The general public, including Johnson's immediate family, had been denied access to the proceedings.[33]

Finally, the defense would argue that Johnson had been denied the assistance of effective counsel during the sentencing phase of his trial. Evidence presented by Parden suggested that some of the committee members who deliberated on Johnson's fate were intimidated by several unnamed citizens who did not want an appeal of the case. At least two of them, Thomas and Brown, were told by a "leading citizen and property owner," that although he was opposed to mob action, if Johnson's case was appealed, he would personally "organize and head a mob to break the jail and hang the petitioner that night." Their open acknowledgment of these threats demonstrated that sufficient motivation existed for Johnson's lawyers to induce him to forego his right of appeal. When Johnson's lawyers chose to abandon him at the time he most needed them, community pressure and intimidation carried the day. "Like a lamb led to the slaughter," declared Parden, "he [Johnson] was dumb."[34]

Despite the compelling case advanced by the defense, Judge Clark ruled in favor of the state. "In the course of his decision," declared the *News*, "Judge Clark exonerates Judge McReynolds and Attorney-General Whitaker of the charges laid at their door in the petition."[35] Anticipating an appeal to the United States Supreme Court, Clark's final ruling contained his recommendation that McReynolds petition a stay of execution to ensure that the defense would be allowed sufficient time to prepare their motions. Governor Cox agreed to grant Johnson a stay of execution for seven days. While Parden and Hutchins hastily prepared a writ of habeas corpus for submission to the United States Supreme Court, the prevailing opinion among the Chattanooga legal profession held that the Court would refuse to hear the case. Lewis Shepherd, one of the original lawyers for Johnson's defense, gave voice to such sentiment when he remarked that "the supreme court of the United States will not interfere in any way with the schedule as now outlined, and I believe the hanging will take place on next Tuesday as now arranged."[36] He was wrong.

On 19 March 1906, when Sheriff Shipp received a telegram from Washington, D.C., officially notifying him of the Supreme Court's decision to hear the merits of Johnson's case, he became accountable for the protection of a federal prisoner. If the habeas corpus motion were to be dismissed, Johnson would immediately be returned to criminal court for resentencing. However, if the Court found that Johnson's civil rights had in fact been violated, he would be ordered released from custody. As the result of such a ruling, the state would be left with the task of securing a new indictment and conducting a new trial.

News of the Court's decision spread swiftly throughout the community. And in the midst of all the open hostility toward the decision, the *News* published an editorial that portended the night's violence: "All of this delay is aggravating the community. The people of Chattanooga believe that Johnson is guilty, and that he ought to suffer the penalty of the law as speedily as possible. If by legal technicality the case is prolonged and the culprit finally escapes, there will be no use to plead with a mob here if another such crime is committed. Such delays are largely responsible for mob violence all over the country."[37]

Even as the news of Johnson's successful appeal circulated during the afternoon of 1 March 1906, small groups of men were observed assembling at several sites near the jail, and they were ready to assume for themselves the role of judge, jury, and executioner, the Supreme Court be damned. As they openly and loudly denounced what they perceived as the Court's interference in a strictly local matter, they were clearly, to a man, committed to nothing less than seeing Ed Johnson dead.[38] At approximately 8:00 P.M. the mob sprang into action. About a dozen men, some "with hand-kerchiefs over the lower part of their faces," confronted deputy Jeremiah Gibson inside the front entrance of the jail and demanded that he deliver Johnson over to them.[39] Within minutes, the jail was occupied by more than twenty men engaged in taking turns swinging a sledgehammer against the doors enclosing the cell block entrance. Offering virtually no resistance to the mob, Gibson managed to telephone Sheriff Shipp within minutes of losing control of the jail. Despite living within blocks of the jail, more than an hour elapsed before Shipp finally arrived. He did arrive on the scene, however, prior to the mob taking Johnson from his cell. According to the eyewitness account of *Chattanooga Daily Times* reporter Joseph R. Curtis, the sheriff offered only perfunctory objections to the mob's activity. When several onlookers asked him how he was going to prevent the lynching, Shipp replied simply, "What can I do, we are over-powered." Shipp was allegedly forced into a first floor bathroom where he remained until Johnson was taken from the jail.[40]

After the incensed mob finally gained entry to the cellblock, they proceeded directly to Johnson's third-floor cell, where they finally came face to face with the man they so desperately wanted to kill. But they did not find a man cowering in fear. Instead, they found a calm and dignified man, seemingly at peace with his fate. Johnson "was the calmest person in the jail. Not a quiver of the lip or utterance of a sound betrayed the slightest fear or terror." After tying his arms against his body with a cotton rope, the mob ushered Johnson from the building through the main entrance where he was confronted by more of the frenzied crowd. As shouts of "kill him now" and "to the county bridge with him" echoed through the crowd, Johnson walked steadily, his face emotionless. Within minutes he would become another victim of vigilante justice in Chattanooga.[41]

As the quiet and resolute mob went about their task in "workmanlike fashion," a large crowd of spectators following them "yelled at the top of their voices and pushed each other from one side of the street to the other." Within minutes, as the crowd reached the County Bridge, one of the spectators shouted that Johnson should be hung from the second span since the first had already been used to lynch a previous victim. Upon discovering that the rope they had used to secure their victim was too short to hang him with, they quickly discarded it for a trolley car cable. Forcing Johnson to stand beneath the menacing noose, his solemn figure illuminated by a single electric light, the mob demanded that he confess to the crime for which he was about to die. Protesting his innocence until the end, Johnson told the mob that they were about to kill the wrong man: "I am going to tell the truth. I am not guilty. I have said it all the time that I did not do it and it is true. I was not there. I know I am going to die and I have no fear to die and I have no fear at all. I was not at St. Elmo that night. Nobody saw me with a strap. They were mistaken and saw somebody else. I was at the Last Chance Saloon just as I said. I am not guilty and that is all I have to say. God Bless You all! I am innocent."[42]

Within seconds the cable was pulled tight around Johnson's neck as two men viciously hoisted him into the air. Their bloodthirsty emotions now uncontrollable, several fired their weapons into Johnson's suspended body and when an errant bullet struck the cable, his lifeless body fell to the bridge floor. Unsure that their victim was dead, several men approached him as they continued to fire into his body. With their deadly task accomplished, the mob "proceeded to disperse as quickly as it had gathered." When Dr. Cooper Holtzclaw inspected Johnson's body within minutes of his death, he stated that at least fifty gunshot wounds had been inflicted. "Anyone of the shots," he noted, "was sufficient to produce death."[43] During the three hours it took for the mob to carry out Johnson's murder, Sheriff Shipp was the only police officer summoned to the scene.

Community reaction following a lynching typically adhered to a pattern of immediate condemnation followed by silence. Chattanooga was no different. But as rumors of a federal investigation into Johnson's murder began to surface, local newspapers rushed to absolve Sheriff Shipp and his department of any wrongdoing. Sheriff Shipp, the editor of the *News* insisted, "was no more to blame for that lynching than the man in the moon."[44] The newspaper instead placed blame on outside interference (another pattern consistent with most lynchings), especially the federal judiciary. The *News* asserted that "it was the appeal to the federal courts that revived the mob spirit and resulted in the lynching." The event, in the newspaper's opinion, should not soil the city's reputation, and as proof it recounted yet again the sordid chain of events that led to Johnson's murder. It seemed irrelevant that Johnson may have been innocent of the crime or that his constitutional rights may have been violated. Quite simply, someone had to pay for the crime, and Ed Johnson was the most accessible target. Had the mob successfully gotten to Johnson during the 25 January attack, the writer commented, "he would have been lynched. However, they were acting under the excitement of the time—when the whole community was stirred by the enormity of the crime." Nothing had changed.[45]

National condemnation of Chattanooga and the lynching was severe. The *New York Times* wrote that the Chattanooga mob's "open defiance of the Supreme court" had "shocked [its] members beyond anything that has ever happened in their experience on the bench." The national publication the *Outlook* was so outraged by the lynching that it publicly appealed to the Supreme Court to take action against the mob. Another article, printed in the *New York Journal*, proved especially embarrassing to Chattanooga since it erroneously described the city as the scene of an uncontrollable race riot. This national humiliation proved to be more than the *Daily Times* could bear. "List, ye lynchers," decried the editorial, "to the outrageous libel perpetrated by the *New York Journal* in its 'Tenth Edition–Night Special' of last Wednesday and realize the enormity of the damage your madness has perpetrated upon the city whose honor, morality, and chivalry you claim to have vindicated."[46]

The Supreme Court assumed a confrontational stance with the city and state courts immediately upon learning that its ruling had been defied by the Chattanooga mob. One justice in particular, unidentified by the *New York Times*, publicly castigated the parochial courts: "Johnson was tried by little better than mob law before the state court. . . . Whether guilty or innocent, he had the right to a fair trial.[47] Johnson's death raised immediate questions relating to violations of sections 5508 and 5509 of the Revised Statutes of the United States, which granted the federal government the authority to prosecute members of the Ku Klux Klan or others who disguised themselves while conspiring to deprive citizens of their constitutional rights.

Within days of Johnson's murder, several court justices met with President Theodore Roosevelt to discuss possible recourse by the federal government. From this meeting came the decision to investigate the lynching and bring the full power of the federal government to bear upon the mob. When Justice Department agents E. P. McAdams and Henry C. Dickey arrived in Chattanooga to conduct the investigation, it soon became clear that Sheriff Shipp would be the primary target of their inquiry. While police forces gained influence in northern cities during the late 1800s, southern police officers resisted the trend. Their resistance, notes Fitzhugh Brundage, was traceable to a belief that their personal authority as "the law" would be undermined. Police complicity during lynchings became a disturbing byproduct of this resistance. Police involvement with mobs was manifested in two ways: by offering only passive protection for their prisoners and by their own participation in the lynching.[48]

The federal agents found that not only had the sheriff's department been derelict in protecting Johnson, but that some of the officers had actually participated in the lynching. From the outset, the Justice Department had intended that its inquiry should proceed under a veil of strict secrecy, but the investigation would not remain secret for very long. Even before it was officially underway, James R. Penland, the U.S. attorney for the Eastern District (Knoxville), received an anonymous note mailed from Knoxville warning him that his department should refrain from investigating the Johnson matter: "If you know yourself, you will let that thing alone. That nigger," the note continued, "was guilty and had made a confession that he was, and what do you want to interfere for? The state courts, like that in Knox County, that of the whole state and of the United States, are corrupt and the people have got to take the affair in their hands."[49]

Chattanooga was the scene of an intense federal inquiry lasting about three weeks. Using information gathered from dozens of interviews, the government built what was in its view a strong case against Shipp and 26 other defendants. Police negligence notwithstanding, substantiating a conspiracy between Shipp's department and the lynch mob became the focus of the government's case. In Penland's view, agents McAdams and Dickey had been successful. Based upon information contained in their final report, he wrote to Moody that Johnson's death "reveals one of the wickedest plots to murder a helpless defenseless man I have ever known." Penland was "clearly of the opinion that Sheriff Shipp of Hamilton County, who had the negro Ed Johnson in his custody, was responsible for the death of said Johnson."[50]

Shipp's own actions prior to the mob assault on 25 January contributed to the government's contention that a conspiracy between the mob and sheriff's department had contributed to Johnson's murder. Rumors of an impending attempt on Johnson's life had prompted Shipp and McReynolds to have him transported to Nashville for safekeeping and to prepare the jail so that the remaining prisoners would be adequately protected. As a result of their actions the jail was protected by a full complement of well-armed officers during the assault. With almost identical circumstances present on the night of Johnson's death, why would Shipp not take similar protective measures? In light of rumors that plans were afoot to kill Johnson, why didn't Shipp remove him to a safer location immediately after receiving the Supreme Court's notification? What the government perceived as Shipp's deliberate failure to protect Johnson, despite his status as a federal prisoner, provided compelling evidence in substantiating a conspiracy case against him.[51]

The investigators concluded that the mob plans were common knowledge throughout the city and had in fact been openly planned throughout the day. Ellen Baker, one of the prisoners that night, told investigators that during the afternoon of 19 March, Deputy George Brown told her that a mob was planning to lynch Johnson that night. During their conversation, he was engaged in transferring several prisoners to another floor, a move that left her and Johnson alone on the third floor. When another prisoner, Arthur Waller, asked Deputy Brown if he expected a mob that night, he replied that "he did not know, [but] that things were looking pretty damned warm." The jail cook, Preston W. Walker, who was himself black, was so distressed by the rumors that he asked Shipp if his own life might be in danger. Walker stated that Shipp responded with "No, they have cool heads and know what they want." Special deputy W. M. Logan told investigators that Deputy Charles A. Baker had alerted him to the mob's plans as early as 11:00 A.M. And seventeen-year-old prisoner William Tarpley claimed that several groups of people had visited the jail throughout the day. They reportedly spoke in loud, argumentative voices proclaiming that Johnson would be taken forcibly from the jail and killed that night. Allegedly, the metal chains securing the cellblock had also been removed sometime during the day. Although the mob was forced to use a sledgehammer to break the door, McAdams and Dickey doubted that they would have gotten to Johnson had these chains been in place. They surmised that "it would have taken the mob hours to have effected an entrance."[52] Had the chains been purposely removed to make it easier for the mob to enter the cellblock? In the government's view they had.

On the night of the lynching, jail operations were not typical of what McAdams and Dickey had established as normal procedure. Deputy Brown, who with his family resided at the jail, left earlier in the day to visit friends in Hill City, because he allegedly knew of the mob's plans. In fact, upon Gibson's arrival to relieve him that evening, Brown told him that a mob was expected later that night. Since it was well known that the jail was usually "made a loafing resort by the Sheriff and his Deputies and that rarely a night passed without some of them being there," the fact that Gibson was the lone officer on duty that night was immediately suspicious to the investigators. According to Penland, Gibson, an "old man," not only failed to resist the attack but "was incapable of offering resistance."[53]

Not only had the lynching been planned throughout the day, further evidence revealed that despite having ample time because of the mob's slow formation, Gibson and Shipp purposely failed to summon additional officers. Carl Rowden and Frank Spurlock, two private citizens, provided affidavits stating that adequate time was available to summon additional officers to the scene. Rowden, watching the mob forming from his home next door to the jail, expressed surprise that additional officers were not called. Spurlock testified that the mob was so slow to form that he walked by it three times within a span of two hours. When Dr. Howard Jones, a Baptist minister, petitioned Shipp to summon officers to "suppress the gathering," his request went unheeded. Furthermore, Judge McReynolds and District Attorney Matt Whitaker were allegedly across the street from the jail listening "at the whole performance, and took no steps whatever to prevent the mob in carrying out its purposes."[54]

Perhaps the government's most disturbing evidence dealt with the allegation that Johnson's death came as the result of Shipp's need to strengthen his political standing for an upcoming election. Agents McAdams and Dickey pointed out that Shipp was running a difficult race for reelection against a "popular competitor for the nomination of his party in one Sam

Bush."[55] But was it Shipp's actions on 25 January or 19 March that made him vulnerable? Would saving Johnson's life or contributing to his death prove to be Shipp's downfall? Shipp maintained that his actions in protecting Johnson and Broaden on 25 January, actions that were met with disdain among some of his supporters, had resulted in the race being closer than anyone had anticipated.[56] Did Bush's surprising challenge prompt Shipp to view his actions through a different lens? The Justice Department believed that it had. The federal investigation named twenty Chattanooga citizens, all of whom were willing to testify that Johnson's death was the result of Shipp's attempt to shore up his faltering campaign.[57]

When the Democratic primary was held on 29 March 1906, the *Daily Times* noted that "various circumstances within recent days combined to change apathy in activity and culminated in the recording of over 3,000 votes," the largest primary voter turnout to that point in Hamilton County history. The race thought too close to call ended in victory for the beleaguered Shipp. His five-hundred-vote majority was far and away a wider margin than anyone expected. The *Daily Times* asserted that Shipp won the election because his supporters wanted to ensure that he was not defeated because of the Johnson affair—an affair for which they considered him blameless. Bush, on the other hand, simply used "too much Johnson."[58] He was defeated because he focused his campaign on an issue that the community would rather forget.

David H. Barker, a thirty-five-year-old Republican and former deputy sheriff, was Shipp's opponent in the general election. During a campaign conducted with an intensity rivaling the primary, the incumbent's renewed popularity proved too great an obstacle for the Republicans to overcome. Shipp won in the outlying districts of Hamilton County, where slightly more than half of the votes were cast, with a 53 percent majority. But his reelection was secured on the strength of his performance in the eight city wards. By carrying all but the predominately black Fourth and Seventh Wards, Shipp won 62 percent of the vote. His 1,518-vote victory was the widest margin for the office to that point in the county's history.[59]

In the end, McAdams and Dickey concluded that Johnson's life had been sacrificed to advance Shipp's political fortunes. Why was it, inquired an anonymous letter writer, that Shipp "made a round to the various factories on the day following the lynching asking the voters if they were going to vote for him now"?[60]

On 28 May 1906, U.S. Attorney General William Moody presented the government's case to the Supreme Court. In doing so, he solicited a ruling from the Court that would require the parties named in the investigation to show cause why they should not be charged with contempt of the Supreme Court. Moody asserted that Shipp and his deputies, in conspiring to murder Ed Johnson, had willfully defied a federal court order.[61] The Court granted Moody's request, executing a show cause ruling that directed Shipp and twenty-six other defendants to appear before the Court during the October 1906 session. The burden of proof now rested with the defendants. In the eyes of the Supreme Court they were considered guilty of contempt until such time as they proved their innocence. Along with Shipp, several other sheriff's department officers were named in the rule. These included Jeremiah Gibson, Matthew Galloway, George Brown, John Vamell, Charles Baker, and Fred Frawley.

Appearing before the Supreme Court on 16 October 1906, the defendants were confident that the charges would be dismissed. From among the several Chattanoogans who attend the proceedings, it was Judge McReynolds who showed the most interest in dispelling what he believed to be the primary issue underlying the Supreme Court's pursuit of Shipp: his alleged political motivation. During an interview for the *New York Times*, McReynolds stated,

> The impression seems to be that the people of Chattanooga are doubtful about the guilt of Johnson and that they condemn Sheriff Shipp. This is not so. That the electors of Hamilton County are loyal to Shipp and believe he did his full duty on the night Johnson was hanged is evidenced by the fact that last August he was re-elected Sheriff by a majority of 1,500, the greatest ever given by a candidate for the office. There was no reason to believe an outbreak would occur the night Johnson was hanged. Inasmuch as no violence had been attempted in the week or more that Johnson had been in Chattanooga, the Sheriff did not take any extraordinary precautions.[62]

McReynolds knew that the conspiratorial aspect of the government's case against Shipp could be undermined if the political element (Shipp's campaign) was eliminated. Later testimony, however, would reveal that his statement claiming that prior knowledge of the lynching did not exist was, in fact, inaccurate. The judge's rationale is flawed in yet another respect. Indeed, Shipp was not required to exercise "extraordinary precautions" because the community was satisfied that Johnson, under a death sentence, would be punished. Having shown no inclination toward violence since the sentence was passed, there was no reason to expect any unless circumstances would intervene to prevent Johnson's sentence from being carried out. But circumstances did intervene, and the government contended that Shipp must be held accountable for failing to protect Johnson when they did.

Was Shipp at all motivated to resist the lynch mob? The sheriff's own answer to this very important question was revealed during an interview with the *Birmingham Age-Herald* on the very day that the Court ordered the show cause ruling. "I am frank to say," stated Shipp, "that I did not attempt to hurt any of them [the mob], and would not have made such an attempt if I could." The Supreme Court, he continued, "was responsible for this lynching," and "not allowing the case to remain in our courts was the most unfortunate thing in the history of Tennessee." The citizens of Chattanooga would not wait several years to have the case heard by the Supreme Court, and this he concluded, "I do not wonder at."[63]

Judson Harmon, former Tennessee attorney general, served as lead attorney for the defendants. In arguing for dismissal Harmon asserted that the Supreme Court had overstepped its jurisdiction by allowing the stay of execution in Johnson's case. The Supreme Court, he maintained, was precluded from intervening in the case because the state appeals process had not been exhausted. In fact, continued Harmon, Judge Clark's ruling must also be set aside because it was rendered prior to exhausting local appeals. The stay of execution was, therefore, "not binding, and failure to obey could not involve contempt." Furthermore, Harmon claimed that the telegram notifying Shipp of the Court's decision did not constitute proper notice nor provide adequate time for him to guarantee Johnson's safety.[64] Harmon's argument was compelling enough that the Court decided to undertake further consideration of its constitutional authority in the case. The decision on Harmon's motion for dismissal would not be rendered until December. The defendants remained confident that the Court would dismiss the case.

On Christmas Eve 1906, the defendants made their second appearance before the Court. In an opinion delivered by Justice Oliver Wendell Holmes, the Court held that despite the merit of Harmon's argument, it possessed the constitutional authority to hear this case. Furthermore, Holmes continued, the actions of these defendants did in fact constitute a contempt of the Supreme Court, and because the result was the murder of a federal prisoner, they would not be permitted to avail themselves of the common practice of denial through affidavit. They would be required to prove their innocence to the Court's satisfaction upon the basis of the evidence. The Court ordered the Justice Department to proceed with hearing the testimony of all defendants and witnesses named in the investigation. "If they do not succeed in exculpating themselves," Holmes concluded, the defendants "are at the mercy of the court, and any penalty can be inflicted."[65]

From February to July 1907, Supreme Court Commissioner James D. Maher presided over three sessions of testimony in Chattanooga. The final transcript, with the accounts of more than 100 witnesses contained therein, was delivered to the Supreme Court for its examination during the fall term of 1907. Citing insufficient evidence and questionable testimony, mostly obtained from jail prisoners and impeachable witnesses, the government dismissed its case against seventeen defendants, including George Brown and deputies Varnell, Baker, and Frawley. Those who remained, Joseph Shipp, Jeremiah Gibson, William Mayes, Nicholas "Nick" Nolan, Luther Williams, Henry Padgett, Matthew Galloway, Bart Justice, and Frank Ward, were ordered to post a one-thousand-dollar bond to guarantee their appearance in May 1909.

In May 1909, the government also dismissed its cases against Bart Justice and Matthew Galloway. Shipp and Gibson, the only officers known to be present during the lynching, remained as the only officers still named as defendants. They, along with private citizens William Mayes, a carpenter, Henry Padgett, a bricklayer, and saloonkeepers Nick Nolan and Luther Williams, were ordered to reappear in November. On 15 November 1909, as these six defendants prepared to depart Chattanooga for what would be their final appearance before the Supreme Court, they stood among an estimated crowd of five hundred supporters who had gathered to see them off. The emotional ex-sheriff was moved to express his appreciation. "With the good wishes and kindly spirit of such a gathering," Shipp told the crowd, "I feel I am ready to face anything."[66] After more than three years of rulings and legal maneuverings, these six men would at last learn their fate.

By a five to three majority, the Supreme Court found Shipp and his five codefendants guilty of contempt. Justice William Moody, recently appointed to the Court by President Theodore Roosevelt, abstained due to his close attachment to the case as attorney general. Justices Rufus Peckham, Edward White, and Joseph McKenna cast dissenting votes. Chief Justice Melville Weston Fuller delivered the Court's opinion on 16 November 1909. The Court agreed with the government's assertion that despite being notified of the Court's decision to stay the proceedings against Johnson, Shipp knowingly and willfully failed to protect him. He neglected to do so in light of "current reports and rumors conveyed to them" which indicated that a mob was planning to abduct Johnson and kill him. Furthermore, the Court found Shipp and Gibson to be "in sympathy with the mob while pretending to perform their official duty of protecting Johnson, and that they aided and abetted the mob in prosecution and performance of the lynching." Their actions constituted an "utter disregard [for] the above mentioned order of this court." The Court dismissed the defendants' fallacious assertion that they were neither prepared for a mob nor expected a mob that night. In fact, Shipp had previously acknowledged that his department did not expect a mob uprising until the following day! Their flimsy excuse was viewed by the Court as "practically conced[ing] the allegation of the information that they were informed" of the impending mob violence.[67]

The Court also concluded that Shipp's political motivations provided compelling evidence of his guilt. By utilizing his remarks from the same *Age-Herald* article, the Court asserted that Shipp's "reference to the 'people' was significant, for he was a candidate for re-election, and had been told that his saving the prisoner from the first attempt to mob him would cost him his place, and he had answered that he wished the mob had got him before he did." The Court interpreted his actions as the product of his resentment of it "as an alien intrusion, and that the court was responsible for the lynching." Shipp, the Court concluded, had been successful in manipulating public emotions and ingratiating himself with "the people" by using the interview as a public forum to blame them for Johnson's death.[68]

For the first time in American history, defendants were incarcerated for being convicted of contempt of the Supreme Court. Of the original twenty-seven defendants, Shipp and five others, Luther Williams, Nick Nolan, Henry Padgett, and William Mayes, were convicted of contempt of "the Supreme Court of the United States in murdering a prisoner under the sentence of death."[69] For the murder of Ed Johnson, Shipp, Williams, and Nolan were sentenced to ninety days, while Gibson, Padgett, and Mayes received sixty-day terms.

The investigation into Ed Johnson's murder proved to be an arduous undertaking for the federal government. Three years and eight months elapsed between the time of Johnson's death and the Supreme Court's decision. Because of Shipp's popularity in the community, the Justice Department feared that as time elapsed a significant portion of their evidence would be undermined. McAdams and Dickey noted that "owing to the hostile atmosphere surrounding our witnesses, threats, intimidation, the fear of assassination, in short, all the obstructions that a diseased public sentiment can invent, being employed, their statement on the stand may vary from the original as reported by us."[70] Indeed, the conspiracy of silence, a phenomenon common to most communities in the aftermath of a lynching, frustrated federal investigators at every turn. As time passed, witnesses became increasingly difficult to locate, threatening letters were received by witnesses summoned to testify against Shipp, and the black community became the subject of intimidation and harassment.

While Shipp served his sentence in federal prison, the citizens of Chattanooga came to view him as a hero. Upon his return, several thousand people turned out to participate in a parade to welcome and honor him. Until his death on 18 September 1925, he continued as an active and highly visible member of the community. While holding various public offices, he was a founding member of the Confederate Veterans Association and was active in restoring the Silverdale Confederate Cemetery. Upon his death, thousands of Chattanoogans turned out to pay their final respects. Clothed in his Confederate army uniform, he was laid to rest in Forest Hills Cemetery under full military honors. His obituary only briefly mentioned his involvement in the Ed Johnson affair.[71]

Judge Samuel D. McReynolds, while representing Tennessee's Third District in the U.S. House of Representatives for eight terms, enjoyed a distinguished national political career. McReynolds was instrumental in passing legislation that led to erecting the Chickamauga Dam in Hamilton County—a major undertaking of the Tennessee Valley Authority. At the time of his death on 11 July 1939, at the age of sixty-three, he served as chairman of the influential House Foreign Affairs Committee. Senators Harry S. Truman of Missouri and Richard Russell of Georgia were among the twenty congressmen who attended his funeral in Chattanooga.

Following more than three years of turmoil, life in Chattanooga was normal once again. But Ed Johnson was dead. Ed Johnson, murdered by a mob that refused to allow him the constitutional protections that Americans hold dear, is now an all but forgotten man. His final resting place—Pleasant Gardens, a long neglected and overgrown black cemetery known only to a handful of local citizens. His grave—marked by a fallen tombstone that proclaims his innocence for the crime that cost his life. His epitaph—the grim reminder of a dark period that echoes from the voices of Chattanooga's past: "God Bless You All, I Am 'A' Innocent Man."[72]

Notes

1. "God Bless You All—I Am Innocent," *Chattanooga Daily Times*, 20 Mar. 1906.
2. "A Horrible Crime," *Chattanooga News*, 24 Jan. 1906.
3. Wilbur J. Cash, *The Mind of the South* (New York, 1941), 302.

4. "Federal Power after Slayers of Ed Johnson," *Atlanta Constitution*, 23 Mar. 1906.

5. Morton Sosna, *In Search of the Silent South: Southern Liberals and the Race Issue* (New York, 1977), 31.

6. "Brutal Crime of Negro Fiend," *Chattanooga News*, 24 Jan. 1906.

7. Charles C. Butler, "Lynching," *American Law Review* 44 (1910): 212.

8. "Negro Now in County Jail; Suspect of St. Elmo Crime," *Chattanooga News*, 25 Jan. 1906.

9. Arthur F. Raper, *The Tragedy of Lynching* (Chapel Hill, 1933), 46.

10. "Brutal Crime of Negro Fiend."

11. "Suspect Arrested and Rushed to Knoxville," *Chattanooga Daily Times*, 26 Jan. 1906; "Negro Now in County Jail," *Chattanooga News*, 25 Jan. 1906.

12. "Wheels of Justice Turn Fast in St. Elmo Assault Case," *Chattanooga Daily Times*, 28 Jan. 1906. Several attempts were made to secure the Chattanooga Police Department's investigation records of Taylor's assault. According to the Chattanooga Police Department, the condition and location of these records, if in fact they still exist, are in such a state of damage and disarray that they are not conducive to examination at this time.

13. The *Chattanooga Daily Times* estimated the crowd to be between 500 and 1,000, 26 Jan. 1906.

14. "Fierce and Frenzied Mob Foiled by Brave and Determined Officers," *Chattanooga News*, 26 Jan. 1906. The agreement restoring order that night was reminiscent of a similar incident in May 1892. Frank Weims, another black prisoner, had been arrested for the attempted assault of a white woman in Hill City. Fearing mob retribution, Sheriff John Skillern ordered Weims removed from Chattanooga. When a mob of Hill City citizens stormed the jail intending to lynch Weims, they were unconvinced of the sheriff's statement that he had been taken from the city. Only after a committee of their members inspected the jail and found Weims absent, did the mob disband without further violence. See James W. Livingood, *A History of Hamilton County, Tennessee* (Memphis, 1981), 338.

15. Editorial, "Last Night's Mob," *Chattanooga Daily Times*, 26 Jan. 1906.

16. "Wheels of Justice Turn Fast in St. Elmo Assault Case," *Chattanooga Daily Times*, 28 Jan. 1906; "Grand Jury Indicts," *Chattanooga News*, 27 Jan. 1906.

17. Editorial, "Judge McReynolds and the Mob," *Chattanooga Daily Times*, 29 Jan. 1906.

18. "Johnson's Trial Is Progressing Rapidly," *Chattanooga News*, 6 Feb. 1906; "Dramatic Incidents at Johnson's Trial," ibid., 8 Feb. 1906.

19. "Johnson's Trial Is Progressing Rapidly."

20. "Johnson Trial Hinges on Alibi for Defendant," *Chattanooga News*, 7 Feb. 1906.

21. Ibid.

22. "Dramatic Incidents at Johnson's Trial."

23. Ibid.

24. "Jury Finds Ed Johnson Guilty; He Will Hang for His Fiendish Crime," *Chattanooga News*, 9 Feb. 1906.

25. *Ed Johnson, Appellant v. State of Tennessee*, Supreme Court of the United States, October Term, 1906. Appeal from the Circuit Court of the United States for the Eastern District of Tennessee, 18; "Ed Johnson Sentenced," *Chattanooga News*, 10 Feb. 1906.

26. "Ed Johnson Sentenced."

27. "Action Deplored by Colored People," *Chattanooga News*, 15 Feb. 1906; editorial, "The Johnson Case," ibid., 10 Mar. 1906; "Effort to Save Johnson's Neck," ibid., 13 Feb. 1906.
28. "Effort to Save Johnson's Neck."
29. "Negro Dies on Day Set," *Chattanooga Daily Times*, 4 Mar. 1906.
30. *Ed Johnson, Appellant v. State of Tennessee*, 3.
31. Ibid.
32. Ibid.
33. Ibid.
34. Ibid.
35. Editorial (untitled), *Chattanooga News*, 12 Mar. 1906.
36. "Last Effort for Johnson," *Chattanooga News*, 14 Mar. 1906.
37. "Justice Harlan Allows Appeal of Ed Johnson," *Chattanooga Daily Times*, 19 Mar. 1906; editorial, *Chattanooga News*, 19 Mar. 1906.
38. "God Bless You All."
39. Ibid.
40. Eyewitness account of Joseph R. Curtis, 28 May 1907. Department of Justice memorandum to Edward T. Sanford, assistant attorney general. General Records of the Department of Justice, subfile 116684, 2, RG 60, College Park, Md.
41. "God Bless You All"; "Johnson Hanged," *Chattanooga News*, 20 Mar. 1906. Johnson was the fourth victim of Hamilton County lynch mobs. Preceding him were Charley Williams (September 1885), lynched inside the Hamilton County Jail; Alfred Blount (February 1893), lynched on the County Bridge; and Charles Brown (1897), lynched from the Chickamauga Creek Bridge near Soddy, Tennessee. For a brief synopsis of these lynchings, see Livingood, *Hamilton County*, 337–41, and John Wilson, *Chattanooga's Story* (Chattanooga, Tenn., 1980), 218–20.
42. "God Bless You All." On 14 February 1893, Alfred Blount, accused of assaulting a white woman in her Chattanooga home, was lynched by a group of 100 to 150 men on the first span. See Livingood, *Hamilton County*, 339–40.
43. "God Bless You All."
44. Fitzhugh N. Brundage, *Lynching in the New South: Georgia and Virginia, 1880–1930* (Chicago, 1993), 32; editorial, "The Mob and What Caused It," *Chattanooga News*, 20 Mar. 1906; editorial, "Sheriff Shipp," ibid., 24 Mar. 1906.
45. "Mob and What Caused It"; editorial (untitled), *Chattanooga News*, 7 Feb. 1906 (emphasis added).
46. "Lynching Mob to Feel Supreme Court's Anger," *New York Times*, 21 Mar. 1906; "An Insult to the Nation," *Outlook*, 31 Mar. 1906, 721; "Aftermath of Lynching— Yellow Peril of Journalism Adds to Our Troubles," *Chattanooga Daily Times*, 25 Mar. 1906.
47. "Lynching Mob to Feel Supreme Court's Anger"; "Re-Elect Sheriff Shipp to Indorse [*sic*] Lynching," *Chattanooga Daily Times*, 3 Aug. 1906.
48. Brundage, *Lynching in the New South*, 4; Butler, "Lynching," 217; Cash, *Mind of the South*, 302.
49. Penland to Moody, 24 Mar. 1906, Department of Justice, subfile 77618, 1; "Federal Power After Slayers," *Atlanta Constitution*, 23 Mar. 1906; "Action in Washington," *Chattanooga Daily Times*, 23 Mar. 1906.

50. Hoyt, acting Attorney General, to Penland, 31 Mar. 1906, Department of Justice, subfile 78772, 1; Penland to Moody, 1 May 1906, Department of Justice, subfile 80598, 1.

51. McAdams and Dickey to John E. Wilkie, U.S. Secret Service. Final Report, 21 Sept. 1906. Department of Justice, subfile 30820R, 6. Johnson officially became a federal prisoner on 19 March 1906, upon Judge S. B. McReynolds's acceptance of U.S. Supreme Court telegram stating that it would hear Johnson's appeal. Department of Justice, subfile 77473.

52. See Emery Gill to Moody, 18 Sept. 1906, O. Gunerius to Bonaparte, 15 Jan. [1907], and O. Johnson to Bonaparte, 10 Apr. 1908, Department of Justice, subfiles 89735, 98075, 135248, respectively; interview with Ellen Baker, McAdams and Dickey to Wilkie, 21 Sept. 1906, Department of Justice, subfile 116684, 6–7; affidavit of Arthur Waller, subfile 116684; interview with Preston W. Walker, subfile 116684, 10–11; interview with W. M. Logan, subfile 116684, 12; interview with William Tarpley, subfile 116684, 9–10. McAdams and Dickey based their opinion upon an interview with John Roach, a prisoner incarcerated on the night of the lynching. McAdams and Dickey to Wilkie, 21 Sept. 1906, subfile 30820R, 16.

53. Penland to Moody, 17 Oct. 1906, Department of Justice, subfile 91658, 2; McAdams and Dickey to Wilkie, 21 Sept. 1906, subfile 30820R, 4; Penland to Moody, 29 Mar. 1906, subfile 78772, 1.

54. Penland to Moody, 29 Mar. 1906, Department of Justice, subfile 78772, 1.

55. McAdams and Dickey to Wilkie, 23 Sept. 1906, Department of Justice, subfile 116684, 17–18; "Democratic Primaries Are On in Earnest Today," *Chattanooga Daily Times*, 29 Mar. 1906.

56. "Wheels of Justice Turn Fast," *Chattanooga Daily Times*, 28 Jan. 1906.

57. Editorial, "Sheriff Shipp's Admirable Conduct," *Chattanooga Daily Times*, 31 Jan. 1906. Such prominent individuals as Milton Ochs, Foster Brown, Chancellor T. M. McConnell, and County Judge Walker were among those named as witnesses by McAdams and Dickey.

58. "Sheriff Shipp the Nominee in Yesterday's Primaries," *Chattanooga Daily Times*, 30 Jan. 1906.

59. Campaign advertisement, "To the Voters of Hamilton County," *Chattanooga Daily Times*, 1 Aug. 1906; editorial, "David H. Barker," ibid., 2 Aug. 1906, "Shipp's Landslide," ibid., 3 Aug. 1906.

60. *United States of America v. Shipp et al.*, 214 U.S. 386, 644; anonymous letter to Sanford, date unknown, Department of Justice, subfile 116684.

61. "Supreme Court Seeks Tennessee Lynchers," *New York Times*, 29 May 1906.

62. "Chattanooga Lynching Before Supreme Court," *New York Times*, 16 Oct. 1906.

63. *United States of America v. Joseph F. Shipp et al.* 214 U.S. 386, 643. Reprinted from *Birmingham Age-Herald*, May 1906.

64. "Chattanooga Lynching Before Supreme Court."

65. "27 Held for Lynching; Supreme Bench Decides It Has Jurisdiction in Chattanooga Case," *New York Times*, 25 Dec. 1906. See also Transcript of Record, Supreme Court of the United States, October Term, 1908. No. 5 Original. *United States of America v. Joseph F. Shipp et al.*, 214 U.S. 386, 128–31.

66. "Shipp off to Washington," *New York Times*, 15 Nov. 1909.

67. *United States of America v. Joseph F. Shipp et al.*, 638–39, 644.

68. Ibid., 643–44.

69. "Sheriff Shipp Now in Washington Jail," *New York Times*, 16 Nov. 1909.

70. McAdams and Dickey to Wilkie, 21 Sept. 1906, Department of Justice, subfile 30820R, 2. Several witnesses did in fact recant or modify their testimony; others simply failed to appear in court, while still others were impeached by the defense. In the end, the government's case was weakened to the extent that charges were dismissed against several participants. Two such examples were charges dropped against deputy sheriffs Matthew Galloway and Joseph Clark, both of whom testimony revealed had been active in the mob. Police officer John Varnell was acquitted despite testimony that he participated and actually cut off Johnson's finger as a souvenir. See also McAdams and Dickey to Wilkie, 23 Sept. 1906. Department of Justice, subfile 11684, 13–14. Additional letters are contained in the Justice Department record. Most notable are those of John N. Stonecypher, who claimed to have received in excess of fifty such letters. His nephew was allegedly murdered by John Pogue shortly after Johnson's lynching, and Stonecypher insisted that it was the result of his agreeing to testify against Pogue.
71. "Funeral Rites for Capt. Shipp Set for Monday," *Chattanooga News*, 19 Sept. 1925.
72. "Gone but Not Forgotten," *Chattanooga News–Free Press*, 13 Apr. 1997.

PART THREE

THE STRUGGLE FOR CIVIL RIGHTS

The Very Best Influence
Josephine Holloway and Girl Scouting in Nashville's African American Community

Elisabeth I. Perry

*I*N HER STUDY OF JOSEPHINE HOLLOWAY AND THE BEGINNINGS OF THE GIRL SCOUT MOVEMENT IN NASHVILLE, ELISABETH PERRY BRIDGES THE JIM Crow era of segregation and the period of integration that began during the Civil Rights movement of the 1960s and 1970s. Like the earlier chapter by Beverly Bond, Perry shows that gender does matter in discussions about race relations in the South. Holloway's determination as a social worker and as a Girl Scout leader produced a generation of followers and, eventually, had an impact on the broader Girl Scout movement in the mid-South. But Perry goes beyond a mere biography of an unknown hero to delve into some of the paradoxes of integration in the late twentieth century. Even as the success of integration was being celebrated, Holloway recalled that her segregated troops exposed girls to "examples of black strength and pride" that they did not receive in the new integrated troops. Separation, in this case, nurtured pride of race and gender and self-esteem, important qualities that Holloway feared would be lost in the next generation. Despite the dilemmas of integration, neither she nor her supporters were ready to step

back from their quest for equality. By integrating the
Girl Scouts, they helped the organization become more
inclusive, more visible, and stronger than before.

G irl Scouting, a program founded in 1912 to prepare girls for citizenship,
came to Nashville in 1917. "Girls' workers" (social workers in charge of
girls attending social settlement programs) and teachers were the first to
adopt the program as a method of organizing extracurricular activities for
girls. In 1923, Josephine Groves, a recent graduate of Fisk University with a
major in sociology, became girls' worker at the Bethlehem Center, a social
settlement in Nashville's African American community. In succeeding
decades, as Josephine Holloway (her married name), she spearheaded the
development of scouting for thousands of black girls and women in the city.
This work led her to make contact with the Nashville Girl Scout Council,
the program's local policy-making body. Organized in 1927, this group
remained exclusively white until the mid-1950s. Holloway's interactions with
the council provide a new perspective on changing patterns in race relations
in the modern mid-South urban environment. They show the ways in which
interracial participation in a women's voluntary association helped prepare
Middle Tennesseans for integration.[1]

Developed by Juliette Gordon Low, a wealthy widow from Savannah,
Georgia, Girl Scouting in the United States had its origins in a British program founded in the early 1900s by Robert Baden-Powell. As an army officer
of the British Empire, Baden-Powell had used scouting techniques (tracking,
woodcraft, and wilderness survival) to train young British soldiers under his
command in India and South Africa. In 1899, when Dutch Boer settlers in
South Africa laid siege to Mafeking, Baden-Powell used these techniques to
hold the city until relief forces arrived. His later reputation as a war hero
gave him a platform from which he promoted a scouting program for boys
based in outdoor living skills and good citizenship. The Boy Scout movement, which began officially in 1907–8, spread rapidly around the world,
reaching the United States in 1910.[2]

The Boy Scouts proved so popular that, shortly after the movement was
founded, British girls approached Baden-Powell with a request to participate. After deciding that scouting could benefit girls as well as boys, Baden-
Powell asked his sister Agnes to head a "Girl Guide" movement. While
shaping the girls' movement along lines similar to that of the boys, Baden-

Powell gave it a distinctly "feminine" cast. He designed blue rather than khaki uniforms for the girls and with his sister produced a handbook, the *British Girl Guide Manual,* which stressed the "guiding" rather than "scouting" nature of traditional female roles. A large part of this manual dwelt on training in domestic skills, such as cleaning, laundering, needlework, nursing, and childcare.[3]

Juliette Low met the Baden-Powells in England and became impressed with the scouting ideal. Until then, she had led a comfortable but troubled life. Neither her marriage nor studies in art and sculpture had fulfilled her. For her, scouting answered a lifelong quest for meaningful work.[4] Her first venture into scouting began in England, where she formed a troop of "Guides." She returned home in 1912, determined to bring scouting to American girls. Telephoning a cousin, she announced, "I've got something for the girls of Savannah and all America and all the world!" On 12 March she enrolled eighteen young family members and their friends into her first American troop.[5]

Low saw her program as doing two things. First, it built moral character by asking girls to honor a "promise" and a set of "laws" regarding behavior.[6] The laws, of which there were ten, inspired honesty, loyalty, usefulness, and helpfulness to others, friendship to all and sisterhood to Girl Scouts, courtesy, kindness to animals, obedience, cheerfulness, thrift, and cleanliness "in thought, word, and deed." Second, her program promoted a range of skills designed to help girls lead socially useful lives as adults. She encouraged girls to learn these skills by adopting Baden-Powell's incentive system of badges, patches, special recognitions, and advancement into higher ranks. She also trained leaders to teach the skills in enjoyable ways, through organized group activities suitable for different age levels. Her early program emphasized the skills of camping, woodcraft (nature study and animal lore), tracking, and crime detection.[7] Low encouraged a scientific approach to domestic work. "To direct her household has always been a woman's work in every century," she wrote in her first independently written handbook of 1920. Because "we no longer believe that housekeeping should take up all a woman's time," her girls would learn to do this work simply and efficiently.[8] Finally, Low adopted Baden-Powell's motto, "Be Prepared," and his slogan, "Do a good turn daily." Over the years, as women's roles have changed, so have the focal points and implementation of Low's program. In general, however, her broad goals for the program have remained in place.

Nashville's first Girl Scout troops arose in connection with the United States' entry into World War I in April 1917. This event spurred interest in patriotism and community service, both central to the scouting ideal. Nashville's troops organized patriotic parades and rallies, sold war bonds, and sponsored war work projects.[9] The troops met in a variety of locales, including schools and denominational social service agencies and community centers. George Peabody College's demonstration School, St. Mary's Orphanage, and the Young Women's Christian Association (YWCA) all sponsored Girl Scout troops. The YWCA's was the largest. In February 1918, 697 Girl Scouts attended thirty-one troop meetings at the "Y"; by 1 May, 1,039 were attending forty-seven meetings.[10]

After the war, other schools and agencies founded Girl Scout troops. Ward-Belmont School and the Nashville section of the Council of Jewish Women (NCJW) started troops, the latter at its Bertha Fensterwald Social Center. The Masonic Home and McNeilly Day Home also sponsored troops.[11] As the Girl Scout movement became more organized on a national basis, however, the cost of participating in it rose. Like Baden-Powell, Juliette Low believed that every girl, regardless of social position, could have fun and get satisfaction in the Girl Scouts. In order to keep costs down, she had sunk personal funds into supporting the national organization. She also inculcated ideals of thrift and entrepreneurship among troops so that they could be self-sustaining. And yet, costs continued to rise. The national program required the payment of dues and the purchase of uniforms, handbooks, and other materials, including food and equipment for camping trips. Later, in developing program-wide events for special fund-raising purposes, the national office put pressure on all Girl Scout troops to contribute. Monetary outlays were relatively small, and middle-class families seldom experienced difficulty raising them. In addition, practical troop leaders often found ways to cover or cut down on expenses. Still, expenses often deterred less privileged girls from joining or from feeling they were full participants.

The cost of Girl Scouting predetermined the type of girl attracted into Nashville's troops. The earliest members were, as far as is known, exclusively white and middle class.[12] In 1919, the members of the local YWCA decided to provide "similar opportunities for the colored girl as for her sisters of the white race." With financial support from its national office, it set up a separate "Colored Branch," called the "Blue Triangle." The Nashville YWCA then abandoned Girl Scouting for a program called the "Girl Reserves." This program had been developed especially for Y clubs, was cheaper than the Girl Scouts, and gave more credit for work "along spiritual lines." Although organizational rivalry between the YWCA and Girl Scouts may have been at the root of the Nashville YWCA's action, its annual report stated that it had given up Girl Scouting because the program had become "much too expensive."[13]

In the fall of 1923, Josephine Groves took the position of girls' worker at the Bethlehem Center.[14] After studying a number of programs for girls, she found herself most attracted to the character building and outdoor emphases of Girl Scouting. When she sought local information about the program, however, she found no evidence that it existed in Nashville. Two circumstances may explain why. First, by 1923, local Girl Scouting had fallen into a decline. Reports sent in 1927 to national Girl Scout headquarters indicate, without further elucidation, that some "unpleasant experiences" had marred early Girl Scout history in Nashville. The remark may refer to the YWCA abandonment of Girl Scouting, or to competition among troops for community support after the patriotic fervor of wartime had waned.[15] In any case, by the time Groves was looking for information, she could find no traces of the early Nashville movement. Second, Josephine Groves was a young, inexperienced social worker in the African American community. Despite the interracial makeup of the Bethlehem Center board, her access to information about Girl Scouting, until then an exclusively white activity in Nashville, was necessarily limited. The local YWCA's Blue Triangle could offer no help, as it had given up its Girl Scout program. Failing to find anyone in town to help her, Groves appealed directly to the national Girl Scout office.

Help came from an authentic source. Despite a diagnosis of cancer, Juliette Low continued to conduct training sessions for Girl Scout leaders. In January 1924, she and several national Girl Scout officials came to a Southern Education Conference on Scouting held at Nashville's George Peabody College.[16] Josephine Groves took her first official training at this conference, receiving at its end her "commission" as a program "captain." Thereafter, Girl Scouting at the Bethlehem Center boomed. With the help of another Girl Scouting enthusiast, Alice B. Collier, Groves organized about 150 to 160 girls into troops.[17] Percie Warner Lea, wife of Luke Lea, the former United States senator and then editor and publisher of the *Nashville Tennessean*, arranged for the girls to camp on family property. By late 1924, ten troops representing over 300 girls were active at the Bethlehem Center. Girl Scouting at the Bethlehem Center continued to thrive. In June 1925, Josephine Groves married Guerney Holloway, the boys' worker at the center. The following fall, the center's director, Martha Nutt, expressing a view shared by most social work professionals of her era, told Josephine that she doubted a married female social worker could devote enough time to her tasks. In response to this pressure, Josephine Holloway resigned to seek employment elsewhere. Although she never lost interest in Girl Scouting, for the time being she had to give it up.[18]

Meanwhile, interest in Girl Scouting was reviving among whites in communities near and in Nashville. Between 1925 and 1928, schoolteachers in Putnam, Dickson, and Maury Counties founded troops. In the city, Girl Scouting took on new life in 1926, when Lillian Weinstein (later Cohen) chose the program for her girls' work at the Young Women's Hebrew Association (YWHA). In addition, Letitia Morgan, formerly active in Tennessee's woman suffrage movement and a leader in Nashville's Unitarian Church, founded a troop to accommodate her daughter Gean. In May 1927 the City Council of the Parent-Teachers Association (PTA) announced that it would sponsor Girl Scout troops in the public schools. Levera Hume, chair of the PTA Council's recreation committee, invited school PTA presidents and recreation committee chairs to meet at Watkins Institute with a representative from the Rockefeller Foundation, who, for six evenings in a row, offered instruction on how to organize and lead troops. As a result of these efforts, Nashville had at least eight active troops by the fall of 1927. At that point, an official from the national Girl Scout office suggested that the troops form a council, a step that would professionalize and make more efficient the training of leaders, fund raising, and the planning of camping activities and city-wide events. On 2 December 1927, Rose Mills (a YWHA activist and also a former suffragist) and Letitia Morgan received a charter for Nashville's first council. Through donations, including one from the Civitan Club, the two women raised enough money to operate nine troops and hire a director.[19]

The program now expanded but still retained its essentially white, middle-class identity. By December 1928, there were 417 registered Girl Scouts. Burk and Company, a clothing outfitter and sporting goods store, gave the council desk space on its mezzanine. Soon it was carrying Girl Scout equipment. A leaders' association formed. Most important, in 1928, the Community Chest recognized the council as an established social service agency and awarded it $3,185 for its next year's operations. This grant enabled the council to hire its first professional director and a half-time assistant director. Future grants from the chest and its successors, the United Givers Fund and the United Way, proved essential to the program's survival.[20]

Despite these grants, funding which might have allowed the council to extend Girl Scout programs to a broader segment of the local population remained inadequate. Consequently, when Josephine Holloway was able to return to Girl Scouting and, in 1933, asked the council to register a troop of

"Negro" girls, council board members used economic reasons to justify turning her down.

Ever since her forced departure from the Bethlehem Center, Holloway had retained her belief in Girl Scouting as the best character-training program for girls. She had supported her husband's pursuit of a medical degree by holding a number of administrative posts, including that of assistant registrar at Fisk University. She had also raised three daughters. In July 1933, the eldest, Nareda, would turn six. Anticipating this event, Holloway decided to form a Girl Scout troop for her. In May she asked the Nashville Girl Scout Council to register the troop and give her access to the required materials. Her request was the council's first for a Negro troop. Unsure how to proceed, the council appointed a committee to study the matter. On 6 June this committee advised the council to turn the request down.[21]

Holloway believed, and oral tradition in Nashville's African American community holds, that racial prejudice lay behind the committee's advice.[22] Prejudice surely existed on the council, but the realities of local race relations and of contemporary economic conditions also influenced the committee recommendation of 6 June. Local race relations required that whites and blacks be kept separate. Just as the YWCA in 1920 had set up a separate "colored" branch and "Colored Girl Reserves," the Girl Scouts could accommodate African American girls only in segregated troops. Unlike the YWCA, however, which received funding for a separate branch from its national organization, Nashville Girl Scouts received no financial aid from the national office. In the summer of 1933, at the depth of the Depression, the Nashville Council believed there was insufficient funding to form a separate branch.[23] The same month that they decided against a Negro troop, board members reported to the national office that a "cut in budget" was "imminent." Two years earlier, the council had boasted a total of 649 members in local programs; by 1933, the number had dropped to 413. Since in the early 1930s only a few visionaries foresaw integrated groups of any kind, the lack of national financial support for a separate program and the decline of local income made Girl Scouting for Nashville's African Americans seem impossible to realize.[24]

Moreover, some council members openly expressed interest in bringing Girl Scouting to African Americans. In a meeting held on 22 June, council founder and board member Letitia Morgan, protesting that racial distinctions were inimical to the Girl Scout laws, moved that two Negro troops be formed "immediately." When her motion failed, to underscore her protest she asked pointedly that a record be made of it.[25] Shortly afterward, another council member, Arlene Ziegler, moved that the formation of Negro troops be deferred until the council had a "definite policy and funds for properly carrying out the work." This motion, which passed, indicated that a majority of council members favored a Girl Scout program for African Americans, at least in principle. Showing further interest in such a program, in September an unidentified board member asked why only one "colored" troop (in Richmond, Virginia) existed in the South. In response, the council instructed Mary A. Moore to write to southern Girl Scout councils to inquire "why this work has not been undertaken among the Negro girls." Although no reply appears in the files, both query and instruction show definite support among council members for Girl Scouting for African Americans.[26]

Although Arlene Ziegler's motion passed, the conditions she hoped for were slow to come. In 1936, a year in which the YWCA's Colored Girl Reserves enrolled six hundred members, the council had to report to the national office, with obvious embarrassment, that the "Negro population is not served by Girl Scouting."[27]

Racial issues arose in an important event that took place among local Girl Scouts in 1938. The Nashville Council invited Eleanor Roosevelt, the president's wife and (like other first ladies before her and since) honorary president of the Girl Scouts, to deliver a lecture in Nashville on 4 October. The city's public accommodations, including Ryman Auditorium where Roosevelt would speak, were segregated. The council, realizing that members of the African American community would wish to hear her, asked her to deliver a separate lecture to a colored audience. Roosevelt refused, insisting that blacks and white attend her single presentation together.[28] In the end, blacks were segregated in the gallery and the Fisk University Jubilee Singers opened the program. The council, which had resisted requests from the local American Association of University Women and Parent-Teachers Association to cosponsor Roosevelt's visit, suffered a two-hundred-dollar deficit from the event. Out of a possible five thousand tickets, only fifteen hundred were sold.

During the 1930s, Girl Scouting expanded in areas around Nashville. Troops formed in Old Hickory in 1933, Pulaski in 1935, Springfield in 1936, and in Lebanon and Murfreesboro in 1938. Troops around Clarksville also formed in the 1930s but later disbanded.[29] As far as is known, no African American girls were members of these troops.

Official status for Negro Girl Scouting finally arrived in Nashville in 1942. Ideological, financial, and personal factors combined to bring it about. First, the United States' entry into World War II highlighted the contradiction between racial exclusions in the Girl Scout program and the democratic values Girl Scouts were pledged to uphold. Accordingly, the national Girl

Scout office began to pressure local councils to combat discrimination. As this campaign soon had a visible impact (between 1942 and 1947, African American Girl Scouting increased 252 percent), Nashville could not have been unaware of this pressure.[30] Second, because of the war, local Girl Scout membership rose. The financial outlay involved in founding a program for African Americans may no longer have seemed as prohibitive as it had in 1933. Third, Josephine Holloway had never given up her quest for official status for her troops. Undaunted by the council's rejection in 1933, she had gone forward on her own to organize a troop. Her husband secured handbooks for her from Chicago, where he was studying medicine, and she taught the girls in her troop to make gingham aprons to serve as uniforms. She also enlisted other African American women to start troops.[31] The growing number of unofficial troops that she inspired may have embarrassed the Nashville Girl Scout Council. At the very least, they were a constant reminder that the council was still failing to serve Negro girls.

In addition, in the spring of 1942 a unique opportunity arose for Holloway's daughter, Nareda, then aged fourteen, to play a role in the issue. On 22 April Eleanor Roosevelt returned to Nashville to present an award at a meeting of the Southern Conference on Human Welfare, an interracial group working for racial harmony in the South. Nareda, a member of its youth section, approached Roosevelt backstage at War Memorial Auditorium and asked for her help in getting official status for African American Girl Scouts in Nashville. Roosevelt promised to do what she could and took down Nareda's name and address. A few weeks later, Roosevelt wrote Nareda that she could do nothing for her but urged her not to give up working toward her goal.[32]

We may never know if Nareda Holloway's bold request in some way influenced the council's acceptance, in the following fall, of African American troops. Most likely, Roosevelt had inquired at the national office and learned that the office could not compel a local council to change its membership policies. No written record has been found between the national and Nashville offices on the issue of race during this period. In light of contemporary developments in antidiscrimination policies, however, it is possible to conclude that, after an inquiry from the First Lady, the national office urged Nashville to accept African Americans. In any case, the proximity of Nareda Holloway's request, Roosevelt's response to her, and the actual policy change support the surmise that the events may have been linked.

After accepting African Americans into local Girl Scouting, the Nashville Council tried to set a cap on the number of their troops, limiting them to one quarter of Nashville's total. Holloway had prepared such a strong foundation for the program that the number of her troops grew too rapidly to keep this cap in place. In 1943, thirty-six African American workers signed up for training through the council and then took additional courses at the Bethlehem Center. Holloway organized camping at Bethlehem Center's campsite on Ashland City Road. By May 1944 Nashville had thirteen African American troops. Out of a total of 1,679 girls in Girl Scouting, 252 were black; of 397 adults, 82 were black. In response to these numbers, in September the council established a branch office in the Morris Memorial Building and hired Holloway as field adviser for Negro troops. Thus, Holloway became Nashville's first African American professional Girl Scout worker. On her return from a professional training course in New York City, Holloway reported that she had been the only person of her race in attendance.[33]

Members of the Nashville Girl Scout Council came to appreciate Holloway's involvement in their work. In 1945, they complimented her for her "humble, gracious manner" when she called scouting "the very best influence for girls" and thanked them "for the privilege of working with Scouting." Council members appreciated her even more when, in 1946, they served as hosts for the annual meeting of the Dixie region to which their council belonged. Planners of the conference, the region's first biracial meeting, had to cope with Nashville hotels, which refused to accept black guests, even for meetings and meals. When the council asked Holloway whether out-of-town black troop leaders should attend at all, she not only replied that they should but said that "her people" would find housing for them in their own homes. A report to the national office on this event indicated that, while council members supported Holloway, they hesitated to set precedents for future biracial meetings. To avoid problems, they held all meetings in the War Memorial Building or the YWCA and planned no social events in places where African American members might be embarrassed.[34]

Girl Scouting for Middle Tennessee's African Americans thrived in the 1940s, but on a separate basis. For greater efficiency, in 1941 the council had divided its jurisdiction into eleven geographical "districts." African American troops were organized under a separate district (District 12) that ignored geographical lines. African American troop leaders developed their own leaders' association and held day camps and celebrations at Tennessee Agricultural and Industrial State College (now Tennessee State University). White troops celebrated at Scarritt College.

Girl Scouting for African Americans began to appear outside of Nashville. Clarksville, which reorganized its troops in 1941 and received a charter for a council in 1943, formed three African American troops. These also met separately, camping at Edith Pettus Park while Clarksville's white troops camped at the farm of Austin Peay State College. In 1945, at Columbia, Cora McFall formed a troop of ten African American fourteen year olds and later expanded her program to include all age levels. By that year, the Nashville Council had removed the restrictions on the number of African American troops. In 1946, forty troops of African Americans were under the jurisdiction of the Nashville Council. The following year it approved sixty, contingent on the hiring of a second field adviser.[35]

Finding camp sites for African American children remained a problem. In 1947, although the Nashville Council voted to buy land for a camp site for African American troops, the purchase was never made. Council minutes from 22 March 1948 indicate that the State of Tennessee Board of Parks asked the Girl Scouts not to request a camp site on state park property for African American troops, as it feared the request might lead to the defeat of legislation for improvements.[36] In 1949, Josephine Holloway was forced to use Camp Henry Koch in Evansville, Indiana, for her troops. Finally, in 1955, she was able to open a camp, which became known as Camp Holloway, on council property near White House in Robertson County. The council made little effort to develop this property, however. The only buildings Holloway could obtain were army barracks, which members of a Fisk University fraternity helped move. Although in 1956 the council voted to contribute five dollars for each African American girl attending Camp Holloway, in 1958 it omitted the camp from its Camp Development Plan. In response to a protest concerning this omission, the council's director, Polly Fessey, reported that, because conditions at the camp were so bad, only thirty-eight girls had attended that year and it had run at a five-hundred-dollar deficit. "I wouldn't go to that camp," Fessey remembers saying. The council eventually realized that it had to address the camp's inadequacies. Improvements made in 1959 in Camp Holloway's buildings and the completion of a pool in 1960 increased the camp's appeal.[37]

The 1950s was a decade of growth for Girl Scouting in Middle Tennessee. Between 1951 and 1964, the council moved to new and larger offices four times.[38] In 1957, in response to national Girl Scout policy to bring nearby "lone" troops under council coverage (known as the "Green Umbrella" plan), sixteen Middle Tennessee and three Kentucky counties merged with Nashville and Davidson County to become the Cumberland Valley Girl Scout Council (CVGSC). Lillian Weinstein Cohen, who had been active in Girl Scouting since 1926, became the first president of the new organization.[39] In 1961, after organizing more troops in outlying counties, the CVGSC accepted the affiliation of the thirteen-county Volunteer Girl Scout Council, which had formed among troops in Shelbyville and Manchester in the 1950s. In 1965, when six counties affiliated with the Highland Rim Girl Scout Council joined, the number of counties in the CVGSC rose to thirty-nine.[40]

As the council expanded its jurisdiction, discussion of racial issues intensified. Other councils in the Dixie region were experiencing similar pressures. Some of them were ahead of Nashville on the path toward integration. Arkansas, for example, discussed incorporating African American troop leaders into the same, instead of a parallel, council structure, in 1949. The Fayetteville Council accomplished the reorganization the next year. A field report in 1950 from the Dixie field director, Lenore Amerman, mentions an integrated troop on an army post. "It can happen here!" she exulted. Integration occurred in the Nashville area as well, but without publicity or advance notice to the national organization. In a report on the progress of integration written many years later, the CVGSC noted that the two military installations within its jurisdiction had integrated troops between 1956 and 1957.[41]

In Nashville, discussions of an integrated council structure began as early as 1950. At a meeting on 28 March, the organization committee reported that since council members representing different races had worked so well together, Nashville felt ready for this move. The committee also feared, however, that the "outside community," by which it meant persons not affiliated with their particular voluntary association, would neither understand nor approve of racial mixing. Arguing that an integrated council might do "more harm than good . . . when the population as a whole is not ready," the members concluded that the move was premature. The committee admitted that such a position was inconsistent with premises "that all Girl Scouts are on an equal level and that world cooperation and understanding is one of our main goals." Still, it advised the council to proceed with caution. In 1951, when the council moved to new offices, it took another step toward integration by taking in the branch office for Negro troops, which until then had been in separate quarters. In 1954, the year the U.S. Supreme Court ruled in *Brown v. Board of Education* against state-mandated school segregation, the council elected its first African American member, Alice Walker, the chair of District 12, under which Negro Girl Scouting had functioned. In 1963, it sent Lula Pointer to Miami as its first African American delegate to a national council meeting.[42]

The civil rights crusade had a powerful Nashville component which surfaced early in the movement. After extensive preparation in 1959, Nashville students organized sit-ins in segregated department-store lunchrooms beginning in February 1960.[43] Many community women, white and black, supported the students. The women protected them during demonstrations, provided transportation, appeared in courtrooms, raised bail for arrested demonstrators, and sent food to the jails. Many of these women had served together on the boards of churches or of voluntary agencies such as the Girl Scouts. Their association with one another as volunteers facilitated their support of local protestors and the integration in the larger community that took place in subsequent years.[44]

The CVGSC's support for integrated troops began officially in July 1960. In September, in accordance with an announced policy, it encouraged the formation of an integrated Brownie troop at Clemons School, which had an integrated student body. The leader of this troop was white, the assistant black. Although the Clemons Men's Club and others phoned the Girl Scouts with threats to withdraw support from the program, the council received sympathetic calls as well. Some calls criticized the council for not going far enough. In response to all of these calls, the council reaffirmed its action, insisting that "no restrictions should exist that would limit the organization of integrated troops."

In October 1962, the council eliminated its twenty-year-old, geographically based district organization and adopted a structure based on "associations." This move abolished District 12, the separate district for African Americans. Integrated troop camps and day camps followed. In the spring of 1963, an integrated troop asked to use the lodge at Percy Warner Park. The council decided to ask the state park board for approval, but promised an alternative site if it refused. Moreover, the council planned to ask the new board coming into office to open the lodge permanently to integrated camping. The following January, it voted to allow integrated troops to use the Warner Park lodge without asking for the park board's permission. Camps Holloway, Sycamore, and Ellington Farm conducted integrated camping in 1963. After these successes, the council voted in the fall of 1964 to end special applications for integrated troops. Fully integrated day camping followed in 1965, along with the integration of four African American senior troops into the Senior Planning Boards. These boards may have been the first biracial experience for some seniors in the program. Finally, when the board of the United Givers Fund required an end to all discrimination in organizations it helped support, the CVGSC passed a general nondiscriminatory resolution.[45]

Josephine Holloway retired in May 1963. By that time she was supervising, by her own report, over two thousand African American Girl Scouts and adult leaders. In addition, Middle Tennessee Girl Scouting was well on its way toward integration.[46] For thirty years, Holloway had devoted herself singlemindedly to the Girl Scout program. As she had said in 1945, she saw it as "the very best influence for girls." In nurturing its growth in Nashville, she herself became an integral part of that influence. After her death, friends, co-workers, and former Girl Scouts recalled her high expectations of both herself and of others, her refusal to be daunted by challenge, and the "sweet" but inflexible determination with which she achieved her goals. According to one of her daughters, Weslia, the Girl Scouts was her life's mission. "We ate, breathed, and slept Girl Scouting," Weslia said. She remembered how her mother went door to door to recruit women as troop leaders, explaining to them their responsibility to help those coming up in the community. Many of these women were so inspired by her enthusiasm that they asked to be buried in their uniforms. Those involved in her program—even those too young to have met her—still describe themselves as "one of Mrs. Holloway's girls," testimony enough to her importance as a stunning community role model.[47]

Racial integration in Girl Scouting brought to a close a special era in the cultural life of Middle Tennessee's African Americans. In recognition of its passing, council member Alice Walker received funding from the CVGSC to produce a souvenir booklet and appreciation event, which was held in the Fisk University Memorial Chapel on 19 May 1963. Josephine Holloway—and perhaps others in the African American community—felt some ambivalence about the end of separate Girl Scouting. When, in 1984, she donated to the council fifty acres of land that adjoined Camp Holloway, she said that separate troops had exposed her girls to "examples of black strength and pride" that they had not received in mixed settings.[48]

Holloway's argument still finds advocates among those who fear the loss of their special identities in integrated clubs, societies, and educational institutions. The debate over separate versus integrated groups continues to resonate. African Americans in particular, and women in general, are especially sensitive to the issue. Both want access to the system of rewards and privileges that whites and men have monopolized. To facilitate such access, they have often asked that attributes such as race and gender be ignored. Yet ignoring those attributes can result in losses for the very groups that make the request. An emphasis on race and gender identity can help minorities or other excluded groups develop greater self-esteem and confidence. Separate associations provide them with opportunities for leadership, which they seldom win in mixed associations. As African Americans began to see these paradoxes, they recognized that integration was only the first step toward the fulfillment of their quest for equality. This recognition later affected racial policies in national as well as local Girl Scouting.[49]

Without study of the record of other southern Girl Scout councils, historians cannot compare racial attitudes in Middle Tennessee with those of its sister councils. The complete separation of white and black programs in the 1920s, the Nashville Council's initial refusal in the 1930s to register African American troops, their acceptance in the 1940s but with separate structures until the mid-1950s, and troop integration in the early 1960s, appear to follow regional patterns. Cumberland Valley Girl Scouts may not have been in the vanguard of integration, but they did not resist the movement once it had begun. Moreover, they openly supported the movement at a relatively early date, taking courageous, even defiant stands in support of nondiscrimination when others in the community disapproved. Further, cordial interracial relations among the girls and women in local Girl Scout programs prepared the ground for the school integration that came later. Ironically, the very trend that Girl Scouting helped facilitate later created organizational nightmares for the program. In the fall of 1971, countywide busing to achieve school integration made after-school troop meetings almost impossible. The council set up workshops and teams to handle the situation. Despite an initial membership loss of 43 percent of the girls and 35 percent of the troops, the community adjusted and the Girl Scout program returned to strong levels.

Integration was only the beginning of efforts by Middle Tennessee Girl Scouts to extend their program to more diverse groups. A survey of the membership taken in 1966 pinpointed inner city and rural areas lacking in social services that could benefit from the program. The council's Membership Extension Project of 1966–67 increased the number of troops in North Nashville from ten to twenty-two. The work to accomplish this growth was not easy. Council administrators had to raise money from public and private sources to cover the costs of extra field staff to form and supervise new troops and to pay for the membership fees, uniforms, handbooks, and camping expenses of disadvantaged girls. No longer able to rely on the services of Josephine Holloway, the council had to find new community volunteers, educating them in program goals and convincing them of the vocational potential of Girl Scout leadership roles. Despite this effort, Girl Scouting could not shake its white, middle-class "stigma."[50] The issue of Girl Scouting's image would arise repeatedly in the next decade as program administrators tried to respond to changing needs in the African American community.

Rising race consciousness among African Americans during the 1970s led eventually to a new multicultural emphasis in Girl Scouting. In the fall of 1970, in response to complaints that the program showed poor under-standing and appreciation of African American culture, Girl Scouts held a national conference on the subject. Delegates from the CVGSC attended. The conference highlighted the insufficient representation of African Americans among both council volunteers and staff and in publicity materials, and the continued "white, upper middle-class" orientation of the organization and its program.[51]

The CVGSC built its response to this report on initiatives begun the previous decade. In 1971, it established the Friendship Troop program to promote understanding between troops of diverse backgrounds. To facilitate greater volunteer participation from the inner city, the council arranged car pools, paid for training in some cases, and scheduled meetings at times more convenient for working women. It encouraged biracial leadership for integrated troops. In the interests of cost reduction, it established a thrift shop for uniform exchange.[52] It applied principles of "affirmative action" to nominations for committee and board posts, taught leaders how to make the program more interesting to African American girls, and won grants to fund new membership initiatives. In 1979, through the Comprehensive Employment Training Act (CETA), the council received funds for inner-city projects, including Project Future Sense, which sought to bring "modern day society's knowledge of job options, particularly for women," to girls in underprivileged communities.[53]

Josephine Holloway's decades of commitment to Girl Scouting for Nashville's African American community built a strong foundation for the integration that followed. In the women's movement spirit of giving greater honor to the work women do, the national Girl Scout office urged local councils in 1974 to select a "Hidden Heroine" for recognition during the bicentennial celebration in 1976. The CVGSC chose Holloway, honoring her in its celebration, which on 19 June 1976 drew six thousand participants to Municipal Auditorium. A special feature of the event was the Hall of Heroines, which saluted "the women of Middle Tennessee and Southern Kentucky who have made vital contributions to their communities but were never properly recognized." Holloway was a principal figure in this hall.

Though now deceased, Holloway is still being honored. In 1990, Nashville's African American community joined with the CVGSC in launching a campaign to raise money for a gallery in her name and a permanent historical exhibit for the program's new headquarters on Granny White Pike at Battery Lane in Nashville. Both are now complete. The gallery preserves some of Holloway's artifacts and memorabilia and the historical exhibit, titled "The Changing Role of Women: The Cumberland Valley Girl Scout Dimension," features Holloway's role in bringing the program to Nashville and making it succeed.[54]

Despite a series of obstacles, before which a less-determined character would have given way, Holloway molded an essentially white, middle-class program into a morale- and confidence-building experience for African American girls. In the process, she herself moved from the program's margins to its very center. Although in forming the Girl Scouts, Juliette Low, a privileged white southerner, most likely never gave much thought to its impact on African American girls, she would have acknowledged that Josephine Holloway had fulfilled her program's goals in "the very best" way possible.

Notes

1. The author acknowledges assistance with some of the primary research for this chapter from the following: Mary Hoffschwelle, Carole Bucy, Linda Dean, and Barbara Mann. The group undertook this work in preparation for the exhibit "The Changing Role of Women: The Cumberland Valley Girl Scout Dimension," which is now on display at the Cumberland Valley Girl Scout Center (CVGSC) headquarters in Nashville. The exhibit was funded in part by the CVGSC and by a grant from the Tennessee Council on the Humanities, a not-for-profit corporation with primary support from the National Endowment for the Humanities. The findings and conclusions of this chapter do not necessarily represent the views of the National Endowment for the Humanities or those of the Tennessee Council on the Humanities.

2. Two critical biographies of Baden-Powell have recently appeared: Michael Rosenthal, *The Character Factory: Baden-Powell and the Origins of the Boy Scout Movement* (New York, 1984, 1986), and Tim Jeal, *The Boy-Man: The Life of Lord Baden-Powell* (New York, 1990).

3. See *The Handbook of the Girl Guides, or How Girls Can Help to Build Up the Empire* (1912). Robert Baden-Powell later updated it (see *Guiding for Girls*, 1918), eliminating, at the Guides' request, those aspects of his sister's advice they found too "lady-like" or "old-fashioned." For a history of Guiding, see two narratives published by the Girl Guide Association: Rose Kerr, *Story of the Girl Guides, 1908–1938* (London, 1976), and Alix Liddell (Kerr's daughter), *Story of the Girl Guides, 1938–1975* (London, 1976).

4. On the relationship between Low's personal crisis and the founding of the Girl Scouts, see Charles E. Strickland, "Juliette Low, the Girl Scouts, and the Role of American Women," in *Woman's Being, Woman's Place: Female Identity and Vocation in American History*, ed. Mary Kelley (Boston, 1979), 252–64.

5. See the Girl Scout–approved biography of Low, Gladys Denny Shultz and Daisy Gordon Lawrence, *Lady from Savannah: The Life of Juliette Low* (New York, c. 1958), chap. 19. Katherine Keena, program specialist at the Juliette Gordon Low National Center, Savannah, Georgia, and Mary Levey and Martha Foley, librarian and former archivist, respectively, at the National Historic Preservation Center, Girl Scouts of the USA, New York, N.Y. (hereafter cited as GS-USA Archives), courteously provided me with information about the early program.

6. In its earliest version, the promise read: "On my honor, I will try: to do my duty to God and my country, to help other people at all times, to obey the Girl Scout laws." A modernized promise from 1972 contained the word "mankind" as a generic term. After protests in the early 1980s, the original wording was restored.

7. Modeled on Baden-Powell's *British Girl Guide Manual*, Low's early program focused on these skills to prepare girls for emergencies or for life on a colonial outpost. Securing a burglar with eight inches of cord was one of its more colorful instructions: "Make a slip-knot at each end of your cord. Tie the burglar's hands behind him by passing each loop over his little fingers. Place him face downwards, and bend his knees, Pass both feet under the string, and he will be unable to get away." See *How Girls Can Help Their Country* (1913), 42, the first American manual.

8. See *Scouting for Girls: Official Handbook of the Girl Scouts*, abridged ed., 1927 (c. 1920), foreword, 14–19, 243.

9. There may have been troops in towns and counties surrounding Nashville, but there is no documentation of their existence until the mid-1920s.

10. Monthly Reports and Board Minutes, Nashville Young Women's Christian Association (YWCA), TSLA, Nashville YWCA Archives; *Nashville Banner*, 1 Sept. 1918.

11. National Council of Jewish Women–Nashville Section, *Yearbook* (1918–19), 28, and *Yearbook* (1919–20), 29, Jewish Federation of Nashville and Middle Tennessee Archives (hereafter cited as JF Archives); Monthly Report, YWCA, Sept. 1919.

12. This was not necessarily true of Girl Scout troops elsewhere. According to Martha Foley, social settlements in northern states reported integrated troops as early as 1913; the first photograph of such a troop dates from 1919.

13. General Secretary's Report for 1919, YWCA, YWCA Archives; Katherine Keena provided information on national competition between the YWCA and Juliette Low in the early 1920s.

14. Around 1912, women leaders of Nashville's Colored Methodist Episcopal Church began social settlement programs for neglected children in Nashville's African American community. Eventually, as the result of an interracial, interdenominational effort among the women of the Methodist Episcopal Church, South, fifty thousand dollars was raised to erect the Bethlehem Center in 1923. See Noreen Dunn Tatum, *A Crown of Service: A Story of Woman's Work in the Methodist Episcopal Church, South, from 1878–1940* (Nashville, 1960), 267–69. *The Annual Report of the Woman's Missionary Council, 1924–25* stated that over five hundred girls took part in Josephine Groves's various programs ("Home Department, Negro Work"). See also Martha Nutt, "Bethlehem Center, Nashville, Tennessee," *Southern Workman* 53 (Sept. 1924): 401–4 (the author is grateful to Jimmie Franklin for this reference); Nutt's claim that the Bethlehem Center sponsored the first colored Girl Scouts of the South is not substantiated, however; there were troops as early as 1914.

15. "Running Record" of relations between Girl Scouts–USA and the Nashville Girl Scout Council, 2 Dec. 1927–7 Dec. 1938, GS-USA Archives.

16. *Nashville Banner*, 30 Jan. 1924.

17. See "You Can Count on Her," program for the Recognition Brunch in honor of Alice Collier, 14 Dec. 1963, CVGSC Archives. One of Collier's daughters had been a member of Groves's Bethlehem Center troops, 1925–26.

18. "Josephine Groves Holloway, Hidden Heroine," typescript, CVGSC Archives. On page 2, this unattributed biography notes that "upon contacting the Council, she [Holloway] was told that black girls were not permitted to join Girl Scouts in

Nashville, that only white girls could belong." Further details about Holloway's life also come from author's interviews with her three daughters, Weslia Holloway and Josephine Holloway Dickson, Nashville, 27 June 1991, and Nareda Holloway Coar, Nashville, 5 Oct. 1991.

19. In August 1920, Tennessee became the thirty-sixth and final state necessary for the ratification of the woman suffrage amendment to the U.S. Constitution. Reports of early Girl Scout troops can be found in the CVGSC Archives. See also Lillian Cohen, Report (n.d.) to the YWHA Board, in Board Records of 1926–28, JF Archives; Gean Morgan, interviews with Carole Bucy, CVGSC Archives, Jan. 1991 (Gean, whose brother was a Boy Scout, wanted to be a Girl Scout "more than anything"), and Adele Mills Schweid, Nashville, July 1991 (Adele found Girl Scouting too "military," but her sister liked it); Sara Fisher, "The Early Days in Girl Scouting in Nashville–Davidson County," 1952, CVGSC Archives. Nashville's first charter gave the council jurisdiction over Nashville, Donelson, Joelton, Goodlettsville, Old Hickory, Bellevue, Antioch, Madison, White's Creek, and Hermitage.

20. Annual Report of the Nashville Girl Scout Council to the National Girl Scouts, Inc., 31 Dec. 1928; "Running Record," GS-USA Archives.

21. "Running Record," GS-USA Archives; Nareda Holloway Coar, interview with author, Nashville, 5 Oct. 1991; Board Minutes, Nashville Girl Scout Council, 6 June 1933, CVGSC Archives.

22. See "Hidden Heroine," CVGSC Archives.

23. The wording of the 6 June Board Minutes is instructive here: "The Committee appointed at a regular meeting May 25th to investigate the advisability of approving the request for organizing Girl Scout troops among the Negroes. Reported as follows: 'That it would be necessary to have a paid, trained Negro worker under the Community Chest; that it was the opinion of the Committee the time was inopportune for the expansion of the work among the Negroes but it was hoped that in much less future time the work would be taken up by the Council with a definite policy along the line of the Girl Reserve.'"

24. Annual Reports of the Nashville Girl Scout Council to the National Girl Scouts, Inc., 1932, 1933; "Running Record," GS-USA Archives.

25. Board Minutes, Nashville Girl Scout Council, 22 June 1933, CVGSC Archives.

26. Ibid., 6 Sept. 1933, CVGSC Archives. Sadly, written evidence of Holloway's own views of these events exists neither in CVGSC files, nor among the artifacts she left at her death.

27. "Running Record," Report for 1936, GS-USA Archives.

28. Board Minutes, Nashville Girl Scout Council, 13 June, 12 Sept., and 17 Oct. 1938; clippings, scrapbook, 1938, CVGSC Archives. Mrs. Roosevelt had of course long been committed to ideals of racial equality. The following year, in a highly publicized event, she resigned from the Daughters of the American Revolution when that group refused to rent its hall for a concert by Marian Anderson. She then helped arrange for the singer to perform in front of the Lincoln Memorial.

29. Karen Spivey Report, Pulaski, Fall 1990; Linda Dean Report, Springfield, Fall 1990; additional notes from Beverly Irene Lawrence, Fall 1990; Mrs. R. W. Weathersby, Clarksville Leaf-Chronicle, 15 Nov. 1958, CVGSC Archives.

30. See Ethel Mockler, Citizenry in Action: The Girl Scout Record, 1912–1947 (New York, 1947), 107. Perhaps in response to this change, after 1953, the national handbook included two women of color in its section on role models in history:

the Native American scout, Sacajawea, and Phyllis Wheatley, America's first published black poet. See *Girl Scout Handbook: Intermediate Program* (1953, 1955), preface.

31. "Hidden Heroine," CVGSC Archives.
32. Coar, interview. Nareda reports that her mother was angry with her for having approached Eleanor Roosevelt on her own. As Roosevelt took a gradualist approach to race issues, her hesitation to push harder on bringing African Americans into the Nashville Council is not surprising. See Lois Scharf, *Eleanor Roosevelt: First Lady of American Liberalism* (Boston, 1987), 107, and Pauli Murray, *The Autobiography of a Black Activist, Feminist, Lawyer, Priest, and Poet* (Knoxville, 1989), 112–13. The *Nashville Banner* and *Tennessean* of 21 April 1942 reported Roosevelt's visit on their society pages.
33. Regional records held at the national office indicate that other black troops existed in the South during the 1940s, particularly in Mississippi and Arkansas. Holloway's unique status at the training session may have been accidental. Information on early relations between the council and black troops appear in the following board minutes: 9 Nov. and 14 Dec. 1942; 12 Feb., 8 Mar., and 14 June 1943; 14 Feb., 23 May, 26 Sept., and 5 Dec. 1944; 24 Apr. and 26 June 1945.
34. Board Minutes, Nashville Girl Scout Council, 25 Sept. 1945; Conferences File, 1946, GS-USA Archives.
35. Board Minutes, Nashville Girl Scout Council, 20 Feb. and 24 Apr. 1945 and 28 Oct. 1947; reports from Clarksville and Columbia, Fall 1990, CVGSC Archives.
36. According to Beverly Coleman ("A History of State Parks in Tennessee" [Ph.D. diss., George Peabody College, 1963], 243, 361), no written policies prevented blacks from using state parks, but blacks were expected to frequent only the two parks built especially for them, one near Chattanooga, the other near Memphis. Neither of these was convenient to Nashville.
37. Board Minutes, Nashville Girl Scout Council, 22 Mar. 1948; 8 July, 20 Aug. 1949; 18 May 1956; 15 Oct. 1958; and 6 July 1960; Polly Fessey and Weslia Holloway, interviews with author, Nashville, 27 June 1991.
38. In 1951, it moved to 819 Second Avenue South; in 1954 to 1531 Demonbreun; in 1959 to 2417 West End Avenue; and in 1964 to 832 Kirkwood Avenue.
39. Board Minutes, 27 Mar. and 22 May 1945, and 24 Oct. 1957, CVGSC Archives.
40. Board Minutes, 19 Feb. 1964 and 15 Sept. 1965; "Outline History," CVGSC Archives.
41. Lenore Amerman, field report, 27 Oct. 1950; the CVGSC report is dated 22 February 1966. At the end of her report, Amerman wrote, "Slowly but surely, our Negroes are being recognized as human beings!" The military installations were not named; one was probably Fort Campbell, located on the state line between Clarksville, Tenn., and Hopkinsville, Kent.
42. Board Minutes, 28 Mar. 1950; Fessey, interview; clipping (n.d.), CVGSC scrapbook, 1954.
43. See Linda T. Wynn, "The Dawning of a New Day: The Nashville Sit-ins, February 13–May 10, 1960," *Tennessee Historical Quarterly* 51 (Spring 1991): 42–54.
44. Emily Walker, "Women and the Nashville Civil Rights Movement," Vanderbilt University graduate student research paper, December 1990, in author's possession.
45. Board Minutes, 21 Sept. 1960, 20 Mar. 1963, 15 Jan. and 16 Sept. 1964, 20 Jan. and 17 Feb. 1965; Fessey, interview; "Outline History."

46. Informal segregation persisted, however. In 1976, the CVGSC had 777 all-white, 21 all-black, and 74 mixed troops. By 1990, the proportion of mixed to single-race troops was much higher: while 890 were all white and 73 all black, 517 were mixed.
47. Holloway, Dickson, and Coar, interviews; videotape, Memorial Tribute to Josephine Holloway, 20 May 1990, CVGSC Archives.
48. See the Fisk Memorial Program and Holloway clippings, Holloway file, CVGSC Archives.
49. To encourage the participation of African Americans in the Girl Scout program, publicity materials from the national office in the late 1970s reemphasized the tradition of blacks in the movement. See "Black Americans Have a History of Helping Each Other," GS-USA brochure, 1979.
50. Reports of the Membership Extension Committee, 1966–67, CVGSC Archives.
51. "Conference on Scouting for Black Girls," Girl Scouts-USA Memorandum, 24 Nov. 1970, copy in CVGSC files. This is a fascinating document. In verbatim transcripts, it captures many of the highly charged emotions and views of African American girls and women on current conditions for their race.
52. Board Minutes, 16 Sept. 1971, CVGSC Archives. The council had expressed concerns about the costs of uniforms earlier in its history. On 28 November 1950, in deploring the "over-emphasis" on uniforms, board members decided to stress to leaders the importance of not excluding a girl who could not afford one.
53. A combined grant from the Werthan Foundation, The Jewish Temple, Calvary Methodist Church, and interested individuals in 1972 resulted in five thousand dollars for a pilot project at the South Street Community Center to extend membership. See also "Recommendations from Conference on Scouting for Black Girls," CVGSC, 17 Apr. 1973.
54. Holloway died on 7 December 1988 at the age of ninety. See videotape, Memorial Tribute to Josephine Holloway, CVGSC Archives.

Few Black Voices Heard
The Black Community
and the 1956 Desegregation
Crisis in Clinton

June N. Adamson

*T*HE PUSH TO DESEGREGATE PUBLIC SCHOOLS FOLLOW-
ING THE SUPREME COURT'S LANDMARK DECISION
IN *BROWN V. BOARD OF EDUCATION* (1954) FIRST
touched Tennessee communities in fall 1956, when a
handful of brave African American students walked with
their adult escorts to enter Clinton High School. The
violence that met this initial attempt at public school
integration temporarily placed Clinton in the national
spotlight, with extensive newspaper and television coverage. But still the blacks came, and later in the spring 1957
Bobby Cain became the first African American to graduate from a white public high school since the nineteenth
century. In brutal retaliation, segregationists dynamited
the school in 1958. June Adamson relates this often-told
story, but does so through the perspective of the African
Americans who actually lived through the experience.
Using hours of interviews conducted with the students
and their surviving parents, Adamson gives an African
American voice to the Clinton crisis, a voice that was
largely missing in the contemporary coverage and later
historical accounts of this pivotal chapter in the history
of Tennessee public education.

One of the nine black students enrolled in East Tennessee's Clinton High School for the first time walked defiantly down the hill with her class-mates on 4 December 1956. School had been in session for three months, but already there had been serious trouble from those who would scare the black students into staying home. But Regina Turner was not afraid. She paid little attention to her classmates, and certainly little to the three white men who accompanied the group to protect them as they walked through the lines of taunting white people on each side. "I didn't want to go to Clinton High School in the first place, but I knew I had a right to be there and I wasn't afraid," she said.

Regina Turner credited her parents, the late Louise and Will Turner, for her lack of fear. "They taught me never to fear anyone or anything, but also not to be a troublemaker. They said the only thing worse than being afraid was death and since no one has been able to talk to a person who has died, no one knows whether that is the worst thing," she explained.[1]

Members of the press, mainly from newspapers at that time, were on the sidelines too. Photographers were particularly visible and the pictures they took of the nine black students and their three white escorts were printed by many newspapers across the country. The students were not identified in most publications, but in some cases, Bobby Cain, the only eligible senior in the group, was named. Readers understood that if he could graduate from a previously all-white southern school, more black graduates would follow. That was the last thing segregationists wanted to happen.

This chapter explains the viewpoint of the black students and others in the black community who, though seriously involved in the process to deseg-regate Clinton schools, were dehumanized in many ways by that process. For example, they were seldom named but ignored entirely or mistakenly identified by the press. True, sometimes reporters avoided naming them for fear they would be singled out for attack, since a number of reporters and pho-tographers were strongly on the side of school desegregation. But too often the attitude was that of Horace Wells, the owner, publisher, and editor of the *Clinton Courier-News* at the time. Answering a question about why no black voices were ever heard in his newspaper in the 1950s he said, "The contro-versy here was between whites about blacks. The Negroes were on the side-lines, even though they were the cause. People assume blacks were involved, but they stayed home."[2]

A study of both local and national newspapers and magazines of the time showed that Regina Turner was one of the few black students sometimes quoted and identified by name, even when it was her mother, Louise, speaking. "Sometimes they [newspapermen] mixed up our quotes. Sometimes they said she was talking when it was me, and they didn't always write exactly what we said." She found journalists generally "pushy and irritating" but did give credit to those reporters who really sought the viewpoint of the black community. The Turner family often got phone calls from out-of-town reporters, but few local queries. Sometimes they talked to reporters; more often they did not. Regina recalled one sympathetic reporter from *Jet* magazine whom she did talk to when he came to the Turner home. She added, "I was never afraid to say what I thought," which may explain why she was quoted more often than other students, several of whom have admitted their fear. She added that she had the ability to "detach myself from conflict" when it was making her too angry, and she said nothing at those times. While her mother taught Regina not to be afraid during the trouble, as head of the household, Louise Turner was prepared to protect them. "She had her gun and her dog, and she could handle that gun," recalled her daughter, adding that she was glad it was never needed.[3]

Along with the Turner family, other Clinton black families were very much involved when the nine made that walk to school as well as at other times of the desegregation crisis because they were so concerned for the safety of their children. Certainly most "stayed home" when their children did not need them because they were a tiny minority in the Anderson County town. Like Regina, they did not want to invite trouble. And certainly some white people besides the three escorts cared about what the students and their families were going through at home and school in their efforts to get equality in education. Most publications, however, said little if anything at all.

The other black students who walked with Regina Turner that December morning were perhaps less defiant, but they held their heads high too. Unlike Regina, they really wanted to go to Clinton High School. They believed they had a right to be there, and knew that some of their families had filed a suit as early as 1950 to give them that right. Besides Regina, Bobby Cain, who would become the first black graduate of any public high school in the South in 1957, was there. Gail Ann Epps, the first black girl to graduate from Clinton High School in 1958, was there. Jo Ann Allen, who appeared with her father on Edward R. Murrow's wonderfully balanced documentary "Clinton and the Law," part of the important *See it Now* series, was there.[4] So were a half a dozen others: Minnie Ann Dickey and Alva J. McSwain, whose parents were among those who filed the original lawsuit to try to desegregate the school in 1950; Ronnie Hayden; Maurice Soles; and Alfred Williams. Edward Lee Soles and Charles Williams may not have come because there was some question about their school records. Theresa Caswell, a freshman who lived in the Claxton community about seven miles away and rode a bus to the school, was not there. Besides the inconvenience, her family's fear must have been greater because she was crippled by polio and an easy target for segregationists.

The three white men who walked to school with the nine blacks who came to school that December day were the Reverend Paul Turner, Sidney Davis, and Leo Burnett. Turner was minister of Clinton's First Baptist Church. Davis was an attorney who once tried to keep Clinton schools segregated but who now was firmly on the side of the black families and the federal law. Burnett was a fair-minded citizen employed at Magnet Mills, a textile factory that was then Clinton's main industry.

Although the crisis now seems virtually forgotten by laymen and journalists alike, the high school in Clinton was the first in the entire South, aside from those on such federally controlled enclaves as army and navy bases, to graduate a black student, not the high school in Little Rock as is so often reported. Almost the same things happened in Clinton in the 1956–57 school year as happened in 1957–58 in Little Rock. Violence was even greater in Clinton, however, when a bomb badly damaged and partly destroyed the high school in October 1958. But this chapter focuses on the beginnings of the struggle to desegregate in 1956. The 1956 turmoil was not the beginning of the Clinton story, however. The original suit filed by Clinton black families asking that their children be allowed to attend Clinton High School was filed in December 1950 in federal district court after they had first visited school Principal D. J. Brittain and Superintendent Frank Irwin. The wheels of justice do grind slowly, and it was not until February 1952 that the case, known first as the *Joheather McSwain v. Anderson County Board of Education*, came to trial. The decision against the blacks was handed down 25 April 1952. During that period the *Brown v. Board of Education, Topeka, Kansas* was also in the courts. The Clinton case went to the Court of Appeals in Cincinnati, Ohio, where it stayed until the 1954 Supreme Court decision.[5]

The National Association for the Advancement of Colored People (NAACP) had been getting bolder in the struggle for civil rights. Some white Clintonians believed that the NAACP wanted to make Clinton the test case. While the NAACP did give support to the families filing the suit, just as the organization gave support in many places, every indication is that Clinton as a "test case" just happened, since it was only one of several pending cases.

The NAACP had been working for the cause of civil rights long before desegregation was finally ordered in Clinton in 1956. In 1952 *Collier's* magazine
carried an article about Thurgood Marshall, who was special counsel for the
NAACP, noting that

> the association has neither the time nor money nor incli-
> nation to go the aid of every Negro in trouble. It is prima-
> rily interested in cases involving a violation of a man's
> constitutional rights, which, in terms of the 14th (or equal
> rights) amendment look as if they can be carried to a suc-
> cessful conclusion in the United States Supreme Court.
> [The] NAACP has won 30 of the 33 cases it has carried to
> that tribunal since 1915, and the ultimate aim is a series of
> Supreme Court rulings that will render null and void all of
> the discriminatory laws now found in the statutes.[6]

Since the local federal district court's negative decision had just been
announced and the decision had yet to come from the court of appeals, the
Clinton case was not mentioned in the *Collier's* article. Clearly the NAACP
or anyone else did not plan it as *the* test case. It never even got to the
Supreme Court, although it was directly affected when the Supreme Court
decision in *Brown v. Board of Education* reversed the local decision.

In 1956 Clinton saw a worse time just after classes began when Frederick
John Kasper, a racial agitator from Washington, D.C., and his segregationist supporters gathered. Taunts, threats, jeering, and rioting brought in the
National Guard to Clinton during the Labor Day weekend. The harassment
in the months that followed had driven all of the black students out of school.
Clinton High School had opened on a desegregated basis just before the holiday weekend. The gathering places for segregationists became the school-
yard and the courthouse square and the white crowds had grown larger and
angrier.

Until Kasper arrived on the scene, desegregation had seemed inevitable
and accepted in Clinton. Black students registered peacefully on 20 August,
then Kasper, a self-styled rabble rouser, arrived in town on 25 August to
begin rounding up followers. The next day, a Sunday, the mayor, police commissioner, sheriff, acting police chief, and a local highway patrol officer met
to plan protection at the school on Monday, 27 August. Classes began that
Monday with black students accepted by most white students. However,
Kasper gathered a crowd at the school the next two mornings and about fifty
in the crowd were identified as "stay-away students." Some wore placards

announcing that they would not go to school with "niggers." Gatherings occurred at night, too, with Kasper shouting that local authorities had no "guts," that people are a higher court than the Supreme Court, and that the desegregation order did not have to be obeyed. A nightly crowd of about eight hundred gathered at the courthouse to hear Kasper speak. On Wednesday, 29 August 1956, he was interrupted as federal marshals served him with papers temporarily restraining his activities and ordering him to appear at a hearing in federal district court the next day. As he left, Kasper told the crowd to continue its work.

His followers did. The next morning several hundred people continued picketing outside the school and the activity of the crowd grew more riotous as the day went on. Inside, with about 600 students out of 732 in attendance, Principal D. J. Brittain announced a 447-to-6 vote of confidence for the desegregated school from parents on the basis of unsigned ballots brought in by students. John Kasper was not in the crowd of picketers that morning, but he stood just down the street to watch. That afternoon Clinton leaders, including newspaper publisher Horace Wells and attorneys Sidney Davis and Bufford Lewallen, appeared in federal district court in Knoxville to present testimony in support of an injunction forbidding interference with desegregation. Kasper told the judge he did not advocate violence or mob rule but was only using his constitutional rights of free speech and freedom of assembly. He was held in jail pending bond and until the hearing could be completed.

The night of 31 August 1956, even without Kasper, crowds swarmed to the courthouse square and impromptu speakers shouted "desegregation means mongrelization." Slurs were made against local, state, and national leaders who were trying to obey the new federal law based on the *Brown v. Board of Education* decision. Little wonder that blacks "stayed home." That day school attendance had dropped sharply because of fear of violence. Only 446, slightly more than half of the student body, attended classes that day. The total included 10 black students.[7] That night two local segregationists began to speak until Asa (Ace) Carter, an outspoken segregationist from the Birmingham, Alabama, White Citizens Council, arrived as a replacement for the jailed Kasper. Carter attacked the Supreme Court, the NAACP and the "carpet-bagging" judge, Robert L. Taylor, who put Kasper in jail.

Carter urged Clintonians to join the White Citizens Council organized by Kasper, and local segregationists immediately formed lines to do so. Sparked by Carter's rhetoric, the crowd marched through the street shouting, "We want Kasper." Groups broke off to march to the mayor's house. They threatened to burn it. Demonstrations continued into the night, with groups in the crowd rocking cars, especially those with black passengers, as they came through the town. A black sailor, who was pulled out of his car by the crowd, was identified by name in a few newspapers as "James Chandler, home on leave and in Clinton to visit a friend. There were no arrests, but young Chandler was taken into 'protective custody' by police. Firecrackers were hurled throughout the night and Mayor W. E. Lewallen tried to reach state authorities to get help."[8]

The next morning the board of aldermen met to declare Clinton in a state of emergency and requested that the governor assist in restoring law and order. Meanwhile a "Home Guard" led by Leo Grant organized a campaign to keep law and order. Grant was an auxiliary policeman chosen for leadership of the hastily organized guard because he had been trained in crowd control as an army infantry officer. As the guard, made up of law-abiding private citizens as well as auxiliary police, and the angry crowd lined up facing each other, guardsmen repelled the crowd with tear gas. At precisely the most tense moment, the highway patrol arrived and made three arrests. Most people in the town—black and white—breathed a sigh of relief and the crowd became more orderly. The rally was allowed to continue. About two thousand people gathered to hear prosegregationist speeches.[9]

Blacks in their homes were surely apprehensive that night. So were leading citizens, for themselves and for the whole town. They feared growing violence would lead to loss of life as well as property. They watched anxiously from their homes into the next morning, said several blacks interviewed, including the Reverend Orville Willis, then pastor of Mount Sinai Baptist Church, who was another of the parents who filed the 1950 suit.

That weekend put Clinton in the news, not just locally but nationally and internationally. But the focus was upon whites. Segregationists were getting far more press attention than the blacks who were so deeply affected by what was happening. When Asa Carter came to Clinton as leader of the violent Northern Alabama White Citizens Council, he brought publicity with him. Radio, television, and newspapers carried the news, so when Carter arrived the crowd was large. Many cars bore license plates from the deeper South states. Wells said, "That night the crowd overturned cars, slashed tires, smashed windows and frightened Negro travelers, some of them servicemen who just happened to be coming through. Youngsters and juvenile-minded [white] adults took over the town threatening to dynamite the mayor's home, the newspaper plant, and even the Courthouse itself."[10] The black residential community was also threatened by segregationists driving through town, but this was only reported later when dynamite was thrown in that neighborhood too. At about noon Sunday, 2 September 1956, six hundred National Guardsmen came rolling into Clinton to organize for immediate duty. The tanks seemed to belong to another time and place. Most residents welcomed the soldiers, but others who had been in the crowd the night before resented the intrusion. Curiosity seekers who tied up traffic on Highway 25W through Clinton that day made the soldiers' work more difficult. No interstates existed in the area then, and only one route bypassed Clinton. By night road blocks were established, with guardsmen checking every car to see who really needed to come into Clinton. Photographers and newsmen were gathering by now, but few if any of them went into the black community to learn what was happening there.

Monday, 3 September 1956, Labor Day, was quieter. National Guard commander Joe Henry had gotten tough. He banned congregations on the square or anywhere else in town. He also banned the use of public address systems for speeches.[11]

Time magazine described the events of the week in dramatic terms:

> In Clinton, Tenn., white mobs rioted in the tree-shaded streets and the old courthouse square to stop the enrollment of twelve Negro students in the local high school. Clinton is the only place in Tennessee [except in the federal enclave of Oak Ridge] to integrate its school, and outsiders came streaming in to lash the little town back into line. . . . Thunder and lightning split the sultry overcast sky as [Leo] Grant's [Home Guard] men fired six tear gas bombs to disperse the mob and keep the peace, but the mob began to move against the vigilantes, shouting, "Let's get the nigger lovers! Let's get their guns and kill them!" Precisely at that moment 100 state highway patrolmen swept into Clinton on orders of Governor Frank Clement, sirens shrieking and searchlights blazing, to restore an uneasy peace. Next day the state rolled 633 troops and seven M-41 tanks of the National Guard into Clinton to button things up, roaring and clanking and chewing up the asphalt of the courthouse square.[12]

So 4 December 1956 was not the first day of divisiveness and violence, nor was it the worst day Clinton had seen since the high school had opened three months before. But it was a day that marked a turning point: the day when most people in Clinton took a firm stand on one side or the other and demonstrated it at the ballot box. A municipal election happened to be held that day, with the White Citizens Council sponsoring one candidate for mayor and two for aldermen. Law abiding citizens, mostly the "establishment" people of the town, that is, those who had lived there for several generations, held offices and owned businesses and had a vested interest in maintaining peace and harmony in the community. They were sponsoring another candidate for mayor. Clinton was a town divided: those for and against the federal law. With the law supporting the three white escorts, the nine black students made it to school that day. But the Reverend Turner did not make it to his office. As he turned down the street away from the school, Turner was beaten and bloodied before friends and police rescued him. Before the day was over, the school was closed for the second time since classes had opened the previous August. Fifteen persons were arrested, and the FBI was asked to take action. The real fight against open segregationist activity in Clinton had begun.[13]

Kasper, the racial agitator, was seen as the catalyst for everything that had happened since September, but was not on the scene in December. Even so, he was arrested following that day on charges of criminal contempt and conspiracy for violating an injunction to prevent interference with peaceful desegregation and for inciting to riot.

Meanwhile, just how did the black students fare as pawns in this small-town social chess game? Although Regina Turner did not share the fear that many in Clinton felt, she said her mother was afraid: "She worried that one of us would be hurt or killed." Regina shared the opinion of many that John Kasper did not come to Clinton to stir up trouble on his own. She explained, "Those first two weeks at school all the kids were great to us. They were just ordinary kids, and we had known a lot of them before coming to the high school. I feel like the segregationists thought things were going too smoothly—they didn't expect that." She added, "I feel like someone big sent for John Kasper," but she had no idea who.[14]

Before the trouble began, Regina Turner attended segregated schools: Green-McAdoo Elementary School in Clinton and then Vine Junior High School in Knoxville, twenty miles away. She greatly enjoyed the latter experience. "I was looking forward to going back to school in Knoxville," she related, admitting that no small part of her enjoyment was the greater freedom she had being away from very strict parents. They would not let her go on a church picnic unless her brothers went along. Years later, she laughed about that. "My son says there was no place to go in Clinton, anyway. He can't believe how strict they were."

Regina Turner stayed at Clinton High School through her sophomore and junior years. "I refused to leave," she said. "People told us, 'If you quit, that will end the idea of desegregation.' I got angry, and I guess I'm stubborn." Nevertheless, after two years she did give up and went to her mother's hometown, Tallahassee, Florida, to live with an aunt and to graduate from a still-segregated black high school. "In Clinton it was just go to school and come home. We couldn't go to football or basketball games or any social event at school. I wanted more than that." Also she remained angry, at times even angrier than she was during that walk through hateful crowds that December day. She had always resented that there "was never enough of anything in the black schools; students always got leftover equipment and books from some white school. Green-McAdoo Elementary School was never even painted inside," she recalled. She also remembered one confrontation between black students and a white student who was "a terrible agitator and a leader of the student White Citizens group." Regina recalled that when one of the black students, whom she did not perceive as a troublemaker, was expelled and not the troublemaker, "I was too angry to be afraid. I hope I never get so angry again. I was angry enough to do something horrible and not care."[15]

Jo Ann Allen, another of the original dozen black students wrote that she was "very afraid." Yet she had ambivalent feelings about her family moving away from the trouble. However, she also recalled that in Clinton her education was being compromised "because of too many days out of school because of the constant threats of violence or death. This bitter struggle was hindering my forward motion. And, although I didn't want to give up 'the fight,' my family packed up and moved." She agreed with Regina Turner that blacks were not treated fairly in Clinton. "There was a time in Clinton when I thought I was pretty smart, but I found myself working twice as hard when we moved here [California]. By classroom standards here, I was very behind. It was probably the second-hand 'Dick and Jane' books and the scarred second-hand desks, and the out-dated educational programs we had to endure when the white children were through with them." Jo Ann did, however, praise one teacher: "I am very grateful to an excellent first grade teacher named Theresa E. Blair who gave most of us Clinton black kids a wonderful start. Without her, things would have been worse, but she got us through, even using those second-hand books."

Jo Ann Allen recalled Edward R. Murrow's "Clinton and the Law" program on which she and her father appeared. She wrote, "Mr. Murrow was a forceful person who spoke out against ill doings in America."[16] She was sixteen years old when she left Clinton with her family just days after the Reverend

Turner was beaten and the high school was closed. Originally the Allens had no intention of leaving. Jo Ann was elated at the idea of attending the newly desegregated school. At the end of August a Knoxville newspaper reported her sentiments: "My classes are real nice and I believe everything would be all right if outsiders left us alone." Three months later the Knoxville newspaper quoted her father, Herbert Allen, who explained the family's planned exodus: "I want my kids to have a better break than I did. No matter how much education they get here, there's no place for them to use it. I don't believe there will ever be an opportunity for my children in Tennessee. I guess you'd call me stubborn for letting the school situation keep me in Clinton this long, but now that integration seems assured, I want to go where my children will have a chance."[17]

Jo Ann Allen and her family often have been asked why they left Clinton, and whether they were afraid. Their friends assumed that, like Regina, the Allens were not afraid since they spoke out publicly the few times they were asked. "But we were afraid; all of us in that tiny black community were afraid," Jo Ann recalled. "Our white neighbors who had shared our food and toys and friendship began to harass us in the night, especially if our parents were away." She wrote of the worn and tattered scrapbook she kept from the Clinton days, noting, "Since most of the articles I clipped were written by the Southern press, there was little or no condemnation of what was happening to us." She added, "And of course, no one wrote that integration was OK and that was the way things should be, simply children going to school with children, and not blacks going to school with whites." She was also aware that there was "little written about the black families (except my family and the family of Bobby Cain) and the impact this had on all of our lives. There has been no follow-up ever as far as I know as to what any of the original twelve children of Clinton are doing, or how their lives changed because of these tumultuous events." Not only black and white youngsters were fearful, she noted, but parents, teachers, school administrators—every citizen trying to obey the new law in the face of mob action.[18]

In Los Angeles Jo Ann was introduced to the *Black Sentinel*, a newspaper that spoke out and condemned segregation. Even acknowledging that few readers subscribed to this newspaper, she wrote, "It was nice to read such things as 'brave black kids.'"[19]

Gail Ann Epps was reared in a white neighborhood in Clinton. The daughter of a respected black Clinton family, the hardest thing for her to understand was the need to be bused to Austin High School in Knoxville "just because of skin color," and then to be shunned in her own community for the same reason—skin color—when the law allowed her to go to Clinton High School. "You see, I didn't play with black kids when I went to grammar school," she explained. Going to the desegregated school meant going across town with the white friends with whom she grew up, but it also meant being uncomfortable around them for the first time in her life.

For Gail Ann, the most horrible feeling came in September 1956, when the National Guard arrived. "It was a Sunday morning and we were in church," she recalled. "Even though we saw them as protectors, it was just like war." Although Gail Ann was grateful for the protection of the guard, she was also grateful that she did not come into contact with its members. One indirect experience made a strong impression upon her. She vividly remembered what happened to James Chandler, a Clinton sailor she had been dating. On one occasion when Chandler came to visit her, he was taken into protective custody after being harassed and threatened. "He was caught up by a mob shouting, 'Let's beat this nigger,' when he was on his way back to Knoxville, and the National Guard had to rescue him." She recalled his fear, both of the mob and of the rather rough guardsmen.

Even though some of her former friends shunned her when the school was desegregated, Gail Ann Epps was fair to them. She retained many friendships even through the crisis. But before 1956 friendships were closer. One of her white friends told her years later, "Those jelly sandwiches your grandmother used to make were the best I ever had." She added, "Yes, I went to their homes to play, and they came to my grandmother's, but we knew the boundaries." That meant sharing the same toys, trading magazines, all the things girls do growing up. It meant going to the same theater, but Gail Ann had to sit upstairs. It meant never attending church or school together. The girls accepted "their place."

A member of a three-generation Clinton family, Gail Ann stayed with her grandmother, Ethel Moore, much of the time because her mother, Anna Mae Hale, and her aunt, Mattie Bell Henley (later Kelley), worked as domestics at the time. Her grandfather, Samuel Moore, was a brakeman for the railroad and therefore away a lot. He had paid room and board to have his Clinton-born daughters attend Austin High School in Knoxville years before Anderson County provided either tuition or a bus so they could commute from home. Later, Mattie Bell Henley, known as a force for good in the community, became one of the directors of Clinton's Green-McAdoo Day Care Center for children of working mothers. Gail Ann's great-grandfather was Aaron Moore, a respected property owner. Her father was the late William Lee Epps, who did construction work for the Tennessee Valley Authority.

Gail Ann recalled many sleepless nights during the years of trouble. Dynamite blasts happened throughout Clinton, and crosses were burned, not just in the black community, but in the white community where she lived. She was often worried about going to school during those first weeks of desegregation. She recalled her fear the day the school was closed in December 1956 and her relief when her mother and aunt came with the police to take her home. And she recalled one early morning when she heard voices outside her bedroom window and saw a strange car parked behind the family's woodshed. "There was a scraping sound on the side of the house right under my window. I woke my mother and my aunt to tell them someone was trying to get in." When they turned the lights on, the car pulled away. "We decided it was someone trying to scare me away from going to school. I didn't go back to sleep that morning."

One way Gail Ann has preserved her experiences of the 1950s is through a scrapbook she made as a project while she was a student at the segregated Tennessee A&I, now the desegregated Tennessee State University in Nashville. The scrapbook helped her recall her reaction to the newsmen and photographers during the worst of the strife in 1956. "They were not abusive; they didn't harass us. They did ask us questions," she recalled, "but mostly they just took pictures." As for how those articles and pictures make her feel now, especially when she was not identified by name, she expressed pride. "I could have left Clinton. I had relatives other places where I could have gone to school. I'm glad I stayed."[20] She has wondered why, when she became the first girl to graduate from a desegregated public high school in Tennessee in the spring of 1958, the press made no mention of her achievement as it had noticed Bobby Cain's graduation the year before. Her question is valid because, along with him, she is a part of the history of the Civil Rights movement in Tennessee.

Bobby Cain and his family probably had the most to fear, since he was the only senior eligible to graduate that first school year. Segregationists knew that if he graduated, their cause was lost. But he never saw himself as a hero and was the most reluctant of all the interviewees for this chapter. He refused to be interviewed "unless you talk with the others." He not only seemed embarrassed to talk about his position in 1956, but he said he just wanted to forget the crisis years. His father, Robert Cain Sr., another respected member of Clinton's black community, talked willingly. Bobby's wife, Margo, said he was even reluctant to talk with her and that she and their children had to learn details in other ways. At the time of the crisis Bobby Cain, a social worker with the Tennessee Department of Human Services in 1994, saw the coverage of the problems as "fair but not full," as the time when he was taken into custody because he had a knife, while those who attacked him were not arrested. "Actually, White Citizens Council members in high school carried knives too," he said, repeating that he didn't want to talk about it.[21]

Bobby's father, Robert Cain described the incident, first asking rhetorically, "Who wouldn't have carried a knife?" The retired Oak Ridge National Laboratory employee, who in retirement turned to carpentry and other craftwork, explained that Bobby was on his way to eat lunch at an ice cream store when segregationists attacked him. A woman clubbed him with an umbrella and men and boys hit him with their fists and threatened him with knives. Bobby, who was walking alone, was outnumbered, but he did try to defend himself, probably with his knife. Fortunately, the police came quickly and separated him from his attackers, but he was the only one taken into custody. "They made it seem like Bobby was looking for trouble with that knife," Mr. Cain said. Bobby was released to his father, and went back to school the next day. The elder Mr. Cain explained that later, "it got so rough on them all Negro parents took them out of school for their own safety." Other black parents pressured Mr. Cain to keep Bobby out and the sheriff told the Cains he didn't know whether he could control the local whites. The sheriff hinted that some would come up the hill with dynamite. But the Cains stood their ground until 4 December 1956, when they were escorted first back to the school and then out again when the school closed after the violence to the Reverend Turner.

Certainly his parents knew some of what Bobby went through. "He would talk about it some, but he kept most of it to himself. We saw him take aspirin when he came home every night. We knew either he needed glasses with all those headaches or it was his nerves jagged and on edge because of the harassment," his father said.

Mr. Cain told of driving Bobby and his friends to the high school during the terrible autumn of 1956, when they were jeered and called "niggers," "coons," and worse. He also told of the night of spring 1957 when Bobby became the first black to graduate from a public high school in the South. Television cameramen, newspaper reporters, and photographers were outside the school, but the school principal refused to allow them in. "Sure we were proud when we saw Bobby marching in the line and when it was all over, but we felt lots of hostility there," his father said. "Bobby had to go it alone after the ceremony when it came time for the graduates to go down into a basement room to change out of their caps and gowns. They didn't really hurt him, but someone cut the lights and hit him in the face," said Cain, recalling that members of the football team recruited by the principal went to his aid. Finally he and his family left the school to walk back to the car. "Mrs. Cain was scared," Cain said, the more so when she saw someone walking away from where their car was parked. "She was afraid someone might have put dynamite in it. I told her to wait until I started the car, and I did, and it was all right."

The Cains knew all about dynamite. They had heard it go off in many places in Clinton during that first year of trouble. There were no cross burnings or dynamite blasts in the Cains' yard, as there had been at other black residences, but "I almost shot a brother-in-law one night and that wasn't funny," Cain recalled. He told of seeing a man come into his yard and lean over to strike a match on a water tap. "I thought it was someone lighting a stick of dynamite, and got my gun and went out to see about it. A neighbor had been watching too, and she called out, 'Robert, don't shoot. It's Herbert.'"[22]

Other students, including Theresa Caswell, Minnie Ann Dickey, Alva McSwain, and others who were in later graduating classes, have similar stories to tell. Although the violence of the Clinton crisis ended following the bombing of the school in 1958, black students had difficulties for several years more. Margaret Anderson taught during the crisis and later became Clinton High School's first real student counselor to help all students move on to do better things following graduation. She is the author of *Children of the South*, the only book so far focused totally on the Clinton crisis, but except for Bobby Cain, she used pseudonyms for the black students. Speaking for opportunities for black students in the 1980s, she termed things "much better. Much easier. Not perfect. It will take a long time, and there may be some slipping back on both sides."[23]

Still, so much of what happened in the Clinton of the 1950s has never been told. The press did a magnificent job of showing what the white folks were doing on both sides of the desegregation issue. It also paid attention to the NAACP, but unfortunately the press largely ignored the black community in Clinton and only now is this side of history becoming known.

Notes

1. Regina Turner (now Smith), interview with author, Oak Ridge, Tenn., 7 Aug. 1980, and subsequent conversations.
2. Horace Wells, interview with author, Oak Ridge, Tenn., 1 July 1978.
3. Turner, interview.
4. Edward R. Murrow, "Clinton and the Law," one episode of the CBS television series *See It Now*, Jan. 1956.

5. *Joheather McSwain v. Anderson County Board of Education*, District Court, Knoxville, Tennessee, 14 Feb. 1952, Federal Archives and Records Center, East Point, Ga. Original transcript. Also, 101 F. Supp. 861, 26 Apr. 1952; County Board of Education, et al. Final decrees as reversed in Sixth Circuit Court of Cincinnati were sent back to Federal District Court in Knoxville to bring about implementation of Supreme Court Decision, 30 June 1954. (Original transcript in Carl Cowan Papers, Knoxville College, Knoxville, Tenn.)

6. James Polling, "Thurgood Marshall and the 14th Amendment," *Collier's*, 23 Feb. 1952, 3.

7. *Clinton Courier-News*, and other area and national newspapers, including the *New York Times*, 6 Dec. 1956, p. 1. Also, Anniversary Edition, *Clinton Courier-News*, 9 Sept. 1975, 4–5. Also Wells, interview, and subsequent conversations, and panel discussion by Wells and others who were involved, May 1984.

8. Ibid. Also, W. Bufford Lewallen, then Clinton attorney and a member of the Home Guard, interview with author, 23 May and 21 June 1990, and subsequent conversations.

9. Ibid.

10. Horace Wells's speech to the Columbus, Ohio, chapter of the Society of Professional Journalists/Sigma Delta Chi, 4 Oct. 1957. Used with Wells's permission.

11. *Clinton Courier-News*, 6 Sept. 1956, p. 1; *New York Times*, 1 Sept. 1956, p. 1, and other area and national newspapers that same week.

12. *Time* 68, no. 11 (10 Sept. 1956): 29–30.

13. *Clinton Courier-News* and other area and national newspapers, including the *New York Times*, 6 Dec. 1956, p. 1.

14. Turner, interview.

15. Ibid.

16. Jo Ann Allen (now Boyce) to author, 28 Aug. 1980; also Highlander Research Center Papers, Civil Rights, 1953–1959, Box 37, file 1, Highlander Center, New Market, Tenn.

17. *Knoxville Journal*, 31 Aug. 1956, p. 1; *New York Times*, 1 Sept. 1956, p. 8.

18. *Knoxville Journal*, 10 Dec. 1956, p. 8.

19. Allen to author, and Clinton Desegregation Papers, Highlander Center, New Market, Tenn.

20. Gail Ann Epps (now Upton), interviews with author, Oak Ridge, Tenn., 19 July 1980 and 1 Oct. 1982.

21. Bobby Cain, interviews with author, Clinton, Tenn., 15 Jan. 1979 and 29 Jan. 1980; Margo Cain, telephone interview with author, 1979.

22. Robert Cain, interview with author, Clinton, Tenn., 12 July 1979, and subsequent conversations.

23. Margaret Anderson, interviews with author, Clinton, Tenn., 23, 31 Aug. 1978, and many subsequent conversations since. Also see Margaret Anderson, *Children of the South* (New York, 1958).

Darwin School and Black Public Education
Cookeville in the Decade of the *Brown* Decision

Wali R. Kharif

ESEGREGATION OF THE STATE'S PUBLIC SCHOOLS DID NOT ALWAYS LEAD TO VIOLENCE AS IT DID IN CLINTON. PUBLIC SCHOOL INTEGRATION occurred peacefully, although at a slow pace, in Cookeville, a small county seat and college town in the eastern part of Middle Tennessee. Part of the reason why, Wali Kharif explains, is the small percentage of the population that African Americans represented in the region. Another reason was that blacks and whites had already mixed in selected community settings before school integration took place. Kharif also found that a large number of Cookeville blacks opposed integration in the mid-1960s. He interprets their actions not as conservative and accommodating (although some certainly fit those categories), but reflecting a fear that they would lose control over their children's education in an integrated school system. Darwin School, even with its inferior facilities and equipment, was at least their school. By fully depicting the central role that Darwin School played in the lives and culture of Cookeville's African Americans, Kharif underscores the loss that accompanied integration for many blacks across Tennessee.

Blending oral interviews, newspaper accounts, and school
board records, he documents an important small-town
example of the Civil Rights movement in action.

In May 1954 the United States Supreme Court ruled, in the case of *Brown
v. Board of Education of Topeka, Kansas*, that there was no place for racial
segregation in schools. This decision established the judicial precedence for
eliminating legal segregation in public schools. Implementing the *Brown*
decision at the community level, however, proved slow and deliberately
delayed by state officials, local governments, and citizens.

Historians have focused much attention on the highly publicized incidents occurring in the aftermath of the *Brown* decision in places like Little
Rock, Arkansas, and Prince Edward County, Virginia.[1] Opposition to integration in some southern communities was not always orchestrated and
sensational. The story of black education and school desegregation in Cookeville, Tennessee, from 1954 to 1963 reveals some unexpected reasons for the
slow desegregation of some schools in the South. Cookeville's experience
raises questions about some of the stereotypes concerning race relations and
desegregation during the decade following the *Brown* decision.

Cookeville is the seat of Putnam County and is located 80 miles east of
Nashville, 110 miles west of Knoxville, and approximately 100 miles north
of Chattanooga. It is the hub of Tennessee's Upper Cumberland, impacting
the surrounding communities of Sparta, Livingston, Gainesboro, and Celina
both economically and culturally. Cookeville is a rural community, but experienced substantial growth between 1950 and 1970. In 1950, Cookeville had
a population of 6,800, and jumped to 7,800 in 1960. By 1970, the city's population had almost doubled to 14,270. Population increase may be attributed, in part, to the growth of Tennessee Technological University, the city's
participation in the Model Cities Program, and the relocation of industry in
the area creating more and better paying jobs. However, the black population over this period was still small and actually declined from 551 in 1950
to 480 in 1970, when it comprised less than 2 percent of the city's total.[2]

At the time of the *Brown* decision, black children in Cookeville
attended Darwin School, located in the black section of the city called
"Bushtown." Darwin was built in 1928 as West Cookeville Junior High
School. The local community raised some funds for school construction,
and received financial support from the Julius Rosenwald Fund. In 1936, a

senior high school department was added, and the school was renamed in honor of J. Claude Darwin, a white Cookeville businessman who promoted black high school education in Putnam County. The first senior class was graduated from Darwin in 1938.[3]

For thirty-five years, Darwin School was the focal point of the local black community, offering African Americans much through social, athletic, and community activities. These afforded blacks outlets for community service and the opportunity to demonstrate leadership qualities. In addition, the positive role models portrayed by black teachers and professionals no doubt motivated and inspired young African Americans who, through their examples, could hope to attain similar positions and advantages. In his work *The Black High School and Its Community*, educator Frederick A. Rodgers observed that, in general, "the black high school was the only long-term publicly supported institution that was pervasive across the black community, and that was controlled, operated, staffed, populated, and maintained by blacks."[4] Darwin School was an institution with regional appeal. The high school facility, by local arrangements, catered to the educational needs of blacks in the surrounding counties. Overton, Clay, and White Counties, which did not have black high schools, bused their black high school students into Cookeville to attend Darwin.[5]

As a rule, the school board was slow to make improvements to Darwin, but the *Brown* decision may have led to the limited upgrading of facilities in 1955. The school building was remodeled and improved with additions of one new classroom, restrooms, a stage, new insulation, installation of a new ceiling and floor in the gymnasium, a new stoker, lighting fixtures, and a new kitchen and cafeteria. Still, in 1961, pressing problems at the school included the need for a science laboratory and fixtures, inadequate sewage disposal (the septic tank overflowed, causing a health hazard on the campus), windows required replacing, and the original frame Rosenwald building needed to be bricked. In addition, the gymnasium floor needed reworking because of normal wear and, perhaps, poor workmanship, where it had either buckled or sagged.[6]

A small, stable, well-educated faculty served the students at Darwin. Principal Isaac Bohannon administered a faculty ranging from three to five.[7] Bohannon held bachelor and master of science degrees from Tennessee Agricultural and Industrial University (later renamed Tennessee State University). A native of Putnam County, he graduated with the first senior class at Darwin in 1938. He was within two semesters of completing his college training when Bohannon was drafted into the U.S. Army. He was stationed in Okinawa when the war ended. Following military service, he completed his college degree and took a position teaching at Darwin in 1946. He assumed the office of principal in 1952. As high school principal, Bohannon held the highest status of any member of the black community. He was the unofficial leader, intermediary with white school officials, spokesman of the black community, and the administrator of the school. His administrative duties required setting school policy, implementing staffing needs, soliciting funds to supplement the school budget, and supervising and counseling teachers and students. Bohannon also taught English and social studies, and coached athletic teams.[8]

Amanda Bohannon, the principal's wife, held a bachelor of science degree from Knoxville College, and taught mathematics and biology. Easter Mays was awarded a bachelor of science degree from Tennessee A&I, and taught home economics and science classes. The elementary department included Agnes Stevens, Edna Beasley, and Gladys Gardenhire (the last addition to the faculty in 1961), each of whom held a bachelor of science degree from Tennessee A&I.[9]

The high school curriculum included three units in mathematics, three in science, three in social studies, two years in home economics and English. Classes were supplemented with field trips and tours. Although course offerings were minimal, the faculty expected students to meet high standards. In a 1961 newspaper interview, Bohannon indicated that "about 30 percent of the graduating class goes to college, usually Tennessee A&I." Some graduates, such as Gladys Adams, went on to teach at Tennessee A&I. Ruby Price, a 1961 A&I graduate, was listed in *Who's Who in American Colleges and Universities*.[10]

The school received much support from the Darwin Parents and Teachers Association (PTA). Bohannon praised the PTA: "They are always doing something to promote the school. This year [1960–61] they bought stage curtains costing from $500 to $600 and have purchased a refrigerator and stove for the home economics department."[11]

Thus, when the *Brown* decision was announced in 1954, Cookeville African American students attended an important and respected, if underfunded, public school. One hundred black youths were enrolled in grades one through twelve at Darwin School: sixty in the high school department and forty in elementary school. Putnam County's remaining thirty-nine blacks enrolled at two one-teacher schools accommodating grades one through eight—25 at Algood's Swallows and 14 at Silver Point Colored. One hundred eight of these black students lived within the county. Another thirty-one black students were bused in from surrounding counties to attend Darwin's high school department. Black students completing Free Hill School in Clay County were bused fifty miles one way to attend high school in Cookeville. Similarly, blacks completing Long View School of Livingston in Overton

County and Sparta's Wallace-Smith School in White County were bused twenty and fifteen miles, respectively, to Cookeville's Darwin High.[12]

In 1963, Putnam County enrolled 7,363 students, of which 182 were blacks attending the county's two black schools (Silver Point Colored School was closed in 1956, and its students and teacher transferred to Darwin). Darwin enrolled 146 of these students (90 in the high school and 56 in elementary school), and the remaining 36 attended Algood's Swallows school.[13]

Darwin School afforded blacks in the region their only chance for a high school education and provided an outlet for participation in activities and organizations. It was also an important social center and fostered a sense of community among blacks in the Upper Cumberland region.

Important events on the Darwin High calendar were baccalaureate and commencement services.[14] Between 1954 and 1963, Darwin graduated eighty-three of its eighty-eight seniors (see table).[15] Though small in number, graduating classes featured the pomp and pageantry deserving of the occasion. Traditionally, on the Sunday before commencement, a well-known black minister delivered a baccalaureate sermon. For example, on 16 May 1954, the speaker was the Reverend W. R. Smith, superintendent of the Murfreesboro

TABLE 2
COMPARISON OF SENIOR CLASS MEMBERS OF
DARWIN SCHOOL AND PUTNAM COUNTY'S WHITE SCHOOLS

Year	Black Seniors	Black Graduates	White Seniors	White Graduates
1954	10	9	209	188
1955	8	7	218	196
1956	6	6	232	210
1957	9	9	252	221
1958	14	14	272	262
1959	5	5	268	240
1960	9	9	302	279
1961	8	8	333	298
1962	11	8	309	270
1963	8	8	285	260

SOURCE: State of Tennessee, Annual Statistical Report of the Department of Education (1954), 74–75, 78–79; (1955), 76, 77, 80–81; (1956), 98–99, 102–3; (1957) 102–3, 106–7; (1958), 106–9, 82–85; (1959), 106–9, 82–85; (1960), 128–31, 98–101; (1961), 116–19, 87–89; (1962), 120–23, 91–93; (1963), 126–29, 93–95.

district of the African Methodist Episcopal Church. The Reverend Marshall Keeble, president of the Nashville Christian Institute, addressed the 1956 graduates. Four years later, the Reverend N. Samuel Jones, editor-in-chief at the National Baptist Publishing Board in Nashville, was guest speaker.[16] Speakers at the graduation ceremonies were equally talented. These included notable representatives from Tennessee Agricultural and Industrial State University, such as Elsie M. Lewis, head of the Graduate History Department, in 1956, and Kermit C. King, coordinator and director of student teaching and professor of education, in 1960.[17]

Darwin School sponsored an array of other activities. Each year, thirty to forty couples attended the junior-senior prom, which was normally held in the school cafeteria.[18] Students annually elected a homecoming queen and court and, in a separate election, Miss Darwin High. The homecoming coronation and ball was a grand occasion, typically held during the basketball season.[19] Other activities included an annual fashion show in which students modeled clothing they made in home economics classes; an awards program recognizing student achievements in music, sports and the elementary and high school departments; and an "operetta" or play performed by the elementary school department.[20]

Darwin students gained valuable experience in various organizations, clubs and extracurricular activities. Darwin had an active chapter of the New Homemakers of America (NHA), which was the black counterpart to the Future Homemakers of America, a yearbook staff, student council, honor society, and a glee club, which sponsored a variety of activities.[21] Darwin also had varsity boys and girls basketball teams, nicknamed the Trojans and Lady Trojans.[22] Because of its small enrollment, Darwin High did not field football and baseball teams.

Several Darwin students were recognized for their achievements in sports and academics. Charles Edward McClellan, a 1953 graduate and son of Edd and Mary Lou McClellan of Cookeville, won an athletic scholarship to Clark College in Atlanta, Georgia. His skills in basketball were featured in the *Atlanta Daily World*, Georgia's daily African American newspaper. As a sophomore, McClellan started on the 1955 basketball team, and was described as "one of the mainstays on Coach Leonadis Epps's 'Race Horse Five.'"[23]

The all-white Cookeville Optimist Club selected Roberta Yvonne Nicholson, daughter of William Nicholson and Inez Holt of Sparta, the January 1963 "Girl Teen of the Month." An honor student interested in science, she was a school leader and member of the 1963 graduating class. Roberta had been on the honor roll (B average or higher) since the ninth grade and was a member of the New Homemakers of America, yearbook staff, and Glee Club, and was co-captain of the Lady Trojan basketball team. Her hobbies included stamp collecting and oil painting. When away from school, Roberta served as president of the Methodist Youth Fellowship of Kynett Chapel in Sparta, where she was also a member of the church choir. Two months later, the Optimist Club chose Danny Wadell Myers, a ninth grader and son of Charles W. and Eleane Myers, the March "Teen of the Month." Danny, a member of the basketball team, was also interested in science. He was an honor student and was voted "most talented" and "most studious" boy in the high school department.[24]

There was no orchestrated attempt by black Cookevillians to desegregate Putnam County schools before 1963. This must not be construed as meaning that blacks were pleased with segregated facilities or were unaware of the *Brown* decision. According to Della Jane Holliday, a black homemaker in the city, the main reasons that many blacks refused to pressure for integration were fear of economic reprisals, concern for what might happen to their children in the white schools, and a fear of upsetting the relatively peaceful race relations in Cookeville.[25] In addition, some blacks did not want to lose autonomy over Darwin School. After all, Darwin School was more than an institution of learning. To black Cookevillians, the school represented a central place for initiating community and regional activities and a refuge from an otherwise white-dominated society. The school building was used for community meetings, church socials and dinners, extracurricular activities, and sports events.

When the 1962–63 academic year commenced, school desegregation was not on the Putnam County school board's agenda. In fact, arrangement for the separate education of blacks and whites continued as usual. The board reaffirmed arrangements with White, Clay, and Overton Counties under which Darwin High would continue accepting blacks bused from Wallace-Smith School of Sparta, Free Hill School, and Long View School of Livingston, respectively. Before the school year ended, however, Putnam, White, Clay, and Overton Counties would be forced to address school desegregation, and the Class of 1963 would be the last to graduate from Darwin High School. Beginning in the fall of 1963, Darwin students would be incorporated into Putnam County schools formerly reserved for whites.

A suspicious fire destroyed Darwin School on 8 January 1963. The fire, believed to be the work of an arsonist, "started in a classroom on the southeast corner . . . and spread fast through the six-classroom building. Soon, the

wood-framed, brick-veneered building was gutted, leaving . . . black students
. . . without a school." The fire destroyed all student performance records.[26]
This single event had a significant impact not only on local Cookevillians
but also on black education in the surrounding counties. When the school
was destroyed, Putnam County had to make plans for black education, and
those counties with arrangements to bus their high school students to Darwin also had to begin finding alternatives.

Following the fire, Darwin School officials worked with both whites and
blacks to make arrangements for completion of the 1962–63 academic year.
Putnam County school superintendent Eddie Watson and Darwin principal
Isaac Bohannon worked with the local black churches to establish makeshift
accommodations for classrooms. They removed desks from the old, white
City School, which had been closed, and placed them in the temporary class-
rooms. Grades one through six were taught in the auditorium of the black
Presbyterian Church; grades seven and eight were taught in Trinity Baptist
Church; and high school classes, grades nine through twelve, were taught in
the Wright Chapel Methodist Church.[27]

Meanwhile, county administrators, school board officials, and representatives of Darwin community pondered long range plans for black education
in Putnam County. Black school officials and parents quickly dismissed a
plan, proposed by Superintendent Watson, to build a "temporary steel building." The blacks argued that was not acceptable since such a structure would
probably become permanent.[28] All parties studied plans for rebuilding the
school, examined strategies for busing black children to schools outside of
Putnam County, and considered integrating black students into all-white
county schools.

The board estimated the cost of rebuilding Darwin School between
$250,000 and $300,000. Board officials looked into several options to reduce
construction costs. They considered combining Algood's Swallows School
with Darwin. From the beginning, however, black parents in Algood voiced
strong disapproval of this option, which would have shut down Swallows
and required busing all Swallows students to Darwin. Another option was to
rebuild only the junior and senior high school departments, grades seven
through twelve, at an estimated cost of $250,000, and integrate grades one
through six. This approach represented a modified version of an integration
strategy utilized in many southern communities (to begin with elementary
students, preferably one grade at a time, thus bringing about gradual desegregation of all classes). Another option was to rebuild the elementary and

junior high school only, grades one through eight, at a cost of $135,000. If this option were taken, the small number of blacks in grades nine and above would have to either be integrated into Putnam County high schools or bused to Carthage in nearby Smith County, where a black high school had been established.[29]

From the very beginning, Superintendent Watson doubted whether the state department of education would agree with plans to rebuild Darwin School. Department rules required a minimum of seventy-five students in any high school department. Furthermore, some parents of black children living outside of Putnam County had suggested that they might not send their children to the new facility, but would rather push for integration of their children in local county schools. Without assurances of students from Overton, Clay, and White Counties, it was doubtful that the state minimum could be achieved.

There were other problems as well. Black Cookevillians were divided over what option to accept. A group of seven blacks, identifying themselves as representatives of the Darwin PTA, attended a 16 January 1963 meeting of the Putnam County school board, where they voiced their support for rebuilding the school exactly as it had been before the fire. Spokesman for the group, Albert Roberts, made the organization's position clear: "When you make statements for publication in the paper, make sure that people understand that we are asking for both the high school and elementary school and that we want the children from the other counties to keep coming here. If they don't know this, they might plan to go somewhere else and we would lose the school." Principal Bohannon concurred and stated forcefully that he expected the school, if rebuilt, "to include cafeteria, library, playroom and science lab."[30]

Support for a black high school among Cookeville's African Americans was not necessarily an objection to integration. Rather, some blacks feared that loss of the black school would lead to elimination of the few professional positions held by black educators (especially the positions of principal and coach), and loss of black community control over an educational institution. The black high school, much like the black church, was a cornerstone of the black community. Darwin School employed a principal, five teachers, a bus driver, occasional substitute teachers, and a janitor. These fears were not without justification. A subsequent U.S. Department of Health, Education and Welfare study indicated that between 1968 and 1971, "over 1,000 black educators in five southern states lost their jobs. . . . During the same period, more than 5,000 white educators were hired." The study concluded that "blacks [professionals] were being made to pay for the opportunity to attend desegregated schools."[31]

The all-white school board, chaired by J. C. Thompson, adopted a resolution on 16 January 1963 recommending that Darwin School be rebuilt contingent upon authorization of funding by the county court and state department of education.[32] These institutions immediately balked, and within three weeks, on 8 February 1963, a special meeting to review "specific" recommendations for replacing Darwin School took place. Isaac Bohannon headed an all-black committee, including Albert Roberts, Melvin Carver, Haskell Carr, and T. B. Maddux, charged with making final recommendations. The committee's decision encouraged construction of a facility in the black neighborhood but reflected an increasing awareness that school integration was forthcoming:

1. With the understanding that construction of a new high school in the community is highly improbable, we recommend that a modern elementary school be built on a suitable site in the immediate community.
2. Said elementary school to include gymnasium and cafeteria facilities, library facilities, in fact, all things necessary in a modern elementary school.
3. Said elementary school should be built on a non-segregated basis, to serve children of the area regardless of race, creed or color.[33]

Between February and April, funding the construction of a new school continued to run into obstacles. The state department of public instruction was reluctant to authorize funds for construction of a high school where less than the state-mandated minimum student requirement of 75 students could be guaranteed. The county court, likewise, was reluctant to spend funds to establish a separate school for blacks when school desegregation might be forthcoming. Plans to completely rebuild Darwin School were shelved in favor of replacing only a part of the school. On 1 April 1963, the school board authorized the superintendent "to furnish figures for a 4-room" elementary school. On 10 April 1963, however, the board rescinded its 1 April action, and instead requested the county court to provide funds for construction of a "three-room elementary school for all children in the Darwin School vicinity."[34] By 25 April 1963, all plans to rebuild Darwin had been abandoned. The *Putnam County Herald* reported that "plans are already set to integrate Darwin high school students" into the existing white schools.

Discussions then turned to establishing a community recreation center on the former Darwin School grounds. Since Darwin School had been more than an institution of learning, the community center could take over the social and community functions once located in the school.[35]

Even as the school board passed its initial resolution for rebuilding Darwin School, another vocal element of the black community, led by Melvin Carver and the Reverend Leroy Jackson, strongly opposed rebuilding the school at all. Integration of Putnam County schools in the fall of 1963, they countered, was the best solution. Jackson, pastor of Trinity Baptist Church, threatened that if the school were rebuilt he would take action to have the Brown decision enforced in Cookeville.[36] Yet Carver and Jackson were initially in a minority. As late as 10 April 1963, eighty-five blacks signed a request that "Darwin School be rebuilt for elementary children." Although it is difficult to assess the group's motivation, the fact that some blacks wanted to rebuild so as to keep a racial center for their own group cannot be dismissed.[37] Superintendent Watson certainly believed that black Cookevillians wanted to hold onto "their" institution. In addition, as indicated above, the 8 February 1963 recommendation of the all-black committee headed by Bohannon specifically called for the construction of a school facility in the black community.[38]

From the very beginning, however, at least four parents of Darwin School students refused to sign a statement presented to the school board in support of rebuilding the school. Among these were the Reverend Jackson and Melvin Carver, who both sent their children to Central High. While most black Cookevillians sent their children to the makeshift church school facilities, some parents had quietly enrolled their children in white Putnam County schools without incident. A 7 February 1963 front-page article in the Putnam County Herald reported that "several former Darwin students already attend Central and Algood highs." In April, Superintendent Watson reported that "several Negro children are now in integrated situations and well adjusted." In fact, on 11 April 1963, Watson went on record as saying, "It should be understood that there is no objection to integration of schools. It is the board's policy to accept any child in any school where he applies."[39]

Tom Deek and Johnny and Elouise Jackson were among that first group of blacks to attend Central High School. Johnny and Elouise, eleventh and tenth graders, respectively, were children of Leroy Jackson. Jackson, one of the most outspoken proponents of compliance with "the law of the land," recalled how he enrolled his children: "Dr. [Lester] King was the principal of the high school at that time. And . . . when I went in . . . he said what do you want? I told him I had two children who were in high school. One who was just about ready to finish. And another one, the girl, I told him was not ready yet, but I told him she was in about the second or third year [the reference is to high school which would mean the ninth or tenth grade]. And he said alright. He'd call someone to take these children on in there and not a word was said."[40] "I didn't experience any [racial problems], as a matter of fact," Elouise Jackson remembers. "I made friends instantly with all kinds of students. . . . I just had a very positive experience and my teachers . . . were supportive, pushed me to do my best to excel."[41]

By 25 April 1963, Jackson and his supporters apparently swayed the opinion of other blacks to oppose rebuilding Darwin School and to support integrating Putnam County schools. In a petition to county court judge Jimmy Mosier, forty-four black citizens argued, "We are for integrating schools. We want to go by the state's placement law and the Supreme Court [*Brown*] decision to integrate."[42]

Blacks in Algood, a small community located a mile or two northeast of Cookeville, attempted to retain their one-teacher school. In April 1963, the Algood black community opposed any action that would eliminate or minimize the role played by Swallows Elementary School. Algood parents vowed that they would not send their children to a rebuilt Darwin School under any conditions. Though the parents did not publicly state their reasons for opposition, they—as did Bohannon and his supporters at Darwin—probably feared loss of a black professional position and a neighborhood icon.

In the fall of 1963, Cookeville's black students attended previously all-white schools. The school board assigned black elementary school students to Parkview, a local elementary school closest to the black neighborhood, but parents were free to transport their children to any school in the county. Seventh-, eighth-, and ninth-graders were assigned to the junior high school department of Central, while senior high students attended Central High. Tenured black faculty members were transferred to various public schools in Cookeville. Principal Bohannon was assigned to Central High School as a teacher, Easter Mays to Jere Whitson Elementary, Edna Beasley to Park View Elementary, and Amanda Bohannon to Sycamore Elementary. Blacks in Algood continued to attend Swallows School, a concession that was short-lived. In 1964, Swallows School was closed, and black students in Algood were integrated into local schools with whites.[43]

Integration of the public schools of Cookeville and Putnam County was, for the most part, uneventful. Certainly a contributing factor was the small number of black students attending school. Perhaps even more important, the smooth transition was due partially to Cookeville's black and white children having had social contacts with each other over the years, which facilitated positive race relations. In spite of the fact that Cookeville and Putnam County were as segregated as other upper South communities, some limited concessions were made in the area of sports. For example, Little League and Babe Ruth League baseball players in Cookeville had played on integrated teams since 1959. Black and white parents and racially mixed crowds had become accustomed to "cheering" and "booing" teams, not individuals. The value of such association and friendship is illustrated in a 1963 episode at Cookeville Junior High involving Herman Peake. Peake was among Cookeville's first black students to enter the junior high school. He was also an outstanding player on racially mixed local Little League and Babe Ruth League baseball teams. Peake had many friends, both black and white. According to Dr. Horace Raper, history professor emeritus at Tennessee Technological University and a longtime recreational league baseball coach, "It so happened that . . . Mr. Carver's grandson [Herman Peake], was assigned over at the junior high to a separate eating table in the cafeteria. Some of Herman's little league players, knowing him as an individual, decided that was not right. So several of them got up and left their seats and went over and ate with Herman. From that time on, it was a smooth operation."[44] This incident involving Peake, though an isolated one, illustrates how prior interracial interaction contributed to less eventful integration of the public schools in Cookeville. After all, people generally tend to feel more comfortable among individuals they know. In addition, unlike Clinton, Tennessee, and Little Rock, Arkansas, where much turmoil took place, there were neither high-profile professional agitators nor vote hungry politicians imploring mass defiance. Desegregation of the public schools in Cookeville may not represent the norm. However, it is safe to say that Cookeville stands as an example of quiet integration, likely similar to other communities. Still, one cannot help but wonder what would have happened if Darwin School had not burned down? Or, if the school had burned down a decade earlier? Or, if the percentage of blacks in the general population was higher? If nothing else, perhaps this study will stimulate further research of isolated southern communities and how these implemented public school desegregation.

Notes

1. There are several books that address the more highly publicized accounts of school desegregation and the Civil Rights movement in general. These include Daisy Bates, A Memoir: The Long Shadow of Little Rock (New York, 1962); Russell H.

Barrett, *Integration at Ole Miss* (Chicago, 1965); George Metcalf, *From Little Rock to Boston: The History of School Desegregation* (Westport, Conn., 1983); J. Harvie Wilkinson, *From Brown to Bakke: The Supreme Court and School Integration* (New York, 1979); Taylor Branch, *Parting the Waters: America in the King Years, 1954–1963* (New York, 1988); Florence Mars, *Witness in Philadelphia* (Baton Rouge, La., 1977); and William Bradford Huie, *3 Lives for Mississippi* (New York, 1965).

2. Seventeenth (1950), Eighteenth (1960), and Nineteenth (1970) Censuses of the United States, Characteristics of Population, Tennessee; Mary Jean Delozier, *Putnam County, Tennessee, 1850–1970* (Cookeville, Tenn., 1979), 265, 300.

3. *Putnam County Herald*, 27 Apr. 1961; 22 Sept. 1960. Refer also to Christine Jones, Tennessee Technological University librarian and archivist, interview with Louie Robbins, Cookeville, Tenn., 21 Apr. 1992, audio recording and transcript in possession of the author. The Rosenwald Fund was created in 1917 by Julius Rosenwald, president of Sears, Roebuck, and required matching funds from grant recipients. The fund "focused on enlarging opportunities for southern African Americans by making funds available for schoolhouse construction, educational programs at high schools and colleges, fellowships for career advancement, support for hospitals and health agencies, development of library services, and improvement of race relations." *Encyclopedia of African-American Civil Rights* (Westport, Conn., 1992), 461. Funding of black school construction was necessary because following the *Cumming v. The School Board of Richmond County, Georgia* (1899) decision, which held that separate facilities for the races did not have to be equal, the disparity in quality between facilities for whites and blacks in the South widened immeasurably. Between 1917 and 1948, the fund aided construction of more than five thousand school facilities for blacks in fifteen southern states. Refer also to James D. Anderson, *The Education of Blacks in the South, 1860–1935* (Chapel Hill, N.C., 1988), and Mary S. Hoffschwelle, "Rebuilding the Rural Southern Community: Reformers, Schools and Homes in Tennessee, 1914–1929" (Ph.D. diss., Vanderbilt University, 1993). Prior to 1936, educational opportunities for blacks were limited throughout Cookeville and the surrounding area. Blacks seeking a high school education had to go outside the county. By 1954, there were three Putnam County schools for blacks, compared with forty-eight for whites. The black schools were Silver Point Colored School and Algood's Swallows, which provided eight grades of education, and Darwin School, which provided grades one through twelve. Silver Point Colored School and Swallows were not Rosenwald schools. Swallows School was built in 1940 on land donated for that purpose by former slave Crusoe Buck. Later, Judge W. L. Swallows was instrumental in acquiring sufficient funds to upgrade the teaching staff and to purchase supplies. It was for him that the school was named. Swallows School was located in a two-room brick building northwest of Algood. The building was constructed in 1940. In 1960, the one-teacher school enrolled thirty-five students, had no window shades, and the large classroom was lighted by only two bulbs. There were thirty-six students attending the school in 1963.

4. Frederick A. Rodgers, *The Black High School and Its Community* (Lexington, Mass., 1975), 73.

5. Minutes, Putnam County Board of Education, 26 Aug. 1953 and 19 July 1956, Office of the Superintendent of Schools, Putnam County, Cookeville, Tennessee. It should be noted that it was not unusual to bus white students in remote areas of adjoining counties to the nearest school in Putnam County and vice versa. In

1953, such arrangements were made for some white high school students in Overton County to attend school in Monterey, and in 1956, similar arrangements were made for Putnam County white students attending Glades Creek School to attend Bondicroft School in White County. Of course, in the case of whites, busing was intended to provide access to the best educational opportunities for those whites in remote areas inconvenient for access to county schools. Blacks were bused to prevent them from attending readily available schools attended by whites.

6. *Putnam County Herald*, 7 May 1955 and 27 Apr. 1991.

7. Ibid., 29 July 1954 and 20 Apr. 1961; *Darwin Trojan* (yearbook) (Cookeville, Tenn., 1959 and 1962).

8. *Putnam County Herald*, 27 Apr. 1961; Rodgers, *Black High School*, 54, 57, 59, and 61–62.

9. *Putnam County Herald*, 29 July 1954 and 20 Apr. 1961; *Darwin Trojan* (1959, 1962). Edna Beasley was formerly principal at the one-teacher Silver Point Colored School, which was phased out in August 1956. Its students were sent to Darwin.

10. *Putnam County Herald*, 27 Apr. 1961 and 24 May 1962.

11. Ibid., 27 Apr. 1961 and 24 May 1962. In May 1962 Albert D. Roberts was elected president of the Darwin PTA. Other elected officers were Inez Sadler, vice president; Easter Mays, secretary; Naomi Strode, assistant secretary; Haskell Carr, treasurer; Gladice Gardenhire, parliamentarian; Edna Beasley, historian; and Agnes Baylor, chairman of program committee. These individuals would bear the distinction of being the last PTA officers for Darwin School.

12. Ibid., 9 Sept. 1954; State of Tennessee, *Annual Statistical Report of the Department of Education* (Nashville, 1954), 44–45.

13. *Putnam County Herald*, 29 Aug. 1963. In September 1963 all but the thirty-six blacks attending Algood's Swallows School would enroll in formerly all-white Putnam County schools.

14. Ibid., 27 Apr. 1961.

15. State of Tennessee, *Annual Statistical Report of the Department of Education* (Nashville, 1954–63). See also *Putnam County Herald*, 7 May 1956 and 19 May 1960.

16. *Putnam County Herald*, 6 May 1954, 7 May 1956, and 19 May 1960.

17. Ibid., 19 May 1960.

18. Ibid., 7 May 1956.

19. *Darwin Trojan*, 1962. Katherine Roberts was the last Darwin High homecoming queen. Members of her court included Rebecca Keeton, Thelia Thompson, Notye Brewington, Barbara Paige, and Glenda Mullins. The last Miss Darwin High was Wilma Carrick.

20. *Putnam County Herald*, 9 May 1957.

21. *Darwin Trojan*, 1959.

22. Ibid., 1959, 1960, 1962.

23. *Putnam County Herald*, 24 Feb. and 10 Mar. 1955.

24. Ibid., 24 Jan., 7 Mar. 1963.

25. Della Jane Holliday, interview with Louie Robbins, Cookeville, Tenn., 21 Apr. 1992, audio recording and transcript in possession of the author.

26. *Cookeville Herald-Citizen*, 6 Jan. 1991.

27. *Putnam County Herald*, 10 Jan. 1963.

28. Ibid.

29. Ibid., 17 Jan. 1963.
30. Ibid.
31. Rodgers, *Black High School*, 54, 57, 59, and 61–62.
32. *Putnam County Herald*, 17 Jan. 1963. Voting for the resolution were board members Hulon Ferrell, Taylor Stout, C. E. Maxwell, J. N. McLouch, and Sue Keller. Thompson did not vote, and member Hubert Slagle was absent.
33. Ibid., 7 Feb. 1963; Minutes, Putnam County Board of Education, 8 Feb. 1963.
34. Minutes, Putnam County Board of Education, 1, 10 Apr. 1963; *Putnam County Herald*, 11 Apr. 1963. Construction of a three-room school was estimated at a cost of ninety-five thousand dollars.
35. *Putnam County Herald*, 18, 25 Apr. 1963; Minutes, Putnam County Board of Education, 19 July 1963.
36. *Putnam County Herald*, 11 Apr. 1963.
37. Horace Raper, emeritus professor of history at Tennessee Technological University, interview with Bill McKibben, Cookeville, Tenn., 30 Apr. 1991, audio recording and transcript in possession of the author. See also Minutes, Putnam County Board of Education, 10 Apr. 1963.
38. *Putnam County Herald*, 11 Apr. 1963.
39. Ibid. Watson's statement is consistent with Putnam County Board of Education sentiments expressed at a 19 January 1963, board meeting: "Board agrees that since no school age child in the county is to be denied entrance in public schools of the county, the superintendent should convey the decision of the board to principals now working in the county system, in order that schools in this county may enjoy a continuing successful operation for all students and teachers." Minutes, Putnam County Board of Education, 19 Jan. 1963.
40. The Reverend Leroy Jackson, late pastor of Trinity Baptist Church, interview with Kayse Buck, Cookeville, Tenn., Apr. 1991, audio recording and transcript in possession of the author.
41. Elouise Jackson, interview with Kelvin L. Morgan, Cookeville, Tenn., Apr. 1991, audio recording and transcript in possession of the author.
42. *Putnam County Herald*, 25 Apr. 1963.
43. Ibid., 11 Apr. 1963. See also Minutes, Putnam County Board of Education, 10, 26 Apr., and 10 May 1963. The board took no action to retain and reassign Agnes L. Stevens (Baylor) and Gladys Gardenhire.
44. Raper, interview. See also Isaac Bohannon, interview with Jeanne C. Potter, Algood, Tenn., 14 Feb. 1991, audio recording and transcript in possession of the author.

White Lunch Counters and Black Consciousness
The Story of the Knoxville Sit-ins

Cynthia Griggs Fleming

*S*IT-IN DEMONSTRATIONS AT SEGREGATED DEPART-
MENT STORE LUNCH COUNTERS AND RESTAURANTS
BECAME A POWERFUL, NONVIOLENT TOOL FOR
change across the South in 1960. Greensboro, North
Carolina, was the site for the first sit-in; a similar demon-
stration soon took place in Nashville. By the summer,
demonstrations were occurring throughout the urban
South. Cynthia Fleming takes a close look at the devel-
opment of a sit-in movement in Knoxville, an Appalachian city that was home to a relatively small African
American population but also the location of Knoxville
College, a solid base that provided many of the demonstrators. Race relations were somewhat more cordial in
Knoxville than in other Tennessee cities; Mayor John
Duncan publicly supported restaurant integration. But
the road to integrate the lunch counters of downtown
Knoxville proved to be a lengthy, although relatively
nonviolent, one. And the sit-in experience became a
"turning point" in how many blacks viewed their own
community, in many cases breaking traditional bonds of
paternalism and accommodation. Fleming presents these
events through the eyes of many participants, effectively
using oral interviews of both whites and blacks along

with contemporary accounts. She concludes that "demonstrators were prepared for the worst, but the worst never came to Knoxville."

It has been over a quarter of a century since thousands of black college students all over the South began the sit-ins: nonviolent direct action that would usher in a new era of civil rights protest in this country. Historians looking back on these student protests often focus on the bitter and violent reactions they provoked. Yet there were some people in the South at that time who thought peaceful change was possible. The story of Knoxville, Tennessee, is the story of a community whose citizens, both black and white, believed in this peaceful possibility. Knoxville's story, which differs from many standard sit-in accounts, serves to emphasize an important reality: each community's response to the sit-ins was different. It was shaped by the particular conditions that existed in that community in 1960. Although there are some basic conclusions that can be drawn about the sit-ins in general, historians will never have a truly clear understanding of the sit-in movement of 1960 until each community has had a chance to tell its own story. This, then, is Knoxville's unique story.

"We don't serve mustard, ketchup, or Negroes."[1] This, remembered Robert Booker, who was a Knoxville College student leader in 1960, was the policy of McDonald's Restaurant in Knoxville at that time. Booker, with other students at the private black Knoxville College, began protesting lunch counter segregation in the early months of 1960. Their actions were patterned after the sit-ins initiated on 1 February 1960 by four freshmen from the black North Carolina Agricultural and Technical College in Greensboro, North Carolina. The action of the Greensboro students captured the imagination of many others in addition to those at Knoxville College. Thus, in the early months of 1960 inspired black students across the South, in concert with their North Carolina colleagues, rushed to the front lines to challenge the very basis of segregation in a number of southern cities.

Booker recalled the feeling among Knoxville College students at the time: "The idea came from them [A&T students], and we watched daily, or whenever the news would give us information—watched what they were doing. And, of course, our activities were patterned after theirs."[2] Yet despite their attempts to follow the guidelines established by A&T students, the events surrounding desegregation in Knoxville differed in some important ways from those in Greensboro. In fact, Knoxville's sit-ins were different from those in most other southern locales. One important difference, for example, involves the issue of length. As the sit-ins spread across the South, they commonly became protracted struggles. In addition, these struggles often involved violence that victimized peaceful black demonstrators. In this regard, Knoxville was an exception.

In Greensboro where the movement started, for example, the sit-ins were not particularly violent, but they were lengthy, and they inspired over-whelming student and community participation and interest. In fact, six months elapsed from the beginning of the sit-ins in February to official deseg-regation at the end of July in Greensboro. The desegregation cause became so popular so quickly that just three days after the demonstrations started, prob-lems of limiting the number of demonstrators to the number of stools to be occupied began to crop up. Joe McNeil, one of the original four demonstra-tors, recalled the strength of commitment that the rapidly growing movement inspired among students and community residents alike in Greensboro. "The movement picked up such strength that personalities were over-looked—that was a good thing, that the meaning of the movement was more important than personalities."[3] Despite the length of the struggle, violence was kept to a minimum since Greensboro, like Knoxville, was "a moderate Southern city, conscious of its image and unwilling to have the students arrested or inflict violence on them."[4]

There were other southern cities, however, where officials were less con-cerned about image than about crushing the demonstrations. In Nashville, for example, the Tennessee state capital located less than two hundred miles west of Knoxville, seventy-six student protestors had been jailed by the fifth day of that city's sit-ins. In addition, James Lawson, a black divinity student at Nashville's white Vanderbilt University, was expelled from school three months before he was scheduled to graduate because he instructed demon-strators in nonviolent passive resistance techniques. By the time Nashville's lunch counters were finally desegregated, hundreds of the thousands of Nashville students who had protested had been arrested.[5]

In sharp contrast to the official attitude in Nashville, Knoxville's mayor in 1960 publicly supported restaurant integration. Prior to the beginning of organized sit-ins Mayor John Duncan attempted to negotiate a desegregation settlement between Knoxville merchants and the city's blacks. He failed. Yet once protestors began demonstrating, Duncan unequivocally articulated his determination to minimize conflict and protect demonstrators from vio-lence. One of the black leaders of the demonstrations recalled the mayor's instructions to him: "Just call me each morning—where you're going to be, and we'll have protection there."[6] This rather unusual southern mayor remembered the reasoning that prompted his actions at that time. "Actually we had very little demonstrations in Knoxville, and I saw the problems going on in Chattanooga, Nashville, and Memphis—bloodshed almost. . . . I made up my mind that I didn't want that in Knoxville. That, a lot of people said, well, you're going to politically cut your throat. . . . I said, I don't care if I do."[7] He didn't: Duncan was later elected to the U.S. House of Representatives. John Duncan remembered that Knoxville's desegregation success prompted officials from other southern cities to ask him how Knoxville was able to accomplish desegregation with such relative ease. The mayor, who firmly believed that his city was unique, advised them, "You have to do it through your own people, I said, we have a different city."[8]

The demonstrations that confronted Mayor Duncan's Knoxville were not only relatively free of violence but also relatively free of students; students of Knoxville College performed very little of the actual sitting-in. They initiated the protest activities, but community members performed more of the actual demonstrating. This reality constitutes another important difference that separates the Knoxville sit-ins from those that occurred in other parts of the South. In most locales, a proportionately larger number of students demonstrated. Dr. Robert Harvey, a member of the Knoxville College faculty in 1960, remembered that he and three others who were the first to sit in and initiate demonstrations in June were older professionals from the black community; Dr. Harvey and Dr. William McArthur were faculty members, while the other two pioneers, the Reverend Robert James, and the Reverend W. T. Crutcher, were local black ministers. Harvey further asserted that an extraordinarily large proportion of the demonstrators were local professionals. "I counted one day in Woolworth's fifteen to twenty Ph.D.s [sitting in]."[9]

Thus, Knoxville's sit-ins involved proportionately fewer black college students and, according to some protestors, comparatively less black community support than similar protests in other southern cities. In addition, the Knoxville sit-ins were short, relatively peaceful, and officially supported by members of the city administration. In contrast, throughout the South cities were being polarized, demonstrators were being brutalized, and emotions were being inflamed. Peace in cities confronted by demonstrations was rare. "More commonly . . . whites responded with violence and savagery."[10] The reason why Knoxville did not follow this general pattern is rooted in the historical circumstances surrounding local race relations. The city is located in a region that has never had a very large black population. Because of mountainous terrain in the eastern part of Tennessee where Knoxville is located, planta-tion slavery never flourished there. Consequently, few slaves were owned by East Tennesseans during the antebellum era. Those slaves who did live in East Tennessee "were house slaves or skilled artisans who worked alongside their masters in trades and businesses. There was, therefore, a very close relation-ship between master and servant in this section of the South."[11]

This "close relationship" that developed because of the kind of slavery practiced in East Tennessee combined with the demographic reality of a rel-atively small black population resulted in the growth of a powerful paternal-ism. That paternalism was practiced by Knoxville whites toward their small black population as early as the antebellum era, and it continued on through the nineteenth and twentieth centuries. In the midst of that paternalism, Knoxville became a segregated city—to a point. This aspect of the city's development was part of the larger developmental pattern enveloping the late-nineteenth-century South. That pattern involved the application of legal segregation to reinforce the preexisting custom of racial separation. It is important to note, however, that the application of legal segregation was uneven from one locale to the next. Rather, as John Cell has suggested in his comparative work, *The Highest Stage of White Supremacy*, each southern region applied the principles of legal segregation with varying degrees of efficiency depending on its particular needs.[12]

Since Knoxville's small black community did not appear to pose a threat to white control of the larger Knoxville community, black Knoxvillians were given privileges that were denied to most blacks in other parts of the South. The perception of Knoxville's black community as an innocuous group rein-forced by a long paternalistic tradition created space for gaps in the city's legal segregation system. In such an atmosphere, the city's blacks, for example, were never denied the right to vote. Yet the fact of their small numbers combined with the reality of the gerrymandering committed by city officials effectively neutralized any potential black political influence. Thus, even though black Knoxvillians were given privileges, their ability to exer-cise those privileges was severely circumscribed.

In the early years following the Civil War, Knoxville's black population grew for a time. With the approach of the twentieth century, however, that pattern of growth was reversed, and the city's black community began to experience serious population decline. The fact of this decline undoubtedly emboldened local whites to increasingly disregard black needs. Yet in 1919 city officials were treated to a rude awakening when their city was rocked by racial violence. Just like a number of other American cities during that Red

Summer following World War I, Knoxville experienced a riot that had racial overtones. "Knoxville's [white] elite was stunned."[13] They had thought their paternalistic city was free from racial strife. Obviously, they were wrong.

Although the emergency of 1919 did engender some interest in blacks, that interest was short-lived. Knoxville's whites soon resumed their previous pattern of disregard for black needs. An example of this later tendency to ignore black issues is offered by the kind of campaigns conducted by white politicians among their black constituents. In 1941, for example, Cas Walker, a candidate for city council, appealed to his black constituency by sponsoring "chittlin' and pigs' feet parties" for black voters. Indeed, Walker was convinced that in the interest of effective campaigning his appearances among Knoxville blacks should be accompanied by free food since "pig ears and snouts sure get a lot of votes."[14] It was, after all, easier to serve free food than address black needs.

The continued decline of the percentage of blacks in the Knoxville population resulted in an exceedingly small black population indeed by the decade of the sit-ins. In 1960 Knoxville's black population was the smallest of the black populations in the state's four largest metropolitan areas: Memphis' 228,028 blacks represented 36.4 percent of that city's total; Nashville's 76,832 blacks accounted for 19.2 percent; some 49,810 blacks resided in Chattanooga, which accounted for 17.6 percent; and finally, Knoxville's 27,772 blacks constituted only 7.5 percent of the total of Knoxville residents in 1960.[15] In the midst of its steady decline Knoxville's increasingly unobtrusive black population was allowed to continue to exercise its limited privileges.

Such circumstances sometimes encouraged a reluctance among some of Knoxville's blacks to push too hard for needed changes. They did not want to upset their city's delicate racial equilibrium. Julian Bell, for example, who was the director of athletics at Knoxville College in 1960, thought the segregated lunch counter situation needed to be changed. "My view is things needed to be changed," he recalled. "No question in my mind about that."[16] Bell, however, thought that the sit-in tactic employed by the demonstrators may not have been the proper way to achieve the goal of desegregation. He believed there were other alternatives since "East Tennessee was not a highly or severely oppressive, in my view, segregated place."[17] Coach Bell is a black native of East Tennessee, and his relatively favorable view of Knoxville's racial climate is rooted in his boyhood experiences. He vividly recalled one of those experiences: "My daddy brought me to Knoxville when I was just a little kid, and the thing that impressed me was a black policeman arresting a white man at Vine and Central."[18] Julian Bell's belief in Knoxville's racial leniency thus prompted him to be less than sympathetic to the sit-in tactics proposed by the students. "Take the kids on the campus," he said. "They used to discuss it [the sit-ins] with me, and I'd look at 'em and laugh."[19]

Others acknowledged Knoxville's differences, but still saw the need to push hard for change. Ann Robinson, for example, another black native East Tennessean, and an Austin High School student in 1960, talked about Knoxville's lenient racial atmosphere: "We here in Knoxville up to that time had been . . . had really not felt the . . . some of the kinds of segregation that some of our other southern cities had."[20] Because of this perception of a relaxed racial atmosphere, Robinson continued, "we expected things to be easier here because we didn't think we had that much of a problem."[21] Despite her agreement with Bell's assessment of the relaxed racial atmosphere, Ann Robinson still aggressively supported the idea of student sit-ins. In fact, she translated her support into action: she sat-in. "Now I wanted to go to the lunch counters and fight."[22]

While native Knoxvillians might have agreed on their city's racial leniency, some outsiders judged the city by a different standard. Harry Wiersma, a northern white engineer employed by the Tennessee Valley Authority who played an active and sympathetic role in the sit-ins, saw Knoxville through the eyes of a transplanted northerner: "Well, it was a segregated city. The restaurants were all segregated, the picture shows were segregated, everything was segregated. It was a typical southern city as a matter of fact."[23] Wiersma thus saw a real need for the demonstrations that erupted in 1960. Although he was sympathetic, Wiersma initially had no intention of becoming involved in the demonstrations. In fact, he recalled that Robert West, the pastor of the Unitarian Church that Wiersma attended, initially discouraged his flock from participating: "He advised his congregation to ignore the sit-ins, pay no attention to it, he said. That the store keepers had a perfect right to serve what clientele they wanted to. And it was nobody's business to interfere—which we did for the first part of the sit-ins."[24] His refusal to become involved was characteristic of a number of Knoxville's white liberals. Many of these people reasoned that the city's racial leniency would solve its racial problems.

Knoxville's apparent racial leniency and paternalistic tradition had a particularly injurious effect on many of the city's black leaders. Because of their attempts to operate within the confines of such a tradition, these leaders found themselves in an awkward position. John Cell succinctly explained the ambiguity inherent in their position: "This structural ambivalence extended deeply into the ranks of the oppressed. To the emerging . . . black elite segregation offered a basis for collaboration that the harder, more inflexible forms of white supremacy could never have permitted or achieved."[25] Thus, these black leaders literally had a foot in both worlds, the black and the white. "The elite of the subjugated caste had a stake in the system."

The ambiguous position of their leadership would distress some later generations of black Knoxvillians. For example, Jerry Pate, one of the student demonstrators in 1960, expressed concern over the cordial relationship between black leaders and Knoxville's white power structure. Pate argued that this relationship hampered their effectiveness. He thought that the occasional breakfasts with the mayor, or the occasional newspaper photos they posed for with local politicians, served to divert black Knoxville leaders' attention from the real problems suffered by their black constituents. Pate reasoned, "I felt that they were too tied in with the power structure of the city to be honest about it."[26]

The relatively permissive paternalistic atmosphere in Knoxville continued and engendered a number of early, though limited attempts at interracial cooperation. In 1951, for example, Fellowship House, an interracial group, sponsored the first in an annual series of interracial day camps for Knoxville youngsters. Fellowship House members were convinced that interracial contact at an early age would reduce any later potential for racial conflict. One member recalled her enthusiasm for the day camp project: "It occurred to me, that while there were a great many things to be done in the world, I had a three year old child growing up (who) I didn't want to go through what I had to go through—to unlearn a great many things that I had to unlearn. I had been thinking it over for about a week, and it occurred to me that one thing we could do legally and physically, within financial limitations, would be to get our children together for a summer day camp."[27] Still another voluntary attempt to reduce racial tension began in 1955. In that year a TVA employee and a member of Fellowship House collaborated to form an organization designed to facilitate school desegregation in Knoxville. Throughout 1955 and 1956 the organization sponsored a series of workshops where black and white teachers could air their desegregation concerns.[28]

In such an atmosphere many Knoxvillians, both black and white, were lulled into believing that Knoxville did not have a real race problem like other areas around it. In the words of Michael Freeman, a black native Knoxvillian, who was a high school student when the sit-ins occurred, "In Knoxville we never had a cause to rally around." Freeman continued, "They always gave us enough in Knoxville to be content, but not ever get ahead. All the things that we aspired to have—they would let a few of us have them."[29] John Cell's analysis corroborates Freeman's eyewitness testimony: "Although they [the black elite] were still confined within the boundaries of caste, a small minority might overcome the barriers of class. In their limited success lay hope, not only for themselves, but ultimately for their people."[30]

Because of this absence of overt racial strife, many Knoxvillians were proud of their community's record on race relations. This pride prompted the Knoxville Area Human Relations Council to devote the 1958 summer issue of its newsletter to a review of voluntary desegregation activities in the city. In that issue, titled *There's Nothing New About Being Fair*, the council praised the racial attitude displayed by members of the Knoxville community: "In the present emotion-charged atmosphere it is helpful to remember that the issue at stake is fairness and equality, and though its application has been spotty, the principles of fairness has [sic] been accepted by people in the Knoxville area."[31] The editor then went on to detail the voluntary desegregation that had occurred in a wide variety of areas that included church groups, schools, professional associations, and public accommodations.

Thus, as sit-ins that were often accompanied by violence began to rock the South in the early months of 1960, many Knoxvillians, both black and white, were convinced that it could not happen in their community. Knoxville College students, many of whom were from other cities, had other ideas. In the early days of February 1960, as news of the events in Greensboro spread, a group of Knoxville College students began visiting downtown retail establishments that maintained lunch counters to ascertain their managers' views on desegregation. None of the merchants indicated a willingness to desegregate at that time. Such intransigence prompted the students to start considering demonstrations.[32] On 15 February interested students met and planned to schedule their first sit-in demonstrations two days later. At this point, however, the students' youthful idealism collided head on with the paralyzing paternalism of the Knoxville community: black and white leaders used every tactic at their disposal to dissuade the students from sitting in.

Dr. James Colston, the president of Knoxville College, was the first adult leader to remind the students that negotiation was possible in Knoxville. He appealed to the students to suspend their protests and allow him to negotiate. Although the students reluctantly agreed, they remained determined to monitor the negotiations in an effort to forestall procrastination. In the meantime, on 1 March, Colston, along with twenty-one other prominent Knoxville leaders, was invited to meet with Knoxville's mayor, John Duncan, to form a biracial citizens committee aimed at solving the lunch counter problem. The Knoxville Area Human Relations Council reported on the sentiments of the committee expressed in that first meeting: "There is a general feeling on the part of committee members that the solution lies in the direction of desegregation, and that desegregation can be accomplished in Knoxville through negotiation. Chamber representatives agree to seek a meeting of merchants concerned, to take place within the next several days."[33]

As interminable meetings were held between the various merchants and the members of the mayor's committee, students became increasingly impatient. By the end of the first week of March this impatience prompted between twenty and twenty-five Knoxville College students to stage a "file-through": they walked past the lunch counters in several downtown stores without sitting down.[34] In the midst of increasing student restlessness, the meetings dragged on without producing any concrete accomplishments. One of the main points of disagreement was the question of national versus local policy. Some of the stores involved in the dispute were part of national chains. The managers of these stores claimed they had no authority to desegregate lunch counters without the approval of their national offices.

As this argument came to be used with increasing frequency, Mayor Duncan decided to take an unprecedented step to combat it. On 6 May, at the mayor's invitation, two Knoxville Chamber of Commerce officials and two Knoxville College students accompanied Mayor Duncan to New York to confer with chain store executives. Robert Booker, one of the Knoxville College students who accompanied the mayor, vividly recalled that "upon arrival in New York, the Committee was told by the National representatives that they would not sit in a meeting with students because they would thus open themselves up to having to meet with student groups from all over the country. They also refused to meet with the Knoxville College president, who was in New York at the time. Even though the Mayor met with these people, it is uncertain what effect, if any, the meeting had on the local situation."[35]

The mayor's journey had been daring and unprecedented. Yet, at home where it should have mattered, the move had been ineffective: Knoxville lunch counters remained segregated and store managers remained recalcitrant. Furthermore, an official report of the results of the trip was not immediately forthcoming. This dearth of official information only served to heighten the frustration experienced by hopeful Knoxville residents. By 12 May the weight of frustration and impatience once again provoked student action: a small group of Knoxville College students staged a sit-in at Cole's Drug Store in the downtown area. This action was only the first of a number of sporadic sit-ins between 12 and 18 May.[36] Although a few adult leaders lodged feeble protests against this student action, most were at least mildly sympathetic since they, too, had begun to wonder whether the merchants were engaging in negotiation or procrastination.

Finally, amid increasing student arrest, Knoxville merchants requested a ten-day cooling-off period. During this time the students reluctantly agreed to refrain from demonstrating. In exchange for this concession, the merchants hinted that they would use the ten days to implement a desegregation plan. The students abided by the agreement, and the ten days passed uneventfully. At the end of the period, however, the merchants flatly refused to desegregate. More important, during this cooling-off period the spring semester at Knoxville College ended, and the majority of students left the campus to return home. Those who remained felt betrayed since they were convinced that the merchants' statements could only be "interpreted as a promise to open after a ten day 'cooling off' period which was to end coincidentally?—one day after school had closed."[37]

Thus, at the end of the spring term Knoxville's lunch counters were segregated, but a majority of black college students had left the city to return home. If, as some have charged, the merchants intended to defuse the lunch counter situation by delaying the announcement of their refusal to desegregate until after school ended, they badly miscalculated. In the absence of a cohesive student movement, some adult members of Knoxville's black community decided to act. They convened and formed the Associated Council for Full Citizenship to direct peaceful sit-ins.

Although they were committed to demonstrating, many Associated Council members were distressed by having to take such a step. They had always thought their city was different, but their city had let them down. "We have arrived at this decision with a deep sense of regret," the noted, "for we have been led to believe that Knoxville was different from most other cities of the south."[38] Their disappointment notwithstanding, council members were unstinting in their praise for Mayor Duncan: "For a time there was ample evidence of the uniqueness of this city. Where else in the South is there a leader of a city administration who has done more than ours to give the merchants an opportunity to do the fair and decent thing."[39] Even as they expressed their disappointment at having to demonstrate, though, some agreed with the Reverend Robert James, who insisted that an adult movement could be more effective. James, the council's co-chairman explained: "Then by adults having it, we had entree to mayor's offices and things like that where the students had a problem. Now the city has to deal with taxpayers and citizens that they looked upon as responsible folk."[40]

On 9 June 1960 members of the Knoxville community began organized sit-ins at downtown lunch counters. The Associated Council exerted tight control over these demonstrations. The council not only scheduled the demonstrations and chose the targets but also screened personnel who wanted to sit in. Ann Robinson, one of the student demonstrators, remembered that the council refused to allow any "hot heads" to participate.[41] This decision was prompted by council concern for the image of the sit-ins. Reverend James remembered the instructions the council gave to demonstrators: "We would meet in the morning at Mt. Olive Baptist Church with the sit-in participants, and we would teach what to do in case the opposition did this or that. So when we went down we were fully prepared to have Coca-Cola thrown in your face, and kicked off the stands, and so forth, and go to jail too."[42]

Some of the demonstrators recalled that maintaining a nonviolent posture was quite an effort even in the comparatively peaceful arena of the Knoxville sit-ins. Demonstrator Ann Robinson remembered how all her pent-up anger and frustration from living a segregated childhood threatened to come through to the surface. "So when this release [the sit-ins] came to get up there, now I wanted to go to the lunch counters and fight. So it's a good thing they counseled me. If somebody hadn't been there to counsel me, I would have been one of the hotheads who would have been hurt, or caused somebody to be hurt."[43] Dr. Robert Harvey, a Knoxville College faculty member, recalled how difficult it was for him to remain nonviolent. Nonviolence was easier while he was demonstrating. Yet "once I came off of the stools, and walking back to my car, if someone had assaulted me, we'd have had a brawl."[44] Jerry Pate, another sit-in participant reflected, "I never was a real big fan of passive resistance, you know."[45] Yet despite his feelings to the contrary, Pate reasonably concluded, "In a sense, that [nonviolence] was the best instrument we could use for our own survival because we just didn't have the numbers."[46]

While a majority of Knoxville's demonstrators saw nonviolence as an effective weapon, its use actually discouraged some potential participants. Black Knoxville high school student Michael Freeman remembered that his interest in the demonstrations prompted him to attend some of the mass meetings sponsored by the Associated Council for Full Citizenship. Despite his support for the cause of desegregation, Freeman did not participate in the demonstrations because he simply could not commit himself to the practice of nonviolence. As demonstrators prepared to leave the mass meetings for the lunch counter battles, Freeman recalled the words of the leaders: "Look, we getting ready to go downtown and do some marching now. All those of you who feel like you can't take these whippings, and these salt shakers, and these harassments, people hitting you, you know, you get in this line over here—so I would always get in the other line."[47]

The potential violence anticipated by some of the participants served to cast a sober aura over this protest undertaking. Yet in the midst of such a sober and serious undertaking, Knoxville's sit-ins still had a lighter side. Michael Freeman recalled that demonstrating became a popular activity because "it became almost a fad."[48] A number of other demonstrators corroborated Freeman's viewpoint of this sit-in characteristic. An example of this corroboration is included in the recollections of Avon Rollins, who was a high school student and demonstrator. "Well, I didn't expect anybody was gonna beat me up, you know," he said. "It was just a kind of fun kind of thing, you know. That here are some young ladies involved and this is how I'll get involved with the young ladies, you know, tag along etc. . . . Not even comprehending the reason for these places denying blacks to really set [sic] down and eat."[49] Despite the frivolous reasons for his initial involvement, this experience, according to Rollins, had a profound effect on him and all those who sat in. "I guess that was a point of awakening for a number of people in the community."[50]

The Associated Council for Full Citizenship made sure that demonstrators were prepared for the worst, but the worst never came to Knoxville. There were a few unpleasant incidents, but for the most part, the sit-ins were peaceful. Curiously enough, on those occasions when the demonstrators were plagued by hecklers, the white demonstrators in the group were often singled out for a special kind of harassment. Ann Robinson remembered that "most of the hostilities of the ones that were coming up there were targeted against the whites that was there."[51] In an attempt to neutralize the efforts of the hecklers and protect their white comrades, black demonstrators instituted a kind of informal buddy system. Robinson remembered, "What we decided was in the morning before we left was that we were not going to let these whites leave by theirselves. . . . Don't let them wander off by themselves because we were afraid these rowdies would gang them."[52]

Harry Wiersma, a white TVA employee, remembered that his wife suffered some harassment while she was sitting in. "The storekeepers and sometimes the waitresses were very indignant when my wife came down to sit in. Once in a while they would throw things at her. They would spray insect powder on her and things of that kind."[53] Wiersma's son, Harry Wiersma Jr., also suffered from the actions of white hecklers. On one occasion, for example, Wiersma Jr. was struck in the face by a young white heckler. As the young man hit Wiersma, he lost his balance and fell. Wiersma recalled the police acted quickly: "As I remember there were some police there who grabbed him and they asked me if I wanted to prosecute, and I told them I didn't."[54]

The incident involving Harry Wiersma Jr. serves to emphasize one of the important differences between Knoxville's sit-ins and those that occurred in other parts of the South. In Knoxville on those occasions when demonstrators were plagued by white hecklers, the hecklers were generally prevented from disrupting the demonstrations. Yet while the Knoxville Police prevented such interference by arresting potential white troublemakers, they never arrested any of those who demonstrated. Thus, unlike many places in the South, the Knoxville Police generally protected demonstrators rather than victimizing them. The Reverend James vigorously applauded this evidence of the city administration's determination to control the white opposition. "The mayor, his influence with the police department—they didn't put us in jail, they put people in jail who bothered us," he recalled.[55] James further insisted that such police action had a powerful impact on some onlookers. One incident in particular stands out in Reverend James's memory: "A little white boy was standing out in front of Walgreen's Drug Store when some whites were arrested for interfering with us. . . . He said, the only way to get anywhere is to be a nigger."[56]

Although Knoxville policemen obeyed their orders to protect the demonstrators, that did not preclude some officers from expressing their own individual opinions. Robert Booker remembered his irritation at negative remarks made by individual policemen: "The only comments we took serious note of were those from our Knoxville Police Department. During the sit-ins the only nasty remarks heard came from certain policemen who were on duty to keep order."[57] Yet certain Knoxville policemen were not the only white Knoxvillians who made negative comments about the sit-ins. During the latter part of the demonstrations members of the Knoxville press also printed some critical sentiments about the demonstrations.

Knoxville newspapers generally contained a curious mix of sympathy for the position of the demonstrators and condemnation of their tactics. An example of such reporting appeared in the 1 July issue of the *Knoxville News-Sentinel*. Under a headline proclaiming that "Sit-ins Violate Individual Rights," the reporter sympathetically asserted, "Nobody can properly dispute the right of all citizens, regardless of race or color, to enjoy the use of public, tax-supported institutions."[58] Despite this promising beginning, the *News-Sentinel* reporter went on to condemn the tactics employed by demonstrators: "But here in Knoxville, and in other cities, pressure groups are in a wholly indefensible position in attempting to force retail merchants to serve Negroes at lunch counters, soda fountains and restaurants."[59] In emphasizing the distinction between public and private property, the reporter claimed that the demonstrators were in a precarious legal position because they were attempting to force desegregation of private facilities. The reporter concluded by scolding those involved in the demonstrations. "We are surprised and disappointed to note that a number of local citizens, of both white and colored races, who have the reputation of being good and solid members of this community, have been encouraging sit-ins and picketing."[60] Furthermore, the *News-Sentinel* reporter's conclusion contained this final warning: "The sooner these demonstrations are abandoned, the quicker the cause of racial parity will win support."[61]

Not all the newspaper coverage of the demonstrations was critical, and what negative reporting there was did not occur until the latter part of the demonstrations. In fact, Knoxville's newspapers did not print anything at all, negative or positive, until the demonstrations were almost over. The local press's failure to cover the sit-in movement was prompted by the instigation of city hall. Because city officials were concerned about attracting outside agitators and polarizing the community, they "requested" that the local press refrain from publicizing the sit-ins. The fact of this press black out that extended throughout much of the sit-in activity in Knoxville at least partially accounts for the reason why Knoxville's sit-ins were such a quiet affair: during the early days of the sit-ins many white Knoxvillians never knew they were occurring. While the blackout served the city administration's purposes, some of the demonstrators maintained that it was inimical to their interests. Demonstrator and organizer Harry Wiersma expressed the frustration many demonstrators felt: "At first we were completely unsuccessful because we got no publicity at all. None in the newspapers, or the radio would report what was happening at all." Wiersma continued, "So it [the tactic of demonstration] was completely unsuccessful at getting our point across."[62]

As they sat in day after day, many of the participants began to agree with Wiersma. They believed the sit-ins were having little effect. In fact, as early as 12 June, in an attempt to force recognition of their efforts, some members of the Associated Council had begun to recommend a black economic boycott. By 24 June black leaders formally announced a boycott of those stores whose lunch counters refused to serve black customers. In an effort to enlist community support, the Associated Council distributed handbills throughout the black community that urged, "Trade With Your Friends." The Reverend W. T. Crutcher, co-chairman of the Associated Council for Full

Citizenship, remembered the boycott well. "We called a boycott, but we wouldn't name any specific stores," he said.[63] The "Trade With Your Friends" campaign was soon followed by the call for a general economic boycott of the downtown area, the "Stay Away from Downtown" campaign. Crutcher emphasized the boycott's importance. "And I think that boycott on the city had more to do with the breakdown than anything else."[64]

In an effort to gain even more visibility, some demonstrators also began picketing outside the stores with segregated lunch counters. This action finally "grabbed" the city's attention. During one demonstration where pickets were involved, for example, "one policeman at the scene called it 'the biggest traffic congestion since Christmas,' as motorists slowed down to look."[65] At the same time, picketers also attracted the attention of increased numbers of white hecklers. At a demonstration in front of Rich's Department Store, for example, "near noon some 75 youths in T-shirts, sport shirts, jeans and such were congregated at Rich's Clinch-Henley corner. One yelled 'Jigaboo, Jigaboo!' at the pickets. Policeman Herman Sloan, ten feet away, turned and moved into the crowd. 'There'll be no cursing and no calling Niggers,' he warned. 'If you think I'm kidding, try me.' The crowd was silent."[66]

On another occasion one picket discovered that this visibility which was calculated to inspire sympathy from moderate white Knoxvillians did not always have the desired effect. Harry Wiersma recalled, "I had a Methodist minister. . . . He was a Kiwanian and I'm a Kiwanian. I knew him very well. And while I was picketing Rich's store, it was hot. . . . Why he called me over to the curb, he was in a car. . . . I walked over to the curb thinking he'd probably congratulate me for engaging in the sit-ins. He said Harry you SOB you ought to be horse-whipped for what you're doing. He called me by name. That's a Methodist minister. That's a Kiwanian too."[67]

Wiersma's Kiwanian acquaintance was not the only one who disapproved of his actions. His employer soon expressed dismay as well. "My TVA people in my office petitioned the board—TVA Board—to fire me because I was engaging in a picketing operation."[68] TVA did not act right away. Later, however, after Wiersma was photographed marching with a picket sign around Rich's Department Store, "the board sent word to me that I had to stop that or I had to be discharged—one or the other."[69] Wiersma only partially yielded to this pressure. He did not sit in or picket after this, but he continued to organize demonstrations.

The picket lines were established not only to attract attention but also as a means of reinforcing the idea of black economic withdrawal. Organizers stated, "We don't think Negroes will cross the lines."[70] While this strategy was largely successful, there were exceptions. Student leader Robert Booker remembered the frustration he felt when he saw others who refused to honor the boycott: "There were some cases where blacks crossed our picket lines and went about their shopping. Or some, under cover of darkness, continued to shop with those stores, making orders and having trucks come to their homes and deliver furniture and what have you."[71] The stores tried to protect the identity of those black citizens who made major purchases that had to be delivered during the boycott. Rather than dispatch their regular delivery trucks, store managers used unmarked vehicles.

Black sit-in supporters exerted pressure on those who were not honoring the boycott. One of the most common tactics they used was to announce in church the names of those who refused to comply with the boycott. At the same time, active participants in the sit-ins were encouraged to speak privately to their recalcitrant neighbors in an effort to change their minds. This black peer pressure was unrelenting, as Theotis Robinson, one of the demonstrators, remembered. "I remember one man who had gone out and made a major purchase at Sears of furniture, and what have you. And Lordy, he caught holy hell."[72] Despite the existence of such pressure, some black Knoxvillians continued to defy the boycott.

This apparent willingness by some blacks to defy peer pressure and patronize businesses that refused to serve blacks at their lunch counters raises an intriguing and important question: To what extent did Knoxville's black community support the idea of the sit-ins? Participant Ann Robinson remembers a unified black community in Knoxville during that period. "And I have never been so proud of Knoxville as I was [of] . . . the Knoxville blacks, because we really did come together."[73] Others involved in the movement disagree with Robinson's perception. Asked whether there was adequate support for the demonstrations from the black community, Knoxville College student leader Robert Booker replied, "No, I don't think so."[74]

At the same time, however, like others in the movement, Booker recalled how full the mass meetings supporting the demonstrations were. Yet he also remembered that the number of people willing to participate in the demonstrations was not nearly as large as the number of people who attended the rallies. An example of this disparity in numbers is offered by the mass meeting on 26 June held at the Mount Olive Baptist Church. Although fifteen hundred supporters attended that meeting to plan a picketing operation for the next day, only about one hundred people actually turned out to demonstrate. Obviously, many members of the large crowds attending the rallies simply went home after the rallies ended rather than on to the lunch counters to demonstrate their concern. It seemed, then, that only a faithful few community members bore a disproportionately large share of the sit-in burden.[75] Thus, unlike sit-in coordinators in Greensboro and other places, Knoxville demonstrators never had to worry about too many participants showing up for the demonstrations.

In addition to this apathy Booker sensed among Knoxville's blacks, he also detected a disconcerting amount of hostility toward the idea of sit-ins. Particularly in the case of some older blacks, Booker remembered, "Well there was some concern on the part of many because, of course, they weren't interested in going to lunch counters, many of them, and they didn't see that that was an important thing in life to be able to do."[76] Such negative sentiments bothered Robert Booker since many of these older blacks were people whose opinions he had been taught to respect. Moreover, Booker became more concerned when some of these same people warned him that "what we were going to do was set back race relations in this town."[77]

Jerry Pate, another student demonstrator, readily agreed with Booker. Pate, who was a native Knoxvillian, was attending Hampton Institute in Virginia when the sit-ins started in Knoxville. Before he returned home for the summer, he participated in sit-ins in Hampton. Upon his arrival in Knoxville once school was over, he was eager to sit-in in his hometown. Fresh from his experience in Virginia, Pate was dismayed by his first view of Knoxville's sit-ins. He questioned the movement's effectiveness because of what he viewed as a lack of community support. That judgment prompted his criticism of the Knoxville demonstrations: "I've never personally felt [it] was a real successful movement."[78] Pate was particularly appalled by the apparent apathy of some Knoxville College students: "But I know that the Knoxville College students . . . didn't participate that much. I don't know why."[79] It is important to reiterate here that a large proportion of the Knoxville College student body consisted of out-of-state students. Since the demonstrations were conducted exclusively during the summer, these students were not even in the city at the time. Thus, this refusal by some local Knoxville College students to sit in further reduced the already restricted number of college student participants locally available.

In an attempt to put the charges of black community apathy in perspective it is necessary to examine the motivations of those who did participate. Dr. Robert Harvey maintained that at least part of the motivation prompting student involvement came from events in Greensboro and the accompanying publicity: "There was a lot of pressure on the part of students to mobilize and to go down and have their sit-ins. . . . There's a follow the leader kind of syndrome, I think, among students in general. That was part of it."[80] Demonstrator Jerry Pate confirmed Harvey's emphasis on imitative behavior as a reason why some became involved. "I'm sure there was a little bit of [that behavior in] me too."[81] Black high school student and native Knoxvillian Michael Freeman divided those who participated into two groups: those who were looking for an adventure and wanted to "raise some sand" and those who were committed to the cause.[82] High school student and demonstrator Ann Robinson remembered that the sit-ins were often a kind of release for the racial tension that had been built up in some over the years.[83]

Whatever the reason for their involvement, the sit-ins were often a turning point for many in terms of the way they viewed their community. This was especially true of high school student participants who were not yet thoroughly schooled in Knoxville's paternalism. Demonstrator Avon Rollins remembered, "I guess that [participation in the sit-ins] was a point of awakening for a number of people in the community."[84] Harvey explained how this awakening led to the formation of a firm commitment to the cause of desegregation for many demonstrators: "Once you participated, you knew it had to happen. Once it got started, you knew that you would never go back to . . . you'd be demonstrating for the rest of your life. There's no way you would accept it [segregation]."[85]

Knoxville's paternalistic tradition had precluded generations of blacks from having an open confrontation with the fact of their segregated lives. While the city's paternalism helped prevent this confrontation, it never prevented black dissatisfaction. According to the Reverend Robert James, the roots of that dissatisfaction ran deep into the black community. "Knoxville was not satisfied," he said. "I mean, the black population was never satisfied with the way things were in Knoxville."[86] This was indeed a turning point since up to this time Knoxville blacks had never had an occasion to articulate their dissatisfaction. The sit-ins changed all that—at least for some.

On the other hand, most Knoxville whites had never realized the existence of any dissatisfaction among the city's blacks. In fact, this lack of white recognition was rooted in Knoxville's historical tradition of disregard for its small group of black citizens. Robert Booker remembered how the sit-ins emphasized the whites' disregard as far as he was concerned: "What we discovered once we got started—we found that many whites really weren't so aware of the [local] segregation policies. They, for example, would pick up a paper and read about the horrible things that were going on in Mississippi, Alabama, or Georgia, or wherever, and didn't realize that blacks couldn't go to the corner drugstore and sit down and drink a coke."[87] Harvey corroborated Booker's assertion: "There were some whites who would walk in and who would be surprised that blacks couldn't eat at the lunch counters."[88]

Robert Booker's realization of this disregard prompted him to test his theory of the invisibility of Knoxville blacks. He went to a lunch counter one day and unceremoniously sat down next to a white man, and "he [the white man] had ordered a hamburger, and when the hamburger came he asked me to pass him the salt. So I passed him the salt, and I said, Now let me test this guy. And I said, 'Pardon me mister, but do you object to sitting beside a Negro at a lunch counter?' He hesitated for a minute, looked at me, and said, 'I sure as hell do, buddy.' And he got up and left."[89]

Although some black Knoxvillians found such disregard distressing, others undoubtedly viewed their invisibility as a positive reality. Invisibility after all, reasoned some, provided a certain amount of protection from the more crude racist activity that occurred in other parts of the South. It could always be worse: "And we have felt that we really haven't been put upon by the white establishment. . . . We didn't want any trouble here."[90] At the same time, many of these pragmatic black Knoxvillians realized that their vulnerable position was reinforced by the fact of their small numbers. Thus, divided black sentiment on their status in Knoxville engendered serious black disagreement on the issue of sit-ins in their community.

Problems with community support notwithstanding, the Knoxville sit-ins were successful in record time. That success was achieved with the aid of influential assistance. Those city officials, such as Mayor Duncan, who had favored desegregation before the demonstrations started, continued to work toward that end even as the protesting was going on. Although they may have been influenced by morality, the actions of these city officials were also undoubtedly influenced by their desire to attract new business and industry to Knoxville. That desire ensured their determination to maintain Knoxville's image as a community free from racial strife.[91] Thus, the activism by some members of the black community combined with city hall's determination to protect Knoxville's image, resulted in victory at the lunch counters. By 12 July, Knoxville's downtown merchants announced their intention to desegregate; the Knoxville sit-ins lasted just over a month—from 9 June to 12 July.[92]

On 17 July, at a mass meeting sponsored by the Associated Council for Full Citizenship, desegregation details were made public. Merchants who agreed to desegregate their lunch counters requested that blacks abide by a ten-day "easing in" period. During that period only two blacks were expected to patronize any one lunch counter at a time. Once the easing-in period ended, desegregated service became a fact of life at Knoxville's downtown lunch counters.[93] Although a few white hecklers had sought to disrupt the desegregation process during the easing-in period, most white customers resumed service as usual at their newly desegregated lunch counters. One of the reasons why peace prevailed could very likely have been rooted in the attitude of many potential black customers. Many black Knoxvillians, for a variety of reasons, displayed absolutely no interest in patronizing the lunch counters. On demonstrator, for example, remembered the disappointment that prompted his refusal to eat downtown. "I waited all this damn time and this is what it's like—all this bland food," he said.[94]

Desegregation did not change black buying patterns—at least not initially. Despite the lack of black patronage at the lunch counters, many demonstrators still maintained that they had won a symbolic victory: "It's dehumanizing to be sent to the back door all the time. So you have to square your shoulders . . . stand a little taller if you can sit down at the table with everybody else and not have to go to the kitchen."[95] Other Knoxvillians judged the outcome of the sit-ins from a quite different perspective. High school student Michael Freeman, for example, saw the outcome of the sit-ins in very personal terms, and what he saw disappointed him. "See, really, for me personally, it didn't change that much," he declared.[96] Freeman was another of the many black Knoxvillians who did not patronize lunch counters even after they were desegregated.

Still others saw in the peace that reigned during the Knoxville demonstrations the seeds of defeat for a push for black civil rights in Knoxville. Those who held this opinion felt that black Knoxvillians should be more concerned about fighting white disregard rather than white hostility. Thus, because the peaceful nature of the sit-ins drew very little attention to black Knoxvillians, some reasoned, they still suffered from the same invisibility after the demonstrations were over that they had suffered from before they began. This point of view prompted demonstrator Jerry Pate to claim, "For some reason blacks in this area tend to have a superior attitude. They feel that because we didn't have this disruption that we were better off than people in other areas."[97] Pate went on to insist, however, that the opposite was true. Rather, he claimed that a more serious and perhaps violent confrontation between blacks and whites would have forced whites to take more notice of blacks. This, in turn, would have set the stage for serious negotiations to effect fundamental change. Instead, according to Pate, things in Knoxville were too easy, and only surface change occurred. Thus, the power relationship between black and white Knoxvillians was not altered by the sit-ins. Demonstrator Avon Rollins claimed that because the power relationship in Knoxville remained the same even after the sit-in victory, "they [the white power structure] dictated the terms in which these facilities would be opened up."[98]

Not only did Knoxville's sit-ins have no effect on the racial balance of power in the city, but they were not even solely responsible for the desegregation of downtown lunch counters. Rather, the importance of the sit-ins in Knoxville is rooted in their effect on the consciousness of black Knoxvillians. These demonstrations finally forced all black Knoxvillians, despite their reluctance, to come to terms with their subordinate status. On the one hand, those who participated became filled with a restlessness that fired them with a desire for social change. Those who chose not to participate, on the other hand, were relieved when demonstrations ended since these sit-ins had served to rivet their attention on their subordinate status. Their ancestors had always been able to avoid this unpleasant reality and seek refuge in their perception of the city's racial leniency. Yet the demonstrations in 1960 stripped away this psychological refuge: at least for a time even the most conservative Knoxville blacks could no longer hide from the truth.

Student leader Robert Booker's agreement with this judgment prompted him to perceive the outcome of the sit-ins not as an end but as a beginning: the beginning of a dawning black awareness that would finally present a starting place for fundamental change to come to Knoxville.[99] Only time would tell. So, amid the swirling undercurrents of an altered black consciousness, surface calm returned to Knoxville after long negotiations, short sit-ins, and city help all worked together and accomplished desegregation of Knoxville's lunch counters in July 1960.

Notes

1. Robert Booker, interview with author, Knoxville, Tenn., 14 Jan. 1984.
2. Ibid.
3. Miles Wolff, *Lunch at the Five and Ten* (New York, 1970), 101.
4. Ibid., 101.
5. Harvard Sitcoff, *The Struggle for Black Equality* (New York, 1981), 76.
6. W. T. Crutcher, interview with author, Knoxville, Tenn., 28 Feb. 1984.
7. John Duncan, interview with author, Knoxville, Tenn., 15 Feb. 1984.
8. Ibid.
9. Robert Harvey, interview with author, Knoxville, Tenn., 14 Feb. 1984.
10. Sitcoff, *Struggle for Black Equality*, 77.
11. Betsey B. Creekmore, *Knoxville* (Knoxville, 1976), 4.
12. John Cell, *The Highest Stage of White Supremacy* (New York, 1982), 134–35.

13. Michael McDonald and William B. Wheeler, *Knoxville, Tennessee: Continuity and Change in an Appalachian City* (Knoxville, 1983), 38.
14. Ibid.
15. J. Harvey Kerns, *Social and Economic Conditions in Knoxville, Tennessee, As They Affect the Negro* (n.p.: Southern Regional Office–National Urban League, 1967), 5.
16. Julian Bell, interview with author, Knoxville, Tenn., 23 Jan. 1984.
17. Ibid.
18. Ibid.
19. Ibid.
20. Theotis Robinson and Ann Robinson, interview with author, Knoxville, Tenn., 2 Feb. 1984.
21. Ibid.
22. Ibid.
23. Harry Wiersma and Harry Wiersma Jr., interview with author, Knoxville, Tenn., 15 Feb. 1984.
24. Ibid.
25. Cell, *Highest Stage of White Supremacy,* 19.
26. Jerry Pate, interview with author, Knoxville, Tenn., 15 Dec. 1983.
27. Thelma Present and Petie Moulder Recording, Fellowship House Collection, Martin Luther King Center for Social Change, Atlanta, May 1960.
28. Leroy Graf, interview with author, Knoxville, Tenn., 15 Feb. 1984.
29. Michael Freeman, interview with author, Knoxville, Tenn., 9 Mar. 1984.
30. Cell, *Highest Stage of White Supremacy,* 19.
31. *Human Relations News* 3 (May–June 1960): n.p.
32. Knoxville Area Human Relations Council, *A Chronology Of Negotiations* (N.p., 18 July 1960), 1.
33. Ibid.
34. Ibid.
35. *Human Relations News* 3 (May–June 1960), n.p.
36. Knoxville Area Human Relations Council, *Chronology of Negotiations,* 4.
37. *Human Relations News* 3 (May–June 1960): n.p.
38. Ibid.
39. Ibid.
40. Robert James, interview with author, Knoxville, Tenn., 14 Mar. 1984.
41. Robinson and Robinson, interview.
42. James, interview.
43. Robinson and Robinson, interview.
44. Harvey, interview.
45. Pate, interview.
46. Ibid.
47. Freeman, interview.
48. Ibid.
49. Avon Rollins, interview with author, Knoxville, Tenn., 27 Feb. 1984.
50. Ibid.
51. Robinson and Robinson, interview.
52. Ibid.
53. Wiersma and Wiersma, interview.
54. Ibid.
55. James, interview.

56. Ibid.
57. *Human Relations News* 3 (May–June 1960): n.p.
58. *Knoxville News-Sentinel*, 1 July 1960.
59. Ibid.
60. Ibid.
61. Ibid.
62. Wiersma and Wiersma, interview.
63. Crutcher, interview.
64. Ibid.
65. *Knoxville News-Sentinel*, 27 June 1960.
66. Ibid.
67. Wiersma and Wiersma, interview.
68. Ibid.
69. Ibid.
70. *Knoxville News-Sentinel*, 27 June 1960.
71. Booker, interview.
72. Robinson and Robinson, interview.
73. Ibid.
74. Booker, interview.
75. Ibid.
76. Ibid.
77. Ibid.
78. Pate, interview.
79. Ibid.
80. Harvey, interview.
81. Pate, interview.
82. Freeman, interview.
83. Robinson and Robinson, interview.
84. Rollins, interview.
85. Harvey, interview.
86. James, interview.
87. Booker, interview.
88. Harvey, interview.
89. Booker, interview.
90. Ibid.
91. McDonald and Wheeler, *Knoxville*, 101, 129–30.
92. Knoxville Area Human Relations Council, *Chronology of Negotiations*, 9.
93. Ibid., 9.
94. Rollins, interview.
95. Harvey, interview.
96. Freeman, interview.
97. Pate, interview.
98. Rollins, interview.
99. Booker, interview.

Toward a Perfect Democracy

The Struggle of African Americans in Fayette County to Fulfill the Unfulfilled Right of the Franchise

Linda T. Wynn

W HILE THE PROCESS OF DESEGREGATION MOVED SLOWLY BUT GENERALLY PEACEFULLY IN COOKEVILLE AND KNOXVILLE, VIOLENCE and determined opposition met the Civil Rights movement at every turn in Fayette County, which has one of the highest percentages of African American population in the state. White farmers kicked black tenants, who dared to register to vote, off their fields; white merchants refused to sell goods and services to blacks who claimed their voting rights. Threats and intimidation were the rule; in fact, the presence of the federal government did little to quell white opposition. Linda Wynn reviews the long process for African Americans to achieve civil and political rights through oral interviews and a wide range of documentary evidence, taken from court records and major national newspapers and magazines. Her story emphasizes that African Americans continued to push for their rights despite the formidable obstacles placed in their way. When tenants were kicked out of their homes, local leaders worked with state and national constituencies to build "Tent City." County officials may have imposed long delays and intolerable conditions for those

who wanted to register to vote; local blacks patiently
waited their turn no matter how uncomfortable it was to
stand all day in the sun. What happened in Fayette
County happened in different degrees wherever blacks
made up either a majority or large minority of the local
population.

Beginning in 1959, African American residents of Fayette County, Tennessee, conducted an organized and successful effort to register as voters.
The desperate struggle to secure voting rights was just one component of the
Civil Rights movement in the twentieth century. The modern movement,
in turn, is best understood as a continuum of this country's oppressive
encumbrance of race, a socioeconomic proposition constructed upon the
foundation of almost two and a half centuries of black slavery. The modern
Civil Rights movement, or "Second Reconstruction," as it dubbed by some
historians, articulated the combined strivings of countless systematized local
struggles for African American equality and justice.[1] When a crusade for
economic, political, and social remedy is universal, any person or group of
persons who can clearly express the concept, conviction, and certitude of
the masses can come to the forefront of that movement.[2] In Tennessee's
southwest county of Fayette and in other local areas across the nation, the
second Reconstruction and its ubiquitous desire for relief from the evil
debasement of racial injustice caused such persons to stand up and assume
the mantle of leadership. Leadership in Fayette County primarily came from
those newly returned black veterans of the Second World War. After fighting to make the world safe for democracy, the racial discrimination they
experienced in their home county, including being denied the right to participate as citizens in the political process, became unbearable.

When African Americans attempted to register and vote in Fayette
County, they discovered that Tennessee's election laws stipulated that a person must be twenty-one years of age and a resident of the state and county
in which one voted. There was no poll tax and no mention of race. Tennessee's poll tax was officially repealed in 1953, eleven years before the
Twenty-fourth Amendment to the United States Constitution prohibited
the tax. However, in Fayette County, politics was a one-party affair controlled by the Democratic Party, whose primary strictly precluded African
Americans from the ballot box.

Fayette County's seat of government is Somerville. During the late 1950s and early 1960s, it was no different than other small provincial boroughs in the South. Its high-reaching water tower upon which the town's name was indelibly marked was crowned by a spectacular illuminated cross that commanded visual attention at night. This emblem of faith and the Creator's love for humankind was incongruent with the invidious deeds committed by its white citizens against persons of African heritage. Rather than being an emblem of faith and love for humankind, perhaps the lighted cross could be interpreted as a segregationist symbol to remind blacks not to cross the racial divide.

The struggles of unsung African Americans in Fayette County to gain the right to vote are only summarily chronicled in the plethora of literature on the modern Civil Rights movement. However, because of the brutal, cruel, and merciless retributions taken against those who participated in the voter-registration campaign, approximately thirty articles appeared in the *New York Times* between 1960 and 1962. The revengeful racial retaliations caused leaders of the national Civil Rights movement to take a closer look at the connection between the economic subservience and political suppression of African American tenant farmers in the rural South. For James Forman of the Emergency Relief Committee of Chicago's Congress of Racial Equality, the plight of blacks in Fayette County exposed the issue of economic exploitation; if they failed, it would be almost impossible to build any type of movement in Mississippi. John Doar, an attorney in the Justice Department's civil rights division during President Dwight Eisenhower's administration, instituted new fact-finding procedures and enforcement of the civil rights laws. Remaining with the Justice Department after the presidential election of John F. Kennedy, Doar enlightened the new administration concerning the problems blacks faced in the rural county. It was this interconnectedness that galvanized African Americans and others to undauntedly seek justice where injustices were wrought. The county's inoculation with black suffrage destroyed its *mos pro lege*, or custom for law, system of immunity to black participation in the political process.

During the late 1950s and early 1960s, Fayette County was the third poorest county in America. Employment opportunities for African Americans primarily consisted of domestic work, farming or sharecropping, and teaching in the county's black schools. Blacks constituted the majority of the county's population and most worked as sharecroppers on white-owned land. Despite the lack of economic means, many Fayette County blacks were not servile. They did not wait for the organized activism of groups like the

National Association for the Advancement of Colored People (NAACP), Congress of Racial Equality (CORE), the Southern Christian Leadership Conference (SCLC), the Student Nonviolent Coordinating Committee (SNCC), or any other organization to stimulate the resurrected conscious-ness of the Civil Rights movement. The inducement came from themselves, people like John and Viola McFerren, Harpman and Minnie Jameson, Square and Wilola Moorman, the Reverend June Dowdy, Shephard Towels Sr., Gertrude Beasley, and others.

The Civil Rights movement of the 1950s and 1960s was not an under-taking set in motion by a group of people who possessed the ability and lead-ership skills to inspire great popular allegiance; in fact, it was a movement that garnered momentum from localized efforts and their multitudinous steadfast participants. Their story is now the missing part of our understand-ing of the national Civil Rights movement. Even in the face of racial recrim-inations, African Americans in Fayette County demonstrated they understood that if progress was to be made, they, as others before them, would have to be proactive in their struggle to gain the ballot.

It was a struggle that began in the era of slavery. Because of the perni-cious practice of slavery, quasi-free persons of color shouldered the weight of their ebony pigmentation as being synonymous with subjugation. To end slavery, the United States Constitution was amended by the Thirteenth, Fourteenth, and Fifteenth Amendments. But the legacy of slavery could not so easily be escaped; there was *de jure* and *de facto* segregation between black and white Americans, and the country's economic, education, judicial, and political systems were pervasively racist. Eventually, numerous cases were lit-igated before the United States Supreme Court to rectify the civil, political, and social wrongs. Yet due to distortions cast by the pernicious practice of slavery and its nefarious customs of racial discrimination and inequality, judicial decisions did not become public policy until there were organized and unorganized struggles for civil rights among the nation's people of African American heritage.

People of African descent have been a part of Fayette County since the opening of the territory in the early 1800s. Numerous pioneers who migrated to the locality brought black slaves with them. According to the census data of 1830, there were 48 free blacks and 3,193 slaves out of a total population of 8,652. Ten years later, the people of African heritage exceeded the white population. In the 1860s, African Americans in Fayette County outnum-bered European Americans by a ratio of two to one. This ratio remained con-stant until 1980, when the census report revealed an African American populace of 51 percent and a white population of 49 percent. Based on the 1990 census data, African Americans constituted 44 percent of Fayette County's populace, as compared to its white populace of 56 percent. Although they were in the majority during most of the nineteenth century, it was 1883 before African American Fayette Countians elected Representative David Foote Rivers to the state legislature. In 1889, Monroe Gooden was the last person of African descent from Fayette County to serve in the Tennessee General Assembly.[3]

Beginning with the passage of suffrage restrictions in 1890, few African Americans voted, and the white power structure allowed almost none to register. At the same time, the repressive and unjust provisos of Jim Crow laws were approved. Support for Republican gubernatorial candidates in the predominantly black county declined from 1,050 votes in 1888 to 339 in 1894, and to 3 in 1906. Restrictive laws and denial of suffrage completed the debasement of blacks and relegated them to a separate and unequal standing, despite the U.S. Supreme Court's rule of a "separate but equal" standard for civil rights in its famous *Plessy v. Ferguson* decision of 1896. The Supreme Court's validation of racial separation and apartheid against African Americans caused the Siamese twins of racial injustice and bigotry to dictate domestic policy in the United States for more than fifty years. *De jure* and *de facto*, the Supreme Court conferred constitutional enforcement to mores and folkways that effectively retracted the civil rights of America's people of African descent. By the early 1900s, most Tennessee blacks were overtly denied the right to vote.

Throughout the annals of this country's history, African Americans have worked concertedly toward the goals of freedom, equality, justice, and political inclusion. Whether isolated actions of an individual or actions of a group, the protest continuum possibly dates as far back as the seventeenth century. To cite a mathematical truism that the whole is equal to the sum of its parts, thus the combined "parts" of the protest movement form the whole and were the bedrock of the protest structure.

In Tennessee, as one civil liberty after another was taken away, blacks continued to seek equality under the newly inaugurated Jim Crow system. They did so by fighting to redress the inequities imposed by Jim Crow streetcar laws, boycotting local streetcar companies, staging freedom rides and organizing transportation companies, and migrating North to escape the inhumanity of southern whites. They formed branches of organizations such as the NAACP and the National Urban League. Blacks and moderate whites organized the Commission on Interracial Cooperation, and a branch of Marcus Garvey's Universal Negro Improvement Association was organized in Chattanooga.

Their struggle was cultural as much as political. Between 1890 and 1920, the subject of black inferiority permeated the pages of American journals. Scholars endorsed, encouraged, and supported the disfranchisement of men of African descent. They acknowledged that differential treatment founded exclusively on the issue of race was unconstitutional but concluded that discrimination grounded on the cornerstone of literacy, ownership of property, and taxation was constitutionally sound and morally imperative.[4] In 1894, Stephen B. Weeks in his article "History of Negro Suffrage" stated, "Nor did the fifteenth amendment give him [the Negro] the right to vote; it merely invested the citizen of the United States with the right to be exempt from discrimination in the exercise of the elective franchise on account of his race, color, or previous condition of servitude."[5]

The highest court in the land validated this conceptual expression of the Fifteenth Amendment in 1898. Two years after sanctioning the legality of segregation in the *Plessy* case, a unanimous Supreme Court ruled in *Williams v. Mississippi* that limiting the right to vote was lawful, even though it might be directed primarily or even restricted to Negroes, as long as the verbiage of the state statute made no direct reference to the issue of race. The state of Mississippi took the forefront in framing legal blueprints to subterfuge African American voting rights and to complete the transformation that was initiated during the 1880s with statutory disfranchisement. Observed historian Richard Kluger, "The black man was reduced to political cipher and the Fifteenth Amendment lay mortally wounded beside him."[6]

The Mississippi model's shrewdest stratagem were its "literacy and understanding test" and the poll tax. The understanding clause, stated historian Steven F. Lawson, provided uneducated whites with a possible escape. If he could "understand any section of the state constitution read to him . . . or give a reasonable interpretation thereof," white election officials might [and in all probability did] exercise their authority with subjectivity and pass the illiterate white. The poll tax impeded economically disadvantaged whites as well as blacks, and it had to be paid before 1 February of the election year. Based on George S. Stoney's observation, "This was like buying a ticket to a show nine months ahead of time . . . before you know who is playing or really what the thing is about."[7]

By upholding literacy tests and poll taxes in the Williams case, the Supreme Court, in effect, also disfranchised illiterate whites. However, crafty Dixie legislators resolved this dilemma with the "grandfather clause,"

which permitted direct descendants of pre-1866 voters to cast ballots without being proficient in reading and writing, therefore allowing ignorant and
uneducated whites to vote, while taking the ballot away from most blacks.[8]

The story in Tennessee was much similar to that in Mississippi. In
1889–90 the Tennessee legislature passed a number of suffrage restrictions
that practically removed the state's African American populace from the
political playing field. These restrictions included precise registration procedures, a secret ballot, and a new and enforceable poll tax requirement. Thousands of Tennessee's blacks were denied right of entry to the voting polls.
The ethnological effect of the newly fashioned statutes almost completely
negated the black vote in the rural counties of West Tennessee.

Thus, for more than the first half of the twentieth century, the right to
vote granted African Americans in 1870 under the Constitution's Fifteenth
Amendment was nothing more than unfulfilled promises drafted on parch-
ment in many states of the South. Passage and ratification of the Reconstruction amendment and its enforcement legislation did not guarantee the
franchise to the African Americans. For almost a century, an array of legislative stratagems obstructed their path to the voting booth. Disfranchisement constituted only a partial mix of the methodology of depoliticalization.
Poll taxes, literacy tests, residence and registration requirements, and grandfather clauses all, in their own way, eradicated equality at the polls. Socio-
logical and psychological ploys such as economic restrictions, intimidations,
and threatened intimidations caused the mass extraction of African Americans from the political life of this nation. Denied the vote, the fundamental
symbol of citizenship in the Republic, representative rule became unavailable and unanswerable to the country's citizens who happened to be of
African descent.

Even when the courts ruled that the Fifteenth Amendment meant that
southern states at least had to maintain the legal pretense of black voting
rights, those rights meant nothing in an electoral process dominated by the
all-white, and private, Democratic Party primary. While African Americans
in theory could cast their ballots in the general election, the private "white
primary" enjoined blacks from engaging effectively in the political process.
The legal argument justifying the white primaries was simple: if the political
party rather than the legislature was discriminatory, the Fourteenth and Fifteenth Amendments did not come into play. These amendments safe-
guarded persons against "state action," and, as long as the courts viewed
political parties as private agencies, southern politicians reasoned they could
legally bar blacks from the party's affairs.[9]

But in *Smith v. Allwright* (1944), the United States Supreme Court overturned *Grovey v. Townsend* (1935), which had supported the discriminatory white primary and signaled that the days of legal stratagems keeping the vote from African Americans were numbered. Associate Justice Stanley Reed spoke for the eight-to-one majority, which put an end to the white primary:

> It may now be taken as a postulate that the right to vote in such a primary for the nomination of candidates without discrimination by the State, like the right to vote in a general election, is a right secured by the Constitution. By the terms of the Fifteenth Amendment that right may not be abridged by any State on Account of race. Under our Constitution the great privilege of the ballot may not be denied a man by the State because of his color. . . . Here we are applying, contrary to the recent decision in *Grovey v. Townsend*, the well-established principle of the Fifteenth Amendment, forbidding the abridgment by a State of a citizen's right vote. *Grovey v. Townsend* is overruled.

The Supreme Court ruled that the state of Texas had specified the primary as an essential characteristic of its election apparatus by barring those unsuccessful office seekers from running in the general election and by compelling election officials to withhold ballots from those not qualified under convention rules. By permitting the Democratic Party to put into effect regulations that prohibited black voting, Texas became party to the disfranchisement of blacks. Justice Reed admonished those who might be tempted to frame a new rendition of the white primary that the right to vote for those running for public office could not be "nullified by a state through casting its electoral process in a form which permits a private organization to practice racial discrimination in that election."[10]

When Texas attempted to establish a new legal basis for the white primary, the Supreme Court in *Terry v. Adams* (1953) again held that Negroes could not be prohibited from voting. Justice Hugo L. Black, in the majority opinion, wrote that "the procedure violated the Fifteenth Amendment's guarantee that the right to vote shall not be denied because of race."[11] Again, the white primary was ruled null and void. Although the white primary was constitutionally nullified, blacks still faced such contrivances as the poll tax, racist registrars, and racial intimidation. Despite these obstacles, the activist role taken by the NAACP to redress political disfranchisement kept them filled with hope, which was sustained by the *Brown v. Board of*

Education of Topeka, et al. (1954) decision; direct nonviolent protest by blacks, exemplified by Rosa Parks's refusal in 1955 to surrender her seat on a Montgomery bus; and the passage of the 1957 Civil Rights Act, the first federal civil rights bill since 1875.

While the 1957 Civil Rights Act "was not a far-reaching measure in substance," wrote Albert P. Blaustein and Robert Zangrando, "it was a clear indication that the legislative branch was undertaking responsibilities that had previously been left to the executive and judiciary branches."[12] The 1957 act established the nonpartisan United States Commission on Civil Rights (CCR), empowered to gather evidence of voting violations. It also strengthened certain civil rights provisos of the United States Code and authorized the Justice Department to initiate action to counter irregularities in federal elections.

Three years later, Congress passed the Civil Rights Act of 1960. Designed to impede interracial violence without ending the power and authority of local and state officials, the act called for the preservation of records in federal elections and established referees who could facilitate voting in concert with the courts and the Justice Department. If a "pattern or practice" of discrimination existed, the Justice Department was empowered to take action on behalf of the injured voter. Most of the litigation on Negro voting involved legislation designed to prohibit blacks from voting in party primaries. The driving forces of vicissitude were charging against the Old South as blacks stepped up their *modus operandi* of activism and no longer viewed themselves as obsequious to whites.

Two years after the passage of the 1957 Civil Rights Act, local blacks directed a voter registration drive in Fayette County. African Americans owned property and contributed to the county's public coffers. However, whites governed the county with an iron hand. In 1959, as blacks in the county fought for the right to vote, the asphyxiating social frame of reference bequeathed from slavery and perpetuated by segregation was about to undergo a revolutionary transformation. Black Fayette Countians' concern for the lack of civil liberties for their race, which were theoretically granted by the United States Constitution, was sparked by the absence of Negro jurors for the Burton Dodson trial of 1958. Dodson, an African American farmer, was on trial for the purported murder of a white man in 1940. Subsequent to a heated discussion between Dodson and a white man over an African American woman with whom both were involved, a physical struggle erupted.[13] The white man became incensed, filed assault charges against Dodson, and in the ensuing period an organized mob was deputized. In the wee hours of the morning on 23 May 1940, Sheriff W. H. Cocke and a number of deputies descended upon Dodson's isolated farmhouse and ordered him to come out and surrender. Dodson refused. In the melee that followed, Dodson escaped and "deputy" Olin Burrow was fatally wounded.[14]

Eighteen years later, Dodson was discovered in East St. Louis, Illinois, and extradited to Fayette County to face charges of homicide. The issues embodied in the Dodson case were not unusual: the reckless, lawless white mob, the sudden ruination of a black family, and the looming threat of southern justice. But in this case, James F. Estes, a black attorney from Memphis, defended Dodson, a "first" in Fayette County. The Legal Defense Fund of the NAACP provided for Dodson's defense. African Americans converged on the Somerville courthouse to witness the trial. Estes attained three notable results. First, he created a new personification for men of African descent in the Somerville courthouse, since he was in the courthouse as an officer of the court. He was not there to clean or care for the facility nor was he there accused of breaking the law. Second, he obtained a complete hearing before the judicial system for his client. Third, although extraneous to the court proceeding, the rejoinder to his questions reverberated with shattering economic, political, and social impact in Fayette County, as well as in the neighboring county of Haywood.[15]

Attorney Estes entered a plea of not guilty for his client. He questioned the lack of African Americans among the possible jurors conscripted from the voter registration rolls. He interrogated every prospective juror about his racial attitude. "Do you believe Negroes should have the right to register and vote?" Estes asked. If they said no, he challenged them as prejudiced against blacks and dismissed them from the jury. After dismissal of a number of prospective jurors, Estes managed to win admissions from some of the prospective jurors that blacks deserved the right to vote. In doing so, he had tied the issue of voting rights to that of a fair trial for Dodson.

Questions about voting rights in Fayette County, at the same time, were being considered in other legal venues. The CCR received complaints that blacks in Fayette and Haywood Counties were being denied the right to vote. Blacks in Fayette County often questioned why they did not have an opportunity to participate in the political process like their black neighbors in Memphis. Said Minnie Jameson, "We wondered why, with Negroes being in the majority in Fayette County, why they never voted? The question often came up and it would often be asked."[16] Based on an examination of the county's voting records by the CCR, between 1952 and 1959 there were 58 registered Negro voters. Twenty registered in 1958, and 11 registered in 1959.

Voting records found for 46 of the 58 Negro registrants showed that three voted in 1952, one in 1953, 12 in 1956, and one in 1958, for a total of 17 or slightly less than 2 per 1,000. However, when the census data for 1960 are taken into account, and with the county black population numbered 16,927, only 1 out of every 1,000 voted. Of the 46 people for whom voting records were found, 13 never voted, and 16 registered after the 1958 elections and had no opportunity to vote.[17] The CCR's report charged that of the 12 Negro war veterans registered in the county, only 1 voted, and "he doubted his ballot was counted for he thought he handed it to someone instead of dropping it in the box." Two others were frightened away when sheriff's deputies approached them. One was told by his banker that something might happen to him if he attempted to participate in the voting process. One who was in the hauling business lost all of his customers, and the police threatened to arrest his drivers found in his trucks on the highway. According to the CCR's field notes taken from interviews, "When a Negro registers[,] the sheriff is quickly informed and he . . . informs the Negro's landowner or employer. Those who register are soon discharged from their positions and ordered to move from their homes. The police arrest them and impose fines. They are unable to secure credit, their wages are garnished, and their GI loan applications to purchase land are turned down by local lenders."[18]

Because African Americans were denied their intrinsic right to participate in the electoral process, they were omitted from the pool of potential jurors. Dodson's future was in the hands of an all-white jury. Encouraged by attorney Estes, the black community under the leadership of John McFerren and Harpman Jameson hired a court reporter.

At the trial, a deputy who was present at the 23 May 1940 incident testified that white men shot at Dodson from trees and the tops of buildings as he attempted to escape. The deputy doubted that Dodson fired the shot that mortally wounded Olin Burrow. According to the deputy, Dodson dashed out of the house fleeing west, returning gunfire while running away. The body of the slain deputy was found on the east side of the house, down the hill behind a tree. In spite of the deputy's testimony, the jury found the defendant guilty of second-degree murder. Southern justice smothered Estes's defense, and Judge Mark A. Walker imposed on Burton Dodson a twenty-year sentence that was later reduced to ten years.[19]

The outcome of the Dodson trial galvanized local black leaders to address the connection between voter-registration rolls and the roster of potential jurors. In the spring of 1959, John McFerren, Harpman Jameson, Rufus Abernathy, Ed Brooks, Roy Brown, Isaiah Harris, John Lewis, Houston

Malone, Williams S. Towels Sr., and Lavearn Towels formed the Fayette County Civic and Welfare League (FCCWL). With assistance from James F. Estes, they filed a charter of incorporation with the secretary of state's office in Nashville, but they did not register it in Fayette County. This later caused a problem for the FCCWL. The purpose of the new organization was "to promote civil and political and economic welfare for the community progress of Fayette County." Although this objective was moderate and within reason, they seemed disputatious and dangerous to the white-power structure of Fayette County. The economic and political order of the rural South depended upon black disempowerment. It was an order that detested change in the status quo, and blacks who defied the southern code and refused to "stay in their place" garnered white castigation. To whites, "political progress" meant blacks pursuing the right to vote, and "economic welfare" meant fair wages, equitable apportioning of revenue from state and federally funded programs, and fair employment practices. The legitimacy of the league's objectives represented a powerful threat to a system assembled upon centuries of racial and prejudicial inequities. Because of familial ties between Burton Dodson and Currie P. Boyd of Haywood County, Estes also had assisted Boyd and others in formally organizing the Haywood County Civic and Welfare League. According to Robert Hamburger's *Our Portion of Hell*, there was no precedent for this in the rural South.

The first project undertaken by the Fayette County league was a voter-registration drive. In June and July 1959, the league's organizers motivated a number of the county's African American residents to register at the Somerville courthouse. Although gripped by fear and encumbered with domestic responsibilities, Viola McFerren became an active participant in the movement. The league's office was maintained in the McFerren home, and Viola worked assiduously seeing to the needs of its members.[20]

When the Democratic primary was held in August to select nominees for the office of sheriff, county trustee, and general sessions judge, registered African Americans were not allowed to cast their ballots. Those persons selected in the primary ran for office in the August 1960 general election. The official announcement for the primary contained a phrase limiting it to "all known white Democrats." White officials of Fayette County tenaciously clung to the ways of the "redeemed South," even if it meant going against the law of the land. They rebuffed the legislative enactments of the United States Congress and the rulings of the United States Supreme Court, and they did not anticipate nor care about the determination of African Americans to participate in the democratic process. As in other southern towns that used the Democratic primary as an electoral tool to prevent access by blacks to the ballot box, when the Fayette County Democratic primary was held, those who won nomination were virtually always chosen in the general election. Election officials were told to strictly enforce the limitation phrase and turn all of the Negro voters away.

On 16 November 1959, a federal lawsuit was filed in Memphis against the Fayette County Democratic Executive Committee, charging its members with failing to let African Americans vote in the 1 August Democratic Primary.[21] The government contended that casting a ballot in the county's Democratic primary was the only mechanism available that allowed voters a voice in selecting persons to fill county offices. According to the 17 November 1959 issue of the *Memphis Commercial Appeal*, "The federal court suit against Fayette County officials to let Negroes vote in county primaries was the first of its kind filed under the Civil Rights Act of 1957. Justice Department officials said, 'other government suits attacked exclusion of African Americans from registering to vote, but not, as in the present case, from taking part in a primary election.'"[22]

The suit was based on a party resolution adopted in June 1959, which stated that "the primary coming up August 1 was strictly a white primary." Disseminated countywide, the resolution was followed by a letter signed by Joe N. Cocke, secretary of the party's central committee, reiterating that the primary was for whites only. In part, the letter stated, "If any Negro should ask to vote in your district, they are to be informed that this is a White Democratic Primary and not a general election. Any further questions . . . should be directed to me." This letter was forwarded along with the ballot boxes to all voter precincts.[23]

As blacks demonstrated their resolve to register and vote, many of the county's whites demonstrated their determination to maintain the status quo. One month before the federal suit was adjudicated, Inez Davis, James Freeland, and J. B. Haddad, members of the Fayette County Election Commission, submitted their letters of resignation along with Mrs. Hugh Starks, county registrar, to Dr. Sam Coward, chairman of the State Elections Board.[24] All four said that "they resigned in protest against what they termed investigation by the Federal Bureau of Investigation of 'unfounded charges by a Negro.'"[25] The desired outcome of their resignations was a countywide shutdown of voter registration.

On 25 April 1960, African American voters in Fayette County received their first taste of victory when Deputy U.S. Attorney General Lawrence E. Walsh announced the entry of a consent judgment to end voting discrimination. The purpose of the consent decree between the federal government and Fayette County election officials was "to prevent the exclusion, on account of race or color, of duly registered voters of Fayette County from effectively participating in all elections." The entry of judgment by consent marked a new approach to the disposition of voting cases under the Civil Rights Act. Said Joseph M. F. Ryan Jr., assistant attorney general in charge of the Justice Department's Civil Rights Division, "I hope that in the future, whenever possible, the right of citizens to vote can be fully vindicated without resorting to extensive and protracted litigation." They Fayette County case marked the first voting rights case under the 1957 Civil Rights Act to be settled by negotiation.[26]

Two months after the consent judgment was signed, new election commissioners were named to replace those who resigned. However, county officials opened the voter registration offices only on Wednesdays. Hundreds of African Americans registrants stood in long lines while only one registrar processed their applications. As if it were not enough for blacks to endure long lines, extremes of weather conditions and the purposely slow registration process, other devices were instituted to make the process unbearable. Blacks had to stand in a perfectly straight line and could not sit or stand on the courthouse lawn. Election officials moved the place of registration within the courthouse. Even when blacks wished to use the segregated restroom facilities, the doors were locked. Acts of cruelty and intimidation threatened the registrants. Courthouse workers showered black registrants with hot coffee and spit on them. While blacks patiently waited in line and minded their own business, courthouse employees went to the roof of the courthouse and propelled showers of red pepper and paint upon them in ninety- and one-hundred-degree weather. Because of the torrid temperatures, people standing in line often fainted. Yet the determined African Americans would not be swayed. By September 1960, approximately one thousand African Americans had registered to vote.[27]

The cyclonic winds of social change were whirling as a series of events focused the nation's attention on Fayette County. As African Americans pursued their constitutional rights to participate in the electoral process, many lost employment, credit, and insurance policies. Some white physicians refused to abide by their Hippocratic Oath and withheld medical treatment from patients of African descent.

Beginning in April 1960, members of the White Citizens' Council, which reportedly met in the courthouse, drew up a list banning blacks and some whites from the marketplace. Approximately 12 African American

leaders made up the nucleus of the list, and others were added as they registered to vote. The main targets on the list were designated with an A. Any
person whose name appeared on the list soon discovered that he or she was
unable to purchase anything anywhere in the county. While some whites
denied the existence of a "blacklist," W. B. Wigglestone, manager of the
local bank, admitted there was such a thing: "The men on that list, I won't
even talk to unless they already owe us money and are coming to pay it off.
My secretary's got the names of the 325 who registered. I told them, anybody
on there, no need in coming into this bank. He'll get no crop loan here."[28]

Harpman Jameson was denied a crop loan. "My credit was good . . . until
I registered," said Jameson. Grocery and drug stores refused to sell food and
medicine to eighty-four-year-old John Lewis, a founder of the FCCWL, and
his wife. Shepherd Towels's insurance was canceled. The Fayette County
board of education refused to renew teacher Allen Yancy's contract. Minnie
Jameson, a substitute teacher in the county school system, lost her job and
to this day has not been called to substitute teach. Viola McFerren had to
travel fifty miles to Memphis to give birth to her third child. John McFerren
said, "They won't sell me a damn thing here. I can't even buy my baby milk."
T. L. Redfearn, a liberal white farmer and store owner who ran for sheriff and
was the candidate of choice supported by African Americans in the 1959
August primary, was boycotted as well. "Merchants in all parts of the county
turned down my business," said Redfearn. "I couldn't get a tire fixed." Scott
C. Franklin, a black grocer, faced the same treatment. Gas dealers, soft drink
distributors, and candy salesmen refused to sell to him. One farmer reported
that because the doctor in Fayette County refused to see black patients, he
had to take his injured child to Memphis for medical attention.[29]

The politics of the white economic boycott not only centered around
race and legal writs but also around simple mathematics. There were nine
thousand blacks of voting age in the county as compared to forty-six hundred whites. Whites feared that blacks would gain political control of the
county. "What we are afraid of is some unscrupulous politician getting the
majority group together and upsetting the welfare of our county, electing a
nigger law-enforcement officer," said Isaac P. Yancey, mayor of Somerville.[30]

The boycott stiffened black resolve. Troops on both sides were determined to secure victory in the county's racial battle. J. L. Howse, a white
Somerville grocer, contended, "We don't care what nobody else out there
thinks. There's nobody can help us and nobody can hurt us." John McFerren,
a grocer, gas station owner, and leader of the Civil Rights movement, said, "I
was born and raised in Fayette County. I was 18 years old [when] taken into

the army. . . . I came back here and made a home. I think it is as important for me to fight a war here as it was for me to go over there and fight. This war is just as important as World War II. I may have been a private in that war but I am a general in this one."[31]

The Nashville branch of the NAACP launched a drive to benefit the African American victims of white economic reprisals. Dr. Vivian Henderson, professor of economics at Fisk University and chairman of the Nashville branch, said that "a real emergency exists among Negro families in the West Tennessee county who have suffered economic reprisals because of their efforts to regis-ter and vote." With the assistance of local churches, the Nashville branch sent food, clothing, and cash resources to aid the black families. Henderson also asked Governor Buford Ellington to order a "thorough and objective investi-gation of the Fayette County situation." The Memphis branch of the NAACP also supplied emergency relief in the form of food and clothing.

Because of the complicity of the oil companies, the national office of the NAACP urged its 350,000 members to boycott the products of oil companies whose Tennessee agents refused to sell fuel to the beleaguered African Amer-ican families in Fayette County. In early August, the national Gulf, Esso, Tex-aco, and Amoco oil companies broke the fuel and gas embargo. Earlier in the year, John McFerren of the FCCWL attended a meeting of the Southern Con-ference Educational Fund (SCEF), a liberal white organization that supported the freedom struggles of blacks. At the Washington meeting, McFerren informed the group that black tenant farmers and sharecroppers faced eco-nomic pressure and intimidation by white landowners of Fayette County. He also told how local gas dealers of major oil companies refused to sell fuel to himself and others. McFerren asked the SCFC to publicize the Fayette County movement and to raise relief funds. Officials of the SCEF contacted support-ers with oil stock to pressure the companies involved.[32]

Roy Wilkins, executive secretary of the national NAACP, called upon the American Red Cross to assist in what he called "a man-made disaster" in Tennessee. He asked the Red Cross to take immediate steps to bring relief to the county's Negro families who met with economic retaliation after regis-tering to vote.[33] Responding to the need of the people, on 5 July 1960 the NAACP delivered seventy-five bags of food and clothing to the black resi-dents. "It's plumb ridiculous," said Mayor Yancey. "There is no need evident in this county." A similar statement came from George Green, chairman of the county's Red Cross chapter.[34]

In August 1960, the incessant racial ferocity endured by African Ameri-cans in Fayette County captivated the attention of Ted Poston. Poston, a veteran newspaperman from Kentucky, served in President Franklin Roosevelt's "Black Cabinet" as racial advisor in the Office of War Information.[35] In a six-article exposé for the *New York Post,* Poston brought the activities of the FCCWL and the oppressive treatment rendered by whites to national attention.

But the negative publicity failed to temper the hostile white response. In September, the Fayette *Falcon* warned that white farm owners would evict Negro tenants off the land, if they registered to vote. Said McFerren, "Once you registered you had to move."[36] As the harvesting season came to a close and the crops were gathered, whites followed through on their threat in November when eight black families were forced off land owned by Ellis Watkins, Bynum Leatherwood, and Mrs. Henry G. McNamee.[37] Without fear and hesitation and with the support of Shepherd Towels, an African American property owner, the FCCWL established a makeshift community with thirteen drab green surplus U.S. Army tents. Said Towels, "These people had nowhere to go. I . . . let them come in free, let them use water from my deep well, as long as it lasts."[38] Known as "Tent City," its new inhabitants prepared themselves to face the bitter winds of winter. The settlement, albeit a locale of merciless misery, became an undaunted declaration of African American self-esteem.

Fifty-eight-year-old Georgia Mae Turner, who was evicted by Mrs. McNamee, exemplifies why African Americans defied the segregationist system of Fayette County. She stated: "The reason I registered. . . . I want to be a citizen and I want my freedom. I registered so that my children could get their freedom. I registered so my children won't have to stand around at the back door in the rain and cold and Mrs. McNamee sat in the front until she got ready to come to the back to see what I wanted. I wouldn't want none of my children, none of my friends, to have to come through it, run, rocking and rolling, over the hills and mountains that I come over."[39]

Shortly after the first city of tents was erected, leaders of the FCCWL established a second camp outside Moscow. It was located off Highway 57 on land owned by an African American woman, Gertrude Beasley. Landowners contended that the mass termination of tenant leases and sharecropper contracts was a result of mechanization. They echoed the sentiments of the mayor, who thought that the Tent City community of evicted Negro tenant farmers was a "propaganda stunt" and that all of the trouble, including the effort to vote, was instigated by northern educators. The property owners also cited the blacks' refusal to accept offers of interstate and intrastate employment in places where they were in a minority and farmhands were needed. "There are more than a half dozen white farmers not fifty miles from here advertising in the local papers," said one white. "But these Negroes don't want a job."[40]

The November election witnessed a larger number of African American voters and more Republican votes than usual. In Fayette County, where John Doar of the Eisenhower Justice Department sued to protect blacks, twelve hundred new black votes helped turn the county Republican for the first time since Reconstruction; they did, however, vote for Democratic senatorial candidate Estes Kefauver. Nationally, the vote was interpreted to mean that blacks in the South would reward those who helped them gain the right to vote.[41]

On 14 December 1960, the U.S, Department of Justice moved to stop the economic reprisals against African Americans who registered and voted in Fayette County. Filed in the federal district court in Memphis, the Justice Department attorneys sought a temporary injunction against the landowners, who evicted four hundred African Americans. Accused of using "intimidation, threats, and coercion," some eighty-two parties were named as defendants in the case, including forty-five landowners, twenty-four merchants, and the Somerville Bank and Trust Company. Some of the county's most influential citizens were named in the suit.[42] Among other practices, they were charged with (1) terminating leases and sharecropper arrangements held by blacks who voted; (2) dismissing black employees involved in the voting campaign; (3) refusing to sell supplies to black registrants, even for cash, and refusing others the credit they had always had; (4) canceling insurance polices of blacks who had registered; and (5) persuading whites to join in the economic pressure by circulating lists of black voters and refusing to deal with white merchants and others believed sympathetic to black voting. In addition to the temporary injunctions to stop the evictions, the suit sought permanent injunctions against any efforts to discourage black voting.[43]

The legal action sought by the Justice Department invoked the 1957 Civil Rights Act, which prohibited intimidations or coercion to discourage registration or voting because of race. This litigation was significant because it sought to alleviate pressures inflicted by individuals in racial matters. All previous lawsuits had been directed at state actions. Anthony Lewis, author of *Portrait of a Decade: The Second American Revolution*, described attorney John Doar's efforts in Haywood and Fayette Counties as "the most imaginative use" of the 1957 civil rights legislation.[44]

Because of the decision by the U.S. Sixth Circuit Court of Appeals in the Haywood County case, which was similar to the Fayette County case, on

30 December 1960, federal district judge Marion S. Boyd issued a temporary restraining order blocking the evictions of the four hundred sharecroppers of African descent. A week earlier, Boyd decided not to hold a hearing, pending the disposition of the Haywood County case.[45] For the first time in almost a century, the U.S. government actively engaged itself in the defense of civil rights for African Americans. The week of hearings, decisions, and appeals culminated in a temporary restraining order prohibiting landowners from executing the evictions scheduled for 1 January 1961. Since the Haywood County eviction case was before the Sixth Circuit Court of Appeals in Cincinnati, Boyd, on 13 January, indefinitely continued the temporary restraining order stopping the eviction of Fayette County black sharecroppers. The appellate court ordered no evictions of Negro sharecroppers "simply because that negro tenant registered to vote." However, the appellate court did state that evictions might occur for "legitimate causes." The judge said, before he took action anywhere in the district court level, he intended to await further appellate court action.[46] Earlier, Boyd ruled the 1957 Civil Rights Act did not give authority to tamper with property and contract rights.[47] In their own defense, white landowners continued to insist that farm mechanization reduced the need for black workers.

Scores of sharecropping families sought sanctuary in Tent City. Not content with having evicted African Americans from the farmlands, hate groups such as the White Citizens' Council and Ku Klux Klan fired shots into the tents to terrorize the residents. On 28 December 1960, armed whites in vehicles shot into Early B. Williams's tent, which faced the road. "It shook the whole tent. . . . I didn't know what happened and my wife said, 'You're shot!' "[48]

White supremacist hoodlums perpetrated acts of violence and physical harm upon black Fayette Countians, but blacks did not retaliate in kind. They, as their student counterparts who were conducting sit-ins in Nashville, Knoxville, Greensboro, North Carolina, and other cities across the South, applied the strategy of nonviolent resistance. Said John McFerren, "The Fayette County Civic and Welfare League is committed to a policy of nonviolence." "Nonviolence is the way," advised Square Moorman. "Just think of our Lord Savior Jesus. On the cross. . . . He turned to his Father and said, 'Father forgive them, they know not what they do.' They crucified Him. . . . He is our example."[49]

In December, Senator Estes Kefauver asked the Red Cross, the U.S. Department of Agriculture, and other agencies to aid evicted blacks. On 29 December, Gen. Alfred M. Gruenther, president of the American Red Cross, said the organization could not come to the aid of the evicted sharecroppers in Fayette County. However, local Red Cross chapters were authorized to join with community organizations "to alleviate suffering." He added, "It has been felt that such problems must necessarily be the responsibility of Government at appropriate levels."[50] Six days later, U.S. Department of Agriculture officials announced that, because "there was no urgent need," they would not send surplus food to sharecroppers in Fayette County. During his visit a week earlier, James W. Hutchens Jr., director of the distribution center, took note that food was being received from other sources across the nation. "I talked with people on both sides of the color line," said the director. "They both told me that there was no emergency." Governor Buford Ellington also implied that residents of Tent City needed no aid,[51] although the "man-made disaster" of Tent City caused a massive food and clothing drive. Food and clothing poured in from across the nation. Individuals, groups, and organizations sent donations in support of Fayette County's black citizens. The AFL-CIO Executive Council voted two thousand dollars to the Tennessee Labor Council to aid the evictees. Food and clothing were donated by Local 259 of the United Automobile Workers and Local 6 of the Hotel and Club Employees Union. Trucks were driven by members of the Teamsters Union, whose services were donated by the New York Joint Council of the International Brotherhood of Teamsters. Other unions and their locals sent assistance into the area as well. The Emergency Relief Committee, a subcommittee of Chicago CORE, organized mass support for evicted black tenant sharecroppers. The Packinghouse Workers pledged help on many fronts of the racial war. They voted to send a delegation to investigate purchasing land for those residing in tents and to send monthly checks to the FCCWL. They wrote a pamphlet on the crisis titled Tent City, "Home of the Brave" and successfully convinced the Industrial Union Department of the CIO to print and widely distribute the pamphlet. Additionally, the AFL-CIO Industrial Union Council of Cook County voted its support.[52]

In July 1960, the executive council of the Highlander Folk School approved the staff's plan to aid black voter registration. Any adult who "lived in the community where a school was to be established and who had at least some high school education, an ability to read well aloud and write clearly on the blackboard, and some familiarity with state voting and election systems and community services could become a teacher."[53] The following spring, the leadership of FCCWL sent fifteen individuals, including women and twelve students from Lane College in Jackson, to teacher-training workshops at Highlander. Most of those who attended the study sessions voted for the first time in the November 1960 elections. The purpose of the workshops was to train individuals to establish Citizenship Schools in their respective communities. The sessions proved beneficial to Fayette County's civil rights leaders. Armed with knowledge acquired from the training sessions, participants returned to the county, and, with funds provided by the staff of Highlander, established a Citizenship School. Of the 141 adults who enrolled in the school, 95 (67 percent) became registered voters by July 1961.[54]

After John F. Kennedy was elected president of the United States in 1960, one of the questions asked at his first press conference concerned the struggle for civil rights in Fayette County: "Does your administration plan to take any steps to solve the problem at Fayette County, Tennessee, where tenant farmers have been evicted from their homes because they voted last November and must now live in tents?" The president responded: "The Congress, of course, enacted legislation, which placed very clear responsibility on the Executive Branch to protect the right of voting. I am extremely interested in making sure that every American is given the right to cast his vote without prejudice to his right as a citizen. And therefore I can state that this Administration will pursue the problems of providing that protection with all vigor."[55]

On 14 June 1961 Kennedy authorized Secretary of Agriculture Orville Freeman to send surplus food to Fayette and Haywood Counties. Kennedy said the food shipments were authorized under Section 416 of the 1939 Agriculture Act as amended. State officials impeded execution and distribution of the program, saying it was not needed. Local landowners insisted that the food distribution program was not needed because of the excellence of the cotton crop and surplus workers would be in demand. Said John Wilder, a wealthy landowner, "I [am] particularly surprised that surplus food was ordered. We are right in the middle of the cotton crop. Cotton chopping will begin shortly and not only will we use all of the surplus labor here, but we will have to import field hands. . . . There is plenty of work available for anyone who wants to work." However, only six months earlier, landowners argued that the labor force surpassed the need. Now the surplus had diminished and the scarcity of workers rendered the federal distribution of food superfluous.[56]

While Wilder was surprised about the federal government's shipment of surplus food to victims of the white-segregationist blockade, he was one of the few landowners who did not evict black tenant farmers from his property, and he refused to call in 365 crop loans against potential voters. His refusals caused him to be subjected to white enmity. Even his fellow Methodist church members urged him to call in the loans. "Members of white churches were involved in trying to stop Blacks from voting," said Wilder. "According to the leadership in the white church, if you were a good white person, you had to do what they said, which was, if they [blacks] registered to vote, you had to move them off the farm and you had to cut-off their finances. I couldn't do what they wanted me to do. And I didn't."[57]

Although the majority of white Fayette Countians supported the economic squeeze placed on African Americans, some whites provided their black neighbors with covert assistance. According to Minnie Jameson, Viola McFerren, and Lavearn Towels, clothing and food sometimes appeared "from nowhere" at the homes of blacks, and they agree that the much-needed articles were given by whites who did not support the "lock out" of blacks from the economic and political systems of the county.[58]

In March 1961, the Reverend Dr. Joseph H. Jackson, president of the nation's largest African American denomination, the National Baptist Convention, USA, announced the February purchase of four hundred acres of land in Fayette County. Part of the "farm aid plan" adopted by the denomination, according to Memphis resident Dr. W. H. Brewster, who served as chairman of the convention's National Education Board, called for relocating Tent City residents into houses on the land and building others.[59]

Often, when grass-roots organizations are established and certain leaders acquire a degree of influence and support, egos, jealously, and mistrust invade the ranks and cause an organizational fissure. Early in 1961, internal organizational conflict developed between John McFerren, chairman, and Scott Franklin, president of FCCWL. As reported by James Forman, Franklin was opposed to many of the things that McFerren was doing. McFerren was unwilling to abandon his organization and become part of the NAACP's Memphis branch. The factional chasm centered around the dismissal of attorney Estes, who manipulated the internal discord and assisted Scott Franklin in surrendering the organization's charter to the secretary of state's office in Nashville. Because the charter was not registered in the county, the Franklin group, led by Estes, stated that the organization was operating illegally. Franklin subsequently filed a new charter and held a press conference to announce John McFerren's ouster. However, upon the advice of their attorney, R. B. J. Campbell of Nashville, McFerren took a group of supporters to Nashville and incorporated another organization under the name of the Original Fayette County Civic and Welfare League (OFCCWL). The incorporators of the new organization were: John and Viola McFerren, Noah McFerren, John Lewis, Leveam Towels, Shephard Towels Sr., Ray Brown, and June Dowdy. The two groups went to court and the monetary assets, food, clothing, and supplies were divided between the OFCCWL and the FCCWL.[60]

Labor unions, churches, and other organizations committed to the movement in Fayette County supported the McFerren group, which was recognized as the coordinating group for the distribution of food, clothing, money, and other commodities to relieve the suffering of people in Tent City. The OFC-CWL continued the movement for African American civil rights in Fayette County. With assistance from various sources across the nation, the OFC-CWL distributed food and clothing on Wednesdays and Saturdays, under a system of districts with district officers who submitted the names of individuals in need. It paid crop loans, medical bills, and purchased sorely needed tents for its army of newly registered black voters. The league secured scholarships for the county's African American children and instituted a program of adult education in reading and writing. An office to handle the league's business affairs was set up with basic equipment and a mimeograph machine.[61]

After almost two years of court battles between the landowners and the United States Justice Department, a consent decree was filed in federal district court in Memphis on 26 July 1962. The decree ended all pending lawsuits against the defendants accused of using economic pressure to prevent the registration of African American voters. Signed by federal district judge Marion S. Boyd and Lucius E. Burch Jr., attorney for the white landowners, the agreement permanently enjoined the defendants from "engaging in any acts . . . for the purpose of interfering with the right of any person to register to vote and to vote for candidates for public office." The decree was identical to an out-of-court settlement reached in Washington on 1 May between the Justice Department and the seventy Haywood County landowners. The order listed seventy-four owners as defendants and dismissed charges against six others, including the Somerville Bank and Trust Company. By agreeing to the final judgment, the Justice Department stated that the landowners were doing so "without constituting evidence of admission . . . with respect to the issues of fact." The defendants bore no cost for the lengthy legal battles. The decree ordered the federal court to retain jurisdiction in the case for the "purpose of enforcement of the provisions."[62]

Brought to the court on 14 December 1960, the lawsuit charged the landowners of using "intimidation, threats, and coercion," including the eviction of African American farmers who attempted to register to vote. Of the seventy-four defendants named, four were women, and only one of the county's public officials was dismissed from the case. The order made no mention of black tenant farmers who were released for reasons other than voting. In addition to the Somerville Bank and Trust Company and John S.

Wilder, the solitary public official, the judgment dismissed action against four others, including two women.[63]

"In 1959, all we had in mind was registering and voting," said Minnie Jameson. "We didn't have an organization, all we wanted was the vote. . . . If they [whites] had left us alone, we would have gone and registered and voted . . . and that might have been the end. We didn't want to control the county, we just wanted to be part of the county."[64] When John S. Wilder was asked where he stood on the issue of blacks in Fayette County being denied the right of franchise, he replied, "Thomas Jefferson said, 'These truths are self-evident, all men are created equal' . . . to pursue life, liberty and happiness. . . . I believe from the depth of my heart all persons under the law are created equally." Continuing, he paraphrased the Apostle Paul's Epistle to the Colossians and further stated, "In love there is neither Greek nor Jew, slave nor free, black nor white, female nor male, Republican nor Democrat. I believe that and so it seems wrong to me that a person's skin should deny them the right to vote."[65]

Even though a settlement was reached between the U.S. Department of Justice and the landowners, Fayette County continued to attract attention from across the nation. In 1963, as residents of Tent City began moving into homes made available through low-interest government loans, student activists from college and universities across the country came to the county and assisted the OFCCWL in setting up summer workshops to further embolden voter-registration. Said Viola McFerren, "Many of the student volunteers were white men and women interested in assisting the Civil Rights movement in Fayette County." The first group arrived in 1962. One of the first white students encountered by members of the league was Charlie Butts from Oberlin College. "This was the first time I worked with a white person, and I didn't know if he could be trusted," said Minnie Jameson. "But after he stayed with us . . . he became . . . one of us. I no longer thought about his color."[66]

In 1964 and 1965, a large contingency of students from Cornell University came to the county and resided in the homes of black families. They and the OFCCWL conducted one of the most rigorous voter-registration drives. These civil rights activists, paired in teams of blacks and whites, crisscrossed the county's fifteen districts and urged blacks to register and vote. Through their efforts, forty-three hundred blacks were added to the registration rolls. Two years after the Justice Department reached a settlement with the landowners in Fayette and Haywood Counties, on 2 July 1964, Congress passed the Civil Rights Act of 1964. The most important civil rights law since 1875, and the most encompassing civil rights legislation ever proposed and enacted, the statute was designed to ensure maximum freedom and equality for African Americans in as many spheres of the public domain as possible. Separate titles covered voting, public accommodations, public facilities, education, and fair employment practices. The powers of the CCR were broadened and provisions were made for the establishment of two other agencies to facilitate the act's implementation.[67]

There were enough registered black voters to dominate the 1964 Fayette County election for tax assessor and sheriff. The Reverend June Dowdy ran for tax assessor, and L. T. Redfearn ran for sheriff. According to Robert Hamburger's *Our Portion of Hell*, the election was stolen at the polls. In one district, 51 whites and 88 blacks were counted voting, but when the votes came, in the white candidate received 201 votes, and Dowdy received 72 votes. In Hamburger's opinion, tallied votes across the county bore little relation to the actual vote.[68] Blacks did not let the county's "business as usual" syndrome deter them from their position of activism. They moved on to the next battle in the war of racial justice.

Impelled by the success of their warfare to register and vote, in 1965, leaders of the OFCCWL led the fight to desegregate the public schools in Fayette County. Viola McFerren became a plaintiff in the county's school desegregation case on behalf of her son, John McFerren Jr. The suit was filed in order to compel local school officials to comply with the desegregation order enunciated in the 1954 *Brown* decision. Nashville civil rights attorney Avon N. Williams Jr. provided legal counsel for the plaintiffs. One year later, the case was adjudicated and the board of education was ordered to desegregate its school system. Because they were the original plaintiffs in the school desegregation case, Viola McFerren and others intervened in 1970 in a federal court case instigated by thirteen African American teachers who were dismissed by the Fayette County board of education. Again, the federal court ruled in favor of the plaintiffs.[69]

Though many of the formal racial barriers had crumbled, African Americans in Fayette County still encountered racist attitudes and behaviors, ranging from police brutality to insulting treatment from white businesses. Because of this, Viola McFerren assisted in organizing a refusal-to-purchase offensive against local white merchants. She not only worked to bring about civil and social changes in the county, but she traveled outside county lines to expose Fayette's callous, cruel, and unfair treatment of its African American residents.[70]

The march from Selma to Montgomery, Alabama, in March 1965, marred by the deaths of Viola Liuzzo and the Reverend James Reeb, convinced the nation that additional legislation was needed to further guarantee the voting rights of African Americans. On 6 August 1965, the United States Congress passed the 1965 Voting Rights Act. In August 1966, the first black men and women were elected to the Fayette County Quarterly Court: Gladys Allen (Oakland community); Gerldine Johnson (Bernard Community, Mason); Sherman Perry (Oakland); Cooper Parks (Rossville); Charlie Minor (Somerville); and William Hayslett (Rossville).[71]

Six years after the 1965 Voting Rights Act was passed, in 1971, the Tennessee Committee to the United States Commission on Civil Rights found ten voting rights violations in Fayette County. These violations ranged from blacks being systematically discriminated against in the appointment of election officials, to 4:00 P.M. poll closings on election day.[72]

Today, seven of Fayette County's commissioners are African Americans, and they serve on the town boards in Oakland, Moscow, and Gallaway. Although they serve on the school board, no person of African American heritage has ever won a countywide election. While many communities in the South battled racial conflicts similar to those that shattered Fayette County in the 1950s and 1960s, most conformed to the changes brought about by the modern Civil Rights movement. However, racial hostilities kindled by the county's warring factions left penetrating wounds that still remain infected and festering. Because of the efforts of Viola McFerren and the OFCCWL, all that remains of Tent City or "Freedom Village," as it was also called, is a historical marker commemorating the challenges overcome by its residents.[73] The battle waged and the byproduct of its consequences are always in the hearts and minds of its participants.

Ever vigilant for their cause, blacks of Fayette County, who possessed extraordinary capabilities and courage, actively pursued their rights as citizens. They did not sit by calmly enduring the racial rigidity and waiting for organized assistance to come from the outside to foster economic, political, and social change. With determined collective action and propelling thrust, they began the process of forging change. As W. E. B. Du Bois declared, "There can be no perfect democracy curtailed by color, race, or poverty. But with all we accomplish all, even peace."

Notes

1. The modern Civil Rights movement refers to that period beginning with the decision handed down by the United States Supreme Court in *Brown v. Board of Education of Topeka, Kansas* (1954) and waning after Congress passed the 1964 Civil Rights Act. According to Alton Hornsby Jr., this ten-year period was a

resurgence of the progress aborted by the end of Reconstruction in the 1870s
and 1880s. The attainments and the advancements that emerged were so
consequential that numerous people believed that the period could be termed
the "Second Reconstruction" See Alton Hornsby Jr., *African American History:
Significant Events and People from 1619 to the Present* (Detroit, 1991), xxxiv–xxxv;
C. Vann Woodward states, "This historic movement falls into two fairly distinctive
periods divided by the Supreme Court decisions of 1954 and 1955 on segregation
in public schools. In the first period the executive and judicial branches of
government took initiative in inaugurating reform, while Congress and public
opinion remained largely unresponsive. In the second period, Civil Rights groups
responded with direct action that eventually aroused public support and stirred
Congress into unprecedented and effective action." See C. Vann Woodward, *The
Strange Career of Jim Crow* (New York, 1965), 135.

2. This sentiment is illustrated in G. Plekhanov, *The Individual's Role in History*,
   quoted in Isaac Deutscher, *The Prophet Outcast: Trotsky, 1929–1940* (New York,
   1963), 242–43.
3. Dorothy Rich Morton, *Fayette County* (Memphis, 1989), 3, 74-75.
4. Bettina Aptheker, *Women's Legacy: Essays on Race, Sex, and Class in American
   History* (Amherst, Mass., 1982), 57.
5. Ibid.; Stephen B. Weeks, "History of Negro Suffrage," *Political Science Quarterly* 9
   (Dec. 1894): 680.
6. Richard Kluger, *Simple Justice: The History of Brown v. Board of Education and Black
   America's Struggle for Equality* (New York, 1976), 67.
7. Steven F. Lawson, *Black Ballots* (New York, 1976), 11; George S. Stoney, "Suffrage
   in the South, Part 1, The Poll Tax," *Survey Graphics* 29 (1940): 8-9.
8. Kermit Hall, William M. Wieck, and Paul Finkleman, *American Legal History:
   Cases and Materials* (New York, 1991), 446.
9. Lawson, *Black Ballots*, 26-29, 35.
10. Hall, Wieck, and Finkleman, *American Legal History*, 447; Lawson, *Black Ballots*,
    45; *Smith v. Allwright*, 321 U.S. 664. In deciding this case the Supreme Court relied
    on the earlier Nixon cases and the *United States v. Classic* (1941) cases. When
    Thurgood Marshall, who litigated the *Smith* and *Brown* cases before the Supreme
    Court, was asked what case was more important, he stated he did not know.
    "Without the ballot you've got no . . . citizenship, no status, no power, in this
    country," Marshall said, "but without the chance to get an education you have no
    capacity to use the ballot effectively." See Carl T. Rowan, *Dream Makers, Dream
    Breakers* (New York, 1993), 129.
11. *Terry v. Adams*, 345 U.S. 461 (1953); According to Steven F. Lawson, the final
    nail that sealed the white primary's coffin was when African Americans in Texas'
    Fort Bend County successfully brought suit against the Jaybird Association in the
    Supreme Court case of *Terry v. Adams*.
12. Albert P. Blaustein and Robert Zangrando, eds., *Civil Rights and African Americans*
    (Evanston, Ill., 1991), 471.
13. Richard A. Couto, *Lifting the Veil: A Political History of the Struggle for Emancipation*
    (Knoxville, 1993), 191-192.
14. Pauline Keller and Bob Koeing, "Tent City Came to Symbolize Blacks' Struggle for
    Equality." *Fayette Falcon*, 12 Apr. 1995.
15. Robert Hamburger, *Our Portion of Hell, Fayette County, Tennessee: An Oral
    History of the Struggle for Civil Rights* (New York, 1973), 4.; Minnie Jameson, Viola
    McFerren, and Lavearn Towels, interview with author, Fayette County, Tenn., 16

June 1995; Couto, *Lifting the Veil*, 192. Couto has written extensively on the voter registration drive and the subsequent establishment of Tent City in Haywood County. In addition to *Lifting the Veil*, see his *Ain't Gonna Let Nobody Turn Me Around: The Pursuit of Racial Justice in the Rural South* (Philadelphia, 1991).

16. Jameson, interview; Hamburger, *Our Portion of Hell*, 32.
17. U.S. Bureau of the Census, *U.S. Census of Population: 1950*, vol. 2, *Characteristics of the Population, Part 42, Tennessee* (Washington, D.C., 1952), 93; U.S. Bureau of the Census, *U.S. Census of Population: 1960*, vol. 2, *Characteristics of the Population, Part 42, Tennessee* (Washington, D.C., 1962); *Report of the United States Commission on Civil Rights* (Washington, D.C., 1959), 64.
18. *Report of the United States Commission on Civil Rights*, 64.
19. "Court Again Bars Negro Evictions," *New York Times*, 6 June 1961; Hamburger, *Our Portion of Hell*, 3; Keller and Koeing, "Tent City."
20. Linda T. Wynn "Viola Harris McFerren: Civil Rights and Social Activist" in *Notable Black American Women*, ed. Jessie Carney (Detroit, 1995), 447. Early in Fayette County's Civil Rights movement, in addition to James Estes, legal assistance was provided by Memphis attorneys Benjamin Hooks, Russell B. Sugarmon Jr. and A. W. Willis Jr. Jameson, McFerren, and Towels, interview. Willis became the first African American in modern times (1965) elected to Tennessee General Assembly. Sugarmon also served in the assembly. See Ilene J. Cornwell, *Biographical Directory of the Tennessee General Assembly, 1951-1971* (Nashville, 1990), 5:431-432; 476-477.
21. "Suit Is First Under New Act," *Memphis Commercial Appeal*, 17 Nov. 1957. Plaintiffs in the case were John McFerren, Charlie Harrison, Harpman Jameson, George F. Jones, Albert L. Murrell, John C. Lewis, Scott F. Franklin, Isaiah Harris, William M. Person, Will Watson, Clinton Murrell, and William S. Towels Sr. Defendants named in the case were Hugh Preston Parks Jr., chairman of the Fayette County Democratic Executive Committee; Joe N. Cocke, secretary; James L. Day; Homer Smith; and James Samuel Rhea, John S. Wilder Sr., Dr. L. D. McAuley, Albert Thomas, Sam F. Dunn, Robert Lee Tacker, Bernard Franklin, Herman K. Crawford, and M. Wilburn Parks Jr., individually and as members of the executive committee. Other defendants were Hugh P. Parks Sr., chairman; Joe N. Cocke, secretary; and William T. Boyd, Dr. John W. Morris, William H. Cocke, and H. Clay McCarley, individually and as members of the central committee of the executive committee.
22. Ibid.
23. Ibid.
24. "Election Aides Quit: Four in Tennessee Protest Investigation by F.B.I.," *New York Times*, 16 Mar. 1960.
25. Ibid.
26. "A Tennessee Area Backs Negro Vote," *New York Times*, 26 Apr. 1960.
27. "156 Negroes Register," *New York Times*, 8 Sept. 1960.
28. "Cold War in Fayette County," *Ebony Magazine*, Sept. 1960, 27-34; *Voting, 1961 Commission on Civil Rights Report* (Washington, D.C., 1961), 36-37.
29. "Cold War in Fayette County," 27-34.
30. "Negroes Plan Counterattack," *Ebony Magazine*, Sept. 1960, 30.
31. "Cold War in Fayette County," 28.
32. Ted Poston, "NAACP Urges Oil Firm Boycott in Tennessee" *New York Post*, 7–8 July 1960; ibid., "The Right to Vote and the Right to Live," ibid., 13 Aug. 1960; Post articles provided by Larry E. Armstrong Jr., White Plains, N.Y.; Dr. Vivian

Henderson of Fisk University was also the impetus behind the economic boycott of white merchants by blacks during the Nashville sit-in movement. See Linda T. Wynn, "The Dawning of a New Day: The Nashville Sit-Ins, February 13–May 10," *Tennessee Historical Quarterly* 50 (Spring 1991): 42-54.

33. "Boycott of Negroes Stirs Plea," *New York Times*, 2 July 1960.

34. "Food Sent to Negroes," *New York Times*, 6 July 1960.

35. John Hope Franklin, *From Slavery to Freedom: A History of Black Americans* (New York, 1994), 351.

36. Hamburger, *Our Portion of Hell*, 8.

37. Keller and Koeing, "Tent City."

38. AFL-CIO, Industrial Union Department, *Tent City "Home of the Brave"* (Washington, D.C.: AFL-CIO, 1961), 12.

39. James Forman, *The Making of Black Revolutionaries* (New York, 1968), 126.

40. "Negroes' Tent City Decried as Stunt," *New York Times*, 29 Dec. 1960; "Negroes Await Eviction Moves," ibid., 1 Jan. 1960.

41. Taylor Branch, *Parting the Water: America in the King Years, 1954-1963* (New York, 1988), 382.

42. Keller and Koeing, "Tent City." Citizens named in the suit included state representative David Givens; Somerville mayor I. P. Yancey; county tax assessor Joseph M. Jordan; and county commissioner John S. Wilder, currently lieutenant governor of Tennessee. For a list of those included in the lawsuit as defendants, see "U.S., Fayette Landowners End Suit," *Memphis Commercial Appeal*, 27 July 1962.

43. "U.S. Fights Abuse of Negro Voters," *New York Times*, 14 Dec. 1960.

44. Anthony Lewis, *Portrait of a Decade: The Second American Revolution* (New York, 1964), 113.

45. "Court Acts Today on Negro Tenants," *New York Times*, 30 Dec. 1960; "Negroes' Eviction Stayed by Courts," ibid., 31 Dec. 1960.

46. "Judge Boyd Waiting on Evictions: Action Now Up to Appellate Court," *Memphis Press Scimitar*, 13 Jan. 1961; "Restraint Extended on Negro Evictions," *New York Times*, 14 Jan. 1961.

47. "Negroes' Tent City Decried as Stunt."

48. "Negro Wounded," *New York Times*, 30 Dec. 1960; Hamburger, *Our Portion of Hell*, 74–75.

49. "Negroes Plan Counterattack," 30; Keller and Koeing, "Tent City."

50. "Negroes' Tent City Decried as Stunt"; "Red Cross Notes Plight," *New York Times*, 30 Dec. 1960.

51. "U.S. Won't Give Food," *New York Times*, 5 Jan. 1961; "Tennessee Governor Doubts Evicted Negroes Need N.Y. Aid," *New York Post*, 13 Jan. 1961.

52. AFL-CIO, *Tent City "Home of the Brave"*; "Sharecroppers Aided: Unions Here Send Ten Tons of Supplies to Tent City," *New York Times*, 16 Feb. 1961; Forman, *Making of Black Revolutionaries*, 133.

53. John M. Glen, *Highlander: No Ordinary School, 1932-1962* (Lexington, 1988), 167–168.

54. Ibid., 169.

55. "Transcript of President Kennedy's First News Conference," *New York Times*, 26 Jan. 1961.

56. "President Orders Food for Negroes," *New York Times*, 14 June 1961; John Wilder, Somerville attorney and one of the largest landowners in the Fayette County quoted, in "West Tennessee Food Seen Kennedy Bid for Support," *Nashville*

Banner, 19 July 1961; "U.S. Pays Grocery Bill for Fayette, Haywood Negroes," ibid., 18 July 1961; "Free Handouts Results in Squabble," ibid., 14 July 1961; Couto, *Lifting the Veil,* 205.

57. Lt. Gov. John S. Wilder, interview with author, 25 July 1995.
58. Jameson, McFerren, and Towels, interview.
59. "Negroes Buy Farm for Evicted Tenants," *New York Times,* 19 Feb. 1961; "Group of Baptist Spurs Farm Plan," ibid., 15 Mar. 1961.
60. Jameson, McFerren, and Towels, interview; Forman, *Making of Black Revolutionaries,* 132-133; "Negro Leader Evicted," *New York Times,* 28 Jan. 1961.
61. Jameson, McFerren, and Towels interview; AFL-CIO, *Tent City;* Forman, *Making of Black Revolutionaries,* 133.
62. "U.S., Fayette Landowners End Suits," *Memphis Commercial Appeal,* 27 July 1962.
63. Ibid.; Wilder, interview.
64. Jameson, interview.
65. Wilder, interview.
66. Jameson, interview.
67. Blaustein and Zangrando, *Civil Rights and African Americans,* 525.
68. Hamburger, *Our Portion of Hell,* 87.
69. Wynn, "Viola Harris McFerren," 447. Other parties to the school desegregation lawsuit included Mr. and Mrs. Houston Gray, Mr. and Mrs. Willie Elsberry, Mr. and Mrs. William H. Ghilchrease, Mr. and Mrs. Simon Wilderson, and Mr. and Mrs. Sanford Wright; Jameson, McFerren, and Towels, interview.
70. Wynn, "Viola Harris McFerren," 447.
71. Keller and Koeing, "Tent City"; Jameson, McFerren, and Towels, interview. In 1966, after blacks registered to vote, whites in Lowndes County, Alabama, evicted African American sharecroppers and the Lowndes County Freedom Organization established a Tent City. As in the Fayette County case, Lowndes County's Tent City was located on black-owned property. See Henry Hampton and Steve Fayer, *Voices of Freedom: An Oral History of the Civil Rights Movement from the 1950s through the 1980s* (New York, 1990), 267-282.
72. *Fear Runs Deep: A Report by the Tennessee State Advisory Committee to the U.S. Commission on Civil Rights,* 17–18 Mar. 1971, Somerville, Tenn.
73. Wynn, "Viola Harris McFerren," 448. A Tennessee Historical Commission marker was approved in 1990 and placed on State Highway 76 and County Road 195 and LaGrange Road, just south of the Somerville city limits.

Contributors

JUNE N. ADAMSON is professor emeritus from the University of Tennessee, Knoxville, where she taught in the School of Journalism. Her chapter originally appeared in the spring 1994 issue of the *Tennessee Historical Quarterly*.

BEVERLY G. BOND is an associate professor of history at the University of Memphis. Her chapter originally appeared in the winter 2000 issue of the *Tennessee Historical Quarterly*.

MARIUS CARRIERE JR. is a professor of history at Christian Brothers University. His chapter originally appeared in the spring 1989 issue of the *Tennessee Historical Quarterly*.

RICHARD COUTO is a professor at the Jepson School for Leadership Studies at the University of Richmond. His chapter originally appeared in the summer 1996 issue of the *Tennessee Historical Quarterly*.

GARY T. EDWARDS is a graduate assistant at the University of Memphis. His chapter originally appeared in the spring/summer 1998 issue of the *Tennessee Historical Quarterly*.

CYNTHIA GRIGGS FLEMING is an associate professor at the University of Tennessee, Knoxville. Her chapter originally appeared in the spring 1990 issue of the *Tennessee Historical Quarterly*.

KENNETH W. GOINGS is chair of the Department of African American and African Studies at the Ohio State University. His chapter originally appeared in the summer 1996 issue of the *Tennessee Historical Quarterly* and has been reprinted in *Tennessee History: The Land, the People, and the Culture*, edited by Carroll Van West (University of Tennessee Press, 1998).

ANITA S. GOODSTEIN was a professor of history at the University of the South. Her chapter appeared in the winter 1979 issue of the *Tennessee Historical Quarterly*.

DOROTHY GRANBERRY is a professor in the Department of Psychology at Tennessee State University. Her chapter originally appeared in the spring 1997 issue of the *Tennessee Historical Quarterly*.

WALI R. KHARIF is a professor of history at Tennessee Technological University. His chapter originally appeared in the spring 1997 issue of the *Tennessee Historical Quarterly*.

BOBBY L. LOVETT is a professor of history at Tennessee State University. His chapter originally appeared in the spring 1982 issue of the *Tennessee Historical Quarterly*.

LARRY MCKEE is the Nashville branch manager and senior archaeologist with Garrow Associates. His chapter originally appeared in the fall 2000 issue of the *Tennessee Historical Quarterly*.

KENNETH B. MOORE received his M.A. in history from Auburn University. His chapter originally appeared in the summer 1995 issue of the *Tennessee Historical Quarterly*.

BRIAN D. PAGE is a graduate assistant at the University of Memphis. His chapter originally appeared in the winter 1999 issue of the *Tennessee Historical Quarterly*.

ELISABETH I. PERRY holds the Bannon Chair in History at St. Louis University. Her chapter originally appeared in the spring 1993 issue of the *Tennessee Historical Quarterly*.

PAUL DAVID PHILLIPS received his doctorate in history from Vanderbilt University and has served as a professor at Tennessee State University and Lipscomb University. His chapter originally appeared in the summer 1987 issue of the *Tennessee Historical Quarterly*.

MECHAL SOBEL is a professor of history and director of Graduate Studies in American Studies at the University of Haifa, Israel. Her chapter appeared in the fall 1979 issue of the *Tennessee Historical Quarterly*.

LOREN SCHWENINGER is a professor of history at the University of North Carolina, Greensboro. His chapter originally appeared in the spring/summer 1998 issue of the *Tennessee Historical Quarterly*.

CHRISTOPHER M. SCRIBNER teaches history at Indian Springs School in Birmingham; his most recent publication is *Renewing Birmingham: Federal Funding and the Promise of Change, 1929–1979* (University of Georgia Press, 2002). His chapter originally appeared in the spring 1995 issue of the *Tennessee Historical Quarterly*.

GERALD L. SMITH is an associate professor of history at the University of Kentucky. His chapter originally appeared in the summer 1996 issue of the *Tennessee Historical Quarterly* and has been reprinted in *Tennessee History: The Land, the People, and the Culture*, edited by Carroll Van West (University of Tennessee Press, 1998).

LISA TOLBERT is an associate professor of history at the University of North Carolina, Greensboro. Her chapter originally appeared in the winter 1998 issue of the *Tennessee Historical Quarterly*.

MICHAEL D. WEBB received his B.A. degree from the University of Tennessee, Chattanooga. His chapter originally appeared in the summer 1999 issue of the *Tennessee Historical Quarterly*.

CARROLL VAN WEST is the senior editor of the *Tennessee Historical Quarterly* and an associate professor of history with the Center for Historic Preservation at Middle Tennessee State University.

LINDA T. WYNN is assistant director for state programs at the Tennessee Historical Commission and an adjunct professor at Fisk University. Her chapter originally appeared in the fall 1996 issue of the *Tennessee Historical Quarterly*.

Index

Trial and Triumph was designed and typeset on a Macintosh computer system using QuarkXPress software. The text and chapter openings are set in Goudy. This book was designed by Cheryl Carrington, typeset by Kimberly Scarbrough, and manufactured by Thomson-Shore, Inc.